ACCA

P
R
A
C
T
I
C
E

&

R
E
V
I
S
I
O
N

K
I
T

PAPER P2

CORPORATE REPORTING
(INTERNATIONAL AND UNITED KINGDOM)

BPP Learning Media is an **ACCA Approved Content Provider** for the ACCA qualification. This means we work closely with ACCA to ensure our products fully prepare you for your ACCA exams.

In this Practice and Revision Kit, which has been reviewed by the **ACCA examination team**, we:

- Discuss the **best strategies** for revising and taking your ACCA exams

- Ensure you are well **prepared** for your exam

- Provide you with **lots of great guidance** on tackling questions

- Provide you with **three** mock exams

- Provide **ACCA exam answers** as well as our own for selected questions

Our **Passcards** support this paper.

FOR EXAMS FROM 1 SEPTEMBER 2015 TO 31 AUGUST 2016

BPP LEARNING MEDIA

First edition 2007
Ninth edition April 2015

ISBN 9781 4727 2693 3
(previous ISBN 9781 4727 1108 3)

e-ISBN 9781 4727 2745 9

British Library Cataloguing-in-Publication Data
A catalogue record for this book
is available from the British Library

Published by

BPP Learning Media Ltd
BPP House, Aldine Place
London W12 8AA

www.bpp.com/learningmedia

Printed in the United Kingdom by

Polestar Wheatons
Hennock Road
Marsh Barton
Exeter
EX2 8RP

We are grateful to the Association of Chartered Certified
Accountants for permission to reproduce past
examination questions. The suggested solutions in the
practice answer bank have been prepared by BPP
Learning Media Ltd, except where otherwise stated.

BPP
LEARNING MEDIA

Contents

A note about copyright

Question index

The headings in this checklist/index indicate the main topics of questions, but questions often cover several different topics.

Questions set under the previous syllabus *Advanced Corporate Reporting* paper are included because their style and content are similar to those which appear in the P2 exam. The questions have been amended to reflect the current exam format.

BPP
LEARNING MEDIA

Topic index

Listed below are the key Paper P2 syllabus topics and the numbers of the questions in this Kit covering those topics.

If you need to concentrate your practice and revision on certain topics or if you want to attempt all available questions that refer to a particular subject, you will find this index useful.

Syllabus topic	Question numbers
Associates	39
Complex groups	40 – 44
Consolidated statement of financial position	50
Consolidated statement of profit or loss and other comprehensive income	43
Consolidated statement of cash flows	58 – 61
Corporate citizenship	65
Disposals	45 – 53
Employee benefits	10 – 12
Environmental issues	62
Ethics	43,44, 49 – 53, 57, 60, 61
Financial instruments	19 – 24
Foreign currency	54 – 57
IAS 1 (revised)	Throughout
Impairment	9, 87
International issues	68
IFRS 2	29 – 31
IFRS 3	38 – 61
IFRS 9	19 – 24
IFRS 10 to 12	38 – 61
IFRS 13	64, throughout
Joint ventures	67
Measurement of performance	32 – 36
Non-current assets	6 – 9
Provisions	13 – 15
Related party transactions	37, 85
Reporting performance	34
Revenue recognition	4, 8
Share-based payment	29 – 31
Small and medium-sized entities	74, 75
Taxation	16 – 18

Helping you with your revision

As ACCA's **Approved Content Provider**, BPP Learning Media gives you the **opportunity** to use **exam team reviewed** revision materials. By incorporating the examination team's comments and suggestions regarding syllabus coverage, the BPP Learning Media Practice and Revision Kit provides excellent, **ACCA-approved** support for your revision.

Tackling revision and the exam

Using feedback obtained from the ACCA exam team review:

- We look at the dos and don'ts of revising for, and taking, ACCA exams

- We focus on Paper P2; we discuss revising the syllabus, what to do (and what not to do) in the exam, how to approach different types of question and ways of obtaining easy marks

Selecting questions

We provide signposts to help you plan your revision.

- A full **question index**

- A **topic index** listing all the questions that cover key topics, so that you can locate the questions that provide practice on these topics, and see the different ways in which they might be examined

Making the most of question practice

At BPP Learning Media we realise that you need more than just questions and model answers to get the most from your question practice.

- Our **Top tips** included for certain questions provide essential advice on tackling questions, presenting answers and the key points that answers need to include

- We show you how you can pick up **Easy marks** on some questions, as we know that picking up all readily available marks often can make the difference between passing and failing

- We include **marking guides** to show you what the examiner rewards

- We include **comments from the examiners** to show you where students struggled or performed well in the actual exam

- We refer to the **BPP Study Text** (for exams between 1 September 2015 and 31 August 2016) for detailed coverage of the topics covered in questions

- In a bank at the end of this Kit we include the **official ACCA answers** to the June and December 2014 papers. Used in conjunction with our answers they provide an indication of all possible points that could be made, issues that could be covered and approaches to adopt.

Attempting mock exams

There are three mock exams that provide practice at coping with the pressures of the exam day. We strongly recommend that you attempt them under exam conditions. **Mock exams 1 and 2** reflect the question styles and syllabus coverage of the exam; **Mock exam 3** is the December 2014 paper.

Revising P2

P2 has the reputation of being a difficult paper. However its pass rate is usually quite high. Although the examiner sets challenging questions, the styles of question used are now familiar. The examiner has also provided a great deal of feedback via examiner's reports and in the very detailed published marking schemes, many of which are included in this Kit.

The examiner has warned very strongly against question-spotting and trying to predict the topics that will be included in the exam. On occasions the same topic has been examined in two successive sittings. The examiner regards few areas as off-limits for questions, and nearly all of the major areas of the syllabus can and have been tested.

That said, exams over the years have shown that the following areas of the syllabus are very important, and your revision therefore needs to cover them particularly well.

- **Group accounts.** You should not omit any aspect of group accounts, as they come up every sitting. We would advise against question spotting, but if a statement of cash flows, say, has not come up for a few sittings, it might be a good bet. Group accounts will always be examined as part of the 50 mark case study question, in which you may also expect a question on some aspect of **ethics**.

- **Emerging issues.** The impact of a change in accounting standards on the financial statements is often examined. Look on the IASB website for details: www.iasb.org

- **Share based payment** usually comes up as part of a question.

- **Financial instruments** was the subject of regular *Student Accountant* articles, and it is regularly tested. IFRS 9 (July 2014) is now fully examinable.

- **Developments in financial reporting**, for example, the exposure drafts on leasing and revenue recognition.

Question practice under timed conditions is essential, so that you can get used to the pressures of answering exam questions in **limited time** and practise not only the key techniques but allocating your time between different requirements in each question. Our list of recommended questions includes compulsory Section A and optional Section B questions; it's particularly important to do all the Section A case-study-style questions in full as a case study involving group accounts will always come up.

Passing the P2 exam

What to expect on the paper

Of course you cannot know in advance what questions are going to come up, but you can have a fair idea of what kind of questions.

Question 1

This will always be a case study, with half or a little more than half on group accounts. It will often involve high speed number crunching. Easy marks, it cannot be said too often, will always be available for basic consolidation techniques. You cannot pass the groups part on these alone, but it can give you a foothold. Question 1 usually has a bit of a twist, for example financial instruments or pensions. This question will also contain an element of written explanation and a question on ethics or corporate social accounting. For example, the June 2014 paper had two disposals; then you were asked to discuss an ethical dilemma for a new financial controller arising from the finance director 's wish to avoid treating a lease as a finance lease.

The examiner has stressed the importance of answering the written parts of Question 1. Many students ignore parts (b) and (c), but marks can be gained for common sense.

Question 1 will always have more than half the marks allocated to the computational part. Generally, it will be in the order of 35 marks.

Questions 2 and 3

These each cover several IFRSs and are very often – although not always – mini-case-studies, involving you in giving advice to the directors on accounting treatment, possibly where the directors have followed the wrong treatment. Being multi-standard, you may be able to answer parts, but not all of a question, so it makes sense to look through the paper to select a question where you can answer most of it. If Part (a) is on an area you are not confident about, do not dismiss the question out of hand.

The examiner is testing whether you can identify the issues. Even if you don't get the accounting treatment exactly right, you will still gain some credit for showing that you have seen what the problem is about. So do not be afraid to have a stab at something, even if you are not sure of the details.

These questions can be on a single standard or theme. Question 3 will usually be the specialised industry question.

Question 4

This question is generally on developments in financial reporting. It may cover an aspect of reporting financial performance – for example the Management Commentary, but it can also be set on just one standard if this standard is undergoing revision. This question can feature criticism of existing standards, as well as aspects of new or proposed standards.

While you certainly cannot bluff your way through Question 4, if you know your material it is a good way of earning marks without high speed number crunching.

Question 4 may now include a computational aspect illustrating the topic you have just discussed. Usually these are fairly straightforward.

Exam technique for P2

Do not be needlessly intimidated

There is no shortcut to passing this exam. It looks very difficult indeed, and many students wonder if they will ever pass. But most students generally do. Why is this?

Easy marks

All the questions are demanding, but there are many easy marks to be gained. Suppose, for example, you had a consolidated statement of cash flows with a disposal, a pension complication and a financial instruments calculation. There will be easy marks available simply for the basic cash flow aspects, setting out the proforma, setting up your workings, presenting your work neatly. If you recognise, as you should, that the disposal needs to be taken into account, of course you will get marks for that, even if you make a mistake in the arithmetic. If you get the pension bit right, so much the better, but you could pass the question comfortably while omitting this altogether. If you're short of time, this is what you should do.

Be ruthless in ignoring the complications

Look at the question. Within reason, if there are complications – often only worth a few marks – that you know you will not have time or knowledge to do, cross them out. It will make you feel better. Then tackle the bits you can do. This is how people pass a seemingly impossible paper.

Be ruthless in allocating your time

At BPP, we have seen how very intelligent students do two almost perfect questions, one averagely good and one sketchy. The first eight to ten marks are the easiest to get. Then you have to push it up to what you think is 15 (30 for the case study question), to get yourself a pass.

Do your best question either first or second, and the compulsory question either first or second. The compulsory question, being on groups, will always have some easy marks available for consolidation techniques.

Exam information

Format of the exam

		Number of marks
Section A:	1 compulsory case study	50
Section B:	Choice of 2 from 3 questions (25 marks each)	50
		100

Section A will consist of one scenario based question worth 50 marks. It will deal with the preparation of consolidated financial statements including group statements of cash flow and with issues in financial reporting.

Students will be required to answer two out of three questions in Section B, which will normally comprise two questions which will be scenario or case-study based and one question which will be an essay. Section B could deal with any aspects of the syllabus.

Additional information

The Study Guide provides more detailed guidance on the syllabus.

Analysis of past papers

December 2014

Section A

1   Business combination in stages with adjustments for non-current asset held for sale and joint venture; share-based payment; ethical issue

Section B

2   Related parties; financial guarantee contracts; interest rate swap; credit risk
3   IFRS 3 and control; IAS 16 application to a scenario
4   Impairment: factors to consider and application to a scenario

The December 2014 Paper is Mock Exam 3 in this Kit.

Examiner's comments

The performance of candidates in this paper was good. Question 1 often determines whether a candidate is successful in the examination because of the detailed and complex nature of the question. Therefore, it is important for candidates to answer all parts of the question. It is often the case in question 1c, which is based around ethical knowledge and application, that candidates do not attempt the question even though marks can readily be gained for a well-argued answer to this part of the question..

The normal problems of providing irrelevant answers, poor time management and lack of application of knowledge to the scenario are generally evident in every examination from an increasingly smaller number of candidates. A candidate is required to apply their knowledge to scenarios affecting issuers of financial statements in an international context and therefore the scenarios are not necessarily going to be typical of a particular region of the world. Further, the questions are not designed as purely an academic exercise.

June 2014

Section A   *Question in this Kit*

1   Consolidated statement of profit or loss and other comprehensive income with two   47
     disposals and various adjustments; fair value in IFRS; ethical issue

Section B

2   Foreign transactions (functional currency, goodwill, deferred tax and a loan)   55
3   Specialised industry question set in the property industry, covering revenue, interim   33
     reporting, asset held for sale, provisions and intangibles
4   Distinction between debt and equity: discussion and scenario   21

December 2013

Section A | *Question in this Kit*

1   Consolidated statement of cash flows with acquisition of subsidiary and adjustments for deferred tax, a government grant and a pension plan; classification of cash flows; ethics — 59

Section B

2   Revenue recognition; impairment loss; sale and leaseback — 26
3   Specialised industry question set in a bank, covering debt versus equity, hedging and the application of IFRS 10 in determining which party is the acquirer — 20
4   IAS 8: use of judgement in selecting accounting policies; prior period errors (three scenarios) — 32

June 2013

Examiner's comments

The examiner stressed again the importance of answering all questions and all parts of questions, and also of exam technique: exam technique consists of a few simple procedures that can help the candidate immeasurably. Answers should have a structure and cover points in an organised way. It may be best to write less on each point, leave out some of the background knowledge but focus on the facts/scenario in the question. The examiner does not need to know, for example, the role of the IASB in standard setting unless specifically asked in the question but often candidates may outline this as an introduction to an answer.

There is always a model solution to the question but in practice there are always opposing viewpoints, and candidates should not be afraid of expressing these viewpoints as they will not be penalised if the rationale is acceptable. The questions are not written to trick candidates but it is important to read the question carefully. Always ask yourself, is what I am including relevant to the question? Successful candidates demonstrate relevant knowledge by using ideas and concepts from recommended accounting practice. Practical examples from reading current articles are important ways of supporting the points made. Many candidates simply set out everything they know, hoping that some of the material is relevant. There is a need for a broader understanding rather than rote-learnt facts.

Candidates should try and use proper sentences and paragraphs rather than bullet points, as this will contribute to the awarding of professional marks. Candidates should never use abbreviations of words such as text language.

December 2012

Examiner's comments

Candidates performed quite well in this session. As usual the paper dealt with a wide range of issues and accounting standards. There are several key principles in each standard, which are the basis of most of the examination questions, and candidates should concentrate on understanding and interpreting these principles. Candidates need to understand the standards, and not just learn their content. Understanding will lead to better application in the examination.

Candidates should practice divergent thinking, which is the ability to think of several possible answers to a question before providing the solution. This is the ability to see potentially different outcomes for a given set of circumstances. This will lead to candidates having the ability to apply the standards to different scenarios. Every examination session produces scenarios, which candidates will not necessarily have met before, and thus there is a need for this type of reasoning.

Candidates often simply recite the standard leaving the marker with the task of determining how applicable the answer actually is to the question. Candidates should adopt a model of learning which suits them and by doing this; candidates will be better prepared for the examination.

June 2012

Section A   *Question in this Kit*

1   Consolidated statement of financial position with business combination achieved in   50
    stages and joint operation; de-recognition of financial asset ; ethics

Section B

2   Sale and leaseback, defined benefit pension plan, cash-settled share-based payment   28
    and contingent liability in the context of a business combination
3   Measuring fair value, impairment of goodwill, deferred tax liabilities and the fair   68
    value option for an accounting mismatch; shares as financial liability or equity
4   Provisions (discussion and calculation)   14

Examiner's comments

Generally candidates performed well on this paper, with Questions 1 and 2 being answered better than Questions 3 and 4.

Candidates approached the examination well and did not appear too time-pressured, but some failed to produce answers of sufficient length and appear to be spending too much time on Question 1. Question 1(a) is designed to test candidates' computational skills and very brief explanations may be useful to the marker but many candidates entered into detailed discussion of the relevant standard, which costs time in the examination, and it is important for candidates to use their time effectively. Very few marks are allocated in Question 1(a) for detailed discussion.

Candidates often wasted time discussing a standard in detail when an application of the standard was required.

Candidates should read the question and formulate an answer in their mind. The answer should be based upon the detail of the question. Simply reading the requirement without application to the scenario does not gain marks.

This examination focussed on application of knowledge and it was application, which often let candidates down. Candidates often do not use the information in the scenario in order to develop their answers. Often the content of the scenario will help students answer the question as the scenario gives candidates direction in terms of their answers. This was particularly true of Question 4.

December 2011

Examiner's comments

The standard of answers varied. Many candidates passed the examination because of strong performance on Q

Question 1 and the questions answered best by candidates were Question 1a, Questions 3(a/c), and Question 4(a)(i).

Answers to Section B questions are often very general in nature with no relationship to the facts given in the scenario. This can involve just repeating information given in the question without explaining how it impacts on the financial statements or just quoting facts from standards without reference to the question. This can result in long answers that often don't address the issues in a scenario and may leave candidates bemused as to why they have failed when they have written so much. Often these scripts bordered on illegibility, which makes marking difficult. It is often better to explain a few points well than trying to regurgitate all the knowledge that the candidate possesses.

There were however many excellent scripts, particularly in answering the technical aspects of group accounting and the issues surrounding intangible assets.

Too many candidates let themselves down by failing to attempt all parts of the questions chosen, or in some cases by answering all four questions.

June 2011

December 2010

Section A	*Question in this Kit*
1 Consolidated statement of cash flows	60

Section B

2 Share-based payment; derivatives	29
3 Provisions, contingent liability, significant influence; share-based payment	30
4 Small and medium-sized entities	75

June 2010

Examiner's comments

The pass rate for this paper was satisfactory, and the examiner was generally pleased with the way candidates responded to a testing paper covering a wide range of accounting issues and standards. Examination techniques were well applied. However yet again there was evidence of candidates only answering two questions rather than the three questions required, and also leaving out the ethics part of Question 1, suggesting that they do not appreciate the importance of attempting all of the examination paper, or perhaps particular problems with ethical instruments. Some candidates still do not have a good understanding of accounting for financial instruments which are examined frequently in this paper. It is essential that candidates get to grips with this topic.

December 2009

Examiner's comments The paper dealt with a wide range of issues and accounting standards. The examiner said that the paper was quite testing but that candidates responded well resulting in a pleasing pass rate. Candidates had benefited from reading articles in *Student Accountant* on specific topics and had built on their knowledge, particularly of the revised IFRS 3 and financial instruments. Candidates also seem to have applied good examination techniques in answering the paper. In particular, candidates were not making the mistake of missing out questions or parts of questions.

June 2009

Examiner's comments. This was the first sitting where the technical aspects of IFRS 3 (Revised) 'Business Combinations' were examined in Question 1. It seemed as though many candidates were not adequately prepared for the question even though several articles had appeared in the student accountant. The results overall were disappointing. The main reasons for this appeared to be lack of a thorough understanding of IFRS 3 (Revised), poor time management and difficulty in applying knowledge to questions. An important aspect of the paper is the current issues question. Generally speaking current issues would comprise those issues being discussed in the accountancy press or those issues being dealt with by the IASB in its current work programme or very recent accounting standards. Candidates do not perform well on current issues questions and in order to improve their performance in this area, they should make sure that they manage their own learning by reading wider than just course notes and manuals. The IASB work programme for example is open for everyone to view and web sites such as www.iasplus.com are available for candidates to read around subjects that are on the programme.

December 2008

Section A	Question in this Kit
1 Group statement of cash flows with adjustments and interpretation; ethics	61

Section B	
2 Changes to accounting for business combinations	38
3 Tangibles, intangibles and revenue recognition	8
4 Accounting standards and disclosure	2

Examiner's comments. The paper was generally well answered and the pass rate was pleasing. However candidates must learn to apply their knowledge and not simply reiterate definitions.

The approach to the examination seems to be improving with little evidence of time pressure although some candidates are still failing to produce answers to all parts of the paper and appear to be spending too much time on Question 1. Also candidates are often not using the information in the question to develop their answers even when the question requires the information to be used. There is a minimum amount of information required in each question in order to gain a pass standard and candidates do sometimes not appreciate this.

Exam update

Examinable documents

The following documents are examinable for sittings up from September 2015 to June 2016.

Knowledge of new examinable regulations issued by 31st August will be required in examination sessions being held in the following exam year. Documents may be examinable even if the effective date is in the future.

The documents listed as being examinable are the latest that were issued prior to 31st August 2014 and will be examinable in examination sessions in September 2015, December 2015, March 2016 and June 2016.

The study guide offers more detailed guidance on the depth and level at which the examinable documents will be examined. The study guide should be read in conjunction with the examinable documents list.

	Title
	International Accounting Standards (IASs)/International Financial Reporting Standards (IFRSs)
IAS 1	Presentation of financial statements
IAS 2	Inventories
IAS 7	Statement of cash flows
IAS 8	Accounting policies, changes in accounting estimates and errors
IAS 10	Events after the reporting period
IAS 12	Income taxes
IAS 16	Property, plant and equipment
IAS 17	Leases
IAS 19	Employee benefits
IAS 20	Accounting for government grants and disclosure of government assistance
IAS 21	The effects of changes in foreign exchange rates
IAS 23	Borrowing costs
IAS 24	Related party disclosures
IAS 27	Separate financial statements
IAS 28	Investments in associates and joint ventures
IAS 32	Financial Instruments: presentation
IAS 33	Earnings per share
IAS 34	Interim financial reporting
IAS 36	Impairment of assets
IAS 37	Provisions, contingent liabilities and contingent assets
IAS 38	Intangible assets
IAS 40	Investment property
IAS 41	Agriculture
IFRS 1	First-time adoption of international financial reporting standards
IFRS 2	Share-based payment
IFRS 3	Business combinations
IFRS 5	Non-current assets held for sale and discontinued operations
IFRS 7	Financial instruments: disclosures
IFRS 8	Operating segments
IFRS 9	Financial instruments (revised July 2014)
IFRS 10	Consolidated financial statements
IFRS 11	Joint arrangements
IFRS 12	Disclosure of interests in other entities
IFRS 13	Fair value measurement
IFRS 15	Revenue from contracts with customers
IFRS	For Small and Medium-sized Entities

Other Statements
Conceptual Framework for Financial reporting
Management Commentary
The International <IR> Framework
EDs, Discussion Papers and Other Documents
ED	Leases
ED	Disclosure initiative: amendments to IAS 1
ED	Equity method: share of other net asset changes
ED	Improvements to IFRS 2012 – 2014 cycle
ED	Recognition of deferred tax assets for unrealized losses
ED	Investment entities
ED	Sale or contribution of assets between an investor and its associate or joint venture
DP	A review of the Conceptual Framework for Financial Reporting

Important note for UK students

If you are sitting the UK P2 paper you will be studying under International standards and up to 20 marks will be for comparisons between International and UK GAAP. The ACCA UK Syllabus and Study Guide gives the following advice:

> International Financial Reporting Standards (IFRS) are the main accounting standards examined in the preparation of financial information. The key differences between UK GAAP and International Financial Reporting Standards are looked at on a subject by subject basis. The comparison between IFRS and UK GAAP will be based on the new UK GAAP as set out in FRSs 100–102, so the standard by standard comparisons that appeared in previous editions of this study guide are now combined in outcome C11 d): *Discuss the key differences between the IFRS for SMEs and UK GAAP.*

This Kit is based on International Financial Reporting Standards. An online supplement will be available at www.bpp.com/learning-media, covering the additional UK issues and providing additional question practice.

Useful websites

The websites below provide additional sources of information of relevance to your studies for *Corporate Reporting*.

- www.accaglobal.com

  ACCA's website. The students' section of the website is invaluable for detailed information about the qualification, past issues of *Student Accountant* (including technical articles) and a free downloadable Student Planner App.

- www.bpp.com

  Our website provides information about BPP products and services, with a link to ACCA's website.

- www.ft.com

  This website provides information about current international business. You can search for information and articles on specific industry groups as well as individual companies.

- www.economist.com

  Here you can search for business information on a week-by-week basis, search articles by business subject and use the resources of the Economist Intelligence Unit to research sectors, companies or countries.

- www.invweek.co.uk

  This site carries business news and articles on markets from *Investment Week* and *International Investment*.

- www.pwc.com

  The PricewaterhouseCoopers website includes UK Economic Outlook.

- www.cfo.com

  Good website for financial officers.

- www.bankofengland.co.uk

  This website is useful for sourcing Bank of England publications.

- www.iasb.org
- www.accountancyfoundation.com
- www.ifac.org
- www.IASPlus.com

Questions

REGULATORY AND ETHICAL FRAMEWORK

Questions 1 to 4 cover Regulatory and Ethical Framework, the subject of Part A of the BPP Study Text for Paper P2.

1 Conceptual framework   45 mins

12/07, amended

The International Accounting Standards Board (IASB) is working on a joint project with the FASB to revisit its conceptual framework for financial accounting and reporting. The goals of the project are to build on the existing frameworks and converge them into a common framework. The first phase has now been published as the *Conceptual Framework for Financial Reporting.*

Required

(a)   Discuss why there is a need to develop an agreed international conceptual framework and the extent to which an agreed international conceptual framework can be used to resolve practical accounting issues.

(14 marks)

(b)   In July 2013, the IASB published a Discussion Paper *Review of the Conceptual Framework,* which addresses areas found to be deficient in the existing *Conceptual Framework.*

How does the Discussion Paper propose to improve reporting in the following areas:

(i)   Recognition and derecognition of assets and liabilities
(ii)   The distinction between equity and liabilities
(iii)   Profit or loss versus other comprehensive income and recycling.   **(9 marks)**

Appropriateness and quality of discussion.   **(2 marks)**

(Total = 25 marks)

2 Accounting standards and disclosure   45 mins

12/08

Whilst acknowledging the importance of high quality corporate reporting, the recommendations to improve it are sometimes questioned on the basis that the marketplace for capital can determine the nature and quality of corporate reporting. It could be argued that additional accounting and disclosure standards would only distort a market mechanism that already works well and would add costs to the reporting mechanism, with no apparent benefit. It could be said that accounting standards create costly, inefficient, and unnecessary regulation. It could be argued that increased disclosure reduces risks and offers a degree of protection to users. However, increased disclosure has several costs to the preparer of financial statements.

Required

(a)   Explain why accounting standards are needed to help the market mechanism work effectively for the benefit of preparers and users of corporate reports.   **(9 marks)**

(b)   Discuss the relative costs to the preparer and benefits to the users of financial statements of increased disclosure of information in financial statements.   **(14 marks)**

Quality of discussion and reasoning.   **(2 marks)**

(Total = 25 marks)

3 Lizzer

(a) Developing a framework for disclosure is at the forefront of current debate and there are many bodies around the world attempting to establish an overarching framework to make financial statement disclosures more effective, coordinated and less redundant. It has been argued that instead of focusing on raising the quality of disclosures, these efforts have placed their emphasis almost exclusively on reducing the quantity of information. The belief is that excessive disclosure is burdensome and can overwhelm users. However, it could be argued that there is no such thing as too much 'useful' information for users.

Required

    (i) Discuss why it is important to ensure the optimal level of disclosure in annual reports, describing the reasons why users of annual reports may have found disclosure to be excessive in recent years.

(9 marks)

    (ii) Describe the barriers, which may exist, to reducing excessive disclosure in annual reports.

(6 marks)

(b) The directors of Lizzer, a public limited company, have read various reports on excessive disclosure in the annual report. They have decided to take action and do not wish to disclose any further detail concerning the two instances below.

    (i) Lizzer is a debt issuer whose business is the securitisation of a portfolio of underlying investments and financing their purchase through the issuing of listed, limited recourse debt. The repayment of the debt is dependent upon the performance of the underlying investments. Debt-holders bear the ultimate risks and rewards of ownership of the underlying investments. Given the debt specific nature of the underlying investments, the risk profile of individual debt may differ.

        Lizzer does not consider its debt-holders as being amongst the primary users of the financial statements and, accordingly, does not wish to provide disclosure of the debt-holders' exposure to risks in the financial statements, as distinct from the risks faced by the company's shareholders, in accordance with IFRS 7 *Financial instruments: disclosures*. **(4 marks)**

    (ii) At the date of the financial statements, 31 January 20X3, Lizzer's liquidity position was quite poor, such that the directors described it as 'unsatisfactory' in the management report. During the first quarter of 20X3, the situation worsened with the result that Lizzer was in breach of certain loan covenants at 31 March 20X3. The financial statements were authorised for issue at the end of April 20X3. The directors' and auditor's reports both emphasised the considerable risk of not being able to continue as a going concern.

        The notes to the financial statements indicated that there was 'ample' compliance with all loan covenants as at the date of the financial statements. No additional information about the loan covenants was included in the financial statements. Lizzer had been close to breaching the loan covenants in respect of free cash flows and equity ratio requirements at 31 January 20X3.

        The directors of Lizzer felt that, given the existing information in the financial statements, any further disclosure would be excessive and confusing to users. **(4 marks)**

Required

Discuss the directors' view that no further information regarding the two instances above should be disclosed in the financial statements because it would be 'excessive'.

Note. The mark allocation is shown against each of the two instances above.

Professional marks will be awarded in this question for clarity and quality of presentation. **(2 marks)**

(Total = 25 marks)

4 Venue

The introduction of IFRS 15 *Revenue from contracts with customers* will have a significant impact on the financial statements of many companies. IFRS 15 significantly reduces an entity's discretion to apply judgement when recognising revenue. This represents an improvement on the old revenue standards, which provided limited revenue recognition guidance and led to divergence in practice.

Required

(a) (i) Discuss the main weaknesses in the old revenue standards which led to the introduction of IFRS 15 *Revenue from contracts with customers.* **(8 marks)**

(ii) Discuss the ways in which IFRS 15 attempts to remedy the disadvantages of the previous standards on revenue. **(11 marks)**

Professional marks will be awarded in part (a) for clarity and expression of your discussion.

(2 marks)

(b) On 1 July 20X6, Venue entered into a contract with Reven for the sale of plant for $500,000. The contract included a call option that gave Venue the right to repurchase the plant for $550,000 on or before 30 June 20X7.

Required

Discuss how the above transaction would be treated in subsequent financial statements of Venue for the year ended 31 July 20X7. **(4 marks)**

(Total = 25 marks)

ACCOUNTING STANDARDS

Questions 5 to 37 cover Accounting Standards, the subject of Part B of the BPP Study Text for Paper P2.

5 Preparation question: sundry standards

(a)   Penn Co has a defined benefit pension plan and wishes to recognise the full deficit in its statement of financial position.

Required

Using the information below, prepare extracts from the statement of financial position and the statement of comprehensive income, together with a reconciliation of plan movements for the year ended 31 January 20X8. Ignore taxation.

(i)   The opening plan assets were $3.6m on 1 February 20X7 and plan liabilities at this date were $4.3m.

(ii)   Company contributions to the plan during the year amounted to $550,000.

(iii)   Pensions paid to former employees amounted to $330,000 in the year.

(iv)   The yield on high quality corporate bonds was 8% and the actual return on plan assets was $295,000.

(v)   During the year, five staff were made redundant, and an extra $58,000 in total was added to the value of their pensions.

(vi)   Current service costs as provided by the actuary are $275,000.

(vii)   The actuary valued the plan liabilities at 31 January 20X8 as $4.54m.

(b)   Sion Co operates a defined benefit pension plan for its employees. The following details relate to the plan.

Present value of obligation at start of 20X8 ($'000)		40,000
Market value of plan assets at start of 20X8 ($'000)		40,000

	20X8	20X9
	$'000	$'000
Current service cost	2,500	2,860
Benefits paid out	1,974	2,200
Contributions paid by entity	2,000	2,200
Present value of obligation at end of the year	46,000	40,800
Market value of plan assets at end of the year	43,000	35,680
Yield on corporate bonds at end of year	8%	9%

During 20X8, the benefits available under the plan were improved. The resulting increase in the present value of the defined benefit obligation was $2 million.

On the final day of 20X9, Sion Co. divested of part of its business, and as part of the sale agreement, transferred the relevant part of its pension fund to the buyer. The present value of the defined benefit obligation transferred was $11.4 million and the fair value of plan assets transferred was $10.8million. Sion also made a cash payment of $400,000 to the buyer in respect of the plan.

Assume that all transactions occur at the end of the year.

Required

(i)   Calculate the net defined benefit liability as at the start and end of 20X8 and 20X9 showing clearly any remeasurement gain or loss on the plan each year.

(ii)   Show amounts to be recognised in the financial statements in each of the years 20X8 and 20X9 in respect of the plan.

(c)   Bed Investment Co entered into a contract on 1 July 20X7 with Em Bank. The contract consisted of a deposit of a principal amount of $10 million, carrying an interest rate of 2.5% per annum and with a maturity date of 30 June 20X9. Interest will be receivable at maturity together with the principal. In addition, a further 3% interest per annum will be payable by Em Bank if the exchange rate of the dollar against the Ruritanian Kroner (RKR) exceeds or is equal to $1.15 to RKR 1.

BPP
LEARNING MEDIA

Bed's functional currency is the dollar.

Required

Explain how Bed should account for the above investment in the financial statements for the year ended 31 December 20X7.

6 Key

(a) Key, a public limited company, is concerned about the reduction in the general availability of credit and the sudden tightening of the conditions required to obtain a loan from banks. There has been a reduction in credit availability and a rise in interest rates. It seems as though there has ceased to be a clear relationship between interest rates and credit availability, and lenders and investors are seeking less risky investments. The directors are trying to determine the practical implications for the financial statements particularly because of large write downs of assets in the banking sector, tightening of credit conditions, and falling sales and asset prices. They are particularly concerned about the impairment of assets and the market inputs to be used in impairment testing. They are afraid that they may experience significant impairment charges in the coming financial year. They are unsure as to how they should test for impairment and any considerations which should be taken into account.

Required

Discuss the main considerations that the company should take into account when impairment testing non-current assets in the above economic climate. **(8 marks)**

Professional marks will be awarded in part (a) for clarity and expression. **(2 marks)**

(b) There are specific assets on which the company wishes to seek advice. The company holds certain non-current assets, which are in a development area and carried at cost less depreciation. These assets cost $3 million on 1 June 20X3 and are depreciated on the straight-line basis over their useful life of five years. An impairment review was carried out on 31 May 20X4 and the projected cash flows relating to these assets were as follows:

Year to	31 May 20X5	31 May 20X6	31 May 20X7	31 May 20X8
Cash flows ($'000)	280	450	500	550

The company used a discount rate of 5%. At 30 November 20X4, the directors used the same cash flow projections and noticed that the resultant value in use was above the carrying amount of the assets and wished to reverse any impairment loss calculated at 31 May 20X4. The government has indicated that it may compensate the company for any loss in value of the assets up to 20% of the impairment loss.

Key holds a non-current asset, which was purchased for $10 million on 1 December 20X1 with an expected useful life of ten years. On 1 December 20X3, it was revalued to $8.8 million. At 30 November 20X4, the asset was reviewed for impairment and written down to its recoverable amount of $5.5 million.

Key committed itself at the beginning of the financial year to selling a property that is being under-utilised following the economic downturn. As a result of the economic downturn, the property was not sold by the end of the year. The asset was actively marketed but there were no reasonable offers to purchase the asset. Key is hoping that the economic downturn will change in the future and therefore has not reduced the price of the asset.

Required

Discuss with suitable computations, how to account for any potential impairment of the above non-current assets in the financial statements for the year ended 30 November 20X4. **(15 marks)**

Note. The following 5% discount factors may be relevant.

Year 1	0.9524
Year 2	0.9070
Year 3	0.8638
Year 4	0.8227

(Total = 25 marks)

7 Prochain

Prochain, a public limited company, operates in the fashion industry and has a financial year end of 31 May 20X6. The company sells its products in department stores throughout the world. Prochain insists on creating its own selling areas within the department stores which are called 'model areas'. Prochain is allocated space in the department store where it can display and market its fashion goods. The company feels that this helps to promote its merchandise. Prochain pays for all the costs of the 'model areas' including design, decoration and construction costs. The areas are used for approximately two years after which the company has to dismantle the 'model areas'. The costs of dismantling the 'model areas' are normally 20% of the original construction cost and the elements of the area are worthless when dismantled. The current accounting practice followed by Prochain is to charge the full cost of the 'model areas' against profit or loss in the year when the area is dismantled. The accumulated cost of the 'model areas' shown in the statement of financial position at 31 May 20X6 is $20 million. The company has estimated that the average age of the 'model areas' is eight months at 31 May 20X6. **(7 marks)**

Prochain acquired 100% of a sports goods and clothing manufacturer, Badex, a private limited company, on 1 June 20X5. Prochain intends to develop its own brand of sports clothing which it will sell in the department stores. The shareholders of Badex valued the company at $125 million based upon profit forecasts which assumed significant growth in the demand for the 'Badex' brand name. Prochain had taken a more conservative view of the value of the company and measured the fair value as being in the region of $108 million to $112 million of which $20 million relates to the brand name 'Badex'. Prochain is only prepared to pay the full purchase price if profits from the sale of 'Badex' clothing and sports goods reach the forecast levels. The agreed purchase price was $100 million plus a further payment of $25 million in two years on 31 May 20X7. This further payment will comprise a guaranteed payment of $10 million with no performance conditions and a further payment of $15 million if the actual profits during this two year period from the sale of Badex clothing and goods exceed the forecast profit. The forecast profit on Badex goods and clothing over the two year period is $16 million and the actual profits in the year to 31 May 20X6 were $4 million. Prochain did not feel at any time since acquisition that the actual profits would meet the forecast profit levels. **(8 marks)**

After the acquisition of Badex, Prochain started developing its own sports clothing brand 'Pro'. The expenditure in the period to 31 May 20X6 was as follows:

Period from	Expenditure type	$m
1 June 20X5 – 31 August 20X5	Research as to the extent of the market	3
1 September 20X5 – 30 November 20X5	Prototype clothing and goods design	4
1 December 20X5 – 31 January 20X6	Employee costs in refinement of products	2
1 February 20X6 – 30 April 20X6	Development work undertaken to finalise design of product	5
1 May 20X6 – 31 May 20X6	Production and launch of products	6
		20

The costs of the production and launch of the products include the cost of upgrading the existing machinery ($3 million), market research costs ($2 million) and staff training costs ($1 million). Currently an intangible asset of $20 million is shown in the financial statements for the year ended 31 May 20X6. **(6 marks)**

Prochain owns a number of prestigious apartments which it leases to famous persons who are under a contract of employment to promote its fashion clothing. The apartments are let at below the market rate. The lease terms are short and are normally for six months. The leases terminate when the contracts for promoting the clothing terminate. Prochain wishes to account for the apartments as investment properties with the difference between the market rate and actual rental charged to be recognised as an employee benefit expense. **(4 marks)**

Assume a discount rate of 5.5% where necessary.

Required

Discuss how the above items should be dealt with in the financial statements of Prochain for the year ended 31 May 20X6 under International Financial Reporting Standards.

(Total = 25 marks)

8 Johan

12/08

Johan, a public limited company, operates in the telecommunications industry. The industry is capital intensive with heavy investment in licences and network infrastructure. Competition in the sector is fierce and technological advances are a characteristic of the industry. Johan has responded to these factors by offering incentives to customers and, in an attempt to acquire and retain them, Johan purchased a telecom licence on 1 December 20X6 for $120 million. The licence has a term of six years and cannot be used until the network assets and infrastructure are ready for use. The related network assets and infrastructure became ready for use on 1 December 20X7. Johan could not operate in the country without the licence and is not permitted to sell the licence. Johan expects its subscriber base to grow over the period of the licence but is disappointed with its market share for the year to 30 November 20X8. The licence agreement does not deal with the renewal of the licence but there is an expectation that the regulator will grant a single renewal for the same period of time as long as certain criteria regarding network build quality and service quality are met. Johan has no experience of the charge that will be made by the regulator for the renewal but other licences have been renewed at a nominal cost. The licence is currently stated at its original cost of $120 million in the statement of financial position under non-current assets.

Johan is considering extending its network and has carried out a feasibility study during the year to 30 November 20X8. The design and planning department of Johan identified five possible geographical areas for the extension of its network. The internal costs of this study were $150,000 and the external costs were $100,000 during the year to 30 November 20X8. Following the feasibility study, Johan chose a geographical area where it was going to install a base station for the telephone network. The location of the base station was dependent upon getting planning permission. A further independent study has been carried out by third party consultants in an attempt to provide a preferred location in the area, as there is a need for the optimal operation of the network in terms of signal quality and coverage. Johan proposes to build a base station on the recommended site on which planning permission has been obtained. The third party consultants have charged $50,000 for the study. Additionally Johan has paid $300,000 as a single payment together with $60,000 a month to the government of the region for access to the land upon which the base station will be situated. The contract with the government is for a period of 12 years and commenced on 1 November 20X8. There is no right of renewal of the contract and legal title to the land remains with the government.

Johan purchases telephone handsets from a manufacturer for $200 each, and sells the handsets direct to customers for $150 if they purchase call credit (call card) in advance on what is called a prepaid phone. The costs of selling the handset are estimated at $1 per set. The customers using a prepaid phone pay $21 for each call card at the purchase date. Call cards expire six months from the date of first sale. There is an average unused call credit of $3 per card after six months and the card is activated when sold.

Johan also sells handsets to dealers for $150 and invoices the dealers for those handsets. The dealer can return the handset up to a service contract being signed by a customer. When the customer signs a service contract, the customer receives the handset free of charge. Johan allows the dealer a commission of $280 on the connection of a customer and the transaction with the dealer is settled net by a payment of $130 by Johan to the dealer being the cost of the handset to the dealer ($150) deducted from the commission ($280). The handset cannot be sold separately by the dealer and the service contract lasts for a 12 month period. Dealers do not sell prepaid phones, and Johan receives monthly revenue from the service contract.

The chief operating officer, a non-accountant, has asked for an explanation of the accounting principles and practices which should be used to account for the above events.

Required

Discuss the principles and practices which should be used in the financial year to 30 November 20X8 to account for:

(a)	The licences	**(8 marks)**
(b)	The costs incurred in extending the network	**(7 marks)**
(c)	The purchase of handsets and the recognition of revenue from customers and dealers	**(8 marks)**

Appropriateness and quality of discussion. **(2 marks)**

(Total = 25 marks)

9 Scramble

45 mins

12/11

Scramble, a public limited company, is a developer of online computer games.

(a) At 30 November 20X1, 65% of Scramble's total assets were mainly represented by internally developed intangible assets comprising the capitalised costs of the development and production of online computer games. These games generate all of Scramble's revenue. The costs incurred in relation to maintaining the games at the same standard of performance are expensed to profit or loss for the year. The accounting policy note states that intangible assets are valued at historical cost. Scramble considers the games to have an indefinite useful life, which is reconsidered annually when the intangible assets are tested for impairment. Scramble determines value in use using the estimated future cash flows which include maintenance expenses, capital expenses incurred in developing different versions of the games and the expected increase in turnover resulting from the above mentioned cash outflows. Scramble does not conduct an analysis or investigation of differences between expected and actual cash flows. Tax effects were also taken into account. **(7 marks)**

(b) Scramble has two cash generating units (CGU) which hold 90% of the internally developed intangible assets. Scramble reported a consolidated net loss for the period and an impairment charge in respect of the two CGUs representing 63% of the consolidated profit before tax and 29% of the total costs in the period. The recoverable amount of the CGUs is defined, in this case, as value in use. Specific discount rates are not directly available from the market, and Scramble estimates the discount rates, using its weighted average cost of capital. In calculating the cost of debt as an input to the determination of the discount rate, Scramble used the risk-free rate adjusted by the company specific average credit spread of its outstanding debt, which had been raised two years previously. As Scramble did not have any need for additional financing and did not need to repay any of the existing loans before 20X4, Scramble did not see any reason for using a different discount rate. Scramble did not disclose either the events and circumstances that led to the recognition of the impairment loss or the amount of the loss recognised in respect of each cash-generating unit. Scramble felt that the events and circumstances that led to the recognition of a loss in respect of the first CGU were common knowledge in the market and the events and the circumstances that led to the recognition loss of the second CGU were not needed to be disclosed. **(7 marks)**

(c) Scramble wished to diversify its operations and purchased a professional football club, Rashing. In Rashing's financial statements for the year ended 30 November 20X1, it was proposed to include significant intangible assets which related to acquired players' registration rights comprising registration and agents' fees. The agents' fees were paid by the club to players' agents either when a player is transferred to the club or when the contract of a player is extended. Scramble believes that the registration rights of the players are intangible assets but that the agents fees do not meet the criteria to be recognised as intangible assets as they are not directly attributable to the costs of players' contracts. Additionally, Rashing has purchased the rights to 25% of the revenue from ticket sales generated by another football club, Santash, in a different league. Rashing does not sell these tickets nor has any discretion over the pricing of the tickets. Rashing wishes to show these rights as intangible assets in its financial statements. **(9 marks)**

Required

Discuss the validity of the accounting treatments proposed by Scramble in its financial statements for the year ended 30 November 20X1.

The mark allocation is shown against each of the three accounting treatments above.

Professional marks will be awarded for clarity and expression of your discussion. **(2 marks)**

(Total = 25 marks)

10 Preparation question: Defined benefit plan

BPP Note. In this question, proformas are given to you to help you get used to setting out your answer. You may wish to transfer them to a separate sheet, or alternatively to use a separate sheet for your workings.

Brutus Co operates a defined benefit pension plan for its employees conditional on a minimum employment period of six years. The present value of the future benefit obligations and the fair value of its plan assets on 1 January 20X1 were $110 million and $150 million respectively.

The pension plan received contributions of $7m and paid pensions to former employees of $10m during the year.

Extracts from the most recent actuary's report show the following:

Present value of pension plan obligation at 31 December 20X1	$116m
Fair value of plan assets at 31 December 20X1	$140m
Present cost of pensions earned in the period	$11m
Yield on high quality corporate bonds at 1 January 20X1	10%

On 1 January 20X1, the rules of the pension plan were changed to improve benefits for plan members. The actuary has advised that this will cost $10 million.

Required

Produce the extracts for the financial statements for the year ended 31 December 20X1.

Assume contributions and benefits were paid on 31 December.

Statement of profit or loss and other comprehensive income notes

Defined benefit expense recognised in profit or loss

	$m
Current service cost	
Past service cost	
Net interest on the net defined benefit asset	___
	===

Other comprehensive income (items that will not be reclassified to profit or loss)
Remeasurement of defined benefit plans

	$m
Actuarial gain on defined benefit obligation	
Return on plan assets (excluding amounts in net interest)	___
	===

Statement of financial position notes

Net defined benefit asset recognised in the statement of financial position

	31 December 20X1 $m	31 December 20X0 $m
Present value of pension obligation		
Fair value of plan assets		
Net asset	___	___
	===	===

Changes in the present value of the defined benefit obligation

	$m
Opening defined benefit obligation	
Interest on obligation	
Current service cost	
Past service cost	
Benefits paid	
Gain on remeasurement of obligation(balancing figure)	___
Closing defined benefit obligation	═══

Changes in the fair value of plan assets

	$m
Opening fair value of plan assets	
Interest on plan assets	
Contributions	
Benefits paid	
Loss on remeasurement of assets (balancing figure)	___
Closing fair value of plan assets	═══

11 Macaljoy
45 mins

12/07, amended

Macaljoy, a public limited company, is a leading support services company which focuses on the building industry. The company would like advice on how to treat certain items under IAS 19 *Employee benefits* and IAS 37 *Provisions, contingent liabilities and contingent assets*. The company operates the Macaljoy Pension Plan B which commenced on 1 November 20X6 and the Macaljoy Pension Plan A, which was closed to new entrants from 31 October 20X6, but which was open to future service accrual for the employees already in the scheme. The assets of the schemes are held separately from those of the company in funds under the control of trustees. The following information relates to the two schemes.

Macaljoy Pension Plan A

The terms of the plan are as follows.

(i)   Employees contribute 6% of their salaries to the plan.
(ii)   Macaljoy contributes, currently, the same amount to the plan for the benefit of the employees.
(iii)   On retirement, employees are guaranteed a pension which is based upon the number of years service with the company and their final salary.

The following details relate to the plan in the year to 31 October 20X7:

	$m
Present value of obligation at 1 November 20X6	200
Present value of obligation at 31 October 20X7	240
Fair value of plan assets at 1 November 20X6	190
Fair value of plan assets at 31 October 20X7	225
Current service cost	20
Pension benefits paid	19
Total contributions paid to the scheme for year to 31 October 20X7	17

Remeasurement gains and losses are recognised in accordance with IAS 19 as revised in 2011.

Macaljoy Pension Plan B

Under the terms of the plan, Macaljoy does not guarantee any return on the contributions paid into the fund. The company's legal and constructive obligation is limited to the amount that is contributed to the fund. The following details relate to this scheme:

	$m
Fair value of plan assets at 31 October 20X7	21
Contributions paid by company for year to 31 October 20X7	10
Contributions paid by employees for year to 31 October 20X7	10

The interest rate on high quality corporate bonds for the two plans are:

1 November 20X6   31 October 20X7
    5%   6%

The company would like advice on how to treat the two pension plans, for the year ended 31 October 20X7, together with an explanation of the differences between a defined contribution plan and a defined benefit plan.

Warranties

Additionally the company manufactures and sells building equipment on which it gives a standard one year warranty to all customers. The company has extended the warranty to two years for certain major customers and has insured against the cost of the second year of the warranty. The warranty has been extended at nil cost to the customer. The claims made under the extended warranty are made in the first instance against Macaljoy and then Macaljoy in turn makes a counter claim against the insurance company. Past experience has shown that 80% of the building equipment will not be subject to warranty claims in the first year, 15% will have minor defects and 5% will require major repair. Macaljoy estimates that in the second year of the warranty, 20% of the items sold will have minor defects and 10% will require major repair.

In the year to 31 October 20X7, the following information is relevant.

	Standard warranty (units)	*Extended warranty* (units)	*Selling price per unit* (both)($)
Sales	2,000	5,000	1,000

	Major repair $	*Minor defect* $
Cost of repair (average)	500	100

Assume that sales of equipment are on 31 October 20X7 and any warranty claims are made on 31 October in the year of the claim. Assume a risk adjusted discount rate of 4%.

Required

Draft a report suitable for presentation to the directors of Macaljoy which:

(a)   (i)   Discusses the nature of and differences between a defined contribution plan and a defined benefit plan with specific reference to the company's two schemes.   **(7 marks)**

      (ii) Shows the accounting treatment for the two Macaljoy pension plans for the year ended 31 October 20X7 under IAS 19 *Employee benefits* (revised 2011).   **(7 marks)**

(b)   (i)   Discusses the principles involved in accounting for claims made under the above warranty provision.
                                                                                                (6 marks)

      (ii) Shows the accounting treatment for the above warranty provision under IAS 37 *Provisions, contingent liabilities and contingent assets* for the year ended 31 October 20X7.   **(3 marks)**

Appropriateness of the format and presentation of the report and communication of advice.   **(2 marks)**

                                                                                        (Total = 25 marks)

12 Smith   45 mins

6/09, amended

(a)   Accounting for defined benefit pension schemes is a complex area of great importance. In some cases, the net pension liability even exceeds the market capitalisation of the company. The financial statements of a company must provide investors, analysts and companies with clear, reliable and comparable information on a company's pension obligations and interest on net plan assets/obligations.

      Required

      (i)   Discuss the problems associated with IAS 19 *Employee benefits* prior to its revision in June 2011 regarding the accounting for actuarial gains and losses, setting out the main criticisms of the approach taken under the old version of the standard.   **(6 marks)**

(ii) Outline the advantages of immediate recognition of such gains and losses. **(4 marks)**

(iii) Discuss the other main changes to IAS 19 when it was revised in June 2011, explaining how the revised treatment differed from the previous treatment. **(5 marks)**

(iv) Outline the likely consequences of the revision of IAS 19. **(5 marks)**

Professional marks will be awarded in part (a) for clarity and quality of discussion. **(2 marks)**

(b) Smith operates a defined benefit pension plan for its employees. At 1 January 20X2 the fair value of the pension plan assets was $2,600,000 and the present value of the plan liabilities was $2,900,000.

The actuary estimates that the current and past service costs for the year ended 31 December 20X2 is $450,000 and $90,000 respectively. The past service cost is caused by an increase in pension benefits and takes effect from 31 December 20X2. The plan liabilities at 1 January and 31 December 20X2 correctly reflect the impact of this increase.

The interest rate on high quality corporate bonds for the year ended 31 December 20X2 was 8%.

The pension plan paid $240,000 to retired members on 31 December 20X2. On the same date, Smith paid $730,000 in contributions to the pension plan and this included $90,000 in respect of past service costs.

At 31 December 20X2 the fair value of the pension plan assets is $3,400,000 and the present value of the plan liabilities is $3,500,000.

In accordance with the 2011 revision to IAS 19 *Employee benefits*, Smith recognises actuarial gains and losses (now called 'remeasurement gains and losses') in other comprehensive income in the period in which they occur.

Required

Calculate the remeasurement gains or losses on pension plan assets and liabilities that will be included in other comprehensive income for the year ended 31 December 20X2. (Round all figures to the nearest $'000.) **(3 marks)**

(Total = 25 marks)

13 Ryder

45 mins

ACR, 12/05

Ryder, a public limited company, is reviewing certain events which have occurred since its year end of 31 October 20X5. The financial statements were authorised on 12 December 20X5. The following events are relevant to the financial statements for the year ended 31 October 20X5:

(a) Ryder disposed of a wholly owned subsidiary, Krup, a public limited company, on 10 December 20X5 and made a loss of $9 million on the transaction in the group financial statements. As at 31 October 20X5, Ryder had no intention of selling the subsidiary which was material to the group. The directors of Ryder have stated that there were no significant events which have occurred since 31 October 20X5 which could have resulted in a reduction in the value of Krup. The carrying value of the net assets and purchased goodwill of Krup at 31 October 20X5 were $20 million and $12 million respectively. Krup had made a loss of $2 million in the period 1 November 20X5 to 10 December 20X5. **(6 marks)**

(b) Ryder acquired a wholly owned subsidiary, Metalic, a public limited company, on 21 January 20X4. The consideration payable in respect of the acquisition of Metalic was 2 million ordinary shares of $1 of Ryder plus a further 300,000 ordinary shares if the profit of Metalic exceeded $6 million for the year ended 31 October 20X5. The profit for the year of Metalic was $7 million and the ordinary shares were issued on 12 November 20X5. The annual profits of Metalic had averaged $7 million over the last few years and, therefore, Ryder had included an estimate of the contingent consideration in the cost of the acquisition at 21 January 20X4. The fair value used for the ordinary shares of Ryder at this date including the contingent consideration was $10 per share. The fair value of the ordinary shares on 12 November 20X5 was $11 per share. Ryder also made a one for four bonus issue on 13 November 20X5 which was applicable to the contingent shares issued. The directors are unsure of the impact of the above on the accounting for the acquisition. **(8 marks)**

(c)   The company acquired a property on 1 November 20X4 which it intended to sell. The property was obtained as a result of a default on a loan agreement by a third party and was valued at $20 million on that date for accounting purposes which exactly offset the defaulted loan. The property is in a state of disrepair and Ryder intends to complete the repairs before it sells the property. The repairs were completed on 30 November 20X5. The property was sold after costs for $27 million on 9 December 20X5. The property was classified as 'held for sale' at the year end under IFRS 5 *Non-current assets held for sale and discontinued operations* but shown at the net sale proceeds of $27 million. Property is depreciated at 5% per annum on the straight-line basis and no depreciation has been charged in the year.   **(6 marks)**

(d)   The company granted share appreciation rights (SARs) to its employees on 1 November 20X3 based on ten million shares. The SARs provide employees at the date the rights are exercised with the right to receive cash equal to the appreciation in the company's share price since the grant date. The rights vested on 31 October 20X5 and payment was made on schedule on 1 December 20X5. The fair value of the SARs per share at 31 October 20X4 was $6, at 31 October 2005 was $8 and at 1 December 20X5 was $9. The company has recognised a liability for the SARs as at 31 October 20X4 based upon IFRS 2 *Share-based payment* but the liability was stated at the same amount at 31 October 20X5.   **(5 marks)**

Required

Discuss the accounting treatment of the above events in the financial statements of the Ryder Group for the year ended 31 October 20X5, taking into account the implications of events occurring after the end of the reporting period.

(The mark allocations are set out after each paragraph above.)   **(Total = 25 marks)**

14 Royan   **27 mins**

6/12, amended

(a)   Discuss the guidance in IAS 37 *Provisions, contingent liabilities and contingent assets* as regards the recognition and measurement of provisions and why it might be felt necessary to replace this guidance.
                                                                                   (10 marks)

(b)   Royan, a public limited company, extracts oil and has a present obligation to dismantle an oil platform at the end of the platform's life, which is ten years. Royan cannot cancel this obligation or transfer it. Royan intends to carry out the dismantling work itself and estimates the cost of the work to be $150 million in ten years' time. The present value of the work is $105 million.

A market exists for the dismantling of an oil platform and Royan could hire a third party contractor to carry out the work. The entity feels that if no risk or probability adjustment were needed then the cost of the external contractor would be $180 million in ten years' time. The present value of this cost is $129 million. If risk and probability are taken into account, then there is a probability of 40% that the present value will be $129 million and 60% probability that it would be $140 million, and there is a risk that the costs may increase by $5 million.

Required

Describe the accounting treatment of the above events under IAS 37.   **(3 marks)**

Professional marks will be awarded for the quality of the discussion.   **(2 marks)**

                                                                                   (Total = 15 marks)

15 Electron   **45 mins**

Pilot paper

Electron, a public limited company, operates in the energy sector. The company has grown significantly over the last few years and is currently preparing its financial statements for the year ended 30 June 20X6.

Electron buys and sells oil and currently has a number of oil trading contracts. The contracts to purchase oil are treated as non-current assets and amortised over the contracts' durations. On acceptance of a contract to sell oil, fifty per cent of the contract price is recognised immediately with the balance being recognised over the remaining life of the contract. The contracts always result in the delivery of the commodity. **(4 marks)**

Electron has recently constructed an ecologically efficient power station. A condition of being granted the operating licence by the government is that the power station be dismantled at the end of its life which is estimated to be 20 years. The power station cost $100 million and began production on 1 July 20X5. Depreciation is charged on the power station using the straight line method. Electron has estimated at 30 June 20X6 that it will cost $15 million (net present value) to restore the site to its original condition using a discount rate of five per cent. Ninety-five per cent of these costs relate to the removal of the power station and five per cent relates to the damage caused through generating energy. **(7 marks)**

Electron has leased another power station, which was relatively inefficient, to a rival company on 30 June 20X6. The beneficial and legal ownership remains with Electron and in the event of one of Electron's power stations being unable to produce energy, Electron can terminate the agreement. The leased power station is being treated as an operating lease with the net present value of the income of $40 million being recognised in profit or loss. The fair value of the power station is $70 million at 30 June 20X6. A deposit of $10 million was received on 30 June 20X6 and it is included in the net present value calculation. **(5 marks)**

The company has a good relationship with its shareholders and employees. It has adopted a strategy of gradually increasing its dividend payments over the years. On 1 August 20X6, the board proposed a dividend of 5c per share for the year ended 30 June 20X6. The shareholders will approve the dividend along with the financial statements at the general meeting on 1 September 20X6 and the dividend will be paid on 14 September 20X6. The directors feel that the dividend should be accrued in the financial statements for the year ended 30 June 20X6 as a 'valid expectation' has been created. **(3 marks)**

The company granted share options to its employees on 1 July 20X5. The fair value of the options at that date was $3 million. The options vest on 30 June 20X8. The employees have to be employed at the end of the three year period for the options to vest and the following estimates have been made:

Estimated percentage of employees leaving during vesting period at:

Grant date 1 July 20X5	5%	
30 June 20X6	6%	**(4 marks)**
Effective communication to the directors		**(2 marks)**

Required

Draft a report suitable for presentation to the directors of Electron which discusses the accounting treatment of the above transactions in the financial statements for the year ended 30 June 20X6, including relevant calculations.

(Total = 25 marks)

16 Cohort

40 mins

ACR, 6/02, amended

is a private limited company and has two 100% owned subsidiaries, Legion and Air, both themselves private limited companies. Cohort acquired Air on 1 January 20X2 for $5 million when the fair value of the net assets was $4 million, and the tax base of the net assets was $3.5 million. The acquisition of Air and Legion was part of a business strategy whereby Cohort would build up the 'value' of the group over a three year period and then list its existing share capital on the stock exchange.

(a)   The following details relate to the acquisition of Air, which manufactures electronic goods.

   (i)   Air has sold goods worth $3 million to Cohort since acquisition and made a profit of $1 million on the transaction. The inventory of these goods recorded in Cohort's statement of financial position at the year end of 31 May 20X2 was $1.8 million.

   (ii)   The balance on the retained earnings of Air at acquisition was $2 million. The directors of Cohort have decided that, during the three years to the date that they intend to list the shares of the company, they will realise earnings through future dividend payments from the subsidiary amounting to $500,000 per year. Tax is payable on any remittance or dividends and no dividends have been declared for the current year. **(10 marks)**

(b)   Legion was acquired on 1 June 20X1 and is a company which undertakes various projects ranging from debt factoring to investing in property and commodities. The following details relate to Legion for the year ending 31 May 20X2.

    (i)   Legion has a portfolio of readily marketable government securities which are held as current assets. These investments are stated at market value in the statement of financial position with any gain or loss taken to profit or loss for the year. These gains and losses are taxed when the investments are sold. Currently the accumulated unrealised gains are $4 million.

    (ii)   Legion has calculated that it requires a specific allowance of $2 million against loans in its portfolio. Tax relief is available when the specific loan is written off.

    (iii)   When Cohort acquired Legion it had unused tax losses brought forward. At 1 June 20X1, it appeared that Legion would have sufficient taxable profit to realise the deferred tax asset created by these losses but subsequent events have proven that the future taxable profit will not be sufficient to realise all of the unused tax loss.

The current tax rate for Cohort is 30% and for public companies is 35%. **(12 marks)**

Required

Write a note suitable for presentation to the partner of an accounting firm setting out the deferred tax implications of the above information for the Cohort Group of companies.

(Total = 22 marks)

17 Panel

45 mins

ACR, 12/05

The directors of Panel, a public limited company, are reviewing the procedures for the calculation of the deferred tax liability for their company. They are quite surprised at the impact on the liability caused by changes in accounting standards such as IFRS 1 *First time adoption of International Financial Reporting Standards* and IFRS 2 *Share-based payment*. Panel is adopting International Financial Reporting Standards for the first time as at 31 October 20X5 and the directors are unsure how the deferred tax provision will be calculated in its financial statements ended on that date including the opening provision at 1 November 20X3.

Required

(a)   (i)   Explain how changes in accounting standards are likely to have an impact on the deferred tax liability under IAS 12 *Income taxes*. **(5 marks)**

    (ii)   Describe the basis for the calculation of the deferred taxation liability on first time adoption of IFRS including the provision in the opening IFRS statement of financial position. **(4 marks)**

Additionally the directors wish to know how the provision for deferred taxation would be calculated in the following situations under IAS 12 *Income taxes*:

(i)   On 1 November 20X3, the company had granted ten million share options worth $40 million subject to a two year vesting period. Local tax law allows a tax deduction at the exercise date of the intrinsic value of the options. The intrinsic value of the ten million share options at 31 October 20X4 was $16 million and at 31 October 20X5 was $46 million. The increase in the share price in the year to 31 October 20X5 could not be foreseen at 31 October 20X4. The options were exercised at 31 October 20X5. The directors are unsure how to account for deferred taxation on this transaction for the years ended 31 October 20X4 and 31 October 20X5.

(ii)   Panel is leasing plant under a finance lease over a five year period. The asset was recorded at the present value of the minimum lease payments of $12 million at the inception of the lease which was 1 November 20X4. The asset is depreciated on a straight line basis over the five years and has no residual value. The annual lease payments are $3 million payable in arrears on 31 October and the effective interest rate is 8% per annum. The directors have not leased an asset under a finance lease before and are unsure as to its treatment for deferred taxation. The company can claim a tax deduction for the annual rental payment as the finance lease does not qualify for tax relief.

(iii) A wholly owned overseas subsidiary, Pins, a limited liability company, sold goods costing $7 million to Panel on 1 September 20X5, and these goods had not been sold by Panel before the year end. Panel had paid $9 million for these goods. The directors do not understand how this transaction should be dealt with in the financial statements of the subsidiary and the group for taxation purposes. Pins pays tax locally at 30%.

(iv) Nails, a limited liability company, is a wholly owned subsidiary of Panel, and is a cash generating unit in its own right. The value of the property, plant and equipment of Nails at 31 October 20X5 was $6 million and purchased goodwill was $1 million before any impairment loss. The company had no other assets or liabilities. An impairment loss of $1.8 million had occurred at 31 October 20X5. The tax base of the property, plant and equipment of Nails was $4 million as at 31 October 20X5. The directors wish to know how the impairment loss will affect the deferred tax liability for the year. Impairment losses are not an allowable expense for taxation purposes.

Assume a tax rate of 30%.

Required

(b) Discuss, with suitable computations, how the situations (i) to (iv) above will impact on the accounting for deferred tax under IAS 12 *Income taxes* in the group financial statements of Panel.   **(16 marks)**

(The situations in (i) to (iv) above carry equal marks.)   **(Total = 25 marks)**

18 Kesare

45 mins

Pilot paper

The following statement of financial position relates to Kesare Group, a public limited company, at 30 June 20X6.

	$'000
Assets	
Non current assets:	
Property, plant and equipment	10,000
Goodwill	6,000
Other intangible assets	5,000
Financial assets (cost)	9,000
	30,000
Current assets	
Trade receivables	7,000
Other receivables	4,600
Cash and cash equivalents	6,700
	18,300
Total assets	48,300
Equity and liabilities	
Equity	
Share capital	9,000
Other reserves	4,500
Retained earnings	9,130
Total equity	22,630
Non-current liabilities	
Long term borrowings	10,000
Deferred tax liability	3,600
Employee benefit liability	4,000
Total non-current liabilities	17,600
Current liabilities	
Current tax liability	3,070
Trade and other payables	5,000
Total current liabilities	8,070
Total liabilities	25,670

Total equity and liabilities   48,300

The following information is relevant to the above statement of financial position:

(i)   The financial assets are classified as 'investments in equity instruments' but are shown in the above statement of financial position at their cost on 1 July 20X5. The market value of the assets is $10.5 million on 30 June 20X6. Taxation is payable on the sale of the assets. As allowed by IFRS 9, an irrevocable election was made for changes in fair value to go through other comprehensive income (not reclassified to profit or loss).

(ii)   The stated interest rate for the long term borrowing is 8%. The loan of $10 million represents a convertible bond which has a liability component of $9.6 million and an equity component of $0.4 million. The bond was issued on 30 June 20X6.

(iii)   The defined benefit plan had a rule change on 1 July 20X5, giving rise to past service costs of $520,000. The past service costs have not been accounted for.

(iv)   The tax bases of the assets and liabilities are the same as their carrying amounts in the draft statement of financial position above as at 30 June 20X6 except for the following:

(1)

	$'000
Property, plant and equipment	2,400
Trade receivables	7,500
Other receivables	5,000
Employee benefits	5,000

(2)   Other intangible assets were development costs which were all allowed for tax purposes when the cost was incurred in 20X5.

(3)   Trade and other payables includes an accrual for compensation to be paid to employees. This amounts to $1 million and is allowed for taxation when paid.

(v)   Goodwill is not allowable for tax purposes in this jurisdiction.

(vi)   Assume taxation is payable at 30%.

Required

(a)   Discuss the conceptual basis for the recognition of deferred taxation using the temporary difference approach to deferred taxation.   **(7 marks)**

(b)   Calculate the deferred tax liability at 30 June 20X6 after any necessary adjustments to the financial statements showing how the deferred tax liability would be dealt with in the financial statements. (Assume that any adjustments do not affect current tax. Candidates should briefly discuss the adjustments required to calculate deferred tax liability.)   **(18 marks)**

(Total = 25 marks)

Two marks will be awarded for the quality of the discussion of the conceptual basis of deferred taxation in (a).

19 Preparation question: Financial instruments

(a)   Graben Co purchases a bond for $441,014 on 1 January 20X1. It will be redeemed on 31 December 20X4 for $600,000. The bond is held at amortised cost and carries no coupon.

Required

Calculate the valuation of the bond for the statement of financial position as at 31 December 20X1 and the finance income for 20X1 shown in profit or loss.

Compound sum of $1: $(1 + r)^n$

Year	2%	4%	6%	8%	10%	12%	14%
1	1.0200	1.0400	1.0600	1.0800	1.1000	1.1200	1.1400
2	1.0404	1.0816	1.1236	1.1664	1.2100	1.2544	1.2996
3	1.0612	1.1249	1.1910	1.2597	1.3310	1.4049	1.4815
4	1.0824	1.1699	1.2625	1.3605	1.4641	1.5735	1.6890
5	1.1041	1.2167	1.3382	1.4693	1.6105	1.7623	1.9254

(b)   Baldie Co issues 4,000 convertible bonds on 1 January 20X2 at par. The bond is redeemable three years later at its par value of $500 per bond, which is its nominal value.

The bonds pay interest annually in arrears at an interest rate (based on nominal value) of 5%. Each bond can be converted at the maturity date into 30 $1 shares.

The prevailing market interest rate for three year bonds that have no right of conversion is 9%.

Required

Show the statement of financial position valuation at 1 January 20X2.

Cumulative three year annuity factors:

5%   2.723
9%   2.531

20 Bental

45 mins

12/13, amended

(a)   Bental, a listed bank, has a subsidiary, Hexal, which has two classes of shares, A and B. A-shares carry voting powers and B-shares are issued to meet Hexal's regulatory requirements. Under the terms of a shareholders' agreement, each shareholder is obliged to capitalise any dividends in the form of additional investment in B-shares. The shareholder agreement also stipulates that Bental agrees to buy the B-shares of the minority shareholders through a put option under the following conditions

(i)   The minority shareholders can exercise their put options when their ownership in B-shares exceeds the regulatory requirement, or

(ii)   The minority shareholders can exercise their put options every three years. The exercise price is the original cost paid by the shareholders.

In Bental's consolidated financial statements, the B-shares owned by minority shareholders are to be reported as a non-controlling interest.   **(7 marks)**

(b)   Bental has entered into a number of swap arrangements. Some of these transactions qualified for cash flow hedge accounting in accordance with IFRS 9 *Financial instruments* (July 2014). The hedges were considered to be effective. At 30 November 20X3, Bental decided it wishes to cancel the hedging relationships and had to pay compensation. The forecast hedged transactions were still expected to occur and Bental wishes to recognise the entire amount of the compensation in profit or loss. The hedging relationships still meet the risk management objective and continue to meet all other qualifying criteria.

Additionally, Bental also has an investment in a foreign entity over which it has significant influence and therefore accounts for the entity as an associate. The entity's functional currency differs from Bental's and in the consolidated financial statements, the associate's results fluctuate with changes in the exchange rate. Bental wishes to designate the investment as a hedged item in a fair value hedge in its individual and consolidated financial statements.   **(6 marks)**

(c)   On 1 September 20X3, Bental entered into a business combination with another listed bank, Lental. The business combination has taken place in two stages, which were contingent upon each other. On 1 September 20X3, Bental acquired 45% of the share capital and voting rights of Lental for cash. On 1 November 20X3, Lental merged with Bental and Bental issued new A-shares to Lental's shareholders for their 55% interest.

On 31 August 20X3, Bental had a market value of $70 million and Lental a market value of $90 million. Bental's business represents 45% and Lental's business 55% of the total value of the combined businesses.

After the transaction, the former shareholders of Bental excluding those of Lental owned 51% and the former shareholders of Lental owned 49% of the votes of the combined entity. The Chief Operating Officer (COO) of Lental is the biggest individual owner of the combined entity with a 25% interest. The purchase agreement provides for a board of six directors for the combined entity, five of whom will be former board members of Bental with one seat reserved for a former board member of Lental. The board of directors nominates the members of the management team. The management comprised the COO and four other members, two from Bental and two from Lental. Under the terms of the purchase agreement, the COO of Lental is the COO of the combined entity.

Bental proposes to account for the transaction as a business combination and identify Lental as the acquirer.

(10 marks)

Required

Discuss whether the accounting practices and policies outlined above are acceptable under International Financial Reporting Standards.

Note. The mark allocation is shown against each of the three issues above.

Professional marks will be awarded in question 3 for clarity and quality of presentation. **(2 marks)**

(Total = 25 marks)

21 Avco   45 mins

6/14 amended

(a)   The difference between debt and equity in an entity's statement of financial position is not easily distinguishable for preparers of financial statements. Some financial instruments may have both features, which can lead to inconsistency of reporting. The International Accounting Standards Board (IASB) has agreed that greater clarity may be required in its definitions of assets and liabilities for debt instruments. It is thought that defining the nature of liabilities would help the IASB's thinking on the difference between financial instruments classified as equity and liabilities.

   Required

   (i)   Discuss the key classification differences between debt and equity under International Financial Reporting Standards.

           Note. Examples should be given to illustrate your answer. **(9 marks)**

   (ii)   Explain why it is important for entities to understand the impact of the classification of a financial instrument as debt or equity in the financial statements. **(5 marks)**

(b)   The directors of Avco, a public limited company, are reviewing the financial statements of two entities which are acquisition targets, Cavor and Lidan.They have asked for clarification on the treatment of the following financial instruments within the financial statements of the entities.

   Cavor has two classes of shares: A and B shares. A shares are Cavor's ordinary shares and are correctly classed as equity. B shares are not mandatorily redeemable shares but contain a call option allowing Cavor to repurchase them. Dividends are payable on the B shares if, and only if, dividends have been paid on the A ordinary shares. The terms of the B shares are such that dividends are payable at a rate equal to that of the A ordinary shares. Additionally, Cavor has also issued share options which give the counterparty rights to buy a fixed number of its B shares for a fixed amount of $10 million. The contract can be settled only by the issuance of shares for cash by Cavor.

   Lidan has in issue two classes of shares: A shares and B shares. A shares are correctly classified as equity. Two million B shares of nominal value of $1 each are in issue. The B shares are redeemable in two years' time. Lidan has a choice as to the method of redemption of the B shares. It may either redeem the B shares for cash at their nominal value or it may issue one million A shares in settlement. A shares are currently valued at $10 per share. The lowest price for Lidan's A shares since its formation has been $5 per share.

Required

Discuss whether the above arrangements regarding the B shares of each of Cavor and Lidan should be treated as liabilities or equity in the financial statements of the respective issuing companies.   **(9 marks)**

Professional marks will be awarded in this question for clarity and quality of presentation.   **(2 marks)**

(Total = 25 marks)

22 Complexity

45 mins

12/09

The definition of a financial instrument captures a wide variety of assets and liabilities including cash, evidence of an ownership interest in an entity, or a contractual right to receive or deliver cash or another financial instrument. Preparers, auditors and users of financial statements have found the requirements for reporting financial assets and liabilities to be very complex, problematical and sometimes subjective. The result is that there is a need to develop new standards of reporting for financial instruments that are principle-based and significantly less complex than current requirements. It is important that a standard in this area should allow users to understand the economic substance of the transaction and preparers to properly apply generally accepted accounting principles.

Required

(a)   (i)   Discuss how the measurement of financial instruments under International Financial Reporting Standards can create confusion and complexity for preparers and users of financial statements.

(9 marks)

(ii)   Set out the reasons why using fair value to measure all financial instruments may result in less complexity in accounting for financial instruments, but may lead to uncertainty in financial statements.   **(9 marks)**

Professional marks will be awarded in part (a) for clarity and expression.   **(2 marks)**

(b)   A company borrowed $47 million on 1 December 20X4 when the market and effective interest rate was 5%. On 30 November 20X5, the company borrowed an additional $45 million when the current market and effective interest rate was 7.4%. Both financial liabilities are repayable on 30 November 20X9 and are single payment notes, whereby interest and capital are repaid on that date.

Required

Discuss the accounting for the above financial liabilities under current accounting standards using amortised cost, and additionally using fair value as at 30 November 20X5.   **(5 marks)**

(Total = 25 marks)

23 Ambush

45 mins

ACR, 12/05, amended

(a)   IFRS 9 *Financial instruments* was published in final form in July 2014. The final version of the standard incorporated the new requirements on impairment of financial assets.

Required

Outline the requirements of IFRS 9 as regards the impairment of financial assets.   **(10 marks)**

(b)   On 1 December 20X4, Ambush sold goods on credit to Tray for $600,000. Tray has a credit limit with Ambush of 60 days. Ambush applies IFRS 9 *Financial instruments*, and uses a pre-determined matrix for the calculation of allowances for receivables as follows.

Days overdue	Expected loss provision
Nil	1%
1 to 30	5%
31 to 60	15%
61 to 90	20%
90 +	25%

Tray had not paid by 31 January 20X5, and so failed to comply with its credit term, and Ambush learned that Tray was having serious cash flow difficulties due to a loss of a key customer. The finance controller of Tray has informed Ambush that they will receive payment.

Ignore sales tax.

Required

Show the accounting entries on 1 December 20X4 and 31 January 20X5 to record the above, in accordance with the expected credit loss model in IFRS 9. **(6 marks)**

(c) Ambush is reviewing the accounting treatment of its buildings. The company uses the 'revaluation model' for its buildings. The buildings had originally cost $10 million on 1 December 20X3 and had a useful economic life of 20 years. They are being depreciated on a straight line basis to a nil residual value. The buildings were revalued downwards on 30 November 20X4 to $8 million which was the buildings' recoverable amount. At 30 November 20X5 the value of the buildings had risen to $11 million which is to be included in the financial statements. The company is unsure how to treat the above events. **(9 marks)**

(Total = 25 marks)

24 Aron

45 mins

6/09, amended

The directors of Aron, a public limited company, are worried about the challenging market conditions which the company is facing. The markets are volatile and illiquid. The central government is injecting liquidity into the economy. The directors are concerned about the significant shift towards the use of fair values in financial statements. IFRS 9 *Financial instruments* in conjunction with IFRS 13 *Fair value measurement* defines fair value and requires the initial measurement of financial instruments to be at fair value. The directors are uncertain of the relevance of fair value measurements in these current market conditions.

Required

(a) Briefly discuss how the fair value of financial instruments is measured, commenting on the relevance of fair value measurements for financial instruments where markets are volatile and illiquid. **(4 marks)**

(b) Further they would like advice on accounting for the following transactions within the financial statements for the year ended 31 May 20X8.

(i) Aron issued one million convertible bonds on 1 June 20X5. The bonds had a term of three years and were issued with a total fair value of $100 million which is also the par value. Interest is paid annually in arrears at a rate of 6% per annum and bonds, without the conversion option, attracted an interest rate of 9% per annum on 1 June 20X5. The company incurred issue costs of $1 million. If the investor did not convert to shares they would have been redeemed at par. At maturity all of the bonds were converted into 25 million ordinary shares of $1 of Aron. No bonds could be converted before that date. The directors are uncertain how the bonds should have been accounted for up to the date of the conversion on 31 May 20X8 and have been told that the impact of the issue costs is to increase the effective interest rate to 9.38%. **(6 marks)**

(ii) Aron held a 3% holding of the shares in Smart, a public limited company, The investment was classified as an investment in equity instruments and at 31 May 20X8 had a carrying value of $5 million (brought forward from the previous period). As permitted by IFRS 9 *Financial instruments*, Aron had made an irrevocable election to recognise all changes in fair value in other comprehensive income (items that will not be reclassified to profit or loss). The cumulative gain to 31 May 20X7 recognised in other comprehensive income relating to the investment was $400,000. On 31 May 20X8, the whole of the share capital of Smart was acquired by Given, a public limited company, and as a result, Aron received shares in Given with a fair value of $5.5 million in exchange for its holding in Smart. The company wishes to know how the exchange of shares in Smart for the shares in Given should be accounted for in its financial records. **(4 marks)**

(iii)   The functional and presentation currency of Aron is the dollar ($). Aron has a wholly owned foreign subsidiary, Gao, whose functional currency is the zloti. Gao owns a debt instrument which is held for trading. In Gao's financial statements for the year ended 31 May 20X7, the debt instrument was carried at its fair value of 10 million zloty.

At 31 May 20X8, the fair value of the debt instrument had increased to 12 million zloty. The exchange rates were:

	Zloti to $1
31 May 20X7	3
31 May 20X8	2
Average rate for year to 31 May 20X8	2.5

The company wishes to know how to account for this instrument in Gao's entity financial statements and the consolidated financial statements of the group. **(5 marks)**

(iv)   Aron granted interest free loans to its employees on 1 June 20X7 of $10 million. The loans will be paid back on 31 May 20X9 as a single payment by the employees. The market rate of interest for a two year loan on both of the above dates is 6% per annum. The company is unsure how to account for the loan but wishes to hold the loans at amortised cost under IFRS 9 *Financial instruments*

(4 marks)

Required

Discuss, with relevant computations, how the above financial instruments should be accounted for in the financial statements for the year ended 31 May 20X8.

Note 1. The mark allocation is shown against each of the transactions above.

Note 2. The following discount and annuity factors may be of use.

	Discount factors			Annuity factors		
	6%	9%	9.38%	6%	9%	9.38%
1 year	0.9434	0.9174	0.9142	0.9434	0.9174	0.9174
2 years	0.8900	0.8417	0.8358	1.8334	1.7591	1.7500
3 years	0.8396	0.7722	0.7642	2.6730	2.5313	2.5142

Professional marks will be awarded for clarity and quality of discussion. **(2 marks)**

(Total = 25 marks)

25 Preparation question: Leases

Sugar Co leased a machine from Spice Co. The terms of the lease are as follows:

Inception of lease	1 January 20X1
Lease term	4 years at $78,864 per annum payable in arrears
Present value of minimum lease payments	$250,000
Useful life of asset	4 years

Required

(a)   Calculate the interest rate implicit in the lease, using the table below.

This table shows the present value of $1 per annum, receivable or payable at the end of each year for n years.

Years (n)	Interest rates		
	6%	8%	10%
1	0.943	0.926	0.909
2	1.833	1.783	1.736
3	2.673	2.577	2.487
4	3.465	3.312	3.170
5	4.212	3.993	3.791

(b) Prepare the extracts from the financial statements of Sugar Co for the year ended 31 December 20X1. Notes to the accounts are not required.

26 Havanna

45 mins

12/13

(a) Havanna owns a chain of health clubs and has entered into binding contracts with sports organisations, which earn income over given periods. The services rendered in return for such income include access to Havanna's database of members, and admission to health clubs, including the provision of coaching and other benefits. These contracts are for periods of between nine and 18 months. Havanna feels that because it only assumes limited obligations under the contract mainly relating to the provision of coaching, this could not be seen as the rendering of services for accounting purposes. As a result, Havanna's accounting policy for revenue recognition is to recognise the contract income in full at the date when the contract was signed.

(6 marks)

(b) In May 20X3, Havanna decided to sell one of its regional business divisions through a mixed asset and share deal. The decision to sell the division at a price of $40 million was made public in November 20X3 and gained shareholder approval in December 20X3. It was decided that the payment of any agreed sale price could be deferred until 30 November 20X5. The business division was presented as a disposal group in the statement of financial position as at 30 November 20X3. At the initial classification of the division as held for sale, its net carrying amount was $90 million. In writing down the disposal group's carrying amount, Havanna accounted for an impairment loss of $30 million which represented the difference between the carrying amount and value of the assets measured in accordance with applicable International Financial Reporting Standards (IFRS).

In the financial statements at 30 November 20X3, Havanna showed the following costs as provisions relating to the continuing operations. These costs were related to the business division being sold and were as follows.

(i) A loss relating to a potential write-off of a trade receivable owed by Cuba Sport, which had gone into liquidation. Cuba Sport had sold the goods to a third party and the division had guaranteed the receipt of the sale proceeds to the Head Office of Havanna

(ii) An expense relating to the discounting of the long-term receivable on the fixed amount of the sale price of the disposal group

(iii) A provision was charged which related to the expected transaction costs of the sale including legal advice and lawyer fees

The directors wish to know how to treat the above transactions.

(9 marks)

(c) Havanna has decided to sell its main office building to a third party and lease it back on a ten-year lease. The lease has been classified as an operating lease. The current fair value of the property is $5 million and the carrying value of the asset is $4.2 million. The market for property is very difficult in the jurisdiction and Havanna therefore requires guidance on the consequences of selling the office building at a range of prices. The following prices have been achieved in the market during the last few months for similar office buildings.

(i) $5 million

(ii) $6 million

(iii) $4.8 million

(iv) $4 million

Havanna would like advice on how to account for the sale and leaseback, with an explanation of the effect which the different selling prices would have on the financial statements, assuming that the fair value of the property is $5 million.   **(8 marks)**

Required

Advise Havanna on how the above transactions should be dealt with in its financial statements with reference to International Financial Reporting Standards where appropriate.

Note. The mark allocation is shown against each of the three issues above.

Professional marks will be awarded in question 2 for clarity and quality of the presentation.   **(2 marks)**

(Total = 25 marks)

27 Holcombe

45 mins

6/10, amended

(a)   Leasing is important to Holcombe, a public limited company as a method of financing the business. The Directors feel that it is important that they provide users of financial statements with a complete and understandable picture of the entity's leasing activities. They believe that the current accounting model is inadequate and does not meet the needs of users of financial statements.

Holcombe has leased plant for a fixed term of six years and the useful life of the plant is 12 years. The lease is non-cancellable, and there are no rights to extend the lease term or purchase the machine at the end of the term. There are no guarantees of its value at that point. The lessor does not have the right of access to the plant until the end of the contract or unless permission is granted by Holcombe.

Fixed lease payments are due annually over the lease term after delivery of the plant, which is maintained by Holcombe. Holcombe accounts for the lease as an operating lease but the directors are unsure as to whether the accounting treatment of an operating lease is conceptually correct.

Required

(i)   Discuss the reasons why the current lease accounting standards may fail to meet the needs of users and could be said to be conceptually flawed.   **(6 marks)**

(ii)   Discuss whether the plant operating lease in the financial statements of Holcombe meets the definition of an asset and liability as set out in *Conceptual Framework for Financial Reporting*.

(7 marks)

(iii) Discuss the IASB's proposals to improve the reporting of leases.   **(4 marks)**

Professional marks will be awarded in part (a) (i) and (ii) for clarity and quality of discussion.   **(2 marks)**

(b) (i)   On 1 May 20X4, Holcombe entered into a short operating lease agreement to lease another building. The lease will last for three years and is currently $5 million per annum. However an inflation adjustment will be made at the conclusion of leasing years 1 and 2. Currently inflation is 4% per annum.

The following discount factors are relevant (8%).

	Single cash flow	Annuity
Year 1	0.926	0.926
Year 2	0.857	1.783
Year 3	0.794	2.577
Year 4	0.735	3.312
Year 5	0.681	3.993

Required

State how the inflation adjustment on this short term operating lease should be dealt with in the financial statements of Holcombe. **(3 marks)**

(ii)   Holcombe is considering entering a three-year lease of a machine from Brooke from 1 May 20X5. The machine has a total economic life of 20 years. The fair value of the machine at 1 May 20X5 is $113,600.

The lease payments are $13,000 per year, and the present value of the lease payments is $21,700, calculated using the rate Brooke charges Holcombe.

The directors of Holcombe have heard about the proposals for revising the classification of leases, and wish to know whether the lease from Brooke would be classified as a 'Type A' lease or a 'Type B' lease under those proposals.

Required

Advise the directors on the appropriate classification. **(3 marks)**
(Total = 25 marks)

28 William
45 mins

6/12

William is a public limited company and would like advice in relation to the following transactions.

(a)   William owned a building on which it raised finance. William sold the building for $5 million to a finance company on 1 June 20X2 when the carrying amount was $3.5 million. The same building was leased back from the finance company for a period of twenty years, which was felt to be equivalent to the majority of the asset's economic life. The lease rentals for the period are $441,000 payable annually in arrears. The interest rate implicit in the lease is 7%. The present value of the minimum lease payments is the same as the sale proceeds.

William wishes to know how to account for the above transaction for the year ended 31 May 20X3.
(7 marks)

(b)   William operates a defined benefit pension plan for its employees. Shortly before the year end of 31 May 20X3, William decided to relocate a division from one country to another, where labour and raw material costs are cheaper. The relocation is due to take place in December 20X3. On 13 May 20X3, a detailed formal plan was approved by the board of directors. Half of the affected division's employees will be made redundant in July 20X3, and will accrue no further benefits under William's defined benefit pension plan. The affected employees were informed of this decision on 14 May 20X3. The resulting reduction in the net pension liability due the relocation is estimated to have a present value of $15 million as at 31 May 20X3. Total relocation costs (excluding the impact on the pension plan) are estimated at $50 million.

William requires advice on how to account for the relocation costs and the reduction in the net pension liability for the year ended 31 May 20X3. **(7 marks)**

(c)   On 1 June 20X0, William granted 500 share appreciation rights to each of its twenty managers. All of the rights vest after two years' service and they can be exercised during the following two years up to 31 May 20X4. The fair value of the right at the grant date was $20. It was thought that three managers would leave over the initial two-year period and they did so. The fair value of each right was as follows.

Year	Fair value at the year-end ($)
31 May 20X1	23
31 May 20X2	14
31 May 20X3	24

On 31 May 20X3, seven managers exercised their rights when the intrinsic value of the right was $21.

William wishes to know what the liability and expense will be at 31 May 20X3. **(5 marks)**

(d)   William acquired another entity, Chrissy, on 1 May 20X3. At the time of the acquisition, Chrissy was being sued as there is an alleged mis-selling case potentially implicating the entity. The claimants are suing for damages of $10 million. William estimates that the fair value of any contingent liability is $4 million and feels that it is more likely than not that no outflow of funds will occur.

William wishes to know how to account for this potential liability in Chrissy's entity financial statements and whether the treatment would be the same in the consolidated financial statements. **(4 marks)**

Required

Discuss, with suitable computations, the advice that should be given to William in accounting for the above events.

Note. The mark allocation is shown against each of the four events above.

Professional marks will be awarded for the quality of the discussion. **(2 marks)**

(Total = 25 marks)

29 Leigh   45 mins

ACR, 6/07

(a)   Leigh, a public limited company, purchased the whole of the share capital of Hash, a limited company, on 1 June 20X6. The whole of the share capital of Hash was formerly owned by the five directors of Hash and under the terms of the purchase agreement, the five directors were to receive a total of three million ordinary shares of $1 of Leigh on 1 June 20X6 (market value $6 million) and a further 5,000 shares per director on 31 May 20X7, if they were still employed by Leigh on that date. All of the directors were still employed by Leigh at 31 May 20X7.

Leigh granted and issued fully paid shares to its own employees on 31 May 20X7. Normally share options issued to employees would vest over a three year period, but these shares were given as a bonus because of the company's exceptional performance over the period. The shares in Leigh had a market value of $3 million (one million ordinary shares of $1 at $3 per share) on 31 May 20X7 and an average fair value of $2.5 million (one million ordinary shares of $1 at $2.50 per share) for the year ended 31 May 20X7. It is expected that Leigh's share price will rise to $6 per share over the next three years. **(10 marks)**

(b)   On 31 May 20X7, Leigh purchased property, plant and equipment for $4 million. The supplier has agreed to accept payment for the property, plant and equipment either in cash or in shares. The supplier can either choose 1.5 million shares of the company to be issued in six months time or to receive a cash payment in three months time equivalent to the market value of 1.3 million shares. It is estimated that the share price will be $3.50 in three months time and $4 in six months time.

Additionally, at 31 May 20X7, one of the directors recently appointed to the board has been granted the right to choose either 50,000 shares of Leigh or receive a cash payment equal to the current value of 40,000 shares at the settlement date. This right has been granted because of the performance of the director during the year and is unconditional at 31 May 20X7. The settlement date is 1 July 20X8 and the company estimates the fair value of the share alternative is $2.50 per share at 31 May 20X7. The share price of Leigh at 31 May 20X7 is $3 per share, and if the director chooses the share alternative, they must be kept for a period of four years. **(9 marks)**

(c)   Leigh acquired 30% of the ordinary share capital of Handy, a public limited company, on 1 April 20X6. The purchase consideration was one million ordinary shares of Leigh which had a market value of $2.50 per share at that date and the fair value of the net assets of Handy was $9 million. The retained earnings of Handy were $4 million and other reserves of Handy were $3 million at that date. Leigh appointed two directors to the Board of Handy, and it intends to hold the investment for a significant period of time. Leigh exerts significant influence over Handy. The summarised statement of financial position of Handy at 31 May 20X7 is as follows.

	$m
Share capital of $1	2
Other reserves	3
Retained earnings	5
	10
Net assets	10

There had been no new issues of shares by Handy since the acquisition by Leigh and the estimated recoverable amount of the net assets of Handy at 31 May 20X7 was $11 million. **(6 marks)**

Required

Discuss with suitable computations how the above share-based transactions should be accounted for in the financial statements of Leigh for the year ended 31 May 20X7.

(Total = 25 marks)

30 Margie

45 mins

12/10

Margie, a public limited company, has entered into several share related transactions during the period and wishes to obtain advice on how to account for the transactions.

(a) Margie has entered into a contract with a producer to purchase 350 tonnes of wheat. The purchase price will be settled in cash at an amount equal to the value of 2,500 of Margie's shares. Margie may settle the contract at any time by paying the producer an amount equal to the current market value of 2,500 of Margie shares, less the market value of 350 tonnes of wheat. Margie has entered into the contract as part of its hedging strategy and has no intention of taking physical delivery of the wheat. Margie wishes to treat this transaction as a share based payment transaction under IFRS 2 *Share-based payment*. **(7 marks)**

(b) Margie has acquired 100% of the share capital of Antalya in a business combination on 1 December 20X3. Antalya had previously granted a share-based payment to its employees with a four-year vesting period. Its employees have rendered the required service for the award at the acquisition date but have not yet exercised their options. The fair value of the award at 1 December 20X3 is $20 million and Margie is obliged to replace the share-based payment awards of Antalya with awards of its own.

Margie issues a replacement award that does not require post-combination services. The fair value of the replacement award at the acquisition date is $22 million. Margie does not know how to account for the award on the acquisition of Antalya. **(6 marks)**

(c) Margie issued shares during the financial year. Some of those shares were subscribed for by employees who were existing shareholders, and some were issued to an entity, Grief, which owned 5% of Margie's share capital. Before the shares were issued, Margie offered to buy a building from Grief and agreed that the purchase price would be settled by the issue of shares. Margie wondered whether these transactions should be accounted for under IFRS 2. **(4 marks)**

(d) Margie granted 100 options to each of its 4,000 employees at a fair value of $10 each on 1 December 20X1. The options vest upon the company' share price reaching $15, provided the employee has remained in the company's service until that time. The terms and conditions of the options are that the market condition can be met in either year 3, 4 or 5 of the employee's service.

At the grant date, Margie estimated that the expected vesting period would be four years which is consistent with the assumptions used in measuring the fair value of the options granted, and maintained this estimate at 30 November 20X2 and 30 November 20X3. The company's share price reached $15 on 30 November 20X4. **(6 marks)**

Required

Discuss, with suitable computations where applicable, how the above transactions would be dealt with in the financial statements of Margie for the year ending 30 November 20X4.

Professional marks will be awarded for clarity and quality of discussion.

(2 marks)

(Total = 25 marks)

31 Greenie

45 mins

12/10

(a)   Greenie, a public limited company, builds, develops and operates airports. During the financial year to 30 November 20X0, a section of an airport collapsed and as a result several people were hurt. The accident resulted in the closure of the terminal and legal action against Greenie. When the financial statements for the year ended 30 November 20X0 were being prepared, the investigation into the accident and the reconstruction of the section of the airport damaged were still in progress and no legal action had yet been brought in connection with the accident. The expert report that was to be presented to the civil courts in order to determine the cause of the accident and to assess the respective responsibilities of the various parties involved, was expected in 20X1.

Financial damages arising related to the additional costs and operating losses relating to the unavailability of the building. The nature and extent of the damages, and the details of any compensation payments had yet to be established. The directors of Greenie felt that at present, there was no requirement to record the impact of the accident in the financial statements.

Compensation agreements had been arranged with the victims, and these claims were all covered by Greenie's insurance policy. In each case, compensation paid by the insurance company was subject to a waiver of any judicial proceedings against Greenie and its insurers. If any compensation is eventually payable to third parties, this is expected to be covered by the insurance policies.

The directors of Greenie felt that the conditions for recognising a provision or disclosing a contingent liability had not been met. Therefore, Greenie did not recognise a provision in respect of the accident nor did it disclose any related contingent liability or a note setting out the nature of the accident and potential claims in its financial statements for the year ended 30 November 20X0.   **(6 marks)**

(b)   Greenie was one of three shareholders in a regional airport Manair. As at 30 November 20X0, the majority shareholder held 60.1% of voting shares, the second shareholder held 20% of voting shares and Greenie held 19.9% of the voting shares. The board of directors consisted of ten members. The majority shareholder was represented by six of the board members, while Greenie and the other shareholder were represented by two members each. A shareholders' agreement stated that certain board and shareholder resolutions required either unanimous or majority decision. There is no indication that the majority shareholder and the other shareholders act together in a common way. During the financial year, Greenie had provided Manair with maintenance and technical services and had sold the entity a software licence for $5 million. Additionally, Greenie had sent a team of management experts to give business advice to the board of Manair. Greenie did not account for its investment in Manair as an associate, because of a lack of significant influence over the entity. Greenie felt that the majority owner of Manair used its influence as the parent to control and govern its subsidiary.   **(10 marks)**

(c)   Greenie has issued 1 million shares of $1 nominal value for the acquisition of franchise rights at a local airport. Similar franchise rights are sold in cash transactions on a regular basis and Greenie has been offered a similar franchise right at another airport for $2.3 million. This price is consistent with other prices given the market conditions. The share price of Greenie was $2.50 at the date of the transaction. Greenie wishes to record the transaction at the nominal value of the shares issued.

Greenie also showed irredeemable preference shares as equity instruments in its statement of financial position. The terms of issue of the instruments give the holders a contractual right to an annual fixed cash dividend and the entitlement to a participating dividend based on any dividends paid on ordinary shares. Greenie felt that the presentation of the preference shares with a liability component in compliance with IAS *32 Financial instruments: presentation* would be so misleading in the circumstances that it would conflict with the objective of financial statements set out in the *IASB's Conceptual Framework.*. The reason given by Greenie for this presentation was that the shares participated in future profits and thus had the characteristics of permanent capital because of the profit participation element of the shares. **(7 marks)**

Required

Discuss how the above financial transactions should be dealt with in the financial statements of Greenie for the year ended 30 November 20X0.

Professional marks will be awarded in question 3 for clarity and quality of discussion. **(2 marks)**

(Total = 25 marks)

32 Zack
45 mins

12/13

(a) Due to the complexity of International Financial Reporting Standards (IFRS), often judgements used at the time of transition to IFRS have resulted in prior period adjustments and changes in estimates being disclosed in financial statements. The selection of accounting policy and estimation techniques is intended to aid comparability and consistency in financial statements. However, IFRS also place particular emphasis on the need to take into account qualitative characteristics and the use of professional judgement when preparing the financial statements. Although IFRS may appear prescriptive, the achievement of all the objectives for a set of financial statements will rely on the skills of the preparer. Entities should follow the requirements of IAS 8 *Accounting policies, changes in accounting estimates and errors* when selecting or changing accounting policies, changing estimation techniques, and correcting errors.

However, the application of IAS 8 is additionally often dependent upon the application of materiality analysis to identify issues and guide reporting. Entities also often consider the acceptability of the use of hindsight in their reporting.

Required

(i) Discuss how judgement and materiality play a significant part in the selection of an entity's accounting policies.

(ii) Discuss the circumstances where an entity may change its accounting policies, setting out how a change of accounting policy is applied and the difficulties faced by entities where a change in accounting policy is made.

(iii) Discuss why the current treatment of prior period errors could lead to earnings management by companies, together with any further arguments against the current treatment.

Credit will be given for relevant examples.

Note. The total marks will be split equally between each part. **(15 marks)**

(b) In 20X3, Zack, a public limited company, commenced construction of a shopping centre. It considers that in order to fairly recognise the costs of its property, plant and equipment, it needs to enhance its accounting policies by capitalising borrowing costs incurred whilst the shopping centre is under construction. A review of past transactions suggests that there has been one other project involving assets with substantial construction periods where there would be a material misstatement of the asset balance if borrowing costs were not capitalised. This project was completed in the year ended 30 November 20X2. Previously, Zack had expensed the borrowing costs as they were incurred. The borrowing costs which could be capitalised are $2 million for the 20X2 asset and $3 million for the 20X3 asset.

A review of the depreciation schedules of the larger plant and equipment not affected by the above has resulted in Zack concluding that the basis on which these assets are depreciated would better reflect the resources consumed if calculations were on a reducing balance basis, rather than a straight-line basis. The revision would result in an increase in depreciation for the year to 30 November 20X2 of $5 million, an increase for the year end 30 November 20X3 of $6 million and an estimated increase for the year ending 30 November 20X4 of $8 million.

Additionally, Zack has discovered that its accruals systems for year-end creditors for the financial year

30 November 20X2 processed certain accruals twice in the ledger. This meant that expenditure services were overstated in the financial statements by $2 million. However, Zack has since reviewed its final accounts systems and processes and has made appropriate changes and introduced additional internal controls to ensure that such estimation problems are unlikely to recur.

All of the above transactions are material to Zack.

Required

Discuss how the above events should be shown in the financial statements of Zack for the year ended 30 November 20X3.   **(8 marks)**

Professional marks will be awarded in question 4 for clarity and quality of presentation.   **(2 marks)**

(Total = 25 marks)

33 Minco   45 mins

`6/14, amended`

(a)   Minco is a major property developer. On 1 June 20X3, Minco entered into a contract with Holistic Healthco for the sale of a building for $3 million. Holistic Healthco intends to use the building as a fitness and leisure centre. The building is located in a busy city, where there are many gyms and leisure centres. Holistic Healthco's experience to date has been in stores selling health foods and aromatherapy oils, and it has no experience of the fitness industry.

Holistic Healthco paid Minco a non-refundable deposit of $150,000 on 1 June 20X3 and entered into a long-term financing agreement with Minco for the remaining 95 per cent of the promised consideration. The terms of the financing arrangement are that if Holistic Healthco defaults, Minco can repossess the building, but cannot seek further compensation from Holistic Healthco, even if the collateral does not cover the full value of the amount owed. The building cost Minco $1.8m to construct. Holistic Healthco obtained control of the building on 1 June 20X3.

Minco argues that this contract falls within the scope of IFRS 15 *Revenue from contracts with customers*, and that the non-refundable deposit should be recognised as revenue.   **(7 marks)**

(b)   Minco often sponsors professional tennis players in an attempt to improve its brand image. At the moment, it has a three-year agreement with a tennis player who is currently ranked in the world's top ten players. The agreement is that the player receives a signing bonus of $20,000 and earns an annual amount of $50,000, paid at the end of each year for three years, provided that the player has competed in all the specified tournaments for each year. If the player wins a major tournament, she receives a bonus of 20% of the prize money won at the tournament. In return, the player is required to wear advertising logos on tennis apparel, play a specified number of tournaments and attend photo/film sessions for advertising purposes. The different payments are not interrelated.   **(5 marks)**

(c)   Minco leased its head office during the current accounting period and the agreement terminates in six years' time.

There is a clause in the operating lease relating to the internal condition of the property at the termination of the lease. The clause states that the internal condition of the property should be identical to that at the outset of the lease. Minco has improved the building by adding another floor to part of the building during the current accounting period. There is also a clause which enables the landlord to recharge Minco for costs relating to the general disrepair of the building at the end of the lease. In addition, the landlord can recharge any costs of repairing the roof immediately. The landlord intends to replace part of the roof of the building during the current period.   **(5 marks)**

(d)   On 1 June 20X1, Minco acquired a property for $5 million and annual depreciation of $500,000 is charged on the straight line basis with no residual value. At the end of the previous financial year of 31 May 20X3, when accumulated depreciation was $1 million, a further amount relating to an impairment loss of $350,000 was recognised, which resulted in the property being valued at its estimated value in use. On 1 October 20X3, as a consequence of a proposed move to new premises, the property was classified as held for sale. At the time of classification as held for sale, the fair value less costs to sell was $3·4 million. At the date of the published interim financial statements, 1 December 20X3, the property market had improved and the fair value less costs to sell was reassessed at $3·52 million and at the year-end on 31 May 20X4 it had improved even further, so that the fair value less costs to sell was $3·95 million. The property was sold on 5 June 20X4 for $4 million. **(6 marks)**

Required

Discuss how the above items should be dealt with in the financial statements of Minco.

Note. The mark allocation is shown against each of the four issues above.

Professional marks will be awarded in this question for clarity and quality of presentation. **(2 marks)**

(Total = 25 marks)

34 Alexandra   45 mins

6/11

Alexandra, a public limited company, designs and manages business solutions and infrastructures.

(a) In November 20X0, Alexandra defaulted on an interest payment on an issued bond loan of $100 million repayable in 20X5. The loan agreement stipulates that such default leads to an obligation to repay the whole of the loan immediately, including accrued interest and expenses. The bondholders, however, issued a waiver postponing the interest payment until 31 May 20X1. On 17 May 20X1, Alexandra felt that a further waiver was required, so requested a meeting of the bondholders and agreed a further waiver of the interest payment to 5 July 20X1, when Alexandra was confident it could make the payments. Alexandra classified the loan as long-term debt in its statement of financial position at 30 April 20X1 on the basis that the loan was not in default at the end of the reporting period as the bondholders had issued waivers and had not sought redemption. **(6 marks)**

(b) Alexandra enters into contracts with both customers and suppliers. The supplier solves system problems and provides new releases and updates for software. Alexandra provides maintenance services for its customers. In previous years, Alexandra recognised revenue and related costs on software maintenance contracts when the customer was invoiced, which was at the beginning of the contract period. Contracts typically run for two years.

During 20X0, Alexandra had acquired Xavier Co, which recognised revenue, derived from a similar type of maintenance contract as Alexandra, on a straight-line basis over the term of the contract. Alexandra considered both its own and the policy of Xavier Co to comply with the requirements of IAS 18 *Revenue* but it decided to adopt the practice of Xavier Co for itself and the group. Alexandra concluded that the two recognition methods did not, in substance, represent two different accounting policies and did not, therefore, consider adoption of the new practice to be a change in policy.

In the year to 30 April 20X1, Alexandra recognised revenue (and the related costs) on a straight-line basis over the contract term, treating this as a change in an accounting estimate. As a result, revenue and cost of sales were adjusted, reducing the year's profits by some $6 million. **(5 marks)**

(c) Alexandra has a two-tier board structure consisting of a management and a supervisory board. Alexandra remunerates its board members as follows:

– Annual base salary
– Variable annual compensation (bonus)
– Share options

In the group financial statements, within the related parties note under IAS 24 *Related party disclosures*, Alexandra disclosed the total remuneration paid to directors and non-executive directors and a total for each of these boards. No further breakdown of the remuneration was provided.

The management board comprises both the executive and non-executive directors. The remuneration of the non-executive directors, however, was not included in the key management disclosures. Some members of the supervisory and management boards are of a particular nationality. Alexandra was of the opinion that in that jurisdiction, it is not acceptable to provide information about remuneration that could be traced back to individuals. Consequently, Alexandra explained that it had provided the related party information in the annual accounts in an ambiguous way to prevent users of the financial statements from tracing remuneration information back to specific individuals. **(5 marks)**

(d)   Alexandra's pension plan was accounted for as a defined benefit plan in 20X0. In the year ended 30 April 20X1, Alexandra changed the accounting method used for the scheme and accounted for it as a defined contribution plan, restating the comparative 20X0 financial information. The effect of the restatement was significant. In the 20X1 financial statements, Alexandra explained that, during the year, the arrangements underlying the retirement benefit plan had been subject to detailed review. Since the pension liabilities are fully insured and indexation of future liabilities can be limited up to and including the funds available in a special trust account set up for the plan, which is not at the disposal of Alexandra, the plan qualifies as a defined contribution plan under IAS 19 *Employee benefits* rather than a defined benefit plan. Furthermore, the trust account is built up by the insurance company from the surplus yield on investments. The pension plan is an average pay plan in respect of which the entity pays insurance premiums to a third party insurance company to fund the plan. Every year 1% of the pension fund is built up and employees pay a contribution of 4% of their salary, with the employer paying the balance of the contribution. If an employee leaves Alexandra and transfers the pension to another fund, Alexandra is liable for, or is refunded the difference between the benefits the employee is entitled to and the insurance premiums paid. **(7 marks)**

Professional marks will be awarded in this question for clarity and quality of discussion.   **(2 marks)**

Required

Discuss how the above transactions should be dealt with in the financial statements of Alexandra for the year ended 30 April 20X1.   **(Total = 25 marks)**

35 Cate   **45 mins**

6/10

(a)   Cate is an entity in the software industry. Cate had incurred substantial losses in the financial years 31 May 20X0 to 31 May 20X5. In the financial year to 31 May 20X6 Cate made a small profit before tax. This included significant non-operating gains. In 20X5, Cate recognised a material deferred tax asset in respect of carried forward losses, which will expire during 20X8. Cate again recognised the deferred tax asset in 20X6 on the basis of anticipated performance in the years from 20X6 to 20X8, based on budgets prepared in 20X6. The budgets included high growth rates in profitability. Cate argued that the budgets were realistic as there were positive indications from customers about future orders. Cate also had plans to expand sales to new markets and to sell new products whose development would be completed soon. Cate was taking measures to increase sales, implementing new programs to improve both productivity and profitability. Deferred tax assets less deferred tax liabilities represent 25% of shareholders' equity at 31 May 20X6. There are no tax planning opportunities available to Cate that would create taxable profit in the near future.
     (5 marks)

(b)   At 31 May 20X6 Cate held an investment in and had a significant influence over Bates, a public limited company. Cate had carried out an impairment test in respect of its investment in accordance with the procedures prescribed in IAS 36, *Impairment of assets*. Cate argued that fair value was the only measure applicable in this case as value-in-use was not determinable as cash flow estimates had not been produced. Cate stated that there were no plans to dispose of the shareholding and hence there was no binding sale agreement. Cate also stated that the quoted share price was not an appropriate measure when considering the fair value of Cate's significant influence on Bates. Therefore, Cate measured the fair value of its interest in Bates through application of two measurement techniques; one based on earnings multiples and the other based on an option-pricing model. Neither of these methods supported the existence of an impairment loss as of 31 May 20X6.   **(5 marks)**

(c)   At 1 April 20X5 Cate had a direct holding of shares giving 70% of the voting rights in Date. In May 20X6, Date issued new shares, which were wholly subscribed for by a new investor. After the increase in capital, Cate retained an interest of 35% of the voting rights in its former subsidiary Date. At the same time, the shareholders of Date signed an agreement providing new governance rules for Date. Based on this new agreement, Cate was no longer to be represented on Date's board or participate in its management. As a consequence Cate considered that its decision not to subscribe to the issue of new shares was equivalent to a decision to disinvest in Date. Cate argued that the decision not to invest clearly showed its new intention not to recover the investment in Date principally through continuing use of the asset and was considering selling the investment. Due to the fact that Date is a separate line of business (with separate cash flows, management and customers), Cate considered that the results of Date for the period to 31 May 20X6 should be presented based on principles provided by IFRS 5 *Non-current assets held for sale and discontinued operations.* **(8 marks)**

(d) In its 20X6 financial statements, Cate disclosed the existence of a voluntary fund established in order to provide a post-retirement benefit plan (Plan) to employees. Cate considers its contributions to the Plan to be voluntary, and has not recorded any related liability in its consolidated financial statements. Cate has a history of paying benefits to its former employees, even increasing them to keep pace with inflation since the commencement of the Plan.

The main characteristics of the Plan are as follows:

(i) The Plan is totally funded by Cate.

(ii) The contributions for the Plan are made periodically.

(iii) The post retirement benefit is calculated based on a percentage of the final salaries of Plan participants dependent on the years of service.

(iv) The annual contributions to the Plan are determined as a function of the fair value of the assets less the liability arising from past services.

Cate argues that it should not have to recognise the Plan because, according to the underlying contract, it can terminate its contributions to the Plan, if and when it wishes. The termination clauses of the contract establish that Cate must immediately purchase lifetime annuities from an insurance company for all the retired employees who are already receiving benefit when the termination of the contribution is communicated. **(5 marks)**

Required

Discuss whether the accounting treatments proposed by the company are acceptable under International Financial Reporting Standards.

Professional marks will be awarded in this question for clarity and quality of discussion. **(2 marks)**

The mark allocation is shown against each of the four parts above.

(Total = 25 marks)

36 Calcula   45 mins

Asha Alexander has recently been appointed as the CEO of Calcula plc. The company develops specialist software for use by accountancy professionals. The specialist software market is particularly dynamic and fast changing. It is common for competitors to drop out of the market place. The most successful companies have been particularly focused on enhancing their offering to customers through creating innovative products and investing heavily in training and development for their employees.

Turbulent times

Calcula has been through a turbulent time over the last three years. During this time there have been significant senior management changes which resulted in confusion among shareholders and employees as to the strategic direction of the company. One investor complained that the annual accounts made it hard to know where the company was headed.

The last CEO introduced an aggressive cost-cutting programme aimed at improving profitability. At the beginning of the financial year the annual staff training and development budget was significantly reduced and has not been reviewed since the change in management.

Future direction

In response to the confusion surrounding the company's strategic direction, Asha and the board published a new mission, the primary focus of which centres on making Calcula the market leader of specialist accountancy software. Asha was appointed as the CEO having undertaken a similar role at a competitor. The board were keen on her appointment as she is renowned in the industry for her creativity and willingness to introduce 'fresh ideas'. In her previous role Asha oversaw the introduction of an integrated approach to reporting performance. This is something she is particularly keen to introduce at Calcula.

During the company's last board meeting, Asha was dismayed by the finance director's reaction when she proposed introducing integrated reporting at Calcula. The finance director made it clear that he was not convinced of the need for such a change, arguing that 'all this talk of integrated reporting in the business press is just a fad, requiring a lot more work, simply to report on things people do not care about. Shareholders are only interested in the bottom line'.

Required

(a)   Discuss what is meant by 'integrated reporting', highlighting how it differs from traditional performance reporting.   **(10 marks)**

(b)   How may integrated reporting help Calcula to communicate its strategy and improve the company's strategic performance? Your answer should make reference to the concerns raised by the finance director.
                                                                              (10 marks)

(c)   Advise on the likely implications of introducing 'integrated reporting' which Calcula should consider before deciding to proceed with its adoption.   **(5 marks)**

                                                                              (Total = 25 marks)

37 Egin Group   45 mins

ACR, 6/06

On 1 June 20X5, Egin, a public limited company, was formed out of the reorganisation of a group of companies with foreign operations. The directors require advice on the disclosure of related party information but are reluctant to disclose information as they feel that such transactions are a normal feature of business and need not be disclosed.

Under the new group structure, Egin owns 80% of Briars, 60% of Doye, and 30% of Eye. Egin exercises significant influence over Eye. The directors of Egin are also directors of Briars and Doye but only one director of Egin sits on the management board of Eye. The management board of Eye comprises five directors. Originally the group comprised five companies but the fifth company, Tang, which was a 70% subsidiary of Egin, was sold on 31 January 20X6. There were no transactions between Tang and the Egin Group during the year to 31 May 20X6. 30% of the shares of Egin are owned by another company, Atomic, which exerts significant influence over Egin. The remaining 40% of the shares of Doye are owned by Spade, which exerts significant influence over Doye.

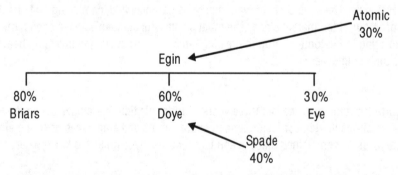

During the current financial year to 31 May 20X6, Doye has sold a significant amount of plant and equipment to Spade at the normal selling price for such items. The directors of Egin have proposed that where related party relationships are determined and sales are at normal selling price, any disclosures will state that prices charged to related parties are made on an arm's length basis.

The directors are unsure how to treat certain transactions relating to their foreign subsidiary, Briars. Egin purchased 80% of the ordinary share capital of Briars on 1 June 20X5 for 50 million euros when its net assets were fair valued at 45 million euros. At 31 May 20X6, it is established that goodwill is impaired by 3 million euros. Additionally, at the date of acquisition, Egin had made an interest free loan to Briars of $10 million. The loan is to be repaid on 31 May 20X7. An equivalent loan would normally carry an interest rate of 6% taking into account Briars' credit rating.

The exchange rates were as follows:

	Euros to $
1 June 20X5	2
31 May 20X6	2.5
Average rate for year	2.3

Financial liabilities of the group are normally measured at amortised cost.

One of the directors of Briars who is not on the management board of Egin owns the whole of the share capital of a company, Blue, that sells goods at market price to Briars. The director is in charge of the production at Briars and also acts as a consultant to the management board of the group.

Required

(a) (i)   Discuss why it is important to disclose related party transactions, explaining the criteria which determine a related party relationship. **(5 marks)**

     (ii) Describe the nature of any related party relationships and transactions which exists:

           (1)   Within the Egin Group including Tang   **(5 marks)**
           (2)   Between Spade and the Egin Group   **(3 marks)**
           (3)   Between Atomic and the Egin Group   **(3 marks)**

           commenting on whether transactions should be described as being at 'arm's length'.

(b) Describe with suitable calculations how the goodwill arising on the acquisition of Briars will be dealt with in the group financial statements and how the loan to Briars should be treated in the financial statements of Briars for the year ended 31 May 20X6. **(9 marks)**

(Total = 25 marks)

GROUP FINANCIAL STATEMENTS

Questions 38 to 61 cover Group Financial Statements, the subject of Part C of the BPP Study Text for Paper P2.

38 Marrgrett

45 mins

Marrgrett, a public limited company, is currently planning to acquire and sell interests in other entities and has asked for advice on the impact of IFRS 3 (Revised) *Business combinations*. The company is particularly concerned about the impact on earnings, net assets and goodwill at the acquisition date and any ongoing earnings impact that the revised standards may have.

The company is considering purchasing additional shares in an associate, Josey, a public limited company. The holding will increase from 30% stake to 70% stake by offering the shareholders of Josey cash and shares in Marrgrett. Marrgrett anticipates that it will pay $5 million in transaction costs to lawyers and bankers. Josey had previously been the subject of a management buyout. In order that the current management shareholders may remain in the business, Marrgrett is going to offer them share options in Josey subject to them remaining in employment for two years after the acquisition. Additionally, Marrgrett will offer the same shareholders, shares in the holding company which are contingent upon a certain level of profitability being achieved by Josey. Each shareholder will receive shares of the holding company up to a value of $50,000, if Josey achieves a pre-determined rate of return on capital employed for the next two years.

Josey has several marketing-related intangible assets that are used primarily in marketing or promotion of its products. These include trade names, internet domain names and non-competition agreements. These are not currently recognised in Josey's financial statements.

Marrgrett does not wish to measure the non-controlling interest in subsidiaries on the basis of the proportionate interest in the identifiable net assets, but wishes to use the 'full goodwill' method on the transaction. Marrgrett is unsure as to whether this method is mandatory, or what the effects are of recognising 'full goodwill'. Additionally the company is unsure as to whether the nature of the consideration would affect the calculation of goodwill.

To finance the acquisition of Josey, Marrgrett intends to dispose of a partial interest in two subsidiaries. Marrgrett will retain control of the first subsidiary but will sell the controlling interest in the second subsidiary which will become an associate. Because of its plans to change the overall structure of the business, Marrgrett wishes to recognise a re-organisation provision at the date of the business combination.

Required

Discuss the principles and the nature of the accounting treatment of the above plans under International Financial Reporting Standards setting out any impact that IFRS 3 (Revised) *Business combinations* might have on the earnings and net assets of the group.

Note. this requirement includes 2 professional marks for the quality of the discussion.

(25 marks)

BPP
LEARNING MEDIA

39 Preparation question: Associate

The statements of financial position of J Co and its investee companies, P Co and S Co, at 31 December 20X5 are shown below.

STATEMENTS OF FINANCIAL POSITION AS AT 31 DECEMBER 20X5

	J Co $'000	P Co $'000	S Co $'000
Assets			
Non-current assets			
Freehold property	1,950	1,250	500
Plant and equipment	795	375	285
Investments	1,500	–	–
	4,245	1,625	785
Current assets			
Inventories	575	300	265
Trade receivables	330	290	370
Cash	50	120	20
	955	710	655
	5,200	2,335	1,440
Equity and liabilities			
Equity			
Share capital ($1 ordinary shares)	2,000	1,000	750
Retained earnings	1,460	885	390
	3,460	1,885	1,140
Non-current liabilities			
12% debentures	500	100	–
Current liabilities			
Bank overdraft	560		
Trade payables	680	350	300
	1,240	350	300
	5,200	2,335	1,440

Additional information

(a) J Co acquired 600,000 ordinary shares in P Co on 1 January 20X0 for $1,000,000 when the accumulated retained earnings of P Co were $200,000.

(b) At the date of acquisition of P Co, the fair value of its freehold property was considered to be $400,000 greater than its value in P Co's statement of financial position. P Co had acquired the property ten years earlier and the buildings element (comprising 50% of the total value) is depreciated on cost over 50 years.

(c) J Co acquired 225,000 ordinary shares in S Co on 1 January 20X4 for $500,000 when the retained profits of S Co were $150,000.

(d) P Co manufactures a component used by J Co only. Transfers are made by P Co at cost plus 25%. J Co held $100,000 of these components in inventories at 31 December 20X5.

(e) It is the policy of J Co to review goodwill for impairment annually. The goodwill in P Co was written off in full some years ago. An impairment test conducted at the year end revealed impairment losses on the investment in S Co of $92,000.

(f) It is the group's policy to value the non-controlling interest at acquisition at fair value. The market price of the shares of the non-controlling shareholders just before the acquisition was $1.65.

Required

Prepare, in a format suitable for inclusion in the annual report of the J Group, the consolidated statement of financial position at 31 December 20X5.

40 Preparation question: 'D'-shaped group

> **BPP note**. In this question, a proforma is given to you for Part (a) to help you get used to setting out your answer. You may wish to transfer it to a separate sheet or to use a separate sheet for workings.

Below are the statements of financial position of three companies as at 31 December 20X9.

	Bauble Co $'000	Jewel Co $'000	Gem Co $'000
Non-current assets			
Property, plant and equipment	720	60	70
Investments in group companies	185	100	–
	905	160	70
Current assets	175	95	90
	1,080	255	160
Equity			
Share capital – $1 ordinary shares	400	100	50
Retained earnings	560	90	65
	960	190	115
Current liabilities	120	65	45
	1,080	255	160

You are also given the following information:

(a)   Bauble Co acquired 60% of the share capital of Jewel Co on 1 January 20X2 and 10% of Gem on 1 January 20X3. The cost of the combinations were $142,000 and $43,000 respectively. Jewel Co acquired 70% of the share capital of Gem Co on 1 January 20X3.

(b)   The retained earnings balances of Jewel Co and Gem Co were:

	1 January 20X2 $'000	1 January 20X3 $'000
Jewel Co	45	60
Gem Co	30	40

(c)   No impairment loss adjustments have been necessary to date.

(d)   It is the group's policy to value the non-controlling interest at acquisition at its proportionate share of the fair value of the subsidiary's identifiable net assets.

Required

(a)   Prepare the consolidated statement of financial position for Bauble Co and its subsidiaries as at 31 December 20X9.

(b)   Calculate the total goodwill arising on acquisition if Bauble Co had acquired its investments in Jewel and Gem on 1 January 20X3 at a cost of $142,000 and $43,000 respectively and Jewel Co had acquired its investment in Gem Co on 1 January 20X2.

(a)   BAUBLE – CONSOLIDATED STATEMENT OF FINANCIAL POSITION AS AT 31 DECEMBER 20X9

	$'000
Non-current assets	
Property, plant and equipment	
Goodwill	_____
	_____
Current assets	_____
	_____
Equity attributable to owners of the parent	
Share capital – $1 ordinary shares	
Retained earnings	_____
	_____
Non-controlling interest	_____
	_____
Current liabilities	_____
	_____

41 Preparation question: Sub-subsidiary

The Exotic Group carries on business as a distributor of warehouse equipment and importer of fruit into the country. Exotic was incorporated in 20X1 to distribute warehouse equipment. It diversified its activities during 20X3 to include the import and distribution of fruit, and expanded its operations by the acquisition of shares in Melon in 20X5 and in Kiwi in 20X7.

Accounts for all companies are made up to 31 December.

The draft statements of profit or loss and other comprehensive income for Exotic, Melon and Kiwi for the year ended 31 December 20X9 are as follows.

	Exotic	Melon	Kiwi
	$'000	$'000	$'000
Revenue	45,600	24,700	22,800
Cost of sales	18,050	5,463	5,320
Gross profit	27,550	19,237	17,480
Distribution costs	(3,325)	(2,137)	(1,900)
Administrative expenses	(3,475)	(950)	(1,900)
Finance costs	(325)	–	–
Profit before tax	20,425	16,150	13,680
Income tax expense	8,300	5,390	4,241
Profit for the year	12,125	10,760	9,439
	Exotic	Melon	Kiwi
	$'000	$'000	$'000
Other comprehensive income for the year			
Items that will not be reclassified to profit or loss			
Revaluation of property	200	100	–
Total comprehensive income for the year	12,325	10,860	9439
Dividends paid and declared for the period	9,500	–	–

The draft statements of financial position as at 31 December 20X9 are as follows.

	Exotic $'000	Melon $'000	Kiwi $'000
Non-current assets			
Property, plant and equipment (at carrying value)	35,483	24,273	13,063
Investments			
Shares in Melon	6,650		
Shares in Kiwi		3,800	
	42,133	28,073	13,063
Current assets	1,568	9,025	8,883
	43,701	37,098	21,946
Equity			
$1 ordinary shares	8,000	3,000	2,000
Reserves (retained earnings and reval'n surplus)	22,638	24,075	19,898
	30,638	27,075	21,898
Current liabilities	13,063	10,023	48
	43,701	37,098	21,946

The following information is available relating to Exotic, Melon and Kiwi.

(a) On 1 January 20X5 Exotic acquired 2,700,000 $1 ordinary shares in Melon for $6,650,000 at which date there was a credit balance on the retained earnings of Melon of $1,425,000. No shares have been issued by Melon since Exotic acquired its interest.

(b) At the date of acquisition, the fair value of the identifiable net assets of Melon was $5m. The excess of the fair value of net assets is due to an increase in the value of non-depreciable land.

(c) On 1 January 20X7 Melon acquired 1,600,000 $1 ordinary shares in Kiwi for $3,800,000 at which date there was a credit balance on the retained earnings of Kiwi of $950,000. No shares have been issued by Kiwi since Melon acquired its interest.

(d) During 20X9, Kiwi had made intragroup sales to Melon of $480,000 making a profit of 25% on cost and $75,000 of these goods were in inventories at 31 December 20X9.

(e) During 20X9, Melon had made intragroup sales to Exotic of $260,000 making a profit of 25% on sales and $60,000 of these goods were in inventories at 31 December 20X9.

(f) An impairment test conducted at the year end did not reveal any impairment losses.

(g) It is the group's policy to value the non-controlling interest at fair value at the date of acquisition. The fair value of the non-controlling interests in Melon on 1 January 20X5 was $500,000. The fair value of the 28% non-controlling interest in Kiwi on 1 January 20X7 was $900,000.

Required

Prepare for the Exotic Group:

(a) A consolidated statement of profit or loss and other comprehensive income for the year ended 31 December 20X9

(b) A consolidated statement of financial position as at that date

42 Glove

ACR, 6/07, amended

The following draft statements of financial position relate to Glove, Body and Fit, all public limited companies, as at 31 May 20X7.

	Glove $m	Body $m	Fit $m
Assets			
Non-current assets			
Property, plant and equipment	260	20	26
Investment in Body	60		
Investment in Fit		30	
Investments in equity instruments	10		
Current assets	65	29	20
Total assets	395	79	46
Ordinary shares	150	40	20
Other reserves	30	5	8
Retained earnings	135	25	10
Total equity	315	70	38
Non-current liabilities	45	2	3
Current liabilities	35	7	5
Total liabilities	80	9	8
Total equity and liabilities	395	79	46

The following information is relevant to the preparation of the group financial statements.

(a) Glove acquired 80% of the ordinary shares of Body on 1 June 20X5 when Body's other reserves were $4 million and retained earnings were $10 million. The fair value of the net assets of Body was $60 million at 1 June 20X5. Body acquired 70% of the ordinary shares of Fit on 1 June 20X5 when the other reserves of Fit were $8 million and retained earnings were $6 million. The fair value of the net assets of Fit at that date was $39 million. The excess of the fair value over the net assets of Body and Fit is due to an increase in the value of non-depreciable land of the companies. There have been no issues of ordinary shares in the group since 1 June 20X5.

(b) Body owns several trade names which are highly regarded in the market place. Body has invested a significant amount in marketing these trade names and has expensed the costs. None of the trade names has been acquired externally and, therefore, the costs have not been capitalised in the statement of financial position of Body. On the acquisition of Body by Glove, a firm of valuation experts valued the trade names at $5 million and this valuation had been taken into account by Glove when offering $60 million for the investment in Body. The valuation of the trade names is not included in the fair value of the net assets of Body above. Group policy is to amortise intangible assets over ten years.

(c) On 1 June 20X5, Glove introduced a defined benefit retirement plan. During the year to 31 May 20X7, loss on remeasurement on the defined benefit obligation was $1m, and gain on remeasurement on the plan assets were $900,000. These have not yet been accounted for and need to be treated in accordance with IAS 19, as revised in 2011. The net defined benefit liability is included in non-current liabilities.

(d) Glove has issued 30,000 convertible bonds with a three year term repayable at par. The bonds were issued at par with a face value of $1,000 per bond. Interest is payable annually in arrears at a nominal interest rate of 6%. Each bond can be converted at any time up to maturity into 300 shares of Glove. The bonds were issued on 1 June 20X6 when the market interest rate for similar debt without the conversion option was 8% per annum. Glove does not wish to account for the bonds at fair value through profit or loss. The interest has been paid and accounted for in the financial statements. The bonds have been included in non-current liabilities at their face value of $30 million and no bonds were converted in the current financial year.

(e) On 31 May 20X7, Glove acquired plant with a fair value of $6 million. In exchange for the plant, the supplier received land, which was currently not in use, from Glove. The land had a carrying value of $4 million and an open market value of $7 million. In the financial statements at 31 May 20X7, Glove had made a transfer of $4 million from land to plant in respect of this transaction.

(f)   Goodwill has been tested for impairment at 31 May 20X6 and 31 May 20X7 and no impairment loss occurred.

(g)   It is the group's policy to value the non-controlling interest at acquisition at its proportionate share of the fair value of the subsidiary's identifiable net assets.

(h)   Ignore any taxation effects.

Required

Prepare the consolidated statement of financial position of the Glove Group at 31 May 20X7 in accordance with International Financial Reporting Standards (IFRS).   **(25 marks)**

43 Case study question: Minny   **90 mins**

12/12

Minny is a company which operates in the service sector. Minny has business relationships with Bower and Heeny. All three entities are public limited companies. The draft statements of financial position of these entities are as follows at 30 November 20X2.

	Minny $m	Bower $m	Heeny $m
Assets			
Non-current assets			
Property, plant and equipment	920	300	310
Investment in subsidiaries:			
Bower	730		
Heeny		320	
Investment in Puttin	48		
Intangible assets	198	30	35
	1,896	650	345
Current assets	895	480	250
Total assets	2,791	1,130	595
Equity and liabilities			
Share capital	920	400	200
Other components of equity	73	37	25
Retained earnings	895	442	139
Total equity	1,888	879	364
Non-current liabilities	495	123	93
Current liabilities	408	128	138
Total liabilities	903	251	231
Total equity and liabilities	2,791	1,130	595

The following information is relevant to the preparation of the group financial statements.

(i)   On 1 December 20X0, Minny acquired 70% of the equity interests of Bower. The purchase consideration comprised cash of $730 million. At acquisition, the fair value of the non-controlling interest in Bower was $295 million. On 1 December 20X0, the fair value of the identifiable net assets acquired was $835 million and retained earnings of Bower were $319 million and other components of equity were $27 million. The excess in fair value is due to non-depreciable land.

(ii)   On 1 December 20X1, Bower acquired 80% of the equity interests of Heeny for a cash consideration of $320 million. The fair value of a 20% holding of the non-controlling interest was $72 million; a 30% holding was $108 million and a 44% holding was $161 million. At the date of acquisition, the identifiable net assets of Heeny had a fair value of $362 million, retained earnings were $106 million and other components of equity were $20 million. The excess in fair value is due to non-depreciable land. It is the group's policy to measure the non-controlling interest at fair value at the date of acquisition.

(iii) Both Bower and Heeny were impairment tested at 30 November 20X2. The recoverable amounts of both cash generating units as stated in the individual financial statements at 30 November 20X2 were Bower, $1,425 million, and Heeny, $604 million, respectively. The directors of Minny felt that any impairment of assets was due to the poor performance of the intangible assets. The recoverable amount has been determined without consideration of liabilities which all relate to the financing of operations.

(iv) Minny acquired a 14% interest in Puttin, a public limited company, on 1 December 20X0 for a cash consideration of $18 million. The investment was accounted for under IFRS 9 Financial instruments and was designated as at fair value through other comprehensive income. On 1 June 20X2, Minny acquired an additional 16% interest in Puttin for a cash consideration of $27 million and achieved significant influence. The value of the original 14% investment on 1 June 20X2 was $21 million. Puttin made profits after tax of $20 million and $30 million for the years to 30 November 20X1 and 30 November 20X2 respectively. On 30 November 20X2, Minny received a dividend from Puttin of $2 million, which has been credited to other components of equity.

(v) Minny purchased patents of $10 million to use in a project to develop new products on 1 December 20X1. Minny has completed the investigative phase of the project, incurring an additional cost of $7 million and has determined that the product can be developed profitably. An effective and working prototype was created at a cost of $4 million and in order to put the product into a condition for sale, a further $3 million was spent. Finally, marketing costs of $2 million were incurred. All of the above costs are included in the intangible assets of Minny.

(vi) Minny intends to dispose of a major line of the parent's business operations. At the date the held for sale criteria were met, the carrying amount of the assets and liabilities comprising the line of business were:

	$m
Property, plant and equipment (PPE)	49
Inventory	18
Current liabilities	3

It is anticipated that Minny will realise $30 million for the business. No adjustments have been made in the financial statements in relation to the above decision.

Required

(a) Prepare the consolidated statement of financial position for the Minny Group as at 30 November 20X2

(35 marks)

(b) Minny intends to dispose of a major line of business in the above scenario and the entity has stated that the held for sale criteria were met under IFRS 5 *Non-current assets held for sale and discontinued operations*. The criteria in IFRS 5 are very strict and regulators have been known to question entities on the application of the standard. The two criteria which must be met before an asset or disposal group will be defined as recovered principally through sale are: that it must be available for immediate sale in its present condition and the sale mustbe highly probable.

Required

Discuss what is meant in IFRS 5 by 'available for immediate sale in its present condition' and 'the sale must be highly probable', setting out briefly why regulators may question entities on the application of the standard.

(7 marks)

(c) Bower has a property which has a carrying value of $2 million at 30 November 20X2. This property had been revalued at the year end and a revaluation surplus of $400,000 had been recorded in other components of equity. The directors were intending to sell the property to Minny for $1 million shortly after the year end. Bower previously used the historical cost basis for valuing property.

Required

Without adjusting your answer to Part (a), discuss the ethical and accounting implications of the above intended sale of assets to Minny by Bower.

(8 marks)

(Total = 50 marks)

44 Case study question: Trailer

Trailer, a public limited company, operates in the manufacturing sector. Trailer has investments in two other companies. The draft statements of financial position at 31 May 20X3 are as follows.

	Trailer $m	Park $m	Caller $m
Assets			
Non-current assets:			
Property, plant and equipment	1,440	1,100	1,300
Investment in subsidiaries			
Park	1,250	–	–
Caller	310	1,270	–
Financial assets	320	21	141
	3,320	2,391	1,441
Current assets	895	681	150
Total assets	4,215	3,072	1,591
Equity and liabilities			
Share capital	1,750	1,210	800
Retained earnings	1,240	930	350
Other components of equity	125	80	95
Total equity	3,115	2,220	1,245
Non-current liabilities	985	765	150
Current liabilities	115	87	196
Total liabilities	1,100	852	346
Total equity and liabilities	4,215	3,072	1,591

The following information is relevant to the preparation of the group financial statements.

(a)   On 1 June 20X1, Trailer acquired 14% of the equity interests of Caller for a cash consideration of $260 million and Park acquired 70% of the equity interests of Caller for a cash consideration of $1,270 million. At 1 June 20X1, the identifiable net assets of Caller had a fair value of $990 million, retained earnings were $190 million and other components of equity were $52 million. At 1 June 20X2, the identifiable net assets of Caller had a fair value of $1,150 million, retained earnings were $240 million and other components of equity were $70 million. The excess in fair value is due to non-depreciable land.

The fair value of the 14% holding of Trailer in Caller was $280 million at 31 May 20X2 and $310 million at 31 May 20X3. The fair value of Park's interest in Caller had not changed since acquisition.

(b)   On 1 June 20X2, Trailer acquired 60% of the equity interests of Park, a public limited company. The purchase consideration comprised cash of $1,250 million. On 1 June 20X2, the fair value of the identifiable net assets acquired was $1,950 million and retained earnings of Park were $650 million and other components of equity were $55 million. The excess in fair value is due to non-depreciable land.

It is the group's policy to measure the non-controlling interest at acquisition at its proportionate share of the fair value of the subsidiary's net assets.

(c)   Goodwill of Park and Caller was impairment tested at 31 May 20X3. There was no impairment relating to Caller. The recoverable amount of the net assets of Park was $2,088 million. This amount includes the cost of Park's investment in Caller. There was no impairment of the net assets of Park before this date and any impairment loss has been determined to relate to goodwill and property, plant and equipment.

(d)   Trailer has made a loan of $50 million to a charitable organisation for the building of new sporting facilities. The loan was made on 1 June 20X2 and is repayable on maturity in three years' time. Interest is to be charged one year in arrears at 3%, but Trailer assesses that an unsubsidised rate for such a loan would have been 6%. The only accounting entries which have been made for the year ended 31 May 20X3 are the cash entries for the loan and interest received which have resulted in a balance of $48.5 million being shown as a financial asset.

(e) On 1 June 20X1, Trailer acquired office accommodation at a cost of $90 million with a 30-year estimated useful life. During the year, the property market in the area slumped and the fair value of the accommodation fell to $75 million at 31 May 20X2 and this was reflected in the financial statements. However, the market recovered unexpectedly quickly due to the announcement of major government investment in the area's transport infrastructure. On 31 May 20X3, the valuer advised Trailer that the offices should now be valued at $105 million. Trailer has charged depreciation for the year but has not taken account of the upward valuation of the offices. Trailer uses the revaluation model and records any valuation change when advised to do so.

(f) Trailer has announced two major restructuring plans. The first plan is to reduce its capacity by the closure of some of its smaller factories, which have already been identified. This will lead to the redundancy of 500 employees, who have all individually been selected and communicated with. The costs of this plan are $9 million in redundancy costs, $4 million in retraining costs and $5 million in lease termination costs. The second plan is to re-organise the finance and information technology department over a one-year period but it does not commence for two years. The plan results in 20% of finance staff losing their jobs during the restructuring. The costs of this plan are $10 million in redundancy costs, $6 million in retraining costs and $7 million in equipment lease termination costs. No entries have been made in the financial statements for the above plans.

(g) The following information relates to the group pension plan of Trailer

	1 June 20X2 ($m)	31 May 20X3 ($m)
Fair value of plan assets	28	29
Actuarial value of defined benefit obligation	30	35

The contributions for the period received by the fund were $2 million and the employee benefits paid in the year amounted to $3 million. The discount rate to be used in any calculation is 5%. The current service cost for the period based on actuarial calculations is $1 million. The above figures have not been taken into account for the year ended 31 May 20X3 except for the contributions paid which have been entered in cash and the defined benefit obligation.

Required

(a) Prepare the group consolidated statement of financial position of Trailer Group as at 31 May 20X3.

(35 marks)

(b) It is the Trailer group's policy to measure the non-controlling interest (NCI) at acquisition at its proportionate share of the fair value of the subsidiary's net assets. The directors of Trailer have used this policy for several years and do not know the implications, if any, of changing the policy to that of accounting for the NCI at fair value. The fair value of the NCI of Park at 1 June 20X2 was $800 million. The fair value of the NCI of Caller, based upon the effective shareholdings, was $500 million at 1 June 20X1 and $530 million at 1 June 20X2.

Required

Explain to the directors, with suitable calculations, the impact on the financial statements if goodwill was calculated using the fair value of the NCI. **(9 marks)**

(c) The directors of Trailer are involved in takeover talks with another entity. In the discussions, one of the directors stated that there was no point in an accountant studying ethics because every accountant already has a set of moral beliefs that are followed and these are created by simply following generally accepted accounting practice. He further stated that in adopting a defensive approach to the takeover, there was no ethical issue in falsely declaring Trailer's profits in the financial statements used for the discussions because, in his opinion, the takeover did not benefit the company, its executives or society as a whole.

Required

Discuss the above views of the director regarding the fact that there is no point in an accountant studying ethics and that there was no ethical issue in the false disclosure of accounting profits. **(6 marks)**

(Total = 50 marks)

45 Preparation question: Part disposal

> **BPP note**. In this question, proformas are given to you to help you get used to setting out your answer. You may wish to transfer them to a separate sheet or to use a separate sheet for your workings.

Angel Co bought 70% of the share capital of Shane Co for $120,000 on 1 January 20X6. At that date Shane Co's retained earnings stood at $10,000.

The statements of financial position at 31 December 20X8, summarised statements of profit or loss and other comprehensive income to that date and movement on retained earnings are given below.

	Angel Co $'000	Shane Co $'000
STATEMENTS OF FINANCIAL POSITION		
Non-current assets		
Property, plant and equipment	200	80
Investment in Shane Co	120	–
	320	80
Current assets	890	140
	1,210	220
Equity		
Share capital – $1 ordinary shares	500	100
Retained reserves	400	90
	900	190
Current liabilities	310	30
	1,210	220
SUMMARISED STATEMENTS OF PROFIT OR LOSS AND OTHER COMPREHENSIVE INCOME		
Profit before interest and tax	100	20
Income tax expense	(40)	(8)
Profit for the year	60	12
Other comprehensive income (not reclassified to P/L) , net of tax	10	6
Total comprehensive income for the year	70	18
MOVEMENT IN RETAINED RESERVES		
Balance at 31 December 20X7	330	72
Total comprehensive income for the year	70	18
Balance at 31 December 20X8	400	90

Angel Co sells one half of its holding in Shane Co for $120,000 on 30 June 20X8. At that date, the fair value of the 35% holding in Shane was slightly more at $130,000 due to a share price rise. The remaining holding is to be dealt with as an associate. This does not represent a discontinued operation.

No entries have been made in the accounts for the above transaction.

Assume that profits accrue evenly throughout the year.

It is the group's policy to value the non-controlling interest at acquisition fair value. The fair value of the non-controlling interest on 1 January 20X6 was $51.4m.

Required

(a) Prepare the consolidated statement of financial position, statement of profit or loss and other comprehensive income and a reconciliation of movement in retained reserves for the year ended 31 December 20X8.

Ignore income taxes on the disposal. No impairment losses have been necessary to date.

PART DISPOSAL PROFORMA

ANGEL GROUP
CONSOLIDATED STATEMENT OF FINANCIAL POSITION
AS AT 31 DECEMBER 20X8 $'000
Non-current assets
Property, plant and equipment
Investment in Shane
                                                                        _____

Current assets   _____

                                                                        _____

Equity attributable to owners of the parent
Share capital
Retained reserves
                                                                        _____

Current liabilities   _____

                                                                        _____

CONSOLIDATED STATEMENT OF PROFIT OR LOSS AND OTHER COMPREHENSIVE INCOME
FOR THE YEAR ENDED 31 DECEMBER 20X8

                                                                          $'000
Profit before interest and tax
Profit on disposal of shares in subsidiary
Share of profit of associate
                                                                        _____
Profit before tax
Income tax expense
                                                                        _____
Profit for the year
                                                                        _____

Other comprehensive income (not reclassified to P/L) net of tax:
Share of other comprehensive income of associate
Other comprehensive income for the year
Total comprehensive income for the year

Profit attributable to:
  Owners of the parent
  Non-controlling interests
                                                                        _____

                                                                        _____

Total comprehensive income attributable to
  Owners of the parent
  Non-controlling interests
                                                                        _____

                                                                        _____

CONSOLIDATED RECONCILIATION OF MOVEMENT IN RETAINED RESERVES
                                                                          $'000

Balance at 31 December 20X7
Total comprehensive income for the year
Balance at 31 December 20X8
                                                                        _____

                                                                        _____

(b)   Explain the accounting treatment that would be required if Angel had disposed of 10% of its holding in Shane.

46 Preparation question: Purchase of further interest

RBE owns 70% of the ordinary share capital of DCA. The total group equity as at 31 December 20X1 was $4,000,000, which included $650,000 attributable to non-controlling interest.

RBE purchased a further 20% of the ordinary share capital of DCA on 1 October 20X2 for $540,000.

During the year to 31 December 20X2, RBE issued 2 million $1 ordinary shares, fully paid, at $1.30 per share.

Dividends were paid by both group entities in April 20X2. The dividends paid by RBE and DCA were $200,000 and $100,000, respectively.

Total comprehensive income for the year ended 31 December 20X2 for RBE was $900,000 and for DCA was $600,000. Income is assumed to accrue evenly throughout the year.

Required

(a)   Explain the impact of the additional 20% purchase of DCA's ordinary share capital by RBE on the equity of the RBE Group.

(b)   Prepare the consolidated statement of changes in equity for the year ended 31 December 20X2 for the RBE Group, showing the total equity attributable to the parent and to the non-controlling interest.

47 Case study question: Marchant   90 mins

6/14

The following financial statements relate to Marchant, a public limited company.

MARCHANT GROUP: STATEMENTS OF PROFIT OR LOSS AND OTHER COMPREHENSIVE INCOME
FOR THE YEAR ENDED 30 APRIL 20X4

	Marchant $m	Nathan $m	Option $m
Revenue	400	115	70
Cost of sales	(312)	(65)	(36)
Gross profit	88	50	34
Other income	21	7	2
Administrative costs	(15)	(9)	(12)
Other expenses	(35)	(19)	(8)
Operating profit	59	29	16
Finance costs	(5)	(6)	(4)
Finance income	6	5	8
Profit before tax	60	28	20
Income tax expense	(19)	(9)	(5)
Profit for the year	41	19	15
Other comprehensive income for the year, net of tax – Items that will not be reclassified to profit or loss:			
Revaluation surplus	10	–	–
Total comprehensive income and expense for year	51	19	15

The following information is relevant to the preparation of the group statement of profit or loss and other comprehensive income:

(i)   On 1 May 20X2, Marchant acquired 60% of the equity interests of Nathan, a public limited company. The purchase consideration comprised cash of $80 million and the fair value of the identifiable net assets acquired was $110 million at that date. The fair value of the non-controlling interest (NCI) in Nathan was $45 million on 1 May 20X2. Marchant wishes to use the 'full goodwill' method for all acquisitions. The share capital and retained earnings of Nathan were $25 million and $65 million respectively and other components of equity were $6 million at the date of acquisition. The excess of the fair value of the identifiable net assets at acquisition is due to non-depreciable land.

Goodwill has been impairment tested annually and as at 30 April 20X3 had reduced in value by 20%. However at 30 April 20X4, the impairment of goodwill had reversed and goodwill was valued at $2 million above its original value. This upward change in value has already been included in above draft financial statements of Marchant prior to the preparation of the group accounts.

(ii) Marchant disposed of an 8% equity interest in Nathan on 30 April 20X4 for a cash consideration of $18 million and had accounted for the gain or loss in other income. The carrying value of the net assets of Nathan at 30 April 20X4 was $120 million before any adjustments on consolidation. Marchant accounts for investments in subsidiaries using IFRS 9 *Financial Instruments,* and has made an election to show gains and losses in other comprehensive income. The carrying value of the investment in Nathan was $90 million at 30 April 20X3 and $95 million at 30 April 20X4 before the disposal of the equity interest.

(iii) Marchant acquired 60% of the equity interests of Option, a public limited company, on 30 April 20X2. The purchase consideration was cash of $70 million. Option's identifiable net assets were fair valued at $86 million and the NCI had a fair value of $28 million at that date. On 1 November 20X3, Marchant disposed of a 40% equity interest in Option for a consideration of $50 million. Option's identifiable net assets were $90 million and the value of the NCI was $34 million at the date of disposal. The remaining equity interest was fair valued at $40 million. After the disposal, Marchant exerts significant influence. Any increase in net assets since acquisition has been reported in profit or loss and the carrying value of the investment in Option had not changed since acquisition. Goodwill had been impairment tested and no impairment was required. No entries had been made in the financial statements of Marchant for this transaction other than for cash received.

(iv) Marchant sold inventory to Nathan for $12 million at fair value. Marchant made a loss on the transaction of $2 million and Nathan still holds $8 million in inventory at the year end.

(v) The following information relates to Marchant's pension scheme:

	$m
Plan assets at 1 May 20X3	48
Defined benefit obligation at 1 May 20X3	50
Service cost for year ended 30 April 20X4	4
Discount rate at 1 May 20X3	10%
Re-measurement loss in year ended 30 April 20X4	2
Past service cost 1 May 20X3	3

The pension costs have not been accounted for in total comprehensive income.

(vi) On 1 May 20X2, Marchant purchased an item of property, plant and equipment for $12 million and this is being depreciated using the straight line basis over 10 years with a zero residual value. At 30 April 20X3, the asset was revalued to $13 million but at 30 April 20X4, the value of the asset had fallen to $7 million. Marchant uses the revaluation model to value its non-current assets. The effect of the revaluation at 30 April 20X4 had not been taken into account in total comprehensive income but depreciation for the year had been charged.

(vii) On 1 May 20X2, Marchant made an award of 8,000 share options to each of its seven directors. The condition attached to the award is that the directors must remain employed by Marchant for three years. The fair value of each option at the grant date was $100 and the fair value of each option at 30 April 20X4 was $110. At 30 April 20X3, it was estimated that three directors would leave before the end of three years. Due to an economic downturn, the estimate of directors who were going to leave was revised to one director at 30 April 20X4. The expense for the year as regards the share options had not been included in profit or loss for the current year and no directors had left by 30 April 20X4.

(viii) A loss on an effective cash flow hedge of Nathan of $3 million has been included in the subsidiary's finance costs.

(ix) Ignore the taxation effects of the above adjustments unless specified. Any expense adjustments should be amended in other expenses.

Required

(a) (i) Prepare a consolidated statement of profit or loss and other comprehensive income for the year ended 30 April 20X4 for the Marchant Group. **(30 marks)**

(ii) Explain, with suitable calculations, how the sale of the 8% interest in Nathan should be dealt with in the group statement of financial position at 30 April 20X4. **(5 marks)**

(b) The directors of Marchant have strong views on the usefulness of the financial statements after their move to International Financial Reporting Standards (IFRSs). They feel that IFRSs implement a fair value model. Nevertheless, they are of the opinion that IFRSs are failing users of financial statements as they do not reflect the financial value of an entity.

Required

Discuss the directors' views above as regards the use of fair value in IFRSs and the fact that IFRSs do not reflect the financial value of an entity. **(9 marks)**

(c) Marchant plans to update its production process and the directors feel that technology-led production is the only feasible way in which the company can remain competitive. Marchant operates from a leased property and the leasing arrangement was established in order to maximise taxation benefits. However, the financial statements have not shown a lease asset or liability to date.

A new financial controller joined Marchant just after the financial year end of 30 April 20X4 and is presently reviewing the financial statements to prepare for the upcoming audit and to begin making a loan application to finance the new technology. The financial controller feels that the lease relating to both the land and buildings should be treated as a finance lease but the finance director disagrees. The finance director does not wish to recognise the lease in the statement of financial position and therefore wishes to continue to treat it as an operating lease. The finance director feels that the lease does not meet the criteria for a finance lease, and it was made clear by the finance director that showing the lease as a finance lease could jeopardise the loan application.

Required

Discuss the ethical and professional issues which face the financial controller in the above situation.

(6 marks)

(Total = 50 marks)

48 Ejoy

54 mins

ACR, 6/06, amended

Ejoy, a public limited company, has acquired two subsidiaries. The details of the acquisitions are as follows:

Company	Date of acquisition	Ordinary share capital of $1 $m	Reserves at acquisition $m	Fair value of net assets at acquisition $m	Cost of investment $m	Ordinary share capital of $1 acquired $m
Zbay	1 June 20X4	200	170	600	520	160
Tbay	1 December 20X5	120	80	310	192	72

Any fair value adjustments relate to non-depreciable land. The draft statements of profit or loss and other comprehensive income for the year ended 31 May 20X6 are:

	Ejoy $m	Zbay $m	Tbay $m
Revenue	2,500	1,500	800
Cost of sales	(1,800)	(1,200)	(600)
Gross profit	700	300	200
Other income	70	10	–
Distribution costs	(130)	(120)	(70)
Administrative expenses	(100)	(90)	(60)
Finance costs	(50)	(40)	(20)
Profit before tax	490	60	50
Income tax expense	(200)	(26)	(20)
Profit for the year	290	34	30
Other comprehensive for the year (not reclassified to profit or loss):			
Gain on property revaluation net of tax	80	10	8
Total comprehensive income for the year	370	44	38
Total comprehensive income for year 31 May 20X5	190	20	15

The following information is relevant to the preparation of the group financial statements.

(a) Tbay was acquired exclusively with a view to sale and at 31 May 20X6 meets the criteria of being a disposal group. The fair value of Tbay at 31 May 20X6 is $344 million and the estimated selling costs of the shareholding in Tbay are $5 million.

(b) Ejoy entered into a joint arrangement with another company on 31 May 20X6, which met the IFRS 11 definition of a joint venture. The joint venture is a limited company and Ejoy has contributed assets at fair value of $20 million (carrying value $14 million). Each party will hold five million ordinary shares of $1 in the joint venture. The gain on the disposal of the assets ($6 million) to the joint venture has been included in 'other income'.

(c) Zbay has a loan asset which was carried at $60 million at 1 June 20X5. The loan's effective interest rate is 6%. On 1 June 20X5 the company felt that because of the borrower's financial problems, it would receive $20 million in approximately two years time, on 31 May 20X7. At 31 May 20X6, the company still expects to receive the same amount on the same date. The loan asset is held at amortised cost.

(d) On 1 June 20X5, Ejoy purchased a five year bond with a principal amount of $50 million and a fixed interest rate of 5% which was the current market rate. The bond is classified as at fair value through profit or loss. Because of the size of the investment, Ejoy has entered into a floating interest rate swap. Ejoy has designated the swap as a fair value hedge of the bond. At 31 May 20X6, market interest rates were 6%. As a result, the fair value of the bond has decreased to $48.3 million. Ejoy has received $0.5 million in net interest payments on the swap at 31 May 20X6 and the fair value hedge has been 100% effective in the period, and you should assume any gain/loss on the hedge is the same as the loss/gain on the bond. No entries have been made in the statement of profit or loss and other comprehensive income to account for the bond or the hedge.

(e) No impairment of the goodwill arising on the acquisition of Zbay had occurred at 1 June 20X5. The recoverable amount of Zbay was $630 million and the value in use of Tbay was $334 million at 31 May 20X6. Impairment losses on goodwill are charged to cost of sales.

(f) Assume that profits accrue evenly throughout the year and ignore any taxation effects.

(g) It is the group's policy to value the non-controlling interest at its proportionate share of the fair value of the subsidiary's identifiable net assets.

Required

Prepare a consolidated statement of profit or loss and other comprehensive income for the Ejoy Group for the year ended 31 May 20X6 in accordance with International Financial Reporting Standards.

(30 marks)

49 Case study question: Traveler

90 mins

12/11

Traveler, a public limited company, operates in the manufacturing sector. The draft statements of financial position of the group companies are as follows at 30 November 20X1.

	Traveler $m	Data $m	Captive $m
Assets			
Non-current assets			
Property, plant and equipment	439	810	620
Investment in subsidiaries:			
Data	820		
Captive	541		
Financial assets	108	10	20
	1,908	820	640
Net defined benefit asset	72		
Current assets	995	781	350
Total assets	2,975	1,601	990

	Traveler $m	Data $m	Captive $m
Equity and liabilities			
Share capital	1,120	600	390
Retained earnings	1,066	442	169
Other components of equity	60	37	45
Total equity	2,246	1,079	604
Non-current liabilities	455	323	73
Current liabilities	274	199	313
Total liabilities	729	522	386
Total equity and liabilities	2,975	1,601	990

The following information is relevant to the preparation of the group financial statements.

(i)   On 1 December 20X0, Traveler acquired 60% of the equity interests of Data, a public limited company. The purchase consideration comprised cash of $600 million. At acquisition, the fair value of the non-controlling interest in Data was $395 million. Traveler wishes to use the 'full goodwill' method. On 1 December 20X0, the fair value of the identifiable net assets acquired was $935 million and retained earnings of Data were $299 million and other components of equity were $26 million. The excess in fair value is due to non-depreciable land.

On 30 November 20X1, Traveler acquired a further 20% interest in Data for a cash consideration of $220 million.

(ii)   On 1 December 20X0, Traveler acquired 80% of the equity interests of Captive for a consideration of $541 million. The consideration comprised cash of $477 million and the transfer of non-depreciable land with a fair value of $64 million. The carrying amount of the land at the acquisition date was $56 million. At the year end, this asset was still included in the non-current assets of Traveler and the sale proceeds had been credited to profit or loss.

At the date of acquisition, the identifiable net assets of Captive had a fair value of $526 million, retained earnings were $90 million and other components of equity were $24 million. The excess in fair value is due to non-depreciable land. This acquisition was accounted for using the partial goodwill method in accordance with IFRS 3 (Revised) *Business combinations*.

(iii) Goodwill was impairment tested after the additional acquisition in Data on 30 November 20X1. The recoverable amount of Data was $1,099 million and that of Captive was $700 million.

(iv) Included in the financial assets of Traveler is a ten-year 7% loan. At 30 November 20X1, the borrower was in financial difficulties and its credit rating had been downgraded. Traveler has adopted IFRS 9 *Financial instruments* and the loan asset is currently held at amortised cost of $29 million. Traveler now wishes to value the loan at fair value using current market interest rates. Traveler has agreed for the loan to be restructured; there will only be three more annual payments of $8 million starting in one year's time. Current market interest rates are 8%, the original effective interest rate is 6.7% and the effective interest rate under the revised payment schedule is 6.3%.

(v) Traveler acquired a new factory on 1 December 20X0. The cost of the factory was $50 million and it has a residual value of $2 million. The factory has a flat roof, which needs replacing every five years. The cost of the roof was $5 million. The useful economic life of the factory is 25 years. No depreciation has been charged for the year. Traveler wishes to account for the factory and roof as a single asset and depreciate the whole factory over its economic life. Traveler uses straight-line depreciation.

(vi) The actuarial value of Traveler's pension plan showed a surplus at 1 December 20X0 of $72 million. Losses of $25 million on remeasurement of the net defined benefit asset are to be recognised in other comprehensive income in accordance with IAS 19 (revised 2011). The aggregate of the current service cost and the net interest cost amounted to a cost of $55 million for the year. After consulting with the actuaries, the company decided to reduce its contributions for the year to $45 million. The contributions were paid on 7 November 20X1. No entries had been made in the financial statements for the above amounts. The present value of available future refunds and reductions in future contributions was $18 million.

Required

(a) Prepare a consolidated statement of financial position for the Traveler Group as at 30 November 20X1.

(35 marks)

(b) Traveler has three distinct business segments. The management has calculated the net assets, turnover and profit before common costs, which are to be allocated to these segments. However, they are unsure as to how they should allocate certain common costs and whether they can exercise judgement in the allocation process. They wish to allocate head office management expenses; pension expense; the cost of managing properties and interest and related interest bearing assets. They also are uncertain as to whether the allocation of costs has to be in conformity with the accounting policies used in the financial statements.

Required

Advise the management of Traveler on the points raised in the above paragraph. **(8 marks)**

(c) Segmental information reported externally is more useful if it conforms to information used by management in making decisions. The information can differ from that reported in the financial statements. Although reconciliations are required, these can be complex and difficult to understand. Additionally, there are other standards where subjectivity is involved and often the profit motive determines which accounting practice to follow. The directors have a responsibility to shareholders in disclosing information to enhance corporate value but this may conflict with their corporate social responsibility.

Required

Discuss how the ethics of corporate social responsibility disclosure are difficult to reconcile with shareholder expectations. **(7 marks)**

(Total = 50 marks)

50 Case study question: Robby

90 mins

The following draft statements of financial position relate to Robby, Hail and Zinc, all public limited companies, as at 31 May 20X3

	Robby $m	Hail $m	Zinc $m
Assets			
Non-current assets			
Property, plant and equipment	112	60	26
Investments in subsidiaries:			
Hail	55		
Zinc	19		
Financial assets	9	6	14
Joint operation	6		
Current assets	5	7	12
Total assets	206	73	52
Equity and liabilities			
Ordinary shares	25	20	10
Other components of equity	11	–	–
Retained earnings	70	27	19
Total equity	106	47	29
Non-current liabilities:	53	20	21
Current liabilities	47	6	2
Total equity and liabilities	206	73	52

The following information is relevant to the preparation of the group financial statements of Robby.

(a) On 1 June 20X1, Robby acquired 80% of the equity interests of Hail. The purchase consideration comprised cash of $50 million. Robby has treated the investment in Hail at fair value through other comprehensive income (OCI).

   A dividend received from Hail on 1 January 20X3 of $2 million has similarly been credited to OCI.

   It is Robby's policy to measure the non-controlling interest at fair value and this was $15 million on 1 June 20X1.

   On 1 June 20X1, the fair value of the identifiable net assets of Hail was $60 million and the retained earnings of Hail were $16 million. The excess of the fair value of the net assets is due to an increase in the value of non-depreciable land.

(b) On 1 June 20X0, Robby acquired 5% of the ordinary shares of Zinc. Robby had treated this investment at fair value through profit or loss in the financial statements to 31 May 20X2.

   On 1 December 20X2, Robby acquired a further 55% of the ordinary shares of Zinc and gained control of the company.

   The consideration for the acquisitions was as follows.

	Shareholding	Consideration $m
1 June 20X0	5%	2
1 December 20X2	55%	16
	60%	18

   At 1 December 20X2, the fair value of the equity interest in Zinc held by Robby before the business combination was $5 million.

   It is Robby's policy to measure the non-controlling interest at fair value and this was $9 million on 1 December 20X2.

BPP
LEARNING MEDIA

The fair value of the identifiable net assets at 1 December 20X2 of Zinc was $26 million, and the retained earnings were $15 million. The excess of the fair value of the net assets is due to an increase in the value of property, plant and equipment (PPE), which was provisional pending receipt of the final valuations. These valuations were received on 1 March 20X3 and resulted in an additional increase of $3 million in the fair value of PPE at the date of acquisition. This increase does not affect the fair value of the non-controlling interest at acquisition. PPE is to be depreciated on the straight-line basis over a remaining period of five years.

(c) Robby has a 40% share of a joint operation, a natural gas station. Assets, liabilities, revenue and costs are apportioned on the basis of shareholding. The following information relates to the joint arrangement activities.

 (i) The natural gas station cost $15 million to construct and was completed on 1 June 20X2 and is to be dismantled at the end of its life of ten years. The present value of this dismantling cost to the joint arrangement at 1 June 20X2, using a discount rate of 5%, was $2 million.

 (ii) In the year, gas with a direct cost of $16 million was sold for $20 million. Additionally, the joint arrangement incurred operating costs of $0.5 million during the year.

Robby has only contributed and accounted for its share of the construction cost, paying $6 million. The revenue and costs are receivable and payable by the other joint operator who settles amounts outstanding with Robby after the year end.

(d) Robby purchased PPE for $10 million on 1 June 20X0. It has an expected useful life of twenty years and is depreciated on the straight-line method. On 31 May 20X2, the PPE was revalued to $11 million. At 31 May 20X3, impairment indicators triggered an impairment review of the PPE. The recoverable amount of the PPE was $7.8 million. The only accounting entry posted for the year to 31 May 20X3 was to account for the depreciation based on the revalued amount as at 31 May 20X2. Robby's accounting policy is to make a transfer of the excess depreciation arising on the revaluation of PPE.

(e) Robby held a portfolio of trade receivables with a carrying amount of $4 million at 31 May 20X3. At that date, the entity entered into a factoring agreement with a bank, whereby it transfers the receivables in exchange for $3.6 million in cash. Robby has agreed to reimburse the factor for any shortfall between the amount collected and $3.6 million. Once the receivables have been collected, any amounts above $3.6 million, less interest on this amount, will be repaid to Robby. Robby has derecognised the receivables and charged $0.4 million as a loss to profit or loss.

(f) Immediately prior to the year end, Robby sold land to a third party at a price of $16 million with an option to purchase the land back on 1 July 20X3 for $16 million plus a premium of 3%. The market value of the land is $25 million on 31 May 20X3 and the carrying amount was $12 million. Robby accounted for the sale, consequently eliminating the bank overdraft at 31 May 20X3.

Required

(a) Prepare a consolidated statement of financial position of the Robby Group at 31 May 20X3 in accordance with International Financial Reporting Standards. **(35 marks)**

(b) (i) In the above scenario (information point (e)), Robby holds a portfolio of trade receivables and enters into a factoring agreement with a bank, whereby it transfers the receivables in exchange for cash. Robby additionally agreed to other terms with the bank as regards any collection shortfall and repayment of any monies to Robby. Robby derecognised the receivables. This is an example of the type of complex transaction that can arise out of normal terms of trade. The rules regarding derecognition are quite complex and are often not understood by entities.

 Describe the rules of IFRS 9 *Financial Instruments* relating to the derecognition of a financial asset and how these rules affect the treatment of the portfolio of trade receivables in Robby's financial statements. **(9 marks)**

 (ii) Discuss the legitimacy of Robby selling land just prior to the year end in order to show a better liquidity position for the group and whether this transaction is consistent with an accountant's responsibilities to users of financial statements. **(6 marks)**

 Note. Your answer should include reference to the above scenario.

(Total = 50 marks)

51 Case study question: Bravado

90 mins

Bravado, a public limited company, has acquired two subsidiaries and an associate. The draft statements of financial position are as follows at 31 May 20X9.

	Bravado $m	Message $m	Mixted $m
Assets			
Non-current assets			
Property, plant and equipment	265	230	161
Investments in subsidiaries:			
Message	300		
Mixted	133		
Investment in associate: Clarity	20		
Investment in equity instruments	51	6	5
	769	236	166
Current assets			
Inventories	135	55	73
Trade receivables	91	45	32
Cash and cash equivalents	102	100	8
	328	200	113
	1,097	436	279
Total assets			
Equity and liabilities			
Share capital	520	220	100
Retained earnings	240	150	80
Other components of equity	17	4	7
Total equity	777	374	187
Non-current liabilities:			
Long-term borrowings	120	15	5
Deferred tax	25	9	3
Total non-current liabilities	145	24	8
Current liabilities			
Trade and other payables	115	30	60
Current tax payable	60	8	24
Total current liabilities	175	38	84
Total liabilities	320	62	92
Total equity and liabilities	1,097	436	279

The following information is relevant to the preparation of the group financial statements.

(a)   On 1 June 20X8, Bravado acquired 80% of the equity interests of Message, a private entity. The purchase consideration comprised cash of $300 million. The fair value of the identifiable net assets of Message was $400 million, including any related deferred tax liability arising on acquisition. The owners of Message had to dispose of the entity for tax purposes by a specified date, and therefore sold the entity to the first company to bid for it, which was Bravado. An independent valuer has stated that the fair value of the non-controlling interest in Message was $86 million on 1 June 20X8. Bravado does not wish to measure the non-controlling interest in subsidiaries on the basis of the proportionate interest in the identifiable net assets, but wishes to use the 'full goodwill' method. The retained earnings of Message were $136 million and other components of equity were $4 million at the date of acquisition. There had been no new issue of capital by Message since the date of acquisition and the excess of the fair value of the net assets is due to an increase in the value of non-depreciable land.

(b) On 1 June 20X7, Bravado acquired 6% of the ordinary shares of Mixted. Bravado had treated this as an as investment in equity instruments at fair value in the financial statements to 31 May 20X8, and had made an irrevocable election (see note (d)) to recognise changes in fair value in other comprehensive income. There were no changes in the fair value of Mixted in the year to 31 May 20X9. On 1 June 20X8, Bravado acquired a further 64% of the ordinary shares of Mixted and gained control of the company. The consideration for the acquisitions was as follows.

	Holding	Consideration $m
1 June 20X7	6%	10
1 June 20X8	64%	118
	70%	128

Under the purchase agreement of 1 June 20X8, Bravado is required to pay the former shareholders 30% of the profits of Mixted on 31 May 20Y0 for each of the financial years to 31 May 20X9 and 31 May 20Y0. The fair value of this arrangement was measured at $12 million at 1 June 20X8 and at 31 May 20X9 this value had not changed. This amount has not been included in the financial statements.

At 1 June 20X8, the fair value of the equity interest in Mixted held by Bravado before the business combination was $15 million, and the fair value of the non-controlling interest in Mixted was $53 million. The fair value of the identifiable net assets at 1 June 20X8 of Mixted was $170 million (excluding deferred tax assets and liabilities), and the retained earnings and other components of equity were $55 million and $7 million respectively. There had been no new issue of share capital by Mixted since the date of acquisition and the excess of the fair value of the net assets is due to an increase in the value of property, plant and equipment (PPE).

The fair value of the PPE was provisional pending receipt of the final valuations for these assets. These valuations were received on 1 December 20X8 and they resulted in a further increase of $6 million in the fair value of the net assets at the date of acquisition. This increase does not affect the fair value of the non-controlling interest. PPE is depreciated on the straight-line basis over seven years. The tax base of the identifiable net assets of Mixted was $166 million at 1 June 20X8. The tax rate of Mixted is 30%.

(c) Bravado acquired a 10% interest in Clarity, a public limited company, on 1 June 20X7 for $8 million. The investment was accounted for as an investment in equity instruments and at 31 May 20X8, its value was $9 million. On 1 June 20X8, Bravado acquired an additional 15% interest in Clarity for $11 million and achieved significant influence. Clarity made profits after dividends of $6 million and $10 million for the years to 31 May 20X8 and 31 May 20X9. An irrevocable election was made to take changes in fair value through other comprehensive income (items that will not be reclassified to profit or loss).

(d) Bravado has made an irrevocable election to hold its investments in Message, Mixted and Clarity at fair value with changes in fair value recognised in other comprehensive income. There were no changes in fair value during the year ended 31 May 20X9.

(e) On 1 June 20X7, Bravado purchased an equity instrument of 11 million dinars which was its fair value. On that date an election was made to hold it at fair value through other comprehensive income. The relevant exchange rates and fair values were as follows:

	$ to dinars	Fair value of instrument – dinars
1 June 20X7	4.5	11
31 May 20X8	5.1	10
31 May 20X9	4.8	7

Bravado has not recorded any change in the value of the instrument since 31 May 20X8. The reduction in fair value as at 31 May 20X9 is deemed to be as a result of impairment.

(f) Bravado manufactures equipment for the retail industry. The inventory is currently valued at cost. There is a market for the part completed product at each stage of production. The cost structure of the equipment is as follows.

	Cost per unit $	Selling price per unit $
Production process: 1st stage	1,000	1,050
Conversion costs: 2nd stage	500	
Finished product	1,500	1,700

The selling costs are $10 per unit, and Bravado has 10,000 units at the first stage of production and 20,000 units of the finished product at 31 May 20X9. Shortly before the year end, a competitor released a new model onto the market which caused the equipment manufactured by Bravado to become less attractive to customers. The result was a reduction in the selling price to $1,450 of the finished product and $950 for 1st stage product.

(g)   The directors have included a loan to a director of Bravado in cash and cash equivalents of $1 million. The loan has no specific repayment date on it but is repayable on demand. The directors feel that there is no problem with this accounting entry as there is a choice of accounting policy within International Financial Reporting Standards (IFRS) and that showing the loan as cash is their choice of accounting policy as there is no IFRS which says that this policy cannot be utilised.

(h)   There is no impairment of goodwill arising on the acquisitions.

Required

(a)   Prepare a consolidated statement of financial position as at 31 May 20X9 for the Bravado Group. **(35 marks)**

(b)   Calculate and explain the impact on the calculation of goodwill if the non-controlling interest was calculated on a proportionate basis for Message and Mixted. **(9 marks)**

(c)   Discuss the view of the directors that there is no problem with showing a loan to a director as cash and cash equivalents, taking into account their ethical and other responsibilities as directors of the company.
(6 marks)

(Total = 50 marks)

52 Case study question: Grange

90 mins

12/09

Grange, a public limited company, operates in the manufacturing sector. The draft statements of financial position of the group companies are as follows at 30 November 20X9.

	Grange $m	Park $m	Fence $m
Assets			
Non-current assets			
Property, plant and equipment	257	311	238
Investment in subsidiaries:			
Park	340		
Fence	134		
Investment in Sitin	16		
	747	311	238
Current assets	475	304	141
Total assets	1,222	615	379
Equity and liabilities			
Share capital	430	230	150
Retained earnings	410	170	65
Other components of equity	22	14	17
Total equity	862	414	232
Non-current liabilities	172	124	38
Current liabilities			
Trade and other payables	178	71	105
Provisions for liabilities	10	6	4
Total current liabilities	188	77	109
Total liabilities	360	201	147
Total equity and liabilities	1,222	615	379

The following information is relevant to the preparation of the group financial statements.

(i)   On 1 June 20X8, Grange acquired 60% of the equity interests of Park, a public limited company. The purchase consideration comprised cash of $250 million. Excluding the franchise referred to below, the fair value of the identifiable net assets was $360 million. The excess of the fair value of the net assets is due to an increase in the value of non-depreciable land.

Park held a franchise right, which at 1 June 20X8 had a fair value of $10 million. This had not been recognised in the financial statements of Park. The franchise agreement had a remaining term of five years to run at that date and is not renewable. Park still holds this franchise at the year-end.

Grange wishes to use the 'full goodwill' method for all acquisitions. The fair value of the non-controlling interest in Park was $150 million on 1 June 20X8. The retained earnings of Park were $115 million and other components of equity were $10 million at the date of acquisition.

Grange acquired a further 20% interest from the non-controlling interests in Park on 30 November 20X9 for a cash consideration of $90 million.

(ii)   On 31 July 20X8, Grange acquired 100% of the equity interests of Fence for a cash consideration of $214 million. The identifiable net assets of Fence had a provisional fair value of $202 million, including any contingent liabilities. At the time of the business combination, Fence had a contingent liability with a fair value of $30 million. At 30 November 20X9, the contingent liability met the recognition criteria of IAS 37 *Provisions, contingent liabilities and contingent assets* and the revised estimate of this liability was $25 million. The accountant of Fence is yet to account for this revised liability.

However, Grange had not completed the valuation of an element of property, plant and equipment of Fence at 31 July 20X8 and the valuation was not completed by 30 November 20X8. The valuation was received on 30 June 20X9 and the excess of the fair value over book value at the date of acquisition was measured at $4 million. The asset had a useful economic life of ten years at 31 July 20X8.

The retained earnings of Fence were $73 million and other components of equity were $9 million at 31 July 20X8 before any adjustment for the contingent liability.

On 30 November 20X9, Grange disposed of 25% of its equity interest in Fence to the non-controlling interest for a consideration of $80 million. The disposal proceeds had been credited to the cost of the investment in the statement of financial position.

(iii)   On 30 June 20X8, Grange had acquired a 100% interest in Sitin, a public limited company, for a cash consideration of $39 million. Sitin's identifiable net assets were fair valued at $32 million.

On 30 November 20X9, Grange disposed of 60% of the equity of Sitin when its identifiable net assets were $36 million. Of the increase in net assets, $3 million had been reported in profit or loss and $1 million had been reported in other comprehensive income as profit on an investment in equity instruments (with irrevocable OCI election). The sale proceeds were $23 million and the remaining equity interest was fair valued at $13 million. Grange could still exert significant influence after the disposal of the interest. The only accounting entry made in Grange's financial statements was to increase cash and reduce the cost of the investment in Sitin.

(iv)   Grange acquired a plot of land on 1 December 20X8 in an area where the land is expected to rise significantly in value if plans for regeneration go ahead in the area. The land is currently held at cost of $6 million in property, plant and equipment until Grange decides what should be done with the land. The market value of the land at 30 November 20X9 was $8 million but as at 15 December 20X9, this had reduced to $7 million as there was some uncertainty surrounding the viability of the regeneration plan.

(v)   Grange anticipates that it will be fined $1 million by the local regulator for environmental pollution. It also anticipates that it will have to pay compensation to local residents of $6 million, although this is only the best estimate of that liability. In addition, the regulator has requested that certain changes be made to the manufacturing process in order to make the process more environmentally friendly. This is anticipated to cost the company $4 million.

(vi)   Grange has a property located in a foreign country, which was acquired at a cost of 8 million dinars on 30 November 20X8 when the exchange rate was $1 = 2 dinars. At 30 November 20X9, the property was revalued to 12 million dinars. The exchange rate at 30 November 20X9 was $1 = 1.5 dinars. The property was being carried at its value as at 30 November 20X8. The company policy is to revalue property, plant and equipment whenever material differences exist between book and fair value. Depreciation on the property can be assumed to be immaterial.

(vii) Grange has prepared a plan for reorganising the parent company's own operations. The board of directors has discussed the plan but further work has to be carried out before they can approve it. However, Grange has made a public announcement as regards the reorganisation and wishes to make a reorganisation provision at 30 November 20X9 of $30 million. The plan will generate cost savings. The directors have calculated the value in use of the net assets (total equity) of the parent company as being $870 million if the reorganisation takes place and $830 million if the reorganisation does not take place. Grange is concerned that the parent company's property, plant and equipment have lost value during the period because of a decline in property prices in the region and feel that any impairment charge would relate to these assets. There is no reserve within other equity relating to prior revaluation of these non-current assets.

(viii) Grange uses accounting policies, which maximise its return on capital employed. The directors of Grange feel that they are acting ethically in using this approach as they feel that as long as they follow 'professional rules', then there is no problem. They have adopted a similar philosophy in the way they conduct their business affairs. The finance director had recently received information that one of their key customers, Brook, a public limited company, was having serious liquidity problems. This information was received from a close friend who was employed by Brook. However, he also learned that Brook had approached a rival company Field, a public limited company, for credit and knew that if Field granted Brook credit then there was a high probability that the outstanding balance owed by Brook to Grange would be paid. Field had approached the director for an informal credit reference for Brook who until recently had always paid promptly. The director was intending to give Brook a good reference because of its recent prompt payment history, as the director felt that there was no obligation or rule which required him to mention the company's liquidity problems. (There is no change required to the financial statements as a result of the above information.)

Required

(a) Calculate the consolidated gain or loss arising on the disposal of the equity interest in Sitin. **(7 marks)**

(b) Prepare a consolidated statement of financial position of the Grange Group at 30 November 20X9 in accordance with International Financial Reporting Standards. **(35 marks)**

(c) Discuss the view that ethical behaviour is simply a matter of compliance with professional rules and whether the finance director should simply consider 'rules' when determining whether to give Brook a good credit reference. **(8 marks)**

(Total = 50 marks)

53 Case study question: Ashanti

90 mins

6/10, amended

The following financial statements relate to Ashanti, a public limited company.

ASHANTI GROUP: STATEMENTS OF PROFIT OR LOSS AND OTHER COMPREHENSIVE INCOME
FOR THE YEAR ENDED 30 APRIL 20X5

	Ashanti $m	Bochem $m	Ceram $m
Revenue	810	235	142
Cost of sales	(686)	(137)	(84)
Gross profit	124	98	58
Other income	31	17	12
Distribution costs	(30)	(21)	(26)
Administrative costs	(55)	(29)	(12)
Finance costs	(8)	(6)	(8)
Profit before tax	62	59	24
Income tax expense	(21)	(23)	(10)
Profit for the year	41	36	14

	Ashanti $m	Bochem $m	Ceram $m
Other comprehensive income for the year, net of tax – Items that will not be reclassified to profit or loss:			
Investment in equity instruments	20	9	6
Gains (net) on PPE revaluation	12	6	–
Actuarial losses on defined benefit plan	(14)	–	–
Other comprehensive income for the year, net of tax	18	15	6
Total comprehensive income and expense for year	59	51	20

The following information is relevant to the preparation of the group statement of profit or loss and other comprehensive income:

(i) On 1 May 20X3, Ashanti acquired 70% of the equity interests of Bochem, a public limited company. The purchase consideration comprised cash of $150 million and the fair value of the identifiable net assets was $160 million at that date. The fair value of the non-controlling interest in Bochem was $54 million on 1 May 20X3. Ashanti wishes to use the 'full goodwill' method for all acquisitions. The share capital and retained earnings of Bochem were $55 million and $85 million respectively and other components of equity were $10 million at the date of acquisition. The excess of the fair value of the identifiable net assets at acquisition is due to an increase in the value of plant, which is depreciated on the straight-line method and has a five year remaining life at the date of acquisition. Ashanti disposed of a 10% equity interest to the non-controlling interests (NCI) of Bochem on 30 April 20X5 for a cash consideration of $34 million. The carrying value of the net assets of Bochem at 30 April 20X5 was $210 million before any adjustments on consolidation. Goodwill has been impairment tested annually and as at 30 April 20X4 had reduced in value by 15% and at 30 April 20X5 had lost a further 5% of its original value before the sale of the equity interest to the NCI. The goodwill impairment should be allocated between group and NCI on the basis of equity shareholding.

(ii) Bochem acquired 80% of the equity interests of Ceram, a public limited company, on 1 May 20X3. The purchase consideration was cash of $136 million. Ceram's identifiable net assets were fair valued at $115 million and the NCI of Ceram attributable to Ashanti had a fair value of $26 million at that date. On 1 November 20X4, Bochem disposed of 50% of the equity of Ceram for a consideration of $90 million. Ceram's identifiable net assets were $160 million and the consolidated value of the NCI of Ceram attributable to Bochem was $35 million at the date of disposal. The remaining equity interest of Ceram held by Bochem was fair valued at $45 million. After the disposal, Bochem can still exert significant influence. Goodwill had been impairment tested and no impairment had occurred. Ceram's profits are deemed to accrue evenly over the year.

(iii) Ashanti has sold inventory to both Bochem and Ceram in October 20X4. The sale price of the inventory was $10 million and $5 million respectively. Ashanti sells goods at a gross profit margin of 20% to group companies and third parties. At the year-end, half of the inventory sold to Bochem remained unsold but the entire inventory sold to Ceram had been sold to third parties.

(iv) On 1 May 20X2, Ashanti purchased a $20 million five-year bond with semi annual interest of 5% payable on 31 October and 30 April. The purchase price of the bond was $21·62 million. The effective annual interest rate is 8% or 4% on a semi annual basis. The bond is held at amortised cost. At 1 May 20X4 the amortised cost of the bond was $21.046 million. The issuer of the bond did pay the interest due on 31 October 20X4 and 30 April 20X5, but was in financial trouble at 30 April 20X5. Ashanti feels that as at 30 April 20X5, the bond is impaired and that the best estimates of total future cash receipts are $2·34 million on 30 April 20X6 and $8 million on 30 April 20X7. The current interest rate for discounting cash flows as at 30 April 20X5 is 10%. No accounting entries have been made in the financial statements for the above bond since 30 April 20X4. (You should assume the annual compound rate is 8% for discounting the cash flows.)

(v) Ashanti sold $5 million of goods to a customer who recently made an announcement that it is restructuring its debts with its suppliers including Ashanti. It is probable that Ashanti will not recover the amounts outstanding. The goods were sold after the announcement was made although the order was placed prior to the announcement. Ashanti wishes to make an additional allowance of $8 million against the total receivable balance at the year end, of which $5 million relates to this sale.

(vi) Ashanti owned a piece of property, plant and equipment (PPE) which cost $12 million and was purchased on 1 May 20X3. It is being depreciated over ten years on the straight-line basis with zero residual value. On 30 April 20X4, it was revalued to $13 million and on 30 April 20X5, the PPE was revalued to $8 million. The whole of the revaluation loss had been posted to other comprehensive income and depreciation has been charged for the year. It is Ashanti's company policy to make all necessary transfers for excess depreciation following revaluation.

(vii)   The salaried employees of Ashanti are entitled to 25 days paid leave each year. The entitlement accrues evenly over the year and unused leave may be carried forward for one year. The holiday year is the same as the financial year. At 30 April 20X5, Ashanti has 900 salaried employees and the average unused holiday entitlement is three days per employee. 5% of employees leave without taking their entitlement and there is no cash payment when an employee leaves in respect of holiday entitlement. There are 255 working days in the year and the total annual salary cost is $19 million. No adjustment has been made in the financial statements for the above and there was no opening accrual required for holiday entitlement.

(viii) As permitted by IFRS 9 *Financial instruments* all group companies have made an irrevocable election to recognise changes in the fair value of investments in equity instruments (excluding shares group entities) in in other comprehensive income (items that will not be reclassified to profit or loss).

(ix)   Ignore any taxation effects of the above adjustments and the disclosure requirements of IFRS 5 *Non-current assets held for sale and discontinued operations*.

Required

(a)   Prepare a consolidated statement of profit or loss and other comprehensive income for the year ended 30 April 20X5 for the Ashanti Group.   **(35 marks)**

(b)   Explain the factors which provide encouragement to companies to disclose social and environmental information in their financial statements, briefly discussing whether the content of such disclosure should be at the company's discretion.   **(8 marks)**

(c)   Discuss the nature of and incentives for 'management of earnings' and whether such a process can be deemed to be ethically acceptable.   **(7 marks)**

(Total = 50 marks)

54 Preparation question: Foreign operation

BPP Note. In this question the proformas are given to you to help you get used to setting out your answer. You may wish to transfer them to a separate sheet, or alternatively use a separate sheet for your workings only.

Standard Co acquired 80% of Odense SA for $520,000 on 1 January 20X4 when the retained reserves of Odense were 2,100,000 Danish Krone.

An impairment test conducted at the year end revealed impairment losses of 168,000 Danish Krone relating to Odense's recognised goodwill. No impairment losses had previously been recognised.

The translation differences in the consolidated financial statements at 31 December 20X5 relating to the translation of the financial statements of Odense (excluding goodwill) were $27,000. Retained reserves of Odense in Odense's separate financial statements in the post-acquisition period to 31 December 20X5 as translated amounted to $138,000. The dividends charged to retained earnings in 20X6 were paid on 31 December 20X6.

It is the group's policy to value the non-controlling interest at acquisition at its proportionate share of the fair value of the subsidiary's net assets.

Exchange rates were as follows:

	Kr to $1
1 January 20X4	9.4
31 December 20X5	8.8
31 December 20X6	8.1
Average 20X6	8.4

Required

Prepare the consolidated statement of financial position, statement of profit or loss and other comprehensive income and statement of changes in equity extract for retained earnings of the Standard Group for the year ended 31 December 20X6.

Set out your answer below, using a separate sheet for workings.

STATEMENTS OF FINANCIAL POSITION AT 31 DECEMBER 20X6

	Standard $'000	Odense Kr'000	Rate	Odense $'000	Consol $'000
Property, plant and equipment	1,285	4,400	8.1	543	
Investment in Odense	520	–		–	
Goodwill	–	–		–	
	1,805	4,400		543	
Current assets	410	2,000	8.1	247	
	2,215	6,400		790	
Share capital	500	1,000	9.4	106	
Retained reserves	1,115				
Pre-acquisition		2,100	9.4	224	
Post-acquisition			Bal	324	
	–	–			
	1,615	5,300		654	
Non-controlling interest					
Loans	200	300	8.1	37	
Current liabilities	400	800	8.1	99	
	600	1,100		136	
	2,215	6,400		790	

STATEMENT OF PROFIT OR LOSS AND OTHER COMPREHENSIVE INCOME FOR YEAR ENDED 31 DECEMBER 20X6

	Standard $'000	Odense Kr'000	Rate	Odense $'000	Consol $'000
Revenue	1,125	5,200	8.4	619	
Cost of sales	(410)	(2,300)	8.4	(274)	
Gross profit	715	2,900		345	
Other expenses	(180)	(910)	8.4	(108)	
Impairment loss	–	–		–	
Dividend from Odense	40				
Profit before tax	575	1,990		237	
Income tax expense	(180)	(640)	8.4	(76)	
Profit for the year	395	1,350		161	
Other comprehensive income for the year:					
Items that may be reclassified to profit or loss					
Exchange differences on translation of foreign operation	–	–			
Total comprehensive income for the year	395	1,350			
Profit attributable to:					
Owners of the parent					
Non-controlling interest					
Total comprehensive income attributable to:					
Owners of the parent					
Non-controlling interest					

STATEMENTS OF CHANGES IN EQUITY FOR THE YEAR (EXTRACT FOR RETAINED RESERVES)

	Standard $'000	Odense Kr'000
Balance at 1 January 20X6	915	3,355
Dividends paid	(195)	(405)
Total comprehensive income for the year	395	1,350
Balance at 31 December 20X6	1,115	4,300

CONSOLIDATED STATEMENT OF CHANGES IN EQUITY FOR YEAR ENDED 31 DECEMBER 20X6 (EXTRACTS)

	Retained Earnings $'000
Balance at 1 January 20X6	1,065
Dividends paid	
Total comprehensive income for the year	
Balance at 31 December 20X6	

55 Aspire

45 mins

6/14

Aspire, a public limited company, operates many of its activities overseas. The directors have asked for advice on the correct accounting treatment of several aspects of Aspire's overseas operations. Aspire's functional currency is the dollar.

(a)   Aspire has created a new subsidiary, which is incorporated in the same country as Aspire. The subsidiary has issued 2 million dinars of equity capital to Aspire, which paid for these shares in dinars. The subsidiary has also raised 100,000 dinars of equity capital from external sources and has deposited the whole of the capital with a bank in an overseas country whose currency is the dinar. The capital is to be invested in dinar denominated bonds. The subsidiary has a small number of staff and its operating expenses, which are low, are incurred in dollars. The profits are under the control of Aspire. Any income from the investment is either passed on to Aspire in the form of a dividend or reinvested under instruction from Aspire. The subsidiary does not make any decisions as to where to place the investments.

Aspire would like advice on how to determine the functional currency of the subsidiary.   **(7 marks)**

(b)   Aspire has a foreign branch which has the same functional currency as Aspire. The branch's taxable profits are determined in dinars. On 1 May 20X3, the branch acquired a property for 6 million dinars. The property had an expected useful life of 12 years with a zero residual value. The asset is written off for tax purposes over eight years. The tax rate in Aspire's jurisdiction is 30% and in the branch's jurisdiction is 20%. The foreign branch uses the cost model for valuing its property and measures the tax base at the exchange rate at the reporting date.

Aspire would like an explanation (including a calculation) as to why a deferred tax charge relating to the asset arises in the group financial statements for the year ended 30 April 20X4 and the impact on the financial statements if the tax base had been translated at the historical rate.   **(6 marks)**

(c)   On 1 May 20X3, Aspire purchased 70% of a multi-national group whose functional currency was the dinar. The purchase consideration was $200 million. At acquisition, the net assets at cost were 1,000 million dinars. The fair values of the net assets were 1,100 million dinars and the fair value of the non-controlling interest was 250 million dinars. Aspire uses the full goodwill method.

Aspire wishes to know how to deal with goodwill arising on the above acquisition in the group financial statements for the year ended 30 April 20X4.   **(5 marks)**

(d)   Aspire took out a foreign currency loan of 5 million dinars at a fixed interest rate of 8% on 1 May 20X3. The interest is paid at the end of each year. The loan will be repaid after two years on 30 April 20X5. The interest rate is the current market rate for similar two-year fixed interest loans.

Aspire requires advice on how to account for the loan and interest in the financial statements for the year ended 30 April 20X4.   **(5 marks)**

Aspire has a financial statement year end of 30 April 20X4 and the average currency exchange rate for the year is not materially different from the actual rate.

	$1 = dinars
Exchange rates	
1 May 20X3	5
30 April 20X4	6
Average exchange rate for year ended 30 April 20X4	5.6

Required

Advise the directors of Aspire on their various requests above, showing suitable calculations where necessary.

Note. The mark allocation is shown against each of the four issues above.

Professional marks will be awarded in this question for clarity and quality of presentation   **(2 marks)**

(Total = 25 marks)

56 Memo   **58 mins**

ACR, 6/04, amended

Memo, a public limited company, owns 75% of the ordinary share capital of Random, a public limited company which is situated in a foreign country. Memo acquired Random on 1 May 20X3 for 120 million crowns (CR) when the retained profits of Random were 80 million crowns. Random has not revalued its assets or issued any share capital since its acquisition by Memo. The following financial statements relate to Memo and Random:

STATEMENTS OF FINANCIAL POSITION AT 30 APRIL 20X4

	Memo	Random
	$m	CRm
Property, plant and equipment	297	146
Investment in Random	48	–
Loan to Random	5	–
Current assets	355	102
	705	248
Equity		
Ordinary shares of $1/1CR	60	32
Share premium account	50	20
Retained earnings	360	95
	470	147
Non current liabilities	30	41
Current liabilities	205	60
	705	248

STATEMENTS OF PROFIT OR LOSS AND OTHER COMPREHENSIVE INCOME FOR YEAR ENDED 30 APRIL 20X4

	Memo $	Random CRm
Revenue	200	142
Cost of sales	(120)	(96)
Gross profit	80	46
Distribution and administrative expenses	(30)	(20)
Profit from operations	50	26
Interest receivable	4	–
Interest payable	–	(2)
Profit before taxation	54	24
Income tax expense	(20)	(9)
Profit/total comprehensive income for the year	34	15

The following information is relevant to the preparation of the consolidated financial statements of Memo.

(a)   Goodwill is reviewed for impairment annually. At 30 April 20X4, the impairment loss on recognised goodwill was CR4.2m.

(b)   During the financial year Random has purchased raw materials from Memo and denominated the purchase in crowns in its financial records. The details of the transaction are set out below:

	Date of transaction	Purchase price $m	Profit percentage on selling price
Raw materials	1 February 20X4	6	20%

At the year end, half of the raw materials purchased were still in the inventory of Random. The intragroup transactions have not been eliminated from the financial statements and the goods were recorded by Random at the exchange rate ruling on 1 February 20X4. A payment of $6 million was made to Memo when the exchange rate was 2.2 crowns to $1. Any exchange gain or loss arising on the transaction is still held in the current liabilities of Random.

(c)   Memo had made an interest free loan to Random of $5 million on 1 May 20X3. The loan was repaid on 30 May 20X4. Random had included the loan in non-current liabilities and had recorded it at the exchange rate at 1 May 20X3.

(d)   The fair value of the net assets of Random at the date of acquisition is to be assumed to be the same as the carrying value.

(e)   The functional currency of Random is the Crown.

(f)   The following exchange rates are relevant to the financial statements:

	Crowns to $
30 April/1 May 20X3	2.5
1 November 20X3	2.6
1 February 20X4	2
30 April 20X4	2.1
Average rate for year to 30 April 20X4	2

(g)   Memo has paid a dividend of $8 million during the financial year and this is not included in profit or loss.

It is the group's policy to value the non-controlling interest at acquisition at its proportionate share of the fair value of the subsidiary's identifiable net assets.

Required

Prepare a consolidated statement of profit or loss and other comprehensive income for the year ended 30 April 20X4 and a consolidated statement of financial position at that date in accordance with International Financial Reporting Standards.

(Candidates should round their calculations to the nearest $100,000.)

(32 marks)

57 Case study question: Rose

90 mins

6/11

Rose, a public limited company, operates in the mining sector. The draft statements of financial position are as follows, at 30 April 20X8.

	Rose $m	Petal $m	Stem Dinars m
Assets			
Non-current assets:			
Property, plant and equipment	370	110	380
Investment in subsidiaries			
Petal	113	–	–
Stem	46	–	–
Financial assets	15	7	50
	544	117	430
Current assets	118	100	330
Total assets	662	217	760
Equity and liabilities			
Share capital	158	38	200
Retained earnings	256	56	300
Other components of equity	7	4	–
Total equity	421	98	500
Non-current liabilities	56	42	160
Current liabilities	185	77	100
Total liabilities	241	119	260
Total equity and liabilities	662	217	760

The following information is relevant to the preparation of the group financial statements.

(a)   On 1 May 20X7, Rose acquired 70% of the equity interests of Petal, a public limited company. The purchase consideration comprised cash of $94 million. The fair value of the identifiable net assets recognised by Petal was $120 million excluding the patent below. The identifiable net assets of Petal at 1 May 20X7 included a patent which had a fair value of $4 million. This had not been recognised in the financial statements of Petal. The patent had a remaining term of four years to run at that date and is not renewable. The retained earnings of Petal were $49 million and other components of equity were $3 million at the date of acquisition. The remaining excess of the fair value of the net assets is due to an increase in the value of land.

Rose wishes to use the 'full goodwill' method. The fair value of the non-controlling interest in Petal was $46 million on 1 May 20X7. There have been no issues of ordinary shares since acquisition and goodwill on acquisition is not impaired.

Rose acquired a further 10% interest from the non-controlling interest in Petal on 30 April 20X8 for a cash consideration of $19 million.

(b)   Rose acquired 52% of the ordinary shares of Stem on 1 May 20X7 when Stem's retained earnings were 220 million dinars. The fair value of the identifiable net assets of Stem on 1 May 20X7 was 495 million dinars. The excess of the fair value over the net assets of Stem is due to an increase in the value of land. The fair value of the non-controlling interest in Stem at 1 May 20X7 was 250 million dinars.

Stem is located in a foreign country and operates a mine. The income of Stem is denominated and settled in dinars. The output of the mine is routinely traded in dinars and its price is determined initially by local supply and demand. Stem pays 40% of its costs and expenses in dollars with the remainder being incurred locally and settled in dinars. Stem's management has a considerable degree of authority and autonomy in carrying out the operations of Stem and is not dependent upon group companies for finance.

Rose wishes to use the 'full goodwill' method to consolidate the financial statements of Stem. There have been no issues of ordinary shares and no impairment of goodwill since acquisition.

The following exchange rates are relevant to the preparation of the group financial statements.

	Dinars to $
1 May 20X7	6
30 April 20X8	5
Average for year to 30 April 20X8	5.8

(c)   Rose has a property located in the same country as Stem. The property was acquired on 1 May 20X7 and is carried at a cost of 30 million dinars. The property is depreciated over 20 years on the straight-line method. At 30 April 20X8, the property was revalued to 35 million dinars. Depreciation has been charged for the year but the revaluation has not been taken into account in the preparation of the financial statements as at 30 April 20X8.

(d)   Rose commenced a long-term bonus scheme for employees at 1 May 20X7. Under the scheme employees receive a cumulative bonus on the completion of five years service. The bonus is 2% of the total of the annual salary of the employees. The total salary of employees for the year to 30 April 20X8 was $40 million and a discount rate of 8% is assumed. Additionally at 30 April 20X8, it is assumed that all employees will receive the bonus and that salaries will rise by 5% per year.

(e)   Rose purchased plant for $20 million on 1 May 20X4 with an estimated useful life of six years. Its estimated residual value at that date was $1.4 million. At 1 May 20X7, the estimated residual value changed to $2.6 million. The change in the residual value has not been taken into account when preparing the financial statements as at 30 April 20X8.

Required

(a)   (i)   Discuss and apply the principles set out in IAS 21 *The effects of changes in foreign exchange rates* in order to determine the functional currency of Stem. **(8 marks)**

        (ii)   Prepare a consolidated statement of financial position of the Rose Group at 30 April 20X8 in accordance with International Financial Reporting Standards (IFRS), showing the exchange difference arising on the translation of Stem's net assets. Ignore deferred taxation. **(35 marks)**

(b)   Rose was considering acquiring a service company. Rose stated that the acquisition may be made because of the value of the human capital and the opportunity for synergies and cross-selling opportunities. Rose measured the fair value of the assets based on what it was prepared to pay for them. Rose further stated that what it was willing to pay was influenced by its future plans for the business.

The company to be acquired had contract-based customer relationships with well-known domestic and international companies and some mining companies. Rose measured that the fair value of all of these customer relationships at zero because Rose already enjoyed relationships with the majority of those customers.

Required

Discuss the validity of the accounting treatment proposed by Rose and whether such a proposed treatment raises any ethical issues. **(7 marks)**

(Total = 50 marks)

58 Preparation question: Consolidated statement of cash flows

BPP Note. In this question, proformas are given to you to help you get used to setting out your answer. You may wish to transfer them to a separate sheet, or alternatively to use a separate sheet for your workings.

On 1 September 20X5 Swing Co acquired 70% of Slide Co for $5,000,000 comprising $1,000,000 cash and 1,500,000 $1 shares.

The statement of financial position of Slide Co at acquisition was as follows:

	$'000
Property, plant and equipment	2,700
Inventories	1,600
Trade receivables	600
Cash	400
Trade payables	(300)
Income tax payable	(200)
	4,800

The consolidated statement of financial position of Swing Co as at 31 December 20X5 was as follows:

	20X5	20X4
Non-current assets	$'000	$'000
Property, plant and equipment	35,500	25,000
Goodwill	1,400	–
	36,900	25,000
Current assets		
Inventories	16,000	10,000
Trade receivables	9,800	7,500
Cash	2,400	1,500
	28,200	19,000
	65,100	44,000
Equity attributable to owners of the parent		
Share capital	12,300	10,000
Share premium	5,800	2,000
Revaluation surplus	350	–
Retained earnings	32,100	21,900
	50,550	33,900
Non-controlling interest	1,750	–
	52,300	33,900
Current liabilities		
Trade payables	7,600	6,100
Income tax payable	5,200	4,000
	12,800	10,100
	65,100	44,000

The consolidated statement of profit or loss and other comprehensive income of Swing Co for the year ended 31 December 20X5 was as follows:

	20X5
	$'000
Profit before tax	16,500
Income tax expense	(5,200)
Profit for the year	11,300
Other comprehensive income (not reclassified to P/L)	
Revaluation surplus	500
Total comprehensive income for the year	11,800
Profit attributable to:	
Owners of the parent	11,100
Non-controlling interest	200
	11,300
Total comprehensive income for the year attributable to	
Owners of the parent	11,450
Non-controlling interest 200 + (500 × 30%)	350
	11,800

Notes:

1   Depreciation charged for the year was $5,800,000. The group made no disposals of property, plant and equipment.

2   Dividends paid by Swing Co amounted to $900,000.

It is the group's policy to value the non-controlling interest at its proportionate share of the fair value of the subsidiary's identifiable net assets.

Required

Prepare the consolidated statement of cash flows of Swing Co for the year ended 31 December 20X5. No notes are required.

CONSOLIDATED STATEMENT OF CASH FLOWS PROFORMA
STATEMENT OF CASH FLOWS FOR THE YEAR ENDED 31 DECEMBER 20X5

	$'000	$'000
Cash flows from operating activities		
Profit before tax		
Adjustments for:		
Depreciation		
Impairment losses	_____	
Increase in trade receivables (W4)		
Increase in inventories (W4)		
Increase in trade payables (W4)	_____	
Cash generated from operations		
Income taxes paid (W3)	_____	
Net cash from operating activities		
Cash flows from investing activities		
Acquisition of subsidiary, net of cash acquired (W2)		
Purchase of property, plant & equipment (W1)	_____	
Net cash used in investing activities		

	$'000	$'000

Cash flows from financing activities
Proceeds from issue of share capital
Dividends paid
Dividends paid to non-controlling interest (W2)

Net cash used in financing activities
Net decrease in cash and cash equivalents
Cash and cash equivalents at the beginning of the period
Cash and cash equivalents at the end of the period

Workings

1   *Assets*

	Property, plant and equipment $'000	Goodwill $'000
b/d		–
OCI (revaluation)		
Depreciation/ Impairment		**(X)** β
Acquisition of sub/assoc		(W5)
Cash paid/(rec'd) β	X	–
c/d		

2   *Equity*

	Share capital $'000	Share premium $'000	Retained earnings $'000	Non-controlling interest $'000
b/d				–
P/L				
Acquisition of subsidiary				(W5)
Cash (paid)/rec'd β	X	X	(X)*	X
c/d				

*Dividend paid is given in question but working shown for clarity.

3   *Liabilities*

	Tax payable $'000
b/d	
P/L	
Acquisition of subsidiary	
Cash (paid)/rec'd	(X) β
c/d	

4   *Working capital changes*

	Inventories $'000	Receivables $'000	Payables $'000
Balance b/d			
Acquisition of subsidiary			
Increase/(decrease) (balancing figure)	X	X	X
Balance c/d			

5   *Purchase of subsidiary*

                                                                                    $'000
         Cash received on acquisition of subsidiary
         Less cash consideration
         Cash outflow   (X)

    Note. Only the **cash** consideration is included in the figure reported in the statement of cash flows. The
    shares issued as part of the consideration are reflected in the share capital working (W2) above.

    Goodwill on acquisition (to show no impairment):

                                                                                    $'000
         Consideration
         Non-controlling interest
         Net assets acquired
         Goodwill
                                                                                    ═════

59 Case study question: Angel   90 mins

12/13

The following draft group financial statements relate to Angel, a public limited company:

ANGEL GROUP: STATEMENT OF FINANCIAL POSITION AS AT 30 NOVEMBER 20X3

	30 Nov 20X3 $m	30 Nov 20X2 $m
Assets		
Non-current assets		
Property, plant and equipment	475	465
Goodwill	105	120
Other intangible assets	150	240
Investment in associate	80	–
Financial assets	215	180
	1,025	1,005
Current assets		
Inventories	155	190
Trade receivables	125	180
Cash and cash equivalents	465	355
	745	725
Total assets	1,770	1,730
Equity and liabilities		
Equity attributable to owners of the parent: to last million		
Share capital	850	625
Retained earnings	456	359
Other components of equity	29	20
	1,335	1,004
Non-controlling interest	90	65
Total equity	1,425	1,069
Non-current liabilities		
Long-term borrowings	26	57
Deferred tax	35	31
Retirement benefit liability	80	74
Total non-current liabilities	141	162

	30 Nov 20X3 $m	30 Nov 20X2 $m
Current liabilities:		
Trade payables	155	361
Current tax payable	49	138
Total current liabilities	204	499
Total liabilities	345	661
Total equity and liabilities	1,770	1,730

ANGEL GROUP: STATEMENT OF PROFIT OR LOSS AND OTHER COMPREHENSIVE INCOME
FOR THE YEAR ENDED 30 NOVEMBER 20X3

	$m
Revenue	1,238
Cost of sales	(986)
Gross profit	252
Other income	30
Administrative expenses	(45)
Other expenses	(50)
Operating profit	187
Finance costs	(11)
Share of profit of equity accounted investees (net of tax)	12
Profit before tax	188
Income tax expense	(46)
Profit for the year	142
Profit/loss attributable to	
Owners of the parent	111
Non-controlling interest	31
	142
Other comprehensive income for the year: items that will not be reclassified to profit or loss	
Financial assets	4
Revaluation of property, plant and equipment	8
Actuarial losses on defined benefit plan	(4)
Tax related to items not reclassified	(3)*
Other comprehensive income (net of tax) for the year	5
Total comprehensive income for the year	147
Total comprehensive income attributable to	
Owners of the parent	116
Non-controlling interest	31
	147

Note. Of the $3m tax, $1m relates to the financial assets.

ANGEL GROUP: STATEMENT OF CHANGES IN EQUITY FOR THE YEAR ENDED 30 NOVEMBER 20X3

	Share capital $m	Retained earnings $m	Other components of equity: financial assets reserve $m	Other components of equity: revaluation reserve $m	Total $m	Non-controlling interest $m	Total equity $m
Balance at 1 December 20X2	625	359	15	5	1,004	65	1,069
Share capital issued	225				225		225
Dividends for year		(10)			(10)	(6)	(16)
Total comprehensive income for the year		107	3	6	116	31	147
Balance at 30 November 20X3	850	456	18	11	1,335	90	1,425

The following information relates to the financial statements of the Angel Group.

(i)   Angel decided to renovate a building which had a zero book value at 1 December 20X2. As a result, $3 million was spent during the year on its renovation. On 30 November 20X3, Angel received a cash grant of $2 million from the government to cover some of the refurbishment cost and the creation of new jobs which had resulted from the use of the building. The grant related equally to both job creation and renovation. The only elements recorded in the financial statements were a charge to revenue for the refurbishment of the building and the receipt of the cash grant, which has been credited to additions of property, plant and equipment (PPE). The building was revalued at 30 November 20X3 at $7 million.

Angel treats grant income on capital-based projects as deferred income.

(ii)   On 1 December 20X2, Angel acquired all of the share capital of Sweety for $30 million. The book values and fair values of the identifiable assets and liabilities of Sweety at the date of acquisition are set out below, together with their tax base. Goodwill arising on acquisition is not deductible for tax purposes. There were no other acquisitions in the period. The tax rate is 30%. The fair values in the table below have been reflected in the year-end balances of the Angel Group.

	Carrying values $m	Tax base $m	Fair values excluding deferred taxation $m
Property, plant and equipment	12.0	10	14
Inventory	5.0	4	6
Trade receivables	3.0	3	3
Cash and cash equivalents	2.0	2	2
Total assets	22.0	19	25
Trade payables	(4.0)	(4)	(4)
Retirement benefit obligations	(1.0)		(1)
Deferred tax liability	(0.6)		
Net assets at acquisition	16.4	15	20

(iii) The retirement benefit is classified as a long-term borrowing in the statement of financial position and comprises the following.

	$m
Net obligation at 1 December 20X2	74
Net interest cost	3
Current service cost	8
Contributions to plan	(9)
Remeasurements – actuarial losses	4
Net obligation 30 November 20X3	80

The benefits paid in the period by the trustees of the plan were $6 million. Angel had included the obligation assumed on the purchase of Sweety in current service cost above, although the charge to administrative expenses was correct in the statement of profit and loss and other comprehensive income. There were no tax implications regarding the retirement benefit obligation. The defined benefit cost is included in administrative expenses.

(iv) The property, plant and equipment (PPE) comprises the following.

	$m
Carrying value at 1 December 20X2	465
Additions at cost including assets acquired on the purchase of subsidiary	80
Gains on property revaluation	8
Disposals	(49)
Depreciation	(29)
Carrying value at 30 November 20X3	475

Angel has constructed a machine which is a qualifying asset under IAS 23 *Borrowing costs* and has paid construction costs of $4 million. This amount has been charged to other expenses. Angel Group paid $11 million in interest in the year, which includes $1 million of interest which Angel wishes to capitalise under IAS 23. There was no deferred tax implication regarding this transaction.

The disposal proceeds were $63 million. The gain on disposal is included in administrative expenses.

(v) Angel purchased a 30% interest in an associate for cash on 1 December 20X2. The net assets of the associate at the date of acquisition were $280 million. The associate made a profit after tax of $40 million and paid a dividend of $10 million out of these profits in the year ended 30 November 20X3.

(vi) An impairment test carried out at 30 November 20X3 showed that goodwill and other intangible assets were impaired. The impairment of goodwill relates to 100% owned subsidiaries.

(vii) The following schedule relates to the financial assets owned by Angel.

	$m
Balance at 1 December 20X2	180
Less sales of financial assets at carrying value	(26)
Add purchases of financial assets	57
Add gain on revaluation of financial assets (investments in equity instruments)	4
Balance at 30 November 20X3	215

The sale proceeds of the financial assets were $40 million. Profit on the sale of the financial assets is included in 'other income' in the financial statements.

The financial assets included a mixture of financial assets measured at fair value through profit or loss and investments in equity instruments for which an irrevocable election had been made to hold them at fair value through other comprehensive income. All the financial assets at fair value through profit or loss were sold, with no revaluation gain arising in the year of sale before the date of sale.

(viii) The finance costs were all paid in cash in the period.

Required

(a) Prepare a consolidated statement of cash flows using the indirect method for the Angel Group plc for the year ended 30 November 20X3 in accordance with the requirements of IAS 7 *Statement of cash flows*.

Note. The notes to the statement of cash flows are not required. **(35 marks)**

(b)   The directors of Angel are confused over several issues relating to IAS 7 *Statement of cash flows*. They wish to know the principles utilised by the International Accounting Standards Board in determining how cash flows are classified, including how entities determine the nature of the cash flows being analysed.

They have entered into the following transactions after the year end and wish to know how to deal with them in a cash flow statement, as they are unsure of the meaning of the definition of cash and cash equivalents.

Angel had decided after the year end to deposit the funds with the bank in two term deposit accounts as follows.

(i) $3 million into a 12-month term account, earning 3.5% interest. The cash can be withdrawn by giving 14 days' notice but Angel will incur a penalty, being the loss of all interest earned.

(ii) $7 million into a 12-month term account earning 3% interest. The cash can be withdrawn by giving 21 days' notice. Interest will be paid for the period of the deposit but if money is withdrawn, the interest will be at the rate of 2%, which is equivalent to the bank's stated rate for short-term deposits.

Angel is confident that it will not need to withdraw the cash from the higher-rate deposit within the term, but wants to keep easy access to the remaining $7 million to cover any working capital shortfalls which might arise.

Required

Discuss the principles behind the classifications in the statements of cash flows whilst advising Angel on how to treat the two transactions above.   **(9 marks)**

(c)   All accounting professionals are responsible for acting in the public interest, and for promoting professional ethics. The directors of Angel feel that when managing the affairs of a company the profit motive could conflict with the public interest and accounting ethics. In their view, the profit motive is more important than ethical behaviour and codes of ethics are irrelevant and unimportant.

Required

Discuss the above views of the directors regarding the fact that codes of ethics are irrelevant and unimportant.   **(6 marks)**

(Total = 50 marks)

60 Case study question: Jocatt

90 mins

12/10

The following draft group financial statements relate to Jocatt, a public limited company.

JOCATT GROUP
STATEMENT OF FINANCIAL POSITION AS AT 30 NOVEMBER

	20X2 $m	20X1 $m
Assets		
Non-current assets		
Property, plant and equipment	327	254
Investment property	8	6
Goodwill	48	68
Intangible assets	85	72
Investment in associate	54	–
Investments in equity instruments	94	90
	616	490

	20X2 $m	20X1 $m
Assets		
Current assets		
Inventories	105	128
Trade receivables	62	113
Cash and cash equivalents	232	143
	399	384
	1,015	874
Equity and Liabilities		
Equity attributable to the owners of the parent:		
Share capital	290	275
Retained earnings	351	324
Other components of equity	15	20
	656	619
Non-controlling interest	55	36
Total equity	711	655
Non-current liabilities		
Long-term borrowings	67	71
Deferred tax	35	41
Long-term provisions: pension liability	25	22
Total non-current liabilities	127	134
Current liabilities		
Trade payables	144	55
Current tax payable	33	30
Total current liabilities	177	85
Total liabilities	304	219
Total equity and liabilities	1,015	874

JOCATT GROUP
STATEMENT OF PROFIT OR LOSS AND OTHER COMPREHENSIVE INCOME
FOR THE YEAR ENDED 30 NOVEMBER 20X2

	$m
Revenue	432.0
Cost of sales	(317.0)
Gross profit	115.0
Other income	25.0
Distribution costs	(55.5)
Administrative expenses	(36.0)
Finance costs paid	(6.0)
Gains on property	10.5
Share of profit of associate	6.0
Profit before tax	59.0
Income tax expense	(11.0)
Profit for the year	48.0
Other comprehensive income after tax (items that will not be reclassified to profit or loss)	
Gain on investments in equity instruments (IEI)	2.0
Losses on property revaluation	(7.0)
Remeasurement losses on defined benefit plan	(6.0)
Other comprehensive income for the year, net of tax	(11.0)
Total comprehensive income for the year	37.0
Profit attributable to	
Owners of the parent	38.0
Non-controlling interest	10.0
	48.0
Total comprehensive income attributable to	
Owners of the parent	27.0
Non-controlling interest	10.0
	37.0

JOCATT GROUP
STATEMENT OF CHANGES IN EQUITY FOR THE YEAR ENDED 30 NOVEMBER 20X2

	Share capital $m	Retained earnings $m	Investments in equity instruments $m	Revaluation surplus (PPE) $m	Total $m	Non-controlling interest $m	Total equity $m
Balance at 1 December 20X1	275	324	4	16	619	36	655
Share capital issued	15				15		15
Dividends		(5)			(5)	(13)	(18)
Rights issue						2	2
Acquisitions						20	20
Total comprehensive income for the year		32	2	(7)	27	10	37
Balance at 30 November 20X2	290	351	6	9	656	55	711

The following information relates to the financial statements of Jocatt.

(i) On 1 December 20X0, Jocatt acquired 8% of the ordinary shares of Tigret. Jocatt had treated this as an investment in equity instruments in the financial statements to 30 November 20X1 with changes in fair value taken to profit or loss for the year. There were no changes in fair value in the year to 30 November 20X1. On 1 January 20X2, Jocatt acquired a further 52% of the ordinary shares of Tigret and gained control of the company. The consideration for the acquisitions was as follows.

	Holding	Consideration
		$m
1 December 20X0	8%	4
1January 20X2	52%	30
	60%	34

At 1 January 20X2, the fair value of the 8% holding in Tigret held by Jocatt at the time of the business combination was $5 million and the fair value of the non-controlling interest in Tigret was $20 million. The purchase consideration at 1 January 20X2 comprised cash of $15 million and shares of $15 million.

The fair value of the identifiable net assets of Tigret, excluding deferred tax assets and liabilities, at the date of acquisition comprised the following.

	$m
Property, plant and equipment	15
Intangible assets	18
Trade receivables	5
Cash	7

The tax base of the identifiable net assets of Tigret was $40 million at 1 January 20X2. The tax rate of Tigret is 30%.

(ii) On 30 November 20X2,Tigret made a rights issue on a 1 for 4 basis. The issue was fully subscribed and raised $5 million in cash.

(iii) Jocatt purchased a research project from a third party including certain patents on 1 December 20X1 for $8 million and recognised it as an intangible asset. During the year, Jocatt incurred further costs, which included $2 million on completing the research phase, $4 million in developing the product for sale and $1 million for the initial marketing costs. There were no other additions to intangible assets in the period other than those on the acquisition of Tigret.

(iv) Jocatt operates a defined benefit scheme. The current service costs for the year ended 30 November 20X2 are $10 million. Jocatt enhanced the benefits on 1 December 20X1. The total cost of the enhancement is $2 million. The net interest on net plan assets was $8 million for the year and Jocatt recognises remeasurement gains and losses in accordance with IAS 19 as revised in 2011.

(v) Jocatt owns an investment property. During the year, part of the heating system of the property, which had a carrying value of $0.5 million, was replaced by a new system, which cost $1 million. Jocatt uses the fair value model for measuring investment property.

(vi) Jocatt had exchanged surplus land with a carrying value of $10 million for cash of $15 million and plant valued at $4 million. The transaction has commercial substance. Depreciation for the period for property, plant and equipment was $27 million.

(vii) Goodwill relating to all subsidiaries had been impairment tested in the year to 30 November 20X2 and any impairment accounted for. The goodwill impairment related to those subsidiaries which were 100% owned.

(viii) Deferred tax of $1 million arose in the year on the gains on investments in equity instruments in the year where the irrevocable election was made to take changes in fair value through other comprehensive income

(ix) The associate did not pay any dividends in the year.

Required

(a) Prepare a consolidated statement of cash flows for the Jocatt Group using the indirect method under IAS 7 *Statements of cash flows.*

Note: Ignore deferred taxation other than where it is mentioned in the question. **(35 marks)**

(b) Jocatt operates in the energy industry and undertakes complex natural gas trading arrangements, which involve exchanges in resources with other companies in the industry. Jocatt is entering into a long-term contract for the supply of gas and is raising a loan on the strength of this contract. The proceeds of the loan are to be received over the year to 30 November 20X3 and are to be repaid over four years to 30 November 20X7. Jocatt wishes to report the proceeds as operating cash flow because it is related to a long-term purchase contract. The directors of Jocatt receive extra income if the operating cash flow exceeds a predetermined target for the year and feel that the indirect method is more useful and informative to users of financial statements than the direct method.

    (i) Comment on the directors' view that the indirect method of preparing statements of cash flow is more useful and informative to users than the direct method. **(8 marks)**

    (ii) Discuss the reasons why the directors may wish to report the loan proceeds as an operating cash flow rather than a financing cash flow and whether there are any ethical implications of adopting this treatment **(7 marks)**

(Total = 50 marks)

61 Case study question: Warrburt

90 mins

12/08, amended

Note: This question has been amended in accordance with issues raised with the examiner.

The following draft group financial statements relate to Warrburt, a public limited company:

WARRBURT GROUP: STATEMENT OF FINANCIAL POSITION AS AT 30 NOVEMBER 20X8

	30 Nov 20X8 $m	30 Nov 20X7 $m
Assets		
Non-current assets		
Property, plant and equipment	350	360
Goodwill	80	100
Other intangible assets	228	240
Investment in associate	100	–
Investment in equity instruments	142	150
	900	850
Current assets		
Inventories	135	198
Trade receivables	92	163
Cash and cash equivalents	288	323
	515	684
Total assets	1,415	1,534
Equity and liabilities		
Equity attributable to owners of the parent: to last million		
Share capital	650	595
Retained earnings	367	454
Other components of equity	49	20
	1,066	1,069
Non-controlling interest	46	53
Total equity	1,112	1,122

BPP LEARNING MEDIA

	30 Nov 20X8	30 Nov 20X7
	$m	$m
Non-current liabilities		
Long-term borrowing	20	64
Deferred tax	28	26
Long-tem provisions	100	96
Total non-current liabilities	148	186
Current liabilities:		
Trade payables	115	180
Current tax payable	35	42
Short-term provisions	5	4
Total current liabilities	155	226
Total liabilities	303	412
Total equity and liabilities	1,415	1,534

WARRBURT GROUP: STATEMENT OF PROFIT OR LOSS AND OTHER COMPREHENSIVE INCOME
FOR THE YEAR ENDED 30 NOVEMBER 20X8

	$m
Revenue	910
Cost of sales	(886)
Gross profit	24
Other income	7
Distribution costs	(40)
Administrative expenses	(35)
Finance costs	(9)
Share of profit of associate	6
Loss before tax	(47)
Income tax expense	(29)
Loss for the year from continuing operations	(76)
Loss for the year	(76)

Other comprehensive income for the year (after tax, not reclassified to P/L)	
Investment in equity instruments (IEI)	27
Gains on property revaluation	2
Actuarial losses on defined benefit plan	(4)
Other comprehensive income for the year (after tax)	25
Total comprehensive income for the year	(51)

Profit/loss attributable to:	
Owners of the parent	(74)
Non-controlling interest	(2)
	(76)

Total comprehensive income attributable to:	
Owners of the parent	(49)
Non-controlling interest	(2)
	(51)

WARRBURT GROUP: STATEMENT OF CHANGES IN EQUITY FOR THE YEAR ENDED 30 NOVEMBER 20X8

	Share capital $m	Retained earnings $m	IEI $m	Revaluation surplus $m	Total $m	Non-controlling interest $m	Total equity $m
Balance at 1 December 20X7	595	454	16	4	1,069	53	1,122
Share capital issued	55				55		55
Dividends		(9)			(9)	(5)	(14)
Total comprehensive income for the year		(78)	27	2	(49)	(2)	(51)
Balance at 30 November 20X8	650	367	43	6	1,066	46	1,112

NOTE TO STATEMENT OF CHANGES IN EQUITY:

	$m
Profit/loss attributable to owners of parent	(74)
Actuarial losses on defined benefit plan	(4)
Total comprehensive income for year – retained earnings	(78)

The following information relates to the financial statements of Warrburt.

(i)   Warrburt holds investments in equity instruments (IEI) which are owned by the parent company. At 1 December 20X7, the total carrying amount of those investments was $150m. In respect of $112m of this $150m, Warrburt had made an irrevocable election under IFRS 9 for changes in fair value to go through other comprehensive income (items that will not be reclassified to profit or loss). The remaining $38m related to an investment in the shares of Alburt, in respect of which changes in fair value had been taken to profit or loss for the year. During the year, the investment in Alburt was sold for $45m, with the fair value gain shown in 'other income' in the financial statements. The following schedule summarises the changes:

	Alburt $m	Other $m	Total $m
Carrying value at 1 December 20X7	38	112	150
Add gain on derecognition/revaluation of IEI	7	30	37
Less sales of IEI at fair value	(45)	–	(45)
Carrying value at 30 November 20X8	–	142	142

Deferred tax of $3 million arising on the $30m revaluation gain above has been taken into account in 'other comprehensive income' for the year.

(ii)   The retirement benefit liability is shown as a long-term provision in the statement of financial position and comprises the following:

	$m
Liability at 1 December 20X7	96
Expense for period	10
Contributions to scheme (paid)	(10)
Actuarial losses	4
Liability at 30 November 20X8	100

Warrburt recognises remeasurement gains and losses in other comprehensive income in the period in which they occur, in accordance with IAS 19 (revised 2011). The benefits paid in the period by the trustees of the scheme were $3 million. There is no tax impact with regards to the retirement benefit liability.

(iii)   The property, plant and equipment (PPE) in the statement of financial position comprises the following:

	$m
Carrying value at 1 December 20X7	360
Additions at cost	78
Gains on property revaluation	4
Disposals	(56)
Depreciation	(36)
Carrying value at 30 November 20X8	350

Plant and machinery with a carrying value of $1 million had been destroyed by fire in the year. The asset was replaced by the insurance company with new plant and machinery which was valued at $3 million. The machines were acquired directly by the insurance company and no cash payment was made to Warrburt. The company included the net gain on this transaction in 'additions at cost' and as a deduction from administrative expenses.

The disposal proceeds were $63 million. The gain on disposal is included in administrative expenses. Deferred tax of $2 million has been deducted in arriving at the 'gains on property revaluation' figure in 'other comprehensive income (items that will not be reclassified to profit or loss)'.

The remaining additions of PPE comprised imported plant and equipment from an overseas supplier on 30 June 20X8. The cost of the PPE was 380 million dinars with 280 million dinars being paid on 31 October 20X8 and the balance to be paid on 31 December 20X8.
The rates of exchange were as follows:

	Dinars to $1
30 June 20X8	5
31 October 20X8	4.9
30 November 20X8	4.8

Exchange gains and losses are included in administrative expenses.

(iv)   Warrburt purchased a 25% interest in an associate for cash on 1 December 20X7. The net assets of the associate at the date of acquisition were $300 million. The associate made a profit after tax of $24 million and paid a dividend of $8 million out of these profits in the year ended 30 November 20X8.

(v)   An impairment test had been carried out at 30 November 20X8, on goodwill and other intangible assets. The result showed that goodwill was impaired by $20 million and other intangible assets by $12 million.

(vi)   The short term provisions relate to finance costs which are payable within six months.

Warrburt's directors are concerned about the results for the year in the statement of profit or loss and other comprehensive income and the subsequent effect on the statement of cash flows. They have suggested that the proceeds of the sale of property, plant and equipment and the sale of investments in equity instruments should be included in 'cash generated from operations'. The directors are afraid of an adverse market reaction to their results and of the importance of meeting targets in order to ensure job security, and feel that the adjustments for the proceeds would enhance the 'cash health' of the business.

Required

(a)   Prepare a group statement of cash flows for Warrburt for the year ended 30 November 20X8 in accordance with IAS 7 *Statement of cash flows*, using the indirect method.   **(35 marks)**

(b)   Discuss the key issues which the statement of cash flows highlights regarding the cash flow of the company.   **(10 marks)**

(c)   Discuss the ethical responsibility of the company accountant in ensuring that manipulation of the statement of cash flows, such as that suggested by the directors, does not occur.   **(5 marks)**

(Total = 50 marks)

DEVELOPMENTS IN REPORTING

Questions 62 to 75 cover Developments in Reporting, the subject of Part D of the BPP Study Text for Paper P2.

62 Glowball

45 mins

ACR, Pilot paper

The directors of Glowball, a public limited company, had discussed the study by the Institute of Environmental Management which indicated that over 35% of the world's largest 250 corporations are voluntarily releasing green reports to the public to promote corporate environmental performance and to attract customers and investors. They have heard that their main competitors are applying the 'Global Reporting Initiative' (GRI) in an effort to develop a worldwide format for corporate environmental reporting. However, the directors are unsure as to what this initiative actually means. Additionally they require advice as to the nature of any legislation or standards relating to environmental reporting, as they are worried that any environmental report produced by the company may not be of sufficient quality and may detract and not enhance their image if the report does not comply with recognised standards. Glowball has a reputation for ensuring the preservation of the environment in its business activities.

Further the directors have collected information in respect of a series of events which they consider to be important and worthy of note in the environmental report but are not sure as to how they would be incorporated in the environmental report or whether they should be included in the financial statements.

The events are as follows.

(a)   Glowball is a company that pipes gas from offshore gas installations to major consumers. The company purchased its main competitor during the year and found that there were environmental liabilities arising out of the restoration of many miles of farmland that had been affected by the laying of a pipeline. There was no legal obligation to carry out the work but the company felt that there would be a cost of around $150 million if the farmland was to be restored.

(b)   Most of the offshore gas installations are governed by operating licenses which specify limits to the substances which can be discharged to the air and water. These limits vary according to local legislation and tests are carried out by the regulatory authorities. During the year the company was prosecuted for infringements of an environmental law in the USA when toxic gas escaped into the atmosphere. In 20X2 the company was prosecuted five times and in 20X1 eleven times for infringement of the law. The final amount of the fine/costs to be imposed by the courts has not been determined but is expected to be around $5 million. The escape occurred over the seas and it was considered that there was little threat to human life.

(c)   The company produced statistics that measure their improvement in the handling of emissions of gases which may have an impact on the environment. The statistics deal with:

   (i)   Measurement of the release of gases with the potential to form acid rain. The emissions have been reduced by 84% over five years due to the closure of old plants.

   (ii)   Measurement of emissions of substances potentially hazardous to human health. The emissions are down by 51% on 20W8 levels.

   (iii)   Measurement of emissions to water that removes dissolved oxygen and substances that may have an adverse effect on aquatic life. Accurate measurement of these emissions is not possible but the company is planning to spend $70 million on research in this area.

(d)   The company tries to reduce the environmental impacts associated with the siting and construction of its gas installations. This is done in the way that minimises the impact on wild life and human beings. Additionally when the installations are at the end of their life, they are dismantled and are not sunk into the sea. The current provision for the decommissioning of these installations is $215 million and there are still decommissioning costs of $407 million to be provided as the company's policy is to build up the required provision over the life of the installation.

Required

Prepare a report suitable for presentation to the directors of Glowball in which you discuss the following elements:

(a)   Current reporting requirements and guidelines relating to environmental reporting.   **(10 marks)**

BPP
LEARNING MEDIA

(b)   The nature of any disclosure which would be required in an environmental report and/or the financial statements for the events (a)–(d) above.   **(15 marks)**

(The mark allocation includes four marks for the style and layout of the report.)   **(Total = 25 marks)**

63 Preparation question: Current issues

BPP Note. Current developments are mainly covered within individual topics, for example all the questions on revenue recognition test the new standard IFRS 15, and any questions on impairment of financial assets apply the expected credit loss model of the July 2014 final version of IFRS 9..

(a)   In July 2014, the IASB published IFRS 9 *Financial instruments* in final form. Among the changes is a new business model requiring certain financial assets to be measured at fair value through other comprehensive income if certain criteria are met.

Required

(i)   What are the criteria which, if met, mean that a financial asset must be measured at fair value through other comprehensive income rather than at amortised cost?

(ii)   Can the financial asset be measured at fair value through profit or loss?

(b)   IFRS 9 *Financial instruments* in final form also made changes to the hedge accounting requirements.

Required

(i)   What problems were identified in the old hedging rules?

(ii)   Summarise the main changes in IFRS 9.

(c)   IFRS 10 *Consolidated financial statements* was published in 2011. It retains control from its predecessor IAS 27 as the key concept underlying the parent/subsidiary relationship but it has broadened the definition and clarified its application.

(i)   Explain the circumstances in which an investor controls an investee according to IFRS 10

(ii)   Twist holds 40% of the voting rights of Oliver and twelve other investors each hold 5% of the voting rights Oliver. A shareholder agreement grants Twist the right to appoint, remove and set the remuneration of management responsible for directing the relevant activities. To change the agreement, a two-thirds majority vote of the shareholders is required. To date, Twist has not exercised its rights with regard to the management or activities of Oliver.

Required

Explain whether Twist should consolidate Oliver in accordance with IFRS 10.

(iii)   Copperfield holds 45% of the voting rights of Spenlow. Murdstone and Steerforth each hold 26% of the voting rights of Spenlow. The remaining voting rights are held by three other shareholders, each holding 1%. There are no other arrangements that affect decision-making.

Required

Explain whether Copperfield should consolidate Spenlow in accordance with IFRS 10.

(d)   Red, a public company, is preparing its financial statements for the year ended 31 December 20X6.The Finance Director of Red has set up a company, Blue, through which Red conducts its investment activities. Red has paid $400 million to Blue during the year and this has been included in dividends paid. The money was invested in a specified portfolio of investments. Ninety five per cent of the profits and one hundred per cent of the losses in the specified portfolio of investments are transferred to Red. An investment manager has charge of the company's investments and owns all of the share capital of Blue. An agreement between the investment manager and Red sets out the operating guidelines and prohibits the investment manager from obtaining access to the investments for the manager's benefit. An annual transfer of the profit/loss will occur on 31 December annually and the capital will be returned in four years' time. The transfer of $400 million cash occurred on 1 July 20X6 but no transfer of profit/loss has yet occurred. The statement of financial position of Blue at 31 December 20X6 is as follows:

BLUE: STATEMENT OF FINANCIAL POSITION AT 31 DECEMBER 20X6

	$m
Investment at fair value through profit or loss	390
	390
Share capital	400
Retained earnings	(10)
	390

Required

Discuss the issues which would determine whether Blue should be consolidated by Red in the group financial statements.

(e)   Briefly outline the current issues in equity accounting.

64 Fair values and IFRS 13   45 mins

Financial statements have seen an increasing move towards the use of fair values in accounting. Advocates of 'fair value accounting' believe that fair value is the most relevant measure for financial reporting whilst others believe that historical cost provides a more useful measure. Issues have been raised over the reliability and measurement of fair values, and over the nature of the current level of disclosure in financial statements in this area.

In 2011 the IASB published IFRS 13 *Fair value measurement,* which sets out to sets out to define fair value, set out in a single IFRS a framework for measuring fair value and require disclosure about fair value measurements.

Required

(a)   Discuss the view that fair value is a more relevant measure to use in corporate reporting than historical cost.

(12 marks)

(b)   Discuss the main changes introduced by IRS 13 *Fair value measurement.*   **(9 marks)**

(c)   Fairview holds shares in Greenfield, which it treats as an equity instrument (a financial asset). Sale of this financial asset is restricted by contract to qualifying investors.

How would the fair value of this instrument be measured?   **(4 marks)**

(Total = 25 marks)

65 Jones and Cousin   45 mins

ACR,12/06

Jones and Cousin, a public quoted company, operate in twenty seven different countries and earn revenue and incur costs in several currencies. The group develops, manufactures and markets products in the medical sector. The growth of the group has been achieved by investment and acquisition. It is organised into three global business units which manage their sales in international markets, and take full responsibility for strategy and business performance. Only five per cent of the business is in the country of incorporation. Competition in the sector is quite fierce.

The group competes across a wide range of geographic and product markets and encourages its subsidiaries to enhance local communities by reinvestment of profits in local education projects. The group's share of revenue in a market sector is often determined by government policy. The markets contain a number of different competitors including specialised and large international corporations. At present the group is awaiting regulatory approval for a range of new products to grow its market share. The group lodges its patents for products and enters into legal proceedings where necessary to protect patents. The products are sourced from a wide range of suppliers, who, once approved both from a qualitative and ethical perspective, are generally given a long term contract for the supply of goods. Obsolete products are disposed of with concern for the environment and the health of its customers, with reusable materials normally being used. The industry is highly regulated in terms of medical and environmental laws and regulations. The products normally carry a low health risk.

The Group has developed a set of corporate and social responsibility principles during the period, which is the responsibility of the Board of Directors. The Managing Director manages the risks arising from corporate and social responsibility issues. The group wishes to retain and attract employees and follows policies which ensure equal opportunity for all the employees. Employees are informed of management policies, and regularly receive in-house training.

The Group enters into contracts for fixed rate currency swaps and uses floating to fixed rate interest rate swaps. The cash flow effects of these swaps match the cash flows on the underlying financial instruments. All financial instruments are accounted for as cash flow hedges. A significant amount of trading activity is denominated in the Dinar and the Euro. The dollar is its functional currency.

Required

(a) Describe the principles and objectives behind the Management Commentary, discussing whether the commentary should be made mandatory or whether directors should be free to use their judgement as to what should be included in such a commentary. **(13 marks)**

(b) Draft a report suitable for inclusion in a Management Commentary for Jones and Cousin which deals with:

(i)   The key risks and relationships of the business **(9 marks)**
(ii) The strategy of the business regarding its treasury policies **(3 marks)**

(Marks will be awarded in Part (b) for the identification and discussion of relevant points and for the style of the report.)

(Total = 25 marks)

66 Lockfine   45 mins

6/11

Lockfine, a public limited company, operates in the fishing industry and has recently made the transition to International Financial Reporting Standards (IFRS). Lockfine's reporting date is 30 April 20X9.

(a) In the IFRS opening statement of financial position at 1 May 20X7, Lockfine elected to measure its fishing fleet at fair value and use that fair value as deemed cost in accordance with IFRS 1 *First time adoption of international financial reporting standards*. The fair value was an estimate based on valuations provided by two independent selling agents, both of whom provided a range of values within which the valuation might be considered acceptable. Lockfine calculated fair value at the average of the highest amounts in the two ranges provided. One of the agents' valuations was not supported by any description of the method adopted or the assumptions underlying the calculation. Valuations were principally based on discussions with various potential buyers. Lockfine wished to know the principles behind the use of deemed cost and whether agents' estimates were a reliable form of evidence on which to base the fair value calculation of tangible assets to be then adopted as deemed cost. **(6 marks)**

(b) Lockfine was unsure as to whether it could elect to apply IFRS 3 *Business Combinations* retrospectively to past business combinations on a selective basis, because there was no purchase price allocation available for certain business combinations in its opening IFRS statement of financial position.

As a result of a major business combination, fishing rights of that combination were included as part of goodwill. The rights could not be recognised as a separately identifiable intangible asset at acquisition under the local GAAP because a reliable value was unobtainable for the rights. The fishing rights operated for a specified period of time.

On transition from local GAAP to IFRS, the fishing rights were included in goodwill and not separately identified because they did not meet the qualifying criteria set out in IFRS 1, even though it was known that the fishing rights had a finite life and would be fully impaired or amortised over the period specified by the rights. Lockfine wished to amortise the fishing rights over their useful life and calculate any impairment of goodwill as two separate calculations. **(6 marks)**

(c) Lockfine has internally developed intangible assets comprising the capitalised expenses of the acquisition and production of electronic map data which indicates the main fishing grounds in the world. The intangible assets generate revenue for the company in their use by the fishing fleet and are a material asset in the statement of financial position. Lockfine had constructed a database of the electronic maps. The costs incurred in bringing the information about a certain region of the world to a higher standard of performance are capitalised. The costs related to maintaining the information about a certain region at that same standard of performance are expensed. Lockfine's accounting policy states that intangible assets are valued at historical cost. The company considers the database to have an indefinite useful life which is reconsidered annually when it is tested for impairment. The reasons supporting the assessment of an indefinite useful life were not disclosed in the financial statements and neither did the company disclose how it satisfied the criteria for recognising an intangible asset arising from development. **(6 marks)**

(d)   The Lockfine board has agreed two restructuring projects during the year to 30 April 20X9:

Plan A involves selling 50% of its off-shore fleet in one year's time. Additionally, the plan is to make 40% of its seamen redundant. Lockfine will carry out further analysis before deciding which of its fleets and related employees will be affected. In previous announcements to the public, Lockfine has suggested that it may restructure the off-shore fleet in the future.

Plan B involves the reorganisation of the headquarters in 18 months time, and includes the redundancy of 20% of the headquarters' workforce. The company has made announcements before the year end but there was a three month consultation period which ended just after the year end, whereby Lockfine was negotiating with employee representatives. Thus individual employees had not been notified by the year end.

Lockfine proposes recognising a provision in respect of Plan A but not Plan B. **(5 marks)**

Professional marks will be awarded in this question for clarity and quality of discussion. **(2 marks)**

Required

Discuss the principles and practices to be used by Lockfine in accounting for the above valuation and recognition issues.

(Total = 25 marks)

67 Seltec   45 mins

6/10

Seltec, a public limited company, processes and sells edible oils and uses several financial instruments to spread the risk of fluctuation in the price of the edible oils. The entity operates in an environment where the transactions are normally denominated in dollars. The functional currency of Seltec is the dollar.

(a)   The entity uses forward and futures contracts to protect it against fluctuation in the price of edible oils. Where forwards are used the company often takes delivery of the edible oil and sells it shortly afterwards. The contracts are constructed with future delivery in mind but the contracts also allow net settlement in cash as an alternative. The net settlement is based on the change in the price of the oil since the start of the contract. Seltec uses the proceeds of a net settlement to purchase a different type of oil or purchase from a different supplier. Where futures are used these sometimes relate to edible oils of a different type and market than those of Seltec's own inventory of edible oil. The company intends to apply hedge accounting to these contracts in order to protect itself from earnings volatility. Seltec has also entered into a long-term arrangement to buy oil from a foreign entity whose currency is the dinar. The commitment stipulates that the fixed purchase price will be denominated in pounds sterling.

Seltec is unsure as to the nature of derivatives and hedge accounting techniques and has asked your advice on how the above financial instruments should be dealt with in the financial statements. **(14 marks)**

(b)   Seltec has decided to enter the retail market and has recently purchased two well-known brand names in the edible oil industry. One of the brand names has been in existence for many years and has a good reputation for quality. The other brand name is named after a famous film star who has been actively promoting the edible oil as being a healthier option than other brands of oil. This type of oil has only been on the market for a short time. Seltec is finding it difficult to estimate the useful life of the brands and therefore intends to treat the brands as having indefinite lives.

In order to sell the oil, Seltec has purchased two limited liability companies from a company that owns several retail outlets. Each entity owns retail outlets in several shopping complexes. The only assets of each entity are the retail outlets. There is no operational activity and at present the entities have no employees.

Seltec is unclear as to how the purchase of the brands and the entities should be accounted for. **(9 marks)**

BPP
LEARNING MEDIA

Required

Discuss the accounting principles involved in accounting for the above transactions and how the above transactions should be treated in the financial statements of Seltec.

Professional marks will be awarded in this question for clarity and quality of discussion. **(2 marks)**

The mark allocation is shown against each of the two parts above.

(Total = 25 marks)

68 Ethan
45 mins

`6/12`

Ethan, a public limited company, develops, operates and sells investment properties.

(a) Ethan focuses mainly on acquiring properties where it foresees growth potential, through rental income as well as value appreciation. The acquisition of an investment property is usually realised through the acquisition of the entity, which holds the property.

In Ethan's consolidated financial statements, investment properties acquired through business combinations are recognised at fair value, using a discounted cash flow model as approximation to fair value. There is currently an active market for this type of property. The difference between the fair value of the investment property as determined under the accounting policy, and the value of the investment property for tax purposes results in a deferred tax liability.

Goodwill arising on business combinations is determined using the measurement principles for the investment properties as outlined above. Goodwill is only considered impaired if and when the deferred tax liability is reduced below the amount at which it was first recognised. This reduction can be caused both by a reduction in the value of the real estate or a change in local tax regulations. As long as the deferred tax liability is equal to, or larger than, the prior year, no impairment is charged to goodwill. Ethan explained its accounting treatment by confirming that almost all of its goodwill is due to the deferred tax liability and that it is normal in the industry to account for goodwill in this way.

Since 20X0, Ethan has incurred substantial annual losses except for the year ended 31 May 20X3, when it made a small profit before tax. In year ended 31 May 20X3, most of the profit consisted of income recognised on revaluation of investment properties. Ethan had announced early in its financial year ended 31 May 20X4 that it anticipated substantial growth and profit. Later in the year, however, Ethan announced that the expected profit would not be achieved and that, instead, a substantial loss would be incurred. Ethan had a history of reporting considerable negative variances from its budgeted results. Ethan's recognised deferred tax assets have been increasing year-on-year despite the deferred tax liabilities recognised on business combinations. Ethan's deferred tax assets consist primarily of unused tax losses that can be carried forward which are unlikely to be offset against anticipated future taxable profits. **(11 marks)**

(b) Ethan wishes to apply the fair value option rules of IFRS 9 *Financial instruments* to debt issued to finance its investment properties. Ethan's argument for applying the fair value option is based upon the fact that the recognition of gains and losses on its investment properties and the related debt would otherwise be inconsistent. Ethan argued that there is a specific financial correlation between the factors, such as interest rates, that form the basis for determining the fair value of both Ethan's investment properties and the related debt. **(7 marks)**

(c) Ethan has an operating subsidiary, which has in issue A and B shares, both of which have voting rights. Ethan holds 70% of the A and B shares and the remainder are held by shareholders external to the group. The subsidiary is obliged to pay an annual dividend of 5% on the B shares. The dividend payment is cumulative even if the subsidiary does not have sufficient legally distributable profit at the time the payment is due.

In Ethan's consolidated statement of financial position, the B shares of the subsidiary were accounted for in the same way as equity instruments would be, with the B shares owned by external parties reported as a non-controlling interest. **(5 marks)**

Required

Discuss how the above transactions and events should be recorded in the consolidated financial statements of Ethan.

Note. The mark allocation is shown against each of the three transactions above.

Professional marks will be awarded for the quality of the discussion. **(2 marks)**

(Total = 25 marks)

69 Norman

45 mins

6/08

(a) Norman, a public limited company, has three business segments which are currently reported in its financial statements. Norman is an international hotel group which reports to management on the basis of region. It does not currently report segmental information under IFRS 8 *Operating segments*. The results of the regional segments for the year ended 31 May 20X8 are as follows.

| | Revenue | | Segment results | Segment | Segment |
Region	External	Internal	profit/(loss)	assets	liabilities
	$m	$m	$m	$m	$m
European	200	3	(10)	300	200
South East Asia	300	2	60	800	300
Other regions	500	5	105	2,000	1,400

There were no significant intra-group balances in the segment assets and liabilities. The hotels are located in capital cities in the various regions, and the company sets individual performance indicators for each hotel based on its city location.

Required

Discuss the principles in IFRS 8 *Operating segments* for the determination of a company's reportable operating segments and how these principles would be applied for Norman plc using the information given above. **(11 marks)**

(b) One of the hotels owned by Norman is a hotel complex which includes a theme park, a casino and a golf course, as well as a hotel. The theme park, casino, and hotel were sold in the year ended 31 May 20X8 to Conquest, a public limited company, for $200 million but the sale agreement stated that Norman would continue to operate and manage the three businesses for their remaining useful life of fifteen years. The residual interest in the business reverts back to Norman after the fifteen year period. Norman would receive 75% of the net profit of the businesses as operator fees and Conquest would receive the remaining 25%. Norman has guaranteed to Conquest that the net minimum profit paid to Conquest would not be less than $15 million. **(4 marks)**

Norman has recently started issuing vouchers to customers when they stay in its hotels. The vouchers entitle the customers to a $30 discount on a subsequent room booking within three months of their stay. Historical experience has shown that only one in five vouchers are redeemed by the customer. At the company's year end of 31 May 20X8, it is estimated that there are vouchers worth $20 million which are eligible for discount. The income from room sales for the year is $300 million and Norman is unsure how to report the income from room sales in the financial statements. **(4 marks)**

Norman has obtained a significant amount of grant income for the development of hotels in Europe. The grants have been received from government bodies and relate to the size of the hotel which has been built by the grant assistance. The intention of the grant income was to create jobs in areas where there was significant unemployment. The grants received of $70 million will have to be repaid if the cost of building the hotels is less than $500 million. **(4 marks)**

Appropriateness and quality of discussion **(2 marks)**

Discuss how the above income would be treated in the financial statements of Norman for the year ended 31 May 20X8.

(Total = 25 marks)

70 Preparation question: Reconstruction scheme

Contemplation is a company that carries on business as film processors. For the past few years it has been making losses owing to the low price competition.

The company's statement of financial position as at 30 June 20X2 was as follows.

	$'000
Non-current assets	3,600
Current assets	4,775
	8,375
Equity	
Ordinary shares of $1 each fully paid	10,000
Retained earnings	(9,425)
	575
Non-current liabilities	
8% cumulative preference shares ((2,500,000 shares of $1 each)	3,300
11% Loan notes redeemable 20X9	3,500
Current liabilities	1,000
	8,375

The company has changed its marketing strategy and is now aiming at the specialist portrait print market. It is expected that the company will earn annual profits after tax of $1,500,000 for the next five years; the figure is before an interest charge. Income tax is assumed to be at a rate of 35%.

The directors are proposing to reconstruct the company and have produced the following proposal for discussion.

(a) To cancel the existing ordinary shares.

(b) The 11% loan notes are to be retired and the loan note holders issued in exchange with:

    (i) $3,000,000 14% redeemable loan notes 20Y5; and

    (ii)   2,000,000 ordinary shares of 25c each, fully paid up.

(c) The carrying value of the preference share capital above includes four years of dividends arrears. Assume that the IAS 32 definition of a liability is met. The preference shareholders are to be issued with 2,000,000 ordinary shares of 25c each fully paid up in exchange for the cancellation of these dividends arrears.

(d) The existing ordinary shareholders will be issued with 3,500,000 ordinary shares of 25c each, fully paid up.

In the event of a liquidation, it is estimated that the net realisable value of the assets would be $3,100,000 for the non-current assets and $3,500,000 for the net current assets.

Required

(a) Prepare a statement of financial position as at 1 July 20X2 after the reconstruction has been effected.

(b) Prepare computations to show the effect of the proposed reconstruction scheme on each of the loan note holders, preference shareholders and ordinary shareholders.

(c) Write a brief report to advise a shareholder who owns 10% of the issued ordinary share capital on whether to agree to the reconstruction as proposed. The shareholder has informed you that he feels the proposals are unfair.

(d) In your capacity as adviser to the shareholder, write a brief report to the directors suggesting any amendments you consider advisable.

Guidance notes

1   Layout a proforma statement of financial position for part (a) and fill in numbers as you work them out. Clearly label and cross reference workings.

2   The acceptability of any scheme to the major parties involved will be the main issue in such reconstructions. You must weigh up how much each group has to lose or gain and then reach a compromise.

71 Plans
27 mins

X, a public limited company, owns 100% of companies Y and Z which are both public limited companies. The X group operates in the telecommunications industry and the directors are considering two different plans to restructure the group. The directors feel that the current group structure is not serving the best interests of the shareholders and wish to explore possible alternative group structures.

The statements of financial position of X and its subsidiaries Y and Z at 31 May 20X7 are as follows:

	X $m	Y $m	Z $m
Property, plant and equipment	600	200	45
Cost of investment in Y	60		
Cost of investment in Z	70		
Net current assets	160	100	20
	890	300	65
Share capital – ordinary shares of $1	120	60	40
Retained earnings	770	240	25
	890	300	65

X acquired the investment in Z on 1 June 20X1 when the company's retained earnings balance was $20 million. The fair value of the net assets of Z on 1 June 20X1 was $60 million. Company Y was incorporated by X and has always been a 100% owned subsidiary. The fair value of the net assets of Y at 31 May 20X7 is $310 million and of Z is $80 million. The fair values of the net current assets of both Y and Z are approximately the same as their book values.

The directors are unsure as to the impact or implications that the following plans are likely to have on the individual accounts of the companies and the group accounts.

Local companies legislation requires that the amount at which share capital is recorded is dictated by the nominal value of the shares issued and if the value of the consideration received exceeds that amount, the excess is recorded in the share premium account. Shares cannot be issued at a discount. In the case of a share for share exchange, the value of the consideration can be deemed to be the book value of the investment exchanged.

The two different plans to restructure the group are as follows:

Plan 1

Y is to purchase the whole of X's investment in Z. The purchase consideration would be 50 million $1 ordinary shares of Y.

Plan 2

The same scenario as Plan 1, but the purchase consideration would be a cash amount of $75 million.

Required

Discuss the key considerations and the accounting implications of the above plans for the X group. Your answer should show the potential impact on the individual accounts of X, Y and Z and the group accounts after each plan has been implemented.

(15 marks)

72 Decany
45 mins

12/11

Decany owns 100% of the ordinary share capital of Ceed and Rant. All three entities are public limited companies. The group operates in the shipbuilding industry, which is currently a depressed market. Rant has made losses for the last three years and its liquidity is poor. The view of the directors is that Rant needs some cash investment. The directors have decided to put forward a restructuring plan as at 30 November 20X1. Under this plan:

(a) Ceed is to purchase the whole of Decany's investment in Rant. The purchase consideration is to be $98 million payable in cash to Decany and this amount will then be loaned on a long-term unsecured basis to Rant.

(b) Ceed will purchase land with a carrying amount of $10 million from Rant for a total purchase consideration of $15 million. The land has a mortgage outstanding on it of $4 million. The total purchase consideration of $15 million comprises both five million $1 nominal value non-voting shares issued by Ceed to Rant and the $4 million mortgage liability which Ceed will assume.

(c) A dividend of $25 million will be paid from Ceed to Decany to reduce the accumulated reserves of Ceed.

The statements of financial position of Decany and its subsidiaries at 30 November 20X1 are summarised below.

	Decany	Ceed	Rant
	$m	$m	$m
Non-current assets			
Property, plant and equipment at cost/valuation	600	170	45
Cost of investment in Ceed	130		
Cost of investment in Rant	95		
Current assets	155	130	20
	980	300	65
Equity and reserves			
Share capital	140	70	35
Retained earnings	750	220	5
	890	290	40
Non-current liabilities			
Long-term loan	5		12
Current liabilities			
Trade payables	85	10	13
	980	300	65

As a result of the restructuring, several of Ceed's employees will be made redundant. According to the detailed plan, the costs of redundancy will be spread over two years with $4 million being payable in one year's time and $6 million in two years' time. The market yield of high quality corporate bonds is 3%. The directors feel that the overall restructure will cost $2 million.

Required

(a) (i) Prepare the individual entity statements of financial position after the proposed restructuring plan.

(13 marks)

(ii) Set out the requirements of IAS 27 (Revised) *Separate financial statements* as regards the reorganisation and payment of dividends between group companies, discussing any implications for the restructuring plan. **(5 marks)**

(b) Discuss the key implications of the proposed plans for the restructuring of the group. **(5 marks)**

Professional marks will be awarded in Part (b) for clarity and expression of your discussion. **(2 marks)**

(Total = 25 marks)

73 Lucky Dairy

45 mins

ACR, 6/02, amended

The Lucky Dairy, a public limited company, produces milk for supply to various customers. It is responsible for producing twenty five per cent of the country's milk consumption. The company owns 150 farms and has a stock of 70,000 cows and 35,000 heifers which are being raised to produce milk in the future. The farms produce 2.5 million kilograms of milk per annum and normally hold an inventory of 50,000 kilograms of milk (Extracts from the draft accounts to 31 May 20X2).

The herds comprise at 31 May 20X2:

70,000 – 3 year old cows (all purchased on or before 1 June 20X1)
25,000 – heifers (average age 1½ years old – purchased 1 December 20X1)
10,000 – heifers (average age 2 years – purchased 1 June 20X1)

There were no animals born or sold in the year. The per unit values less estimated point of sale costs were as follows.

	$
2 year old animal at 1 June 20X1	50
1 year old animal at 1 June 20X1 and 1 December 20X1	40
3 year old animal at 31 May 20X2	60
1½ year old animal at 31 May 20X2	46
2 year old animal at 31 May 20X2	55
1 year old animal at 31 May 20X2	42

The company has had a difficult year in financial and operating terms. The cows had contracted a disease at the beginning of the financial year which had been passed on in the food chain to a small number of consumers. The publicity surrounding this event had caused a drop in the consumption of milk and as a result the dairy was holding 500,000 kilograms of milk in storage.

The government had stated, on 1 April 20X2, that it was prepared to compensate farmers for the drop in the price and consumption of milk. An official government letter was received on 6 June 20X2, stating that $1.5 million will be paid to Lucky on 1 August 20X2. Additionally on 1 May 20X2, Lucky had received a letter from its lawyer saying that legal proceedings had been started against the company by the persons affected by the disease. The company's lawyers have advised them that they feel that it is probable that they will be found liable and that the costs involved may reach $2 million. The lawyers, however, feel that the company may receive additional compensation from a government fund if certain quality control procedures had been carried out by the company. However, the lawyers will only state that the compensation payment is 'possible'.

The company's activities are controlled in three geographical locations, Dale, Shire and Ham. The only region affected by the disease was Dale and the government has decided that it is to restrict the milk production of that region significantly. Lucky estimates that the discounted future cash income from the present herds of cattle in the region amounts to $1.2 million, taking into account the government restriction order. Lucky was not sure that the fair value of the cows in the region could be measured reliably at the date of purchase because of the problems with the diseased cattle. The cows in this region amounted to 20,000 in number and the heifers 10,000 in number. All of the animals were purchased on 1 June 20X1. Lucky has had an offer of $1 million for all of the animals in the Dale region (net of point of sale costs) and $2 million for the sale of the farms in the region. However, there was a minority of directors who opposed the planned sale and it was decided to defer the public announcement of sale pending the outcome of the possible receipt of the government compensation. The board had decided that the potential sale plan was highly confidential but a national newspaper had published an article saying that the sale may occur and that there would be many people who would lose their employment. The board approved the planned sale of Dale farms on 31 May 20X2.

The directors of Lucky have approached your firm for professional advice on the above matters.

Required

Advise the directors on how the biological assets and produce of Lucky should be accounted for under IAS 41 *Agriculture* and discuss the implications for the published financial statements of the above events.

(Candidates should produce a table which shows the changes in value of the cattle stock for the year to 31 May 20X2 due to price change and physical change excluding the Dale region, and the value of the herd of the Dale region as at 31 May 20X2. Ignore the effects of taxation. Heifers are young female cows.) **(25 marks)**

74 IFRSs and SMEs

45 mins

ACR, 6/06, amended

International Financial Reporting Standards (IFRSs) are primarily designed for use by publicly listed companies and in many countries the majority of companies using IFRSs are listed companies. In other countries IFRSs are used as national Generally Accepted Accounting Practices (GAAP) for all companies including unlisted entities. It has been argued that the same IFRSs should be used by all entities or alternatively a different body of standards should apply to small and medium entities (SMEs) and recently the IASB published an IFRS for SMEs.

Required

(a) Discuss whether it was necessary to develop a set of IFRSs specifically for SMEs. **(7 marks)**

(b) Discuss the nature of the following issues in developing IFRSs for SMEs.

    (i) The purpose of the standards and the type of entity to which they should apply. **(7 marks)**
    (ii) How existing standards could be modified to meet the needs of SMEs. **(6 marks)**
    (iii) How items not dealt with by an IFRS for SMEs should be treated. **(5 marks)**

(Total = 25 marks)

75 Whitebirk

40 mins

12/10, amended

(a) The main argument for separate SME accounting standards is the undue cost burden of reporting, which is proportionately heavier for smaller firms.

    Required

    Discuss the main differences and modifications to IFRS which the IASB made to reduce the burden of reporting for SME's, giving specific examples where possible and include in your discussion how the Board has dealt with the problem of defining an SME. **(9 marks)**

    Professional marks will be awarded in part (a) for clarity and quality of discussion. **(2 marks)**

(b) Whitebirk has met the definition of a SME in its jurisdiction and wishes to comply with the *IFRS for Small and Medium-sized Entities*. The entity wishes to seek advice on how it will deal with the following accounting issues in its financial statements for the year ended 30 November 20X2. The entity already prepares its financial statements under full IFRS.

    (i) Whitebirk purchased 90% of Close, a SME, on 1 December 20X1. The purchase consideration was $5.7 million and the value of Close's identifiable assets was $6 million. The value of the non-controlling interest at 1 December 20X1 was measured at $0.7 million. Whitebirk has used the full goodwill method to account for business combinations and the life of goodwill cannot be estimated with any accuracy. Whitebirk wishes to know how to account for goodwill under the *IFRS for SMEs*.

    (ii) Whitebirk has incurred $1 million of research expenditure to develop a new product in the year to 30 November 20X2. Additionally, it incurred $500,000 of development expenditure to bring another product to a stage where it is ready to be marketed and sold.

    (iii) Whitebirk purchased some properties for $1.7m on 1 December 20X1 and designated them as investment properties under the cost model. No depreciation was charged as a real estate agent valued the properties at $1.9m at the year end.

    (iv) Whitebirk has an intangible asset valued at $1m on 1 December 20X1. The asset has an indefinite useful life, and in previous years had been reviewed for impairment. As at 30 November 20X2, there are no indications that the asset is impaired.

    Required

    Discuss how the above transactions should be dealt with in the financial statements of Whitebirk, with reference to the *IFRS for Small and Medium-sized Entities*. **(11 marks)**

(Total = 22 marks)

Answers

1 Conceptual framework

Marking scheme

		Marks
(a)	Subjective	14
(b)	Up to 3 marks per key issue	9
	(i) Recognition and de-recognition	
	(ii) Equity v liabilities	
	(iii) P/L v OCI	
	Appropriateness and quality of discussion	2
	Maximum	25

(a)   **The need for a conceptual framework**

The financial reporting process is concerned with providing information that is useful in the business and economic decision-making process. Therefore a conceptual framework will form the theoretical basis for determining which events should be accounted for, how they should be measured and how they should be communicated to the user.

Although it is theoretical in nature, a conceptual framework for financial reporting has highly practical final aims.

The **danger of not having a conceptual framework** is demonstrated in the way some countries' standards have developed over recent years; standards tend to be produced in a **haphazard and fire-fighting approach**. Where an agreed framework exists, the standard-setting body act as an architect or designer, rather than a fire-fighter, building accounting rules on the foundation of sound, agreed basic principles.

The lack of a conceptual framework also means that fundamental principles are tackled more than once in different standards, thereby producing contradictions and inconsistencies in basic concepts, such as those of prudence and matching. This leads to ambiguity and it affects the true and fair concept of financial reporting.

Another problem with the lack of a full conceptual framework has become apparent in the USA. The large number of highly detailed standards produced by the Financial Accounting Standards Board (FASB) has created a financial reporting environment governed by specific rules rather than general principles. FASB has 'concept statements' but a full conceptual framework would be better.

A conceptual framework can also bolster standard setters against political pressure from various 'lobby groups' and interested parties. Such pressure would only prevail if it was acceptable under the conceptual framework.

Can it resolve practical accounting issues?

A framework cannot provide all the answers for standard setters. It can provide **basic principles** which can be used when deciding between alternatives, and can narrow the range of alternatives that can be considered. In the UK, the *Statement of Principles* has provided **definitions that have formed the basis of definitions in accounting standards,** as has the IASB's conceptual framework in areas such as financial instruments and provisions. A framework can also provide guidance in the absence of an accounting standard. For example, there is no IFRS dealing specifically with off balance sheet finance, so the IASB *Conceptual Framework* must form the basis for decisions.

However, a conceptual framework is **unlikely**, on past form, to **provide all** the **answers to practical accounting problems**. There are a number of reasons for this:

(i)   Financial statements are intended for a variety of users, and it is not certain that a single conceptual framework can be devised which will suit all users.

(ii)   Given the diversity of user requirements, there may be a need for a variety of accounting standards, each produced for a different purpose (and with different concepts as a basis).

(iii)   It is not clear that a conceptual framework makes the task of preparing and then implementing standards any easier than without a framework.

The IASB's *Conceptual Framework for Financial Reporting* was criticised by the UK Accounting Standards Board at least partly on grounds of practical utility – it is thought to be **too theoretical,** and also for focusing on **some users (decision makers) at the expense of others (shareholders).** Perhaps it is not possible to satisfy all users.

(b)   **Discussion paper**

(i)   **Recognition and derecognition of assets and liabilities**

Generally all assets and liabilities are to be recognised unless recognising an asset or a liability is considered irrelevant or not sufficiently relevant to justify the costs for doing so or no measurement of the item would lead to a sufficiently faithful representation. For the first time, the *Conceptual Framework* will give guidance on derecognition. Generally entities should derecognise an asset or liability, or part of an asset or liability, when it no longer meets the recognition criteria.

(ii)   **Equity versus liabilities**

The distinction between equity and liabilities is clarified through **focus on the definition of a liability**. The paper identifies **two types** of approach: **narrow equity and strict obligation**.

(1)   **Narrow equity approach.** Equity is treated as being only the residual class issued, with changes in the measurement of other equity claims recognised in profit or loss.

(2)   **Strict obligation approach.** All equity claims are classified as equity with obligations to deliver cash or assets being classified as liabilities. Any changes in the measurement of equity claims would be shown in the statement of changes in equity.

Under the strict obligation approach, certain transactions now classified as liabilities would now be classified as equity because they do not involve an obligation to transfer cash or assets. An example of this is an issue of shares for a fixed monetary amount.

(iii)   **Profit or loss versus other comprehensive income**

Currently, the *Conceptual Framework* does not contain principles to determine:

(1)   What items are recognised in **profit or loss**

(2)   What items are recognised in **other comprehensive income**

(3) Whether, and when, items can be **recycled** from other comprehensive income to profit or loss.

In response, the Discussion Paper proposes that the *Conceptual Framework* should:

(1) Require a **profit or loss total or subtotal** that also **results, or could result**, in some items of income or **expense being recycled**

(2) **Limit the use of OCI** (only to income and expenses resulting from remeasurements of assets and liabilities).

The Discussion Paper proposes a **narrow and broad approach** to what should be included in other comprehensive income, but the IASB has not yet decided which approach it will use. Under the **narrow approach**. Other comprehensive income would **include bridging items and mismatched remeasurements**. In addition to the narrow approach, the **broad approach** would also include **transitory remeasurements**.

Bridging items are items of income or expense which represent the difference between measurement used in determining profit or loss and remeasurement used in the statement of financial position. An example would be investments in equity instruments with changes in fair value recorded in other comprehensive income. Such items would have to be **recycled as a consequence of the measurement basis presented in profit or loss**.

Mismatched remeasurements represent the effects of part of a linked set of assets, liabilities or past or planned transactions. It represents their effect so incompletely that, in the opinion of the IASB, the item provides little relevant information about the return that the entity has made on its economic resources in the period. An example would be a cash flow hedge, where fair value gains and losses are accumulated in other comprehensive income until the hedged transaction affects profit or loss. These amounts should **be recycled when the item can be presented with the matched item**.

2 Accounting standards and disclosure

Text reference. Issues covered here are dealt with in Chapters 1, 18 and 21 of the Study Text.

Top tips. This is an open-ended question. Part (a) asked why accounting standards help the 'market mechanism'. Your answer should deal with matters of consistency and comparability, which make the information more transparent than would be the case in a 'free for all'. Part (b), on the costs and benefits of disclosure is rather topical in the light of the 'credit crunch'. Arguments both for and against disclosure could be made, as well as the case that too much disclosure means that the user cannot see the wood for the trees.

You would be advised to do a quick answer plan before you start, otherwise there is a danger of rambling.

Easy marks. There are no easy marks as such; the trick is to keep on writing and backing up everything you say.

Examiner's comments. There were a variety of answers which were quite good, but very few candidates made reference to the *Framework*. The *Framework* is always a useful reference point for answers to discursive questions. In answering the part of the question dealing with the costs and benefits of disclosure, very few candidates mentioned possible litigation and competitive disadvantage and advantage. Also information asymmetry and its link with the liquidity of the market were seldom mentioned. Particularly in these current times, this point has particular relevance.

		Marks
(a)	Common understanding	2
	Neutral, unbiased	2
	Comparability	1
	Credibility	2
	Consistency	2
		9
(b)	Investment process	4
	Risk	2
	Protection	2
	Costs	2
	Competitive disadvantage	2
	Other criteria	2
		14
	Professional marks	2
	Available	25

(a)   **Accounting standards and the market mechanism**

Independently from financial reporting standards, the marketplace for capital encourages entities to invest time and thought into the quality of their reports. Companies have a vested interest in providing quality reports to potential lenders and investors, and if such information is not forthcoming, the cost of capital will be higher. However, **accounting standards play a key role in the effective functioning of the market mechanism** in the following ways.

(i)   **Consistency.** Accounting standards are generally developed in accordance with an agreed conceptual framework. For example International Financial Reporting Standards use definitions of assets and liabilities that are found in the IASB's *Conceptual Framework for Financial Reporting,* and UK Financial Reporting Standards use the *Statement of Principles.* In consequence, there is consistency in the presentation of financial information, and a common understanding of terms used for the elements of financial statements. This aids efficiency and decision-making, since users do not need to learn a new set of concepts for each reporting entity.

(ii)   **Neutrality.** While companies have an incentive to provide information in order to gain access to capital, they do not necessarily have an incentive to be unbiased. On the contrary, they may wish to portray their performance and financial position in a misleadingly favourable light. Users are aware of the potential bias, but if accounting standards are in place, compelling a company to present the information fairly, they can have more confidence in the financial statements. This increased trust helps decision making and efficiency, while too much scepticism is as bad as too little.

(iii)   **Comprehensiveness.** Reports prepared in accordance with, say, International Financial Reporting Standards or UK Financial Reporting Standards, and generally accepted accounting principles, are required to contain certain information. As a minimum, certain financial statements and notes are required, for example a statement of cash flows. Potential lenders and companies are aware of these requirements, and therefore know that reports prepared under accounting standards will meet certain of their information needs. In the absence of accounting standards, lenders would have to request information on an *ad hoc* basis, or speculate as to why certain information was missing.

(iv)   **Comparability.** If accounting standards are in force, the financial statements of companies can be compared effectively, which makes the decision-making process more efficient. Without them, companies could use very different bases for the preparation of accounts, and the user would not be comparing like with like. This is particularly important in the context of a global economy, where comparisons cross national borders, and was one of the main reasons why International Financial Reporting Standards were developed.

(v)   **Verification.** Auditors verify that financial statements have been prepared in accordance with applicable accounting standards. While an audit report is not a guarantee of a good investment, it lends credibility to the financial statements in a report.

(b)   **Costs and benefits of increased disclosure**

Benefits of disclosure

Users of financial statements need **as much relevant information as possible** in order to make or retain wise investments and to avoid less prudent uses of capital. Companies also benefit from providing this information as it means that they do not take on debt that they cannot afford. There are, then, obvious advantages to increased disclosure.

(i)   **Lenders** need to know if a company has **liquidity problems**. Disclosure of reasons for a large bank overdraft, or changes in gearing, may help allay any concerns, or alternatively may help the lender avoid a bad decision.

(ii)   Users need to know the full extent of **any risk** they are taking on in investing in – or indeed trading with – a company. Risk is not automatically a bad thing, if potential returns are good, and information on both profitability and gearing can help the decision-making process along. A venture capitalist may be more willing to take on risk than a high street bank, but both will need full disclosure of relevant information. A better understanding of risk may lower the cost of capital.

(iii)   **Investors** and potential investors will need to know which companies are the most **profitable**, and whether those profits are sustainable. Their job is to maximise returns. It is not in the long-term interests of either companies or potential investors to withhold information.

An article by KPMG's Andrew Vials *(Accountancy,* December 2008) emphasised the **importance of disclosure in a recession,** specifically the 'credit crunch' of 2008. Profits or cash balances may have fallen, but a user needs to know why:

> 'Now, more than ever, companies in their business review and in the accounts should be providing full disclosures around their business risks and the factors and assumptions that have featured in the going concern assessments.'

Costs of disclosure

Companies are sometimes reluctant to increase the level of disclosure, not because they have anything to hide, but because of the associated costs. These include the following.

(i)   **Costs to collate and prepare the required information.** These costs are principally time-costs of senior and junior staff, but may include fees to external consultants or lawyers. Training of staff – for example in moving to IFRS – may be required, or staff may need to be moved from other, revenue generating projects.

(ii)   **Costs of disseminating information.** This may simply mean a thicker annual report, or the cost of more time to present the information on the web. The annual report and accounts may not be adequate, and additional reports may be used.

(iii)   **Cost of lost competitive advantage.** Extra information on marketing strategies, planned products or locations for expansion can give competitors an advantage that they might not otherwise have. In particular, disclosure of problems, weaknesses and strategies for improvement may give the competitor an idea of areas to target. This disadvantage should not be overstated, however. A company does not need to give away trade secrets, and if the competitor is, for the benefits outlined above, also providing increased disclosure, there is no advantage to either party.

(iv)   **Potential litigation.** The additional information disclosed needs to be accurate, as misleading disclosure runs the risk of litigation. Time – and therefore money – needs to be spent checking the information to avoid this risk. That said, there is also a risk of litigation arising from incomplete or inadequate disclosure, so potential litigation should not, in itself be a reason to avoid increased disclosure.

Even in a recession, **enhanced disclosures are arguably worth the extra cost.** Even if the news is bad, it is better that users know, rather than find out later when it gets worse. A company with a reputation for full disclosure will earn the trust of potential investors. There are indeed costs to increased disclosure, but the **cost of non-disclosure may be greater**.

It is noticeable that there has been little opposition to the introduction of the IASB's *Management Commentary,* or, in the UK, the *Operating and Financial Review,* which requires disclosures above and beyond what is in the financial statements. Clearly companies and users are in agreement that the **benefits of disclosure outweigh the costs**.

3 Lizzer

Text reference. Disclosure and usefulness of reports are covered in Chapter 18 of the Study Text. Disclosures relating to financial instruments are covered in Chapter 7.

Top tips. Part (a) asks for a discussion about the optimal level of disclosure, and barriers to reducing disclosure. Arguments both for and against extensive disclosure could be made, as well as the case that too much disclosure means that the user cannot see the wood for the trees. Part (b) asks for application of specific disclosures, namely those in IFRS 7 relating to financial instruments.

You would be advised to do a quick answer plan before you start, otherwise there is a danger of rambling.

Easy marks. There are no obvious easy marks as such. However, Part (a) is rather open ended, so the trick is to keep on writing and backing up your arguments.

Examiner's comments. In answering Part (a) of this question, candidates were able to draw upon their own experiences and examples. However, this was not always forthcoming and thus it demonstrated the lack of wider reading by candidates. Having stated this fact the question was quite well answered. Part b required candidates to apply their knowledge of this area in determining whether disclosure should be made in two instances where the directors' view was that no further information regarding the two instances should be disclosed in the financial statements because it would be 'excessive'. The instances concerned IFRS 7 *Financial instruments: disclosures.* This is not a frequently examined part of the syllabus but candidates did not require a detailed knowledge of the IFRS to be able to answer the question. Marks could be gained for a logical discussion of the scenario involved. This question was well answered in the main.

Marking scheme

			Marks
(a)	Subjective: disclosure		9
	barriers		6
(b)	Subjective		8
	Professional marks		2
		Available	25

(a)   (i)   **Optimal level of disclosure**

Users of financial statements need **as much relevant information as possible** in order to make or retain wise investments and to avoid less prudent uses of capital. Companies also benefit from providing this information as it means that they do not take on debt that they cannot afford. There are, then, obvious advantages to increased disclosure.

(1)   **Lenders** need to know if a company has **liquidity problems**. Disclosure of reasons for a large bank overdraft, or changes in gearing, may help allay any concerns, or alternatively may help the lender avoid a bad decision.

(2)   Users need to know the full extent of **any risk** they are taking on in investing in – or indeed trading with – a company. Risk is not automatically a bad thing, if potential returns are good, and information on both profitability and gearing can help the decision-making process along. A venture capitalist may be more willing to take on risk than a high street bank, but both will

need full disclosure of relevant information. A better understanding of risk may lower the cost of capital.

(3) **Investors** and potential investors will need to know which companies are the most **profitable**, and whether those profits are sustainable. Their job is to maximise returns. It is not in the long-term interests of either companies or potential investors to withhold information.

(4) **Other stakeholders,** such as employees, customers, suppliers and environmentalists need to be informed of issues that concern them.

However, the key word here is **relevant. Too much disclosure can obscure**, rather than inform, as the key points are buried under excessive detail and less important points. Information overload may even mean that users stop reading altogether. Clear presentation helps – a summary of key points with cross references to more detailed analysis can save the user from the need to read through information that is not relevant to his or her needs.

Preparers of annual reports **do not, however, have full discretion** over how the reports are presented, because they are subject to the following **constraints**.

(1) Legal requirements, such as the Companies Acts in the UK

(2) International Financial Reporting Standards and local financial reporting standards

(3) Corporate governance codes

(4) Listing requirements, both local and overseas for companies with an overseas listing

(5) *Management Commentary,* although this has more flexibility than the others

These requirements have been **developed for different purposes,** which may add to the disclosure burden because entities must make **separate sets of disclosures on the same topic.** For example, an international bank in the UK may have to disclose credit risk under IFRS 7 *Financial instruments: disclosures,* the Companies Acts, the Disclosure and Transparency Rules, the SEC rules and Industry Guide 3, and the Basel Accords.

While the IASB has **reduced the level of disclosures for small and medium-sized enterprises** with the *IFRS for SMEs,* in general the **tendency** has been for **annual reports to expand,** and this is set to continue as stakeholders become increasingly demanding.

(ii) **Barriers to reducing disclosure**

Companies are sometimes reluctant to reduce the level of disclosure. These barriers are behavioural and include the following.

(1) **The perception that disclosing everything will satisfy all interested parties.** Many of the disclosures will not be applicable to the needs of any one user.

(2) **The threat of criticism or litigation.** Preparers of financial statements err on the side of caution rather than risk falling foul of the law by omitting a required disclosure. Removing disclosures is seen as creating a risk of adverse comment and regulatory challenge.

(3) **Cut and paste mentality.** If items were disclosed in last year's annual report and the issue is still on-going, there is a tendency to copy the disclosures into this year's report. It is thought that, if such disclosures are removed, stakeholders may wonder whether the financial statements still give a true and fair view. Disclosure is therefore the safest option and the default position.

(4) **Standard disclosures should be easy to find.** It has been suggested that the 'clutter' problem could be alleviated by segregating standing data in a separate section of the annual report (an appendix) or putting it on the company's website. A valid objection to this approach, however, is that even though explanatory information does not change much from year to year, its inclusion remains necessary to an understanding of aspects of the report. Users will benefit from being able to find all this information in one place in the hard copy, rather than having to go to a website to gain a full understanding of a particular point. An appendix may not be the

best place for the standing information, as the reader has to hunt in the small print in order to understand a point.

(5) **Not all users have access to the internet.** Relegating points of detail or standing information to the company's website would disadvantage such users.

(6) **Segregation of information may appear arbitrary.** Preparers (and users) may disagree as to what is important enough to be included in the main body of an annual report and what may be published in an appendix or on the website.

(7) **Checklist approach.** While materiality should determine what is disclosed, because what is material is what may influence the user, the assessment of what is material can be a matter of judgement. The purpose of checklists is to include all possible disclosures that could be material. Users may not be know which of the checklist disclosures is actually material in the context of their specific needs.

(b) (i) **Disclosure of debt risk**

It is not for Lizzer alone to determine who are the primary users of financial statements and what disclosures are necessary. The entity **needs to consider the requirements of IFRS 7** *Financial instruments: disclosures,* and apply them more broadly, to include debt-holders as well as just shareholders. More generally, IAS 1 *Presentation of financial statements* states that the objective of financial statements is to provide information about an entity's financial performance, financial position and cash flows that is useful to a wide range of users in making economic decisions. These users are defined by the *Conceptual Framework* as 'existing and potential investors, lenders and **other creditors**' which would **include debt-holders**.

The objective of IFRS 7 is to require entities to provide disclosures in their financial statements that enable users to evaluate:

(1) The significance of financial instruments for the entity's financial position and performance

(2) The nature and extent of risks arising from financial instruments to which the entity is exposed during the period and at the reporting date, and how the entity manages those risks

The disclosures required by IFRS 7 **show the extent to which an entity is exposed to different types of risk,** relating to both recognised and unrecognised financial instruments. **Credit risk** is one such risk, defined by the standard as:

'The risk that one party to a financial instrument will cause a financial loss for the other party by failing to discharge an obligation.'

Clearly disclosures about credit risk are important to debt-holders, Such disclosures are **qualitative** (exposure to risk and objectives, policies and processes for managing risk) and **quantitative**, based on the information provided internally to management personnel, enhanced if this is insufficient.

More important, in this context is **market risk**. The debtholders are exposed to the risk of the underlying investments whose value could go up or down depending on market value. Market risk is defined as:

'The risk that the fair value or future cash flows of a financial instrument will fluctuate because of changes in market prices. Market risk comprises three types of risk: currency risk, interest rate risk and other price risk.'

Disclosures required in connection with market risk are:

(1) **Sensitivity analysis**, showing the effects on profit or loss of changes in each market risk

(2) If the sensitivity analysis reflects interdependencies between risk variables, such as interest rates and exchange rates the method, **assumptions and limitations** must be disclosed

(ii)   **Potential breach of loan covenants**

The applicable standards here are IFRS 7 Financial instruments: disclosures, and IAS 10 Events after the reporting period.

According to IFRS 7, Lizzer **should have included additional information** about the loan covenants **sufficient to enable the users of its financial statements to evaluate the nature and extent of risks arising from financial instruments** to which the entity is exposed at the end of the reporting period. Such disclosure is particularly important in Lizzer's case because there was considerable risk at the year end (31 January 20X3) that the loan covenants would be breached in the near future, as indicated by the directors' and auditors' doubts about the company continuing as a going concern. Information should have been given about the **conditions attached to the loans and how close the entity was at the year-end to breaching** the covenants.

IFRS 7 requires disclosure of additional information about the covenants relating to each loan or group of loans, including headroom (the difference between the amount of the loan facility and the amount required).

The **actual breach of the loan covenants** at 31 March 20X3 was a **material event after the reporting period** as defined in IAS 10. The breach, after the date of the financial statements but before those statements were authorised, represents a **non-adjusting event**, which should have given rise to further disclosures in accordance with IAS 10.

Although the breach is a non-adjusting event, there appears to be some **inconsistency** between the information in the directors' and auditors' reports (which express going-concern doubts) and the information in the financial statements, which are prepared on a going-concern basis. **If any of the figures** in the statement of financial position are **affected,** these will **need to be adjusted.**

4 Venue

> **Text reference.** Revenue recognition is covered in Chapter 1 of your Study Text.
>
> **Top tips.** This is a topical issue and the subject of a new standard, IFRS 15, which is covered in your Study Text. You should not just give the details of the new approach, but explain why it was needed. Our answer is longer than you would be expected to write in the examination. The examiner has indicated that there will be a computational element in his current issues question. As here, it is not too complex. This question has been largely re-written to take account of the requirements of IFRS 15.
>
> **Easy marks.** Credit will be given for valid arguments in Part (a), which has a generous mark allocation.
>
> **Examiner's comment.** Part (a) of this question was well answered and discussions were good. However some candidates wrote general comments about recognition criteria for revenue and again these answers did not relate to the requirements of the question and were not in sufficient detail to justify full marks and the length and depth of the answers were often too short given the mark allocation for this question. Part (b) of the original question was well answered.

Marking scheme

		Marks
(a)	Main weaknesses of IAS 18 and IAS 11 – up to	8
	IFRS 15 improvements – up to	11
	Professional marks	2
(b)	Control not obtained by customer	3
	Option lapses	1
		25

(a) (i) **Main weaknesses of previous standards on revenue recognition**

The previous revenue recognition standards, IAS 18 *Revenue* and IAS 11 *Construction contracts*, were criticised because an entity applying the standards might recognise amounts in the financial statements that do not faithfully represent the nature of the transactions.

IAS 18 *Revenue* was criticised for being **vague** and this led to inconsistency in how it was applied by different entities. IAS 11 *Construction contracts* was also criticised, and there was sometimes uncertainty about which standard to apply. It was further argued that those standards were inconsistent with principles used in other accounting standards

Specifically, the weaknesses of the old standards were as follows.

(1) **Timing of revenue recognition.**

Many companies were uncertain about when they should recognise revenue because there is a lack of clear and comprehensive guidance in IAS 18 and IAS 11. This was particularly the case for goods and services because goods are sold at a point in time whereas services may be provided over time. This meant that the revenue recognised did not represent fairly the pattern of transfer to the customer of the goods and services.

(2) **Conflict with the IASB *Conceptual Framework***

Under the *Conceptual Framework*, income is recognised when an increase in future economic benefits related to an increase in an asset or a decrease of a liability has arisen that can be measured reliably. This means, in effect, that recognition of income occurs simultaneously with the recognition of increases in assets or decreases in liabilities (for example, the net increase in assets arising on a sale of goods or services or the decrease in liabilities arising from the waiver of a debt payable). It was not clear how this applied in the case of construction contracts.

(3) **Distinguishing between goods and services**

IAS 18 and IAS 11 did not clearly distinguish between goods and services, so some companies were not entirely sure whether to account for some transactions under IAS 18 or IAS 11. The standards are very different as regards the timing of recognition

(4) **Variable consideration**

Some contracts will have variable terms for the consideration paid to company by its customer. However, IAS 18 and IAS 11 did not include comprehensive guidance for measuring how much revenue should be recognised in such cases.

(5) **Multi-element arrangements**

Some transactions, often called multi-element arrangements, involve the delivery of more than one good or service. **The previous standards did not give sufficient guidance on dealing with such transactions.** IAS 18 stated that in certain circumstances the revenue recognition criteria must be applied to the separately identifiable components of a transaction. However, it did not explain the circumstances when a transaction could be broken down into separate components or the basis for identifying those components.

Under the standard proposed in the Exposure Draft *Revenue from contracts with customers*, distinct performance obligations would be accounted for separately. Goods or services are distinct if they are sold separately by the company, or if it provides benefits to the company's customer.

(6) **Disclosures**

Disclosures in current standards on revenue recognition were seen as inadequate when compared to disclosures in other standards.

(ii)   **Improvements brought about by IFRS 15**

IFRS 15 was published in May 2014. It is the result of a joint IASB and FASB project on revenue recognition. It seeks to strike a balance between the IASB rules in IAS 18, which were felt to be too general, leading to a lot of diversity in practice, and the FASB regulations, which were too numerous.

The core principle of IFRS 15 is that an entity should **recognise revenue to depict the transfer of promised goods or services to customers in an amount that reflects the consideration to which the entity expects to be entitled in exchange for those goods or services.**

To apply this core principle, IFRS 15 requires the following five step process:

(1)   **Identify the contract with a customer.** A contract can be written, oral or implied by customary business practices.

(2)   **Identify the separate performance obligations in the contract.** If a promised good or service is not distinct, it can be combined with others.

(3)   **Determine the transaction price.** This is the amount to which the entity expects to be 'entitled'. For variable consideration, the probability – weighted expected amount is used. The effect of any credit losses shown as a separate line item (just below revenue).

(4)   **Allocate the transaction price to the separate performance obligations in the contract.** For multiple deliverables, the transaction price is allocated to each separate performance obligation in proportion to the **stand-alone selling price** at contract inception of each performance obligation.

(5)   **Recognise revenue when (or as) the entity satisfies a performance obligation,** that is when the entity **transfers** a promised good or service to a customer. The good or service is only considered as transferred when the customer obtains **control** of it.

Addressing each of the criticisms in turn:

(1)   **Timing of revenue recognition.**

IFRS 15 is clear about when revenue should be recognised. Revenue from a contract may be recognised in accordance with IFRS 15 *Revenue from contracts with customers* when all of the following criteria are met.

- The **parties** to the contract have **approved the contract.**

- **Each party's rights** in relation to the goods or services to be transferred **can be identified.**

- The **payment terms and conditions** for the goods or services to be transferred **can be identified.**

- The contract has **commercial substance.**

- The **collection of an amount of consideration** to which the entity is entitled to in exchange for the goods or services is **probable.**

(2)   **Conflict with the IASB *Conceptual Framework***

IFRS 15 adopts an **asset/liability-driven approach**, consistent with the *Conceptual Framework*. Further, in the definition of ordinary activities. Reference is made to the description of revenue in the IASB's *Conceptual Framework*.

(3)   **Distinguishing between goods and services**

Step 2 of the five-stage process above addresses this criticism by requiring the entity to **identify the separate performance obligations in the contract.** The key point is distinct goods or services. A contract includes promises to provide goods or services to a customer. Those promises are called performance obligations. A company would account for a performance obligation separately only if the promised good or service is distinct. A good or service is distinct if it is sold separately or if it could be sold separately because it has a distinct function and a distinct profit margin.

(4) **Variable consideration**

This criticism is addressed by Step 3 above, which requires the entity to **determine the transaction price**. The transaction price is the amount of consideration a company expects to be entitled to from the customer in exchange for transferring goods or services. The transaction price would reflect the company's probability-weighted estimate of **variable consideration** (including reasonable estimates of contingent amounts) in addition to the effects of the customer's credit risk and the time value of money (if material). Examples of where a variable consideration can arise include: discounts, rebates, refunds, price concessions, credits and penalties.

(5) **Multi-element arrangements**

Under IFRS 15, **distinct performance obligations must be accounted for separately**. Goods or services are distinct if they are sold separately by the company, or if it provides benefits to the company's customer.

(6) **Disclosures**

The disclosures in IFRS 15 are clear and comprehensive. Entities must disclose sufficient information to enable users of financial statements to understand the **nature, amount, timing and uncertainty of revenue and cash flows arising from contract with customers.**

(b) **Plant**

Reven does not obtain control of the plant, because the repurchase option means that it is limited in its ability to use and obtain benefit from the plant.

As **control has not been transferred**, Venue must account for the transaction as a **financing arrangement**, because the exercise price is above the original selling price. Venue must continue to recognise the plant and recognise the cash received as a financial liability. The difference of $50,000 is recognised as interest expense.

If, on 31 July 20X7, the **option lapses** unexercised, Reven will then obtain control of the plant. In this case, **Venue must will derecognise the plant and recognise revenue of $550,000** (the $500,000 already received plus the $50,000 charged to interest).

5 Preparation question: Sundry standards

(a) **Curtailment**

Statement of financial position extract

	$'000
Non-current liabilities (4,115 – 4,540)	425

	$'000
Statement of comprehensive income extract	
Charged to profit or loss	
Current service cost	275
Net interest on net defined benefit liability (344 – 288)	56
Curtailment cost	58
	389

Other comprehensive income	
Actuarial gain on obligation	107
Return on plan assets (excluding amounts in net interest)	7

	$'000
Reconciliation of pension plan movement	
Plan deficit at 1 Feb 20X7 (3,600 – 4,300)	(700)
Company contributions	550
Profit or loss total	(389)
Other comprehensive income total (107 + 7)	114
Plan deficit at 31 Jan 20X8 (4,115 – 4,540)	(425)

	$'000
Changes in the present value of the defined benefit obligation	
Defined benefit obligation at 1 Feb 20X7	4,300
Interest cost @ 8%	344
Pensions paid	(330)
Curtailment	58
Current service cost	275
Remeasurement gain through OCI (bal. Fig.)	(107)
Defined benefit obligation at 31 Jan 20X8	4,540

Changes in the fair value of plan assets	
Fair value of plan assets at 1 Feb 20X7	3,600
Contributions	550
Pensions paid	(330)
Interest on plan assets 8% × 3,600	288
Remeasurement gain through OCI (295 – 288)	7
Fair value of plan assets at 31 Jan 20X8 (bal. fig.)	4,115

(b) **Settlement**

(i) *Calculation of net defined benefit liability*

Changes in the present value of the defined benefit obligation

	Obligation
	$'000
20X8 b/f	40,000
Interest at 8%	3,200
Current service cost	2,500
Past service cost	2,000
Benefits paid	(1,974)
	45,726
Remeasurement losses through OCI	274
20X8 c/f	46,000

20X9 b/f	46,000
Interest at 9%	4,140
Current service cost	2,860
Settlement	(11,400)
Benefits paid	(2,200)
	39,400
Remeasurement losses	1,400
20X9 c/f	40,800

Changes in the fair value of plan assets

	Assets
	$'000
20X8 b/f	40,000
Interest at 8%	3,200
Benefits paid	(1,974)
Contributions paid in	2,000
	43,226
Remeasurement losses	(226)
20X8 c/f	43,000
20X9 b/f	43,000
Interest at 9%	3,870
Settlement	(10,800)
Benefits paid	(2,200)
Contributions paid in	2,200
	36,070
Remeasurement losses	(390)
20X9 c/f	35,680

- During 20X8, there is an improvement in the future benefits available under the plan and as a result there is a past service cost of $1million, being the increase in the present value of the obligation as a result of the change.

- During 20X9, Sion sells part of its operations and transfers the relevant part of the pension plan to the purchaser. This is a settlement. The overall gain on settlement is calculated as:

	$'000
Present value of obligation settled	11,400
Fair value of plan assets transferred on settlement	(10,800)
Cash transferred on settlement	(400)
Gain	200

(ii) *Financial statements extracts*

STATEMENT OF FINANCIAL POSITION

	20X8	20X9
	$'000	$'000
Net defined benefit liability:(46,000 – 43,000)/(40,800 – 35,680)	3,000	5,120

STATEMENT OF PROFIT OR LOSS AND OTHER COMPREHENSIVE INCOME

	20X8 $'000	20X9 $'000
Profit or loss		
Current service cost	2,500	2,860
Past service cost	2,000	–
Gain on settlement	–	(200)
Net interest: (3,200 – 3,200)/(4,140 – 3,870)	–	270
Other comprehensive income		
Remeasurement loss on defined pension plan: (274 + 226)/(1,400 +390)	500	1,790

(c) **Classification of financial assets**

Bed's investment is a financial asset. According to IFRS 9 *Financial instruments*, financial assets are classified as measured at either amortised cost or fair value depending on:

(i)   The entity's business model for managing the financial assets and

(ii) the contractual cash flow characteristics of the financial assets.

In particular, a financial asset is measured at amortised cost where:

(i)   The asset is held within a business model where the objective is to hold assets in order to collect contractual cash flows

(ii) The contractual terms of the financial asset give rise on specified dates to cash flows that are solely payments of principal and interest on the principal outstanding.

For this purpose, interest is consideration for the time value of money and for the credit risk associated with the principal amount.

Embedded derivatives

Derivatives embedded within a host which is a financial asset within the scope of IFRS 9 are not separated out for accounting purposes; instead the entire hybrid contract is accounted for as one and classified as measured at amortised cost or fair value through profit or loss in accordance with the guidelines above.

Deposit with Em Bank

The deposit is considered a financial asset classified as held at amortised cost.

The additional 3% interest is an example of an embedded derivative. However, as the host contract is a financial asset, the derivative is not separated out for the purposes of accounting and the entire hybrid contract is accounted for together.

6 Key

Marking scheme

		Marks
(a)	Impairment processes	4
	General considerations	4
	Professional marks	2
(b)	Non-current asset at cost	6
	Non-current asset at valuation	6
	Non-current asset held for sale	3
		25

(a) The basic principle of IAS 36 *Impairment of assets* is that an asset should be carried at no more than its recoverable amount, that is the amount to be recovered through use or sale of the asset. If an **asset's value** is **higher than its recoverable amount**, an **impairment loss** has occurred. The impairment loss should be **written off** against profit or loss for the year.

Entities must determine, **at each reporting date**, whether there are any indications that impairment has occurred. Indicators of impairment may be internal or external. Where it is not possible to measure impairment for individual assets, the loss should be measured for a **cash generating unit. Internal factors** may apply in any economic climate, and include such matters as physical damage, adverse changes to the methods of use of the asset, management restructuring and over-estimation of cash flows. In an adverse economic climate, additional, **external indicators** of impairment are more likely to be evident. Such factors include:

(i) A **significant decrease** in the **market** value of an asset in excess of **normal passage of time**
(ii) Significant **adverse changes** in the **markets** or **business** in which the asset is used
(iii) Adverse changes to the **technological, economic or legal environment** of the business
(iv) Increase in **market interest rates** likely to affect **the discount rate** used in calculating value in use
(v) Where **interest rates increase**, adversely affecting **recoverable amounts**
(vi) The **carrying amount** of an entity's assets exceeding its **market capitalisation**

The **recoverable amount** is **defined** as the **higher** of:

(i)   The **asset's fair value less costs of disposal**. This is the price that would be received to sell the asset in an orderly transaction between market participants at the measurement date under current market conditions, net of costs of disposal.

(ii)   The asset's **value in use**. This is the present value of estimated future cash flows (inflows minus outflows) generated by the asset, including its estimated net disposal value (if any) at the end of its useful life. A number of factors must be reflected in the calculation of value in use (variations, estimates of cash flows, uncertainty), but the most important is the **time value of money** as value in use is based on **present value calculations**.

Impairment testing is difficult whether the recoverable amount is based on fair value less costs of disposal, because of the uncertainties surrounding **assumptions** that must be made. IAS 36 requires that these **are 'reasonable and supportable'**. Cash flow projections up to five years should be based on the most recent budgets and financial forecasts, but in a recession, these **should not be overly optimistic**. Longer term cash flow projections should be based on a steady or declining growth rate. Discount rates should reflect the specific risks of the asset or cash generating unit.

In an adverse economic climate, the entity will need to **consider the market** in which it operates in making its assumptions about recoverable amounts, because the market affects recoverable amounts. If **comparable industries** are taking impairment losses, then the entity will need to **explain the absence of such impairment charges**. Industry analysts will expect this. The market also needs to be informed about how the entity is reflecting the economic downturn in its impairment calculations, and what market information is being used in the impairment testing.

Clearly, testing for impairment will be a **time-consuming activity**. Cash flow assumptions may need to be reassessed, and **discount rates** must be scrutinised to see if they are **still valid** in a time of rising risk premiums and poor liquidity. Detailed calculations must be made and revised as necessary. Estimates and calculations may also need to be **revised** in the light of **information** becoming available only **after the end of the reporting period**. Last but not least, **extensive disclosures** will be required of discount rates, long-term growth rate assumptions and the reasons behind such assumptions.

(b)   **Impairment loss for year ended 31 May 20X4**

IAS 36 states that if an **asset's value** is **higher than** its **recoverable amount**, an **impairment loss** has occurred. The impairment loss should be written off to profit or loss for the year.

The carrying value of the non-current assets of Key at 31 May 20X4 is cost less depreciation:

$3m – ($3m ÷ 5) = $2.4m.

This needs to be compared to value in use at 31 May 20X4, which, using a discount rate of 5%, is calculated as:

Year ended	31 May 20X5	31 May 20X6	31 May 20X7	31 May 20X8	Total
Cash flows	280	450	500	550	
Discount factors	0.9524	0.9070	0.8638	0.8227	
Discounted cash flows ($'000)	267	408	432	452	1,559

The value in use of $1,559,000 is below the carrying value, so the carrying value must be written down, giving rise to an **impairment loss**:

$2,400,000 – $1,559,000 = $841,000

Value in use at 30 November 20X4

The directors wish to reverse the impairment loss calculated as at 31 May 20X4, on the grounds that, using the same cash flows, the value in use of the non-current assets is now above the carrying value. However, while IAS 36 requires an assessment at each reporting date of whether an impairment loss has decreased, this does not apply to the unwinding of the discount (or goodwill). Since the **same cash flows** have been used, the increase in value in use is **due to the unwinding of the discount, and so cannot be reversed**.

Government reimbursement

The treatment of compensation received in the form of reimbursements is governed by IAS 37 *Provisions, contingent liabilities and contingent assets*. Reimbursements from governmental indemnities are recorded in profit or loss for the year **when the compensation becomes receivable,** and the receipt is **treated as a separate economic event** from the item it was intended to compensate for. In this particular case, receipt is by no means certain, since the government has merely indicated that it may compensate.

Thus **no credit can be taken** for compensation of 20% of the impairment loss.

Revalued asset

When an **impairment loss occurs** for a **revalued asset**, the **impairment loss** should be first be charged to other comprehensive income (that is, treated as a **revaluation decrease**). Any **excess** is then charged to **profit or loss**.

The revaluation gain and impairment loss will be accounted for as follows:

	Revalued carrying value
	$m
1 December 20X1	10.0
Depreciation (10 × 2/10)	(2.0)
Revaluation (bal. fig.)	0.8
1 December 20X3	8.8
Depreciation (1 year) (8.8 × 1/8)	(1.1)
Impairment loss (bal. fig.)	(2.2)
Recoverable amount at 30 November 20X4	5.5

The impairment loss of $2.2m is charged to **other comprehensive income** until the revaluation surplus has been eliminated, and the rest is charged to profit or loss. Therefore the impairment **loss charged to other comprehensive income** will be **$0.8m.** The **remainder**, $2.2m − $0.8m = $1.4m will be **charged to profit or loss**.

It is possible that the company would transfer an amount from revaluation surplus to retained earnings to cover the excess depreciation of $0.1m. If so, the impairment loss charged to OCI would be $(0.8 − 0.1m) = $0.7m.

Property to be sold

The fact that management plans to sell the property because it is being under-utilised may be an **indicator** of **impairment**. Such assets (or cash generating units) must be tested for impairment when the decision to sell is made.

IFRS 5 *Non-current assets held for sale and discontinued operations* may apply in such cases, but the decision to sell the asset is generally made well before the IFRS 5 criteria are met. IFRS requires an asset or disposal group to be classified as held for sale where it is **available for immediate sale** in its **present condition** subject only to **terms that are usual** and customary and the sale is **highly probable**. For a sale to be highly probable:

- Management must be **committed** to the sale.
- An **active programme to locate a buyer** must have been initiated.
- The **market price** must be **reasonable** in relation to the asset's current fair value.
- The sale must be **expected to be completed within one year** from the date of classification.

An asset (or disposal group) that is held for sale should be measured at the **lower of** its **carrying amount** and **fair value less costs to sell**. Immediately before classification of the asset as held for sale, the entity must update any impairment test carried out. **Once** the asset has been **classified as held for sale**, any **impairment loss** will be based on the **difference between the adjusted carrying amounts and the fair value less cost to sell**. The impairment loss (if any) will be **recognised in profit or loss**.

A **subsequent increase** in fair value less costs of disposal may be **recognised** in profit or loss **only to the extent of any impairment previously recognised**.

In the case of the property held by Key, it is likely that **IFRS 5 would not apply** because **not all the criteria for a highly probable sale** have been met. Management is committed to the sale, and there is an active programme to locate a buyer. However, **Key has not reduced the price of the asset, which is in excess of its market value** – one of the IFRS 5 criteria is that the market price must be reasonable in relation to the asset's current fair value. In addition, the asset has remained unsold for a year, so it **cannot be assumed that the sale will be completed within one year** of classification.

The property does not meet the IFRS 5 criteria, so it **cannot be classified as held for sale**. However, an **impairment** has taken place and, in the circumstances, the **recoverable amount** would be **fair value less costs to sell**.

7 Prochain

Text reference. This topic is covered in Chapters 4 and 1 of your text.

Top tips. This question was a case study that dealt with the accounting issues for an entity engaged in the fashion industry. The areas examined were fundamental areas of the syllabus: non-current assets, intangible assets, determination of the purchase consideration for the subsidiary, and research and development expenditure. Tricky bits to get right were:

(a)   A provision for dismantling the 'model areas' would need to be set up and discounted back to the present.
(b)   Contingent consideration that is not probable would not be included in the cost of acquisition.
(c)   Investment properties do not include properties owned and occupied by the entity.

 When discussing the development expenditure, the criteria for capitalisation may be remembered using the mnemonic PIRATE.

Easy marks. Stating the obvious – that the model areas are items of property, plant and equipment and need to be depreciated will earn you easy marks, as will mentioning the basic distinction between research and development expenditure and listing the criteria when talking about the brand.

Examiner's comment. Generally, candidates answered the question quite well, obtaining a pass mark, although accounting for the non-current assets did confuse some candidates.

Marking scheme

	Marks
Model areas	7
Purchase of Badex	8
Research and Development	6
Apartments	4
Maximum/Available	25

Model areas

IAS 16 *Property, plant and equipment* is the relevant standard here. The model areas are held for use in the supply of goods and are used in more than one accounting period. The company should recognise the costs of setting up the model areas as **tangible non-current assets** and should **depreciate** the costs over their useful lives. **Subsequent measurement should be based on cost**. In theory the company could measure the model areas at fair value if the revaluation model of IAS 16 was followed, but it would be difficult to measure their fair value reliably.

IAS 16 states that the initial cost of an asset **should include** the initial estimate of the **costs of dismantling and removing the item and restoring the site** where the entity has an obligation to do so. A **present obligation appears to exist**, as defined by IAS 37 *Provisions, contingent liabilities and contingent assets* and therefore the entity should also **recognise a provision** for that amount. The provision should be **discounted to its present value** and the unwinding of the discount recognised in profit or loss.

At 31 May 20X6, the entity should recognise a non-current asset of $15.7 million (cost of $23.6 million (W) less accumulated depreciation of $7.9 million (W)) and a provision of $3.73 million (W).

Working

	$m
Cost of model areas	20.0
Plus provision ($20 \times 20\% \times \dfrac{1}{1.055^2}$ (= 0.898))	3.6
Cost on initial recognition	23.6
Less accumulated depreciation ($23.6 \times 8/24$)	(7.9)
Net book value at 31 May 20X6	15.7
Provision: on initial recognition ($20 \times 20\% \times 0.898$)	3.6
Plus unwinding of discount ($3.6 \times 5.5\% \times 8/12$)	0.13
Provision at 31 May 20X6	3.73

Purchase of Badex

IFRS 3 *Business Combinations* states that the consideration transferred in a business combination shall be measured at **fair value at the acquisition date**.

The **$100 million cash paid** on the acquisition date, 1 June 20X5 is **recognised as purchase consideration**. The **$25 million payable on 31 May 20X7** (two years after acquisition) should be **split** into the **$10 million deferred consideration** which should be **discounted to its present value** by two years ($10m \times 1/1.055^2 = $8.98m$) and the **contingent consideration** of $15 million. The contingent consideration should be measured at its **acquisition-date fair value**. Here, as the profit forecast targets are unlikely to be met, **the fair value would be significantly less than $15 million** but as the percentage chance of the targets being met and other relevant information are not given, it is not possible to establish a fair value.

Prochain should also recognise a corresponding **financial liability for the deferred and contingent consideration** (rather than equity) as they meet the definition of a financial liability in IAS 32 *Financial Instruments: Presentation*. This is because Prochain has a **contractual obligation to deliver cash** on 31 May 20X7 providing the conditions of the contingent consideration are met. At the year end 31 May 20X6, any **changes in the contingent consideration** as a result of changes in expectations of the targets being met will be recognised in **profit or loss** (rather than adjusting goodwill).

Under IFRS 3, any associated **transaction costs** should be **expensed to profit or loss**.

A further issue concerns the valuation and treatment of the 'Badex' brand name. IAS 38 *Intangible Assets* prohibits the recognition of internally generated brands and therefore the brand will not **be recognised in Badex's individual statement of financial position** prior to the acquisition. However, **IFRS 3 requires intangible assets** of an acquiree to be **recognised in a business combination if they meet the identifiability criteria** in IAS 38. For an intangible to be identifiable, the asset must be separable or it must arise from contractual or legal rights. Here, these **criteria appear to have been met** as the brand could be sold separately from the entity. Therefore, the 'Badex' brand should be **recognised as an intangible asset at $20m in the consolidated statement of financial position**.

Development of own brand

IAS 38 *Intangible assets* divides a development project into a research phase and a development phase. In the research phase of a project, an entity cannot yet demonstrate that the expenditure will generate probable future economic benefits. Therefore expenditure on **research** must be **recognised as an expense when it occurs**.

Development expenditure is capitalised when an entity demonstrates **all** the following.

(a)   The **technical feasibility** of completing the project

(b)   Its **intention to complete** the asset and use or sell it

(c)   Its **ability to use or sell** the asset

(d)   That the asset will generate **probable future economic benefits**

(e)   The availability of **adequate technical, financial and other resources** to complete the development and to use or sell it

(f)   Its ability to **reliably measure** the expenditure attributable to the asset.

Assuming that all these criteria are met, the cost of the development should comprise **all directly attributable costs** necessary to **create the asset** and to make it **capable of operating in the manner intended by management**.

Directly attributable costs **do not include selling or administrative costs,** or **training costs** or market research. The **cost of upgrading** existing machinery can be recognised as **property, plant and equipment**. Therefore the expenditure on the project should be treated as follows:

	Expense (P/L) $m	Recognised in statement of financial position	
		Intangible Assets $m	Property, plant and equipment $m
Research	3		
Prototype design		4	
Employee costs		2	
Development work		5	
Upgrading machinery			3
Market research	2		
Training	1		
	6	11	3

Prochain should **recognise $11 million** as an intangible asset.

Apartments

The apartments are leased to persons who are under contract to the company. Therefore they **cannot be classified as investment property**. IAS 40 *Investment property* specifically states that **property occupied by employees** is not investment property. The apartments must be treated as **property, plant and equipment**, carried at cost or fair value and depreciated over their useful lives.

Although the rent is below the market rate the difference between the actual rent and the market rate is simply **income foregone** (or an opportunity cost). In order to recognise the difference as an employee benefit cost it would also be necessary to **gross up rental income** to the market rate. The financial statements would **not present fairly** the financial performance of the company. Therefore the company **cannot recognise the difference** as an employee benefit cost.

8 Johan

Text reference. Intangibles and PPE are covered in Chapter 4 of the Study Text, and leasing in Chapter 10. Revenue recognition is covered in Chapter 1. This could also be viewed as a specialised industry question, as covered in Chapter 20 of the text.

Top tips. Although this question is set in a specialised industry, it draws on principles relating to intangibles, tangibles, leases and revenue recognition that are applicable in most industries. It is important to consider basic points, such as: does the licence meet the definition of an intangible asset, and how are such assets carried in the SOFP? In Part (c), a hint is given in the question that the prepaid phones and the service contracts should be treated differently: if you treat them both the same, you must have got one of them wrong.

Easy marks. These are available for identifying which standards apply and outlining the principles applicable, and you will gain these marks whether or not you come to the correct conclusion about the accounting treatment.

Examiner's comment. The question was not well answered with candidates failing to recognise the key accounting principles required. The main areas where candidates had problems was determining when the intangible asset should be recognised, determining the amortisation period for the asset, recognising that there was a lease and not a contingent liability, allocating the lease premium, determining when the revenue should be recognised on the sale of the handsets on the agency agreement and recognising the write down of inventory. Candidates did not appear to be able to draft answers where the main purpose of the question is to advise clients. Candidates seemed to be able to produce definitions but not to apply them.

		Marks
Intangible assets:	Licence	2
	Amortisation	2
	Impairment	2
	Renewal	2
		8
Tangible fixed assets:	Cost	1
	Feasibility study	1
	Location and condition	1
	Capitalised costs	1
Leases:	Operating lease	2
	Prepayment	1
		7
Inventory		2
IFRS 15:	Recognition	2
	Agency	2
	Separability	2
		8
Discussion		2
	Available	25

(a) **Licences**

The relevant standard here is IAS 38 *Intangible assets.* An intangible asset may be **recognised if it meets the identifiability criteria** in IAS 38, if it is probable that future economic benefits attributable to the asset will flow to the entity and if its fair value can be **measured reliably**. For an intangible asset to be identifiable the asset must be separable or it must arise from contractual or other legal rights. It appears that these **criteria have been met**. The licence has been acquired separately, and its value can be measured reliably at $120 million (cost). It is also expected that future economic benefits will flow to Johan. Therefore **the licence will be recognised as an intangible asset at cost**.

Regarding **subsequent valuation,** IAS 38 has two models: the **cost model** and the **revaluation model**. The revaluation model can only be used if intangible assets are traded in an active market. As Johan cannot sell the licence, this is not the case here, so Johan **cannot use the revaluation model**.

Under the **cost model,** intangible assets must be carried at **cost less amortisation and impairment losses**. The depreciable amount of an asset is cost less residual value; since the licence has no residual value, the depreciable amount is the cost. However, an impairment review should have been undertaken at 30 November 20X7, before amortisation commenced, and the licence written down, if necessary to its recoverable amount.

The **depreciable amount** must be **allocated over the useful life of the licence on a systematic basis.** The basis of allocation should reflect the **pattern of consumption** of the asset's benefit, unless this cannot be reliably determined, in which case the straight line basis would be used. The **straight line basis is appropriate**, in any case, for this licence, because the economic benefit is Johan's ability to earn income from the licence which accrues on a time basis and is not affected by wear and tear as some assets would be.

The **amortisation starts on the day that the network is available for use,** that is 1 December 20X7. Although the licence runs for six years from the date of purchase, 1 December 20X6, economic benefits cannot flow to the entity before the network assets and infrastructure are ready for use.

Other licences have been renewed at a nominal cost. It could therefore be argued that the licence should be amortised over two periods totalling eleven years: a period of five years from 1 December 20X7 to the renewal date, followed by six years from the renewal date. However, Johan does not know for certain what charge the regulator will make on renewal, so it would be more **appropriate to amortise the licence over a five year period,** that is $24 million per annum.

For the purposes of any **impairment review**, the licence and network assets should be classified as a single cash generating unit. They cannot be used separately from one another. There are **indications that the licence may be impaired:** disappointing market share, fierce competition and difficulty in retaining customers. Therefore the cash generating unit (licence and network assets) **must be tested for impairment**.

(b) **Costs incurred in extending the network**

The applicable standards here are IAS 16 *Property, plant and equipment,* and IAS 17 *Leases.*

IAS 16 states that the **cost** of an item of property, plant and equipment should be **recognised when two conditions** have been fulfilled:

It is probable that future economic benefits associated with the item will flow to the entity.

The cost of the item can be measured reliably.

The cost, according to IAS 16, includes **directly attributable costs of bringing the asset to the location and condition necessary for it to be capable of operating in a manner intended by management**. Examples of such directly attributable costs are site preparation costs and installation and assembly costs.

Applying the first criterion (probability of economic benefits) would **exclude the costs of the feasibility study**, both internal and external, because by definition, the economic benefits of a feasibility study are uncertain. These costs, $250,000 in total, should be **expensed as incurred**.

Applying the IAS 16 definition of directly attributable costs, the selection of the base station site is critical for the optimal operation of the network, and is part of the process of bringing the network assets to the location and condition necessary for operation. The **$50,000 paid to third party consultants** to find a suitable site is part of the cost of constructing the network, and **may thus be capitalised**.

The other costs – a payment of $300,000 followed by $60,000 a month for twelve years – is a **lease**, and is governed by IAS 17. IAS 17 defines a lease as an agreement whereby the lessor conveys to the lessee, in return for a payment or series of payments, the right to use an asset for an agreed period of time.

The question arises as to whether the payments are to be treated as **a finance lease or as an operating lease**. IAS 17 defines a finance lease as a lease that transfers substantially all the risks and rewards incidental to ownership of the leased asset to the lessee. An operating lease is a lease other than a finance lease.

In the case of the contract with the government for access to the land, there is **no transfer of ownership**. The term of the lease is **not for the major part of the asset's life**, because the land has an indefinite economic life. The lease **cannot therefore be said to transfer substantially all the risks and rewards of ownership** to Johan. Accordingly, the contract should be treated as an operating lease. The initial payment of $300,000 should be treated as a prepayment in the statement of financial position, and charged to profit or loss for the year on a straight line basis over the life of the contract. The monthly payments of $60,000 should be expensed. No value will be shown for the lease contract in the statement of financial position.

(c) **Purchase of handsets and revenue recognition**

The applicable standards in this case are IAS 2 *Inventories* and IAS 18 *Revenue.*

Inventory of handsets

IAS 2 states that inventories must be valued at the lower of cost and net realisable value. The handsets cost $200, and the net realisable value is selling price of $150 less costs to sell of $1, which is $149. All handsets in inventory – whether they are to be sold to prepaid customers or dealers – must be written down to $149 per handset.

Call cards and prepaid phones

IFRS 15 *Revenue from contracts with customers* has a **five-step process for** recognising revenue.

(i)   Identify the contract with the customer.
(ii)   Identify the separate performance obligations.
(iii)   Determine the transaction price.
(iv)   Allocate the transaction price to the performance obligations.
(v)   Recognise revenue when (or as) a performance obligation is satisfied.

Of these steps, (i) and (iii) are uncontroversial – there is a contract and the price is $21 per card. Step (ii) **'identify the separate performance obligations'** needs to be considered. A company would account for a performance obligation separately only if the promised good or service is distinct. A good or service is distinct if it is sold separately or if it could be sold separately because it has a distinct function and a distinct profit margin.

In the case of the call cards, **revenue is generated by the provision of services, not the sale of the card itself. The card is not a separate performance obligation** – the performance obligation is the provision of services. All of the transaction price is allocated to the services (step (iv)). Revenue should be recognised as the services are provided (step (v)). Step (v) would treat this as a **performance obligation satisfied over time** because the customer simultaneously receives and consumes the benefits as the performance takes place. The $21 received per call card should therefore be treated as deferred revenue at the point of sale. Of this, $18 per card should be recognised over the six month period from the date of the sale. The $3 of unused credit – an average figure may be used rather than the figure for each card – should be recognised when the card expires, that is when Johan has no further obligation to the customer.

Sales to dealers

IFRS 15 gives guidance on whether an entity acts as a **principal or agent.**

It is a principal if it controls the promised good or service before it is transferred to the customer. When the performance obligation is satisfied, the entity recognises revenue in the gross amount of the consideration for those goods or services.

It is acting as an agent if its performance obligation is to arrange for the provision of goods or services by another party. **Satisfaction of this performance obligation will give rise to the recognition of revenue in the amount of any fee or commissio**n to which it expects to be entitled in exchange for arranging for the other party to provide its goods or services.

Further relevant factors addressed by IFRS 15 are as follows.

(i)   **Johan bears the risk of loss** in value of the handset, as the dealer may return any handsets before a service contract is signed with a customer.

(ii)   **Johan sets the price** of the handset.

In conclusion, the **dealer, in this case, is acting as an agent for the sale of the handset and service contract**. Step (ii) of the IFRS 15 revenue recognition process, **'Identify the separate performance obligations'**, must be considered. The **handset cannot be sold separately** from the service contract, so the two transactions must be taken together because the commercial effect of either transaction cannot be understood in isolation. Johan earns revenue from the service contract with the final customer, not from the sale of the handset to the dealer. The service contract with the final customer is thus the performance obligation.

From Johan's point of view **revenue is not earned when the handsets are sold to the dealer, so revenue should not be recognised at this point**. Instead the net payment of $130 (commission paid to the agent less cost of the handset) should be recognised as a customer acquisition cost, which may qualify as an intangible asset under IAS 38. If it is so recognised, it will be amortised over the twelve month contract. **Revenue from the service contract will be recognised as the performance obligations (over time) are satisfied, that is as the service is rendered.**

9 Scramble

Marking scheme

	Marks
Intangible assets – subjective assessment	7
Cash generating units – subjective assessment	7
Intangible assets – subjective assessment	9
Professional	2
	25

(a) **Internally developed intangibles**

IAS 38 *Intangible assets* **allows internally developed intangibles such to be capitalised** provided certain criteria (technological feasibility, probable future benefits, intent and ability to use or sell the software, resources to complete the software, and ability to measure cost) are met. It is assumed, in the absence of information to the contrary, that they have; accordingly Scramble's treatment is correct in this respect.

Scramble is also correct in expensing the maintenance costs. These should not be capitalised as they do not enhance the value of the asset over and above the original benefits.

As regards subsequent measurement, IAS 38 requires that **an entity must choose either the cost model or the revaluation** model for each class of intangible asset. Scramble has chosen cost, and this is acceptable as an accounting policy.

Intangible assets **may have a finite or an indefinite useful life**. IAS 38 states that an entity may treat an intangible asset as having an indefinite useful life, when, having regard to all relevant factors there is no foreseeable limit to the period over which the asset is expected to generate net cash inflows for the entity.

'Indefinite' is not the same as 'infinite'. Computer software is mentioned in IAS 38 as an intangible that is prone to technological obsolescence and whose life may therefore be short. Its **useful life should be reviewed each reporting period** to determine whether events and circumstances continue to support an indefinite useful life assessment for that asset. If they do not, the change in the useful life assessment from indefinite to finite should be accounted for as a change in an accounting estimate.

The asset should also be **assessed for impairment in accordance with IAS 36** *Impairment of assets*. Specifically, the entity must test the intangible asset for impairment annually, and whenever there is an indication that the asset may be impaired. The asset is tested by **comparing its recoverable amount with its carrying amount**.

The **cash flows** used by Scramble to determine value in use for the purposes of impairment testing **do not comply with IAS 36**. Scramble does not analyse or investigate the differences between expected and actual cash flows, but this is an important way of testing the reasonableness of assumptions about expected cash flows, and IAS 36 requires such **assumptions to be reasonable and supported by evidence**.

Scramble is also **incorrect** to include in its estimate of future cash flows those **expected to be incurred in improving the games and the expected increase in revenue** resulting from that expense. IAS 36 requires cash flow projections to relate to the asset in its current condition. Nor should cash flow estimates include tax payments or receipts as here.

(b) **Discount rate for impairment**

While the cash flows used in testing for impairment are specific to the entity, the **discount rate is supposed to appropriately reflect the current market assessment of the time value of money and the risks specific to the asset or cash generating unit.** When a specific rate for an asset or cash generating unit is not directly available from the market, which is usually the case, the discount rate to be used is a surrogate. An estimate should be made of a **pre-tax rate that reflects the current market assessment of the time value of money and the risks specific to the asset** that have **not been adjusted** for in the estimate of future cash flows. According to IAS 36, this rate is the return that the investors would require if they chose an investment that would generate cash flows of amounts, timing and risk profile equivalent to those that the entity expects to derive from the assets.

Rates that should be considered are the entity's weighted average cost of capital, the entity's incremental borrowing rate or other market rates. The objective must be to obtain a rate which is sensible and justifiable. Scramble should not use the risk free rate adjusted by the company specific average credit spread of outstanding debt raised two years ago. Instead the credit spread input applied **should reflect the current market assessment of the credit spread at the time of impairment testing**, even though Scramble does not intend raising any more finance.

Disclosures

With regard to the impairment loss recognised in respect of each cash generating unit, IAS 36 would disclosure of:

- The amount of the loss
- The events and circumstances that led to the loss
- A description of the impairment loss by class of asset

It is **no defence** to maintain that this information was **common knowledge in the market**. The disclosures are still needed. It should be noted that IAS 1 requires disclosure of material items, so this information needs to be disclosed if the loses are **material,** with materiality determined using a suitable measure such as percentage of profit before tax.

(c) **Recognition of intangible assets**

Registration rights and agents' fees

The relevant standard here is IAS 38 *Intangible assets*. An **intangible asset may be recognised** if it gives control (the power to benefit from the asset), if it meets the identifiability criteria in IAS 38, if it is probable that future economic benefits attributable to the asset will flow to the entity and if its fair value can be measured reliably. For an intangible asset to be identifiable the asset must be separable or it must arise from contractual or other legal rights. It appears that these **criteria have been met**:

(i) The registration rights are contractual.

(ii) Scramble has control, because it may transfer or extend the rights.

(iii) Economic benefits will flow to Scramble in the form of income it can earn when fans come to see the player play.

IAS 38 specifies the items that make up the **cost** of separately acquired assets:

(i) Its purchase price, including import duties and non-refundable purchase taxes, after deducting trade discounts and rebates, and

(ii)   Any directly attributable cost of preparing the asset for its intended use.

IAS 38 specifically mentions, as an example of directly attributable costs, 'professional fees arising directly from bringing the asset to its working condition'. In this business, **the players' registration rights meet the definition of intangible assets**. In addition, **Scramble is incorrect** in believing that the **agents' fees** paid on extension of players' contracts do not meet the criteria to be recognised as intangible assets. The fees are incurred to service the player registration rights, and **should therefore be treated as intangible assets**.

Rights to revenue from ticket sales

Whether Rashing can show these rights as intangible assets depends on whether the IAS 38 criteria have been met. Since Rashing has no discretion over the pricing of the tickets and cannot sell them, it cannot be said to control the asset. Accordingly, the rights **cannot be treated as an intangible asset**.

The entity is only entitled to cash generated from ticket sales, so the issue is one of a **contractual right to receive cash**. The applicable standard is therefore not IAS 38 but IFRS 9 *Financial instruments,* under which the rights to ticket revenue represent a **financial asset**.

IFRS 9 has two classifications for financial assets: amortised cost and fair value. Financial assets are classified as being at **amortised cost** if **both** of the following apply.

(i)   The asset is held within a business model whose objective is to hold the assets to collect the contractual cash flows.

(ii)   The contractual terms of the financial asset give rise, on specified dates, to cash flows that are solely payments of principal and interest on the principal outstanding.

All other financial assets are measured at fair value.

Rashing's receipts are regular cash flows, but they are based on ticket revenues, which are determined by match attendance. Therefore they are not solely payments of principal and interest, and **do not meet the criteria for classification at amortised cost**. Consequently, the financial asset should be classified as being **at fair value** under IFRS 9.

10 Preparation question: Defined benefit plan

Statement of profit or loss and other comprehensive income notes

Defined benefit expense recognised in profit or loss

	$m
Current service cost	11
Past service cost	10
Net interest on the net defined benefit asset $(10\% \times (110 + 10)) - (10\% \times 150)$	(3)
	18

Other comprehensive income (items that will not be reclassified to profit or loss)
 Remeasurement of defined benefit plans

	$m
Actuarial gain on defined benefit obligation	17
Return on plan assets (excluding amounts in net interest)	(22)
	(5)

Statement of financial position notes

Net defined benefit asset recognised in the statement of financial position

	31 December 20X1 $m	31 December 20X0 $m
Present value of pension obligation	116	110
Fair value of plan assets	(140)	(150)
Net asset	(24)	(40)

Changes in the present value of the defined benefit obligation

	$m
Opening defined benefit obligation	110
Interest on obligation (10% × (110 + 10))	12
Current service cost	11
Past service cost	10
Benefits paid	(10)
Gain on remeasurement through OCI (balancing figure)	(17)
Closing defined benefit obligation	116

Changes in the fair value of plan assets

	$m
Opening fair value of plan assets	150
Interest on plan assets (10% × 150)	15
Contributions	7
Benefits paid	(10)
Loss on remeasurement through OCI (balancing figure)	(22)
Closing fair value of plan assets	140

11 Macaljoy

Marking scheme

				Marks
(a)	Pensions	(i)	Explanation	7
		(ii)	Calculation	7
(b)	Provisions	(i)	Explanation	6
		(ii)	Calculation	3
Structure of report				2
Maximum				25

To: The Directors
         Macaljoy

Date: 1 November 20X7

Subject: **Pension plans and warranty claims**

The purpose of this report is to explain the difference between defined benefit and defined contribution pension plans, and to show the accounting treatment of Macaljoy's pension schemes. It also discusses the principles of accounting for warranty claims and shows the accounting treatment of Macaljoy's warranty claims.

(a)   (i)   **Defined contribution plans and defined benefit plans**

With **defined contribution** plans, the employer (and possibly, as here, current employees too) pay regular contributions into the plan of a given or 'defined' amount each year. The contributions are invested, and the size of the post-employment benefits paid to former employees depends on how well or how badly the plan's investments perform. If the investments perform well, the plan will be able to afford higher benefits than if the investments performed less well.

The B scheme is a defined contribution plan. The employer's liability is limited to the contributions paid.

With **defined benefit** plans, the size of the post-employment benefits is determined in advance, ie the benefits are 'defined'. The employer (and possibly, as here, current employees too) pay contributions into the plan, and the contributions are invested. The size of the contributions is set at an amount that is expected to earn enough investment returns to meet the obligation to pay the post-employment benefits. If, however, it becomes apparent that the assets in the fund are insufficient, the employer will be required to make additional contributions into the plan to make up the expected shortfall. On the other hand, if the fund's assets appear to be larger than they need to be, and in excess of what is required to pay the post-employment benefits, the employer may be allowed to take a 'contribution holiday' (ie stop paying in contributions for a while).

The **main difference** between the two types of plans lies in **who bears the risk**: if the employer bears the risk, even in a small way by guaranteeing or specifying the return, the plan is a defined benefit plan. A defined contribution scheme must give a benefit formula based solely on the amount of the contributions.

A defined benefit scheme may be created even if there is no legal obligation, if an employer has a practice of guaranteeing the benefits payable.

The A scheme is a defined benefit scheme. Macaljoy, the employer, guarantees a pension based on the service lives of the employees in the scheme. The company's liability is not limited to the amount of the contributions. This means that the employer bears the investment risk: if the return on the investment is not sufficient to meet the liabilities, the company will need to make good the difference.

(ii) **Accounting treatment: B scheme**

No assets or liabilities will be recognised for this defined contribution scheme. The **contributions** paid by the company of $10m will be **charged to profit or loss**. The contributions paid by the employees will be part of the wages and salaries cost.

Accounting treatment: A scheme

The accounting treatment is as follows:

Statement of profit or loss and other comprehensive income notes

Expense recognised in profit or loss for the year ended 31 October 20X7

	$m
Current service cost	20.0
Net interest on the net defined benefit liability (10 – 9.5)	0.5
Net expense	20.5

Other comprehensive income: remeasurement of defined benefit plans (for the year ended 31 October 20X7)

	$m
Actuarial loss on defined benefit obligation	(29.0)
Return on plan assets (excluding amounts in net interest)	27.5
Net actuarial loss	(1.5)

STATEMENT OF FINANCIAL POSITION NOTES

Amounts recognised in statement of financial position

	31 October 20X7 $m	1 November 20X6 $m
Present value of defined benefit obligation	240	200
Fair value of plan assets	(225)	(190)
Net liability	15	10

Change in the present value of the defined benefit obligation

	$m
Present value of obligation at 1 November 20X6	200
Interest on obligation: 5% × 200	10
Current service cost	20
Benefits paid	(19)
Loss on remeasurement through OCI (balancing figure)	29
Present value of obligation at 31 October 20X7	240

Change in the fair value of plan assets

	$m
Fair value of plan assets at 1 November 20X6	190.0
Interest on plan assets: 5% × 190	9.5
Contributions	17.0
Benefits paid	(19.0)
Gain on remeasurement through OCI (balancing figure)	27.5
Fair value of plan assets at 31 October 20X7	225.0

(b) **Warranty provisions**

(i) **Principles**

Under IAS 37 *Provisions, contingent liabilities and contingent assets,* provisions must be recognised in the following circumstances.

(1) There is a **legal** or **constructive obligation** to transfer benefits as a result of past events.
(2) It is probably that **an outflow of economic resources** will be required to **settle** the **obligation**.
(3) A **reasonable estimate** of the amount required to settle the obligation can be made.

If the company can **avoid expenditure by its future action, no provision** should be recognised. A legal or constructive obligation is one created by an **obligating event**. Constructive obligations arise when an entity is committed to certain expenditures because of a pattern of behaviour which the public would expect to continue.

IAS 37 states that the amount recognised should be the **best estimate of the expenditure required to settle the obligation at the end of the reporting period**. The estimate should **take the various possible outcomes into account** and should be the **amount that an entity would rationally pay** to settle the obligation at the reporting date or to transfer it to a third party. In the case of warranties, the provision will be made at a probability weighted expected value, taking into account the risks and uncertainties surrounding the underlying events.

The amount of the provision should be **discounted to present value** if the time value of money is material using a **risk adjusted rate**. If some or all of the expenditure is expected to be **reimbursed** by a third party, the reimbursement should be **recognised as a separate asset,** but only if it is virtually certain that the reimbursement will be received.

(ii) **Accounting treatment**

In Macaljoy's case, the past event giving rise to the obligation is the sale of the product with a warranty. A provision for the warranty will be made as follows:

	$
Re year 1 warranty	280,000
Re year 2 warranty	350,000
	630,000

If material, the provisions may be discounted:

	$
Re year 1 warranty	269,000
Re year 2 warranty	323,000
	592,000

Calculations are shown below.

Macaljoy may be able to **recognise the asset and income from the insurance claim,** but only if the insurance company has validated the claim and **receipt is virtually certain**. In general contingent assets are not recognised, but disclosed if an inflow of economic benefits is probable.

Calculations

Year 1: warranty

	Expected value $'000	Discounted expected value (4%) $'000
80% × Nil	0	
15% × 7,000 × $100	105	
5% × 7,000 × $500	175	
	280	$280,000/1.04 = $269,000*

Year 2: extended warranty

	Expected value $'000	Discounted expected value (4%) $'000
70% × Nil	0	
20% × 5,000 × $100	100	
10% × 5,000 × $500	250	
	350	$350,000/(1.04)^2 = $323,000*

*Note. These figures are rounded

12 Smith

(a) (i) **Problems with the previous version of IAS 19**

An entity's defined benefit pension scheme can be a significant net asset or liability. The size of some schemes, together with the complexity of the accounting, meant that IAS 19 *Employee benefits* (prior to its revision in June 2011) came **in for criticism**.

One area that was particularly problematic was the **treatment of actuarial gains and losses**. The old IAS 19 treatment did not provide clear, full and understandable information to users. Specifically, IAS 19 gave a number of options for recognition of actuarial gains and losses: immediate recognition through profit or loss, immediate recognition through other comprehensive income and delaying recognition using the so-called 'corridor method'. This element of choice meant that the figures in the statement of financial position (and profit or loss for the year) were misleading.

The **main problems with the deferred recognition** model were:

(1) It was **inconsistent** the treatment of other assets and liabilities.

(2)   It meant that the employer was **not matching** the cost of providing post-employment benefits (as represented by the changes in plan assets and benefit obligations) to the periods in which those changes take place.

(3)   The accounting was **complex** and required complex records to be kept.

(4)   The statement of financial position figure could be **misleading**, for example, the plan might be in surplus and a liability shown in the financial statements or the plan might be in deficit with an asset shown.

(ii)   **Immediate recognition** has the following **advantages**:

(1)   By eliminating the options it **improves consistency** and comparability between accounting periods between different entities.

(2)   It gives a more **faithful representation** of the entity's financial position. A surplus in the pension plan will result in an asset being recognised and a deficit in a liability being recognised.

(3)   The financial statements are **easier to understand** and more transparent than if deferred recognition is used.

(4)   The income and expense recognised in profit or loss (or in other comprehensive income) **correspond** to changes in the fair value of the plan assets or the defined benefit obligation.

(5)   It is **consistent with the IASB** *Conceptual Framework for Financial Reporting*, which requires that 'the effects of transactions and other events are recognised when they occur ... and recorded ... and reported in the financial statements of the periods to which they relate.'

(6)   It is **consistent with IAS 8** *Accounting policies, changes in accounting estimates and errors* (changes in estimates must be included in the period in which the assets and liabilities change as a result) **and IAS 37** *Provisions, contingent liabilities and contingent assets* (changes in long term liabilities must be recognised in the period in which they occur).

(iii)   **Other changes to IAS 19**

(1)   **Remeasurements.** The revised standard introduced the term **'remeasurements'**. This is made up of the actuarial gains and losses on the defined benefit obligation, the difference between actual investment returns and the return implied by the net interest cost and the effect of the asset ceiling. Remeasurements are recognised immediately in other comprehensive income and **not** reclassified to profit or loss. This reduces diversity of presentation that was possible under the previous version of the standard.

(2)   **Net interest cost.** The revised standard requires interest to be calculated on **both** the plan assets and plan obligation at the same rate and the **net** interest to be recognised in the profit or loss. The rationale for this is the view that the **net** defined benefit liability/(asset) is equivalent to an amount owed by the company to the plan (or vice versa). The difference under the previous version of the standard was that an 'Expected return on assets' was calculated, based on assumptions about the long term rates of return on the particular classes of asset held within the plan.

(3)   **Past service costs.** The revised standard requires all past service costs to be recognised in the period of plan amendment. The previous standard made a distinction between past service costs that were **vested** (all past service costs relating to former employees and those relating to current employees that were not subject to any condition relating to further service) and those that were **not vested** (relating to current employees and where the entitlement was subject to further service). Only **vested** past service costs were recognised in profit or loss, and unvested benefits were deferred, and spread over remaining service lives.

(iv)   **Likely consequences of the revision to IAS 19**

(1)   **Increased comparability but increased volatility.** The new rules on recognition of gains and losses will increase comparability and bring increased transparency to the statement of financial position. However, companies that have the corridor approach may find that the new

rules bring increased volatility to the statement of profit or loss and other comprehensive income.

(2) **Pension funds invested differently.** The removal of the corridor method may result in changes in the way in which pension fund assets are invested. Pension companies have been able to take risks by investing in equities in the knowledge that gains and losses could be smoothed over the working lives of employees if the reporting entity chose to do so. Now that this option is no longer available, they may choose to invest in bonds, which are more stable.

(3) **Expenses will be more visible.** Under the previous version of the standard, the cost of running post-employment plans was accounted for either as a reduction to the expected return on plan assets or reserved for as an addition to the present value of the liabilities. Under the revised IAS 19, expenses will be split into those relating to the management of plan assets (charged to other comprehensive income) and those relating to the administration of the scheme (charged to profit or loss).

(4) More extensive disclosures will be required particularly relating to risk.

(5) **Change to the type of assets invested in because of the requirement to use the discount rate as for liabilities.** The replacement of the expected return on plan assets with an interest credit based on the discount rate will affect all companies, as the nature of the assets held in the scheme's investment portfolio will no longer influence the credit to the profit and loss account. This may lead to a reduction in investment risk as companies move to asset classes which tend to provide more stable returns and provide a better correlation with the scheme's liabilities, albeit at a higher expected long-term cost.

(b) **Gains or loss on plan assets**

	$
Fair value of plan assets at 1.1.20X2	2,600
Interest on plan assets (8% × $2,600,000)	208
Contributions	730
Benefits paid	(240)
Gain on remeasurement through OCI (balancing figure)	102
Fair value of plan assets at 31.12.20X2	3,400

Gains or loss on obligation

	$'000
Present value of obligation at 1.1.20X2	2,900
Current service cost	450
Past service cost	90
Interest cost (8% × $2,900,000)	232
Benefits paid	(240)
Loss on remeasurement through OCI (balancing figure)	68
Present value of obligation at 31.12.20X2	3,500

The net gain on remeasurement that will be recognised in other comprehensive income is $34,000 ($102,000 – $68,000).

13 Ryder

Text reference. IAS 10 is in Chapter 9, IAS 36 in Chapter 4 and IFRS 5 in Chapter 15.

Top tips. This is a mixed standard question, of the kind that the examiner generally likes.

Easy marks. Parts (a) and (b) are fairly straightforward. You should be familiar with IAS 10 and 36, even if you missed the IFRS 5 aspect.

(a) **Disposal of subsidiary**

The issue here is the value of the subsidiary at 31 October 20X5. The directors have stated that there has been no significant event since the year end which could have resulted in a reduction in its value. This, taken together with the loss on disposal, indicates that the subsidiary had **suffered an impairment at 31 October 20X5**. IAS 10 requires the sale to be treated as an **adjusting event** after the reporting period as it provides **evidence of a condition that existed at the end of the reporting period**.

The assets of Krup should be **written down to their recoverable amount**. In this case this is the eventual sale proceeds. Therefore the value of the net assets and purchased goodwill of Krup should be **reduced by $11 million** (the loss on disposal of $9 million plus the loss of $2 million that occurred between 1 November 2005 and the date of sale). IAS 36 *Impairment of assets* states that an impairment loss should be allocated to goodwill first and therefore the **purchased goodwill of $12 million is reduced to $1 million**. The impairment loss of $11 million is **recognised in profit or loss**.

Because there was no intention to sell the subsidiary at 31 October 20X5, **IFRS 5 *Non current assets held for sale and discontinued operations* does not apply**. The disposal is **disclosed** in the notes to the financial statements in accordance with IAS 10.

(b) **Issue of shares at fair value**

IFRS 3 *Business combinations* (revised 2008) recognises that, by entering into an acquisition, the acquirer becomes obliged to make additional payments. The revised IFRS 3 **requires recognition of contingent consideration, measured at fair value, at the acquisition date**.

The treatment of **post-acquisition changes** in the fair value of the contingent consideration **depends on the circumstances**.

(i) If the change is due to **additional information** that affects the position at the acquisition date, **goodwill should be re-measured, as a retrospective adjustment**. The additional information must come to light **within the measurement period,** a maximum of one year after acquisition.

(ii) If the change is **due to events which took place after the acquisition date,** for example meeting earnings target, an **equity instrument is not re-measured**. Other instruments are re-measured, with changes to total comprehensive income.

Ryder has **correctly included** an estimate of the amount of consideration in the cost of the acquisition on 21 January 20X4. This would have been based on the fair value of the ordinary shares at that date of $10 per share, giving a total of 300,000 × $10 = $3,000,000:

DEBIT Investment $3,000,000
CREDIT Equity $3,000,000

As the consideration is in the form of shares, and the change is due to an event which took place after the acquisition date (the rise in share price), **the consideration is not remeasured.**

The value of the contingent shares should be included in a **separate category of equity** in the statement of financial position at 31 October 20X5. They should be transferred to share capital and share premium after the actual issue of the shares on 12 November 20X5.

IAS 10 requires **disclosure of all material share transactions** or potential share transactions entered into after the reporting period end, excluding the bonus issue. Therefore **details of the issue of the contingent shares should be disclosed** in the notes to the financial statements.

(c)   **Property**

The property appears to have been **incorrectly classified** as 'held for sale'. Although the company had always intended to sell the property, IFRS 5 states that in order to qualify as 'held for sale' an asset must be **available for immediate sale in its present condition**. Because **repairs were needed** before the property could be sold and these were **not completed until after the reporting period end**, this was clearly **not the case at 31 October 20X5**.

In addition, even if the property had been correctly classified, it has been **valued incorrectly**. IFRS 5 requires assets held for sale to be valued at **the lower of their carrying amount or fair value less costs to sell**. The property **should have been valued at its carrying amount of $20 million**, not at the eventual sale proceeds of $27 million.

The property **must be included within property, plant and equipment** and must be **depreciated**. Therefore its **carrying amount at 31 October 20X5 is $19 million** ($20 million less depreciation of $1 million). The **gain of $7 million** that the company has previously recognised **should be reversed**.

Although the property cannot be classified as 'held for sale' in the financial statements for the year ended 31 October 2005, it **will qualify for the classification after the end of the reporting period**. Therefore details of the sale should be **disclosed** in the notes to the financial statements.

(d)   **Share appreciation rights**

The granting of share appreciation rights is a **cash settled share based payment transaction** as defined by IFRS 2 *Share based payment*. IFRS 2 requires these to be **measured at the fair value of the liability** to pay cash. The liability should be **re-measured at each reporting date and at the date of settlement**. Any **changes in fair value** should be **recognised in profit or loss** for the period.

However, the company has **not remeasured the liability since 31 October 20X4**. Because IFRS 2 requires the expense and the related liability to be recognised over the two-year vesting period, the rights should be measured as follows:

	$m
At 31 October 20X4: ($6 × 10 million × ½)	30
At 31 October 20X5 ($8 × 10 million)	80
At 1 December 20X5 (settlement date) ($9 × 10 million)	90

Therefore at 31 October 20X5 the liability **should be re-measured to $80 million** and an **expense of $50 million** should be recognised in profit or loss for the year.

The additional expense of $10 million resulting from the remeasurement at the settlement date is not included in the financial statements for the year ended 31 October 20X5, but is recognised the following year.

14 Royan

Marking scheme

	Marks
Existing guidance and critique	10
IAS 37 treatment	3
Communication skills	2
	15

(a) **Guidance in IAS 37**

Under IAS 37 *Provisions, contingent liabilities and contingent assets,* provisions must be recognised in the following circumstances.

(i)   There is a **legal** or **constructive obligation** to transfer benefits as a result of past events.

(ii)   It is **probable** that **an outflow of economic resources** will be required to **settle** the **obligation**.

(iii)   The obligation can be **measured reliably**.

IAS 37 considers an outflow to be probable if the event is **more likely than not** to occur.

If the company can **avoid expenditure by its future action, no provision** should be recognised. A legal or constructive obligation is one created by an **obligating event**. Constructive obligations arise when an entity is committed to certain expenditures because of a pattern of behaviour which the public would expect to continue.

IAS 37 states that the amount recognised should be the **best estimate of the expenditure required to settle the obligation at the end of the reporting period**. The estimate should **take the various possible outcomes into account** and should be the **amount that an entity would rationally pay** to settle the obligation at the reporting date or to transfer it to a third party. Where there is s **large population of items,** for example in the case of warranties, the provision will be made at **a probability weighted expected value,** taking into account the risks and uncertainties surrounding the underlying events. Where there is a **single obligation**, **the individual most likely outcome** may be the best estimate of the liability.

The amount of the provision should be **discounted to present value** if the time value of money is material using a **risk adjusted rate**. If some or all of the expenditure is expected to be **reimbursed** by a third party, the reimbursement should be **recognised as a separate asset,** but only if it is virtually certain that the reimbursement will be received.

Why replace IAS 37?

IAS 37 has provided useful guidance over the years that it has been in force, and is generally consistent with the *Conceptual Framework*. However, for the following reasons, it has been considered necessary to replace it.

(i)   IAS 37 requires recognition of a liability only if it is **probable,** that is more than 50% likely, that the obligation will result in an outflow of resources from the entity. This is **inconsistent with other standards,** for example IFRS 3 *Business combinations* and IFRS 9 *Financial instruments* which do not apply the probability criterion to liabilities. In addition, probability is not part of the *Conceptual Framework* definition of a liability.

(ii)   There is **inconsistency with US GAAP** as regards how they treat the **cost of restructuring** a business. US GAAP requires entities to recognise a liability for individual costs of restructuring only when the entity has incurred that particular cost, while IAS 37 requires recognition of the total costs of restructuring when the entity announces or starts to implement a restructuring plan.

(ii)   The **measurement rules** in IAS 37 are **vague and unclear**. In particular, 'best estimate' could mean a number of things: the mot likely outcome the most likely outcome, the weighted average of all possible outcomes or even the minimum/maximum amount in a range of possible outcomes. IAS 37 does not clarify which costs need to be included in the measurement of a liability, and in practice different entities include different costs. It is also unclear if 'settle' means 'cancel', 'transfer' or 'fulfil' the obligation.

(b)   **Treatment under IAS 37**

The IAS 37 criteria for recognising a **provision** have been met as there is a present obligation to dismantle the oil platform, of which the present value has been measured at **$105m**. Because Royan cannot operate the oil without incurring an obligation to pay dismantling costs at the end of ten years, the expenditure also enables it to acquire **economic benefits** (income from the oil extracted). Therefore Royan should **recognise an asset of $105m** (added to the 'oil platform' in property, plant and equipment) and this should be **depreciated** over the life of the oil platform, which is ten years. In addition, there will be an adjustment charged in profit or loss each year to the present value of the obligation for the **unwinding of the discount.**

15 Electron

Text reference. Environmental provisions are covered in Chapter 9; share schemes in Chapter 8.

Top tips. This is a multi-standard question on environmental provisions, leases, proposed dividend and a share option scheme. The question on the power station is similar to one you will have already met in this kit, and you have come across longer, more complicated questions on share-based payment, a favourite topic with this examiner.

Easy marks. The proposed dividend is straightforward, as is the explanation (if not the calculations) for the provision. The treatment of share options provides 4 easy marks for nothing much in the way of complications.

Marking scheme

	Marks
Oil contracts	4
Power station	7
Operating leases	5
Proposed dividend	3
Share options	4
Effective communication	2
Available/Maximum	25

REPORT

To: The Directors, Electron   Date: July 20X6
From: Accountant

Accounting treatment of transactions

Oil trading contracts

The first point to note is that the contracts always result in the delivery of the commodity. They are therefore correctly treated as normal sale and purchase contracts, **not financial instruments**.

The adoption of a policy of **deferring recognising revenue and costs is appropriate** in general terms because of the duration of the contracts. Over the life of the contracts, costs and revenues are equally matched. However, there is a mismatch between costs and revenues in the early stages of the contracts.

In the first year of the contract, 50% of revenues are recognised immediately. However, costs, in the form of amortisation, are recognised evenly over the duration of the contract. This means that **in the first year, a higher proportion of the revenue is matched against a smaller proportion of the costs**. It could also be argued that revenue is inflated in the first year.

While there is no detailed guidance on accounting for this kind of contract, IAS 18 *Revenue* and the IASB *Conceptual Framework* give general guidance. IAS 18 states that revenue and expenses that relate to the same transaction or event should be recognised simultaneously, and the *Conceptual Framework* says that the 'measurement and display of the financial effect of like transactions must be carried out in a consistent way'

It would be advisable, therefore, to match revenue and costs, and to **recognise revenue evenly** over the duration of the contract.

Power station

IAS 37 *Provisions, contingent liabilities and contingent assets* states that a provision should be recognised if:

- There is a present obligation as a result of a past transaction or event and
- It is probable that an outflow of resources embodying economic benefits will be required to settle the obligation
- A reliable estimate can be made of the amount of the obligation

In this case, the obligating event is the **installation of the power station**. The **operating licence** has created a **legal obligation** to incur the cost of removal, the expenditure is **probable,** and a **reasonable estimate** of the amount can be made.

Because Electron cannot operate its power station without incurring an obligation to pay for removal, **the expenditure also enables it to acquire economic benefits** (income from the energy generated). Therefore Electron correctly **recognises an asset** as well as a provision, and **depreciates this asset over its useful life of 20 years**.

Electron should recognise a provision for the cost of removing the power station, but should not include the cost of rectifying the damage caused by the generation of electricity until the power is generated. In this case the cost of rectifying the damage would be 5% of the total discounted provision.

The accounting treatment is as follows:

STATEMENT OF FINANCIAL POSITION AT 30 JUNE 20X6 (EXTRACTS)

	$m
Property, plant and equipment	
Power station	100.0
Decommissioning costs (W)	13.6
	113.6
Depreciation (113.6 ÷ 20)	(5.7)
	107.9
Provisions	
Provision for decommissioning at 1 July 20X5	13.6
Plus unwinding of discount (13.6 × 5%)	0.7
	14.3
Provision for damage (0.7(W)÷20)	0.1
	14.4

BPP
LEARNING MEDIA

STATEMENT OF PROFIT OR LOSS AND OTHER COMPREHENSVIE INCOME
FOR THE YEAR ENDED 30 JUNE 20X6 (EXTRACTS)

	$m
Depreciation	5.7
Provision for damage	0.1
Unwinding of discount (finance cost)	0.7

Working

	$m
Provision for removal costs at 1 July 20X5 (95% × (15 ÷ 1.05))	13.6
Provision for damage caused by extraction at 30 June 20X6 (5% (15 ÷ 1.05))	0.7

Operating lease

One issue here is the **substance** of the lease agreement. IAS 17 *Leases* classifies leases as either finance leases or operating leases. A finance lease **transfers substantially all the risks and rewards of ownership to the lessee**, while an operating lease does not. The company **retains legal ownership of the equipment** and also **retains the benefits of ownership** (the equipment remains available for use in its operating activities). In addition, the **present value of the minimum lease payments is only 57.1% of the fair value of the leased assets** ($40 million ÷ $70 million). For a lease to be a finance lease, the present value of the minimum lease payments should be **substantially all** the fair value of the leased assets. Therefore the lease **appears to be correctly classified as an operating lease**.

A further issue is the **treatment of the fee received**. The company has recognised the whole of the net present value of the future income from the lease in profit or loss for the year to 30 June 20X6, despite the fact that only a deposit of $10 million has been received. In addition, the date of inception of the lease is 30 June 20X6, so **the term of the lease does not actually fall within the current period**. IAS 17 states that **income from operating leases should be recognised on a straight line basis over the lease term** unless another basis is more appropriate. IAS 18 *Revenue* applies here. It does not allow revenue to be recognised **before an entity has performed under the contract** and therefore **no revenue should be recognised** in relation to the operating leases for the current period.

Proposed dividend

The dividend was **proposed after the end of the reporting period** and therefore IAS 10 *Events after the reporting period* applies. This **prohibits the recognition of proposed dividends** unless these are declared before the end of the reporting period. The directors **did not have an obligation** to pay the dividend **at 31 October 20X5** and therefore there **cannot be a liability**. The directors seem to be arguing that their past record creates a constructive obligation as defined by IAS 37 *Provisions, contingent liabilities and contingent assets*. A constructive obligation may exist as a result of the proposal of the dividend, but this had **not arisen at the end of the reporting period**.

Although the proposed dividend is not recognised it was **approved before the financial statements were authorised for issue** and should be **disclosed** in the notes to the financial statements.

Share options

The share options granted on 1 July 20X5 are **equity-settled transactions**, and are governed by IFRS 2 *Share based payment*. The aim of this standard is to recognise the cost of share based payment to employees over the period in which the services are rendered. The options are generally **charged to profit or loss** on the basis of their **fair value at the grant date**. If the equity instruments are traded on an active market, market prices must be used. Otherwise an option pricing model would be used.

The conditions attached to the shares state that the share options will vest in three years' time provided that the employees remain in employment with the company. Often there are other conditions such as growth in share price, but here **employment is the only condition**.

The **treatment** is as follows:

- Determine the fair value of the options at grant date.
- Charge this fair value to profit or loss equally over the three year vesting period, making adjustments at each accounting date to reflect the best estimate of the number of options that will eventually vest. This will depend on the estimated percentage of employees leaving during the vesting period.

For the year ended 30 June 20X6, the charge to profit or loss is $3m × 94% × 1/3 = $940,000. Shareholders' equity will be increased by an amount equal to this profit or loss charge.

16 Cohort

Text reference. Taxation is in Chapter 6 of the text.

Top tips. This question required a knowledge of deferred tax (IAS 12). The question focused on the key areas of the Standard and required an understanding of those areas. It did not require detailed computational knowledge but the ability to take a brief outline scenario and advise the client accordingly. Rote knowledge would be of little use in this situation.

Examiner's comment. Some candidates scored quite well on the question but again guessing at the answer was a fruitless exercise. The key areas were intragroup profit in inventory, unremitted earnings of subsidiaries, revaluation of securities, general provisions and tax losses. Basically an appreciation was required of how to deal with each of these areas but unfortunately most candidates struggled to deal with the issues involved.

Marking scheme

		Marks
Air	– Acquisition	5
	– Intra group profit	3
	– Unremitted earnings	3
Legion	– Long term investments	4
	– Loan provision	4
	– Deferred tax asset	4
	Maximum	**23**

Acquisition of the subsidiaries – general

Fair value adjustments have been made for consolidation purposes in both cases and these will **affect the deferred tax charge for the year**. This is because the deferred tax position is viewed **from the perspective of the group** as a whole. For example, it may be possible to recognise deferred tax assets which previously could not be recognised by individual companies, because there are now sufficient tax profits available within the group to utilise unused tax losses. Therefore a **provision** should be made for **temporary differences between fair values of the identifiable net assets acquired and their carrying values** ($4 million less $3.5 million in respect of Air). **No provision should be made for the temporary difference** of $1 million **arising on goodwill** recognised as a result of the combination with Air.

Future listing

Cohort plans to seek a listing in three years' time. Therefore it will become a **public company** and will be subject to a **higher rate of tax**. IAS 12 states that deferred tax should be measured at the **average tax rates expected to apply in the periods in which the timing differences are expected to reverse**, based on current enacted tax rates and laws. This means that Cohort may be paying tax at the higher rate when some of its timing differences reverse and this should be taken into account in the calculation.

Acquisition of Air

(a) The intra-group transaction has resulted in an **unrealised profit** of $0.6 million in the group accounts and this will be **eliminated on consolidation**. The tax charge in group profit or loss includes the tax on this profit, for which **the group will not become liable to tax until the following period. From the perspective of the group, there is a temporary difference**. Because the temporary difference arises in the financial statements of Cohort, **deferred tax should be provided** on this difference (an asset) using the rate of tax payable by Cohort.

(b)   **Deferred tax should be recognised on the unremitted earnings of subsidiaries** unless the parent is able to **control the timing of dividend payments** and it is **unlikely that dividends will be paid for the foreseeable future**. Cohort controls the dividend policy of Air and this means that there would normally be no need to make a provision in respect of unremitted profits. However, the profits of Air **will be distributed** to Cohort over the next few years and **tax will be payable** on the dividends received. Therefore a **deferred tax liability should be shown**.

Acquisition of Legion

(a)   A **temporary difference arises** where non-monetary assets are **revalued upwards** and the **tax treatment of the surplus is different from the accounting treatment**. In this case, the revaluation surplus has been **recognised in profit or loss** for the current period, rather than in equity but no corresponding adjustment has been made to the tax base of the investments because the gains will be taxed in future periods. Therefore the company **should recognise a deferred tax liability on the temporary difference of $4 million**.

(b)   A temporary difference arises when the provision for the loss on the loan portfolio is first recognised. The general allowance is expected to increase and therefore it is unlikely that the temporary difference will reverse in the near future. However, a **deferred tax liability should still be recognised**. The temporary difference gives rise to a **deferred tax asset**. IAS 12 states that **deferred tax assets should not be recognised unless it is probable that taxable profits will be available** against which the taxable profits can be utilised. **This is affected by the situation in point (c) below**.

(c)   In theory, unused tax losses give rise to a deferred tax asset. However, IAS 12 states that **deferred tax assets should only be recognised to the extent that they are regarded as recoverable**. They should be regarded as recoverable to the extent that on the basis of all the evidence available it is **probable that there will be suitable taxable profits against which the losses can be recovered**. The future taxable profit of Legion **will not be sufficient to realise all the unused tax loss. Therefore the deferred tax asset is reduced to the amount that is expected to be recovered**.

This reduction in the deferred tax asset implies that it was **overstated at 1 June 20X1**, when it was acquired by the group. As these are the first post-acquisition financial statements, **goodwill should also be adjusted**.

17 Panel

> **Text reference.** Tax is covered in Chapter 6 of the text.
>
> **Top tips.** This is a single topic question, which is a departure from the examiner's usual mixed standard question. The IFRS 1 aspects are likely to become less frequent over time.
>
> **Easy marks.** Part (b) (iii) and (iv) are easier than (i) and (ii), though they carry the same number of marks.
>
> **Examiner's comment.** Part (a) was quite well answered albeit often in a very general way. Part (b) was answered far better than when this area was tested in June 2005. The other three areas were a leasing transaction, an inter company sale and an impairment of property plant and equipment. These elements of the question were quite well answered although the discussion of the topic areas was generally quite poor whilst the computations were quite good. Deferred tax is a key area and must be understood.

(a)   (i)   **The impact of changes in accounting standards**

IAS 12 *Income taxes* is based on the idea that all **changes in assets and liabilities** have unavoidable **tax consequences**. Where the recognition criteria in IFRS are different from those in tax law, the **carrying amount of an asset or liability in the financial statements is different from the amount at which it is stated for tax purposes (its 'tax base')**. These differences are known as **'temporary differences'**. The practical effect of these differences is that a transaction or event occurs in a different accounting period from its tax consequences. For example, income from interest receivable is recognised in the financial statements in one accounting period but it is only taxable when it is actually received in the following accounting period.

IAS 12 requires a company to make **full provision** for the tax effects of temporary differences. Where a change in an accounting standard results in a change to the carrying value of an asset or liability in the financial statements, the **amount of the temporary difference** between the carrying value and the tax base **also changes**. Therefore the amount of the deferred tax liability is affected.

(ii) **Calculation of deferred tax on first time adoption of IFRS**

IFRS 1 *First time adoption of International Financial Reporting Standards* requires a company to **prepare an opening IFRS statement of financial position** and to **apply IAS 12 to temporary differences** between the carrying amounts of assets and liabilities and their tax bases at that date. Panel prepares its opening IFRS statement of financial position sheet **at 1 November 20X3**. The carrying values of its assets and liabilities are **measured in accordance with IFRS 1** and **other applicable IFRSs** in force at 31 October 20X5. The deferred tax provision is based on **tax rates that have been enacted or substantially enacted by the end of the reporting period**. Any **adjustments** to the deferred tax liability under previous GAAP are **recognised directly in equity (retained earnings)**.

(b) (i) **Share options**

Under IFRS 2 *Share based payment* the company **recognises an expense** for the employee services received in return for the share options granted over the vesting period. The related tax deduction **does not arise until the share options are exercised**. Therefore a **deferred tax asset arises**, based on the difference between the intrinsic value of the options and their carrying amount (normally zero).

At 31 October 20X4 the tax benefit is as follows:

	$m
Carrying amount of share based payment	–
Less: tax base of share based payment (16 ÷ 2)	(8)
Temporary difference	(8)

The **deferred tax asset is $2.4 million** (30% × 8). This is recognised at 31 October 20X4 provided that taxable profit is available against which it can be utilised. Because the tax effect of the remuneration expense is greater than the tax benefit, the tax benefit is **recognised in profit or loss**. (The tax effect of the remuneration expense is 30% × $40 million ÷ 2 = $6 million.)

At 31 October 20X5 there is **no longer a deferred tax asset** because the options have been exercised. The **tax benefit receivable is $13.8 million** (30% × $46 million). Therefore the deferred tax asset of $2.4 million is no longer required.

(ii) **Leased plant**

An asset leased under a finance lease is **recognised as an asset** owned by the company and the **related obligation** to pay lease rentals is **recognised as a liability**. Each instalment payable is treated partly as interest and partly as repayment of the liability. The **carrying amount** of the plant for accounting purposes is the **net present value of the lease payments less depreciation**.

A **temporary difference** effectively arises between the value of the plant for accounting purposes and the equivalent of the outstanding obligations, as the annual rental payments quality for the relief. The tax base of the asset is the amount deductable for tax in future, which is zero. The tax base of the liability is the carrying amount less any future tax deductible amounts, which will give a **tax base of zero**.

Therefore at 31 October 20X5 a **net temporary difference** will be as follows:

	$m	$m
Carrying value in financial statements:		
Asset:		
Net present value of future lease payments at inception of lease	12	
Less depreciation (12 ÷ 5)	(2.4)	
		9.60
Less finance lease liability		
Liability at inception of lease	12.00	
Interest (8% × 12)	0.96	
Lease rental	(3.00)	
		(9.96)
		0.36
Less tax base		(0.00)
Temporary difference		0.36

A **deferred tax asset of $108,000** (30% × 360,000) arises.

(iii) **Intra-group sale**

Pins has **made a profit of $2 million** on its sale to Panel. Tax is **payable on the profits of individual companies**. Pins is liable for tax on this profit in the current year and will have provided for the related tax in its individual financial statements. However, **from the viewpoint of the group** the profit **will not be realised until the following year**, when the goods are sold to a third party and must be **eliminated** from the consolidated financial statements. Because the group **pays tax before the profit is realised** there is a **temporary difference of $2 million** and a **deferred tax asset of $600,000** (30% × $2 million).

(iv) **Impairment loss**

The impairment loss in the financial statements of Nails **reduces the carrying value** of property, plant and equipment, but is **not allowable for tax**. Therefore the **tax base** of the property, plant and equipment **is different from its carrying value** and there is a **temporary difference**.

Under IAS 36 *Impairment of assets* the impairment loss is allocated first to goodwill and then to other assets:

	Goodwill $m	Property, plant and equipment $m	Total $m
Carrying value at 31 October 20X5	1	6.0	7.0
Impairment loss	(1)	(0.8)	(1.8)
	–	5.2	5.2

IAS 12 states that **no deferred tax should be recognised on goodwill** and therefore **only the impairment loss relating to the property, plant and equipment affects the deferred tax position.**

The effect of the impairment loss is as follows:

	Before impairment $m	After impairment $m	Difference $m
Carrying value	6	5.2	
Tax base	(4)	(4)	
Temporary difference	2	1.2	0.8
Tax liability (30%)	0.6	0.36	0.24

Therefore the impairment loss reduces deferred the tax liability by $240,000.

18 Kesare

Marking scheme

		Marks
(a)	Quality of discussion	2
	Conceptual Framework	1
	Temporary difference	2
	Liability	1
	Weakness	1
		7
(b)	Adjustments: Investment in equity instruments	2
	Convertible bond	2
	Defined benefit plan	2
	Property, plant and equipment	1
	Deferred tax: Goodwill	1
	Other intangibles	1
	Financial assets	1
	Trade receivables	1
	Other receivables	1
	Long-term borrowings	1
	Employee benefits	1
	Trade payables	1
	Calculation	3
		18
	Available	25
	Professional communication	2

(a)   IAS 12 *Income taxes* is based on the idea that **all changes in assets and liabilities** have **unavoidable tax consequences**. Where the recognition criteria in IFRS are different from those in tax law, **the carrying amount of an asset or liability in the financial statements is different from its tax base** (the amount at which it is stated for tax purposes). These differences are known as **temporary differences**. The practical effect of these differences is that a transaction or event occurs in a different accounting period from its tax consequences. For example, depreciation is recognised in the financial statements in different accounting periods from capital allowances.

IAS 12 requires a company to make **full provision** for the tax effects of temporary differences. Both **deferred tax assets**, and **deferred tax liabilities** can arise in this way.

It may be argued that deferred tax assets and liabilities **do not meet the definition of assets and liabilities** in the IASB *Conceptual Framework for Financial Reporting*. Under the *Conceptual Framework* an asset is the right to receive economic benefits as a result of past events, and a liability is an obligation to transfer economic benefits, again as a result of past events.

Under IAS 12, the tax effect of transactions are recognised in the same period as the transactions themselves, but in practice, tax is paid in accordance with tax legislation when it becomes a legal liability. There is a **conceptual weakness** or inconsistency, in that only one liability, that is tax, is being provided for, and not other costs, such as overhead costs.

(b)

	$'000	Adjustments to financial statements $'000	Adjusted financial statements $'000	Tax base $'000	Temporary difference $'000
Property, plant and equipment	10,000		10,000	2,400	7,600
Goodwill	6,000		6,000	6,000	
Other intangible assets	5,000		5,000	0	5,000
Financial assets (cost)	9,000	1,500	10,500	9,000	1,500
Total non-current assets	30,000		31,500		
Trade receivables	7,000		7,000	7,500	(500)
Other receivables	4,600		4,600	5,000	(400)
Cash and cash-equivalents	6,700		6,700	6,700	–
Total current assets	18,300		18,300		
Total assets	48,300		49,800		
Share capital	(9,000)		(9,000)		
Other reserves	(4,500)	(1,500)	(6,400)		
		(400)			
Retained earnings	(9,130)	520	(8,610)		
Total equity	(22,630)		(24,010)		
Long term borrowings	(10,000)	400	(9,600)	(10,000)	400
Deferred tax liability	(3,600)		(3,600)	(3,600)	–
Employee benefits	(4,000)	(520)	(4,520)	(5,000)	480
Current tax liability	(3,070)		(3,070)	(3,070)	–
Trade and other payables	(5,000)		(5,000)	(4,000)	(1,000)
Total liabilities	(25,670)		(25,790)		13,080
Total equity and liabilities	48,300		49,800		

Deferred tax liability			$'000
Liability b/fwd (per draft SOFP)			3,600
Charge: OCI ($1,500 × 30%			
(note (i))		450	
P/L (bal. fig)		(126)	
			324
Deferred tax liability c/fwd	14,980 × 30%	4,494	
Deferred tax asset – c/fwd	1,900 × 30%	(570)	
Net deferred tax liability	13,080 × 30%		3,924

Notes on adjustments

(i) The investments in equity instruments are shown at cost. However, per IFRS 9, they should instead be valued at fair value, with the increase ($10,500 – $9,000 = $1,500) going to other comprehensive income (items that will not be reclassified to profit or loss) as per the irrevocable election.

(ii) IAS 32 states that convertible bonds must be split into debt and equity components. This involves reducing debt and increasing equity by $400.

(iii) The defined benefit plan needs to be adjusted to reflect the change. The liability must be increased by $520,000. The same amount is charged to retained earnings.

(iv) The development costs have already been allowed for tax, so the tax base is nil. No deferred tax is recognised on goodwill.

(v) The accrual for compensation is to be allowed when paid, ie in a later period. The tax base relating to trade and other payables should be reduced by $1m.

19 Preparation question: Financial instruments

(a) STATEMENT OF PROFIT OR LOSS AND OTHER COMPREHENSIVE INCOME

	$
Finance income	
(441,014 × (W1) 8%)	35,281

STATEMENT OF FINANCIAL POSITION

	$
Non-current assets	
Financial asset (441,014 + 35,281)	476,295

Working: Effective interest rate

$$\frac{600,000}{441,014} = 1.3605 \therefore \text{from tables interest rate is 8\%}$$

(b) **Compound instrument**

Presentation

	$
Non-current liabilities	
Financial liability component of convertible bond (Working)	1,797,467
Equity	
Equity component of convertible bond (2,000,000 – (Working) 1,797,467)	202,533

Working

	$
Fair value of equivalent non-convertible debt	
Present value of principal payable at end of 3 years	1,544,367

$$(4,000 \times \$500 = \$2m \times \frac{1}{(1.09)^3})$$

	$
Present value of interest annuity payable annually in arrears	
for 3 years [(5% × $2m) × 2.531]	253,100
	1,797,467

20 Bental

Text reference. Specialised industries are covered in general terms in Chapter 20 of your Study Text. Financial instruments (including hedging) are covered in Chapter 7, and IFRS 10 (control) is covered in Chapter 12.

Top tips. Part (a), on the distinction between debt and equity, was the subject of an article by the examiner in *Student Accountant* magazine. Part (b), on hedging, contained some elements that were textbook knowledge, but only for the very well prepared students. In Part (c), you could have made some points about control using IFRS 10, thereby making inroads into a rather obscure topic area. The examiner has stated in a recent report: 'in practice there are always opposing viewpoints, and candidates should not be afraid of expressing these viewpoints as they will not be penalised if the rationale is acceptable.' This part of the question is an example of a case where arguments can be made in support of opposing viewpoints, reflecting the fact that decisions are often finely balanced in practice.

Easy marks. There were no easy marks – this was a very difficult question.

Examiner's comment. The examiner noted that this question was based on a 'real life' example, as are many of the scenario questions. The question was seen as difficult, but the knowledge assumed was not particularly complex – it was application of the knowledge that let candidates down. In Part (a), candidates seemed to understand the definitions but could not apply them. If the application was not exactly correct, candidates scored marks for a sensible discussion. Part (b) was challenging, but candidates could score reasonably well if they approached the question sensibly. The second element of part b again dealt with hedging and again the above principles applied. Knowledge of the equity method was required and its application in a hedging situation. This part of the question was not well answered. Part (c) of the question dealt with the situation where it was difficult to determine an acquirer. The knowledge required was that of IFRS 3 and IFRS 10. This type of question has been asked in the past and because of the introduction of IFRS 10, it was pertinent to ask candidates to apply the new standard. The key aspect of this question was the discussion of the principles and applying it to the scenario.

Marking scheme

	Marks
(a) Financial instrument explanation up to	7
(b) Hedged items	6
(c) IFRS 3 explanation	10
Professional marks	2
	25

(a)   **Classification of B-shares**

It is not always easy to **distinguish between debt and equity in an entity's** statement of financial position, partly because many financial instruments have elements of both. The distinction is important, since the classification of a financial instrument as either debt or equity **can have a significant impact on the entity's reported earnings and gearing ratio**, which in turn can affect debt covenants. Companies may wish to classify a financial instrument as equity, in order to give a favourable impression of gearing, but this may in turn have a negative effect on the perceptions of existing shareholders if it is seen as diluting existing equity interests.

IAS 32 *Financial instruments: presentation* brings clarity and consistency to this matter, so that the **classification is based on principles** rather than driven by perceptions of users.

Bental has classified the B-shares as **non-controlling interest** (equity) but this **does not comply with IAS 32**. IAS 32 defines an equity instrument as: 'any contract that evidences a residual interest in the assets of an entity after deducting all of its liabilities'. It must first be established that an instrument is not a financial liability, before it can be classified as equity.

A key feature of the **IAS 32 definition of a financial liability** is that it **is a contractual obligation to deliver cash or another financial asset to another entity**. A financial instrument is an **equity instrument** there is an **unconditional right to avoid delivering cash or another financial asset** to another entity. An instrument may be classified as an equity instrument if it contains a **contingent settlement provision** requiring settlement in cash or a variable number of the entity's own shares **only on the occurrence of an event which is very unlikely to occur** – such a provision is **not considered to be genuine.** If the **contingent payment condition** is **beyond the control of** both the entity and the holder of the instrument, then the instrument is classified as a **financial liability**.

The shareholders' agreement imposes on Bental a **clear contractual obligation to buy B-shares** from the non-controlling shareholders on the terms set out in the agreement. It **does not have an unconditional right to avoid delivering cash or another financial asset** to settle the obligation. The circumstance above, where the contingent settlement provision is not considered genuine because an event is unlikely to occur, does not apply here: the minority shareholders' can exercise their put option at least every three years, and more frequently if their ownership in B-shares exceeds the regulatory requirement.

Accordingly, the minority shareholders' holdings of B shares **should be treated as a financial liability** in the consolidated financial statements of Bental.

(b) **Hedging**

Swap arrangements

IFRS 9 *Financial instruments* (July 2014) sets out requirements for when hedge accounting is discontinued.

An entity cannot voluntarily discontinue hedge accounting as it could under the old IAS 39. Under IFRS 9, an entity is **not allowed to discontinue hedge accounting where the hedging relationship still meets the risk management objective and continues to meet all other qualifying criteria.**

This includes instances when the hedging instrument expires or **is sold, terminated or exercised or if a forecast transaction is no longer expected to occur.**

Discontinuing hedge accounting can either affect a hedging relationship in its entirety or only a part of it If only part of the hedging relationship is affected, hedge accounting continues for the remainder of the hedging relationship.

If hedge accounting ceases for a cash flow hedge relationship because the forecast transaction is no longer expected to occur, gains and losses deferred in other components of equity must be recognised in profit or loss immediately. If the **transaction is still expected to occur and the hedge relationship ceases, the amounts accumulated in equity will be retained in equity until the hedged item affects profit or loss.**

In the case of **Bental,** the forecast hedged transactions are still expected to occur. In any case, under the revised IFRS 9, Bental **cannot opt to discontinue the hedge accounting.**

Investment in foreign entity

The foreign entity is an **associate** and Bental will therefore account for it using the **equity method** in its consolidated accounts.

Under IFRS 9, an **equity method investment cannot be a hedged item in a fair value hedge** because the **equity method recognises in profit or loss the investor's share of the associate's profit or loss,** rather than changes in the investment's fair value. For a similar reason, an investment in a consolidated subsidiary cannot be a hedged item in a fair value hedge because consolidation recognises in profit or loss the subsidiary's profit or loss, rather than changes in the investment's fair value. A hedge of a net investment in a foreign operation is different because it is a hedge of the foreign currency exposure, not a fair value hedge of the change in the value of the investment.

Bental may, however, be able to **designate the investment as a hedged item** in a fair value hedge in its **individual financial statements,** provided its fair value can be **measured reliably.**

(c) **Business combination**

IFRS 10 *Consolidated financial statements* requires an acquirer to be identified in all business combinations, even where the business combination looks like a merger of equals. The acquirer is the combining entity which obtains **control** of the entity with which it is combined. It is not always easy to determine which party is the acquirer, and IFRS 10 gives guidance on the matter. The key point is **control,** rather than mere ownership, but this may not be easy to assess.

IFRS 10 states that an investor **controls** an investee if and only if it has all of the following.

(i)   **Power** over the investee

(ii)   Exposure, or rights, to **variable returns** from its involvement with the investee, and

(iii)   The **ability to use its power** over the investee to affect the amount of the investor's returns.

Power is defined as **existing rights that give the current ability to direct the relevant activities of the investee**. There is no requirement for that power to have been exercised.

Relevant activities may include selling and purchasing goods or services, managing financial assets, electing, acquiring and disposing of assets, researching and developing new products and processes and determining a funding structure or obtaining funding.

In some cases assessing power is straightforward, for example, where power is obtained directly and solely from having the majority of voting rights or potential voting rights, and as a result the ability to direct relevant activities.

In other cases, assessment is more complex and more than one factor must be considered. IFRS 10 gives the following examples of **rights**, other than voting or potential voting rights, which individually, or alone, can give an investor power.

(i)   Rights to appoint, reassign or remove key management personnel who can direct the relevant activities

(ii)   Rights to appoint or remove another entity that directs the relevant activities

(iii)   Rights to direct the investee to enter into, or veto changes to transactions for the benefit of the investor

(iv)   Other rights, such as those specified in a management contract.

If it is not clear which is the acquirer from applying IFRS 10, IFRS 3 *Business combinations* gives a number of other factors to consider; in particular the acquirer is usually the entity which transfers cash or other assets.

Applying the above criteria produces **arguments in favour of either party being the acquirer**.

Arguments in favour of Bental being the acquirer

(i)   Bental is the entity **giving up cash** amounting to 45% of the purchase price, which is a **significant share** of the total purchase consideration.

(ii)   In a business combination effected primarily by exchanging equity interests, as here, the acquirer is usually the **entity that issues its equity interests**. Thus Bental appears to be the acquirer.

(ii)   Other factors need to be taken into consideration in determining which of the combining entities has the power to govern the financial and operating policies of the other entity. Usually that is the one whose shareholders retain or receive the largest proportion of the voting rights in the combined entity, here **Bental which has 51%** immediately after the transaction.

(iv)   A controlling share does not always mean that the party that has it has the power to govern the combined entity's financial and operating policies so as to obtain benefits from its activities. Power may also be given by rights to appoint, reassign or remove key management personnel who can direct the relevant activities of the combined entity. **Five out of the six directors** of the combined entity are former board members of Bental, which points to Bental being the acquirer.

Arguments in favour of Lental being the acquirer

(i)   Despite the above, arguably the **former management of Lental has greater representation on the management team**. The management team consists of the Chief Operating Officer and two former employees of Lental, while Bental has only two former employees on the management team.

(ii)   The **Chief Operating Officer** of Lental has, as an individual, the **largest share** of the combined entity, which at 25%, gives him a great deal of **influence** over the team, especially taking into account the composition of the team. Although the board nominates the team, this individual influence points towards Lental being the acquirer.

(iii)   Lental may also be seen as the acquirer when the **relative size** of the combining entities is taken into account, for example in terms of assets, revenue or profit.. The fair value of Lental is $90m, which is significantly greater than that of Bental, ($70m) and this is an indication of control.

Conclusion

Identifying the acquirer is not easy, and there are **arguments on both sides**. In the case of Lental, the Chief Operating Officer of Lental is the source of much of Lental's power, **whereas Bental has a balance of other factors** in its favour, the most important of which are:

(i)   Bental is the entity transferring the cash
(ii)   Bental issued the equity interest
(iii)   Bental has the marginal controlling interest.

It is possible to conclude that Bental is the acquirer, but this is not a clear-cut case.

21 Avco

Text reference. The distinction between debt and equity is covered in Chapter 7 of your Study Text.

Top tips. While this question, on the distinction between debt and equity, was quite narrow in focus, the topic has featured in an article by the examining team. The issue has been flagged by the examining team as topical. The distinction between debt and equity is fundamental to any set of financial statements, and it is essential that you can explain it with reference to such matters as debt being determined where redemption is at the option of the instrument holder, where there is a limited life to the instrument and dividends being non-discretionary. Part (b) required you to apply the principles in Part (a) to two scenarios, discussing whether the instruments were debt or equity. It was not possible, therefore, to do Part (b) if you could not do Part (a), because you need to understand the principles in order to apply them. Unless you were sure of your ground, you would have been advised to tackle another optional question, in which the parts were more standalone.

Easy marks. It is difficult to find much in the way of easy marks in this challenging question. However, if you had practised the December 2013 question Bental, you might have found that Part (a) dealt with some of the same arguments, and this might have made the question easier.

Examiner's comment. The key message from the examiner is that the final decision as to whether the instrument was debt or equity was not as important as the ability to discuss the scenario. Obviously the answer should be correct but if candidates can discuss the relevant issues then they will score a good proportion of the marks.

ACCA Examiner's answer. The Examiner's answer to this question is included at the back of this Kit.

Marking scheme

		Marks
(a)(i)	1 mark per point up to maximum	9
(ii)	Effects	5
(b)	1 mark per point up to maximum	9
Professional marks		2
		25

(a)   (i)   **Classification differences between debt and equity**

It is not always easy to **distinguish between debt and equity in an entity's** statement of financial position, partly because many financial instruments have elements of both.

IAS 32 *Financial instruments: presentation* brings clarity and consistency to this matter, so that the **classification is based on principles** rather than driven by perceptions of users.

IAS 32 defines an **equity instrument** as: 'any contract that evidences a residual interest in the assets of an entity after deducting all of its liabilities'. It must first be **established that an instrument is not a financial liability,** before it can be classified as equity.

A key feature of the **IAS 32 definition of a financial liability** is that it **is a contractual obligation to deliver cash or another financial asset to another entity**. The contractual obligation may arise from a requirement to make payments of principal, interest or dividends. The contractual obligation may be explicit, but it may be implied indirectly in the terms of the contract. An example of a debt instrument is a bond which requires the issuer to make interest payments and redeem the bond for cash.

A financial instrument is an **equity instrument** only if there is no obligation to deliver cash or other financial assets to another entity and if the instrument will or may be settled in the issuer's own equity instruments. An example of an equity instrument is **ordinary shares, on which dividends are payable at the discretion of the issuer.** A less obvious example is preference shares required to be converted into a fixed number of ordinary shares on a fixed date or on the occurrence of an event which is certain to occur.

An instrument may be classified as an equity instrument if it contains a **contingent settlement provision** requiring settlement in cash or a variable number of the entity's own shares **only on the occurrence of an event which is very unlikely to occur** – such a provision is **not considered to be genuine.** If the **contingent payment condition** is **beyond the control of** both the entity and the holder of the instrument, then the instrument is classified as a **financial liability**.

A **contract resulting in the receipt or delivery of an entity's own shares is not automatically an equity instrument.** The classification depends on the so-called **'fixed test'** in IAS 32. A contract which will be settled by the entity receiving or delivering a **fixed number of its own equity instruments in exchange for a fixed amount of cash is an equity instrument**. The reasoning behind this is that by fixing upfront the number of shares to be received or delivered on settlement of the instrument in concern, the holder is exposed to the upside and downside risk of movements in the entity's share price.

In contrast, if the **amount of cash or own equity shares to be delivered or received is variable,** then the contract is a **financial liability or asset.** The reasoning behind this is that using a variable number of own equity instruments to settle a contract can be similar to using own shares as 'currency' to settle what in substance is a financial liability. Such a contract does not evidence a residual interest in the entity's net assets. Equity classification is therefore inappropriate.

IAS 32 gives two **examples** of contracts where the number of own equity instruments to be received or delivered varies so that their fair value equals the amount of the contractual right or obligation.

(1)   A contract to deliver a variable number of own equity instruments equal in value to a fixed monetary amount on the settlement date is classified as a financial liability.

(2)   A contract to deliver as many of the entity's own equity instruments as are equal in value to the value of 100 ounces of a commodity results in liability classification of the instrument.

There are **other factors** which might result in an instrument being **classified as debt.**

(1)   Dividends are non-discretionary.

(2)   Redemption is at the option of the instrument holder.

(3)   The instrument has a limited life.

(4)   Redemption is triggered by a future uncertain event which is beyond the control of both the issuer and the holder of the instrument.

Other factors which might result in an instrument being **classified as equity** include the following.

(1)   Dividends are discretionary.
(2)   The shares are non-redeemable.
(3)   There is no liquidation date.

(ii)   **Significance of debt/equity classification for the financial statements**

The distinction between debt and equity is very important, since the classification of a financial instrument as either debt or equity **can have a significant impact on the entity's reported earnings and gearing ratio**, which in turn can affect debt covenants. Companies may wish to classify a financial instrument as **equity,** in order to give a **favourable impression of gearing,** but this may in turn have a **negative effect** on the perceptions of existing shareholders if it is seen **as diluting existing equity interests.**

The distinction is also relevant in the context of a **business combination** where an entity **issues financial instruments as part consideration, or to raise funds to settle a business combination in cash.** Management is often called upon to **evaluate different financing options**, and in order to do so must **understand the classification rules and their potential effects**. For example, **classification as a liability** generally means that **payments are treated as interest** and charged to profit or loss, and this may, in turn, **affect the entity's ability to pay dividends** on equity shares.

(b)   (i)   **Cavor**

B shares

The classification of Cavor's B shares will be made by applying **the principles-based definitions of equity and liability in IAS 32**, and considering the **substance,** rather than the legal form of the instrument. 'Substance' here relates only to consideration of the contractual terms of the instrument. Factors outside the contractual terms are not relevant to the classification. The following factors demonstrate that Cavor's B shares are **equity instruments.**

(1)   **Dividends are discretionary** in that they need only be paid if paid on the A shares, on which there is no obligation to pay dividends. Dividends on the B shares will be paid at the same rate as on the A shares, which will be variable.

(2)   Cavor has **no obligation to redeem** the B shares.

Share options

The 'fixed test' must be applied. If the amount of cash or own equity shares to be delivered is variable, then the contract is a debt instrument. Here, however, the contract is to be settled by Cavor issuing a fixed number of its own equity instruments for a fixed amount of cash. Accordingly there is **no variability, and the share options are classified as an equity instrument.**

(ii)   **Lidan**

A financial liability under IAS 32 is **a contractual obligation to deliver cash or another financial asset to another entity**. The contractual obligation may arise from a requirement to make payments of principal, interest or dividends. The contractual obligation may be explicit, but it may be implied indirectly in the terms of the contract.

In the case of Lidan, the **contractual obligation is not explicit**. At first glance it looks as if Lidan has a choice as to how much it pays to redeem the B shares. However, the conditions of the financial instrument are such that the value of the **settlement in own shares is considerably greater than the cash settlement obligation**. The effect of this is that **Lidan is implicitly obliged to redeem the B shares at for a cash amount of $1 per share**. The own-share settlement alternative is uneconomic in comparison to the cash settlement alternative, and cannot therefore serve as a means of avoiding classification as a liability.

IAS 32 states further that where a derivative contract has settlement options, **all of the settlement alternatives must result in it being classified as an equity instrument**, otherwise it is a financial asset or liability.

In conclusion, **Lidan's B shares must be classified as a liability.**

22 Complexity

Marking scheme

			Marks
(a)	(i)	1 mark per point up to maximum	9
	(ii)	1 mark per point up to maximum	9
	Professional marks		2
(b)	Identical payment		2
	Carrying amount		1
	Fair value		2
			25

(a)   (i)   Many users and preparers of accounts have found financial instruments to be **complex**. There are a number of reasons for this complexity and resulting confusion, many of which were covered in a Discussion Paper, *Reducing Complexity in Reporting Financial Instruments*, issued by the IASB as long ago 2008.

The main reason for complexity in accounting for financial instruments is the **many different ways in which they can be measured**. The measurement method depends on:

(1)   The **applicable financial reporting standard.** A variety of IFRS and IAS apply to the measurement of financial instruments. For example, financial assets may be measured using consolidation for subsidiaries (IFRS 10), the equity method for associates and joint ventures (IAS 28 and IFRS 11) or IFRS 9 for most other financial assets.

(2)   The **categorisation of the financial instrument**. IAS 39 *Financial instruments: recognition and measurement* had four categories: fair value through profit or loss, available for sale financial assets, loans and receivables and held to maturity.

While IFRS 9 simplifies these categories so that financial assets are classified as measured at **either amortised cost or fair value,** the final (July 2014) introduced another category of **fair value through other comprehensive income,** in addition to fair value through profit or loss. A financial asset may only be classified as measured at amortised cost if the object of the business model in which it is held is to collect contracted cash flows and its contractual terms give rise on specified dates to cash flows that are solely payments of principal and interest.

(3)   Whether **hedge accounting** has been applied. Hedge accounting is **complex**, for example when cash flow hedge accounting is used, gains and losses may be split between profit or loss for the year and other comprehensive income (items that may subsequently be reclassified to profit or loss). In addition, there may be mismatches when hedge accounting applies reflecting the underlying mismatches under the non-hedging rules.

Some measurement methods use an estimate of **current value, and others use historical cost.** Some include impairment losses, others do not.

The different measurement methods for financial instruments creates a number of **problems for preparers and users** of accounts:

(1)   The treatment of a particular instrument **may not be the best**, but may be determined by other factors.

(2)   Gains or losses resulting from different measurement methods may be combined in the same line item in the statement of profit or loss and other comprehensive income. **Comparability** is therefore compromised.

(3)   Comparability is also affected when it is **not clear** what measurement method has been used.

(4)   It is **difficult to apply the criteria** for deciding which instrument is to be measured in which way. As new types of instruments are created, the criteria may be applied in ways that are not consistent.

(ii)   There is pressure to reduce complexity in accounting for financial instruments. One idea, put forward in the 2008 Discussion Paper, is that **fair value is the only measure that is appropriate for all types of financial instruments**, and that a full fair value model would be much simpler to apply than the current mixed model. A single measurement method would, it is argued:

(1)   Significantly **reduce complexity in classification**. There would be no need to classify financial instruments into the four categories of fair value through profit or loss, available for sale financial assets, loans and receivables and held to maturity. This simplification has already been partially achieved by IFRS 9.

(2)   **Reduce complexity in accounting**. There would be no need to account for transfers between the above categories, or to report how impairment losses have been quantified.

(3)   **Eliminated measurement mismatches** between financial instruments and reduce the need for fair value hedge accounting.

(4)   Eliminate the need to identify and separate **embedded derivatives**.

(5)   **Better reflect the cash flows** that would be paid if liabilities were transferred at the re-measurement date.

(6)   Make reported information **easier to understand**.

(7)   **Improve the comparability** of reported information between entities and between periods.

However, while fair value has some obvious advantages, it has problems too. **Uncertainty** may be an issue for the following reasons

(1)   Markets are not all liquid and transparent.

(2)   Many assets and liabilities do not have an active market, and methods for estimating their value are more subjective.

(3)   Management must exercise judgement in the valuation process, and may not be entirely objective in doing so.

(4)   Because fair value, in the absence of an active market, represents an estimate, additional disclosures are needed to explain and justify the estimates. These disclosures may themselves be subjective.

(5)   Independent verification of fair value estimates is difficult for all the above reasons.

(b)   Different valuation methods bring comparability problems, as indicated in Part (a), and this can be seen with the examples in this part of the question.

Amortised cost

Using amortised cost, both the initial loan and the new loan result in **single payments that are almost identical** on 30 November 20X9:

Initial loan: $47m × 1.05 for 5 years = $59.98m

New loan: $45m × 1.074 for 4 years = $59.89m

However, the **carrying amounts at 30 November 20X5 will be different:**

Initial loan: $47m + ($47m × 5%) = $49.35m

New loan: $45m

Fair value

If the two loans were carried at fair value, both **the initial loan and the new loan would have the same value,** and be carried at $45m. There would be a net profit of $2m, made up of the interest expense of $47m × 5% = $2.35m and the unrealised gain of $49.35m – $45m = $4.35m.

Arguably, since the obligation on 30 November 20X9 will be the same for both loans, fair value is a more appropriate measure than amortised cost.

23 Ambush

Text reference. Financial instruments are covered in Chapter 7 of your text.

Top tips. Impairment is now covered by IFRS 9.

Easy marks. These are available for the discursive aspects, which are most of the question.

(a)   **Impairment of financial assets**

The impairment model in IFRS 9 *Financial instruments* (July 2014) is based on the premise of providing for **expected losses.** The **financial statements should reflect the general pattern of deterioration or improvement in the credit quality of financial instruments** within the scope of IFRS 9. This is a **forward-looking** impairment model.

IFRS 9 requires entities to base their measurement of expected credit losses on **reasonable and supportable information** that is available **without undue cost or effort.** This will include **historical, current and forecast information.**

Expected credit losses are **updated at each reporting date** for new information and changes in expectations, even if there has not been a significant increase in credit risk.

On initial recognition, the entity must **create a credit loss allowance/provision equal to twelve months' expected credit losses.** This is calculated by **multiplying the probability of a default occurring in the next twelve months by the total lifetime expected credit losses that would result from that default.** (This is not the same as the expected cash shortfalls over the next twelve months.)

In subsequent years, the **credit risk increases** significantly since initial recognition this amount will be replaced **by lifetime expected credit losses**. If the credit quality subsequently improves and the lifetime expected credit losses criterion is no longer met, the twelve-month expected credit loss basis is reinstated.

The amount of the impairment to be recognised on these financial instruments **depends on whether or not they have significantly deteriorated** since their initial recognition.

Stage 1 Financial instruments whose credit quality has not significantly deteriorated since their initial recognition

Stage 2 Financial instruments whose credit quality has significantly deteriorated since their initial recognition

Stage 3 Financial instruments for which there is objective evidence of an impairment as at the reporting date

For stage 1 financial instruments, the impairment represents the present value of expected credit losses that will result if a default occurs in the 12 months after the reporting date **(12 months expected credit losses).**

For financial instruments classified as stage 2 or 3, an impairment is recognised at the present value of expected credit shortfalls over their remaining life **(lifetime expected credit loss)**. Entities are required to reduce the gross carrying amount of a financial asset in the period in which they no longer have a reasonable expectation of recovery.

Expected credit losses would be recognised in **profit or loss** and held in a **separate allowance account** (although this would not be required to be shown separately on the face of the statement of financial position)

Assets at **fair value** are **not subject to impairment testing**, because **changes in fair value are automatically recognised immediately** in profit or loss (or other comprehensive income for investments in equity instruments where the election was made to report all gains and losses in other comprehensive income).

(b) **Trade receivable**

In the case of **trade receivables** such as this, that is trade receivables that **do not have an IAS 18 financing element**, IFRS 9 allows a **simplified approach** to the expected credit loss method. The loss allowance is measured at the **lifetime expected credit losses, from initial recognition**.

On 1 December 20X4

The entries in the books of Ambush will be:

DEBIT	Trade receivables	$600,000	
CREDIT	Revenue		$600,000

Being initial recognition of sales

An expected credit loss allowance, based on the matrix above, would be calculated as follows:

DEBIT	Expected credit losses	$6,000	
CREDIT	Allowance for receivables		$6,000

Being expected credit loss: $600,000 \times 1\%$

On 31 January 20X5

Applying Ambush's matrix, Tray has moved into the 5% bracket, because it has exhausted its 60-day credit limit. Despite assurances that Ambush will receive payment, the company should still increase its credit loss allowance to reflect the increased credit risk. Ambush will therefore record the following entries on 31 January 20X5

DEBIT	Expected credit losses	$24,000	
CREDIT	Allowance for receivables		$24,000

Being expected credit loss: $600,000 \times 5\% - $6,000

(c) **Buildings**

Under IAS 16 *Property, plant and equipment,* as amended by IAS 1 (revised), an **increase** in the carrying amount of an asset must be **recognised in other comprehensive income (items that will not be reclassified to profit or loss) and accumulated in equity under the heading of revaluation surplus**. The decrease should **be recognised in profit or loss** to the extent that **it reverses a revaluation** decrease of the same asset previously recognised in profit or loss. If an asset's carrying value is decreased as a result of a revaluation, the **decrease must be recognised in profit or loss**. However, the decrease must be recognised in other comprehensive income to the extent of any credit balance existing in the revaluation surplus in respect of that asset. The decrease recognised in other comprehensive income reduces the amount accumulated in equity under the heading of revaluation surplus.

The buildings would be treated as follows:

	Year ended 30 Nov 20X4 $m	Year ended 30 Nov 20X5 $m
Cost/valuation	10.0	8.00
Depreciation (Note 1)	(0.5)	(0.42)
	9.5	7.58
Impairment charged to profit or loss	(1.5)	–
Reversal of impairment charged to profit or loss (Note 2)	–	1.42
Gain on revaluation to revaluation surplus		2.00
Carrying amount	8.0	11.00

Notes

1. Depreciation charged in the year to 30 November 20X5 is based on the carrying amount at 30 November 20X4 spread over the remaining life of 19 years: $8m ÷ 19 = $421,053 rounded to $420,000.

2. The gain on revaluation in 20X5 is recognised in profit or loss to the extent that it reverses the revaluation loss charged in 20X4. However, this amount ($1.5m) is adjusted for the additionally depreciation that would have been recognised in 20X54had the revaluation loss not been recognised. This is $1.5m ÷ 19 = $0.8m.

24 Aron

Text reference. Financial instruments are covered in Chapter 7 of the BPP Study Text.

Top tips. Part (a) required a brief discussion of how the fair value of financial instruments is determined with a comment on the relevance of fair value measurements for financial instruments where markets are volatile and illiquid. Part (b) required you to discuss the accounting for four different financial instruments. The financial instruments ranged from a convertible bond to transfer of shares to a debt instrument in a foreign subsidiary to interest free loans. Bear in mind that you need to discuss the treatment and not just show the accounting entries. And while you may not have come across the specific treatment of interest-free loans before, you can apply the principles of IFRS 9 (what is fair value in this case?) and the *Conceptual Framework*.

Easy marks. These are available for the discussion in Part (a) and the convertible bond.

Examiner's comment. This was the best answered question on the paper. Part (a) was quite well answered although the answers were quite narrow and many candidates simply described the classification of financial instruments in loans and receivables, fair value through profit or loss etc. In Part (b) many candidates simply showed the accounting entries without any discussion. If the accounting entries were incorrect then it was difficult to award significant marks for the attempt. The treatment of the convertible bond was quite well done except for the treatment of the issue costs and the conversion of the bond. This part of the question often gained good marks. Again the treatment of the transfer of shares and interest free loans was well done but the exchange and fair value gains were often combined and not separated in the case of the debt instrument of the foreign subsidiary.

			Marks
(a)	Fair value – subjective		4
(b)	Convertible bond:	explanation	2
		Calculation	4
	Shares in Smart:	explanation	2
		Calculation	2
	Foreign subsidiary:	explanation of principles	2
		accounting treatment	3
	Interest free loan:	explanation of principles	2
		accounting treatment	2
	Quality of explanations		2
		Available/Maximum	25

(a) **Fair value**

The **fair value** of an asset the price that would be received to sell an asset or paid to transfer a liability in an orderly transaction between market participants at the measurement date (IFRS 13 *Fair value measurement).* IFRS 13 states that valuation techniques must be those which are appropriate and for which sufficient data are available. Entities should maximise the use of relevant **observable inputs** and minimise the use of **unobservable inputs**. The standard establishes a three-level hierarchy for the inputs that valuation techniques use to measure fair value.

Level 1 Quoted prices (unadjusted) in active markets for identical assets or liabilities that the reporting entity can access at the measurement date

Level 2 Inputs other than quoted prices included within Level 1 that are observable for the asset or liability, either directly or indirectly, eg quoted prices for similar assets in active markets or for identical or similar assets in non-active markets or use of quoted interest rates for valuation purposes

Level 3 Unobservable inputs for the asset or liability, ie using the entity's own assumptions about market exit value

The IASB believes that fair value is the **most appropriate measure** for most financial instruments because it is the **most relevant**. However, it, may be **less reliable**. There is more scope for manipulation. Particular difficulties arise where quoted prices are unavailable. If this is the case – and it frequently is – there is more reliance on estimates.

Not all markets are liquid and transparent. Where a market is **illiquid**, it is particularly difficult to apply fair value measurement, because the information will not be available. In addition, not all markets are stable; some are volatile. Fair valuing gives a measurement at a particular point in time, but in a **volatile** market this measure may not apply long term. It needs to be considered whether an asset is to be actively traded or held for the long term.

Disclosure is important in helping to deal with some of the problems of fair value, particularly as it provides an indicator of a company's risk profile.

(b) (i) **Convertible bond**

Some financial instruments contain both a liability and an equity element. In such cases, IAS 32 requires the component parts of the instrument to be **classified separately**, according to the substance of the contractual arrangement and the definitions of a financial liability and an equity instrument.

One of the most common types of compound instrument, as here, is **convertible debt**. This creates a primary financial liability of the issuer and grants an option to the holder of the instrument to convert it into an equity instrument (usually ordinary shares) of the issuer. This is the economic equivalent of the issue of conventional debt plus a warrant to acquire shares in the future.

Although in theory there are several possible ways of calculating the split, the following method is recommended:

(1) Calculate the value for the liability component.
(2) Deduct this from the instrument as a whole to leave a residual value for the equity component.

The reasoning behind this approach is that an entity's equity is its residual interest in its assets amount after deducting all its liabilities.

The **sum of the carrying amounts** assigned to liability and equity will always be equal to the carrying amount that would be ascribed to the instrument **as a whole**.

The **equity component is not re-measured**. However, the **liability component** is measured at amortised cost using an **effective interest rate** (here 9.38%).

It is important to note that the issue costs (here $1million) are allocated in proportion to the value of the liability and equity components when the initial split is calculated.

Step 1 — Calculate liability element

A 9% discount rate is used, which is the market rate for similar bonds without the conversion rights:

Present value of interest at end of:

Year 1 (31 May 20X6) ($100m × 6%) × 0.9174	5,505
Year 2 (31 May 20X7) ($100m × 6%) × 0.8417	5,050
Year 3 (31 May 20X8) ($100m × ($100m × 6%)) × 0.7722	81,852
Total liability component	92,407
Total equity element	7,593
Proceeds of issue	100,000

Step 2 — Allocate issue costs

	Liability $'000	Equity $'000	Total $'000
Proceeds	92,407	7,593	100,000
Issue cost	(924)	(76)	(1,000)
	91,483	7,517	99,000

The double entry is:

		$'000	$'000			$'000	$'000
DEBIT	Cash	100,000		CREDIT	Cash		1,000
CREDIT	Liability		92,407	DEBIT	Liability	924	
CREDIT	Equity		7,593	DEBIT	Equity	76	

Step 3 — Re-measure liability using effective interest rate

	$'000
Cash – 1.6.20X5 (net of issue costs per Step 2)	91,483
Effective interest to 31.5.20X6 (9.38% × 91,483)	8,581
Coupon paid (6% × $100m)	(6,000)
At 31.5.20X6	94,064
Effective interest to 31.5.20X7 (9.38% × 94,064)	8,823
Coupon paid (6% × $100m)	(6,000)
At 31.5.20X7	96,887
Effective interest to 31.5.20X8 (9.38% × 96,887)	9,088
Coupon paid (6% × $100m)	(6,000)
At 31.5.20X8	100,000*

Step 4   **Conversion of bond**

On conversion of the bond on 31 May 20X8, Aron will issue 25 million ordinary shares. The consideration for these shares will be the original equity component (net of its share of issue costs) together with the balance on the liability.

	$'000
Share capital – 25 million at $1	25,000
Share premium	82,517
Equity and liability components (100,000 + 7,593 – 76)	107,517

(ii) **Shares in Smart**

Firstly, the carrying value of the investment in shares in Smart of $5m (which is the fair value as at 31 May 20X7) needs updating to the fair value at 31 May 20X8. The fair value of the investment in shares in Smart at 31 May 20X8 is $5.5m – this is because Given are prepared to buy the shares in Smart and pay with consideration in the form of shares in Given with a fair value of $5.5m. IFRS 13 *Fair value measurement* defines fair value as the 'price that would be received to sell an asset...between market participants at the measurement date'. Here the price that Aron receives for shares in Smart is in the form of shares in Given worth $5.5m.

Aron should therefore recognise a gain on remeasurement of the investment in shares in Smart of $0.5m ($5.5m - $5m) in other comprehensive income(items that will not be reclassified to profit or loss):

DEBIT   Financial Asset: Investment in shares in Smart $0.5m
CREDIT   Remeasurement gain (in OCI: not reclassified to profit or loss) $0.5m.

The second issue here is whether the investment in shares in Smart should be **derecognised**. Derecognition is the removal of a previously recognised financial instrument from an entity's statement of financial position.

An entity should derecognise a **financial asset** when:

(a)   The **contractual rights** to the cash flows from the financial asset **expire**, or

(b)   The entity **transfers substantially all the risks and rewards of ownership** of the financial asset to another party.

In this case, Aron no longer retains any risks and rewards of ownership in the investment in shares in Smart (instead Aron now has access to the risks and rewards of ownership in the investment in shares in Given). Accordingly the financial asset 'Investment in shares in Smart' should be derecognised and instead a financial asset for the 'Investment in shares in Given' should be recognised. No gain or loss on derecognition will arise.

The investment in shares in Smart of $5.5m is then derecognised and an investment in Shares in Given is recognised instead:

DEBIT   Financial asset: shares in Given $5.5m
CREDIT   Financial asset: shares in Smart $5.5m.

Tutorial note. Both the revaluation gain at the date of derecognition taken to other comprehensive income (not reclassified to profit or loss) of $500,000 and the cumulative gain of $400,000 previously recognised in other comprehensive income (not reclassified to profit or loss), and therefore held in other components of equity may be transferred to retained earnings as a reserves movement.

(iii) **Foreign subsidiary**

Two International Accounting Standards apply to this transaction:

(1)   The debt instrument in the foreign subsidiary's financial statements is dealt with under IFRS 9 *Financial instruments*.

(2)   The translation of the financial statements of the foreign subsidiary is governed by IAS 21 *The effects of changes in foreign exchange rates*.

Under IAS 21, **all exchange differences resulting from translation are recognised in other comprehensive income (items that may subsequently be reclassified to profit or loss) until the subsidiary is disposed of**. This includes exchange differences that arise on financial instruments carried at fair value through profit or loss and investments in equity instruments. It is important to distinguish gains that result from increases in fair value from gains that result from changes in exchange rates.

The debt instrument owned by Gao is held for trading, and will therefore be carried at **fair value through profit or loss** in Gao's financial statements. At 31 May 20X8, there will be a gain in the financial statements of Gao 12m – 10m = 2 million zloty. In accordance with IFRS 9, this will be credited to profit or loss for the year in Gao's statement of profit or loss and other comprehensive income.

In the consolidated financial statements, the carrying value of the debt at 1 June 20X7 would be calculated using the exchange rate at that date as: 10 million zloty ÷ 3 = $3.3m. By 31 May 20X8, the carrying value will have increased to: 12 million zloty ÷ 2 = $6m. **Part of the increase** in value of $6m – $ 3.3m = $2.7m is attributable to a **change in the exchange rate**, and **part** of it to an **increase in fair value**. Only the latter can be recognised in profit or loss for the year.

Aaron will use the average rate for the year of 2.5 to translate the statement of profit or loss and other comprehensive income, giving a gain of 2 million zloty ÷ 2.5 = $800,000 to be taken to profit or loss for the year. The remaining part of the increase in value, $2.7m - $0.8m = $1.9m will be **classified in other comprehensive income** until Gao is disposed of.

The accounting is as follows:

	$m
Balance at 1 June 20X7	3.3
Increase in year	2.7
Balance at 31 May 20X8	6.0

DEBIT	Debt instrument	$2.7m	
CREDIT	Profit or loss		$0.8m
CREDIT	Equity		$1.9m

(iv) **Interest free loans**

IFRS 9 *Financial instruments* requires financial assets to be measured on initial recognition at **fair value** plus transaction costs. Usually the fair value of the consideration given represents the fair value of the asset. However, this is not necessarily the case with an interest-free loan. An interest free loan to an employee is not costless to the employer, and the **face value may not be the same as the fair value**.

To arrive at the fair value of the loan, Aaron needs to consider **other market transactions** in the same instrument. The market rate of interest for a two year loan on the date of issue (1 June 20X7) and the date of repayment (31 May 20X9) is 6% pa, and this is rate should be used in valuing the instrument. The **fair value** may be measured as the **present value of future receipts using the market interest rate**. There will be a difference between the face value and the fair value of the instrument, calculated as follows:

	$m
Face value of loan at 1 June 20X7	10.0
Fair value of loan at 1 June 20X7: 10 × 0.8900	8.9
Difference	1.1

The **difference** of $1.1m is the extra cost to the employer of not charging a market rate of interest. It will be treated as **employee compensation** under IAS 19 *Employee benefits*. This employee compensation must be charged over the two year period to the statement of profit or loss and other comprehensive income, through profit or loss for the year.

With regard to subsequent measurement Aron wishes to hold the loan at amortised cost. For this to be possible, two criteria must be met under IFRS 9:

(1) **Business model test.** The objective of the entity's business model is to hold the financial asset to collect the contractual cash flows (rather than to sell the instrument prior to its contractual maturity to realise its fair value changes).

(2) **Cash flow characteristics test:** The contractual terms of the financial asset give rise on specified dates to cash flows that are solely payments of principal and interest on the principal outstanding.

These criteria have been met. Accordingly, the loan may be measured at 31 May 20X8 at **amortised cost** using the effective interest method. The **effective interest rate** is 6%, so the value of the loan in the statement of financial position is: $8.9m × 1.06 = $9.43m. Interest will be credited to profit or loss for the year of: $8.9 × 6% = $53m.

The **double entry** is as follows:

At 1 June 20X7

DEBIT	Loan	$8.9m	
DEBIT	Employee compensation	$1.1m	
CREDIT	Cash		$10m

At 31 May 20X8

DEBIT	Loan	$0.53m	
CREDIT	Profit or loss – interest for the year $8.9m × 6%		$0.53m

25 Preparation question: Leases

(a) Interest rate implicit in the lease

PV = annuity × cumulative discount factor

$250,000 = 78,864 × CDF$

$$\therefore CDF = \frac{250,000}{78,864}$$

$$= 3.170$$

∴ Interest rate is 10%

(b) *Property, plant and equipment*

Net book value of assets held under finance leases is $187,500.

Non-current liabilities

	$
Finance lease liabilities (W)	136,886

Current liabilities

	$
Finance lease liabilities (W) (196,136 – 136,886)	59,250

Statement of profit or loss and other comprehensive income (profit or loss section)

Depreciation on assets held under finance leases	62,500
Finance charges	25,000

Working

		$
Year ended 31 December 20X1:		
1.1.20X1	Liability b/d	250,000
1.1.20X1 – 31.12.20X1	Interest at 10%	25,000
31.12.20X1	Instalment in arrears	(78,864)
31.12.20X1	Liability c/d	196,136
Year ended 31 December 20X2:		
1.1.20X2 – 31.12.20X2	Interest at 10%	19,614
31.12.20X2	Instalment in arrears	(78,864)
31.12.20X2	Liability c/d	136,886

26 Havanna

Text reference. Revenue recognition (the new IFRS 15) is covered in Chapter 1 of your Study Text, IFRS 5 in Chapter 15 and sale and leaseback in Chapter 11.

Top tips. Revenue recognition (Part (a)) is a popular topic with this examiner, partly because the rules have recently changed, and partly because it is an area in which preparers of accounts may wish to bend the existing rules to present the results in a favourable light. You need to explain why their proposed treatment is unacceptable, not just state that it is. IFRS 5 (Part (b)) requires clear, logical thinking: there are two potential impairments, the first in calculating the adjusted carrying value of the disposal group at the time of classification as held for sale, and then again on comparison of this adjusted carrying value with fair value less costs to sell. You are not given any figures for the provisions incorrectly charged to continued operations, but be aware that the adjusted carrying value and fair value less costs to sell would need to be further adjusted once these were treated correctly. In Part (c), do not waste time discussing the different treatments for sale and leaseback resulting in a finance lease versus one resulting in an operating lease – you are told it is to be treated as an operating lease.

Easy marks. There are marks for textbook definitions in Part (a), and Part (c) gives pointers by using the different sales prices to help structure your answer.

Examiner's comment. The level of knowledge needed to answer Part (a) of this question was quite basic but candidates had to apply that knowledge to gain the marks and again this was where any problem arose. However, this part of the question was answered quite well. The main problem with answers to Part (b) was that candidates found reasons as to why the disposal group was incorrectly classified as such, when there was no evidence in the question of this fact. The main problem was the measurement of the disposal group but many candidates failed to recognise this fact. The main problem in Part (c) (sale and leaseback) was that some candidates simply showed the accounting entries without discussing the implications. However, candidates scored well on this part of the question.

Marking scheme

	Marks
(a) Revenue recognition up to	6
(b) IFRS 5 explanation	9
(c) Leases	8
Professional marks	2
	25

(a) **Contracts with sports organisations**

The applicable standard relating to the contracts is IFRS 15 *Revenue from contracts with customers.* This standard has a **five-step process for** recognising revenue.

(i)   Identify the contract with the customer.
(ii)   Identify the separate performance obligations.
(iii)   Determine the transaction price.
(iv)   Allocate the transaction price to the performance obligations.
(v)   Recognise revenue when (or as)a performance obligation is satisfied.

It is assumed that (i) and (iii) are satisfied – the contracts are binding, and there is no indication in the question that the transaction price is undetermined. Step (ii) **'identify the separate performance obligations'** needs to be considered. Despite Havanna's claims, the performance obligation under IFRS 15 is **the provision of services.**)). Revenue should be recognised as the services are provided (step (v). Step (v) would treat this as a **performance obligation satisfied over time** because the customer simultaneously receives and consumes the benefits as the performance takes place.

A performance obligation satisfied over time meets the criteria in Step (v) above and, if it entered into more than one accounting period, as here for some of the contracts, would previously have been described as a long-term contract.

In this type of contract an entity has an enforceable right to payment for performance completed to date. The standard describes this as an amount that approximates the selling price of the goods or services transferred to date (for example recovery of the costs incurred by the entity in satisfying the performance plus a reasonable profit margin).

Methods of measuring the amount of performance completed to date encompass **output methods** and **input methods**.

(i)   **Output methods** recognise revenue on the basis of the value to the **customer** of the goods or services transferred. They include surveys of performance completed, appraisal of units produced or delivered etc.

(ii)   **Input methods** recognise revenue on the basis of the **entity's** inputs, such as labour hours, resources consumed, costs incurred. If using a cost-based method, the costs incurred must contribute to the entity's progress in satisfying the performance obligation.

Havanna argues that the **'limited obligations'** under the contracts (coaching and access to its membership database) **do not constitute rendering of services**, and that it is therefore acceptable to recognise the contract revenue in full. However, this treatment contravenes IFRS 15

In the case of these contracts, the services are performed by an indeterminate number of acts over a specified period of time. Under IFRS 15, the best measure of progress towards complete satisfaction of the performance obligation over time is a **time-based measure** and Havanna should recognise revenue on a **straight-line basis over the specified period.**

There is **no justification for Havanna's treatment**, that is recognising the contract income in full when the contract is signed. The 'limited obligations' argument is not supported by IFRS 15. Accordingly, Havanna **must apportion the income arising from the contracts over the period of the contracts**, as required by the standard.

(b) **Sale of division**

Impairment loss

The division to be sold meets the criteria in IFRS 5 *Non-current assets held for sale and discontinued operations* to be classified as held for sale, and has been classified as a **disposal group** under IFRS 5.

A disposal group that is held for sale should be measured at the **lower of** its **carrying amount** and **fair value less costs to sell**. Immediately before classification of a disposal group as held for sale, the entity must recognise impairment in accordance with applicable IFRS. Any impairment loss is generally recognised in profit or loss, but if the asset has been measured at a revalued amount under IAS 16 *Property, plant and*

equipment or IAS 38 *Intangible assets,* the impairment will be treated as a revaluation decrease. **Once** the disposal group has been **classified as held for sale**, any **impairment loss** will be based on the **difference between the adjusted carrying amounts and the fair value less cost to sell**. The impairment loss (if any) will be **recognised in profit or loss**. For assets carried at fair value prior to initial classification, the requirement to deduct costs to sell from fair value will result in an immediate charge to profit or loss.

Havanna has calculated the impairment as $30m, being the difference between the carrying amount at initial classification and the value of the assets measured in accordance with IFRS.

Step 1   Calculate carrying value under applicable IFRS: $90m – $30m = $60m

Step 2   Classified as held for sale. Compare the adjusted carrying amount under applicable IFRS ($60m) with fair value less costs to sell ($40m). Measure at the lower of carrying value and fair value less costs to sell, here $40m.

Step 3   Determine whether any additional impairment loss is needed to write the division down to fair value less costs to sell. It is clear that an additional impairment loss is needed of $60m – $40m = $20m

Therefore **an additional impairment loss of $20m should be recognised.**

Other costs

Certain other costs relating to the division being sold are currently shown as provisions relating to continuing operations. This treatment is not correct:

(i)   The trade receivable from Cuba Sports should have **been tested for impairment immediately before classification** of the division as held for sale. An **impairment loss** for the amount of the trade receivable should have been **recognised** and would have **reduced the carrying amount of the division on the initial classification as held for sale**. In addition, the division has guaranteed the sale proceeds to Havanna's Head Office, so as the amount owing has not been collected a **refund** would be needed, and the **sales price of the division** (and hence the fair value less costs to sell) would need to be **adjusted** to reflect the amount of the potential refund.

(ii)   The discounting expense for the sales price of the disposal group reflects the fact that payment is deferred until 30 November 20X5. This **discount** should not have been recognised in continuing operations, but **should have been taken into account in calculating the fair value less costs to sell** of the disposal group.

(iii)   The provision for **transaction costs** should not have been recognised in continuing operations. The costs (legal advice and lawyers' fees) should be considered as **part of 'costs to sell'** when calculating fair value less costs to sell.

All three items affect fair value less costs to sell, and item (i), the trade receivable, also affects the carrying value of the division on classification as held for sale.

(c)   **Sale and leaseback**

Where, as here, a lessee enters a sale and leaseback transaction resulting in an **operating lease**, then the original asset should be treated as sold. If the transaction is at fair value then immediate recognition of the profit/loss should occur.

If the transaction is above fair value, then the profit based on fair value should be recognised. The balance in excess of fair value should be deferred and amortised over the period for which the asset is expected to be used.

If the sales value is below fair value, the operating lease rentals may have been adjusted downwards to compensate for the loss. However, whether this is the case depends on the extent of the difference.

Havanna had been given a range of selling prices, and should in each case **compare the potential sales proceeds with the fair value in order to determine the accounting treatment** as well as comparing the sales price with the carrying value ($4.2m) to determine the gain.

(i)   **Sales price $5 million**

In this case the **sales price matches the fair value**. In effect, there has been a **normal sales transaction** and the **whole of the gain** of $0.8m ($5m – $4.2m) should be **recognised immediately** in profit or loss.

(ii) **Sales price $6 million**

Here the **sales price would be above fair value**, then the **profit based on fair value** of $0.8m (see (i) above) should be **recognised**. The **balance in excess** of fair value of $1m ($6m – $5m) should be **deferred and amortised** over the period for which the asset is expected to be used (ten years) ie $100,000 per annum.

In the current market, the sales price is unlikely to be above fair value, and would imply the creation of an artificial gain.

(iii) **Sales price $4.8 million**

Here the **sales price is below fair value**. However, the **difference is small**, and given that property valuations are estimates, $4.8m may simply be a better reflection of genuine fair value than $5m. In this case, therefore, the **sales proceeds are recognised in full** and a **gain of $0.6m** ($4.8m – $4.2m) would be **recognised.**

(iv) **Sales price $4 million**

Here the **sales price is also below fair value**. However, the **difference is significant,** and cannot be explained by estimation tolerances in the valuation. The **price appears to be artificially low**, and it is likely that the **lease rentals are low to reflect this**. Therefore it is appropriate to recognise the sales proceeds of $4m, but the $200,000 **loss on disposal is not recognised**, being an artificial loss. Instead, it is **deferred and amortised** over the ten year life of the lease, that is at $20,000 per annum.

27 Holcombe

Text reference. Leasing is covered in Chapter 11. The *Conceptual Framework* is covered in Chapter 1.

Top tips. This was an untypical and rather demanding question. It is best to focus on Part (a), where marks are available for reasonable arguments. **Easy marks.** The definitions of asset and liability come straight from the *Conceptual Framework,* and should give some easy marks.

Examiner's comment. In discussing the weakness of current accounting standards in Part (a), candidates' answers were often quite narrow. Candidates scored well on the definitions of asset and liability, however. The question was well answered and candidates scored well generally on this question.

Marking scheme

			Marks
(a)	(i)	Subjective	6
	(ii)	Subjective	7
	(iii)	Subjective	4
		Professional marks	2
(b)	(i)	Contingent rentals	3
	(ii)	Lease classification	3
			25

(a) (i) **Problems with current standards on lease accounting**

The different accounting treatment of finance and operating leases has been **criticised** for a number of reasons.

(1) Many users of financial statements believe that **all lease contracts give rise to assets and liabilities that should be recognised in the financial statements of lessees**. Therefore these users routinely adjust the recognised amounts in the statement of financial position in an attempt to assess the effect of the assets and liabilities resulting from operating lease contracts.

(2) The split between finance leases and operating leases can result in **similar transactions being accounted for very differently,** reducing comparability for users of financial statements.

(3) The difference in the accounting treatment of finance leases and operating leases also provides **opportunities to structure transactions so as to achieve a particular lease classification**.

It is also argued that the current accounting treatment of operating leases is **inconsistent with** the definition of assets and liabilities in the **IASB's** *Conceptual Framework*. An operating lease contract confers a valuable right to use a leased item. This right meets the *Conceptual Framework's* definition of an asset, and the liability of the lessee to pay rentals meets the *Conceptual Framework's* definition of a liability. However, the right and obligation are not recognised for operating leases.

Lease accounting is **scoped out of IAS 32 and IFRS 9,** which means that there are considerable differences in the treatment of leases and other contractual arrangements.

The IASB is addressing this matter. An Exposure Draft *Leases* was issued in 2013, based on a 2010 ED whose proposals were found to be too complex. The proposed changes would **require recognition of a right-of-use asset and a lease liability** for **all leases of more than 12 months**, thus providing more complete and useful information to investors and other users of financial statements.

(ii) **Holcombe's lease and framework definitions**

The IASB *Conceptual Framework* defines an **asset** as 'a resource controlled by the entity as a result of past events and from which future economic benefits are expected to flow to the entity'. Holcombe's leased plant would appear to meet this definition:

(1) Holcombe has the right to use the leased plant as an economic resource, that is to generate cash inflows or reduce cash outflows.

(2) Holcombe can be said to control the resource because the lessor does not have the right of access to the plant until the end of the contract without Holcombe's permission.

(3) The control results from past events, that is the signing of the lease contract.

(4) Future economic benefits are expected to flow to Holcombe during the lease term.

In conclusion, the leased plant meets the *Framework's* definition of an asset.

The *Conceptual Framework* defines a **liability** as 'a present obligation of the entity arising from past events, the settlement of which is expected to result in an outflow from the entity of resources embodying economic benefits'. Applying this to Holcombe's lease of plant:

(1) There is a present obligation to pay rentals.

(2) The lessor has no contractual right (unless Holcombe breaches the contract) to take possession of the plant before the end of the contract, and similarly. Holcombe has no contractual right to terminate the contract and avoid paying rentals.

(3) The obligation to pay rentals arises from a past event, namely the signing of the lease.

(4) The obligation is expected to result in an outflow of economic benefits in the form of cash payments.

In conclusion, the leased plant meets the *Conceptual Framework's* definition of a liability.

(iii) **Recent developments: 2013 ED**

Many believe that the current lease accounting is too reliant on bright lines and subjective judgements that may result in economically similar transactions being accounted for differently. The IASB and FASB published an Exposure Draft *Leases*, issued in 2010, which, in effect, **required all leases to be shown on the statement of financial position**. The proposals were seen as too complex, so a revised ED was issued in 2013.

The basic principle of the 2013 ED is that of **recognition in the statement of financial position**. A lessee is **required to recognise a right-of-use asset and a lease liability** for **all leases of more than 12 months**.

For leases of 12 months or less, a lessee is not required to recognise a right-of-use asset and a lease liability, but may choose to do so.

A single accounting model for lessees would not reflect the true economics of different assets. Accordingly, the IASB developed a dual approach, where the type of lease is based on the amount of consumption of the underlying asset.

Type A leases

Type A leases are leases where the **lessee pays for the part of the asset that it consumes**. They are leases of depreciating assets, for example vehicles or equipment, whose value declines over its useful life, generally faster in the earlier years. Type A leases **normally** mean that the underlying asset is **not property**. However, property will be classified as a Type A lease in either of the following circumstances.

(1) The lease term is for the major part of the remaining economic life of the underlying asset.

(2) The present value of the lease payments accounts for substantially all of the fair value of the underlying asset at the commencement date.

Type B leases

Type B leases are leases for which the lessee **pays for use,** consuming only an insignificant part of the asset. Type B leases **normally** mean the underlying asset is **property**. However, leases other than property leases will be classified as type B leases in either of the following circumstances.

(1) The lease term is for an insignificant part of the total economic life of the underlying asset.

(2) The present value of the lease payments is insignificant relative to the fair value of the underlying asset at the commencement date of the lease.

(b) (i) **Inflation adjustment**

Inflation adjustments are not included in the minimum lease payment calculations. Instead they are effectively **contingent rent**, defined in IAS 17 *Leases* as 'that part of the rent that is not fixed in amount, but based on the future amount of a factor that changes other than with the passage of time'. They should be **recognised in the period in which they are incurred**.

Holcombe would recognise operating rentals as follows:

Year 1

$5 million

Year 2

$5 million plus ($5m × 4%) = $5.2m

Year 3

$5.2 million plus ($5.2m × 4%) = $5.408m

(ii) **Lease classification**

Under the proposals of the 2013 Exposure Draft, Holcombe should classify the lease as a Type A lease for the following reasons.

(1)   The underlying asset (the machine) is not property.

(2)   The present value of the lease payments is more than insignificant relative to the fair value of the machine at the commencement date.

(3)   The lease term is for more than an insignificant part of the total economic life of the machine.

28 William

Text reference. Sale and leaseback is covered in Chapter 11 of your BPP Study Text. Employee benefits are in Chapter 5. Share-based payment is covered in Chapter 8 and contingent liabilities in Chapter 9 and Chapter 12 (in the context of business combinations).

Top tips. Part (a), on sale and leaseback, is more straightforward than some of the past exam questions on this subject. We have amended Part (b) on the defined benefit pension plan as it referred to an IAS 19 treatment prior to its 2011 revision, and now only the revised version is examinable. Part (c) deals with a a cash-settled share-based payment, a popular topic with this examiner. Part (d) tested a contingent liability: candidates needed to know that the treatment is different in the individual financial statements of the acquiree and in the consolidated financial statements, where the liability is recognised whether or not it is probable that an outflow of economic benefits will take place.

Easy marks. The structure of the question, which is broken down into manageable chunks, should make it easy to pick up the first few marks on each topic. There are some very easy marks for explaining when a lease is a finance lease in Part (a).

Examiner's comment. In Part (a), candidates generally dealt correctly with the treatment of the finance lease and the nature of the transfer of substantially the entire risks and rewards incident to ownership and understood the situations that would normally lead to a lease being classified as a finance lease. Candidates recognised that the building is derecognised at its carrying amount and then reinstated at its fair value but often took the disposal gain entirely to profit or loss, instead of it being deferred over the new lease term. Answers to Part (c) were often confused. Part (d) was well answered on the whole, but some candidates were confused over the treatment of the two situations and stated that the treatment was the same in both scenarios.

Marking scheme

		Marks
(a)	Definition of lease	3
	Leaseback principle	1
	Accounting	3
(b)	Provision for relocation costs	3
	Curtailment (past service cost) of defined benefit pension plan	4
(c)	Cash-settled share-based payments	2
	Calculation	3
(d)	Contingent liability – discussion	4
Communication skills		2
		25

(a)   **Sale and leaseback**

The accounting treatment for this transaction will be depend, in the first instance, on whether it is a finance lease. A finance lease is a lease that **transfers substantially all the risks and rewards incidental to ownership of an asset**. All other leases are classified as operating leases. The classification, which is made at the inception of the lease, depends on the substance rather than the form, and could include the following situations.

(i)   The lease transfers ownership of the asset to the lessee by the end of the lease term.

(ii)   The lessee has the option to purchase the asset at a price which is expected to be sufficiently lower than the fair value at the date the option becomes exercisable for it to be reasonably certain, at the inception of the lease, that the option will be exercised.

(iii)   The lease term is for the major part of the economic life of the asset even if title is not transferred.

(iv)   At the inception of the lease, the present value of the minimum lease payments amounts to at least substantially all of the fair value of the leased asset.

(v)   The leased assets are of such a specialised nature that only the lessee can use them without major modifications.

William's lease of the building is for the **majority of the asset's life,** ie twenty years (criterion (iii) and the **present value of the minimum lease payments amounts to all the fair value** (sales proceeds) of the leased building of $5m. The lease should therefore be accounted for as a **finance lease**.

The **form** of this transaction is a **sale and leaseback,** but **in substance there has been no disposal** because William has **retained the risks and rewards of ownership**. A liability must be set up for the finance lease On 1 June 20X2:

DEBIT   Cash $5m
CREDIT   Finance lease liability $5m

The apparent gain (that is, the difference between the sale price and the previous carrying value) should be deferred and amortised in the financial statements of the seller/lessee over the lease term. It should not be recognised as income immediately:

DEBIT   Property, plant and equipment ($5m – $3.5m) $1.5m
CREDIT   Deferred income   (SOFP) $1.5m

The building is depreciated over the shorter of its useful life and the lease term, both twenty years, $5m ÷ 20 years = $0.25m:

DEBIT   Depreciation expense $0.25m
CREDIT   Accumulated depreciation $0.25m

The finance cost on the lease liability is charged at the implicit rate of 7% to profit or loss for the year ended 31 May 20X3. The amount is calculated as follows:

Finance lease liability

	$m
1 June 20X2 b/f	5.000
Finance cost: 5m × 7%	0.350
Instalment	(0.441)
31 May 20X3 c/f	4.909
Finance cost: 4.909m × 7%	0.344
Instalment	(0.441)
31 May 20X4 c/f	4.812

The finance lease liability at 31 May 20X3 is split between current and non-current:

	$m
Non-current liability (owed at 31 May 20X4)	4.812
Current liability (bal. fig.) = instalment (0.441) less finance cost (0.344)	0.097
Total liability at 31 May 20X3	4.909

The gain on the 'sale' is released over the twenty year period, $1.5m ÷ 20 years = $0.075m:

DEBIT	Deferred income	(SOFP)	$0.075m	
CREDIT	Deferred income	(P/L)		$0.075m

(b) **Relocation costs and reduction to net pension liability**

A **provision for restructuring** should be recognised in respect of the relocation of the provision during the year ended 31 May 20X3 in accordance with IAS 37 *Provisions, contingent liabilities and contingent assets*. This is because William's board of directors authorised a **detailed formal plan** for the relocation shortly before the year end (13 May 20X3) and William has **raised a valid expectation in affected employees** that it will carry out the restructuring by informing them of the main features of the plan. As the relocation is due to take within two months of the year end (July 20X3), the time value of money is likely to be immaterial. Therefore no discounting is required and a provision should be recognised at the estimated relocation costs of $50 million.

The reduction in the net pension liability as a result of the employees being made redundant and no longer accruing pension benefits is a **curtailment** under IAS 19 *Employee benefits (revised 2011)*. IAS 19 defines a curtailment as occurring when an entity significantly reduces the number of employees covered by a plan. It is **treated as a type of past service costs**. The past service cost may be negative (as is the case here) when the benefits are withdrawn so that the present value of the defined benefit obligation decreases. IAS 19 requires the past service cost to be **recognised in profit or loss** at the earlier of:

- When the plan curtailment occurs, and
- When the entity recognises the related restructuring costs.

Here the restructuring costs (and corresponding provision) are recognised in the year ended 31 May 20X3 and the plan curtailment will not take place until after the year end in July 20X3 when the employees are made redundant. Therefore the reduction in the net pension liability and corresponding income in profit or loss should be recognised at the earlier of these two dates, ie when the restructuring costs are recognised in the year ended 31 May 20X3.

Both the relocation costs and income from the reduction in the net pension liability are likely to require **separate disclosure** in the statement of profit or loss and other comprehensive income or in the notes to the accounts per IAS 1 *Presentation of financial statements* due to their materiality.

(c) **Share-based payment**

Share appreciation rights are **cash-settled share-based-payments**. IFRS 2 *Share-based payment* requires that the entity should measure the goods or services acquired and the liability incurred at the **fair value of the liability**. The fair value of the liability should be **measured at each reporting date** until the liability is settled and at the date of settlement. Any **changes** in fair value are recognised in profit or loss for the period.

	$
1 June 20X2 liability b/f: (20 – 3 (managers)) × 500 SARS × $14 (fair value) × 2/2 (vested)	119,000
Cash paid on exercise: 7 managers × 500 SARS × $21 (intrinsic value)	(73,500)
Expense (balancing figure)	74,500
31 May 20X3 liability c/f: (20 – 3 – 7 (managers)) × 500 SARS × $24 (fair value)	120,000

The expense for the year is accounted for as follows:

DEBIT	Expense	(P/L)	$74,500	
CREDIT	Cash			$73,500
CREDIT	Liability			$1,000

(d)   **Contingent liability**

The legal claim against Chrissy will be treated differently in Chrissy's individual financial statements as compared with the consolidated accounts of the William group.

Chrissy's individual financial statements

The legal claim against Chrissy **does not meet the definition of a provision** under IAS 37 *Provisions, contingent liabilities and contingent assets.* One of IAS 37's requirements for a provision is that an outflow of resources embodying economic benefits should be probable, and William believes that it is more likely than not that such an **outflow will not occur**.

However, the possible payment does fall within the IAS 37 definition of a **contingent liability,** which is:

- A possible obligation depending on whether some uncertain future event occurs, or
- A present obligation but payment is not probable or the amount cannot be measured reliably.

Therefore as **a contingent liability** the details of the claim and the $4 million estimated fair value of the contingent liability would be **disclosed** in the notes to the financial statements.

Consolidated financial statements

Under IFRS 3 *Business combinations*, an acquirer must allocate the cost of a business combination by recognising the acquiree's identifiable assets, liabilities and contingent liabilities that satisfy the recognition criteria at their **fair values** at the date of the acquisition. Contingent liabilities where there is only a possible obligation which, under IAS 37, depend on the occurrence or non-occurrence of some uncertain future event are not recognised under IFRS 3. However, the **IAS 37 probability criterion does not apply under IFRS 3**: a contingent liability is recognised **whether or not it is probable that an outflow** of economic benefits will take place, where there is a present obligation and its fair value can be measured reliably.

Consequently, William should **recognise the contingent liability as part of the business combination at its fair value** of $4 million. This will reduce net assets at acquisition, and therefore increase goodwill.

29 Leigh

Text reference. See Chapters 8 and 12 of the text.

Top tips. This was a difficult question, as all three parts included peripheral areas of the syllabus. This question dealt with several share-based payment transactions. However, not all such transactions were dealt with by a single accounting standard. Part (a) dealt with the cost of a business combination and the issue of shares as purchase consideration. It also dealt with shares given to employees as remuneration. The events are dealt with under the separate accounting standards IFRS 2 and IFRS 3. Part (b) dealt with the purchase of property, plant and equipment, and the grant of rights to a director when there is a choice of settlement. This part of the question was quite technically demanding. Part (c) dealt with the issue of shares to acquire an associate and the subsequent accounting for the associate.

Easy marks. It is difficult to identify easy marks for this question. Unless share-based payment is your 'pet topic', it would have been best avoided in an exam.

Examiner's comment. The question was poorly answered. Parts (a) and (c) were very straightforward but candidates did not seem to recognise the issues or accounting standards which should be used. The question required an application of some basic knowledge but candidates failed to do this. Part (b) required some detailed knowledge of IFRS 2 and again candidates did not have such knowledge. It appears that unless the examiner details the accounting standard to be used in answering the question, candidates have difficulty in applying knowledge to scenarios.

		Marks
(a)	Hash	7
	Employees	3
(b)	Property, plant and equipment	5
	Director	4
(c)	Handy	6
	Available/Maximum	25

(a) **Shares issued to the directors**

The three million $1 shares issued to the directors **on 1 June 20X6** as part of the **purchase consideration** for Hash are accounted for under **IFRS 3** *Business combinations* rather than under IFRS 2 *Share-based payment.* This is because they are not remuneration or compensation, but simply part of the purchase price of the company. The cost of the business combination will be the total of the fair values of the consideration given by Leigh plus any attributable costs. The total fair value here is $6m, of which $3m is share capital and $3m is share premium.

The **contingent consideration** – 5,000 shares per director to be received on 31 May 20X7 if the directors are still employed by Leigh – may, however, be seen as compensation and thus fall to be treated under IFRS 2. The fact that the additional payment of shares is **linked to continuing employment** suggests that it is a compensation arrangement, and therefore **IFRS 2 will apply**.

Under IFRS 2, the fair value used is that at the **grant date,** rather than when the shares vest. The market value of each share at that date is $2. (Three million shares are valued at $6m.) So the total value of the compensation is $5 \times 5,000 \times \$2 = \textbf{\$50,000}$.

The $50,000 is charged to profit or loss with a corresponding increase in equity.

Shares issued to employees

These shares are remuneration and are **accounted for under IFRS 2**.

The fair value used is that at the **date of issue,** as the grant date and issue date are the same, **that is $3 per share**. Because the shares are given as a bonus they vest immediately and are presumed to be consideration for past services.

The total of $3m would be changed to profit or loss and included in equity.

(b) **Purchase of property, plant and equipment**

Under IFRS 2, the purchase of property, plant and equipment would be treated as a share-based payment in which the counterparty has a **choice of settlement**, in shares or in cash. Such transactions are **treated as cash-settled** to the extent that the entity has incurred a **liability**. It is treated as the issue of a compound financial instrument, with a debt and an equity element.

Similar to IAS 32 *Financial instruments: presentation,* IFRS 2 requires the **determination of the liability element and the equity element**. The fair value of the equity element is the fair value of the goods or services (in this case the property) less the fair value of the debt element of the instrument. The fair value of the property is $4m (per question). The share price of $3.50 is the expected share price in three months' time (assuming cash settlement). The fair value of the liability component at 31 May 20X7 is its present value: $1.3 \times \$3 = \$3.9$.

The journal entries are:

DEBIT	Property, plant and equipment	$4m	
CREDIT	Liability		$3.9m
CREDIT	Equity		$0.1m

In three months' time, the debt component is remeasured to its fair value. Assuming the estimate of the future share price was correct at $3.50, the liability at that date will be 1.3 million × $3.5 = $4.55. An adjustment must be made as follows:

DEBIT	Expense (4.55 – 3.9)	$0.65m	
CREDIT	Liability		$0.65m

Choice of share or cash settlement

The share-based payment to the new director, which offers a choice of cash or share settlement, is also treated as the issue of a compound instrument. In this case, the **fair value of the services is determined by the fair value of the equity instruments given**. The fair value of the equity alternative is $2.50 × 50,000 = $125,000. The cash alternative is valued at 40,000 × $3 = $120,000. The **difference** between these two values – $5,000 – is deemed to be the **fair value of the equity component**. At the settlement date, the liability element would be measured at fair value and the method of settlement chosen by the director would determine the final accounting treatment.

At 31 May 20X7, the accounting entries would be:

DEBIT	Profit or loss – directors' remuneration	$125,000	
CREDIT	Liability		$120,000
CREDIT	Equity		$5,000

In effect, the director surrenders the right to $120,000 cash in order to obtain equity worth $125,000.

(c) **Investment in Hardy**

The investment in Hardy should be treated as an **associate under** IAS 28 *Investments in associates and joint ventures.* Between 20% and 50% of the share capital has been acquired, and significant influence may be exercised through the right to appoint directors. Associates are accounted for as cost plus post acquisition change in net assets, **generally cost plus share of post-acquisition retained earnings**. The cost is the fair value of the shares in Leigh exchanged for the shares of Handy. However, negative goodwill arises because the fair value of the net assets of Hardy exceeds this. The negative goodwill must be added back to determine the cost to be used for the carrying value, and, following a reassessment, credited to profit or loss. (Dr Cost 0.2, Cr P/L 0.2)

	$m
Cost: 1m × $2.50	2.5
Add back negative goodwill: (2.5 + (9 × 70% 'NCI') – 9)	0.2
	2.7
Post acquisition profits: (5 – 4) × 30%	0.3
Carrying value at 31 May 20X7	3.0

Note. The 0.2 is not part of post acquisition retained earnings. It is adjustment to the original cost to remove the negative goodwill.

Because negative goodwill has arisen, the investment must be **impairment tested**. A comparison must be made with the estimated recoverable amount of Hardy's net assets. The investment must not be carried above the recoverable amount:

Recoverable amount at 31 May 20X7: $11m × 30% = $3.3m

The recoverable amount is above the carrying value, so the investment at 31 May 20X7 will be shown at $3m.

30 Margie

Text reference. Share-based payment is covered in Chapter 8. Derivatives are covered in Chapter 7.

Top tips. This is a multi-part question, set in the context of share-related transactions. However, you should not assume that all transactions should be accounted for under IFRS 2. Part (a), a contract for the purchase of wheat, could be settled in the entity's own shares, but is intended to be settled net in cash, and is therefore a derivative rather than a share-based payment. Part (b) deals with the situation where share-based payment award is exchanged for awards held by the acquiree's employees as part of the business combination, so IFRS 3 is relevant. Part (c) deals with two share issues, one of which is outside the scope of IFRS 2. Part (d) is an equity-settled share-based payment with a variable vesting period based on a market condition.

Easy marks. There aren't any obvious easy marks here, but if you attempt all parts of the question you can gain the first few marks of each part.

Examiner's comment. In Part (a), Many candidates did not recognise the fact that the transaction should be dealt with under IFRS 9.This type of transaction has been examined recently but candidates did not seem to recognise the nature of the transaction. In Part (b), candidates had to understand the interaction of IFRS 2 and IFRS 3 in order to answer the question. The question was not well answered although candidates did seem to realise that there was a post combination expense to be taken into account. In Part (c), candidates often felt that the first transaction was within the scope of IFRS 2 and the second was not. Unfortunately this assumption was incorrect with the correct answer being that the first transaction was outside the scope and the second was within the scope. Part (d) was well answered. Candidates generally seemed to understand the effect of a market condition.

Marking scheme

		Marks
(a)	Discussion IFRS 9	5
	Conclusion	2
(b)	Discussion of IFRS 3/IFRS 2	4
	Calculation	2
(c)	Discussion	4
(d)	Discussion	4
	Calculation	2
Professional		2
		25

(a) **Contract for the purchase of wheat**

Although the amount paid to settle the contract will be equal to the value of 2,500 of Margie's shares, this is **not a share-based payment** within the scope of IFRS 2. There are two main reasons for this:

(i) The contract may be **settled net in cash.**

(ii) The contract has **not been entered into be entered into in order to satisfy Margie's normal sales and purchases requirements**. Margie has no intention of taking delivery of the wheat; this is a financial contract to pay or receive a cash amount.

Contracts for purchase or sale of non-financial items that meet certain conditions are accounted for under under IFRS 9 *Financial instruments.* Specifically, contracts to buy or sell non-financial items are within the scope of IFRS 9 if they can be settled net in cash or another financial asset, and are not entered into and held for the purpose of the receipt or delivery of a non-financial item in accordance with the entity's expected purchase, sale, or usage requirements. Contracts to buy or sell non-financial items are inside the scope if **net settlement** occurs.

Any one of the following situations constitutes **net settlement**

(i)   The terms of the contract permit either counterparty to settle net.

(ii)   There is a past practice of settling similar contracts net.

(iii)   There is a past practice, for similar contracts, of taking delivery of the underlying and selling it within a short period after delivery to generate a profit from short-term fluctuations in price, or from a dealer's margin.

(iv)   The non-financial item is readily convertible to cash.

Contracts that allow net settlement in cash can be entered into for satisfying the normal sales and purchases requirements of the two parties but this is not such a contract.

The contract to purchase the wheat will be accounted for as a **derivative** and valued at fair value (an **asset or liability at fair value** according to IFRS 9). **On inception the fair value of the contract will be nil** because the value of 350 tonnes of wheat will be equivalent to 2,500 of Margie's shares. This will not be the case at subsequent period ends because factors affecting the market price of wheat will not be the same as those affecting the market price of Margie's shares. Accordingly, differences will arise and there will be a **gain or loss, which must be taken to profit or loss for the year**.

Margie wishes to use this contract as part of its **hedging strategy**. However, **this would not be appropriate**. There is no firm commitment to purchase the wheat (in fact Margie has no intention of purchasing it), and it is not a highly probable forecast transaction.

(b)   **Replacement award**

In a business combination, an acquirer may exchange its share-based payment awards for awards held by employees of the acquiree. This may be termed a **replacement award,** and must be measured using IFRS 2 *Share-based payment.* Part of the fair value of the replacement award may, depending on the circumstances, be treated in accordance with IFRS 3 *Business combinations.*

IFRS 3 provides guidance on whether share-based payment awards in a business combination are part of the consideration transferred to obtain control (accounted for under IFRS 3) or as a post-combination expense (accounted for under IFRS 2). **If the acquirer is obliged to replace the acquiree's award, then all or part of the acquirer's award is part of the consideration transferred. If not, then it is a post-combination expense.**

Margie obliged to replace Antalya's award

If the Margie is obliged to replace Antalya's award, all or a portion of the fair value of Margie's replacement award must be included in the measurement of the consideration transferred by Margie. **The amount included in the consideration transferred is the fair value of Antalya's award at the acquisition date of $20 million.**

The **difference** between the fair value of Margie's replacement award and the fair value of the reward replaced, $22m – $20m = $2m is **recognised as an expense in the post-combination profit or loss**. This is the case even though no post-combination services are required.

Margie not obliged to replace Antalya's award

If Margie is not obliged to replace Antalya's award, then **Margie should not adjust the consideration**, whether or not it actually does replace Antalya's award. **All** of the fair value of Margie's award would be recognised immediately as a **post-combination expense,** despite the fact that no post-combination services are required.

(c)   **Issue of shares to employees**

Margie's issue of shares to its employees who are already shareholders **does not fall within the scope of IFRS 2 *Share-based payment*.** The issue was made to the employees in their capacity as shareholders, not as employees. There are **no service or performance requirements** demanded in exchange for the shares.

The employees are therefore just shareholders like any other, and the issue of shares will be accounted for like any other, with a debit to cash and a credit to share capital and to share premium for any excess over the nominal value.

Issue of shares to Grief

The issue of the shares to Grief does come within the scope of IFRS 2 *Share-based payment.* Share-based payment occurs when an entity purchases goods or services from another party such as a supplier or employee and rather than paying directly in cash, settles the amount owing in shares, share options or future cash amounts linked to the value of shares.

In this case, **Grief is acting as a supplier** (of the building), the payment is in shares, and the purpose of issuing the shares was to buy the building. **In accordance with IFRS 2, the building will be shown at fair value on the statement of financial position, with a corresponding credit to equity.**

(d)   **Share-based payment with variable vesting period**

The grant of the options to employees clearly falls within the scope of IFRS 2. In this case there is a **market condition** which must be met before the shares vest. The vesting period may change as a result of a vesting condition being met. IFRS 2 makes a distinction between the handling of market based performance features from non-market features. Market conditions are those related to the market price of any entity's equity, such as achieving a specified share price or a specified target based on a comparison of the entity's share price with an index of share prices of other entities. Market based performance features should be included in the grant-date fair value measurement. However, the fair value of the equity instruments should not be reduced to take into consideration non-market based performance features or other vesting features.

An entity needs **to estimate, at grant date, the expected vesting period** over which the charge should be spread, on the assumption that services will be rendered by employees over this vesting period in exchange for the equity instruments.

If the vesting period turns out to be **shorter** than estimated, the charge will be **accelerated** in the period in which the entity must fulfil its obligations by delivering shares or cash to the employee or supplier. If the actual vesting period is **longer** than estimated, the expense **is recognised over the original vesting period**.

At the grant date (1 December 20X1), Margie estimated the vesting period to be four years, the assumption being that the market condition would be met four years later in 20X5. Thus the charge over the four years was calculated as (100 × 4,000 × $10) ÷ 4 years = $1m per year.

The market condition was actually **met a year early**, on 30 November 20X4. The **expense therefore needs to be accelerated** and charged in the year ended 30 November 20X4. The charge for the year is calculated as:

	$m
Total charge: 100 × 4,000 × $10	4
Less already charged in the two years to 30.11. 20X3: 2 × $1m	(2)
Charge in the year ended 30.11.20X4	2

31 Greenie

Text reference. Specialised entities are covered in general terms in Chapter 20. The specific issues are covered as follows: share-based payment in Chapter 8, provisions and contingencies in Chapter 9, associates in Chapter 12 and preference shares in Chapter 7.

Top tips. This question is set in the airport industry. In keeping with the examiner's guidance, no specific knowledge of this industry is required. Part (a) covered provisions, contingent liabilities and contingent assets. There is a lot of information, but this part is more straightforward than it looks. In Part (b) you need to consider whether IAS 28 should be applied, that is whether there is significant influence. The percentage holding is not the only determining factor. Part (c) covered purchase of a franchise by issuing shares. This is a form of share-based payment. This part asked for the treatment of irredeemable preference shares with a fixed cash dividend. This meets the definition of a financial liability (in this case a contractual obligation to deliver cash) but also has an equity component, so needs to be accounted for as a compound instrument.

Marking scheme

		Marks
(a)	Provision discussion	3
	Contingent liability discussion	3
(b)	Significant influence discussion and application	10
(c)	Intangible assets	3
	Preference shares	4
	Professional	2
		25

(a) **Provision or contingent liability?**

A **provision** is defined by IAS 37 *Provisions, contingent liabilities and contingent assets* as **a liability of uncertain timing or amount.** IAS 37 states that a provision should only be recognised if:

- There is a **present obligation** as the result of a **past event**
- An **outflow of resources embodying economic benefits is probable**, and
- A **reliable estimate** of the amount can be made

If these conditions apply, a provision must be recognised.

The past event that gives rise, under IAS 37, to a present obligation, is known as the **obligating event.** The obligation may be legal, or it may be constructive (as when past practice creates a valid expectation on the part of a third party). The entity must have no realistic alternative but to settle the obligation.

As at 30 November 20X0, Greenie **has no legal obligation to pay compensation** to third parties. No legal action has been brought in respect of the accident. Nor can Greenie be said to have a constructive obligation at the year end, because the investigation has not been concluded, and the expert report will not be presented to the civil courts until 20X1.Therefore under IAS 37 *Provisions, contingent liabilities and contingent assets* no provision would be recognised for this amount.

However, the possible payment does fall within the IAS 37 definition of a **contingent liability,** which is:

- A possible obligation depending on whether some uncertain future event occurs, or
- A present obligation but payment is not probable or the amount cannot be measured reliably

There is uncertainty as to the outcome of the investigation and findings of the report, and the extent of the damages and any compensation arising remain to be confirmed. However, the uncertainty over these details is not so great that the possibility of an outflow of economic benefits is remote.

Therefore as **a contingent liability** the details and, if possible an estimate of the amount payable, would be **disclosed** in the notes to the financial statements.

The question arises as to whether the **possible recovery of the compensation costs from the insurance company** constitutes a contingent asset under IAS 37. A contingent asset is a possible asset that arises from past events, and whose existence will be confirmed only by the occurrence or non-occurrence of one or more uncertain future events not wholly within the control of the entity.

BPP
LEARNING MEDIA

Because any insurance claim will only be made after the courts have determined compensation, and will then need to be assessed on its merits, any payout is one step removed from the potential payment of compensation. In other words it is merely possible rather than probable, and **disclosure of a contingent asset would not be appropriate**.

(b) **Significant influence**

In accounting for Manair, Greenie needs to have regard to IAS 28 *Investments in associates and joint ventures*. IAS 28 defines an associate as 'an entity in which an investor has significant influence but not control or joint control'.

Significant influence is the power to participate in the financial and operating policy decisions of an economic activity but is not control or joint control over those policies.

Significant influence can be determined by the holding of voting rights (usually attached to shares) in the entity. IAS 28 states that if an investor holds **20% or more** of the voting power of the investee, it can be presumed that the investor has significant influence over the investee, *unless* it can be clearly shown that this is not the case.

Significant influence can be presumed *not* to exist if the investor holds **less than 20%** of the voting power of the investee, unless it can be demonstrated otherwise.

The **existence of significant influence** is evidenced in one or more of the following ways.

(i)   Representation on the **board of directors** (or equivalent) of the investee

(ii)   Participation in the **policy making process**

(iii) **Material transactions** between investor and investee

(iv)   Interchange of management personnel

(v)   Provision of essential technical information

The fact that Greenie holds 19. 9% of the voting shares of Manair suggests that it **wishes to keep just below the threshold** at which significant influence would be presumed in order to avoid accounting for Manair as an associate. The percentage of shares held is only one factor to consider, and the other factors above need to be considered in turn.

(i)   Greenie does have representation on the board of directors.

(ii)   Greenie **can participate in some decisions**. It is not clear whether these are financial and operating decisions, but the fact that the shareholders' agreement requires a unanimous or majority decision suggests that Greenie is more than just an ordinary investor.

(ii)   During the year, Greenie has sold Mainair a software licence for $5m, which is **at least one material transaction**.

(iv)   There is **no evidence** of interchange of management personnel.

(v)   Greenie has provided Manair with **maintenance and technical services**, another indication of significant influence.

The fact that so many indications of significant influence appear to be present, together with the holding of just under the threshold, suggests that Greenie does have significant influence over Manair. Accordingly, IAS 28 applies: **Manair must be treated as an associate and equity accounted** in the financial statements.

Related party

As an associate, Manair is a related party of Greenie under IAS 24 *Related party disclosures*. IAS 24 requires disclosure in the financial statements of Greenie of the **related party relationship** between Greenie and Manair and also of **transactions** between the two companies, the total value of those transactions and outstanding balances and, if applicable, debts deemed irrecoverable.

(c)   **Franchise rights**

The issue of shares for the acquisition of franchise rights falls to be accounted for under IFRS 2 *Share-based payment*. **Share-based payment** occurs when an entity purchases goods or services from another party such as a supplier or employee and rather than paying directly in cash, settles the amount owing in shares (as here), share options or future cash amounts linked to the value of shares.

Greenie's proposal to record the transaction at the **nominal value** of the shares issued, that is $1m, is **incorrect.** IFRS 2 requires that the asset (franchise rights) should be recorded at **the fair value of the rights acquired.** The fair value can be established, according to IFRS 2, **by reference to prices for similar transactions.** In this case a similar franchise was acquired for $2.3m, and this can be taken as the fair value of the asset:

DEBIT   Intangible assets $2.3m
CREDIT   Equity $2.3m

In some cases the fair value of the asset acquired in a share-based payment **cannot be reliably measured.** If so, the **asset is recorded at the fair value of the equity instrument issued.** In this case, the fair value would be $2.5m.

Irredeemable preference shares

IAS 32 *Financial instruments: presentation* **normally treats irredeemable preference shares as equity** because there is normally no obligation to deliver cash or other financial assets to another entity. However, in the case of Greenie there appears to be **both an equity and a liability element:**

(i)   The **right to participate in profits** in the form of a participating dividend based on dividends paid on ordinary shares is an **equity element**.

(ii)   The contractual obligation to pay an **annual fixed cash dividend** is a **liability component**.

IAS 32 required that the preference shares should be treated as **compound instruments,** with both a liability and an equity component. The equity component is determined by deducting the liability component from the fair value of the instrument and taking the residual figure as the equity component.

Greenie has invoked the IASB *Framework* in arguing that compliance with IAS 32 would **not give a fair presentation**. The contention is that the profit participation element of the shares gives them the characteristic of permanent capital.

The motive for wishing the preference shares to be classified solely as equity may be to reduce gearing. This is **not acceptable** under IAS 1 *Presentation of financial statements.* IAS 1 allows **departure from IFRS only in exceptional circumstances** where compliance would not give a fair presentation. This is not one such circumstance. It would be misleading not to present the liability component of the preference shares.

IAS 1 does, however, allow **additional disclosures** where compliance with an IFRS gives insufficient information for a clear understanding of the impact of a transaction on an entity's financial performance or position. The appropriate course of action for Greenie to take would be to **record the preference shares as compound instruments** with an equity and a liability element in accordance with IAS 32, and **to provide disclosures** explaining the participative nature of the shares which make them akin to equity.

32 Zack

Text reference. IAS 8 *Accounting policies, changes in accounting estimates and errors* is covered in Chapter 18 of your study text. IAS 23 *Borrowing costs* is covered in Chapter 4.

Top tips. As Question 4 on the paper, this was different from the usual current issues question in the topic it tested (IAS 8), although not in structure, being a discussion followed by application to a scenario. While IAS 8 is brought forward knowledge from F7, the depth of discussion required is greater, and the scenario requires more thought.

Easy marks. There are marks available for textbook knowledge of IAS 8 and IAS 23, which you should have from your earlier studies, and also the fact that there is much subjectivity in the marking scheme means a variety of valid arguments may be acceptable. Note the word 'valid', however: you **must** apply the knowledge to the scenario and you will get no credit for 'waffle'.

Marking scheme

		Marks
(a)	Subjective	15
(b)	Subjective	8
Professional marks		2
		25

(a) (i) **Judgement and materiality in selecting accounting policies**

The selection of accounting policies in the preparation of financial statements is important in providing consistency, comparability and clarity to users of those statements. In general entities do not have a great deal of discretion, but must follow the accounting policies required by IFRS that are relevant to the particular circumstances of the entity. In certain circumstances, however, IFRS offers a choice or does not give guidance. In these situations, management should select appropriate accounting policies.

Judgement

Management is required to exercise judgement in developing and applying an accounting policy that results in information that is relevant and reliable. If there is **no IFRS** standard or interpretation that is specifically applicable, management should consider the applicability of the requirements in IFRS on **similar and related issues**, and then the definitions, recognition criteria and measurement concepts for assets, liabilities, income and expenses in the **Conceptual Framework**. Management may also consider the most recent pronouncements of **other standard-setting bodies** that use a similar conceptual framework to develop accounting standards, other accounting literature and accepted industry practices, to the extent that these do not conflict with IFRS.

Unless a standard permits or requires otherwise, accounting policies should be applied **consistent**ly to similar transactions and events. For example, it is permissible to carry some items of property, plant and equipment at fair value and some at historical cost, but items within any one class of property, plant and equipment must be treated in the same way.

Management's judgement will be constrained as regards its selection of accounting policies (or changes in accounting policies or estimates) by the need to **follow the requirements of IAS 8** *Accounting policies, changes in accounting estimates and errors.*

Materiality

IAS 8 states that omissions or misstatements of items 'are material if they could, by their size or nature, individually or collectively, influence the economic decisions of users taken on the basis of the financial statements'.

In general, IFRS **only apply to material items,** and an accounting policy need not be applied if its effect would be immaterial. Similarly, a **change** in accounting policy or estimate **would only be necessary if the item was material.** Specifically in the context of IAS 8 and errors, materiality 'depends on the size and nature of the omission or misstatement judged in the surrounding circumstances. The size or nature of the item, or a combination of both, could be the determining factor'.

In addition, IAS 8 notes that it is **inappropriate to make, or leave uncorrected, immaterial departures** from IFRSs to **achieve a particular presentation**, so the principle of materiality cannot be abused to present the results in an artificially favourable light.

(ii) **Change in accounting policy**

IAS 8 allows a change in accounting policy **only where required by a standard** or if it results in financial statements providing reliable and **more relevant information** about the effects of transactions, other events or conditions on the entity's financial position, financial performance, or cash flows. Changes in accounting policy **should be very rare,** because IFRS specifies the accounting policies for most of the transactions an entity will make. Changes in accounting **estimates**, on the other hand, will be **more frequent**. A change in accounting estimate is 'an adjustment of the carrying amount of an asset or liability, or related expense, resulting from reassessing the expected future benefits and obligations associated with that asset or liability'. Such changes may be needed to estimate the figures correctly in order to comply with an accounting policy.

IAS 8 notes that changes in accounting policies **do not include applying an accounting policy to a kind of transaction or event that did not occur previously or were immaterial**. Such a policy would be applied **prospectively,** that is prior period figures would not be adjusted. For example, if an entity begins to let out its head office to residents to earn rental income, this change of use of the building would mean that it should be accounted for as an investment property under IAS 40. However, this is not a change of accounting policy, rather it is the application of a standard to an asset to which it did not apply previously, and so there would be no retrospective application.

If a change in accounting policy is required by a new IFRS or interpretation, the change is accounted for as required by that new pronouncement if the new pronouncement includes specific transition provisions. Not all new standards and interpretations include transition provisions, and if none are included then the change in accounting policy is applied retrospectively.

Retrospective application means that an entity **adjusts the opening balance of each component of equity that is affected for the earliest prior period presented in the financial statements**. It also adjusts the other comparative amounts, that is, amounts in the statement of profit or loss and other comprehensive income, and the statements of financial position, cash flows and changes in equity and related notes. The **comparative amounts** disclosed for each prior period presented **as if the new policy had always applied**. This rule applies except where it is impracticable to determine either the period-specific effects of the change or the cumulative effects of the change.

It is sometimes **difficult to compare** the current period with prior periods because there is **insufficient data** relating to the prior period. Perhaps it was not foreseen that such data would be needed. Even if the data is available, restatement of prior information often requires **complex and detailed estimates** to be made, although this does not mean that reliable adjustments cannot be made.

The further in the past the prior period adjustment relates to, the harder it is for estimates to reflect the circumstances existing at the time. Judgement may be clouded by hindsight, that is influenced by knowledge of events which have occurred since the prior period. **IAS 8 does not permit the use of hindsight** in estimations of amounts to be recognised, measured or disclosed in a prior period, or in making assumptions about management intentions at that time.

If it is impracticable to determine the cumulative effect, at the beginning of the current period, of applying a new accounting policy to all prior periods, an entity must adjust the comparative information to apply the new accounting policy prospectively from the **earliest date practicable**. This may in practice be the current period.

(iii) **IAS 8 and earnings management**

IAS 8 requires the correction of prior period errors to be carried out retrospectively by restating the comparative amounts for the prior period(s) presented in which the error occurred, or if the error occurred before the earliest prior period presented, restating the opening balances of assets, liabilities and equity for the earliest prior period presented. The effect is to restate the comparatives **as if the error had never occurred**. The impact of any prior period errors will not be included in the current period's profit or loss, but will be shown – or perhaps hidden – in retained earnings.

It could be argued that this gives managers an **incentive to use prior period corrections under IAS 8** as a form of **earnings management,** because it allows them to **manipulate current earnings**.

Expenses could be miscalculated and the correction treated as a prior period error in the following year, with an **adjustment through retained earnings rather than profit or loss**. Earnings per share could be miscalculated, or liabilities reported as non-current rather than current. IAS 8 allows such misstatements to be **corrected the following year without any long-term negative effects in the statement of financial position**.

While IAS 8 does not permit **hindsight,** in practice this may be **difficult to prove**, and inappropriate hindsight may be used to relegate bad news to prior periods once the bad news has passed. **Errors are not given the prominence** which users of financial statements might need in order to assess management's competence and integrity, as well as how good the results are. Use of reserves instead of profit or loss has long been seen as undesirable this very reason.

(b) (i) **Borrowing costs**

IAS 23 *Borrowing costs* requires that borrowing costs directly attributable to the acquisition, construction or production of a 'qualifying asset' (one that necessarily takes a substantial period of time to get ready for its intended use or sale) are included in the cost of the asset. Other borrowing costs are recognised as an expense.

IAS 23 would therefore require capitalisation of the borrowing costs of $3m incurred while the shopping centre is under construction. In the case of the borrowing costs of $2m incurred on the 20X2 asset, it has been found that there would be a material misstatement of the asset balance if borrowing costs were not capitalised, so IAS 23 requires capitalisation of those borrowing costs.

The accounting treatment previously used by Zack was incorrect because it did not comply with IAS 23. Consequently, the change to the new, correct policy is **the correction of an error rather than a change of accounting policy** as regards the 20X2 asset. This is a prior period error, which **must be corrected retrospectively**. This involves restating the financial statements for the year ended 30 November 20X2, when the contract was completed, and **restating the opening balances** for 20X3 so that the financial statements are presented as if the error had never occurred. In 20X3, the $3m of borrowing costs should be capitalised in accordance with IAS 23; this is compliance with IFRS rather than a change of accounting policy. It can be assumed that there will be no depreciation, as the asset is under construction.

The **effects of the restatement** for the year ended 30 November 20X2 are:

(1) The carrying amount of property, plant and equipment is **restated upwards** by $2m, less depreciation for the year.

(2) There is a corresponding **increase in profit or loss** for the year of the same amount.

(3) **Disclosures** are required relating to the prior period error:

- The nature of the prior period error

- For each prior period presented, to the extent practicable, the amount of the correction, for each financial statement line item affected, and for basic and diluted earnings per share

- The amount of the correction at the beginning of the earliest prior period presented

- If retrospective restatement is impracticable, an explanation and description of how the error has been corrected.

(ii) **Change in depreciation method**

Changing from straight line depreciation to reducing balance is a **change in accounting estimate, not a change in accounting policy**. A change in accounting estimate is 'an adjustment of the carrying amount of an asset or liability, or related expense, resulting from reassessing the expected future benefits and obligations associated with that asset or liability.'

Changes in accounting estimates are **not applied retrospectively** and accordingly, financial information presented for prior periods is not restated. Instead, the effect of a change in an accounting estimate is recognised **prospectively** (that is, from the date of change) by including it in profit or loss in the period of change, if the change affects only that period, or in the period of change and future periods, where the change also affects future periods.

Where the effect on future periods is not disclosed because it is not practicable, that fact should be disclosed.

The revision to the depreciation figures calculated by management are not correct, because they include an adjustment of **$5m for the year to 30 November 20X2**, that is a **retrospective adjustment**. The carrying amount as at 1 December 20X2 will be depreciated based on **prospective** reducing balance application.

(iii) **Accruals error**

This systems error would be treated as a **prior period error** in accordance with IAS 8. Zack must correct this by **restating the prior period information** for the year ended 30 November 20X2:

(1) Increase profit or loss for 20X2 by $2m.
(2) Adjust trade payables for 20X2 by $2m, to eliminate the overstatement.
(3) Restate the movement in reserves note.

This is the correction of an error, not an accounting estimate.

33 Minco

Text reference. Revenue recognition is covered in Chapter 1 of your Study Text. Intangible assets, property, plant and equipment, and impairment are covered in Chapter 4. IFRS 5 is covered in Chapter 15 and IAS 34 is covered in Chapter 18.

Top tips. This was a specialised industry question, set in the property industry. As the examiner has stated, no specialist knowledge of the industry was required. The question covered a number of standards and issues (revenue, interim reporting, asset held for sale, provisions, intangibles and the treatment of an annual retainer). Both the question and the answer to Part (a) have been amended to reflect the different emphasis of the new IFRS 15 from its predecessor, IAS 18. Part (d) has also been amended.

Easy marks. Although IFRS 15 is new, there are some easy marks to be had in Part (a) for showing knowledge of the criteria for identifying the contract with a customer.

Marking scheme

		Marks
(a)	1 mark per point up to maximum	7
(b)	1 mark per point up to maximum	5
(c)	1 mark per point up to maximum	5
(d)	1 mark per point up to maximum	6
Professional marks		2
Maximum		25

(a) **Contract for sale of the building**

Revenue from a contract may be recognised in accordance with IFRS 15 *Revenue from contracts with customers* when all of the following criteria (Paragraph 9) are met.

(i) The **parties** to the contract have **approved the contract**.

(ii) **Each party's rights** in relation to the goods or services to be transferred **can be identified**.

(iii) The **payment terms and conditions** for the goods or services to be transferred **can be identified**.

(iv) The contract has **commercial substance**.

(v) The **collection of an amount of consideration** to which the entity is entitled to in exchange for the goods or services is **probable**.

Criteria (i) to (iv) have been met, but **criterion (v)**, relating to Holistic Healthco's ability and intention to pay, is **in doubt**. The following factors need to be taken into consideration.

(i) Holistic Healthco's liability under the loan is limited because the **loan is non-recourse**. If the customer defaults Minco is not entitled to full compensation for the amount owed, but only has the right to repossess the building.

(ii) Holistic Healthco intends to repay the loan (which has a significant balance outstanding) primarily from income derived from its fitness and leisure centre. This is a **business facing significant risks** because of high competition in the industry and because of the customer's limited experience.

(iii) Holistic Healthco has **no other income or assets** that could be used to repay the loan.

It is therefore **not probable that Minco will collect the consideration** to which it is entitled in exchange for the transfer of the building and so the IFRS 15 (Paragraph 9) criteria have not been met. Minco must then consider whether either of the criteria in IFRS 15 Paragraph 15 have been met, that is:

(a) Has Minco has received **substantially all** of the consideration?

(b) Has Minco **terminated the contract?**

The answer to both of these is **no**, therefore, in accordance with Paragraph 16 of the standard, **Minco must account for the non-refundable $150,000 payment as a deposit liability.** Minco must continue to account

BPP
LEARNING MEDIA

for the initial deposit, as well as any future payments of principal and interest, as a deposit liability, until such time that the company concludes that the criteria in Paragraph 9 are met, specifically that it will recover the consideration owing, or until it has received substantially all of it, or terminated the contract. Minco must **continue to assess the situation** to see if these changes have occurred.

(b) **Promotional expenditure**

There are three types of payment involved in the arrangement with the tennis player. The question states that the payments are not interrelated, so the interactions between them do not need to be examined and the expense recognition pattern may be different for each.

Signing bonus

The contract is for advertising and promotional expenditure to improve Minco's brand image. IAS 38 *Intangible assets* requires **that these costs must be expensed when the services are received**. The signing bonus is paid in advance of the services being received, those services being wearing Minco's logo, taking part in a specified number of tournaments and attending photo/film sessions for advertising. The signing bonus of $20,000 is paid to the player at the start of the contract, but relates to the full three-year contract term. It must therefore be treated as a **prepayment at the start of the contract and expensed on a straight-line basis** over the three-year contract period.

If the **contract is terminated** before the end of the three-year period, Minco should **expense immediately any amount not recovered** from the player.

It has been assumed in specifying the above treatment that separate services cannot be identified. However, **if the terms of the contract allow separate services to be identified and measured reliably**, then Minco should **recognise the expense once the separate service is rendered.**

Annual retainer

Minco has also contracted to pay the player an annual retainer of $50,000 provided she has competed in all the specified tournaments for that year. IFRS 9 *Financial instruments* requires this arrangement to be treated as a **financial liability** because Minco has a **contractual obligation to deliver cash** to the player. The financial liability is recognised at the **present value of the expected cash flows.**

Minco incurs this obligation on the date **when the player has competed in all the specified tournaments** and it is at this point that the **liability should be recognised.**

Performance bonus

Minco must also pay a performance bonus to the player whenever she wins a tournament. These payments are **related to specific events,** and therefore they are treated as **executory contracts.** (An executory contract is a contract in which something remains to be done by one or both parties.) They are **accrued and expensed when the player has won** a tournament.

(c) **Head office**

Additional floor

IAS 16 *Property, plant and equipment* is the relevant standard here. The standard requires that Minco should capitalise the costs of the extra floor, which is an improvement to the building, and amortise these costs over the six-year lease period.

IAS 16 states that the initial cost of an asset **should include** the initial estimate of the **costs of dismantling and removing the item and restoring the site** where the entity has an obligation to do so. This is the case here: Minco has an obligation to remove the floor at the end of the lease because of the clause in the lease requiring the building's condition to be identical at the end of the lease to its condition at the beginning of the lease. A **present obligation exists**, as defined by IAS 37 *Provisions, contingent liabilities and contingent assets* and therefore the entity should also **recognise a provision** for that amount. The provision should be **discounted to its present value** and the unwinding of the discount recognised in profit or loss.

This arrangement is, in substance, a decommissioning liability. The **asset** recognised for the cost of removal should be **amortised over the six-year period of the lease**. Minco may recover the cost from the benefits generated by the new floor over the remainder of the lease.

General disrepair of the building

A **present obligation** arises for the repair costs under IAS 37 *Provisions, contingent liabilities and contingent assets* because the lease agreement states that the landlord can re-charge these costs to Minco. The **obligating event is the wear and t**ear to the building, which arises gradually over the period of the lease and which will result in an outflow of economic benefits. The **estimated costs should be spread over the six-year lease** period. A **reliable estimate** of the yearly obligation can be made, although this may not necessarily be one sixth per year, for example if exceptional wear and tear arises in any given year.

Roof repair

The lease states clearly that the landlord can re-charge any costs of repairing the roof immediately. Accordingly, **an obligation exists** and a **provision needs to be made for the whole of the roof repair work** on the date on which the requirement was identified.

(d) **Property**

IAS 34 requirement

In accordance with IAS 34 *Interim financial reporting,* an entity must apply the same accounting policies in its interim financial statements as in its annual financial statements. Measurements should be made on a 'year to date' basis. Minco's interim financial statements are for the six months to 30 November 20X3.

Minco must apply the provisions of IFRS 5 *Non-current assets held for sale and discontinued operations* to the valuation of the property.

Application of IFRS 5

In accordance with IFRS 5, an asset held for sale should be measured at the **lower of** its **carrying amount** and **fair value less costs to sell**. Immediately before classification of the asset as held for sale, the entity must recognise impairment in accordance with applicable IFRS. Any impairment loss is generally recognised in profit or loss, but if the asset has been measured at a revalued amount under IAS 16 *Property, plant and equipment* or IAS 38 *Intangible assets,* the impairment will be treated as a revaluation decrease. **Once** the asset has been **classified as held for sale**, any **impairment loss** will be based on the **difference between the adjusted carrying amounts and the fair value less cost to sell**. The impairment loss (if any) will be **recognised in profit or loss**.

A **subsequent increase** in fair value less costs to sell may be **recognised** in profit or loss **only to the extent of any impairment previously recognised**. To summarise:

Step 1   Calculate carrying value under applicable IFRS, here IAS 16:

Depreciation for the four months to 1 October 20X3, the date of classification as held for sale is calculated on the carrying amount net of the impairment loss incurred on 31 May 20X3, over the remaining useful life of eight years, ($1m is two years' depreciation out of 5m/0.5 – ten years):

$(5m - 1m - 0.35m) \div 8 \times 4/12 = \$152,083$

So the carrying value at 1 October 20X3 is $5m - 1m - 0.35m - 0.15m = \$3.5m$

Step 2   Classified as held for sale. Compare the carrying amount ($3.5m) with fair value less costs to sell ($3.4m). Measure at the lower of carrying value and fair value less costs to sell, here $3.4m, giving an initial write-down of $100,000.

Step 3   Determine fair value less costs to sell at the date of the interim financial statements, 1 December 20X3, here given as $3.52m and compare with carrying value of $3.4m. This gives a gain of $120,000.

The impairment previously recognised is: $350,000 + $100,000 = $450,000. The gain of $120,000 is less than this, and may therefore be credited to profit or loss, and the property is carried at $3.52m.

Step 4   On 31 May 20X4, fair value less costs to sell is $3.95m. The change in fair value less cost to sell is recognised but the gain recognised cannot exceed any impairment losses to date. Impairment losses to date are $350,000 + $100,000 – $120,000 = $330,000, and this is less than the change in fair value less costs to sell of $430,000. This restricted gain of $330,000 is recognised, and the property is carried at $3.85m.

Step 5   On 5 June 20X4, the property is sold for $4m, at which point a gain of $150,000 is recognised. If material, this sale would be a non-adjusting event under IAS 10 *Events after the reporting period*.

34 Alexandra

Text reference. IAS 1 and IAS 8 are covered in Chapter 18 of your Study Text. IFRS 15 is covered in Chapter 1. Related parties are covered in Chapter 10. Pension plans are covered in Chapter 5.

Top tips. Part (a) was on reclassification of long-term debt as current. Part (b) had a correction of an error (IAS 8) arising from an incorrect application of IFRS 15 *Revenue from contracts with customers*. Thus you have the interaction of two standards, so don't just concentrate on one. Part (c) was on related party disclosures for key management personnel, which needed to be broken down by category, and part (d) required candidates to explain why a pension plan needed to be accounted for as a defined benefit plan. As this is a multi-topic standard question, you can always have a respectable go at the parts where your knowledge is strongest. As the examiner often says, all information in the question is included for a purpose, so there are plenty of pointers in Part (d).

Easy marks. Part (c) has some easy marks for reproducing definitions from IAS 24. Unusually, the employee benefits question (Part (d)) could be a source of easy marks, as it contains a number of hints, and gives you an opportunity to reproduce knowledge about the differences between the two types of plan without any complicated calculations.

Examiner's comment. In Part (a), only a few candidates mentioned that according to IAS 1 *Presentation of financial statements*, a liability should be classified as current if it is due to be settled within 12 months after the date of the statement of financial position. In Part (b), most candidates had a good understanding of the nature of IAS 18 *Revenue*, but few treated the change in accounting treatment as a correction of an error in accordance with IAS 8 *Accounting policies, changes in accounting estimates and errors*. The previous policy applied was not in accordance with IAS 18, which requires revenue arising from transactions involving the rendering of services to be recognised with reference to the stage of completion at the date of the statement of financial position. Most scored well on Part (c), realising that that the exclusion of the remuneration of the non-executive directors from key management personnel disclosures did not comply with the requirements of IAS 24 *Related party disclosures*. Part (d) was well answered, with most candidates coming to the right conclusion.

Marking scheme

		Marks
(a)	1 mark per question up to maximum	6
(b)	1 mark per question up to maximum	5
(c)	1 mark per question up to maximum	5
(d)	1 mark per question up to maximum	7
	Professional marks	2
	Maximum	25

(a)   **Default on loan**

Under IAS 1 *Presentation of financial statements*, a **long-term financial liability** due to be **settled within twelve months** of the year end date should be classified as a **current liability**. Furthermore, a **long-term financial liability** that is payable on **demand** because the entity **breached** a **condition** of its loan agreement should be classified as **current** at the year end even if the **lender** has agreed **after the year end**, and **before** the financial statements are **authorised for issue**, **not** to **demand payment** as a consequence of the breach.

November 20X0	30 April 20X1	17 May 20X1	Date financial statements approved for issue
Condition of loan agreement breached. Long-term liability becomes payable on demand	Year end	Lender agrees not to enforce payment resulting from breach	

However, if the **lender** has **agreed** by the **year end** to provide a **period of grace** ending **at least twelve months after the year end** within which the entity can rectify the breach and during that time the lender cannot demand immediate repayment, the liability is classified as **non-current**.

In the case of Alexandra, the waiver was given before the year end, but only for the loan to be repaid a month after the year end, then a further waiver was agreed, but again only for a few weeks. It would **not therefore be appropriate for Alexandra to classify the bond as long-term debt** in the statement of financial position as at 30 April 20X1.

The fact that Alexandra has defaulted and sought two loan waivers may cast doubt on its ability to continue as a going concern, especially as the loan waivers may not be renewed. If there is uncertainty regarding Alexandra's going concern status, IAS 1 requires Alexandra to disclose these uncertainties. If Alexandra ceases to be a going concern, then the financial statements would need to be prepared on a break-up basis.

(b) **Maintenance contracts**

There are two aspects to consider:

(i) What is the correct way to recognise the revenue from the maintenance contracts?
(ii) What adjustments does Alexandra need to make, having changed its method of recognition?

Correct IFRS 15 treatment

IFRS 15 *Revenue from contracts with customers* has a five-stage process for recognising revenue. Step (ii) **'identify the separate performance obligations'** would classify the performance obligations in the maintenance contracts as the provision of services. Step (v) of the IFRS 15 process requires the entity to would treat this as a **performance obligation satisfied over time** because the customer simultaneously receives and consumes the benefits as the performance takes place.

Revenue should be recognised as the services are provided (step (v)).

Under IFRS 15, the best measure of progress towards complete satisfaction of the performance obligation over time is a **time-based measure** and Alexander should recognise revenue on a **straight-line basis over the specified period.**

Accordingly, **the new treatment**, and the one used to date by Xavier Co, is the **correct** accounting treatment under IFRS 15, and the **previous treatment,** of recognising the revenue on invoicing at the beginning of the contract, was **incorrect**.

Adjustments under IAS 8

The accounting treatment previously used by Alexandra was incorrect because it did not comply with IAS 18. Consequently, the change to the new, correct policy is **the correction of an error rather than a change of accounting policy**.

IAS 8 *Accounting policies, changes in accounting estimates and errors* states that changes in accounting estimates result from changes in circumstances, new information or more experience, which is not the case here. This is a prior period error, which **must be corrected retrospectively**. This involves **restating the opening balances** for that period so that the financial statements are presented as if the error had never occurred.

In the opening balance of retained earnings, the maintenance contract income that was recognised in full in the year ended 30 April 20X0 must be split between the revenue due for that year (on an IAS 18 basis as described above) and that which should be deferred to subsequence periods. There will be less revenue recognised in the prior year, resulting in a **net debit to opening retained earnings**.

In the year ended 30 April 20X1, the correct accounting policy has been applied. Since the maintenance contracts typically run for two years, it is likely that most of the **income deferred from the prior year relating to this period will also be recognised** in the current period. The effect of this for the year ended 30 April 20X1 is that the reduction in profits of $6m will be mitigated by the recognition of income deferred from last year.

(c) **Directors' remuneration**

The disclosures that Alexandra has provided are insufficient to comply with IAS 24 *Related party disclosures* on two counts:

(i) No breakdown of directors' remuneration
(ii) Exclusion of remuneration of non-executive directors

Breakdown of directors' remuneration

IAS 24 *Related party disclosures* requires that entities should **disclose** key management personnel compensation **not only in total** but also **for each of the** following **categories:**

- Short-term employee benefits
- Post-employment benefits
- Other long-term benefits
- Termination benefits
- Share-based payment

The remuneration for the directors of Alexandra fits into the categories of 'short-term benefits' (ie salary and bonus) and 'share-based payment' (ie share options), and should be disclosed accordingly. Only totals for each category need to be disclosed, not the earnings of individual board members, so no cultural protocol will be breached by these disclosures. However, Alexandra is a public limited company, and so local legislation and corporate governance rules may require more detailed disclosure.

Non-executive directors

By excluding the non-executive directors from the remuneration disclosures, **Alexander is in breach of IAS 24**.

IAS 24 defines **key management personnel** as those persons having authority and responsibility for planning, directing and controlling the activities of the entity, directly or indirectly, including any director **(whether executive or otherwise)** of that entity.

Thus, the remuneration of the non-executive directors, who are key management personnel, should have been disclosed along with that of the executive directors.

(d) **Pension plan**

Alexander wishes to account for its pension plan as a defined contribution scheme, probably because the accounting is more straightforward and the risk not reflected in the figures in the financial statements. These figures were material in the case of Alexandra. However, although the entity's plan has some features in common with a defined contribution plan, it needs to be considered whether this is really the case.

With **defined contribution** plans, the employer (and possibly, as here, current employees too) pay regular contributions into the plan of a given or 'defined' amount each year. The contributions are invested, and the size of the post-employment benefits paid to former employees depends on how well or how badly the plan's investments perform. If the investments perform well, the plan will be able to afford higher benefits than if the investments performed less well.

With **defined benefit** plans, the size of the post-employment benefits is determined in advance, ie the benefits are 'defined'. The employer (and possibly, as here, current employees too) pay contributions into the plan, and the contributions are invested. The size of the contributions is set at an amount that is expected to earn enough investment returns to meet the obligation to pay the post-employment benefits. If, however, it becomes apparent that the assets in the fund are insufficient, the employer will be required to make additional contributions into the plan to make up the expected shortfall. On the other hand, if the fund's assets appear to be larger than they need to be, and in excess of what is required to pay the post-employment benefits, the employer may be allowed to take a 'contribution holiday' (ie stop paying in contributions for a while).

The **main difference** between the two types of plans lies in **who bears the risk**: if the employer bears the risk, even in a small way by guaranteeing or specifying the return, the plan is a defined benefit plan. A defined contribution scheme must give a benefit formula based solely on the amount of the contributions.

Alexandra's is, in reality, a defined benefit plan. Alexandra, the employer, guarantees a pension based on the average pay of the employees in the scheme. The entity's liability is not limited to the amount of the contributions to the plan, but is supplemented by an insurance premium which the insurance company can increase if required in order to fulfil the plan obligations. The trust fund which the insurance company is building up, is in turn dependent on the yield on investments. If the insurer has insufficient funds to pay the guaranteed pension, Alexandra has to make good the deficit. Indirectly, through insurance premiums, the employer bears the investment risk. The employee's contribution, on the other hand is fixed.

A further indication that Alexander bears the risk is the provision that if an employee leaves Alexandra and transfers the pension to another fund, Alexandra is liable for, or is refunded the difference between the benefits the employee is entitled to and the insurance premiums paid. Alexandra thus **has a legal or constructive obligation** to make good the shortfall if the insurance company does not pay all future employee benefits relating to employee service in the current and prior periods.

In conclusion, even though the insurance company limits some of the risk, Alexandra, rather than its employees, bears the risk, so this is a **defined benefit plan**.

35 Cate

Text references. Deferred tax covered in Chapter 6, impairment in Chapter 4, discontinuation in Chapter 15, disposals in Chapter 14 and employee benefits in Chapter 5.

Top tips. This question is unusual in not having any calculations. It is important that you express your answers clearly. Part (a) is fairly straightforward. In Part (b) it should be apparent that Cate is unwilling to recognise an impairment loss, so you need to explain how fair value and value in use could be calculated and compared. Deemed disposals (Part (c)) are not specifically examinable in P2, but it should be clear that there is a dilution of control. In Part (d), you need to look at the substance of what is going on, rather than Cate's assertion that the pension scheme is a 'voluntary' fund.

Easy marks. As a multi-standard question, this offers easy marks by making sure you attempt all parts – it is always easier to get the first few marks of any question, or part of question. Part (a) on deferred tax is (unusually!) quite easy if you know the rule about tax losses – essentially you just need to make the case from the information in the question that future taxable profit will not be available.

Examiner's comment. Parts (a) and (b) were well answered. It is important to apply knowledge to the scenario, not just repeat it. In part (c), which was well answered, the key was to set out the principles in the standard and then to apply them to the case in point. Part (d) contained lots of 'clues' pointing to not accepting Cate's proposed treatment.

	Marks
Deferred tax	5
Investment in associate	5
IFRS 5 Discussion and conclusion	8
IAS 19 Discussion and conclusion	5
Professional marks	2
	25

(a) **Deferred tax**

In principle, IAS 12 *Income taxes* allows recognition of **deferred tax assets**, if material, for deductible temporary differences, unused tax losses and unused tax credits. However, IAS 12 states that **deferred tax assets should only be recognised to the extent that they are regarded as recoverable**. They should be regarded as recoverable to the extent that on the basis of all the evidence available it is **probable that there will be suitable taxable profits against which the losses can be recovered**. There is evidence that this is not the case for Cate:

(i) While Cate has made a small profit before tax in the year to 31 May 20X6, this includes **significant non-operating gains**. In other words the profit is not due to ordinarily business activities.

(ii) In contrast, **Cate's losses were due to ordinary business activities**, not from identifiable causes unlikely to recur (IAS 12).

(iii) The fact that there are **unused tax losses** is strong evidence, according to IAS 12, that future taxable profits may not be available against which to offset the losses.

(iv) When considering the likelihood of future taxable profits, Cate's forecast cannot be considered as sufficient evidence. These are **estimates which cannot be objectively verified**, and are based on possible customer interest rather than confirmed contracts or orders.

(v) Cate **does not** have available any **tax planning opportunities** which might give rise to taxable profits.

In conclusion, **Cate should not recognise deferred tax assets on losses carried forward**, as there is insufficient evidence that future taxable profits can be generated against which to offset the losses.

(b) **Investment in Bates**

Cate's approach to the valuation of the investment in Bates is open to question, and shows that Cate may **wish to avoid showing an impairment loss**.

There is an established principle that **an asset should not be carried at more than its recoverable amount**. If the carrying value is not recoverable in full, the asset must be written down to the recoverable amount. It is said to be impaired. The recoverable amount is the highest value to the business in terms of the cash flows that the asset can generate, and is the higher of:

(i) The asset's fair value less costs of disposal, and
(ii) The asset's value in use

Cate appears to be **raising difficulties** about both of these measures in respect of Bates.

(i) **Fair value less costs of disposal**

An asset's fair value less costs of disposal is the amount net of incremental costs directly attributable to the disposal of an asset (excluding finance costs and income tax expense). Costs of disposal include transaction costs such as legal expenses.

Cate argues that there is no binding sale agreement and that the quoted share price is not an appropriate measure of the fair value or its significant influence over Bates. IFRS 13 *Fair value measurement* defines fair value as 'the price that would be received to sell an asset...in an orderly transaction between market participants'. Just because there is no binding sale agreement does not mean that Cate cannot measure fair value. IFRS 13 has a 3 level hierarchy in measuring fair value:

- Level 1 inputs = quoted prices (unadjusted) in active markets for identical assets

- Level 2 inputs = inputs other than quoted prices included within Level 1 that are observable for the asset or liability, either directly or indirectly (eg quoted prices for similar assets)

- Level 3 inputs = unobservable inputs for the asset

The measurement techniques proposed by Cate (earnings multiple and option-pricing model) are both Level 3 inputs. Therefore, if better Level 1 or 2 inputs are available, they should be used instead. A Level 1 input is available ie the quoted share price of Bates. Paragraph 69 of IFRS 13 requires a premium or discount to be considered when measuring fair value when it is a characteristic of the asset that market participants would take into account in a transaction. Therefore, the premium attributable to significant influence should be taken into account and this adjusted share price used as fair value (rather than the earnings multiple or option pricing model).

Costs of disposal will be fairly easy to estimate. Accordingly, **it should be possible to arrive at a figure for fair value less costs of disposal**.

(ii)   **Value in use**

IAS 36 states that the value in use of an asset is measured as the present value of estimated future cash flows (inflows minus outflows) generated by the asset, including its estimated net disposal value (if any). IAS 28 *Investments in associates and joint ventures* gives some more specific guidance on investments where there is significant influence. In determining the value in use of these investments an entity should estimate:

(1)   Its share of the present value of the estimated future cash flows expected to be generated by the associate (including disposal proceeds)

(2)   The present value of future cash flows expected to arise from dividends to be received from the investment.

Cate has not produced any cash flow estimates, but it could, and should do so.

Conclusion

Cate is able to produce figures for fair value less cost to sell and for value in use, and it should do so. If the carrying amount exceeds the higher of these two, then the **asset is impaired** and must be written down to its recoverable amount.

(c)   **IFRS 5 and investment in Date**

IFRS 10 *Consolidated financial statements* views a **group as an economic entity**. This means that it treats all providers of equity as shareholders in the group, even if they are not shareholders of the parent company. To be consistent with this, IFRS 5 *Non-current assets held for sale and discontinued operations* was amended: if a parent intends to dispose of a controlling interest in a subsidiary which meets the definition of 'held for sale', then the net assets are classified as 'held for sale', even if the parent retains an interest. Where there is a partial disposal, from subsidiary (control) to an associate (significant influence) or an investment in equity instruments (no significant influence), a gain arises on the both the part disposed of and the interest retained.

IFRS 5 *Non-current assets held for sale and discontinued operations* requires an asset or disposal group to be classified as held for sale where it is **available for immediate sale** in its **present condition** subject only to **terms that are usual** and customary and the sale is **highly probable**. For a sale to be highly probable:

*   Management must be **committed** to the sale.
*   An **active programme to locate a buyer** must have been initiated.
*   The **market price** must be **reasonable** in relation to the asset's current fair value.
*   The sale must be **expected to be completed within one year** from the date of classification.

While Date does not meet all the IFRS 5 criteria, it could still be argued that **Cate's presentation is correct** because:

(i)   The issue of new shares to a new investor has **reduced Cate's holding** from 75% to 35%.

(ii)   Cate **has agreed to this reduction** and decided not to subscribe to the issue of new shares, and to step down from the management of Date. This represents a change of strategy with regard to its investment.

(iii)   The effect of (i) and (ii) is **equivalent to the sale of a controlling interest** and the retention of an investment that does not give control.

(iv)   Date represents **a separate line of business** and information disclosed in accordance with IFRS 5 highlights the impact of Date on Cate's financial statements.

(v)   IFRS 5 does not address the issue of dilution of control (a 'deemed disposal'). In the absence of direct guidance, IAS 8 *Accounting policies, changes in accounting estimates and errors* requires management **to use judgement** and apply other IFRSs and the *Conceptual Framework.*

In conclusion, while there is no specific guidance for this situation, the **principles of relevant standards are consistent with Cate's presentation.** The events should be treated as a partial disposal. Cate should **stop consolidating Date on a line-by-line basis f**rom the date that control was lost. The remaining holding should be treated as an **investment in equity instruments** (trade investment) rather than an associate, because although Cate has a holding of 35%, it no longer has significant influence over Date.

(d)   **'Voluntary' post-retirement benefit plan**

Cate emphasises that the fund to provide post-retirement benefits is voluntary, and perhaps wishes to avoid accounting for the liability. However, there is evidence that in fact the **scheme should be accounted for as a defined benefit plan:**

(i)   While the plan is voluntary, IAS 19 *Employee benefits* says that an entity must account for **constructive as well as legal obligations**. These may arise from informal practices, where an entity has no realistic alternative but to pay employee benefits, because employees have a valid expectation that they will be paid.

(ii)   The plan is **not a defined contribution plan**, because if the fund does not have sufficient assets to pay employee benefits relating to service in the current or prior periods, Cate has a legal or constructive obligation to make good the deficit by paying further contributions.

(iii)   The post-retirement benefit is based on final salaries and years of service. In other words it is **not linked solely to the amount that Cate agrees to contribute** to the fund. This is what 'defined benefit' means.

(iv)   Should Cate decide to terminate its contributions to the plan, it **is contractually obliged to discharge the liability** created by the plan by purchasing lifetime annuities from an insurance company.

Cate must account for the scheme as a defined benefit plan and recognise, as a minimum, its net present obligation for the benefits to be paid.

36 Calcula

Text reference

The concept of integrated reporting is covered in Chapter 5 of your BPP Study Text.

Top tips

Part (a): A good technique to answering part (a) was to consider the key differences between integrated reporting and traditional approaches to reporting performance. Remember the aim of integrated reporting is to show users how the company has created value using the resources at its disposal. By contrast traditional methods of reporting performance are focused on financial metrics such as profitability. Part (b): The second requirement builds upon part (a). Part (a) requires you to illustrate that you understand the theory of integrated reporting in general. There were easy marks going for this part of the question provided you had read Chapter 5 of your BPP Study Text which explores the role of integrated reporting. Part (b) required the application of these points to the scenario, with particular emphasis on how integrated reporting could help Calcula improve its strategic performance.

To score well on this requirement it is critical that your answer is related to Calcula. The scenario is provided to give you the opportunity to show two things. Firstly, that you understand the theory – ie what integrated reporting is – and secondly, for you to show that can apply your knowledge. A good approach to dealing with such questions is to set the scene by identifying what has gone wrong in the scenario. In this case stakeholders (shareholders and employees) are confused as to the strategic direction that Calcula is trying to pursue.

Next, use your knowledge to explain how integrated reporting can help Calcula to communicate its strategy. Integrated reporting places a strong emphasis on relaying what the company stands for through setting out its objectives and strategy to realise these. The introduction of integrated reporting would therefore provide the company with a great opportunity to convey Asha Alexander's new mission.

BPP
LEARNING MEDIA

Easy marks: Three marks were available for incorporating a discussion of the finance director's views. Failure to comment on a particular matter when a question directs you – in this case, making reference to the finance director's statement – loses you easy marks.

Part (c): Was a fairly straightforward requirement. Provided you were able to generate a range of practical implications you should have picked up the 5 easy marks on offer.

Marking scheme

	Marks
Part a:	
Integrated reporting:	
Up to 2 marks for a discussion of how integrated reporting allows for a wider performance appraisal	2
Up to 3 marks for a discussion of value creation	3
Up to 2 marks for a discussion on how short term decisions have long term Implications	2
Up to 2 marks for a discussion of monetary values and the use of KPIs in integrated reporting	2
1 mark for a discussion of materiality	1
	10
Part b:	
1 mark for explaining the current stakeholder confusion at Calcula	1
Up to 3 marks for a discussing how integrated reporting may help communicate Strategy	3
Up to 3 marks for a discussion on how integrated reporting may improve Calcula's Performance	3
Up to 3 marks for a discussion of the finance director's comments	3
	10
Part c:	
1 mark per implication raised related to Calcula	5
	25

(a)   **Integrated reporting**

Wider performance appraisal

Integrated reporting is concerned with conveying a wider message on an entity's performance. It is not solely centred on profit and the company's financial position but aims to focus on how the organisations activities interact to create value over the short, medium and long term. It is thought that by producing a holistic view of organisational performance that this will lead to improved management decision making as business decisions are not taken in isolation.

Value creation

In the context of integrated reporting an organisation's resources are referred to as 'capitals'. The International Integrated Reporting Council have identified six capitals which can be used to assess value creation. Increases or decreases in these capitals indicate the level of value created or lost over a period. Capitals cover various types of resources found in a standard organisation. These may include financial capitals, such as the entity's financial reserves, through to its intellectual capital which is concerned with intellectual property and staff knowledge.

Performance evaluation of the six capitals is central to integrated reporting. Throughout time these capitals continually interact with one another, an increase in one may lead to a decrease in another. A decision to purchase a new IT system would improve an entity's 'manufactured' capital while decreasing its financial capital. By contrast the decision to purchase a patent for a new production technology would increase intellectual capital and may also boost financial capital if it reduces costs and increases output. It is important to note that due to the voluntary nature of integrated reporting, organisations are free to report only on those 'capitals' felt to be most relevant.

Short term v long term

In many ways, integrated reporting forces management to balance its short term objectives against its longer term plans. Business decisions which are solely dedicated to the pursuit of increasing profit (financial capital) at the expense of building good relations with key stakeholders such as customers (social capital) are likely to hinder value creation in the longer term.

Performance measures

Integrated reporting is not aimed at attaching a monetary value to every aspect of the organisation's operations. It is fundamentally concerned with evaluating value creation, and uses qualitative and quantitative performance measures to help stakeholders assess how well an organisation is creating value.

The use of KPIs to convey performance is an effective way of reporting. For example when providing detail on customer satisfaction, this can be communicated as the number of customers retained compared to the previous year. Best practice in integrated reporting requires organisations to report on both positive and negative movements in 'capital'. This ensures the entity's performance is fully communicated and not just those favourable movements. Stakeholders are likely to be as interested (if not more so) in understanding what an organisation has not done well as opposed to only considering the entity's achievements. Integrated reporting ensures that a balanced view of performance is presented.

Materiality

When preparing an integrated report, management should disclose matters which are likely to impact on an organisation's ability to create value. Internal weaknesses and external threats regarded as being materially important are evaluated and quantified. This provides users with an indication of how management intend to combat such instances should they materialise.

(b) **Integrated reporting at Calcula**

Confusion

As a result of the recent management changes at Calcula, the company has struggled to communicate its 'strategic direction' to key stakeholders. The company's annual accounts have made it hard for shareholders to understand Calcula's strategy which in turn has led to confusion. Uncertainty among shareholders and employees is likely to increase the risk of investors selling their shares and talented IT developers seeking employment with competitors.

Communicating strategy

The introduction of integrated reporting may help Calcula to overcome these issues as it places a strong focus on the organisation's future orientation. An integrated report should detail the company's mission and values, the nature of its operations, along with features on how it differentiates itself from its competitors.

Including Calcula's new mission to become the market leader in the specialist accountancy software industry would instantly convey what the organisation stands for.

In line with best practice in integrated reporting, Calcula could supplement its mission with how the board intend to achieve this strategy. Such detail could focus on resource allocations over the short to medium term. For example, plans to improve the company's human capital through hiring innovative software developers working at competing firms would help to support the company's long term mission. To assist users in appraising the company's performance, Calcula should provide details on how it will measure value creation in each 'capital'. 'Human capital' could be measured by the net movement in new joiners to the organisation compared to the previous year.

A key feature of integrated reporting focuses on the need for organisations to use non-financial customer-oriented performance measures (KPI's) to help communicate the entity's strategy. The most successful companies in Calcula's industry are committed to enhancing their offering to customers through producing innovative products. Calcula could report through the use of KPI's how it is delivering on this objective, measures could be set which for example measure the number of new software programs developed in the last two years or report on the number of customer complaints concerning newly released software programs over the period.

Improving long term performance

The introduction of integrated reporting may also help Calcula to enhance its performance. Historically, the company has not given consideration to how decisions in one area have impacted on other areas. This is clearly indicated by former CEO's cost cutting programme which served to reduce the staff training budget. Although, this move may have enhanced the company's short term profitability, boosting financial capital, it has damaged long term value creation.

The nature of the software industry requires successful organisations to invest in staff training to ensure that the products they develop remain innovative in order to attract customers. The decision to reduce the training budget will most likely impact on future profitability if Calcula is unable to produce software customers' demand.

Finance director's comments

As illustrated in the scenario, the finance director's comments indicate a very narrow understanding of how the company's activities and 'capitals' interact with each other in delivering value. To dismiss developments in integrated reporting as simply being a 'fad', suggest that the finance director is unaware of the commitment of ACCA in promoting its introduction. The ACCA's support for integrated reporting may lead to backing from other global accountancy bodies thereby reducing the scope for it be regarded as a passing 'fad'.

However, some critics refute this and argue that the voluntary nature of integrated reporting increases the likelihood that companies will choose not to pursue its adoption. Such individuals highlight that until companies are legally required to comply with integrated reporting guidelines, many will simply regard it as an unnecessary effort and cost.

The finance director's assertion regarding shareholders is likely to some degree to be correct. Investors looking for short term results from an investment might assess Calcula's performance based on improvements in profitability. However, many shareholders will also be interested in how the board propose to create value in the future. Ultimately, Calcula's aim to appease both groups is its focus on maximising shareholder value, the achievement of which requires the successful implementation of both short and long term strategies.

Furthermore, unlike traditional annual accounts, integrated reports highlight the importance of considering a wider range of users. Key stakeholder groups such as Calcula's customers and suppliers are likely to be interested in assessing how the company has met or not met their needs beyond the 'bottom line'. Integrated reporting encourages companies to report performance measures which are closely aligned to the concepts of sustainability and corporate social responsibility. This is implied by the different capitals used: consideration of social relationships and natural capitals do not focus on financial performance but instead are concerned, for example, with the impact an organisation's activities have on the natural environment.

Ultimately as integrated reporting provides senior management with a greater quantity of organisational performance data this should help in identifying previously unrecognised areas which are in need of improvement.

Clearly, a major downside to generating extensive additional data concerns determining which areas to report on. This is made especially difficult as there is no recognised criteria for determining the level of importance of each 'capital'. As we shall explore in part (c), the finance director's remark regarding the increase in the Calcula's workload to comply with integrated reporting practices may have some merit.

It is debatable as to whether the production of an integrated report necessarily leads to an improvement in organisational performance or whether it simply leads to an improvement in the reporting of performance. However, focusing management's attention on the non-financial aspects of Calcula's performance as well as its purely financial performance, could be expected to lead to performance improvements in those areas. For example, if innovation is highlighted as a key factor in sustaining Calcula's long term value, a focus on innovation could help to encourage innovation within the company.

(c) **Implications of implementing integrated reporting**

IT and IS costs

The introduction of integrated reporting at Calcula will most likely require significant upgrades to be made to the company's IT and information system infrastructure. Such developments will be needed to assist Calcula in capturing both financial and non-financial KPI data. Due to the broad range of business activities reported on using integrated reporting (customer, finance and human resources) the associated costs in improving the infrastructure to deliver relevant data about each area is likely to be significant. It may, however, be the case that Calcula's existing information systems are already capable of producing the required non-financial performance data needed in which case it is likely that the focus here will be on investigating which data sets should be included in the integrated report.

Time implications

The process of gathering and collating the data to include in an integrated report is likely to require a significant amount of staff time. This may serve to decrease staff morale especially if staff are expected to undertake this work in addition to completing existing duties. In some cases this may require Calcula to pay employees overtime to ensure all required information is published in the report on time.

Staff costs

To avoid overburdening existing staff the board may decide to appoint additional staff to undertake the work of analysing data for inclusion in the integrated report. This will invariably lead to an increase in staff costs.

Consultancy costs

As this will be Calcula's first integrated report the board may seek external guidance from an organisation which provides specialist consultancy on reporting. Any advice is likely to focus on the contents of the report. The consultant's fees are likely to be significant and will increase the associated implementation costs of introducing integrated reporting.

Disclosure

A potential downside of adopting integrated reporting centres on Calcula potentially volunteering more information about its operations than was actually needed. In the event that Calcula fully disclosed the company's planned strategies it is likely that this could be used by competitors. Such a move is likely to undermine any future moves to out-manoeuvre other industry players. In the event that Calcula have hired an external consultant to support the introduction of integrated reporting it is likely that the advice given by the consultant will stress the need to avoid disclosure of commercially sensitive information.

37 Egin Group

Text reference. Related parties are covered in Chapter 10 of the text.

Top tips. This question dealt with the importance of the disclosure of related party transactions and the criteria determining a related party. Additionally, it required candidates to identify related parties, and to account for goodwill and a loan made to one of the related parties which was a foreign subsidiary. Don't forget, from your group accounting knowledge, that goodwill relating to the foreign subsidiary is treated as a foreign currency asset and translated at the closing rate of exchange.

Easy marks. Part (a) should earn you five very easy marks, as it is basic knowledge. Part (b) is application, but very straightforward. This leaves only nine marks for the more difficult aspects.

Examiner's comment. The importance of related parties and their criteria was quite well answered, although candidates often quoted specific examples rather than the criteria for establishing related parties. The identification of related party relationships was well answered, but the accounting for the goodwill of the foreign subsidiary (and the loan made to it) were poorly answered.

			Marks
(a)	(i)	Reasons and explanation	5
	(ii)	Egin	5
		Spade	3
		Atomic	3
(b)		Goodwill	5
		Loan	5
		Available	26
		Maximum	25

(a) (i) **Why it is important to disclose related party transactions**

The directors of Egin are correct to say that related party transactions are a normal feature of business. However, where entities are members of the same group, for example parent and subsidiary, the **financial performance and position of both entities can be affected**. An obvious instance of this is where one group company sells goods to another at artificially low prices. Even where there are no actual transactions between group companies, **a parent normally influences the way in which a subsidiary operates**. For example, a parent may instruct a subsidiary not to trade with particular customers or suppliers or not to undertake particular activities. In the absence of other information, users of the financial statements **assume that a company pursues its interests independently** and undertakes transactions on an **arm's length basis** on terms that could have been obtained in a transaction with a third party. Knowledge of related party relationships and transactions affects the way in which users assess a company's operations and the risks and opportunities that it faces. Therefore **details of an entity's controlling party and transactions with related parties should be disclosed**. Even if the company's transactions and operations have not been affected by a related party relationship, **disclosure puts users on notice that they may be affected in future**.

Under IAS 24 *Related party disclosures* a related party is a person or entity that is related to the entity that is preparing its financial statements (the 'reporting entity').

Persons

IAS 24 states that a person or a close member of that person's family is related to a reporting entity if that person:

(1) Has **control** or **joint control** over the reporting entity;

(2) Has **significant influence** over the reporting entity; or

(3) Is a member of the **key management personnel** of the reporting entity or of a parent of the reporting entity.

Entities

An entity is related to a reporting entity if any of the following conditions applies:

(1) The entity and the reporting entity are **members of the same group** (which means that each parent, subsidiary and fellow subsidiary is related to the others).

(2) One entity is an **associate* or joint venture*** of the other entity (or an associate or joint venture of a member of a group of which the other entity is a member).

(3) Both entities are **joint ventures* of the same third party**.

(4) One entity is a **joint venture* of a third entity** and the other entity is an **associate of the third entity**.

(5)   The entity is a **post-employment benefit plan** for the benefit of employees of either the reporting entity or an entity related to the reporting entity.

(6)   The entity is **controlled** or **jointly controlled** by a person identified in the definition above.

(7)   A person identified above as having control or joint control over the reporting entity has **significant influence** over the entity or is a member of the **key management personnel** of the entity (or of a parent of the entity).

*Including subsidiaries of the associate or joint venture.

(ii)   **Nature of related party relationships**

Within the Egin Group

Briars and Doye are related parties of Egin because they are **members of the same group** (both subsidiaries of Egin). For the same reason, as fellow subsidiaries, **Briars and Doye** are also **related parties of each other. Eye is also a related party of Egin** because it is an **associate of Egin.** (Egin has **significant influence** over Eye.)

Briars and Doye may be related parties of Eye. There is only one director in common and IAS 24 states that entities are not necessarily related simply because they have a director (or other member of key management personnel) in common, or because a member of key management personnel of one entity has significant influence over the other entity. However, **Eye is an associate of Egin**, and therefore **a member of the group** that Briars and Doye are members of (see (2) under 'Entities' above).

Although Tang was sold several months before the year end it was a **related party of Egin, Briars and Doye until then**. Therefore the related party relationship between Tang and the Egin group **should be disclosed** even though there were no transactions between them during the period.

Blue is a related party of Briars as a **director of Briars controls it.** Because the director is not on the management board of Egin it is **not clear whether Blue is also a related party of Egin group**. This would depend on whether the director is considered key management personnel at a group level. The director's services as a consultant to the group may mean that a related party relationship exists. The issue would depend on whether this role meant that this person was directing or controlling a major part of the group's activities and resources.

Between Spade and the Egin Group

Spade is a related party of Doye because it exertss **significant influence** over Doye. This means that the **sale** of plant and equipment **to Spade must be disclosed. Egin is not necessarily a related party of Spade** simply because both have an investment in Doye. A related party relationship will only exist if one party **exercises influence** over another **in practice**.

The directors have proposed that disclosures should state that prices charged to related parties are set on an **arm's length basis**. Because the transaction took place **between related parties** by definition it **cannot have taken place on an arm's length basis** and this description would be **misleading**. Doye sold plant and equipment to Spade at **normal selling prices** and this is the information that should be disclosed, provided the terms can be substantiated.

Between Atomic and the Egin Group

Atomic is a related party of Egin because it can exercise **significant influence** over it. Atomic's significant influence over Egin gives it **significant influence over Briars and Doye** as they are controlled by Egin. **Eye is not a related party of Atomic** as atomic has no ability to exercise control or significant influence over Eye

(b)   **Goodwill arising on the acquisition of Briars**

IAS 21 *The effect of changes in foreign exchange rates* states that goodwill arising on the acquisition of a foreign subsidiary should be expressed in the functional currency of the foreign operation and **retranslated at the closing rate at each year-end**. Goodwill is calculated and translated as follows:

	Euros m	Rate	$m
Consideration transferred	50		25.0
Non-controlling interests (45 × 20%)	9	2	4.5
Less fair value of identifiable net assets at acquisition	(45)		(22.5)
Goodwill at acquisition	14		7.0
Impairment	(3)	2.5	(1.2)
Exchange loss (balancing figure)			(1.4)
At 31 May 20X6	11	2.5	4.4

Goodwill is measured at **$4.4 million** in the statement of financial position. An impairment loss of **$1.2 million** is **recognised in profit or loss** and an **exchange loss of $1.4 million** is **recognised in other comprehensive income (items that may subsequently be reclassified to profit or loss,** and taken to the translation reserve in equity.

Loan to Briars

The loan is a **financial liability measured at amortised cost**. The loan is measured at **fair value** on initial recognition. Fair value **the price that would be received to sell an asset or paid to transfer a liability in an orderly transaction between market participants at the measurement date**. This would normally be the actual transaction price. However, Egin and Briars are **related parties** and the transaction **has not taken place on normal commercial terms**.

IFRS 9 states that it is necessary to **establish what the transaction price would have been** in an orderly transaction between market participants at the measurement date. The amount that will eventually be repaid to Egin is $10 million and the normal commercial rate of interest is 6%. Therefore the fair value of the loan is its **discounted present value**, which is **retranslated at the closing rate** at each year-end.

Therefore the loan is measured at the following amounts in the statement of financial position:

	$'000	Rate	Euros 000
At 1/6/20X5 ($10 \times \dfrac{1}{1.06^2}$)	8,900	2	17,800
Interest (unwinding of discount) (8,900 × 6%)	534	2.3	1,228
Exchange loss			4,557
At 31/5/20X6 ($10 \times \dfrac{1}{1.06}$)	9,434	2.5	23,585

The **unwinding of the discount** is recognised as a **finance cost** in profit or loss for the year and the **exchange loss** is also **recognised in profit or loss**.

Note. It would also be possible to calculate the finance cost for the year ended 31 May 20X6 at the closing rate. This would increase the exchange loss and the total expense recognised in profit and loss would be the same.

38 Marrgrett

Text reference. These topics are covered in Chapter 12 of the BPP Study Text, apart from disposals, which is covered in Chapter 14.

Top tips. This question required a discussion of the impact of the revisions to IFRS 3 *Business combinations* on various aspects of group accounting. These topics are covered in the BPP Study Text, but unless you were very familiar with the changes from old to new, you would not have been advised to attempt this question. That said, it was not technically demanding. Note that since this question was set there have been further revisions to group accounting, covered where relevant elsewhere in this kit.

Easy marks. There are no marks that are easier to gain than others – either you know the subject or you don't!

Examiner's comment. Answers were generally quite good but the main issue was that candidates found it difficult to assimilate relevant information.. Particular issues included failing to recognise that the existing 30% interest in the associate should be fair valued when control of the subsidiary is gained, also dealing with the payments to the subsidiary's directors created a problem and a minority of candidates stated that the full goodwill method was mandatory.

	Marks
Consideration	6
IFRS 3 and consideration	5
Consideration	2
Intangible assets	2
NCI	5
Finalisation and reorganisation provision	2
IFRS 10	3
Professional marks	2
Available	25

Revision of IFRS 3 Business combinations

IFRS 3 Business combinations was extensively revised, and the revised standard issued in 2008. The revised IFRS 3 views **the group as an economic entity.** This means that it treats all providers of equity – including non-controlling interests – as shareholders in the group, even if they are not shareholders of the parent.

All business combinations are accounted for as **acquisitions**. The revisions to IFRS 3 affect both the consideration, and the business acquired. Specifically, **all consideration is now measured at fair value,** and there are implications for the valuation of the non-controlling interest.

Marrgrett is proposing to purchase additional shares in its associate, Josey. An increase from 30% to 70% will **give control,** as the holding passes the all-important 50% threshold. The changes to IFRS 3 have far-reaching implications for various aspects of the acquisition, which is what the standard calls a 'business combination achieved in stages'.

Equity interest already held

Consideration includes cash, assets, contingent consideration, equity instruments, options and warrants. It also includes the **fair value of any equity interest already held**, which marks a departure from the previous version of IFRS 3. This means that **the 30% holding must be re-measured to fair value** at the date of the acquisition of the further 40% holding. The revalued 30% stake, together with the consideration transferred in the form of cash and shares, is compared to the fair value of Josey's net assets at the date control was obtained, in order to arrive at a figure for goodwill.

Any **gain or loss** on the revaluation of the associate is taken to **profit or loss for the year**.

Transaction costs

The original IFRS 3 required fees (legal, accounting, valuation etc) paid in relation to a business acquisition to be included in the cost of the acquisition, which meant that they were measured as part of goodwill.

Under the revised IFRS 3 **costs relating to the acquisition must be recognised as an expense** at the time of the acquisition. They are not regarded as an asset. (Costs of issuing debt or equity are to be accounted for under the rules of IFRS 9.)

Share options

As an incentive to the shareholders and employees of Josey to remain in the business, Marrgrett has offered share options in Josey. These are conditional on them remaining in employment for two years after the acquisition, that is they are contingent on future events. The question arises of whether they are **contingent consideration**, for which the treatment is specified in the revised IFRS 3, **or as compensation** for services after the acquisition, for which the treatment is given in IFRS 2 Share-based payment.

The conditions attached to the share options are employment based, rather than contingent on, say, the performance of the company. Accordingly the options must be treated as **compensation and valued under the rules of IFRS 2. The charge will be to post-acquisition earnings**, since the options are given in exchange for services after the acquisition.

Contingent consideration

The additional shares being offered to Josey's shareholders to the value of $50,000 are contingent on the achievement of a certain level of profitability. These are contingent consideration, defined in IFRS 3 as:

> Usually, an obligation of the acquirer to transfer additional assets or equity interests to the former owners of an acquiree as part of the exchange for control of the acquiree if specified future events occur or conditions are met.

The original IFRS 3 required contingent consideration to be accounted for **only if it was probable that it would become payable** and could be measured reliably. Subsequent changes in the amount of the contingent consideration were accounted for as adjustments to the cost of the business combination, and therefore generally as changes to goodwill.

However, the revised IFRS 3 recognises that, by entering into an acquisition, the acquirer becomes obliged to make additional payments. Not recognising that obligation means that the consideration recognised at the acquisition date is not fairly stated. Accordingly, the revised IFRS 3 **requires recognition of contingent consideration, measured at fair value, at the acquisition date**.

The shares worth up to $50,000 meet the IAS 32 *Financial instruments: presentation* definition of a financial liability. This contingent consideration will be **measured at fair value,** and any **changes** to the fair value on subsequent re-measurement will be taken to **profit or loss for the year**.

Intangible assets

Josey's intangible assets, which include trade names, internet domain names and non-competition agreements, will be **recognised on acquisition** by Marrgrett of a controlling stake. IFRS 3 revised gives more detailed guidance on intangible assets than did the previous version; as a result, more intangibles may be recognised than was formerly the case. The more intangibles are recognised, the lower the figure for goodwill, which is consideration transferred less fair value of assets acquired and liabilities assumed.

Non-controlling interest

As indicated above, the revised IFRS views the group as an economic entity and so non-controlling shareholders are also shareholders in the group. This means that goodwill attributable to the non-controlling interest needs to be recognised.

The non-controlling interest now forms part of the calculation of goodwill. The question now arises as to how it should be valued.

The 'economic entity' principle suggests that the non-controlling interest should be valued at fair value. In fact, IFRS 3 gives a **choice**:

> For each business combination, the acquirer shall measure any non-controlling interest in the acquiree **either at fair value or at the non-controlling interest's proportionate share of the acquiree's identifiable net assets**. *(IFRS 3)*

IFRS 3 revised suggests that the closest approximation to fair value will be the market price of the shares held by the non-controlling shareholders just before the acquisition by the parent.

Non-controlling interest at fair value will be different from non-controlling interest at proportionate share of the acquiree's net assets. The difference is goodwill attributable to non-controlling interest, which may be, but often is not, proportionate to goodwill attributable to the parent.

Effect of type of consideration

The nature of the consideration transferred – cash, shares, contingent, and so on – **does not affect the goodwill**. However, the structure of the payments may affect post-acquisition profits. For example if part of the consideration is contingent (as here), changes to the fair value will be reflected in profit or loss for the year in future years.

Partial disposal

Under the revised IFRS 3, the treatment of a partial disposal depends on whether or not control is retained. Generally, control is lost when the holding is decreased to less than 50%.

On disposal of a controlling interest, any retained interest (an associate or trade investment) is measured at fair value on the date that control is lost. This fair value is used in the calculation of the gain or loss on disposal, and also becomes the carrying amount for subsequent accounting for the retained interest.

If the 50% boundary is not crossed, as when the interest in a subsidiary is reduced, the event is treated as a transaction between owners.

Whenever the 50% boundary is crossed, the existing interest is revalued, and a gain or loss is reported in profit or loss for the year. If the 50% boundary is not crossed, no gain or loss is reported; instead there is an adjustment to the parent's equity.

Margrett intends to retain control of the first subsidiary, so in this case there will be no gain or loss, but an adjustment to the Margrett's equity to reflect the increase in non-controlling interest. In the case of the second subsidiary, however, control is lost. A gain will be recognised on the portion sold, and also on the portion retained, being the difference between the fair value and the book value of the interest retained.

Re-organisation provision

IFRS 10 *Consolidated financial statements* explains that a plan to restructure a subsidiary following an acquisition is not a present obligation of the acquiree at the acquisition date, unless it meets the criteria in IAS 37 *Provisions, contingent liabilities and contingent assets*. This is very unlikely to be the case at the acquisition date. Therefore Margrett should not recognise a liability for the re-organisation of the group at the date of the acquisition.

This prevents creative accounting. An acquirer cannot set up a provision for restructuring or future losses of a subsidiary and then release this to profit or loss in subsequent periods in order to reduce losses or smooth profits.

39 Preparation question: Associate

J GROUP CONSOLIDATED STATEMENT OF FINANCIAL POSITION AS AT 31 DECEMBER 20X5

Assets	$'000
Non-current assets	
Freehold property (1,950 + 1,250 + 370 (W7))	3,570
Plant and equipment (795 + 375)	1,170
Investment in associate (W3)	480
	5,220
Current assets	
Inventories (575 + 300 – 20 (W6))	855
Trade receivables (330 + 290))	620
Cash at bank and in hand (50 + 120)	170
	1,645
	6,865

	$'000
Equity and liabilities	
Equity attributable to owners of the parent	
Issued share capital	2,000
Retained earnings	1,785
	3,785
Non-controlling interests (W5)	890
Total equity	4,675
Non-current liabilities	
12% debentures (500 + 100)	600
Current liabilities	
Bank overdraft	560
Trade payables (680 + 350)	1,030
	1,590
Total liabilities	2,190
	6,865

Workings

1   *Group structure*

```
                              J
         600/1,000   60%   /     \   30%   225/750
                        /         \
                      P             S
       Pre acquisition
          profits     $200k              $150k
```

2   Goodwill

	$'000	$'000
Consideration transferred		1,000
NCI (at 'full' FV: 400 × $1.65)		660
Net assets acquired:		
Share capital	1,000	
Retained earnings at acquisition	200	
Fair value adjustment (W7)	400	
		(1,600)
		60
Impairments to date		(60)
Year-end value		–

3   *Investment in associate*

	$'000
Cost of associate	500.0
Share of post acquisition retained reserves (W4)	72.0
Less impairment of investment in associate	(92.0)
	480.0

4   *Retained earnings*

	J Co $'000	P Co $'000	S Co $'000
Retained earnings per question	1,460	885	390
Unrealised profit (W6)		(20)	
Fair value adjustment movement (W6)		(30)	
Retained earnings at acquisition		(200)	(150)
		635	240
P Co: share of post acquisition retained earnings 60% × 635	381		
S Co: share of post acquisition retained earnings 30% × 240	72		
Goodwill impairments to date			
P Co: 60 (W2) × 60%	(36)		
S Co	(92)		
	1,785		

5   *Non-controlling interests*

	$'000
NCI at acquisition (W2)	660
NCI share of post acq'n ret'd earnings ((W4) 635 × 40%)	254
NCI share of impairment losses ((W2) 60 × 40%)	(24)
	890

6   *Unrealised profit on inventories*

P Co ⟶ J Co $100k × 25/125 = $20,000

7   Fair value adjustment table

	At acquisition $'000	Movement $'000	At reporting date $'000
Land	200		200
Buildings	200	(30)	170 (200 × 34/40)
	400	(30)	370

40 Preparation question: 'D'-shaped group

(a)   BAUBLE GROUP
CONSOLIDATED STATEMENT OF FINANCIAL POSITION AS AT 31 DECEMBER 20X9

	$'000
Non-current assets	
Property, plant and equipment (720 + 60 + 70)	850
Goodwill (W2)	111
	961
Current assets (175 + 95 + 90)	360
	1,321
Equity attributable to owners of the parent	
Share capital – $1 ordinary shares	400
Retained earnings (W3)	600
	1,000
Non-controlling interest (W4)	91
	1,091
Current liabilities (120 + 65 + 45)	230
	1,321

Workings

1   *Group Structure*

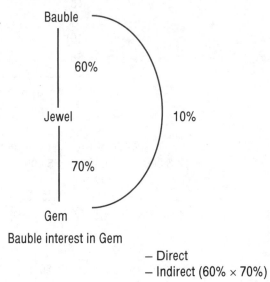

Bauble interest in Gem

– Direct	10%
– Indirect (60% × 70%)	42%
	52%
Non-controlling interest in Gem	48%

2 Goodwill

	Jewel		Gem	
	$'000	$'000	$'000	$'000
Consideration transferred: Bauble		142		43.0
Consideration transferred: Jewel			(100 × 60%)	60.0
NCI	(145 × 40%)	58	(90 × 48%)	43.2
Net assets at acq'n as represented by:				
Share capital	100		50	
Ret'd earnings	45		40	
		(145)		(90.0)
Goodwill		55		56.2

Total goodwill = $111,200

3 Consolidated retained earnings

	B	J	G
	$'000	$'000	$'000
Per Q	560	90	65
Less: pre-acquisition ret'd earnings		(45)	(40)
		45	25
J – share of post acquisition ret'd earnings (45 × 60%)	27		
G – share of post acquisition ret'd earnings (25 × 52%)	13		
	600		

4 Non-controlling interests

	Jewel	Gem
	$'000	$'000
NCI at acquisition (W2)	58	43.2
NCI share of post acquisition retained earnings:		
Jewel ((W3) 45 × 40%)	18	
Gem ((W3) 25 × 48%)		12
NCI in investment in Gem (100 × 40%)	(40)	
	36	55.2

91.2

(b) **Goodwill**

	Jewel		Gem	
	$'000	$'000	$'000	$'000
Consideration transferred: Bauble		142		43.0
Consideration transferred: Jewel			(100 × 60%)	60.0
NCI	(160 × 40%)	64	(90 × 48%)	43.2
Net assets at acq'n as represented by:				
Share capital	100		50	
Ret'd earnings	60		40	
		(160)		(90)
Goodwill		46		56.2

102.2

41 Preparation question: Sub-subsidiary

Text reference. Complex groups are covered in Chapter 13.

Top tips. This question is quite straightforward as long as you remember how to calculate the NCI of a sub-subsidiary. Points to watch in this question are the treatment of intragroup transactions and the calculation of non-controlling interest.

Easy marks. With complex groups, remember to sort out the group structure first. There are enough straightforward marks available here if you remember your basic rules for consolidations. The consolidation is quite straightforward as long as you remember how to calculate the NCI of a sub-subsidiary.

(a)   EXOTIC GROUP
        CONSOLIDATED STATEMENT OF PROFIT OR LOSS AND OTHER COMPREHENSIVE INCOME
        FOR THE YEAR ENDED 31 DECEMBER 20X9

	$'000
Revenue: 45,600 + 24,700 + 22,800 – (W6) 740	92,360
Cost of sales: 18,050 + 5,463 + 5,320 – (W6) 740+ (W6) 15 + (W6) 15(W6)	(28,123)
Gross profit	64,237
Distribution costs (3,325 + 2,137 + 1,900)	(7,362)
Administrative expenses (3,475 + 950 + 1,900)	(6,325)
Finance costs	(325)
Profit before tax	50,225
Income tax expense (8,300 + 5,390 + 4,241)	(17,931)
Profit for the year	32,294

Other comprehensive income for the year (items that will not be reclassified to P/L)	
Revaluation of property (200 + 100)	300
Total comprehensive income	32,594

Profit attributable to:	
Owners of the parent	28,581
Non-controlling interest (W4)	3,713
	32,294

Total comprehensive income attributable to:	
Owners of the parent	28,871
Non-controlling interest (W4)	3723
	32,594

(b)   EXOTIC GROUP
        CONSOLIDATED STATEMENT OF FINANCIAL POSITION AS AT 31 DECEMBER 20X9

	$'000
Non-current assets	
Property, plant and equipment: 35,483 + 24,273 + 13,063 + (W7) 575	73,394
Goodwill (W2)	3,520
	76,914
Current assets :1,568 + 9,025 + 8,883 – (W6) 15 – (W6) 15	19,446
	96,360
Equity attributable to owners of the parent	
Share capital	8,000
Retained earnings (W3)	56,642
	64,642
Non-controlling interest (W4)	8,584
	73,226
Current liabilities (13,063 + 10,023 + 48)	23,134
	96,360

Workings

1   Group structure

Exotic
| 90%
Melon
| 80%
Kiwi   Effective interest (90% × 80%)   72%
              ∴ Non-controlling interest   28%
                                                 100%

2   Goodwill

	Melon	Kiwi	
	$000	$000	$000
Consideration transferred	6,650	3,800 × 90%	3,420
Non-controlling interests (at 'full' fair value)	500		900
FV of identifiable net assets at acq'n:			
Per qu/ 2,000 (SC) + 950 (RE)	(5,000)		(2,950)
	2,150		1,370

3,520

3   Retained earnings

	Exotic	Melon	Kiwi
	$'000	$'000	$'000
Retained earnings per question	22,638	24,075	19,898
Less: PUP (W6)		(15)	(15)
Pre-acquisition retained earnings		(1,425)	(950)
		22,635	18,933
Share of Melon (22,635 × 90%)	20,372		
Share of Kiwi (18,933 × (W1) 72%)	13,632		
	56,642		

4   Non-controlling interest (SOCI)

	Melon		Kiwi	
	PFY	TCI	PFY	TCI
	$'000	$'000	$'000	$'000
Per question	10,760	10,860	9,439	9,439
Less intragroup trading (W6)	(15)	(15)	(15)	(15)
	10,745	10,845	9,424	9,424
× 10%	1,074	1,084		
× 28% (W1)			2,639	2,639

3,713

3,723

5   Non-controlling interests (statement of financial position)

	Melon	Kiwi
	$000	$000
NCI at acquisition (W2)	500	900
NCI share of post acquisition retained earnings:		
Melon ((W3) 22,635 × 10%)	2,263.5	
Kiwi ((W3) 18,933 × (W1) 28%)		5,301.2
NCI in investment in Kiwi (3,800 × 10%)	(380)	
	2,383.5	6,201.2

8,584.7

6   *Intragroup trading*

    (i)   Cancel intragroup sale/purchase:

        DEBIT group revenue (260 + 480) $740,000

        CREDIT group cost of sales $740,000

    (ii)   Unrealised profit

	$'000
Melon (60 × 25/100)	15
Kiwi (75 × 25/125)	15

        Adjust in books of seller:

        DEBIT Cost of sales/retained earnings

        CREDIT Group Inventories

7   *Fair value adjustment*

Melon:

	At acqn 1Jan 20X5 $'000	Movement $'000	At year end 31Dec 20X9 $'000
Land: 5,000.000 − (3,000,000 + 1,425,000)	575	–	575

8   *Revenue* *

	$'000
Exotic	45,600
Melon	24,700
Kiwi	22,800
Less intragroup sales (W6)	(740)
	92,360

9   *Cost of sales* *

		$'000
Exotic		18,050
Melon		5,463
Kiwi		5,320
Add PUP (W6):	Melon	15
	Kiwi	15
		28,123

* **Note**. Workings 8 and 9 are included for completeness. You should do the workings on the face of the SPLOCI.

42 Glove

Text reference. Complex groups are covered in Chapter 13.

Top tips. This question required the preparation of a consolidated statement of financial position of a group which contained a sub-subsidiary. In addition, candidates had to account for brand names, a retirement benefit plan, a convertible bond, and an exchange of plant. The question was a little easier than in previous exams, and you should not have been alarmed at getting both pensions and financial instruments, since only the straightforward aspects were being tested.

Easy marks. There are marks for standard consolidation calculations (goodwill, NCI, retained earnings) which should be familiar to you from your earlier studies, and for setting out the proforma, even if you didn't have time to do the fiddly adjustments. The convertible bond – don't be scared because it is a financial instrument! – is something you have covered at an earlier level.

Marking scheme

	Marks
Equity	7
Reserves	6
Non-current liabilities	3
Defined benefit plan	4
Convertible bond	4
Plant	2
Trade name	3
Available	29
Maximum	25

GLOVE GROUP
CONSOLIDATED STATEMENT OF FINANCIAL POSITION AS AT 31 MAY 20X7

	$m
Non-current assets	
Property, plant and equipment	
260 + 20 + 26 + 6 (W6) + 5(W6) + 3 (W9)	320.0
Goodwill (W2)	10.1
Other intangibles: trade name (W6)	4.0
Investments in equity instruments	10.0
	344.1
Current assets: 65 + 29 + 20	114.0
Total assets	458.1
Equity and liabilities	
Equity attributable to owners of parent	
Ordinary shares	150.0
Other reserves (W4)	30.7
Retained earnings (W3)	150.9
Equity component of convertible debt (W8)	1.6
	333.2
Non-controlling interests (W5)	28.9
	362.1
Non-current liabilities (W10)	
45 + 2 + 3 + 0.1 (W7) – 30 + 28.9 (W8)	49.0
Current liabilities: 35 + 7 + 5	47.0
	96.0
Total equity and liabilities	458.1

Workings

1   *Group structure*

	Glove		
1 June 20X5 80%		Retained earnings	$10m
		Other reserves	$4m
	Body		
1 June 20X5 70%		Retained earnings	$6m
		Other reserves	$8m
	Fit		

	%
Effective interest: 80% × 70%	56
∴ Non-controlling interest	44
	100

2   *Goodwill*

	Glove in Body		Body in Fit	
	$m	$m	$m	$m
Consideration transferred		60	(30 × 80%)	24.00
Non-controlling interests	(65 × 20%)	13	(39 × 44%)	17.16
Fair value of net assets at acq'n:				
Per question	60		39	
Trade name (W6)	5		–	
		(65)		(39.00)
		8		2.16

$$10.16$$

3   *Retained earnings*

	Glove $m	Body $m	Fit $m
Per question	135.00	25	10
Fair value movement (W6)	–	(1)	–
Convertible bonds (W8) (2.3 – 1.8)	(0.50)		
Assets exchange:			
Adjustment to plant (W9)	3.00		
Less pre-acquisition		(10)	(6)
		14	4
Share of Body			
80% × 14			
	11.20		
Share of Fit			
56% × 4	2.24		
	150.94		

4   *Other reserves*

	Glove $m	Body $m	Fit $m
Per question	30.0	5	8
Pension scheme (W7)	(0.1)		
Less pre-acquisition		(4)	(8)
		1	–
Share of body			
80% × 1	0.8		
Share of Fit			
56% × 0	0.0		
	30.7		

5   *Non-controlling interests*

	Body $m	*Fit* $m
NCI at acquisition (W2)	13	17.16
NCI share of post acquisition retained earnings:		
Body ((W3) 14 × 20%)	2.8	
Fit ((W3) 4 × 44%)		1.76
NCI share of post acquisition other reserves:		
Body ((W4) 1 × 20%)	0.2	
Fit ((W4) 0 × 44%)		0
NCI in investment in Fit (30 × 20%)	(6)	
	10	18.92
		28.92

6   *Fair value adjustments*

	At acquisition $m	*Movement* *(2 years)* $m	*At reporting* *date* *(31 May 20X7)* $m
Body			
Land: 60 – (40 + 10 + 4)	6	–	6
Brand name (note)	5	(1)	4
	11	(1)	10
Fit			
Land: 39 – (20 + 8 + 6)	5	–	5

Note. The trade name is an internally generated intangible asset. While these are not normally recognised under IAS 38 *Intangible assets*, IFRS 3 *Business combinations* allows recognition if the fair value can be measured reliably. Thus this Glove should recognise an intangible asset on acquisition (at 1 June 20X5). This will reduce the value of goodwill.

The trade name is amortised over ten years, of which two have elapsed: $5m × 2/10 = $1m.

So the value is $(5 – 1)m = $4m in the consolidated statement of financial position.

7   *Defined benefit pension scheme*

The amount to be recognised is as follows

	$m
Loss on remeasurement through OCI on defined benefit obligation	(1.0)
Gain on remeasurment through OCI on plan assets	0.9
	(0.1)

Accounting entries:

DEBIT	Other comprehensive income	$0.1m	
CREDIT	Net defined benefit liability		$0.1m

8   *Convertible bond*

Under IAS 32, the bond must be split into a liability and an equity component:

	$m	$m
Proceeds: 30,000 × $1,000		30

Present value of principal in three years' time

$\$30m \times \dfrac{1}{1.08^3}$ 23.815

Present value of interest annuity
$30m × 6% = $1,800,000

$\times\dfrac{1}{1.08}$	1.667
$\times\dfrac{1}{(1.08)^2}$	1.543
$\times\dfrac{1}{(1.08)^3}$	1.429

	$m
Liability component	(28.454)
∴ Equity component	1.546

Rounded to $1.6m

Balance of liability at 31 May 20X7

	$'000
Balance b/d at 1 June 20X6	28,454
Effective interest at 8%	2,276
Coupon interest paid at 6%	(1,800)
Balance c/d at 31 May 20X7	28,930

9   *Exchange of assets*

The cost of the plant should be measured at the fair value of the asset given up, rather than the carrying value. An adjustment must be made to the value of the plant, and to retained earnings.

	$
Fair value of land	7
Carrying value of land	(4)
∴ Adjustment required	3

DEBIT	Plant	$3m	
CREDIT	Retained earnings		$3m

10   *Non-current liabilities*

Note. This working is for additional information. To save time, you should do yours on the face of the consolidated position statement

	$m	$m
Non-current liabilities per question:		
Glove	45	
Body	2	
Fit	3	
		50.0
Unrecognised actuarial losses (W7)		0.1
Proceeds of convertible bond		(30.0)
Value of liability component		28.9
		49.0

43 Case study question: Minny

Text reference. Complex groups are covered in Chapter 14, associates in Chapter 12 and IFRS 5 in Chapter 15. Ethical issues are covered in Chapter 2.

Top tips. In Part (a), don't let the term 'complex group' put you off – here it just means that there is a sub-subsidiary. Spend a short time sketching out the group structure (see our Working 10) and working out the effective interest and non-controlling interest. Once you have done that, much of the consolidation is the same as for the simple group. Remember to deduct the cost of the subsidiary's investment in the sub-subsidiary in the NCI working. Of the adjustments, the associate (which becomes an associate only part-way through the year), the disposal group, the intangible asset and the impairment are the most fiddly. Study our answer carefully if you missed these. Part (b) requires detailed knowledge of the IFRS 5 criteria, but is otherwise straightforward. Part (c) requires you to think about the substance and purpose of the transaction – is the motive to manipulate the financial statements?

Easy marks. There are some standard consolidation workings here, and you could slot in the caption for, say, 'disposal group held for sale' even if you get the calculation wrong. Leave enough time for Parts (b) and (c)– the examiner has commented in the past that candidates often do not. Part (b) is straightforward knowledge and Part (c) allows scope for interpretation – it is more important that you show awareness of the ethical issues than come up with a 'correct' answer.

Examiner's comment. In Part (a), candidates dealt with the group structure quite well and the calculations of goodwill arising on acquisition were generally accurate. It is important to take time in the examination to determine the nature of the group structure as marks are allocated for this in the marking guide. Often candidates calculate retained earnings and non-controlling interest inaccurately but the marking guide gives credit for candidates own figures as long as the principle is correct. This latter point also enhances the importance of candidates showing full and clear workings. Another important consideration is the completion of the 'double entry' in the workings. The main problems that arose were the treatment of the impairment of goodwill, the gain arising on the accounting for the associate, and the treatment of the disposal group. Additionally, candidates often find it difficult to deal with the volume of information in the question. This skill can be improved by exam practice and technique. In Part (b), Many candidates simply repeated the information in the question, which did not gain marks. In the introduction to this report, the ability to think widely was alluded to. This question required candidates to do just that. If candidates read widely and learn to formulate opinions, then this type of question would not pose problems. There were two elements to Part (c) of the question: the ethical implications and the accounting implications. There were a surprising number of candidates who did not discuss the accounting implications and also many candidates did not see any ethical issues.If candidates do not deal with every element of the question, then they are significantly restricting the number of marks that they are likely to achieve.

Marking scheme

	Marks
(a)	
Property, plant and equipment	5
Goodwill	5
Intangible assets	1
Investment in Puttin	4
Current assets	1
Disposal group	5
Retained earnings	6
Other components of equity	4
Non-controlling interest	3
Current liabilities	1
	35

(b)

Definition – 1 mark per point up to maximum	4
Discussion	3

(c)

Accounting treatment	4
Ethical considerations	4
	50

(a)   MINNY GROUP
CONSOLIDATED STATEMENT OF FINANCIAL POSITION
AS AT 30 NOVEMBER 20X2

	$m
Non-current assets	
Property, plant and equipment: 920 + 300 + 310 + 89(W7) + 36(W7) – 49(W10)	1,606.0
Goodwill (W2)	190.0
Intangible assets: 198 + 30 + 35 – 27(W8) – 9(W9)	227.0
Investment in associate (W3)	50.5
	2,073.5
Current assets: 895 + 480 + 250 – 18(W10)	1,607.0
Disposal group held for sale (W10): 49 + 18 – 34	33.0
Total assets	3,713.5

	$m
Equity and liabilities	
Equity attributable to owners of the parent	
Share capital	920.00
Retained earnings (W4)	936.08
Other components of equity (W5)	77.80
	1,933.88
Non-controlling interests (W6)	394.62
	2,328.50
Non-current liabilities: 495 + 123 + 93	711.00
Current liabilities: 408 + 128 + 138 – 3 (W10)	671.00
Current liabilities associated with disposal group (W10)	3.00
Total equity and liabilities	3,713.50

Workings

1   *Group structure*

Minny			
1 Dec 20X0	70% (Consideration = $730m)	FV NA	$835m
		Retained earnings	$319m
		OCE	$27m
		FV NCI	$295m

Bower			
1 Dec 20X1	80% (Consideration = $320m)	FV NA	$362m
		Retained earnings	$106m
		OCE	$20m
		FV NCI	$161m

Heeny

	%
Effective interest: 70% × 80%	56
∴ Non-controlling interest	44
	100

2 Goodwill

	Bower $m		Heeny $m
Consideration transferred	730	320 × 70%	224
Non-controlling interests	295		161
FV of identifiable net assets at acq'n:	(835)		(362)
	190		23
Impairment losses (W8)	–		(23)
	190		–

190

3 Investment in associate

	$m	$m	
'Cost' at 1 June 20X2:			
Fair value of 14% holding per qu	21		
Cost of additional 16%	27		
		48.0	
Share of profit for 6 months to 30 Nov 20X2: 30 × 6/12 × 30%		4.5	} $2.5m post sig. inf.
Dividends paid		(2.0)	
		50.5	

Notes

(i) The investment had been designated per IFRS 9 *Financial instruments* as being at fair value through other comprehensive income. The gain of $21m – $18m = $3m now realised is not reclassified to profit or loss for the year, but may be transferred as a reserve movement from other components of equity (W5) to retained earnings (W4).

(ii) The dividend should have been credited to Minny's profit or loss for the year rather than to other comprehensive income. The associate is not impaired as the carrying amount in the separate financial statements of Minny does not exceed the carrying amount in the consolidated financial statement, and the dividend does not exceed the total comprehensive income of the associate in the period in which it is declared.

4 Retained earnings

	Minny $m	Bower $m	Heeny $m
Per question	895.00	442	139
Reclassification of gain on Puttin (W3)	3.00		
Reclassification of dividend from Puttin* (W5)	2.00		
Investigation and marketing of intangible (W10)	(9.00)		
Impairment loss on disposal group (W10)	(34.00)		
Pre-acquisition (W1)		(319)	(106)
		123	33
Group share			
Bower: 123 × 70%	86.10		
Heeny: 33 × 56%	18.48		
Share of post-acqn. profit of Puttin (W3)	2.50		
Impairment loss on Heeny (W8) (50 × 56%)	(28.00)		
	936.08		

5   *Other components of equity*

	Minny $m	Bower $m	Heeny $m
Per question	73.0	37	25
Reclassification of gain on Puttin (W3)	(3.0)		
Reclassification of dividend from Puttin (W4)	(2.0)		
Pre-acquisition (W1)		(27)	(20)
		10	5
Group share post acqn:			
Bower: 10 × 70 %	7.0		
Heeny: 5 × 56%	2.8		
	77.8		

6   *Non-controlling interests*

	Bower $m	Heeny $m
At acquisition (FV per qu (W2))	295.0	161.00
Post acquisition share of retained earnings		
Bower: 123 (W4) × 30%	36.9	
Heeny: 33 (W4) × 44%		14.52
Post acquisition share of other components of equity		
Bower: 10 (W5) × 30%	3.0	
Heeny: 5 (W5) × 44%		2.20
NCI share of investment in Heeney: 320 × 30%	(96.0)	–
Heeny impairment losses: 50 (W8) × 44%	–	(22.00)
	238.9	155.72

394.62

7   *Fair value adjustments*

Bower:

	At acqn 1.12.20X0 $m	Movement $m	At year end 30.11.20X2 $m
Land: 835 – (400 + 319 + 27)	89	–	89

Heeny:

	At acqn 1.12.20X1 $m	Movement $m	At year end 30.11.20X2 $m
Land: 362– (200 + 106+ 20)	36	–	36

8   *Impairment test*

	Bower $m	Heeny $m
Carrying amount		
Assets	1,130	595
Fair value adjustments (W7)	89	36
Goodwill (W2)	190	23
	1,409	654
Recoverable amount	(1,425)	(604)
Impairment loss	–	50
Allocated to: goodwill		23
intangible assets (bal. fig.)		27
		50

Note. Bower is not impaired as the carrying amount is below the recoverable amount, but Heeny's assets are impaired. The impairment loss is allocated first to goodwill and then to the intangible assets, because the directors believe that it is the poor performance of the intangible assets which is responsible for the reduction in the recoverable amount.

9   *Development costs*

	$m	
Patent	10	Intangible asset
Investigation phase	7	Profit or loss
Prototype	4	} Intangible asset:
Preparation for sale	3	} development costs
Marketing	2	Profit or loss

The adjustment required to eliminate the items which should be expensed to profit or loss is:

DEBIT	Profit or loss (retained earnings)	$9m	
CREDIT	Intangible assets		$9m

10   *Disposal group held for sale*

Assets and liabilities of the disposal group are re-classified as current and shown as separate line items in the statement of financial position. The disposal group is impaired, and the impairment loss is calculated as follows.

	$m
Property, plant and equipment	49
Inventory	18
Current liabilities	(3)
Carrying value	64
Anticipated proceeds (FV less costs to sell)	30
Impairment loss	34

(Deduct from assets and retained earnings

(b)   **Held for sale criteria under IFRS 5** *Non-current assets held for sale and discontinued operations*

The held for sale criteria in IFRS 5 *Non-current assets held for sale and discontinued operations* are very strict, and often decision to sell an asset or disposal group is made well before they are met. It may be difficult for regulators, auditors or users of accounts to determine whether an entity **genuinely intends to dispose** of the asset or group of assets.

IFRS requires an asset or disposal group to be classified as held for sale where it is **available for immediate sale** in its **present condition** subject only to **terms that are usual** and customary and the sale is **highly probable**.

The standard does not give guidance on **terms that are usual and customary** but the guidance notes give examples. Such terms may include, for example, a specified period of time for the seller to vacate a headquarters building that is to be sold, or it may include contracts or surveys. However, they would not include terms imposed by the seller that are not customary, for example, a seller could not continue to use its headquarters building until construction of a new headquarters building had taken place.

For a sale to be **highly probable:**

- Management must be **committed** to the sale.
- An **active programme to locate a buyer** must have been initiated.
- The asset must be **marketed at a price** that is **reasonable in relation to its own fair value**.
- The sale must be **expected to be completed within one year** from the date of classification.
- It is **unlikely** that **significant changes** will be made to the plan **or the plan withdrawn**.

Regulators may question entities' application of this standard because the definition of highly probable as 'significantly more likely than probable' is **subjective**. Entities may wish to separate out an unprofitable/impaired part of the business in order to **show a more favourable view of continuing operations,** and so regulators have reason look very closely at whether the classification as held for sale is genuine.

(c)   **Transfer of property**

The proposed transfer of property from Bower to its parent Minny is not a normal sale. The property's carrying value of $2m probably reflects the current value as it was revalued at the year end, but the 'sale' price is only $1m. In effect, this is a distribution of profits of $1m, the shortfall on the transfer.

Distributions of this kind are not necessarily wrong or illegal. Bower's retained earnings of $442m, plus the 'realised' revaluation surplus of $400,000 more than cover the distribution, so, depending on the distributable profits rules in the jurisdiction in which it operates, it is likely to be legal.

Certain IFRS may apply to the transfer.

(i)   If the asset **meets the held for sale** criteria under IFRS 5 *Non-current assets held for sale and discontinued operations,* it will **continue to be included** in the consolidated financial statements, but it will be **presented separately** from other assets in the statement of financial position. An asset that is held for sale should be measured at the **lower of** its **carrying amount** and **fair value less costs to sell**. Immediately before classification of the asset as held for sale, the entity must update any impairment test carried out.

(ii)   As the transfer is from a subsidiary to its parent, **IAS 24 *Related party disclosures*** will apply and in the **individual financial statements of Bower and Minny, although it would be eliminated on consolidation**. Knowledge of related party relationships and transactions affects the way in which users assess a company's operations and the risks and opportunities that it faces. Even if the company's transactions and operations have not been affected by a related party relationship, disclosure puts users on notice that they may be affected in future, but in this case the related party relationship clearly has affected the price of the transfer.

Even though the transfer is likely to be legal, and even if it is correctly accounted for and disclosed in accordance with IAS 24 and IFRS 5 (or IAS 16 if the IFRS 5 criteria are not met) the transaction raises ethical issues. **Ethical behaviour** in the preparation of financial statements, is of **paramount importance**. This applies equally to preparers of accounts, to auditors and to accountants giving advice to directors.

Financial statements may be manipulated for all kinds of reasons, for example to enhance a profit-linked bonus or to disguise an unfavourable liquidity position. In this case, suspicion might be aroused by the fact that **the transfer of the property between group companies at half the current value has no obvious logical purpose**, and looks like a cosmetic exercise of some kind, although its motives are unclear. Accounting information should be truthful and neutral, and while the transaction is probably permissible, the **directors need to explain** why they are doing it.

44 Case study question: Trailer

Text reference. Complex groups are covered in Chapter 13; financial instruments in Chapter 2; provisions in Chapter 9; impairment and non-current assets in Chapter 4; employee benefits in Chapter 5; ethics in Chapter 2.

Top tips. Part (a) of this question required candidates to prepare a consolidated statement of financial position of a complex (D-shaped) group and various adjustments (PPE, loan, pension and impairment). The key to this question is the group structure and the dates – use the retained earnings/non-controlling interest from the date control is gained. For Caller, this is 1 June 20X2, when Trailer acquires 60% of Park; once Park is a subsidiary, then Caller is a sub-subsidiary. In Part (b) candidates had to explain (with numbers) what would be different had the full goodwill method of valuing non-controlling interest been used. Part (c) was on ethical issues arising from a scenario relating to the same company. Do not rush this part, and do not waffle. While a variety of arguments may be acceptable, they **must** relate to the question requirement, in particular the director's comment.

Easy marks. Do not be put off by the term 'complex group'. Once you have established the group structure, there are easy marks to be gained for adding across and other basic consolidation aspects. The pension working is straightforward too, more so than in the past. Easy marks are also to be had in Part (b), where you essentially do the same calculations but with a different figure. And do not get bogged down with the loan or the impairment – there are easier marks to be had elsewhere.

Examiner's comment. Candidates generally score well on question 1. In Part (a), the goodwill calculations were invariably correct as was the nature of the group relationships. The treatment of the office accommodation was well answered as was the pension element. Surprisingly the restructuring costs were not particularly well dealt with by candidates. Only those costs that result directly from and are necessarily entailed by the restructuring may be included, such as employee redundancy costs or lease termination costs. Expenses that relate to ongoing activities, such as relocation and retraining are excluded. Part (b) required candidates to explain to the directors, with suitable calculations, the impact on the financial statements if goodwill was calculated using the fair value of the NCI as opposed to the partial recognition of goodwill. The question was quite well answered in terms of the calculations of goodwill but the majority of marks were allocated to the explanation being what was asked in the question. It was in this area where candidates lost marks. Candidates answered Part (c) of the question very well. However, it is also this part of the question that often candidates leave out and do not answer. Ethics is a critical part of the syllabus and as such every candidate should be capable of answering this question.

Marking scheme

		Marks
(a)	Property, plant and equipment	5
	Goodwill	6
	Financial assets	5
	Current assets/total non-current liabilities	1
	Retained earnings	6
	Other components of equity	3
	Non-controlling interest	3
	Current liabilities	1
	Pension plan	5
		35
(b)	Subjective assessment of discussion	
	Up to 2 marks per element	4
	Calculations	5
		9
(c)	Subjective assessment: 1 mark per point	6
	Maximum	50

(a) TRAILER
CONSOLIDATED STATEMENT OF FINANCIAL POSITION AT 31 MAY 20X3

	$m
Non-current assets	
Property, plant and equipment: 1,440 + 1,100 + 1,300 + 35(W6) + 40(W6) + 32.59(W8) – 167(W11)	3,780.59
Goodwill (W2)	398.00
Financial assets: 320 + 21 + 141 –4.01(W7) + 2.76(W7)	480.75
	4,659.34
Current assets: 895 + 681 + 150	1,726.00
	6385.34
Equity attributable to owners of the parent	
Share capital	1,750.00
Retained earnings (W3)	1,254.64
Other components of equity (W4)	170.10
	3,174.74
Non-controlling interests (W5)	892.60
Total equity	4,067.34
Non-current liabilities: 985 +765 +150 + 6(W10)	1,906.00
Current liabilities: 115 + 87 +196 + 14(W9)	412.00
Total liabilities	2,318.00
	6385.34

Workings

1 *Group structure*

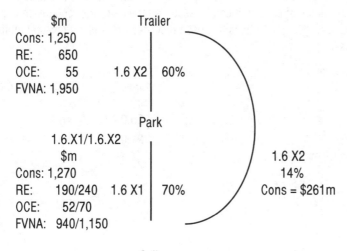

	$m	Trailer
Cons:	1,250	
RE:	650	
OCE:	55	1.6 X2 60%
FVNA:	1,950	

Park
1.6.X1/1.6.X2
$m   1.6 X2
Cons: 1,270   14%
RE: 190/240 1.6 X1 70%   Cons = $261m
OCE: 52/70
FVNA: 940/1,150

Caller

Effective interest [(60% × 70% = 42% indirect + 14% direct]	56%
∴ NCI	44%
	100%

2 *Goodwill*

	Park $m	Caller $m
Consideration transferred : Trailer	1,250	
Consideration transferred: Park (1,270 × 60%)		762
Fair value of previously held interest		280
Non-controlling interests (1,950 × 40%)/(1,150 × 44%)	780	506
FV of identifiable net assets at date of control (1.6.X2)	(1,950)	(1,150)
	80	398
Impairment loss (W11)	(80)	–
	–	398

3 *Retained earnings*

	Trailer $m	Park $m	Caller $m
Per question	1,240.00	930	350
Reversal of investment gain: 310 – 280(W2)*	(30.00)		
Loan: 4.01 (W7) – 2.76 (W7)	(1.25)		
Impairment reversal (W8)	11.59		
Restructuring provision (W9)	(14.00)		
Pension plan (W10)	(1.10)		
Less pre-acquisition		(650)	(240)
		280	110
Group share of Park: 280 × 60%	168.00		
Group share of Caller: 110 × 56%(W1)	61.60		
Less impairment losses on Park			
Goodwill: 133.33 (W11) × 60%	(80.00)		
Property, plant and equipment: 167(W11) × 60%	(100.20)		
	1,254.64		

*Note. The gain in Trailer's books on Trailer's investment in Caller since Caller has been a subsidiary must be reversed on consolidation. As the question does not mention adoption of the irrevocable election to recognise gains or losses on investments in equity instruments in other comprehensive income (and other components of equity), it can be assumed the gain was recognised in profit or loss (and retained earnings). (No gain or loss has been recorded on Trailer's investment in Park nor Park's investment in Caller.)

4 Other components of equity

	Trailer $m	Park $m	Caller $m
Per question	125.0	80	95
Revaluation gain (W8)	21.0		
Pension plan remeasurement (W10)	(4.9)		
Less pre-acquisition		(55)	(70)
		25	25
Group share of Park: 25 × 60%	15.0		
Group share of Caller: 25 × 56%(W1)	14.0		
	170.1		

5 Non-controlling interests

	Park $m	Caller $m
NCI at acquisition (W2)	780.0	506.0
NCI share of post-acquisition retained earnings:		
Park: 280 (W3) × 40%	112.0	
Caller: 110 (W3) × 44%		48.4
NCI share of post-acquisition other components of equity:		
Park: (W4) 25 × 40%	10.0	
Caller: (W4) 25 × 44%		11.0
Less impairment loss on PPE: 167(W11) × 40%	(66.8)	
Less NCI share of investment in Caller (1,270 × 40%)	(508.0)	
	327.2	565.4
		892.6

6 Fair value adjustment

	At acqn 1 June 20X2 $m	Movement $m	At year end 31 May 20X3 $m
Park: land 1,950 – (1,210 + 650+ 55)	35	–	35
Caller*: land: 1,150 – (800 + 240+ 70)	40	–	40

*Note. Use the values at the date Trailer achieves control of Caller, ie when it buys its 60% stake in Park.

7   *Loan receivable*

The loan is at a discounted interest rate of 3%, which means that Trailer will **effectively incur a loss on interest receivable over the life of the loan**. The fair value of the instrument will be lower than the amount advanced and should be measured by calculating the present value of all future cash receipts **discounted using the 'unsubsidised' rate of 6%,** which is the market rate for similar interest. The loss is the difference between amount advanced and the fair value. Effective interest income at the market rate of 6% should then be recognised annually in profit or loss and the financial asset should be held at amortised cost in the statement of financial position.

	$m
1 June 20X2 fair value: $50 \times 3\% \times \dfrac{1}{1.06}$	1.42
$50 \times 3\% \times \dfrac{1}{1.06^2}$	1.33
$((50 \times 3\%) + 50) \times \dfrac{1}{1.06^3}$	43.24
	45.99
Effective interest: $45.99 \times 6\%$	2.76
31 May 20X3 cash received: $50 \times 3\%$	(1.50)
31 May 20X3 Balance c/d	47.25

Correcting double entries:

Initial recognition:

DEBIT	Profit or loss (retained earnings)	$4.01m	
	($50m − $45.99m)		
CREDIT	Financial asset		$4.01m

Effective interest:

DEBIT	Financial asset	$2.76m	
CREDIT	Profit or loss (retained earnings)		$2.76m

8   *Office accommodation*

		$m
1 June 20X1	Cost	90.00
	Depreciation ($90/30 \text{ years}$)	(3.00)
		87.00
	Impairment loss (bal.fig.)	(12.00)
31 May 20X2	Impaired value	75.00
	Depreciation for year ($75/29 \text{ years}$)	(2.59)
		72.41
	Reversal/revaluation (bal. fig.)	32.59
31 May 20X3	Revalued amount	105.00

Carrying value at 31 May 20X3 had impairment not occurred: $90 - (90 \times 2/30 \text{ years}) = \$84m$

Reversal/revaluation:

DEBIT	Property, plant and equipment	$32.59m	
CREDIT	Profit or loss (retained earnings): 84 – 72.41		$11.59m
CREDIT	Other comprehensive income (OCE): 32.59 – 11.59		$21m

The credit to profit or loss is made up of the reversal of the $12m less the difference between the depreciation charged on the impaired amount and the depreciation that would have been charged had the impairment not occurred ($12/29 \text{ years}$ = 0.41). The remainder of the upward valuation, $21m, is credited to the revaluation surplus.

9   *Provision for restructuring*

Plan 1:

A **provision for restructuring** should be recognised in respect of the closure of the factories in accordance with IAS 37 *Provisions, contingent liabilities and contingent assets*. The plan has been **communicated** to the relevant employees (those who will be made redundant) and factories have already been identified. A provision should **only be recognised for directly attributable costs** that will not benefit on-going activities of the entity. Thus, a provision should be recognised for the redundancy costs and the lease termination costs, but none for the retraining costs:

	$m
Redundancy costs	9
Retraining	–
Lease termination costs	5
Liability	14

DEBIT	Profit or loss (retained earnings)	$14m	
CREDIT	Current liabilities		$14m

Plan 2:

No provision should be recognised for the **reorganisation of the finance and IT department**. Since the reorganisation is not due to start for two years, the plan may change, and so a **valid expectation that management is committed to the plan has not been raised**. As regards any provision for redundancy, individuals have not been identified and communicated with, and so no provision should be made at 31 May 20X3 for redundancy costs.

10   *Pension plan assets and obligation*

The defined benefit pension plan is treated in accordance with IAS 19 *Employee benefits*.

The defined benefit expense recognised in profit or loss for the year includes:

	$m
Current service cost	1.0
Net interest cost (30 × 5%) – (28 × 5%)	0.1
	1.1

The defined benefit remeasurement included in other comprehensive income for the year (not to be reclassified to profit or loss), in accordance with IAS 19 (revised 2011), is a net loss of $4.9m ($0.6m – $5.5m), see below for calculation.

Changes in fair value of plan assets

	$m
Opening fair value of plan assets	28.0
Interest on plan assets: 28 × 5%	1.4
Contributions	2.0
Benefits paid	(3.0)
Gain on remeasurement through OCI (balancing figure)	0.6
Closing fair value of plan assets	29.0

Changes in present value of the defined benefit obligation

	$m
Opening defined benefit obligation	30.0
Interest cost on defined benefit obligation: 30 × 5%	1.5
Current service cost	1.0
Benefits	(3.0)
Loss on remeasurement through OCI (balancing figure)	5.5
Closing defined benefit obligation	35.0

Adjustment to the group accounts:

	$m	$m
DEBIT Profit or loss (retained earnings)	1.1	
DEBIT Other comprehensive income (other components of equity)	4.9	
CREDIT Non-current liabilities (1.1 + 4.9)		6

11   *Impairment test: Park*

	Park
	$m
'Notional' goodwill: 80 (W2) × 100%/60%	133.33
Carrying amount of consolidated net assets: 2,220 + 35 (W6)	2,255.00
	2,388.33
Recoverable amount	(2,088.00)
Impairment loss: gross	300.33

Allocated to

Goodwill: 133.33 × 60%	133.33	× 60% = 80m
Property, plant and equipment (bal. fig.)	167.00	
	300.33	

(b)   **Non-controlling interest at fair value**

Non-controlling interest at fair value (the 'full goodwill' method) will be different from non-controlling interest at proportionate share of the acquiree's net assets. The difference is **goodwill attributable to the non-controlling interest,** which may be, but often is not, proportionate to goodwill attributable to the parent. The full goodwill method increases reported net assets, which means that any impairment of goodwill will be greater. The relevant calculations are as follows.

Goodwill

	Park	*Caller*
	$m	*$m*
Consideration transferred : Trailer	1,250	
Consideration transferred: Park (1,270 × 60%)		762
Fair value of previously held interest		280
Non-controlling interests (at fair value)	800	530
FV of identifiable net assets at date of control (1.6.X2)	(1,950)	(1,150)
	100	422
Impairment loss (see below)	(100)	–
	–	422

Impairment of goodwill: Park

	Park
	$m
Goodwill	100.00
Carrying amount of consolidated net assets: 2,220 + 35 (W6)	2,255.00
Less cost of investment in Caller	(1,270.00)
	1,085.00
Recoverable amount	(818.00)
Impairment loss	267.00

Allocated to

Goodwill	100.00
Property, plant and equipment (bal. fig.)	167.00
	267.00

Goodwill (before impairment) in Park has increased to $100m, from $80m under the partial goodwill method, and in Caller the increase is from $398m to $422m. The increase of $20m in Park and $24m in

Caller related to goodwill attributable to the non-controlling interest. (NCI). NCI at acquisition has increased correspondingly by the same amount ie from $780m to $800m in Park and from $506m to $530m in Caller.

The impairment of the goodwill in Park is now $100m, as opposed to $80m under partial goodwill. The group share, $60m, is charged to retained earnings, and the NCI share, $40m, to the NCI. Whereas under the partial method, as there was no goodwill for NCI, no impairment was charged to NCI . (The NCI working would show the NCI share of goodwill at $40m [included in the NCI at acquisition figure] less the NCI share of impairment at $40m.)

The impairment allocated to property, plant and equipment will be $167m using either method, and the charge will be split in the same way under both methods between group retained earnings and non-controlling interest in the proportion 60:40.

While measuring the non-controlling interest at fair value may be difficult, **one complication is avoided**: that of **grossing up the goodwill**. Where the proportionate share of net assets method is used, the carrying amount of a cash generating unit comprises the parent and non-controlling share of the identifiable net assets of the unit and only the parent's share of the goodwill. For the purpose of calculating the impairment loss, the carrying amount of the cash generating unit is therefore notionally adjusted to include the non-controlling share in the goodwill by grossing it up. The consequent impairment loss calculated is only recognised to the extent of the parent's share. Where the **fair value method** is used to value the non-controlling interest, **no adjustment is required**.

(c)   **Ethical issues**

The study of ethics forms an important part of the ACCA qualification because ethics have practical application in the accountant's professional life. One of the directors of Trailer has been dismissive of the importance of ethics to accountants, but his arguments can be countered as follows.

All accountants have their individual moral beliefs

This is certainly true, but it **does not follow that those beliefs are sufficiently developed or adequate** to the dilemmas the accountant may face in the workplace. Personal and professional ethics often overlap, but there may be a conflict, particularly where the **accounting issues are complex**. For example, an individual auditor may believe that it is right to hold shares in an audit client, because he or she knows better than to exploit any inside knowledge. But from the point of view of professional ethics it is better to avoid any potential conflict of interest and to be seen to avoid it.

The **study of ethics** cannot provide ready-made solutions to all potential conflicts, but it **can provide a set of principles on which to base judgements**. A vague wish to 'do the right thing' will be of little use when faced with a decision to report a colleague or member of the client's staff who is acting unethically. The study of ethics can direct the accountant's thinking and reasoning and help him or her make the right decision, even if it does not make that decision any easier. An example of ethical guidance serving this purpose is the ACCA's *Code of Ethics and Conduct,* which requires its members to adhere to a set of fundamental principles in the course of their professional duty, such as confidentiality, objectivity, professional behaviour, integrity, professional competence and due care.

Compliance with GAAP is enough

Compliance with GAAP is **always necessary but not always sufficient**. There are **different ways of complying with GAAP,** some more ethical than others. For example, both the direct and the indirect method of preparing statements of cash flow comply with GAAP, but if a director suddenly wished to change from one to the other, it could be questioned whether this was ethical, if one method gives a more favourable picture of liquidity. Similarly, a director may wish to delay a charge to profit or loss for the year in order to secure a bonus that depends on profit.

The takeover would not benefit the company and other stakeholders, so false disclosure is acceptable

This argument shows the inadequacy of individual morality as the sole guide to what a professional should do. An individual may feel that a takeover would be wrong, and wish to defend the company from it by manipulating financial information. In doing so, he or she may not be motivated by personal gain, and may be thinking of the good of the company's stakeholders (employees, and the local community as well as shareholders). However, such actions would be **unethical and unprofessional, regardless of the motives.**

In the long term, relationships with stakeholders are built on **trust and honesty,** and there can be **no justification for false disclosure**.

To summarise:

- **Personal ethics are necessary but not enough** – reasoning and sound ethical principles are needed to deal with complex issues and conflicts of interest.

- **Compliance with GAAP is necessary but not enough** – some accounting treatments are allowed under GAAP but unacceptable in certain contexts.

- **Good motives are no substitute for sound professional ethics** and no excuse for false or 'creative' accounting.

45 Preparation question: Part disposal

(a) ANGEL GROUP
CONSOLIDATED STATEMENT OF FINANCIAL POSITION AS AT 31 DECEMBER 20X8

	$'000
Non-current assets	
Property, plant and equipment	200.00
Investment in Shane (W3)	133.15
	333.15
Current assets (890 + 120 (cash on sale))	1,010.00
	1,343.15
Equity attributable to owners of the parent	
Share capital	500.00
Retained reserves (W4)	533.15
	1,033.15
Current liabilities	310.00
	1,343.15

ANGEL GROUP
CONSOLIDATED STATEMENT OF PROFIT OR LOSS AND OTHER COMPREHENSIVE INCOME
FOR THE YEAR ENDED 31 DECEMBER 20X8

	$'000
Profit before interest and tax [100 + (20 × 6/12)]	110.00
Profit on disposal of shares in subsidiary (W6)	80.30
Share of profit of associate (12 × 35% × 6/12)	2.10
Profit before tax	192.40
Income tax expense [40 + (8 × 6/12)]	(44.00)
Profit for the year	148.40
Other comprehensive income (not reclassified to P/L) net of tax [10 + (6 × 6/12)]	13.00
Share of other comprehensive income of associate (6 × 35% × 6/12)	1.05
Other comprehensive income for the year	14.05
Total comprehensive income for the year	162.45
Profit attributable to:	
Owners of the parent	146.60
Non-controlling interests (12 × 6/12 × 30%)	1.80
	148.40
Total comprehensive income attributable to:	
Owners of the parents	159.75
Non controlling interests (18 × 6/12 × 30%)	2.70
	162.45

ANGEL GROUP
CONSOLIDATED RECONCILIATION OF MOVEMENT IN RETAINED RESERVES

	$'000
Balance at 31 December 20X7 (W5)	373.40
Total comprehensive income for the year	159.75
Balance at 31 December 20X8 (W4)	533.15

Workings

1   *Timeline*

	1.1.X8	30.6.X8	31.12.X8
SOCI	Subsidiary – 6/12	Associate – 6/12	
		Group gain on disposal	Equity account in SOFP

2   *Goodwill – Shane*

	$'000	$'000
Consideration transferred		120.0
Non-controlling interests (FV)		51.4
Less:		
Share capital	100	
Retained reserves	10	
		(110.0)
		61.4

3   *Investment in associate*

	$'000
Fair value at date control lost	130.00
Share of post 'acquisition' retained reserves (W4)	3.15
	133.15

4   *Group retained reserves*

	Angel	Shane 70%	Shane 35% retained
Per qu/date of disposal (90 – (18 × 6/12))	400.00	81	90
Group profit on disposal (W4)	80.30		
Less retained reserves at acquisition/date of disposal		(10)	(81)
		71	9
Shane: 70% × 71	49.70		
Shane: 35% × 9	3.15		
	533.15		

5   *Retained reserves s b/f*

	Angel $'000	Shane $'000
Per Q	330.0	72
Less: Pre-acquisition retained reserves		(10)
	330.0	62
Shane – Share of post acquisition ret'd reserves (62 × 70%)	43.4	
	373.4	

6   *Group profit on disposal of Shane*

	$'000	$'000
Fair value of consideration received		120.0
Fair value of 35% investment retained		130.0
Less share of carrying value when control lost		
Net assets 190 – (18 × 6/12)	181.0	
Goodwill (W2)	61.4	
Less non-controlling interests (W7)	(72.7)	
		(169.7)
		80.3

7   *Non-controlling interests at date of disposal*

	$'000	$'000
Non-controlling interest at acquisition (FV)		51.4
NCI share of post-acqn retained earnings (30% × 71(W4))		21.3
		72.7

(b)   **Angel disposes of 10% of its holding**

If Angel disposes of 10% of its holding in Shane, Shane goes from being a 70% subsidiary to a 60% subsidiary. In other words **control is retained**. No accounting boundary has been crossed, and the event is treated as a transaction between owners.

The accounting treatment is as follows:

Statement of profit or loss and other comprehensive income

(i)   The subsidiary is **consolidated in full** for the whole period.

(ii)   The **non-controlling interest in the statement of profit or loss and other comprehensive income** will be based on percentage before and after disposal, ie time apportion.

(iii)   There is **no profit or loss on disposal**.

Statement of financial position

(i)   The **change (increase) in non-controlling interests** is shown as an **adjustment to the parent's equity**.

(ii)   **Goodwill** on acquisition **is unchanged** in the consolidated statement of financial position.

In the case of Angel and Shane you would time apportion the non-controlling interest in the statement of profit or loss and other comprehensive income, giving 30% for the first half the year and 40% for the second half. You would also calculate the adjustment to the parent's equity as follows:

	$'000
Fair value of consideration received	X
Increase in NCI in net assets and goodwill at disposal	(X)
Adjustment to parent's equity	X

46 Preparation question: Purchase of further interest

(a)   **RBE already controls DCA** with its 70% investment, so **DCA is already a subsidiary** and would be fully consolidated. In substance, this is **not an acquisition**. Instead, it is treated in the group accounts as a **transaction between the group shareholders** ie the parent has purchased a 20% shareholding from NCI. No goodwill is calculated on the additional investment.

The value of the NCI needs to be worked out at the date of the additional investment (1 October 20X2), and the **proportion purchased by the parent needs to be removed from NCI**. The difference between the consideration transferred and the amount of the reduction in the NCI is included as an **adjustment to parent equity**.

(b) RBE GROUP CONSOLIDATED STATEMENT OF CHANGES IN EQUITY
FOR THE YEAR ENDED 31 DECEMBER 20X2

	Equity attributable to owners of the parent $'000	Non-controlling interest $'000	Total $'000
Balance at 1 January 20X2	3,350	650	4,000
Total comprehensive income for the year (W2)	1,350	150	1,500
Share issue (2m × $1.30)	2,600	–	2,600
Dividends paid (100 × 30%)	(200)	(30)	(230)
Adjustment to equity (on additional purchase of 20% of DCA's shares) (W3 and 4)	(37)	(503)	(540)
Balance at 31 December 20X2	7,063	267	7,330

Workings

1 *Group structure*

RBE

70%	originally
20%	1/10/X2
90%	

DCA

2 *Total comprehensive income*

NCI share:

	$'000
To 1 October 20X2 (30% × 600 × 9/12)	135
To 31 December 20X2 (10% × 600 × 9/12)	15
NCI share of TCI	150

Parent share:

	$'000
Parent share of TCI of DCA (600 – 150)	450
TCI of RBE	900
NCI share of TCI	1,350

3 *Decrease in NCI*

	$'000
NCI b/f 1 January 20X2	650
Share of TCI to 1 October 20X2 (W2)	135
Less share of dividend paid (April 20X2) (30% × 100)	(30)
NCI at 1 October 20X2	755
Decrease in NCI on transfer of shares to parent (755 × 20/30)	503

4 *Adjustment to equity*

	$'000
Consideration transferred	(540)
Decrease in NCI on acquisition (W3)	503
Adjustment to parent's equity	(37)

In RBE's individual statement of financial position, the purchase of the 20% in DCA would have been recorded as follows:

	$'000	$'000
DEBIT Investment	540	
CREDIT Cash		540

Then in the group accounts, the adjustment to equity would be recorded as follows:

	$'000	$'000
DEBIT (reduce) NCI	503	
DEBIT (reduce) Parent's retained earnings	37	
CREDIT(cancel) Investment *		540

47 Case study question: Marchant

Text references. Disposals are covered in Chapter 14 of your Study Text. Pensions are covered in Chapter 5 and share-based payment in Chapter 8. Fair value is covered in Chapters 7 and 12. Ethical issues are covered in Chapter 2.

Top tips. Question 1 part (a) was a consolidated statement of profit or loss and other comprehensive income, with two disposals, one where control was lost and one where control was retained. It is important that you know the difference in the treatment, so be sure to revise this if you had difficulty. Adjustments were required for intragroup sale of inventory (with a 'twist' in that the sale was at fair value so the unrealised loss was genuine), a pension plan, PPE, share-based payment and classification of a hedging loss.

You needed to know, at least in general terms, how to answer Part (a)(ii) in order to treat the gain on the sale of Nathan correctly in Part (a)(i).

Part 1(b) required a discussion of the extent to which fair values are used in IFRS and the impact of this on the usefulness of financial statements. Part (c), as usual, contained an ethical issue – as in a number of past questions, the issue concerned the tension between judgement and conflict of interest, in the (topical) context of lease classification. It is important to tailor your answer to the requirements in discussion parts of questions – the examiner has criticised candidates in the past for failure to *apply* their knowledge.

Easy marks. Once you have established the group structure, there are some very easy marks to be had for multiplying numbers given in the question by $^6/_{12}$. Part (b) allows for flexibility in the arguments made, and IFRS 13 *Fair value measurement,* is also topical, so you should have covered it in detail.

Examiner's comment. Once again, the examiner stressed that candidates should show their workings: 'markers will look to see if there are recognisable figures in such a working but it is important to describe the calculation so that the marker can establish the principle'. Marks are given for correct principles with inaccurate calculations.

Candidates did not deal particularly well with the impairment of goodwill as they did not understand that any subsequent increase in the recoverable amount is likely to be internally generated goodwill rather than a reversal of purchased goodwill impairment. IAS 38 *Intangible assets* prohibits the recognition of internally generated goodwill, thus any reversal of impairment is not recognised. Candidates dealt successfully with the revaluation of non-current assets, the share option scheme and the wrong classification of a cash flow hedge.

In Part (a)(ii) of the question candidates were asked to explain, with suitable calculations, how the sale of the 8% interest in a subsidiary should be dealt with in the group statement of financial position at 30 April 2014. Marks were allocated for the explanation and the calculation. Thus if a candidate simply showed the calculation, marks were lost. Candidates generally answered this part of the question quite well.

Part (b) required candidates to answer across a range of standards and not just focus on IFRS 13. This part of the question was not well answered. In Part (c), candidates had to make reference to more than simply the rules as they had to comment on the fact that subjectivity and professional judgement were involved. The rest of the marks were allocated for the ethical discussion, which many candidates were quite poor at, choosing to spend a significant amount of time discussing the rules underlying IAS 17 rather than using professional and ethical insight.

ACCA Examiner's answer. The Examiner's answer to this question is included at the back of this Kit.

		Marks
(a)	Impairment adjustment	4
	Nathan	6
	Option	6
	Inventory	1
	Share options	4
	PPE	3
	Employee benefits	4
	NCI	2
	Sale of equity interest in Nathan	5
		35
(b)	1 mark per valid point, maximum	9
(c)	1 mark per valid point, maximum	6
		50

(a)(i) MARCHANT GROUP
STATEMENT OF PROFIT OR LOSS AND OTHER COMPREHENSIVE INCOME
FOR THE YEAR ENDED 30 APRIL 20X4

	$m
Revenue: $400 + 115 + (70 \times \frac{6}{12}) - 12$ (W4)	538.00
Cost of sales: $312 + 65 + (36 \times \frac{6}{12}) - 12$ (W4)	(383.00)
Gross profit	155.00
Other income: $21 + 7 + (2 \times \frac{6}{12}) - 5$ (W3) $+ 22$(W9) $- 5.33$ (W10)	40.67
Administrative expenses: $15 + 9 + (12 \times \frac{6}{12})$	(30.00)
Other expenses: $35 + 19 + (8 \times \frac{6}{12}) + 7.5$ (W5) $+ 2.36$ (W6) $+ 2.13$ (W7)	(69.99)
Finance costs: $5 + 6 + (4 \times \frac{6}{12}) - 3$ (W8)	(10.00)
Finance income: $6 + 5 + (8 \times \frac{6}{12})$	15.00
Share of profit of associate: $15 \times \frac{6}{12} \times 20\%$	1.50
Profit before tax	102.18
Income tax expense: $19 + 9 + (5 \times \frac{6}{12})$	(30.50)
Profit for the year	71.68
Other comprehensive income (items that will not be reclassified to profit or loss)	
Gain on property revaluation: $10 - 2.2$ (W7)	7.80
Loss on investments in equity instruments: 5 (W10)	(5.00)
Remeasurement of defined benefit plan (W5)	(2.00)
	0.80
Other comprehensive income (items that may subsequently be reclassified to profit or loss)	
Cash flow hedge (W8)	(3.00)
Other comprehensive income for the year	(2.20)
Total comprehensive income for the year	69.48
Profit attributable to:	
Owners of the parent (bal. fig.)	59.88
Non-controlling interests (W2)	11.80
	71.68
Total comprehensive income attributable to:	
Owners of the parent	58.88
Non-controlling interests (W2)	10.60
	69.48

Workings

1   *Group structure*

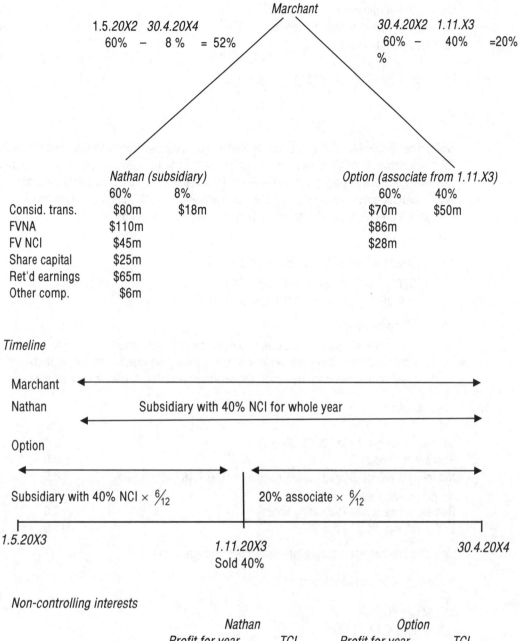

                                              Marchant
       1.5.20X2 30.4.20X4   30.4.20X2 1.11.X3
        60% − 8 % = 52%   60% − 40% =20%
                                                              %

              Nathan (subsidiary)   Option (associate from 1.11.X3)
                  60%   8%   60%   40%
Consid. trans. $80m $18m $70m $50m
FVNA $110m $86m
FV NCI $45m $28m
Share capital $25m
Ret'd earnings $65m
Other comp. $6m

Timeline

Marchant   ⟷

Nathan   Subsidiary with 40% NCI for whole year

Option

Subsidiary with 40% NCI × $^6/_{12}$ 20% associate × $^6/_{12}$

1.5.20X3   1.11.20X3   30.4.20X4
                            Sold 40%

2   *Non-controlling interests*

	Nathan		Option	
	Profit for year	TCI	Profit for year	TCI
	$m	$m	$m	$m
Per question	19.0	19.0		
15 × $^6/_{12}$			7.5	
15 × $^6/_{12}$				7.5
Reclassification of cash flow hedge (W8)	3.0	–	–	–
	22.0	19.0	7.5	7.5
NCI share	× 40%	× 40%	× 40%	× 40%
	8.8	7.6	3.0	3.0
	$11.8		$10.6	

BPP
LEARNING MEDIA

3   *Goodwill*

	Nathan	*Option*
	$m	$m
Consideration transferred	80.0	70.0
Fair value of non-controlling interest	45.0	28.0
Fair value of net assets	(110.0)	(86.0)
	15.0	12.0
Impairment loss to 30.4.20X5: 44 × 5%	(3.0)	–
	12.0	12.0

Note. The impairment of the goodwill in Nathan had been reversed and the goodwill increased to $2m more than its original value, giving an increase of $(3m + 2m) = $5m. However, after the goodwill has been impaired, any subsequent increase is likely to be internally generated goodwill rather than a genuine reversal of goodwill impairment. The $3m uplift and $2m increase cannot be recognised and must be eliminated, so $5m is charged to profit or loss.

4   *Intragroup trading*

(i)   Cancel intra group sales/purchases:

DEBIT	Revenue ($10m + $5m)	$12m	
CREDIT	Cost of sales (purchases)		$12m

(ii)   Unrealised profit:

The unrealised loss on the sale of the inventory is not cancelled. The sale is at fair value, which indicates that the inventory was impaired. The loss on the sale is therefore genuine, and must remain realised. However, the revenue and cost of sales will be eliminated.

5   *Pension plan*

	$m	
Net obligation b/d 1 May 20X3: 50 – 48	2.0	
Past service costs	3.0	
Net interest on net defined benefit obligation: (50 – 48 + 3*) × 10%	0.5	→ P/L
Current service cost	4.0	
Remeasurement loss (balancing figure)	2.0	→ OCI
Net obligation c/d 30 April 20X4	11.5	

*Note that the interest includes interest on past service costs.

6   *Property, plant and equipment*

	$m	
At 1 May 20X2	12.00	
Depreciation: 12/10 years	(1.20)	
31 October 20X4 cash received (20 × 5%) → OCI	2.20	→ OCI
At 30 April 20X3	13.00	
		already
Depreciation 20X3 to 20X4: 13/(10 – 1) years	(1.44)	accounted for
Revaluation loss	(4.56)	
	7.00	

DEBIT	Other comprehensive income	$2.20m	
DEBIT	Profit or loss	$2.36m	
CREDIT	Property, plant and equipment		$4.56m

7 Share options

	$m
30 April 20X3 Equity b/d: 8,000 × 4 × $100 × $\frac{1}{3}$	1.07
Profit or loss (balancing figure)	2.13
30 April 20X4 Equity c/d: 8,000 × 6 × $100 × $\frac{2}{3}$	3.20

8 Cash flow hedge

As the hedge is effective, the loss is taken to other comprehensive income:

DEBIT	Other comprehensive income	$3m	
CREDIT	Finance costs (profit or loss)		$3m

9 Group profit on disposal of Option (control lost)

	$m	$m
Fair value of consideration received		50
Fair value of 20% investment retained		40
Less share of consolidated carrying value when control lost		
Net assets	90	
Goodwill (W3)	12	
Less non-controlling interests	(34)	
		(68)
		22

10 Investment in Nathan

A fair value gain has been recorded on the investment in Nathan of $95m − $90m = $5m. This gain must be eliminated on consolidation because the calculation of goodwill is based on the fair value of the consideration at the date of acquisition, not at the date of the current financial statements. The double entry for the reversal is:

DEBIT	Other comprehensive income	$5m	
CREDIT	Investment in Nathan.		$5m

Reversal of fair value gain recognised in parent's separate financial statements

The sale of the 8% equity in Nathan does not result in loss of control, and is shown as a movement in equity in the consolidated financial statements, with no profit or loss arising. Accordingly, the gain on the sale recognised in the parent's separate financial statements must be reversed:

		$m	$m
DEBIT	Other income (18 − (95 × 8%/60%))	5.33	
DEBIT	Investment in Nathan (95 × 8%/60%)	12.67	
CREDIT	Other components of equity		18

Reversal of gain on sale recognised in parent's separate financial statements

(ii) Sale of 8% interest in Nathan

When Marchant disposed of 8% of its holding in Nathan, Nathan went from being a 60% subsidiary to a 52% subsidiary. In other words **control is retained**. No accounting boundary has been crossed, and the event is treated as a transaction between owners.

The accounting treatment is as follows:

Statement of profit or loss and other comprehensive income

(1) The subsidiary is **consolidated in full** for the whole period.

(2) The **non-controlling interest in the statement of profit or loss and other comprehensive income** is based on percentage before and after disposal, ie time apportion. In this case, the sale took place on the last day of the year, so there is a 40% non-controlling interest for the whole year.

(3) There is **no profit or loss on disposal**.

Statement of financial position

(1) The **change (increase) in non-controlling interests** is shown as an **adjustment to the parent's equity**.

(2) **Goodwill** on acquisition **is unchanged** in the consolidated statement of financial position.

The adjustment to the parent's equity is as follows:

	$m
Fair value of consideration received	18.00
Increase in NCI in net assets and goodwill at disposal:	
[$120m (per qu) + $14m FV adj* + $12m (W3)] × 8%	(11.68)
Adjustment to parent's equity	6.32

*The fair value adjustment is calculated as $110m – $(25 + 65 + 6)m = $14m

(b) **Fair value in financial statements**

It is not entirely accurate to say that IFRS implement a fair value model. While IFRS use fair value (and present value) more than other accounting frameworks, and more than they, and the old IAS did in the past, it is **not a complete fair value system.** IFRS are based on the **business model of the entity** and on the probability of realising the asset- and liability-related cash flows through operations or transfers. In fact the IASB favours a mixed measurement system, with some items being measured at fair value and others at historical cost. Historical cost has a number of **advantages** over fair values, mainly as regards reliability.

(i)   It is **easy to understand**.

(ii) It is grounded in **real transaction amounts**, and is therefore **objective** and objectively verifiable.

(iii) There is **less scope for manipulation**.

Before the publication of IFRS 13 *Fair value measurement* in 2011, there were a number of definitions of fair value, and there was considerable inconsistency. IFRS 13 was developed to solve some of these problems. 13 defines fair value as **'the price that would be received to sell an asset or paid to transfer a liability in an orderly transaction between market participants at the measurement date.'** The price which would be received to sell the asset or paid to transfer (not settle) the liability is described as **the 'exit price'**.

IFRS 13 has brought consistency to the definition and application of fair value, and this consistency is applied across other IFRS, which are generally required to measure fair value 'in accordance with IFRS 13'. This **does not mean, however, that IFRS requires all assets and liabilities to be measured at fair value.** On the contrary, many entities measure most items at depreciated historical cost, a notable exception being in the case of business combinations, where assets and liabilities are recorded at fair value at the acquisition date. In other cases, the use of fair value is restricted. For example:

(i)   IAS 16 *Property, plant and equipment* **allows revaluation** through other comprehensive income, provided it is **carried out regularly**.

(ii) While IAS 40 *Investment properties* allows the **option** of measuring investment properties **at fair value** with corresponding changes in profit or loss, and this arguably reflects the business model of some property companies, **many companies still use historical cost**.

(iii)   IAS 38 *Intangible assets* **permits the measurement of intangible assets at fair value** with corresponding changes in equity, but **only** if the assets can be measured reliably through the existence of an **active market** for them.

IFRS 9 *Financial Instruments*, issued in final form in July 2014, makes **more extensive use of fair value.** The standard requires that on initial recognition, financial assets are classified as measured at either:

(i)   Amortised cost, or

(ii)   Fair value through other comprehensive income, or

(ii)   Fair value through profit or loss

A financial asset is classified as measured at amortised cost where:

(i)   The objective of the business model within which the asset is held is to hold assets in order to collect contractual cash flows and

(ii)   The contractual terms of the financial asset give rise on specified dates to cash flows that are solely payments of principal and interest on the principal outstanding.

An application of these rules means that **equity investments may not be classified as measured at amortised cost** and must be measured at fair value. This is because contractual cash flows on specified dates are not a characteristic of equity instruments. By default, gains and losses on equity investments within the scope of IFRS 9 are recognised in profit or loss for the year. However, if the equity investment is not held for trading **an irrevocable election can be made at initial recognition to measure it at fair value through other comprehensive income** with only dividend income recognised in profit or loss. The amounts recognised in OCI are not re-classified to profit or loss on disposal of the investment although they may be reclassified in equity.

A **debt instrument** may be classified as measured at either amortised cost or fair value **depending on whether it meets the criteria above**. Even where the criteria are met at initial recognition, a debt instrument may be classified as measured at fair value through profit or loss if doing so eliminates or significantly reduces a measurement or recognition inconsistency (sometimes referred to as an 'accounting mismatch') that would otherwise arise from measuring assets or liabilities or recognising the gains and losses on them on different bases. An example of this may be where an entity holds a fixed rate loan receivable that it hedges with an interest rate swap that swaps the fixed rates for floating rates. Measuring the loan asset at amortised cost would create a measurement mismatch, as the interest rate swap would be held at FVTPL. In this case, the loan receivable could be designated at FVTPL under the fair value option to reduce the accounting mismatch that arises from measuring the loan at amortised cost. In practice only banks make a limited use of such transactions.

A financial asset **must** be classified and measured **at fair value through other comprehensive income** (unless the asset is designated at fair value through profit or loss under the fair value option) if it meets both the following criteria:

(i)   The financial asset is held within a business model whose objective is achieved by both collecting contractual cash flows and selling financial assets.

(ii)   The contractual terms of the financial asset give rise on specified dates to cash flows that are solely payments of principal and interest on the principal amount outstanding.

This business model is **new to the July 2014 version of IFRS 9.**

All derivatives are measured at **fair value.** Most **derivatives**, for example swaps, options and futures contracts, do not have a cost when signed and their historical cost is not relevant. **Embedded derivatives** must be classified in their entirety as either amortised cost or fair value, depending on whether they meet the definition of a financial asset within the scope of the standard. Other embedded derivatives must be separated from their host contracts and each part considered separately.

While IFRS makes some use of fair values in the measurement of assets and liabilities, **financial statements prepared under IFRS are not,** as is sometimes believed, **intended to reflect the aggregate value of an entity.** On the contrary, the *Conceptual Framework for Financial Reporting* specifically states that general purpose financial reports are not designed to show the value of a reporting entity. Such an attempt would be incomplete, **since IFRS disallows the recognition of internally generated intangibles**. Rather, the objective identified by the IASB is to provide financial information about a reporting entity which is useful to existing and potential investors, lenders and other creditors in making decisions about providing resources to the entity.

It is only when an entity is **acquired by another entity and consolidated** in group accounts that an entity's **net assets are reported at market value.**

(c)   **Treatment of lease**

IAS 17 distinguishes between operating leases and finance leases. A finance lease is a lease that **transfers substantially all the risks and rewards incidental to ownership of an asset**. All other leases are classified as operating leases.

The classification, which is made at the inception of the lease, depends on the **substance** rather than the form. The distinction often **involves judgement and may be subjective**, particularly in the case of a lease of land. Such a lease may be classified as a finance lease, even if title is not transferred to the lessee, where the value of the land is negligible and the risks and rewards pass to the lessee.

The difference of opinion has arisen between the financial controller and the finance director, both presumably professionally qualified, and is best resolved by the **financial controller seeking expert, independent advice.**

The treatment chosen should be that which presents fairly the substance of the transaction, taking into account all the facts of the case and the advice taken. The **choice should be driven by technical and professional standards, not by the desire to present a favourable picture for a particular purpose**. Thus, if the features of the lease meet the IAS 17 *Leases* criteria for a finance lease, the lease should not be treated as an operating lease in order to understate the liabilities of the entity for the purpose of raising a loan. If the finance director is **trying to compel the financial controller to change what would be the appropriate treatment because of business pressures**, then this presents the financial controller with an ethical dilemma. The pressure will be greater because the financial controller is new.

The **ACCA Code of Ethics** (or professional accountants' code of ethics) will be an essential point of reference in this situation, since it sets out boundaries outside which accountants should not stray. If the financial controller is convinced, after taking advice and in the light of all relevant factors, that the lease is a finance lease, then he or she **should disclose this to the appropriate internal governance authority**, and thus feel confident that his/her actions were ethical.

48 Ejoy

Text reference. Changes in group structure are covered in Chapter 14.

Top tips. This question required the production of a consolidated statement of profit or loss and other comprehensive income of a group. Candidates were expected to calculate and impairment test the investment in a subsidiary, to account for a joint venture, to deal with impairment and hedging of financial assets, and account for a discontinued operation.

Easy marks. Do not spend too long on the discontinued operation. You would not be penalised too heavily if you got this wrong and there are easy marks to be gained for adding across and other basic consolidation aspects.

Examiner's comment. Overall the question was quite well answered, with the majority of candidates achieving a pass mark. However, candidates answered the financial instruments part of the question quite poorly. The main problem seemed to be the application of knowledge; candidates could recite the principles of accounting for financial instruments but could not deal with the practical application thereof. The calculation of the goodwill was done well. However, the impairment testing of the investment in the subsidiary was poorly answered. Candidates need to understand this procedure as it will be a regular feature of future papers.

	Marks
Goodwill	7
Joint venture	2
Financial assets	7
Statement of profit or loss and other comprehensive income	8
Tbay	4
Non-controlling interest	2
Maximum	30

EJOY: CONSOLIDATED STATEMENT OF PROFIT OR LOSS AND OTHER COMPREHENSIVE INCOME
FOR THE YEAR ENDED 31 MAY 20X6

	$m
Continuing operations	
Revenue (2,500 + 1,500)	4,000
Cost of sales (1,800 + 1,200 + 34 (W8))	(3,034)
Gross profit	966
Other income (70 + 10 – 3 (W11)	77
Distribution costs (130 + 120)	(250)
Administrative expenses (100 + 90)	(190)
Finance income (W6)	6
Finance costs (W7)	(134)
Profit before tax	475
Income tax expense (200 + 26)	(226)
Profit for period from continuing operations	249
Discontinued operations	
Profit for the year from discontinued operations ((30 × 6/12) – 2 (W8))	13
Profit for the year	262
Other comprehensive income for the year (not reclassified to P/L):	
Gain on property revaluation net of tax: 80 + 10 + (8 × 6/12)	94
Total comprehensive income for the year	356
Profit attributable to:	
Owners of the parent	257
Non-controlling interest (W2)	5
	262
Total comprehensive income for the year attributable to:	
Owners of the parent (bal. fig.)	348
Non-controlling interest (W2)	8
	356

Workings

1 *Group structure*

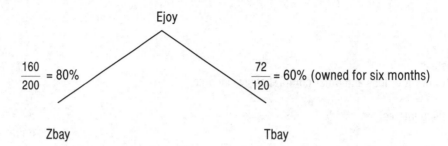

Ejoy

$\dfrac{160}{200} = 80\%$ $\dfrac{72}{120} = 60\%$ (owned for six months)

Zbay   Tbay

Tbay is a discontinued operation (IFRS 5).

Timeline

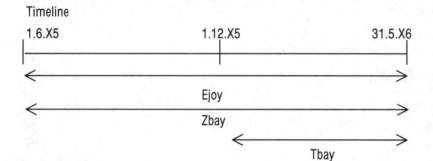

1.6.X5   1.12.X5   31.5.X6

Ejoy

Zbay

Tbay

2 *Non-controlling interest*

	Profit for the year		Total comp income	
	Zbay $m	Tbay $m	Zbay $m	Tbay $m
PFY/TCI per question	34.0		44	
(30 × 6/12)/(38 × 6/12)		15		19
Less impairment loss on loan asset (W4)	(42.2)		(42.2)	
Interest income on loan asset (W4)	1.1		1.1	
	(7.1)	15	2.9	19
	× 20%	×40%	× 20%	× 40%
	(1.4)	6	0.6	7.6
	4.6		8.2	

3 *Goodwill*

		Zbay $m		Tbay $m
Consideration transferred		520		192
Non-controlling interests	(600 × 20%)	120	(310 × 40%)	124
Fair value of net assets at acquisition		(600)		(310)
		40		6

4 *Loan asset held by Zbay*

	$m
Carrying value of loan at 1.6.X5 (a financial asset)	60.0
Impairment loss (balancing figure)	(42.2)
Present value of expected future cash flows $\left(20 \times \dfrac{1}{1.06^2}\right)$ at 1.6.X5 (note)	17.8
Interest income (6% × 17.8)	1.1
At 31.5.X6	18.9

Note. The $20 million is expected to be received on 31 May 20X7, ie. in two years' time.

5 Hedged bond (Ejoy)

	$m
1.6.X5	50.0
Interest income (5% × 50)	2.5
Interest received	(2.5)
Fair value loss (balancing figure)	(1.7)
Fair value at 31.5.X6 (per question)	48.3

Because the interest rate swap is 100% effective as a fair value hedge, it exactly offsets the loss in value of $1.7 million on the bond. The bond is classified at fair value through profit or loss. Both the gain on the swap and the loss on the bond are recognised in profit or loss as income and expense. The net effect on profit or loss is nil.

6 Finance income

	$m
Interest income on loan asset held by Zbay (W4)	1.1
Interest receivable on bond held by Ejoy (W5)	2.5
Interest received on interest rate swap held by Ejoy	0.5
Fair value gain on interest rate swap	1.7
	5.8

7 Finance costs

	$m
Per draft statements of profit or loss and other comprehensive income (50 + 40)	90.0
Impairment loss (loan asset held by Zbay) (W4)	42.2
Fair value loss on hedged bond (W5)	1.7
	133.9

8 Impairment losses

	Zbay $m	Tbay $m
Notional goodwill (40 × 100%/80%) (6 × 100%/60%) (W3)	50.0	10.0
Carrying amount of net assets (W9)/(W10)	622.9	329.0
	672.9	339.0
Recoverable amount	(630.0)	
Fair value less costs of disposal (344 − (5 × 100%/60%))		(335.7)
Impairment loss: gross	42.9	3.3
Impairment loss recognised: all allocated to goodwill		
(80% × 42.9)/(60% × 3.3)	34.3	2.0

9 Carrying amount of net assets at 31 May 20X6 (Zbay)

	$m
Fair value of identifiable assets and liabilities acquired (1 June 20X4)	600.0
TCI for year to 31 May 20X5	20.0
TCI for year to 31 May 20X6 per draft statement of profit or loss and other comprehensive income	44.0
Less impairment loss (loan asset) (W4)	(42.2)
Interest income (loan asset) (W4)	1.1
	622.9

10 Carrying amount of net assets (Tbay)

	$m
Carrying value of investment in Tbay at 31 May 20X6:	
Fair value of net assets at acquisition (1 December 20X5)	310
Post acquisition TCI(38 × 6/12)	19
	329

11   *Joint venture*

	$m	$m
Elimination of Ejoy's share of gain on disposal (50% × 6)		3
DEBIT Other income	3	
CREDIT Investment in joint venture		3

49 Case study question: Traveler

Text reference. Business combinations achieved in stages are covered in Chapter 14. Employee benefits are covered in Chapter 5. Segment reporting is covered in Chapter 18. Ethical issues are covered in Chapter 2.

Top tips. This question has been amended to reflect the revision to IAS 19 in 2011. This is still one of the trickier adjustments in Part (a), together with the impairment of the loan. You should have recognised straightaway that one of the acquisitions is of a further controlling interest (going from 60% to 80%) so there will be an adjustment to parent's equity and no need to revalue the existing interest.

Easy marks. There are some standard consolidation workings here, and you could slot in the caption for, say, adjustment to parent's equity even if you get the calculation wrong. Leave enough time for Parts (b) and (c) – the examiner has commented in the past that candidates often do not. Part (b) is straightforward knowledge and Part (c) allows a variety of valid points to be made .

Examiner's comment. In general, candidates demonstrated a good knowledge of the consolidation process together with calculation skills for the accounting adjustments needed to the parent's financial statements. Some candidates struggled with the impairment testing of the partial goodwill, forgetting to gross up for the non-controlling interest. Other common weaknesses in Part (a) of answers included ignoring the change in ownership interest, calculating impairment by simply comparing goodwill to recoverable amount without considering the net assets or fair value adjustment, not calculating a movement in equity for the non controlling interest change and including OCI changes in retained earnings rather than other components of equity. In addition, some candidates spent too long on Part (a) at the expense of readily available marks in Parts (b) and (c). Parts 1(b) and 1(c) can mean the difference between pass and fail.

Marking scheme

		Marks
(a)		
	Property, plant and equipment	4
	Goodwill	7
	Financial assets	4
	Defined benefit asset	4
	Current assets/total non-current liabilities	1
	Share capital	1
	Retained earnings	7
	Other components of equity	3
	Non-controlling interest	3
	Current liabilities	1
		35
(b)		
	Subjective assessment	8
	Up to 2 marks per element	
(c)		
	Subjective assessment	7
		50

BPP
LEARNING MEDIA

(a)   TRAVELER GROUP
      CONSOLIDATED STATEMENT OF FINANCIAL POSITION
      AS AT 30 NOVEMBER 20X1

	$m
Non-current assets	
Property, plant and equipment: 439 + 810 + 620 + 10(W6) + 22(W6) − 56(W7) − 2.7(W9)	1,842.3
Goodwill (W2)	69.2
Financial assets: 108 + 10 + 20 − 7.9(W8)	130.1
Net defined benefit asset (W10): 72 − 25 − 55 + 45 − 19	18.0
	2,059.6
Current assets: 995 + 781 + 350	2,126.0
Total assets	4,185.6

Equity and liabilities	
Equity attributable to owners of the parent	
Share capital	1,120.0
Retained earnings (W3)	973.4
Other components of equity (W4)	66.7
	2,160.1
Non-controlling interests (W5)	343.5
	2,503.6
Non-current liabilities: 455 + 323 + 73	851.0
Current liabilities: 274 + 199 + 313 + 45 (W10)	831.0
Total equity and liabilities	4,185.6

Workings

1   Group structure

	1.12.2010 60%	30.11.2010 + 20% − 80%		80%		1.12.2010
Consideration	$600m	$220m			Consideration	$541m
FVNA	$935m				FVNA	$526m
Ret'd earnings	$299m				Ret'd earnings	$90m
OCE	$26m				OCE	$24m

Traveler

Data   Captive

2   Goodwill

	Full method Data $m	Partial method Captive $m
Consideration transferred − for 60%	600	
Consideration transferred − for 80%		541.0
Non-controlling interests		
Fair value per qu	395	
526 × 20%		105.2
FV of identifiable net assets at acq'n:	(935)	526.0)
	60	120.2
Impairment losses (W12)	(50)	(61.0)
	10	59.2

69.2

3   Retained earnings

	Traveler $m	Data $m	Captive $m
Per question	1,066.0	442	169
Consideration (W7)	(56.0)		
Impairment of loan (W8)	(7.9)		
Depreciation of factory (W9)	(2.7)		
Defined benefit pension charge (W10)	(55.0)		
Pre-acquisition (W1)		(299)	(90)
		143	79

Group share

Data: 143 × 60%	85.8
Captive: 79 × 80%	63.2
Impairment losses(W12) (50 × 80%) +61	(101.0)
	992.4

4   Other components of equity

	Traveler $m	Data $m	Captive $m
Per question	60.0	37	45
Loss on remeasurement of defined benefit plan (W10)	(25.0)		
Impairment of pension plan (W10)	(19.0)		
Pre-acquisition (W1)		(26)	(24)
		11	21

Group share post acqn:

Data: 11 × 60 %	6.6
Captive : 21 × 80%	16.8
Adjustment to parent's equity (W11)	8.3
	47.7

5   Non-controlling interests

	Data $m	Captive $m
At acquisition (FV/W2)	395.0	105.2
Post acquisition share of retained earnings		
Data: 143 (W3) × 40%	57.2	
Captive: 79 (W3) × 20%		15.8
Post acquisition share of other components of equity		
Data: 11 (W4) × 40%	4.4	
Captive: 21 (W4) × 20%		4.2
	456.6	125.2
Acquisition of additional 20% of Data (W11)	(228.3)	–
	228.3	125.2
Impairment losses: 50(W12) × 20%	(10.0)	–
	218.3	125.2

343.5

6   Fair value adjustments

Data:

	At acqn 1.10.20X0 $m	Movement $m	At year end 30.11.20X1 $m
Land: 935 – (600 + 299 + 26)	10	–	10
Captive:			
Land: 526– (390 + 90+ 24)	22	–	22

7   *Consideration transferred: Captive*

This has been incorrectly treated as:

DEBIT	Cost of investment in Captive	$541m	
CREDIT	Profit or loss		$64m
CREDIT	Cash		$477m

The land transferred as part of the consideration needs to be removed from non-current assets, the $64m sales proceeds removed from profit or loss and a gain on disposal calculated. The gain is $64m sale consideration, less carrying value of $56m = $8m. The correct entries should have been:

DEBIT	Cost of investment in Captive	$541m	
CREDIT	Profit or loss (gain on disposal		$8m
CREDIT	Land		$56m
CREDIT	Cash		$477m

To correct, the entries are:

DEBIT	Profit or loss	$56m	
CREDIT	Land		$56m

8   *Impairment of loan*

The loan is a financial asset held at amortised cost under IFRS 9 *Financial instruments.* Traveler wishes to value the loan at fair value. However, IFRS 9 states that the classification of an instrument is determined on initial recognition and that reclassifications, which are not expected to occur frequently, are permitted only if the entity's business model changes.

Financial assets are subsequently measured at amortised cost if **both** of the following apply.

(i)   The asset is held within a business model whose objective is to hold the assets to collect the contractual cash flows.

(ii)   The contractual terms of the financial asset give rise, on specified dates, to cash flows that are solely payments of principal and interest on the principal outstanding.

All other financial assets are measured at fair value.

Traveler's objective for holding the debt instrument has not changed, and so it cannot measure it at fair value but must continue to measure it at amortised cost.

The impairment loss on the loan is calculated using the original effective interest rate as:

	$m	$m
Carrying value		29.00
Present value of future cash flows		
Year 1: $8m $\times \dfrac{1}{1.067}$	7.50	
Year 2: $8m $\times \dfrac{1}{1.0672^2}$	7.03	
Year 3: $8m $\times \dfrac{1}{1.0672^3}$	6.59	
	21.12	
		7.88

Round to $7.9m

DEBIT	Profit or loss (and Traveler's retained earnings (W3)	$7.9m	
CREDIT	Financial assets		$7.9m

BPP
LEARNING MEDIA

9   *Depreciation of factory*

Traveler wishes to account for the factory as a single asset. However, the roof and the building must be treated separately for the purposes of depreciation. The roof will be depreciated over five years and the remainder of the factory will be depreciated over 25 years taking into account the residual value of $2m:

	Building $m	Roof $m	Total $m
Cost	45.0	5	50.0
Depreciation:			
$(45 – 2) ÷ 25years/ 5 ÷ 5years$	(1.7)	(1)	(2.7)
	43.3	4	47.3

DEBIT	Profit or loss (and Traveler's retained earnings (W3))	$2.7m	
CREDIT	Property, plant and equipment		$2.7m

10   *Defined benefit pension plan*

According to IAS 19 *Employee benefits* (revised 2011), losses on remeasurement of the net defined benefit asset (previously called actuarial losses) must be recognised immediately in other comprehensive income. There will also be a ceiling placed on the amount to be recognised as an asset, which is the present value of available future refunds and reductions in future contributions of $18m. The adjustments are as follows:

	$m		$m
Net defined benefit asset b/d	72 Dr		
Charges to profit or loss			Dr Profit or loss (and retained earnings)
	(55) Cr	→	
Loss on remeasurement of defined benefit asset			Dr Other comprehensive income(and other components of equity)
	(25) Cr	→	
Contributions	45 Dr	→	Cr Current liabilities
	37 Dr		
Impairment loss (β)	(19) Cr	→	Dr Other comprehensive income
Asset ceiling (see above)	18 Dr		

11   *Adjustment to parent's equity on acquisition of additional 20% of Data*

This is an increase in the controlling interest and therefore a reduction in the non-controlling interest, of 20%/40%:

DEBIT	Non-controlling interest (W5) $456.6m × 20%/40%	$228.3m	
CREDIT	Investment		$220m
CREDIT	Parents equity (other components of equity (W4))		$8.3m

12   *Impairment of goodwill*

	Data $m	Captive $m
Net assets at year end per question	1,079	604.0
Fair value adjustments (W6)	10	22.0
	1,089	626.0
Goodwill (W2) Data 60, Captive 120.2 × 100%/80% (see note(i))	60	150.3
	1,149	776.3
Recoverable amount per question	(1,099)	(700.0)
Impairment loss gross	50	76.3
Impairment loss recognised (see note (ii)): 100%/80%	50	61.0

Notes

(i)   Because the non-controlling interest in Data is at fair value, goodwill arises on this non-controlling interest, which bears its share of any impairment using the proportions in which profits and losses are shared at the year end when the impairment review arose, that is 20%.

The gross impairment of $50m is taken to the goodwill working and the 20% ($10m) to the NCI working (W5). In the case of Captive, where the partial goodwill method is used, only 80% of the impairment is taken to the goodwill working.

(ii) Because the non-controlling interest in Data is at fair value, the goodwill is already grossed up, but Captive uses the partial goodwill method, so the goodwill needs to be grossed up for an unrecognised NCI of 20%.

(b) **Allocation of common costs under IFRS 8 *Operating segments***

If segment reporting is to fulfil a useful function, costs need to be appropriately assigned to segments. Centrally incurred expenses and central assets can be significant, and the basis chosen by an entity to allocate such costs **can therefore have a significant impact** on the financial statements. In the case of Traveler, head office management expenses, pension expenses, the cost of managing properties and interest and related interest bearing assets could be material amounts, whose misallocation could mislead users.

IFRS 8 *Operating segments* **does not prescribe a basis** on which to allocate common costs, but it does require that that basis should be **reasonable**. For example, it would not be reasonable to allocate the head office management expenses to the most profitable business segment to disguise a potential loss elsewhere. Nor would it be reasonable to allocate the pension expense to a segment with no pensionable employees.

A reasonable basis on which to allocate common costs for Traveler might be as follows:

(i) **Head office management costs.** These could be allocated on the basis of turnover or net assets. Any allocation might be criticised as arbitrary – it is not necessarily the case that a segment with a higher turnover requires more administration from head office – but this is a fairer basis than most.

(ii) **Pension expense.** A reasonable allocation might be on the basis of number of employees or salary expense of each segment.

(iii) **Costs of managing properties.** These could be allocated on the basis of the value of the properties used by each business segment, or the type and age of the properties (older properties requiring more attention than newer ones).

(iv) **Interest and interest-bearing assets.** These need not be allocated to the same segment – the interest receivable could be allocated to the profit or loss of one segment and the related interest bearing asset to the assets and liabilities of another.

The **amounts reported under IFRS 8 may differ from those reported in the consolidated financial statements** because IFRS 8 requires the information to be presented on the same basis as it is reported internally, even if the accounting policies are not the same as those of the consolidated financial statements. For example, segment information may be reported on a cash basis rather than an accruals basis. Such differences might include allocation of centrally incurred costs that are necessary for an understanding of the reported segment information.

IFRS 8 requires **reconciliations** between the segments' reported amounts and those in the consolidated financial statements. Entities must provide an explanation of such differences, and of the basis of accounting for transactions between reportable segments.

(c) **Ethical issues and conflict of interest**

Increasingly businesses are expected to be **socially responsible as well as profitable**. Strategic decisions by businesses, particularly global businesses nearly always have wider social consequences. It could be argued, as Henry Mintzburg does, that a company produces two outputs: goods and services, and the social consequences of its activities, such as pollution.

The requirement to be a **good corporate citizen goes beyond the normal duty of ethical behaviour** in the preparation of financial statements. To act ethically, the directors must put the interests of the company and its shareholders first, for example they must not mislead users of financial statements and must exercise competence in their preparation. Corporate citizenship, on the other hand, is concerned with a company's **accountability to a wide range of stakeholders**, not just shareholders. There may well be a **conflict of interest between corporate social responsibility and maximising shareholder wealth**; for example it may be cheaper to outsource abroad, but doing so may have an adverse effect on the local economy.

In the context of **disclosure**, a company might prefer not to give information – for example segment information – away, as it could be useful to competitors and have a negative impact on profit and bonuses.

However, the two goals **need not conflict**. It is possible that being a good corporate citizen can **improve business performance. Customers may buy from a company that they perceive as environmentally friendly,** or which avoids animal testing, and **employees may remain loyal** to such a company, and both these factors are likely to increase shareholder wealth in the long term. If a company engages constructively with the country or community in which it is based, it may be seen by shareholders and potential shareholders as being a **good long- term investment** rather than in it for short-term profits. As regards disclosure, a company that makes **detailed disclosures,** particularly when these go beyond what is required by legislation or accounting standards, will be seen as **responsible and a good potential investment**.

50 Case study question: Robby

Text reference. Business combinations achieved in stages are covered in Chapter 14. Non-current assets are covered in Chapter 4. Joint operations are covered in Chapter 13 and financial instruments in Chapter 7.

Top tips. Part (a) required a consolidated statement of financial position with two subsidiaries, one of which was acquired in stages. Included in this part of the question was a joint operation, and there were adjustments for the revaluation of property, plant and equipment, impairment of receivables and sale and repurchase of land. The joint operation was fiddly and time-consuming, although not conceptually difficult as you are told what kind of joint arrangement it was. If you struggled with the details of the step acquisition of Zinc given in Note (b) of the question, look carefully at our goodwill calculation in (W3). The investment in Zinc was made up of the 55% investment at its cost and the 5% investment at its 31 May 20X2 fair value, with a gain on revaluation of the 5% taking place in the current year (to 31 May 20X3). Part (b)(i) was textbook knowledge of a topical issue. Note the examiner's comment for Part (b)(ii) on the ethical implications of the sale of land just before the year end. This type of question is in line with the examiner's pattern of applying ethical principles to transactions that might be designed to manipulate the financial statements. It is not enough just to discuss the accounting treatment without considering the ethical issues.

Easy marks. There are some standard consolidation workings here, and you could slot in the caption for, say, joint operation, even if you get the calculation wrong or do not have time to do it all. Leave enough time for Part (b) – the examiner has commented in the past that candidates often do not.

Examiner's comment. In Part 1(a), candidates showed themselves to be very good at preparing group accounts using the full goodwill method, and coped well with the impairment of the PPE. However, they had problems determining the fair value of the consideration as some candidates did not take into account the increase in the fair value of the equity interest. They also struggled with the joint operation. In Part 1(b), candidates did not seem to know the de-recognition rules of IFRS 9 and often described the nature of a financial instrument, when a financial instrument should be recognised and the valuation methods utilised, which was correct but did not answer the question. Answers to Part 1(b)(ii) were good, although many candidates spent a disproportionate amount of time discussing the accounting treatment with little time spent on the ethical aspect of the transaction.

Marking scheme

	Marks
(a)	
Property, plant and equipment	6
Goodwill	6
Non-controlling interest	4
Financial assets	1
Current assets	3
Other components of equity	3
Retained earnings	6
Non-current liabilities	2
Current liabilities	4
	35

(b)

(i) 1 mark per point up to max   9

(ii) Manipulation   2

     Ethical discussion   4

                                             50

(a)   ROBBY GROUP

CONSOLIDATED STATEMENT OF FINANCIAL POSITION AS AT 31 MAY 20X3

	$m
Assets	
Non-current assets	
Property, plant and equipment: 112 + 60 + 26 + 24 (W8) + 3.6 (W9) + 6.12	
(W10) − 2.59 (W11) + 12 (W13)	241.13
Goodwill: 5 (W2) + 1 (W3)	6.00
Financial assets: 9 + 6 + 14	29.00
Jointly controlled operation: 6 − 6 (W10)	–
	276.13
Current assets: 5 + 7 + 12 + 8 (W10) + 4 (W12)	36.00
Total assets	312.13
Equity and liabilities	
Equity attributable to owners of the parent	
Ordinary shares	25.00
Other components of equity (W4)	2.00
Retained earnings (W5)	81.45
	108.45
Non-controlling interests (W6)	27.64
	136.09
Non-current liabilities: 53 + 20 + 21 + 0.84 (W10)	94.84
Current liabilities: 47 + 6 + 2 +6.6 (W10) + 3.6 (W12) + 16 (W13)	81.20
Total equity and liabilities	312.13

Workings

1   *Group structure*

	1 June X1	Robby		1 June X0	1 Dec X2
	80% (sub)			5% (IEI) +	55% = 60%
Pre-acquisition retained earnings	$16m	Hail Zinc	Pre-acquisition retained earnings	N/A	$15m

2   *Goodwill (Hail)*

	$m
Consideration transferred	50*
Non-controlling interest (fair value per question)	15
FV of identifiable net assets at acq'n	(60)
	5

*Note. Hail is valued at $55m as at 31 May 20X3, so there is a revaluation gain of $55m − $50m = $5m which needs to be reversed out in the calculation of consolidated other components of equity (W4).

3   *Goodwill (Zinc)*

	$m
Consideration transferred – for 55%	16
Non-controlling interest at fair value (per question)	9
Fair value of previously held interest (for 5% at 1 December 20X2)	5*
FV of identifiable net assets at acq'n: 26 + 3	(29)
	1

*Note.** There will be a revaluation gain on the previously held interest, calculated as follows:

	$m
Fair value of 5% at date control achieved (1 December 20X2)	5
Fair value of 5% per SOFP, ie at 31 May 20X2: $19m per Robby's SOFP, less $16m consideration for 55%	(3)
Revaluation gain (1 June 20X2 to 1 December 20X2)	2

This gain on revaluation of the previously held interest is taken to profit or loss for the year, and hence to retained earnings (W5).

4   *Other components of equity*

	$m
Robby (per question)	11.00
Dividend income from Hail transferred to retained earnings (W7)	(2.00)
Reserve transfer on property, plant and equipment (W11)	(0.11)
Impairment loss on property, plant and equipment (W11)	(1.89)
Revaluation gain on investment in Hail (W2)	(5.00)
Pre-acquisition (W1)	2.00

5   *Retained earnings*

	Robby $m	Hail $m	Zinc $m
Per question	70.00	27.0	19.0
Gain on revaluation of 5% investment in Zinc (W3)	2.00		
Dividend income from Hail (W7)	2.00		
Fair value depreciation (W9)	–		(0.4)
Profit from joint operation (W10)	0.68		
Reserve transfer on PPE (W11)	0.11		
Impairment loss on PPE (W11)	(0.70)		
Reverse loss on debt factoring (W12)	0.40		
Reverse gain on sale and repurchase (W13)	(4.00)		
Pre-acquisition (W1)		(16.0)	(15.0)
		11.0	3.6

Group share of post-acquisition profits of:

Hail: 11 × 80%	8.80
Zinc: 3.6 × 60%	2.16
	81.45

6   *Non-controlling interests*

	Hail $m	Zinc $m
At acquisition (W2/W3)	15.0	9.00
Post acquisition share of retained earnings		
Hail: 11 (W5) × 20%	2.2	
Zinc: 3.6 (W5) × 40%		1.44
	17.2	10.44

27.64

7 Dividend

The $2m dividend income has been incorrectly recorded in other comprehensive income for the year, and therefore in other components of equity. It should have been recorded in profit or loss for the year, and therefore in retained earnings.

To correct, the entries are:

DEBIT Other components of equity $2m
CREDIT   Retained earnings $2m

8 *Fair value adjustment: Hail*

Hail:

	At acqn 1June 20X1 $m	Movement (2 years) $m	At year end 31 May 20X3 $m
Land: 60 – (20 + 16)	24	–	24
	Goodwill (FV of NA)	Retained earnings	PPE in year end

9 *Fair value adjustment: Zinc*

Hail:

	At acqn 1 Dec 20X2 $m	Movement (6 months) $m	At year end 31 May 20X3 $m
PPE: (26 + 3) – (10 + 15)	4	(0.4)	3.6
	Goodwill (FV of NA)	Retained earnings	PPE in year end

***Note.** The fair value movement is the additional depreciation caused by the fair valuing for consolidation purposes: $4m \times 1/5 \times 6/12 = \$0.4m$

10 *Joint operation (in Robby's books)*

The treatment of the joint operation is set out in IFRS 11 *Joint arrangements.* Robby must recognise on a line-by-line basis its assets, liabilities, revenues and expenses plus its share (40%) of the joint assets, liabilities, revenue and expenses. The figures are calculated as follows:

Statement of financial position

	$m
Property, plant and equipment:	
1 June 20X2 cost: gas station (15 × 40%)	6.00
dismantling provision (2 × 40%)	0.80
	6.80
Accumulated depreciation: 6.8/10	(0.68)
31 May 20X3 NBV	6.12
Trade receivables (from other joint operator): 20 (revenue) × 40%	8.00
Trade payables (to other joint operator): 16 + 0.5 (costs) × 40%	6.60
Dismantling provision:	
At 1 June 20X2	0.80
Finance cost (unwinding of discount): 0.8 × 5%	0.04
At 31 May 20X3	0.84

Profit or loss for the year

	$m
Revenue: 20 × 40%	8.00
Cost of sales: 16 × 40%	(6.40)
Operating costs: 0.5 × 40%	(0.20)
Depreciation	(0.68)
Finance cost (unwinding of discount)	(0.04)
Profit from joint operation (to retained earnings (W10)	0.68

Robby has accounted only for its share of the construction cost of $6m. The journals to correct this are therefore as follows:

			$m	$m
DEBIT	Property, plant and equipment		6.12	
DEBIT	Trade receivables		8.00	
CREDIT	Joint operation	×		6.00
CREDIT	Trade payables			6.60
CREDIT	Provision			0.84
CREDIT	Retained earnings (Robby)			0.68

11   *Property, plant and equipment*

		Carrying amount $m	Revaluation surplus $m
1 June 20X0	Cost	10.00	
	Acc. depreciation $\frac{2}{10}$ × 10	(1.00)	
		9.00	
	Revaluation gain(bal. fig)	2.00	2.00
31 May 20X2	Revalued PPE c/d	11.00	
	Depreciation for year $\frac{1}{18}$ × 11	(0.61)	
	Transfer to retained earnings: 0.61 – 0.50		(0.11)
31 May 20X3	Balance	10.39	1.89
	Impairment loss (bal. fig.)	(2.59)	
	Recoverable amount	7.80	

The impairment loss is charged to other comprehensive income and therefore to other components of equity to the extent of the revaluation surplus. The remainder is taken to profit or loss and therefore to retained earnings. Thus $1.89 is taken to other components of equity and $2.59 – $1.89 = $0.7 to retained earnings.

Journals in Robby's books

Reserve transfer:

DEBIT	Other components of equity	$0.11m	
CREDIT	Retained earnings		$0.11m

Impairment loss:

DEBIT	Other components of equity	$1.89m	
DEBIT	Retained earnings	$0.70	
CREDIT	Property, plant and equipment		$2.89m

12   *Debt factoring*

Robby should not have derecognised the receivables because the risks and rewards of ownership have not been transferred. The receivables must therefore be reinstated and the loss reversed:

DEBIT	Trade receivables	$4.0m	
CREDIT	Current liabilities		$3.6m
CREDIT	Retained earnings (to reverse loss)		$0.4m

13   *Sale and repurchase of land*

Robby should not have derecognised the land from the financial statements because the risks and rewards of ownership have not been transferred. The substance of the transaction is a loan of $16m, and the 5% 'premium' on repurchase is effectively an interest payment. This is an attempt to manipulate the financial statements in order to show a more favourable cash position. The sale must be reversed and the land reinstated at its carrying amount before the transaction. The repurchase, ie the repayment of the loan takes place one month after the year end, and so this is a current liability:

DEBIT	Property, plant and equipment	$12m	
DEBIT	Retained earnings (to reverse profit on disposal (16 – 12)	$4m	
CREDIT	Current liabilities		$16m

(b)   (i)   **Derecognition of a financial asset**

Derecognition is the removal of a previously recognised financial instrument from an entity's statement of financial position.

An entity should derecognise a **financial asset** when:

(1)   The **contractual rights** to the cash flows from the financial asset **expire**, or

(2)   The entity **transfers the financial asset or substantially all the risks and rewards of ownership** of the financial asset to another party.

IFRS 9 gives **examples of where an entity has transferred substantially all the risks and rewards of ownership**. These include:

(1)   An unconditional sale of a financial asset

(2)   A sale of a financial asset together with an option to repurchase the financial asset at its fair value   at the time of repurchase.

The standard also **provides examples of situations where the risks and rewards of ownership have not been transferred**:

(1)   A sale and repurchase transaction where the repurchase price is a fixed price or the sale price plus a lender's return

(2)   A sale of a financial asset together with a total return swap that transfers the market risk exposure back to the entity

(3)   A sale of short-term receivables in which the entity guarantees to compensate the transferee for credit losses that are likely to occur.

It is possible for only **part** of a financial asset or liability to be derecognised. This is allowed if the part comprises:

(1)   Only specifically identified cash flows, or

(2)   Only a fully proportionate (pro rata) share of the total cash flows

For example, if an entity holds a bond it has the right to two separate sets of cash inflows: those relating to the principal and those relating to the interest. It could sell the right to receive the interest to another party while retaining the right to receive the principal.

In the case of Robby, the substance of the transaction needs to be considered rather than its legal form. Robby has transferred the receivables to the factor in exchange for $3.6m cash, but it is liable for any shortfall between $3.6m and the amount collected. In principle, Robby is liable for the whole $3.6m, although it is unlikely that the default would be as much as this. **Robby therefore retains the credit risk.** In addition, Robby is entitled to receive the benefit (less interest) of repayments in excess of $3.6m once the $3.6m has been collected. Therefore for amounts in excess of $3.6m Robby also retains the late payment risk. **Substantially all the risks and rewards** of the financial asset **therefore remain with Robby**, and the receivables should **continue to be recognised.**

(ii)   **Sale of land**

Ethical behaviour in the preparation of financial statements, and in other areas, is of **paramount importance**. This applies equally to preparers of accounts, to auditors and to accountants giving advice to directors. Financial statements may be manipulated for all kinds of reasons, for example to enhance a profit-linked bonus. In this case, the purpose of the sale and repurchase is **to present a misleadingly favourable picture of the cash position**, which **hides** the fact that the Robby Group **has severe liquidity problems**. The extent of the liquidity problems can be seen in the current ratio of $36m/$81.2m = 0.44:1, and the gearing ratio of 0.83, calculated as follows:

$$\frac{53 + 20 + 21 \text{ (non-current liabilities)} + 3.6 \text{ (factored receivables)} + 16 \text{ (land option)}}{\text{Equity interest (including NCI)}} = \frac{113.60}{136.09} = 0.83$$

The effect of the sale just before the year end was to **eliminate the bank overdraft** and improve these ratios, although once the sale of land has been correctly accounted for as a loan, there is no improvement in gearing. The sale as originally accounted for might forestall proceedings by the bank, but as the substance of the transaction is a loan, it does not alter the true position and gives a **misleading impression** of it.

Company accountants act unethically if they use 'creative' accounting in accounts preparation to make the figures look better. To act ethically, the directors must put the interests of the company and its shareholders first, and must also have regard to other stakeholders such as potential investors or lenders. **If a treatment does not conform to acceptable accounting practice, it is not ethical.** Acceptable accounting practice includes conformity with the qualitative characteristics set out in the *Conceptual Framework* particularly fair presentation and verifiability. Conformity with the *Conceptual Framework* precludes **window-dressing transactions** such as this, and so the land needs to be reinstated in the accounts and a current liability set up for the repurchase.

51 Case study question: Bravado

Text reference. Business combinations achieved in stages are covered in Chapter 14. Ethics are covered in Chapter 2.

Top tips. This question required the preparation of a consolidated statement of financial position where the non-controlling interest on acquisition was at fair value. This is often called the full goodwill method. There was also a calculation and explanation of the impact on the calculation of goodwill if the non-controlling interest was calculated on a proportionate basis and a discussion of the ethics of showing a loan to a director as cash and cash equivalents. The main body of the question required candidates to deal with the calculation of goodwill in a simple situation, the calculation of goodwill where there was a prior holding in the subsidiary, an investment in an associate, a foreign currency transaction, deferred tax and impairment of inventory. Don't be put off by the fact that the goodwill on Message is negative (gain on a bargain purchase). This is unusual, and can sometimes mean your calculation is wrong, but you don't lose many marks for arithmetical mistakes

Easy marks. Part (b) is very generously marked, since the calculation is similar to that in part (a) – you just need the NCI share of the subsidiary's net assets. If you're pushed for time you should ignore the foreign currency investment, as it's fiddly and only carries 3 marks.

Examiner's comment. In general the basic calculation of goodwill under the full goodwill method was well done by candidates. However, they dealt less well with the business combination achieved in stages, the contingent consideration and the deferred tax. Many candidates did not complete the retained earnings calculation and often there was doubt over where the gain on bargain purchase should be recorded. (Group retained profits) The calculation of the impairment of inventories was dealt with quite well by candidates, as was the increase in the value of PPE and land. Often the increase in the depreciation charge as a result of the revaluation of PPE was not calculated correctly, nor was the deferred taxation effect. Many candidates got muddled with Part (b) and omitted Part (c) altogether, but those who attempted Part (c) did well on it.

Marking scheme

		Marks
(a)	Message	5
	Mixted	6
	Clarity	4
	Investment in equity instrument	4
	Retained earnings	3
	Post acquisition reserves	2
	Other components of equity	2
	Current liabilities	1
	NCI	2
	Inventories	2
	PPE	2
	Deferred tax	1
	Trade receivables	1
		35
(b)	Message	3
	Mixted	3
	Explanation	3
		9
(c)	Subjective	6
	Available	50

(a)   BRAVADO GROUP
CONSOLIDATED STATEMENT OF FINANCIAL POSITION AS AT 31 MAY 20X9

	$m
Non-current assets	
Property, plant and equipment: 265 + 230 + 161 + 40 (W7) + 12 (W7)	708.0
Goodwill (W2)	25.0
Investment in associate (W3)	22.5
Investment in equity instruments: 51 + 6 + 5 – 17.4 (W8)	44.6
	800.1
Current assets	
Inventories: 135 + 55 + 73 – 1.8 (W9)	261.2
Trade receivables: 91 + 45 + 32	168.0
Director's loan (W10)	1.0
Cash and cash equivalents: 102 + 100 + 8 – 1 (W10)	209.0
	639.2
	1,439.3

	$m
Equity attributable to owners of the parent	
Share capital	520.0
Retained earnings (W4)	282.3
Other components of equity (W5)	(0.4)
	801.9
Non-controlling interests (W6)	148.8
	950.7
Non-current liabilities	
Long-term borrowings: 120 + 15 + 5	140.0
Deferred tax: 25 + 9 + 3 + 2.6 (W7)	39.6
	179.6
Current liabilities	
Trade and other payables: 115 + 30 + 60 + 12 (W2)	217.0
Current tax payable: 60 + 8 + 24	92.0
	309.0
	1,439.3

Workings

1   *Group structure*

```
                                          1.6. 20X7   1.6. 20X8
                                           10%    +    15%      = 25%

                      Bravado ─────────── Clarity

        1.6. 20X8      80%
                                              1.6. 20X7   1.6. 20X8
                                               6%     +    64% = 70%

          Message                    Mixted
   Retained earnings: $136m   Retained earnings:        $55m
            OCE:    $4m            OCE:                  $7m
```

2   *Goodwill*

	Message		*Mixted*	
	$m	$m	$m	$m
Consideration transferred				
Cash		300		118
Contingent (at FV)		–		12
		300		130
Non-controlling interest (at fair value)		86		53
Fair value of previously held equity interest				15
Less fair value of net assets at acquisition				
Per question/170 + 6	400		176	
Deferred tax liability (W7)	–		(3)	
		(400)		(173)
(Gain on bargain purchase)/Goodwill		(14)*		25

*Note. This is a gain on a bargain purchase and should be recorded in profit or loss for the year attributable to the parent (W4).

3   *Investment in associate*

	$m
Cost = fair value at date significant influence achieved: $9m + $11m	20.0
Share of post 'acquisition' retained earnings $10m* × 25%	2.5
	22.5

*Note. The profit for the year to 31 May 20X9 is the relevant figure, as the investment only became an associate at the beginning of that year.

4   *Retained earnings*

	Bravado $m	Message $m	Mixted $m
Per question	240.0	150	80.0
Fair value movement (W7)			(1.6)
Loss on inventory (W10)	(1.8)		
Gain on bargain purchase (W2)	14.0		
Pre-acquisition		(136)	(55.0)
		14	23.4

Group share

	Bravado $m
Message: 80% × 14	11.2
Mixted: 70% × 23.4	16.4
Clarity: 25% × 10*	2.5
	282.3

***Note.** The $10m profit for the year to 31 May 20X9 is the post-acquisition figure as Clarity became an associate on 1 June 20X8.

5   *Other components of equity*

	Bravado $m	Message $m	Mixted $m
Per question	17.0	4	7
Foreign IEI (W9)	(17.4)		
Pre-acquisition		(4)	(7)
Group share post acqn: Message	0.0	0	0
Mixted	0.0		
	(0.4)		

6   *Non-controlling interests*

	Message $m	Mixted $m
At date of control (FV/W2)	86.0	53
Post acquisition share of reserves		
Message: 14 (W4) × 20%	2.8	
Mixted: 23.4 (W4) × 30%		7
	88.8	60
	148.8	

7   *Fair value adjustments*

Message:

	At acqn 1.6.X8 $m	Movement $m	At year end 31.5 X9 $m
Land: 400 − (220 + 136 + 4)	40	–	40

Mixted:

	At acqn 1.6.X8	Movement	At year end 31.5 X9
		$\left(\frac{1}{7}\right)$	
Property, plant & equipment:170 + 6 − (100 + 55 + 7)	14	(2.0)	12.0
Deferred tax liability: (176 − 166) × 30%	(3)	0.4	(2.6)
	11	(1.6)	9.4

8   *Foreign currency investment in equity instrument*

	$m
Value on initial recognition: 11m dinars × 4.5 =	49.50
Value at 31 May 20X8: 10m dinars × 5.1 =	51.00
Gain	1.50

At 31 May 20X8, this gain would be recorded in other comprehensive income (not reclassified to profit or loss).

DEBIT	Investment in equity instrument	$1.5m	
CREDIT	Other components of equity (via OCI)		$1.5m

	$m
Value at 31 May 20X8	51.00
Value at 31 May 20X9: 7 × 4.8	(33.60)
Impairment	17.40

This is recorded as follows		$m	$m
DEBIT	Other components of equity (via OCI)	17.4	
CREDIT	Investment in equity instrument		17.4

9   *Inventories*

	$m	$m
Cost in financial statements		
1st stage (10,000 × 1,000)	10.0	
2nd stage (20,000 × 1,500)		30.0
Net realisable value		
1st stage (10,000 × (950 – 10))	(9.4)	
2nd stage (20,000 × (1,450 – 10))		(28.8)
	(0.6)	(1.2)
	(1.8)	

10   *Director's loan*

DEBIT	Loan receivable	$1m	
CREDIT	Cash		$1m

(b)   **Goodwill if non-controlling interest is calculated on a proportionate basis**

	Message		*Mixted*	
	$m	$m	$m	$m
Consolidated transferred				
Cash		300		118.0
Contingent (at FV)		–		12.0
		300		130.0
Non-controlling interest (20% × 400)/(30% × 173)		80		51.9
Fair value of previously held equity interest				15.0
Less fair value of net assets at acquisition				
Per question	400		176	
Deferred tax liability (W7)	–		(3)	
		400		(173.0)
(Gain on bargain purchase)/goodwill		(20)		23.9

In the case of **Message**, if non-controlling interest is valued on a **proportionate basis**, the **gain on the bargain purchase is greater**. This is logical if the fair value of the non-controlling interest is seen as part of the cost of the acquisition, and the fair value of this NCI is greater than the NCI's proportionate share of the subsidiary's net assets.

In the case of **Mixted**, the **goodwill is less** because, as for Message, Bravado has 'paid' less. The non-controlling interest is, as for Message, seen as part of the cost of the acquisition.

(c)   **Treatment of loan to director**

Although there is no specific prohibition against this treatment in IFRS, there is a requirement not to be misleading. The treatment is in **breach of certain concepts** prescribed in the IASB's *Framework for the Preparation and Presentation of Financial Statements,* namely:

(i)   **Understandability.** If the loan is shown in cash, it hides the true nature of the practices of the company, making the financial statements less understandable to users.

(ii)   **Relevance.** The information should be disclosed separately as it is relevant to users.

(iii)   **Reliability.** The reliability concept states that information must be free from bias and faithfully represent transactions. Clearly this is not the case if a loan to a director is shown in cash.

(iv)   **Comparability.** For financial statements to be comparable year-on-year and with other companies, transactions must be correctly classified, which is not the case here. If the cash balance one year includes a loan to a director and the next year it does not, then you are not comparing like with like.

In some countries, loans to directors are **illegal**, with directors being personally liable. Even if this is not the case, there is a potential **conflict of interest** between that of the director and that of the company, which is why separate disclosure is required as a minimum. Directors are responsible for the financial statements required by statute, and thus it is their responsibility to put right any errors that mean that the financial statements do not comply with IFRS. There is generally a legal requirement to maintain proper accounting records, and recording a loan as cash conflicts with this requirement.

There is, in addition, an **ethical aspect**. In obscuring the nature of the transaction, it is possible that the directors are **motivated by personal interest**, and are thus failing in their duty to act honestly and ethically. If one transaction is misleading, it casts doubt on the credibility of the financial statements as a whole.

In conclusion, the treatment is problematic and **should be rectified**.

52 Case study question: Grange

Text reference. Changes in group structures are covered in Chapter 14 of your BPP Study Text. Foreign transactions are covered in Chapter 16. Ethics are covered in Chapter 2.

Top tips. This question requires a thorough understanding of IFRS 3 revised and the importance of crossing – or not crossing – the 'control' boundary. There is a lot to do: you have a disposal where control is lost (subsidiary to associate), a disposal where control is retained (subsidiary to subsidiary) and a business combination in stages where the parent already has a controlling interest and is increasing its share. None of these should present problems if you have learned and practised this topic thoroughly. Remember that an increase or decrease in controlling interest that does not cross the control boundary goes to equity, not to profit or loss for the year, as it is a transaction between the owners.

There are a few other adjustments too, including a foreign investment, a contingent liability and an investment property.

Easy marks. Part (a) is very straightforward if you have learned the proforma for such calculations – and you should have. In Part (b) there are some easy marks for basic consolidation aspects. Part (c) is fairly open ended, and marks will be awarded for valid points.

Examiner's comments. Candidates generally performed well in Part (a) of this question. The calculation of the loss arising on the disposal of the equity interest was extremely well answered with many candidates scoring full marks for that. The main issues that candidates had in part (b) were the calculations of the negative and positive movements in equity arising from the sale and purchase of equity holdings. Candidates also struggled with the calculation of post acquisition reserves, which was quite complex. Markers gave credit for the method and workings shown. The non-consolidation adjustments (investment property, provisions for environmental claims, restructuring provisions etc) were generally well tackled, although a major failing often involved the non-recognition of the restructuring provision, as a constructive obligation did not exist.

Part (c) of the question required candidates to discuss the relationship between ethical behaviour and professional rules. The question required candidates to comment on the ethical behaviour of a director where the director possessed confidential information. The examiner was pleased with candidates' performance on this part, but emphasised that it is important to refer to the information in the question when writing the answer.

Marking scheme

		Marks
(a)	Fair value of consideration	1
	Fair value of residual interest	2
	Gain reported in comprehensive income	1
	Net assets	1
	Goodwill	2
		7
(b)	Property, plant and equipment	6
	Investment property	2
	Goodwill	3
	Retained earnings	7
	Other components of equity	5
	Non-controlling interest	2
	Non-current liabilities/trade and other payables	1
	Provisions for liabilities	3
	Intangible assets	2
	Current assets/investments in equity instruments	1
	Investment in associate	2
	Share capital	1
		35
(c)	Subjective up to	8
		50

(a) **Gain on disposal of equity interest in Sitin**

	$m
Fair value of consideration received	23
Fair value of equity interest retained	13
Less share of net assets and goodwill at date of disposal	
Net assets	(36)
Goodwill (W2)	(7)
Loss on disposal	(7)

(b) GRANGE GROUP
CONSOLIDATED STATEMENT OF FINANCIAL POSITION AS AT 30 NOVEMBER 20X9

	$m
Non-current assets	
Property, plant and equipment	
257 + 311 + 238 + 5(W7) + 3.47(W7) − 6(W8) + 4(W10) − 28(W11)	784.47
Investment property (W8): 6 + 2	8.00
Goodwill (W2)	38.00
Intangible assets (W7)	7.00
Investment in associate (W3)	13.00
	850.47
Current assets: 475 + 304 + 141	920.00
	1770.47
Equity attributable to owners of the parent	
Share capital	430.00
Retained earnings (W4)	400.67
Other components of equity (W5)	58.98
	889.65
Non-controlling interests (W6)	140.82
Non-current liabilities: 172 + 124 +38	1030.47
	334.00
Current liabilities	
Trade and other payables: 178 + 71 + 105	354.00
Provisions: 10 + 6 + 4 + 25(W7) + 7(W9)	52.00
	406.00
	1770.47

Workings

1   *Group structure*

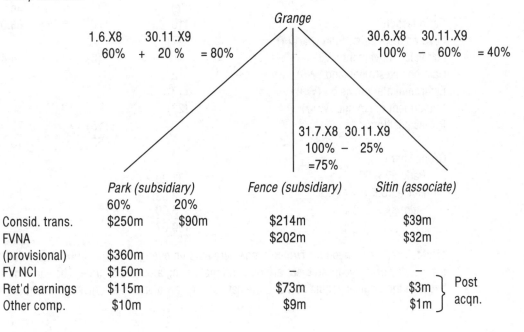

	Park (subsidiary)		Fence (subsidiary)	Sitin (associate)
	60%	20%		
Consid. trans.	$250m	$90m	$214m	$39m
FVNA			$202m	$32m
(provisional)	$360m			
FV NCI	$150m		–	–
Ret'd earnings	$115m		$73m	$3m } Post
Other comp.	$10m		$9m	$1m } acqn.

2   Goodwill

	Park $m	Fence $m	Sitin $m
Consideration transferred	250	214	39
Non-controlling interests (at FV)	150	–	–
Less fair value of net assets acquired			
Per question	(360)	(202)	(32)
Adjustments (W7)	(10)	(4)	–
	30	8	7
		38	
Derecognised on disposal (Part (a))			(7)
			–

3   Investment in associate

	$m
Cost = fair value at date control lost	13*
Share of post 'acquisition' profits	0**
	13

Notes

* The associate is held at $16m in the SOFP of Grange, therefore the effect of the part disposal and fair value exercise has been to impair the investment by $16m – $13m = $3m.

** The disposal was made at the year end so no post 'acquisition' reserves have arisen since it became an associate.

4   Retained earnings

	Grange $m	Park $m	Fence $m	Sitin $m
Per question	410	170	65.00	–
Loss on disposal of Sitin (Part (a))	(7)			
Fair value movement (W7)		(3)	4.47	
Gain on investment land (W8)	2			
Environmental provision (W9)	(7)			
Impairment of Grange (W11)	(28)			
Pre-acquisition		(115)	(73.00)	
		52	(3.53)	
Group share				
Park: 52 × 60%	31.20			
Fence: (3.53) × 100%	(3.53)			
Sitin: 3* × 100%	3.00			
	400.67			

***Note.** There is no need for two columns here as Sitin changed from a subsidiary to an associate on the last day of the year, so there are no earnings arising after the change. The earnings for the period between the original acquisition and the date of the part disposal are given in the question as $3m.

5   *Other components of equity*

	Grange $m	Park $m	Fence $m	Sitin* $m
Per question	22.00	14	17	–
Revaluation of property (W10)	4.00			
Pre-acquisition		(10)	(9)	
		4	8	
Change in controlling interest				
Park (W12)	(3.80)			
Fence (W13)	25.38			
Group share				
Park: 4 × 60%	2.40			
Fence: 8 × 100%	8.00			
Sitin: 1 × 100%	1.00			
	58.98			

*Notes

1   There is no need for two columns here as Sitin changed from a subsidiary to an associate on the last day of the year, so there is no other comprehensive income after the change.

2   The now realised gain of $1m, previously recognised in other comprehensive income (and therefore held in other components of equity), may be transferred to retained earnings as a reserves movement. This transfer is not required and not shown here.

6   *Non-controlling interest*

	Park $m	Fence $m	Sitin* $m
NCI at acquisition	150.0	–	–
NCI share of post-acquisition:			
Retained earnings: 52(W4) × 40%	20.8		
Other components: 4(W5) × 40%	1.6		
NCI at 30.11.X9 before changes	172.4		
Change in NCI on 30.11.X9			
Park (W12)	(86.2)		
Fence (W13)		54.62	
	86.2	54.62	–

140.82

*Note. There is no NCI in Sitin because it goes from being a 100% subsidiary to being an associate.

7   *Fair value adjustments*

Park

	At acqn (1.6.X8) $m	Movement $m	Year-end (30.11.X9) $m
Land*			
360 – (230 + 115 + 10)	5	–	5
Franchise: at 1.6.X8	10		
Depn. $10 \times 1\frac{1}{2}/5$		(3)	7
	15	(3)	12

*Note. For the purposes of the goodwill calculation, the fair value uplift is already included in the $360m given in the question for the fair value of the net assets of Park on acquisition.

Fence

	At acqn $m	Movement $m	Year-end (30.11.X9) $m
Contingent liability* at 31.7.X8	(30)	5	(25)
Property, plant and equipment excess at acquisition per qu.	4		
Depreciation 16 months ÷ 120 months	–	–	–
	–	(0.53)	3.47
	(26)	4.47	(21.53)

Note. For the purposes of the goodwill calculation, the contingent liability of $30 million is already included in the fair value of the net assets.

8   *Investment land (Grange)*

The land should be re-classified as investment property. IAS 40 states that land held for indeterminate use (Grange has not decided what to do with it) is investment property. The entries to re-classify are:

DEBIT   Investment property $6m
CREDIT   Property, plant and equipment $6m

As Grange's policy is to maximise return on capital employed, it will use the fair value model, and the gain for the year end of $8m – $6m = $2m will be taken to profit or loss for the year shown in retained earnings.

DEBIT   Investment property $2m
CREDIT   Profit or loss (retained earnings) $2m

The fall in value after the year end to $7m will be disclosed as a non-adjusting event after the reporting period.

9   *Provision for environmental claim*

The environmental obligations of $1m and $6m are a present obligation arising from past events and should be provided for:

DEBIT   Profit or loss (retained earnings) $7m
CREDIT   Provision $7m

However, no provision should be made for the costs of changing the manufacturing process because the events to date do not provide sufficient detail to recognise a constructive obligation. Grange still has the option of making other changes such as buying a new machine, shutting down production or changing the product.

10   *Foreign property*

	$m
Value at 30 November 20X8 ($8m/2$)	4
Value at 30 November 20X9 ($12m/1.5$)	8
Gain	4

DEBIT   Property, plant and equipment $4m
CREDIT   Other comprehensive income (other $4m
             components of equity)

11 *Restructuring*

No provision should be recognised for the restructuring because there is no constructive obligation.
A constructive obligation arises when an entity:

(i)   Has a formal plan, and

(ii) Makes an announcement of the plan to those affected. There is insufficient detail to recognise
      a constructive obligation. However, there is evidence that Grange's property, plant and
      equipment (and Grange itself) is impaired. An impairment test should be performed on
      Grange.

	$m
Net assets per question	862
Revaluation of investment property (W8)	2
Provision (W9)	(7)
Revaluation of property (W10)	4
Impairment of Sitin (W3)	(3)
	858
Value in use at y/e if not restructured	(830)
Impairment loss	28

All the loss of $28m is taken to profit or loss for the year (in retained earnings) as none of it relates to
previously revalued assets.

12 *Decrease in non-controlling interest in Park*

	$m
Non-controlling interest at 30.11.X9 before changes*(W6)	172.4

***Note.** A 20% share owned by the non-controlling interest passes to the parent at that date.

Increase: $172.4m \times 20\%/40\% = \$86.2m$

The gain is taken to equity (other components)

		$m	$m
DEBIT	NCI	86.2	
DEBIT	Parents' equity (bal. fig.)	3.8	
CREDIT	Cash		90

13 *Increase in non-controlling interest in Fence*

Non-controlling interest in Fence:

	$m
Net assets per question	232.00
Fair value adjustment (W7)	(21.53)
Goodwill (W2)	8.00
	218.47

The NCI arising on the part disposal is $218,470,000 \times 25\% - \$54,620,000$

The adjustment is taken to equity (other components)

		$m	$m
DEBIT	Cost of investment	80	
CREDIT	NCI		54.62
CREDIT	Parents' equity (other components of equity), balancing figure		25.38

(c) **Ethical behaviour and rules**

The **compliance-based approach** to ethics requires companies and individuals to act within the **letter of the
law,** or in conformity to the letter of a professional code of conduct. In essence, it says: follow the rules and
that is enough. Certainly rules are an important part of ethics. A professional code of conduct such as the
ACCA's is an effective and efficient way to communicate expectations as to what behaviour is expected and
what is unacceptable.

The **advantages of rules-based approaches** can be summarised as follows:

(i)   They can be **enforced** through penalties for non-compliance, which makes compliance more likely.

(ii)   The rules are usually **clear and unambiguous**, and companies or individuals can generally provide evidence of compliance.

(iii)   They are usually **specific,** where a requirement for 'integrity' is too general.

There are disadvantages to rules-based approaches, the most important of which are:

(i)   **Rigidity.** The rules-based approach allows no leeway or deviation, irrespective of how illogical the situation is.

(ii)   **Limited scope.** Enforcement can be difficult in situations not covered explicitly by the rules. Accountants who view rules as the sole determinant of ethical behaviour will be unable to cope in situations where there is no rule.

(iii)   A director who lacks integrity may try to find **loopholes**.

(iv)   A **rule may be unfair or inappropriate** – even unethical. Ethical principles and values may be used to judge the appropriateness of a rule, and whether it should be changed.

(v)   Too much emphasis on rules, and on sanctions for non-compliance, means that ethics are perceived as **punitive**. A more positive view of ethics is required if public trust is to be maintained.

In deciding whether to disclose Brook's liquidity problems to Field, the finance director of Grange should consider more than simple compliance with rules. He needs to act ethically. However, even without confining himself to rules, he will be faced with a number of **conflicting demands** and questions to which there are no easy answers.

(i)   Should the finance director **betray his friend's confidence?** Does he have a duty to disclose, or is this **'inside information'** which should not be disclosed?

(ii)   What about the finance director's **duty to other stakeholders**, including the shareholders of Grange? Grange may not be paid if the poor liquidity position of Brook is disclosed, and the shareholders stand to lose.

(iii)   If he discloses the information, the finance director could be perceived as being **responsible f**or Brook going into liquidation.

(iv)   Should the information passed to him by his friend be seen as an accurate assessment of Brook's creditworthiness, or is it a **subjective opinion?**

As can be seen, following rules is not the be all and end all of ethics, but even once it is accepted that integrity must play a role, the **questions are not always straightforward**.

53 Case study question: Ashanti

Text references. Complex groups are covered in Chapter 13 of your Study Text. Disposals are covered in Chapter 14. Financial instruments are covered in Chapter 7. Management of earnings is covered in Chapter 18 and also in Chapter 1 in the context of revenue recognition.

Top tips. This is an exceptionally demanding question, so don't worry too much if you didn't get it all. However, it is really important that you get the group structure. It is complicated. First you have a complex group. Then there are two disposals, one where control is lost (sub-subsidiary to sub-associate) and one where control is retained (70% to 60% subsidiary). In fact the adjustment on the disposal of the interest in Bochem does not belong in the statement of profit or loss and other comprehensive income, but we include it for completeness.

There are also a number of adjustments, some of which relate to financial instruments.

In Part (b), don't be tempted to waffle.

Easy marks. There are a surprising number of easy marks for such a complicated question. First there are the usual straightforward consolidation aspects – adding across, intragroup trading, setting up workings, revaluation of property. And part (c) is reasonably flexible, with credit available for sensible comments.

Examiner's comment. Candidates generally did well on this question. They showed a good understanding of the full goodwill method. Some made the mistake of showing a gain on disposal of the interest in Bochem in the statement of profit or loss and other comprehensive income, when it should be an adjustment to equity. The examiner stressed the importance of showing workings in a clear, concise manner, so that marks can be allocated for principles and method, even if mistakes are made in the calculations.

Marking scheme

		Marks
(a)	Consolidated statement of profit or loss and other comprehensive income	5
	Bochem	8
	Ceram	6
	Inventory	2
	Bond	4
	PPE	3
	Impairment of customer	2
	Employee benefits	2
	NCI	3
		35
(b)	1 mark per valid point, maximum	8
(c)	Description of management of earnings	4
	Moral/ethical considerations	3
		7
		50

(a) ASHANTI GROUP
STATEMENT OF PROFIT OR LOSS AND OTHER COMPREHENSIVE INCOME
FOR THE YEAR ENDED 30 APRIL 20X5

	$m
Revenue: $810 + 235 + (142 \times \frac{6}{12}) - 15$ (W4) $- 5$ (W6)	1,096.00
Cost of sales: $686 + 137 + (84 \times \frac{6}{12}) - 15$ (W4) $+ 1$ (W4)	(851.00)
Gross profit	245.00
Other income: $31 + 17 + (12 \times \frac{6}{12}) + 3.8$ (W10)	57.80
Distribution costs: $30 + 21 + (26 \times \frac{6}{12})$	(64.00)
Administrative expenses: $55 + 29 + (12 \times \frac{6}{12}) + 2$ (W3)	
$\quad + 1.6$ (W7) $+ 0.21$ (W8) $+ 2.2$ (W9)	(96.01)
Finance income: (W5) $0.842 + 0.836$	1.68
Finance costs: $8 + 6 + (8 \times \frac{6}{12}) + 11.699$ (W5) $+ 3$ (W6)	(32.70)
Share of profit of associate: $14 \times \frac{6}{12} \times 30\%$	2.10
Profit before tax	113.87
Income tax expense: $21 + 23 + (10 \times \frac{6}{12})$	(49.00)
Profit for the year	64.87
Other comprehensive income (items that will not be reclassified to profit or loss)	
Gain on investments in equity instruments: $20 + 9 + (6 \times \frac{6}{12})$	32.00
Gain/loss on property revaluation: $12 + 6 + 1.6$ (W7)	19.60
Actuarial loss on defined benefit plan: 14	(14.00)
Share of other comprehensive income of associate: $6 \times \frac{6}{12} \times 30\%$	0.90
Other comprehensive income for the year net of tax	38.5
Total comprehensive income for the year	103.37
Profit attributable to:	
$\quad$ Owners of the parent (bal. fig.)	50.48
$\quad$ Non-controlling interests (W2)	14.39
	64.87
Total comprehensive income attributable to:	
$\quad$ Owners of the parent	82.89
$\quad$ Non-controlling interests (W2)	20.48
	103.37

Workings

1   *Group structure*

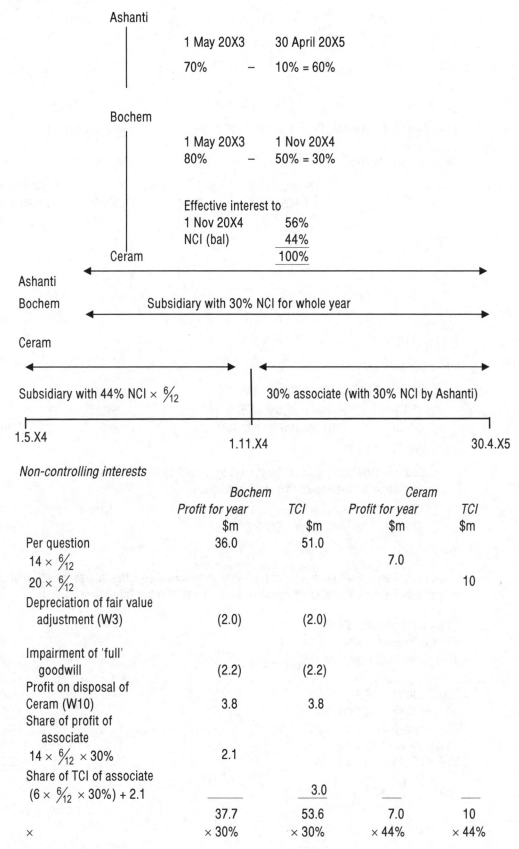

                                  Ashanti

                                  1 May 20X3   30 April 20X5
                                  70%   –   10% = 60%

                                  Bochem

                                  1 May 20X3   1 Nov 20X4
                                  80%   –   50% = 30%

                                  Effective interest to
                                  1 Nov 20X4   56%
                                  NCI (bal)   44%
                                                    100%

Ashanti   Ceram

Bochem   Subsidiary with 30% NCI for whole year

Ceram

Subsidiary with 44% NCI × 6/12   30% associate (with 30% NCI by Ashanti)

1.5.X4   1.11.X4   30.4.X5

2   *Non-controlling interests*

| | Bochem | | Ceram | |
| | Profit for year | TCI | Profit for year | TCI |
	$m	$m	$m	$m
Per question	36.0	51.0		
14 × 6/12			7.0	
20 × 6/12				10
Depreciation of fair value adjustment (W3)	(2.0)	(2.0)		
Impairment of 'full' goodwill	(2.2)	(2.2)		
Profit on disposal of Ceram (W10)	3.8	3.8		
Share of profit of associate 14 × 6/12 × 30%	2.1			
Share of TCI of associate (6 × 6/12 × 30%) + 2.1		3.0		
	37.7	53.6	7.0	10
×	× 30%	× 30%	× 44%	× 44%

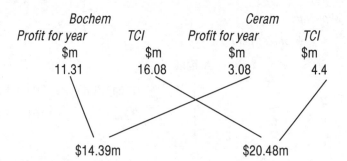

	Bochem		Ceram	
	Profit for year	TCI	Profit for year	TCI
	$m	$m	$m	$m
	11.31	16.08	3.08	4.4

$14.39m $20.48m

Note. There is no profit on the part disposal of Bochem because control is not lost.

3   *Fair value adjustments*

Bochem	At acquisition 1 May 20X3 $m	Movement 20X4 $m	20X5 $m	At year end 30 April 20X5 $m
Plant (160 – (55 + 85 + 10))	10	$^{10}\!/_{5}$ = (2)	(2)	6

(4)

Ceram 115 – 115	–	–	–

4   *Intragroup trading*

(i)   Cancel intra group sales/purchases:

DEBIT	Revenue ($10m + $5m)	$15m	
CREDIT	Cost of sales (purchases)		$15m

(ii)   Unrealised profit:

Note. The inventory sold to Ceram has been sold to third parties, so the unrealised profit arises only on the unsold inventory of Bochem.

DEBIT	Cost of sales (10 × ½ × 20%)	$1m	
CREDIT	Inventories (SOFP)		$1m

5   *Bond*

First calculate amortised cost using the original semi-annual effective interest of 4%, then compare with impaired value calculated using the original annual effective interest of 8%.

	$m
1 May 20X4 amortised cost	21.046
Effective interest @ 4%	0.842
31 October 20X4 cash received (20 × 5%)	(1.000)
	20.888
Effective interest @ 4%	0.836
30 April 20X5 cash received	(1.000)
30 April 20X5 c/d	20.724
Impairment loss (bal. fig.)	(11.699)
30 April 20X5 impaired value*	9.025

$$*2.34 \times \frac{1}{1.08} + 8 \times \frac{1}{(1.08)^2}$$

Double entries:

DEBIT	Profit or loss	$11.698m	
CREDIT	Bond		$11.698m

6   *Allowance for receivables*

The revenue of $5m should not have been recorded, as it is not probable that future economic benefits from the sale will flow to Ashanti. The revenue should only be recorded when the customer pays for the goods.

It is not appropriate to include the $5m in the allowance for doubtful debts of $8m, and so the allowance must be limited to $3m.

DEBIT	Revenue	$5m	
CREDIT	Receivables		$5m
DEBIT	Finance costs (impairment of receivable)	$3m	
CREDIT	Allowance for doubtful debts		$3m

7   *Property, plant and equipment*

		SOFP $m	Revaluation surplus $m	
1 May 20X3	Cost	12.000		
	Depreciation $^{12}\!/_{10}$	(1.200)		To OCI (not re-classified on disposal)
	Revaluation (bal. fig)	2.200	2.2	
30 April 20X4	Revalued PPE c/d	13.000		
	Depreciation for year $^{13}\!/_{9}$	(1.444)		
	Transfer to retained earnings: 1.444 – 1.2		(0.244)	
			1.956	and 1.6 to P/L
	Revaluation loss (bal. fig.)	(3.556)	(1.956)	
30 April 20X5	Revalued PPE c/d	8.000	0.000	

Original entries:

DEBIT	Other comprehensive income	$3.56m	
CREDIT	Property, plant and equipment		$3.56m

Correct entries:

DEBIT	Other comprehensive income	$1.96m	
DEBIT	Profit or loss (bal. fig.)	$1.6m	
CREDIT	Property, plant and equipment		$3.56m

To correct:

DEBIT	Profit or loss	$1.6m	
CREDIT	Other comprehensive income		$1.6m

8   *Holiday pay accrual*

IAS 19 *Employee benefits* requires that an accrual be made for holiday entitlement carried forward to next year.

Number of days c/fwd: $900 \times 3 \times 95\% = 2,565$ days
Number of working days: $900 \times 255 = 229,500$

$$\text{Accrual} = \frac{2,565}{229,500} \times \$19m = \$0.21m$$

DEBIT	Administrative expenses	$0.21m	
CREDIT	Accruals		$0.21m

9 *Goodwill*

	Bochem $m	*Ceram* $m
Consideration transferred: per question/136 × 70%	150.0	95.2
Fair value of non-controlling interest	54.0	26.0
Fair value of net assets	(160.0)	(115.0)
	44.0	6.2
Impairment loss to 30.4. 20X4: 44 × 15%	(6.6)	(−)
	37.4	
Impairment loss to 30.4.20X5: 44 × 5%	(2.2)	
	35.2	6.2

10 *Profit on sale of Ceram*

	$m	$m
Fair value of consideration received		90.0
Fair value of equity interest retained		45.0
Consolidated value of Ceram at date of disposal		
Net assets	160.0	
Goodwill	6.2	
	166.2	
Less NCI per question	(35.0)	
		(131.2)
		3.8

11 *Sale of 10% of Bochem*

As control is not lost, there is **no effect on the consolidated statement of profit or loss and other comprehensive income**. The sale is, in effect, a **transfer between owners** (Ashanti and the non-controlling interest). It is accounted for as an equity transaction directly in equity, and only reflected in the statement of changes in equity.

DEBIT	Cash	$34m	
CREDIT	Non-controlling interest (251.2 * × 10%)		$25.12m
CREDIT	Adjustment to parent's equity (not OCI)		$8.88m

* Net assets of Bochem at date of sale:

	$m
Net assets at 30 April 20X5	210.0
FV adjustments (W3)	6.0
	216.0
Goodwill (W9)	35.2
	251.2

BPP note. Because there is no effect on the consolidated statement of profit or loss and other comprehensive income, it was not necessary to do this working in order to obtain full marks. Nevertheless, it is good practice, so we have included it for completeness.

(b) **Social and environmental information**

There are a number of factors which encourage companies to disclose social and environmental information in their financial statements.

Public interest in corporate social responsibility is steadily increasing. Although financial statements are primarily intended for investors and their advisers, there is growing recognition that companies actually have **a number of different stakeholders**. These include **customers, employees and the general public,** all of whom are **potentially interested** in the way in which a company's operations affect the natural environment and the wider community. These stakeholders can have a **considerable effect on a company's performance**. As a result many companies now deliberately attempt to build a **reputation for social and environmental responsibility**. Therefore the disclosure of environmental and social information is essential. There is also growing recognition that **corporate social responsibility is actually an important part of an entity's overall performance.** Responsible practice in areas such as reduction of damage to the environment and recruitment **increases shareholder value**. Companies that act responsibly and make social and environmental disclosures are **perceived as better investments** than those that do not.

Another factor is **growing interest by governments and professional bodies**. Although there are **no IFRSs** that specifically require environmental and social reporting, it may be required by **company legislation**. There are now a number of **awards for environmental and social reports** and high quality disclosure in financial statements. These provide further encouragement to disclose information.

At present companies are normally able to disclose **as much or as little information as they wish in whatever manner that they wish**. This causes a number of **problems**. Companies tend to disclose information **selectively** and it is difficult for users of the financial statements to **compare the performance of different companies**. However, there are **good arguments** for continuing to allow companies a certain amount of freedom to determine the information that they disclose. If detailed rules are imposed, **companies are likely to adopt a 'checklist' approach** and will **present information in a very general and standardised way**, so that it is of very little use to stakeholders.

(c) **Management of earnings**

'Earnings management' involves exercising judgement with regard to financial reporting and structuring transactions so as to give a **misleadingly optimistic picture** of a company's performance. This is done with the intention, whether consciously or not, of **influencing outcomes that depend on stakeholders' assessments**. For example, a bank, or a supplier or customer may decide to do business with a company on the basis of a favourable performance or position. A director may wish to delay a hit to profit or loss for the year in order to secure a bonus that depends on profit. Indeed earnings management, sometimes called 'creative accounting' may be described as manipulation of the financial reporting process for private gain.

A director may also wish to present the company favourably in order to maintain a **strong position within the market**. The motive is not directly private gain – he or she may be thinking of the company's stakeholders, such as employees, suppliers or customers – but in the long term earnings management is not a substitute for sound and profitable business, and cannot be sustained.

'Aggressive' earnings management is a form of fraud and differs from reporting error. Nevertheless, all forms of earnings management may be **ethically questionable**, even if not illegal.

A more positive way of looking at earnings management is to consider the **benefits of not manipulating earnings:**

(I) Stakeholders can rely on the data. Word gets around that the company 'tells it like it is' and does not try to bury bad news.

(ii) It encourages management to safeguard the assets and exercise prudence.

(iii) Management set an example to employees to work harder to make genuine profits, not arising from the manipulation of accruals.

(iv) Focus on cash flow rather than accounting profits keeps management anchored in reality.

Earnings management goes against **the principle of corporate social responsibility**. Companies have duty not to mislead stakeholders, whether their own shareholders, suppliers, employees or the government.

BPP
LEARNING MEDIA

Because the temptation to indulge in earnings management may be strong, particularly in times of financial crisis, it is important to have **ethical frameworks and guidelines** in place. The letter of the law may not be enough.

54 Preparation question: Foreign operation

CONSOLIDATED STATEMENT OF FINANCIAL POSITION

	Standard $'000	Odense Kr'000	Rate	Odense $'000	Consol $'000
Property, plant and equipment	1,285	4,400	8.1	543	1,828
Inv in Odense	520	–		–	–
Goodwill (W2)	–	–		–	277
	1,805	4,400		543	2,105
Current assets	410	2,000	8.1	247	657
	2,215	6,400		790	2,762
Share capital	500	1,000	9.4	106	500
Retained earnings (W3)	1,115				1,395
Pre-acq'n		2,100	9.4	224	
Post acq'n	–	2,200	Bal fig	324	
	1,615	5,300		654	1,895
Non-controlling interest (W6)					131
					2,026
Loans	200	300	8.1	37	237
Current liabilities	400	800	8.1	99	499
	600	1,100		136	736
	2,215	6,400		790	2,762

CONSOLIDATED STATEMENT OF PROFIT OR LOSS AND OTHER COMPREHENSIVE INCOME

	Standard $'000	Odense Kr'000	Rate	Odense $'000	Consol $'000
Revenue	1,125	5,200	8.4	619	1,744
Cost of sales	(410)	(2,300)	8.4	(274)	(684)
Gross profit	715	2,900		345	1,060
Other expenses	(180)	(910)	8.4	(108)	(288)
Impairment loss (W2)					(21)
Dividend from Odense	40				–
Profit before tax	575	1,990		237	751
Income tax expense	(180)	(640)	8.4	(76)	(256)
Profit for the year	395	1,350		161	495

OTHER COMPREHENSIVE INCOME
Items that may subsequently be reclassified to profit or loss

	Standard $'000	Odense Kr'000	Rate	Odense $'000	Consol $'000
Exchange difference on translating foreign operations (W4)	–	–		–	72
TOTAL COMPREHENSIVE INCOME FOR THE YEAR	395	1,350		161	567

Profit attributable to:
Owners of the parent	463
Non-controlling interest (161 × 20%)	32
	495

Total comprehensive income for the year attributable to:
Owners of the parent	525
Non-controlling interest (161 + 48) × 20%	42
	567

CONSOLIDATED STATEMENT OF CHANGES IN EQUITY (EXTRACT)

	Retained earnings $'000
Balance at 20X5	1,065
Dividends paid	(195)
Total comprehensive income for the year (per SPLOCI)	525
Balance at 31/12/X6 (W3)/(W5)	1,395

Workings

1   *Group structure*

        Standard

1.1.X4 | 80%

                Pre-acquisition ret'd earnings 2,100,000 Krone
        Odense

2   *Goodwill*

	Kr'000	Kr'000	Rate	$'000
Consideration transferred (520 × 9.4)		4,888		520
Non-controlling interests (3,100 × 20%)		620		66
Share capital	1,000		9.4	
Reserves	2,100			
		(3,100)		(330)
		2,408		256
Exchange differences 20X4-20X5		–	β	18
At 31.12.X5		2,408	8.8	274
Impairment losses 20X6		(168)	8.1	(21)
Exchange differences 20X6		–	β	24
At 31.12.X6		2,240	8.1	277

3   *Consolidated retained earnings carried forward*

	Standard $'000
Standard	1,115
Group share of post acquisition reserves at Odense (324 × 80%)	259
	1,374
Less goodwill impairment losses (W2)	(21)
Exchange on differences on goodwill (18 + 24)	42
	1,395

4   *Consolidated retained earnings b/f proof*

	$'000
Standard	915
Add post-acquisition retained earnings of Odense (4,355 @ 8.8 – 3,100 @ 9.4) × 80%	132
Less goodwill impairment losses (W2)	0
Exchange differences on goodwill (W2)	18
	1,065

5   Exchange differences

	$'000	$'000
On translation of net assets:		
Closing NA @ CR	654	
Opening NA @ OR (5,300 – 1,350 + 405 = 4,355 @ 8.8)	(495)	
Less retained profit as translated (161 (SOCI) – 405 @ 8.1)	(111)	
Exchange gain		48
On goodwill (W2)		24
		72

6   Non-controlling interests (statement of financial position)

	$'000
NCI at acquisition (W2)	66
NCI share of post acquisition reserves of Odense (324 × 20%)	65
	131

55 Aspire

Text reference. Foreign currency transactions are covered in Chapter 16 of your Study Text, and deferred tax is covered in Chapter 6.

Top tips. This question dealt with a number of foreign transactions (functional currency, goodwill, deferred tax and a loan), and contained a balanced mixture of discussion and computation. Unusually, this was not in the group accounts case study question, but as this topic is not covered at F7, it is to be expected that it will come up quite regularly in P2. Part (b), on deferred tax issues, was somewhat tricky. The treatment of goodwill (Part (c)) is fundamental to the understanding of accounting for an overseas subsidiary. Goodwill arising on acquisition of foreign operations and any fair value adjustments are both treated as the foreign operation's assets and liabilities. They are expressed in the foreign operation's functional currency and translated at the closing rate. Exchange differences arising on the retranslation of foreign entities' financial statements are recognised in other comprehensive income and accumulated as a separate component of equity.

Easy marks. There are some easy marks in Part (a) for a discussion of how to determine the functional currency – this issue has been examined in the past questions Ribby and Rose.

Examiner's comment. In Part (a), it was important for candidates to use the information in the question. The decision as to the functional currency was subjective and was based upon the candidate's interpretation of the information in the question. Candidates scored well on this part. Many found Part (b) difficult, ignoring the fact that a discussion was required and simply calculating the deferred taxation amount. In Part (c), candidates often calculated goodwill correctly but found the retranslation of goodwill quite difficult. Part (d) (loan and interest) were dealt with satisfactorily by most candidates.

ACCA Examiner's answer. The Examiner's answer to this question is included at the back of this Kit.

Marking scheme

		Marks
(a)	1 mark per point up to maximum	7
(b)	1 mark per point up to maximum	6
(c)	1 mark per point up to maximum	5
(d)	1 mark per point up to maximum	5
Professional marks		2
Maximum		25

(a)   **Factors to consider in determining functional currency of Aspire**

IAS 21 *The effects of changes in foreign exchange rates* defines functional currency as 'the currency of the primary economic environment in which the entity operates'. Each entity, whether an individual company, a parent of a group, or an operation within a group, should determine its functional currency and **measure its results and financial position in that currency**. If it is not obvious what the functional currency is, management will need to use its judgement in determining the currency which most faithfully represents the economic effects of the underlying transactions, events and conditions.

An entity should generally consider the following factors:

(i)   What is the currency that mainly **influences sales prices** for goods and services (this will often be the currency in which sales prices for its goods and services are denominated and settled)?

(ii)   What is the currency of the country whose **competitive forces and regulations** mainly determine the sales prices of its goods and services?

(iii)   What is the currency that **mainly influences labour, material and other costs** of providing goods or services? (This will often be the currency in which such costs are denominated and settled.)

Other factors may also provide evidence of an entity's functional currency:

(i)   It is the currency in which **funds from financing activities** are generated.

(ii)   It is the currency in which **receipts from operating activities** are usually retained.

Aspire's subsidiary does not make investment decisions; these are under Aspire's control, and consideration of the currency which influences sales and costs is not relevant. Costs are incurred in dollars, but these are low and therefore not material in determining which is the subsidiary's functional currency. It is necessary, therefore to consider other factors in order to determine the functional currency of the subsidiary and whether its functional currency is the same as that of Aspire.

(i)   The **autonomy** of a foreign operation from the reporting entity

(ii)   The **level of transactions** between the reporting entity and the foreign operation

(iii)   Whether the foreign operation **generates sufficient cash flows** to meet its cash needs

(iv)   Whether **its cash flows directly affect those of the reporting entity**

The **subsidiary has issued 2 million dinars of equity to Aspire. Although this is in a different currency from that of Aspire, Aspire has controlled how the proceeds were to be invested** – in dinar-denominated bonds, suggesting that the **subsidiary is merely a vehicle for Aspire to invest in dinar-related investments.** Only 100,000 dinars of equity capital is from external sources, and this amount is insignificant compared to the equity issued to Aspire. The lack of autonomy of the subsidiary is confirmed by the fact that income from investments is either remitted to Aspire, or reinvested on instructions from Aspire, and by the fact that the subsidiary does not have any independent management or significant numbers of staff.

It appears that the subsidiary **is merely an extension of Aspire's activities rather than an autonomous entity.** Its purpose may have been to avoid reporting Aspire's exposure to the dinar/dollar exchange rate in profit or loss – it would be reported in other comprehensive income through the translation of the net investment in the subsidiary. These matters would lead to the conclusion that the **subsidiary's functional currency is the dollar.**

Operations are financed in dinars, and any income not remitted to Aspire is in dinars, and so the dinar represents the currency in which the subsidiary's economic activities are primarily carried out. However, in the absence of the benefit of presenting the dollar/dinar exchange rate fluctuations in other comprehensive income, Aspire could have invested the funds directly, and so **Aspire's functional currency should determine that of the subsidiary.**

(b)   **Deferred tax charge**

Investments in foreign branches (or subsidiaries, associates or joint arrangements) are affected by **changes in foreign exchange rates**. In this case, the branch's taxable profits are determined in dinars, and changes in the dinar/dollar exchange rate may give rise to temporary differences. These differences can arise where the carrying amounts of the non-monetary assets are translated at historical rates and the tax base of those assets are translated at the closing rate. The **closing rate** may be used to translate the tax base because the resulting figure is an **accurate measure of the amount that will be deductible in future periods. The deferred tax is charged or credited to profit or loss.**

The deferred tax arising will be calculated **using the tax rate in the foreign branch's jurisdiction**, that is **20%.**

Property	Dinars ('000)	Exchange rate	Dollars (($'000)
Carrying amount:			
Cost	6,000	5	1,200
Depreciation for the year	(500)		(100)
Carrying amount	1,500		1,100
Tax base:			
Cost	6,000		
Tax depreciation	(750)		
Carrying amount	5,250	6	875
Temporary difference			225
Deferred tax at 20%			45

The **deferred tax charge in profit or loss will therefore increase by $45,000.**

If the tax base had been translated at the historical rate, the tax base would have been $(5.25m ÷ 5m) = $1.05m. This gives a temporary difference of $1.1m - $1.05m = $50,000, and therefore a deferred tax liability of $50,000 × 20% = $10,000. This is considerably lower than when the closing rate is used.

(c)   **Goodwill on acquisition**

Goodwill on acquisition of a foreign subsidiary or group, and any fair value adjustments, are treated as **assets and liabilities of the foreign entity**. They are expressed in the foreign operation's functional currency and translated at the closing rate. This means that an exchange difference will arise between goodwill translated at the opening rate and at the closing rate. Even though the goodwill arose through a consideration paid in dollars, it is treated as a foreign currency asset, which means that it is translated into dinars at the rate ruling on the date of acquisition and then re-translated at the year-end rate.

Any **gain or loss** on translation is taken to **other comprehensive income.**

	Dinars (m)	Rate	$m
Consideration transferred			200
Non-controlling interests translated at 1 May 20X3	250	5	50
Less fair value of net assets at acq'n translated at 1 May 20X3	(1,100)	5	(220)
Goodwill			30
Exchange loss to other comprehensive income	-	ß	(5)
Goodwill as re-translated at 30 April 20X4: 30 × 5 ÷ 6	150	6	25

The exchange loss of $5m is recognised in other comprehensive income with the corresponding credit entries to a separate translation reserve (70%) and non-controlling interest (30%) in the statement of financial position:

DEBIT	Other comprehensive income	$5m	
CREDIT	Translation reserve (SOFP): $5m × 70%		$
CREDIT	Non-controlling interest (SOFP): $5m × 30%		$

(d)   **Foreign currency loan**

On 1 May 20X3

On initial recognition (at 1 May 20X3), the loan is measured at the transaction price translated into the functional currency (the dollar), because the interest is at a market rate for a similar two-year loan. The loan is translated at the rate ruling on 1 May 20X3.

DEBIT	Cash 5m ÷ 5	$1m
CREDIT	Financial liability (loan payable)	$

Being recognition of loan

As a monetary item, the loan balance at the year-end is translated at the spot rate at the year end.

Year ended 30 April 20X4

Because there are no transaction costs, the effective interest rate is 8%. Interest on the loan is translated at the average rate because this is an approximation for the actual rate

DEBIT	Profit or loss (interest expense): 5m × 8% ÷ 5.6	$71,429	
CREDIT	Financial liability (loan payable)		$71,429

Being recognition of interest payable for the year ended 30 April 20X4

On 30 April 20X4

The interest is paid and the following entry is made, using the rate on the date of payment of $1 = 6 dinars

DEBIT	Financial liability (loan payable)5m × 8% ÷ 6	$66,667	
CREDIT	Cash		$66,667

Being recognition of interest payable for the year ended 30 April 20X4

In addition, as a monetary item, the loan balance at the year-end is translated at the spot rate at the year end: 5m dinars ÷ 6 = $833,333. This gives rise to an exchange gain of £1,000,000 - $833,333 = $166,667. There is a further exchange gain on the interest paid of $71,429 - $66,667 = $4,762. This gives a total exchange gain of $4,762 + $166,667 = $171,429.

56 Memo

Text reference. Foreign currency is covered in Chapter 16.

Top tips. In this question, you had to produce a consolidated statement of profit or loss and other comprehensive income and statement of financial position for a parent company and its foreign subsidiary. Adjustments had to be made for intragroup items such as loans and inventory, and candidates had to deal with the treatment of goodwill as a foreign currency asset. Exchange gains and losses had to be recognised in the financial statements.

Easy marks. Just setting out the proforma and doing the mechanics of translation will earn you easy marks, even if you struggle with more difficult aspects.

Examiner's comment. This question was well answered. Candidates generally made good attempts at the translation of the foreign subsidiary, the calculation of goodwill, intragroup profit in inventory, and the gain on translation. At the same time, there were problems with the treatment of goodwill as a foreign currency asset, and the exchange gain on the intra group loan.

	Marks
Consolidated statement of financial position	7
Translation of subsidiary's statement of financial position	5
Goodwill	1
Non-controlling interest	2
Post acquisition reserves	5
Consolidated statement of profit or loss and other comprehensive income	5
Unrealised profit	4
Loan	3
Available	32
Maximum	32

(Movement on reserves and exchange gain analysis not asked for)

MEMO
CONSOLIDATED STATEMENT OF FINANCIAL POSITION AT 30 APRIL 20X4

	$m
Assets	
Property, plant and equipment: 297 + 70(W5)	367
Goodwill (W2)	8
Current assets (355 + 48.6 – 0.6) (W7)	403
	778
Equity and liabilities	
Equity attributable to owners of the parent:	
Share capital	60
Share premium	50
Retained earnings (W3)	372
	482
Non-controlling interest (W4)	18
	500
Non-current liabilities (30 + 18.6 – 5)	44
Current liabilities: 6205 + 29 (W5)	234
	778

MEMO
CONSOLIDATED STATEMENT OF PROFIT OR LOSS AND OTHER COMPREHENSIVE INCOME
FOR THE YEAR ENDED 30 APRIL 20X4

	$m
Revenue (200 + 71 – 6)	265
Cost of sales (120 + 48 – 6 + 0.6 (W8)	(163)
Gross profit	102
Distribution costs and administrative expenses: 30 + 10 (W6)	(40)
Impairment of goodwill (W2)	(2)
Interest receivable	4
Finance costs (W6)	(1)
Exchange gains (W8)	1
Profit before tax	64
Income tax expense: 20 + 4.5 (W6)	(24)
Profit for the year	40
Other comprehensive income (items that may subsequently be reclassified to profit or loss)	
Exchange differences on foreign operations (W9) (9.7 + 1.6)	11
Total comprehensive income for the year	51

	$m
Profit attributable to	
Owners of the parent	38
Non-controlling interest (25% × 7.9) (W4)	2
	40
Total comprehensive income for the year attributable to	
Owners of the parent	47
Non-controlling interest (7.9 + 9.7) × 25%	4
	51

Workings

1   *Group structure*

	Memo		
1 May 20X3	│	75%	Cost = 120m crowns
	Random		PAR = 80m crowns

2   *Goodwill*

	CRm	CRm	Rate	$m
Consideration transferred		120.0	⎫	48
Non-controlling interests (132 × 25%)		33.0	⎪	13.2
			⎪	
Less fair value of net assets at acq'n:			⎪	
Share capital	32		2.5	
Share premium	20		⎬	
Retained earnings	80		⎪	
		(132.0)	⎪	(52.8)
		21.0	⎭	8.4
Impairment losses		(4.2)	2.1	(2.0)
FX gain		–	β	1.6
At 30.4.X4		16.8	2.1	8.0

3   *Retained earnings*

	$m
Memo	360.0
Random (75% × 17.6 (W6))	13.2
Provision for unrealised profit (W7)	(0.6)
Impairment of goodwill (W2)	(2.0)
Exchange differences on goodwill (W2)	1.6
	372.2

4   *Non-controlling interests*

	$m
NCI at acquisition (W1)	13.2
NCI share of post acquisition reserves of Random ((W3) 17.6 × 25%)	4.4
	17.6

5   *Translation of statement of financial position*

	CRm	Rate	$m
Property, plant and equipment	146.0	2.1	69.5
Current assets	102.0	2.1	48.6
	248.0		118.1
Share capital	32.0	2.5	12.8
Share premium	20.0	2.5	8.0
Retained earnings:			
Pre-acquisition	80.0	2.5	32.0
	132.0		52.8

	CRm	Rate	$m
Post-acquisition: 15 + (2 – 1.2) (W8)	15.8	β	17.6
	147.8		70.4
Non-current liabilities (41 – 2 (W8))	39.0	2.1	18.6
Current liabilities (60 + 1.2 (W8))	61.2	2.1	29.1
	248.0		118.1

6   *Translation of statement of profit or loss and other comprehensive income*

	CRm	Rate	$m
Revenue	142	2	71
Cost of sales	(96)	2	(48)
Gross profit	46		23
Distribution and administrative expenses	(20)	2	(10)
Interest payable	(2)	2	(1)
Exchange gain (2 – 1.2) (W8)	0.8	2	0.4
Profit before tax	24.8		12.4
Income tax expense	(9)	2	(4.5)
Profit/total comprehensive income for the year	15.8		7.9

7   *Provision for unrealised profit*

	$m
Sale by parent to subsidiary (6 million × 20% × ½)	0.6

8   *Exchange gains and losses in the accounts of Random*

Loan to Random (non-current liabilities)

	CRm
At 1 May 20X3 ($5 million × 2.5)	12.5
At 30 April 20X4 ($5 million × 2.1)	(10.5)
Gain	2.0

Intro-group purchases (current liabilities)

	CRm
Purchase of goods from Memo ($6 million × 2)	12
Payment made ($6 million × 2.2)	(13.2)
Loss	(1.2)

Exchange differences in statement of profit or loss (retranslated to dollars)

	$m
Gain on loan (2 ÷ 2)	1.0
Loss on current liability/purchases (1.2 ÷ 2)	(0.6)
	0.4

(*Note.* This has been rounded up to $1 million.)

9   *Exchange differences arising during the year year to be recorded in other comprehensive income (items that may subsequently be reclassified to profit or loss)*

	$m	$m
Closing net assets at closing rate (W5)	70.4	
Less opening net assets at opening rate (W5)	(52.8)	
		17.6
Less retained profit as translated (W6)		(7.9)
		9.7
Exchange gain on retranslation of goodwill (W2)		1.6
		11.3

57 Case study question: Rose

Text reference. Foreign currency transactions are covered in Chapter 16 of the text. Ethics is covered in Chapter 3.

Top tips. Part (a) of this question is similar to Ribby, elsewhere in this Kit. Part (a) (i) asked you to determine the functional currency of an overseas subsidiary. Make sure you produce arguments for and against your decision, as it is not clear cut. In Part (a)(ii), you were asked to prepare a consolidated statement of financial position for a simple group structure involving an overseas subsidiary and several adjustments for an additional interest acquired, a long-term bonus (current service cost), revaluation of a foreign property and change in residual value of plant. It is important to grab the easy marks for basic consolidation workings, and not get bogged down in the adjustments. It is a good idea to provide a brief explanation of the adjustments, in case the figures are wrong. **Note that although you are asked to show the exchange difference arising on the translation of Stem's net assets, the examiner has stated that it is acceptable to combine the translation reserve with retained earnings, as we do here.** Part (b) concerned fair values in a business combination and the ethical implications of the directors valuing customer relationships in a way that was not in accordance with IFRSs. Since this question was set, IFRS 13 *Fair value measurement* has been issued.

Easy marks. These are available for simply translating the statement of financial position at the correct rate, and setting out the proforma and the basic workings for group structure, non-controlling interest and retained earnings. If the bonus and foreign property revaluation adjustments worry you, ignore them and make some figures up – if you make a good attempt at the easy bits you will still pass comfortably.

Examiner's comment. Part (a)(i) was generally well answered, although some candidates did not use the information in the question. Part ((a)(ii)) was also well answered. Some candidates used incorrect exchange rates to translate the statement of financial position of the subsidiary but most candidates managed to compute goodwill correctly using the full goodwill method. The cumulative bonus payable on the long term bonus scheme was often incorrectly calculated with the main problem being the present value calculation. The main problem with Part (b) was that candidates focussed on the accounting treatment at the expense of the ethical considerations.

			Marks
(a)	(i)	1 mark per point up to maximum	8
	(ii)	Amortisation of patent	1
		Acquisition of further interest	5
		Stem – translation and calculation of goodwill	7
		Retained earnings and other equity	8
		Non-controlling interest	3
		Property, plant and equipment	6
		Non-current liabilities	1
		Employee bonus scheme	4
			35
(b)		Accounting treatment	4
		Ethical consideration	3
		Maximum	50

(a)   (i)   **Factors to consider in determining functional currency of Stem**

IAS 21 *The effects of changes in foreign exchange rates* defines functional currency as 'the currency of the primary economic environment in which the entity operates'. Each entity, whether an individual company, a parent of a group, or an operation within a group, should determine its functional currency and **measure its results and financial position in that currency**.

An entity should consider the following factors:

(1)   What is the currency that mainly **influences sales prices** for goods and services (this will often be the currency in which sales prices for its goods and services are denominated and settled)?

(2)   What is the currency of the country whose **competitive forces and regulations** mainly determine the sales prices of its goods and services?

(3)   What is the currency that **mainly influences labour, material and other costs** of providing goods or services? (This will often be the currency in which such costs are denominated and settled.)

Applying the first of these, it appears that **Stem's functional currency is the dinar**. The price is denominated and settled in dinars and is determined by local supply and demand. However, when it comes to **costs and expenses**, Stem pays in a mixture of dollars, dinars and the local currency, so that aspect is less clear cut.

Other factors may also provide evidence of an entity's functional currency:

(1)   It is the currency in which **funds from financing activities** are generated.
(2)   It is the currency in which **receipts from operating activities** are usually retained.

Stem **does not depend on group companies for finance.** Furthermore, Stem operates with a considerable degree of autonomy, and is not under the control of the parent as regards finance or management. It also generates sufficient cash flows to meet its cash needs. These aspects point away from the dollar as the functional currency.

The position is **not clear cut**, and there are arguments on both sides. However, **on balance it is the dinar** that should be considered as the functional currency, since this most faithfully represents the economic reality of the transactions, both operating and financing, and the autonomy of Stem in relation to the parent company.

(ii)   ROSE GROUP
        CONSOLIDATED STATEMENT OF FINANCIAL POSITION AS AT 30 APRIL 20X8

	$m
Non-current assets	
Property, plant and equipment: 370 + 110 + 76 (W2) + 30 (W8) + 15 ((W8) 2.25 (W9) + 0.4 (W11)	603.65
Goodwill: 16 (W3) + 6.2 (W4)	22.20
Intangible assets (W8)	3.00
Financial assets: 15 + 7 + 10 (W2)	32.00
	660.85
Current assets: 118 + 100 + 66 (W2)	284.00
	944.85
Equity and liabilities	
Share capital	158.00
Retained earnings (W5)	277.39
Other components of equity (W6)	6.98
	442.37
Non-controlling interests (W7)	89.83
	532.20
Non-current liabilities: 56 + 42 + 32 (W2) + 0.65 (W10)	130.65
Current liabilities: 185 + 77 + 20 (W2)	282.00
	412.65
	944.85

Workings

1   *Group structure*

Rose

	1 May 20X7	30 April 20X8				1 May 20X7
	70%	10% = 80%				52%
Cost	$94m +	$19m			Cost	$46m
FV NCI	$46m		80%	52%	FV NCI	250m dinars
FV NA	$120m				FV NA	495m dinars
RE	$49m				RE	220m dinars
OCE	$3m		Petal	Stem	OCE	

2   *Translation of SOFP of Stem at 30 April 20X8*

	Dinars (m)	Rate	$m
Property, plant and equipment	380	5	76.00
Financial assets	50	5	10.00
Current assets	330	5	66.00
	760		152.00
Share capital	200	6	33.33
Retained earnings			
Pre-acqn	220	6	36.67*
	420		70.00
Post-acqn. (300 – 220 (including FX differences	80	ß	30.00*
	500		100.00
Non-current liabilities	160	5	32.00
Current liabilities	100	5	20.00
	760		152.00

*$36.67m + *$30.00m = $66.67m total retained earnings.

3   *Goodwill: Petal*

	$m
Consideration transferred	94
Fair value of non-controlling interests	46
Fair value of identifiable net assets at acq'n (120 + 4 (W8))	(124)
	16

4   *Goodwill: Stem*

	Dinars (m)	Rate	$m
Consideration transferred (46 × 6)	276	6	46.00
Non-controlling interests	250	6	41.67
Less fair value of net assets at acq'n per question	(495)	6	(82.50)
At 1 May 20X7	31		5.17
Exchange gain	-	ß	1.03
At 30 April 20X8	31	5	6.20

5   *Retained earnings*

	Rose $m	Petal $m	Stem $m
Per question/as translated (W2)	256.00	56	66.67
Adjustments			–
Fair value movement (W8)		(1)	
Exchange gain on fair values (W8)			2.5
Bonus (W10)	(0.65)		
Depreciation adjustment (W11)	0.40		
Pre-acquisition: per question		(49)	
as translated (W2)			(36.67)
		6	32.50

		Rose $m
Group share:	Petal: 6 × 70%	4.20
	Stem: 32.5 × 52%	16.90
Exchange gain on goodwill ((W4) 1.03 × 52%)		0.54
		277.39

6 *Other components of equity*

	Rose $m	Petal $m
Per question	7.00	4.00
Adjustments		
Revaluation of foreign property (W9)	2.25	
Pre acquisition		(3.00)
		1.00
Group share: Petal: 1 × 70%	0.70	
Acquisition of 10% of NCI (W12)	(2.97)	
	6.98	

7 *Non-controlling interests*

	Petal $m	Stem $m
NCI at acquisition (W3)/(W4)	46.00	41.67
NCI share of post acquisition retained earnings:		
Petal ((W5) 6 × 30%)	1.80	
Stem ((W5) 32.5 × 48%)		15.60
NCI share of post-acquisition other components of equity (W6): 1 × 30%	0.3	
Exchange gain on goodwill ((W4) 1.03 × 48%)		0.49
	48.10	57.76
Acquisition of 10% of Petal	(16.03)	
	32.07	57.76

89.83

8 *Fair value adjustments*

Petal:

	Acquisition 1 May 20X7 $m	Movement 1 year $m	Year end 30 April 20X8 $m
Land: 120 – 38 (SC) –49 (RE) – 3 (OCE	30	–	30
Patent	4	(¼ ×4)=(1)	3
	34	(1)	33

Stem:	Acquisition 1 May 20X7	Movement (exchange diff)	Year-end 30 April 20X8 $m
Land (in dinars (m)) 495 – 200 (SC) – 220 (RE) = 75			
In dollars: 75/6(75/5)	12.5	2.5 (ß)	15

Note. The land is non-depreciable so the movement for Stem is the change in exchange rate.

9 *Foreign property revaluation (Rose)*

		$m
Cost at 1 May 20X7	30m dinars ÷ 6	5.00
Depreciation	5 ÷ 20	(0.25)
		4.75
Revaluation ß		2.25
Revalued amount at 30 April 20X8	35m dinars ÷ 5	7.00

Note. The revaluation surplus goes to other components of equity (W6) and is added to property, plant and equipment.

10 *Long-term bonus scheme*

The cumulative bonus payable is $4.42m, calculated as follows, with a 5% annual increase:

Bonus as at:		$m
30 April 20X8	$40m × 2%	0.800
30 April 20X9	$0.8m × 1.05	0.840
30 April 20Y0	$0.8m × 1.05^2	0.882
30 April 20Y1	$0.8m × 1.05^3	0.926
30 April 20Y2	$0.8m × 1.05^4	0.972
		4.420

This is $884,000 ($4.42/5 years) per year. The current service cost is the present value of $884,000 at 30 April 20X8: $884,000 × $1/1.08^4$ = $0.65m

The double entry to record this is as follows.

DEBIT	Profit or loss/retained earnings (W5)	$0.65m	
CREDIT	Non-current liabilities		$0.65m

11 *Residual value of plant*

		$m	$m
Depreciation based on original residual value	(20 − 1.4) ÷ 6		3.10
Depreciation based on revised amount	(20 − (3.1 × 3 years) − 2.6) ÷ 3 years		2.70
Adjustment to depreciation in retained earnings and add back to PPE			0.40

12 *Acquisition of additional 10% interest in Petal*

Rose acquired an additional 10% interest on 30 April 20X8, going from 70% to 80%, so the non-controlling interests decreased by one third on that date, going from 30% to 20%. The amount of the decrease is calculated in W7 as $16.03m. The adjustment to parent's equity, which goes through other components of equity (W6), is calculated as follows.

DEBIT	Non-controlling interest (W7)	$16.03m
DEBIT	Other components of equity (ß)	$2.97m
CREDIT	Consideration transferred	$19m

(b) **Acquisition of service company**

Rose's proposed valuation of the service company's assets (based on what it is prepared to pay for them, which is, in turn, influenced by future plans for the business) **does not comply with IFRS**.

Such a valuation needs to be based on the following IFRS:

(i) IFRS 3 *Business combinations.* Under IFRS 3, an acquirer must allocate the cost of a business combination by recognising the acquiree's identifiable assets, liabilities and contingent liabilities that satisfy the recognition criteria at their **fair values** at the date of the acquisition.

(ii) IFRS 13 *Fair value measurement,* published in May 2011, which defines fair value as as **'the price that would be received to sell an asset or paid to transfer a liability in an orderly transaction between market participants at the measurement date.'** This is also known as 'exit price'.

(iii) IAS 38 *Intangible assets,* which states that intangible assets acquired in business combinations can normally be measured sufficiently reliably to be **recognised separately from goodwill**.

Valuing the service company's assets on the basis of their value to Rose does not accord with the above standards. First, **the standards may recognise as assets items that Rose does not identify**. Secondly, there has been **no attempt to apply the IFRS 13 definition of fair value,** which specifies the price that would be paid by **market participants,** and implies that **Rose's judgement alone would not be sufficient**.

Turning to the **contract-based customer relationships** that the service company has, in proposing to value these at zero on the grounds that Rose already has good relationships with customers, Rose is **failing to apply IAS 38**. Under IAS 38, part of the cost of the acquisition should be allocated to these relationships, which will **have a value separate from goodwill** at the date of the acquisition. The fair value of the customer relationships should not be based on Rose's judgement of their worth but on that of a market participant such as a well informed buyer.

Ethical behaviour in the preparation of financial statements, and in other areas, is of **paramount importance**. Directors and company accountants act unethically if they use 'creative' accounting in accounts preparation to make the figures look better, in particular if their treatment would mislead users, as here. Motivation for misleading treatments can include market expectations, market position or expectation of a bonus.

To act ethically, the directors must put the interests of the company and its shareholders first, and must also have regard to other stakeholders such as potential investors or lenders. **If a treatment does not conform to acceptable accounting practice, it is not ethical**.

If the aim of the proposed treatment is to **deliberately** mislead users of financial statements, then it is **unethical**, and should not be put into practice. It is possible that non-compliance with IFRS 3, IFRS 13 and IAS 38 is a genuine **mistake.** If so, the mistake **needs to be corrected** in order to act ethically. There is, in any case a duty of professional competence in the preparation of financial statements, which would entail keeping up to date with IFRS and local legislation.

58 Preparation question: Consolidated statement of cash flows

STATEMENT OF CASH FLOWS FOR THE YEAR ENDED 31 DECEMBER 20X5

	$'000	$'000
Cash flows from operating activities		
Profit before tax	16,500	
Adjustments for:		
Depreciation	5,800	
Impairment losses (W1)	240	
	22,540	
Increase in trade receivables (W4)	(1,700)	
Increase in inventories (W4)	(4,400)	
Increase in trade payables (W4)	1,200	
Cash generated from operations	17,640	
Income taxes paid (W3)	(4,200)	
Net cash from operating activities		13,440
Cash flows from investing activities		
Acquisition of subsidiary net of cash acquired	(600)	
Purchase of property, plant and equipment (W1)	(13,100)	
Net cash used in investing activities		(13,700)
Cash flows from financing activities		
Proceeds from issue of share capital (W2)	2,100	
Dividends paid (W2)	(900)	
Dividends paid to non-controlling interest (W2)	(40)	
Net cash from financing activities		1,160
Net increase in cash and cash equivalents b/f		900

	$'000	$'000
Net increase in cash and cash equivalents c/f		900
Cash and cash equivalents at the beginning of the period		1,500
Cash and cash equivalents at the end of the period		2,400

Workings

1   Assets

	Property, plant and equipment $'000	Goodwill $'000
b/d	25,000	–
OCI (revaluation)	500	
Depreciation/ Impairment	(5,800)	**(240)** β
Acquisition of sub/assoc	2,700	1,640 (W5)
Cash paid/(rec'd) β	**13,100**	–
c/d	35,500	1,400

2   Equity

	Share capital $'000	Share premium $'000	Retained earnings $'000	Non-controlling interest $'000
b/d	10,000	2,000	21,900	--
SPLOCI			11,100	350
Acquisition of subsidiary	1,500	2,500		1,440 (W5)
Cash (paid)/rec'd β	**800**	**1,300**	**(900)***	**(40)**
c/d	12,300	5,800	32,100	1,750

*Dividend paid is given in question but working shown for clarity.

3   Liabilities

	Tax payable $'000
b/d	4,000
P/L	5,200
Acquisition of subsidiary	200-
Cash (paid)/rec'd	**(4,200) β**
c/d	5,200

4   Working capital changes

	Inventories $'000	Receivables $'000	Payables $'000
Balance b/d	10,000	7,500	6,100
Acquisition of subsidiary	1,600	600	300
	11,600	8,100	6,400
Increase/(decrease) (balancing figure)	**4,400**	**1,700**	**1,200**
Balance c/d	16,000	9,800	7,600

5   Purchase of subsidiary

	$'000
Cash received on acquisition of subsidiary	400
Less cash consideration	(1,000)
Cash outflow	(600)

Note. Only the **cash** consideration is included in the figure reported in the statement of cash flows. The **shares** issued as part of the consideration are reflected in the share capital working (W2) above.

Goodwill on acquisition (before impairment):

	$'000
Consideration: 55 + 695 (W3) + 120 (W2) + 216	5,000
Non-controlling interest: 4,800 × 30%	1,440
Net assets acquired	(4,800)
Goodwill	1,640

59 Case study question: Angel

Text reference. Group statements of cash flow are covered in Chapter 17 of the text. Retirement benefits are covered in Chapter 5 and deferred tax in Chapter 6. Ethics is covered in Chapter 3.

Top tips. This question has been slightly amended from the original. There are many straightforward, non-group aspects to this group statement of cash flows, so make sure you don't get bogged down in the detailed adjustments at the expense of these. The adjustments to the net profit before tax include retirement benefit expense because only the contributions paid are included in the SOCF. We have set up workings for some cash payments and receipts even though the amounts are given to you in the question. It is good practice to set up standard workings in case there is something missing from the information in the question, or you have to calculate the figures from scratch.

Don't skimp on Part (b) – it has nine marks.

Easy marks. These are available for setting out the proforma and workings, and also for valid points made in Part (b) on cash flow and Part (c) on ethical matters. Do not spend too much time on the fiddly PPE working at the expense of these much easier marks.

Examiner's comment. The examiner stress the importance of showing all workings. For example, very few candidates correctly calculated the income taxes paid figure but there were several marks for this calculation, which were often awarded in the workings in the scripts. Several candidates did not adjust for the purchase of the subsidiary .This of course affects several items in the consolidated statement of cash flows. However the marking scheme treated the non-adjustment of the various balances as a single error. While there are complex elements to all consolidates statement of cash flow questions, there are some basic marks too, and candidates nearly always get those. Candidates found Part (b) of this question difficult to answer satisfactorily as many candidates simply outlined the headings in the statement rather than discussing the cause or reason for the classification. Part (c) required candidates to discuss a comment by the Directors of Angel that codes of ethics were irrelevant and unimportant. Worryingly, some candidates actually agreed with the directors' comment, stating that the profit motive was more important than ethical behaviour. This shows a lack of knowledge or a failure to apply the knowledge. This part of the question normally attracts high marks if candidates apply their knowledge and therefore it is a part of the paper, which should never be omitted.

			Marks
(a)	Net profit before taxation		4
	Cash generated from operations		16
	Cash flow from investing activities		10
	Cash flow from financing activities		5
			35
(b)	Subjective assessment of discussion		9
(c)	Subjective assessment – 1 mark per point		6
		Available	50

(a)   ANGEL GROUP
       STATEMENT OF CASH FLOWS FOR THE YEAR ENDED 30 NOVEMBER 20X3

	$m	$m
Operating activities		
Profit before tax (W1)/Note 2	197.0	
Adjustments for		
Profit on sale of financial assets ($40m –$26m)	(14.0)	
Retirement benefit expense (W6)	10.0	
Depreciation	29.0	
Profit on sale of property plant and equipment: $63m – $49m	(14.0)	
Share of profit of associate (W1)	(12.0)	
Impairment of goodwill and intangible assets (W1): $26.5m + $90m	116.5	
Interest expense: $11m less $1m capitalised	10.0	
	322.5	
Decrease in trade receivables(W4)	58.0	
Decrease in inventories (W4)	41.0	
Decrease in trade payables(W4)	(210.0)	
Cash generated from operations	211.5	
Retirement benefit contributions*(W3)	(9.0)	
Interest paid: $11m less $1m capitalised	(10.0)	
Income taxes paid (W2)	(135.5)	
Net cash from operating activities c/f		57
Net cash from operating activities b/f		57
Investing activities		
Purchase of property, plant and equipment (W1)	(76)	
Proceeds from sale of property, plant and equipment	63	
Cash grant for property, plant and equipment (W2)	1	
Proceeds from sale of financial assets (per question)	40	
Acquisition of subsidiary, net of cash acquired: $30m – $2m	(28)	
Purchase of financial assets (per question/(W1))	(57)	
Acquisition of associate (W1)	(71)	
Dividend received from associate (W1)	3	
Net cash used in investing activities		(125)
Financing activities		
Proceeds from issue of share capital (W2)	225	
Repayment of long-term borrowings (W3)	(31)	
Dividends paid (W2)	(10)	
Dividends paid to non-controlling shareholders (W2)	(6)	
Net cash generated by financing activities		178
Net increase in cash and cash equivalents		110
Cash and cash equivalents at beginning of year		355
Cash and cash equivalents at end of year		465

Notes

1   *Building renovation*

     The building renovation has been incorrectly accounted for, and this needs to be corrected in order to
     produce the workings for the statement of cash flows. The correcting entries are:

     DEBIT   Property, plant and equipment $3m
     CREDIT   Revenue $3m

     Being revaluation of building and correction of charge to revenue.

     Angel treats grant income on capital-based projects as deferred income. However, the grant of $2m
     needs to be split equally between renovation (capital) and job creation (revenue). The correcting
     entries for this are:

DEBIT	Property, plant and equipment	$2m	
CREDIT	Retained earnings		$1m
CREDIT	Deferred income		$1m

2   *Adjustments to profit before tax*

Profit before tax needs to be adjusted to take account of the correcting entries for the building refurbishment and grant.

The construction costs for the machine have been incorrectly charged to other expenses, and the interest needs to be capitalised: Correcting entries are:

DEBIT	Property, plant and equipment	$4m	
CREDIT	Profit or loss		$4m

Being correction of construction costs charge

DEBIT	Property, plant and equipment	$1m	
CREDIT	Profit or loss		$1m

Being capitalisation of interest

Profit before tax

	$m
Per question	188
Correction of rebuilding costs	3
Share of cash grant	1
Correction of construction costs	4
Capitalisation of interest	1
	197

Workings

1   *Assets*

	PPE $m	Goodwill $m	Intangible assets $m	Associate $m	Financial assets $m
b/d	465	120.0	240	0	180
				40 × 30%	
P/L				12	4
OCI (8 – 3)	5				
Dep'n/Impairment/Amort'n (non-cash)	(29)	(26.5) β	(90) β		
Acquisition of sub/assoc	14	(W4) 11.5		71 β	
Disposals/derecognition	(49)				(26)
				40 × 30%	
Cash paid/(rec'd)	76 β	0.0		(3)	57
c/d	482	105.0	150	80	215

2 Equity

	Share capital	Retained earnings	NCI
	$m	$m	$m
b/d	625	359	65
P/L		111	31
OCI		(4)	
Cash (paid)/rec'd	**225** *	(10) *	(6) *
c/d	850	456	90

* cash flow given in question, but working shown for clarity

3 Liabilities

	Long-term borrowings	Tax payable	Retirement benefit	Deferred income
	$m	$m	$m	$m
b/d	57	(31 + 138) 169.0	74	0
P/L		46.0	(W6) 10	
OCI		(2 + 1) 3.0	4	
Acquisition of subsidiary		(W5)1.5	1	
Cash (paid)/rec'd	**(31)** β	**(135.5)** β	(9)*	2 × 50% 1
c/d	26	84.0 (35 + 33)	80	1

* cash flow given in question, but working shown for clarity

4 Working capital changes

	Inventories	Trade receivables	Trade payables
	$m	$m	$m
b/d	190	180	361
Acquisition of subsidiary	6	3	4
∴ **Increase/(decrease)**	**(41)** β	**(58)** β	**(210)** β
c/d	155	125	155

5 Goodwill on acquisition of Sweety

	$m	$m
Consideration transferred		30.0
Fair value of net assets (net of deferred tax)	20.0	
	(1.5)	
Deferred tax*		(18.5)
		11.5

*Deferred tax:

	$m
Fair values of Sweety's identifiable net assets excluding deferred tax $15m + $15m	20
Tax base	(15)
Temporary difference arising on acquisition	5

Temporary difference arising on acquisition: $5m × 30% = $1.5m

6   *Retirement benefit*

The total net pension cost charged to profit or loss is:

	$m
Current service cost	8
Net interest cost	3
Less obligation assumed on the purchase of Sweety	(1)
	10

The remeasurement (actuarial) losses are charged to other comprehensive income. The amounts paid by the trustees are not included, because they are not paid by the company.

(b)   **Classification of cash flows**

IAS 7 *Statement of cash flows* requires the classification of cash flows under three main headings: operating activities, investing activities and financing activities. The classification is, however, **not always straightforward**. Some cash flows which look similar may be **classified differently, depending on the nature of the business**. For example, an investment company might classify dividends received as a cash inflow from operating activities because investment is its operation, whereas a retail company would classify dividends received as an investing activity.

IAS 7 favours classification which **reflects the nature of an entity's activities** over classification in accordance with the underlying item in the statement of financial position.

To identify the nature of the cash inflow or outflow, the following questions should be considered:

(i)   Why is the cash flow being paid or received?
(ii)   Who receives or pays the cash flow?
(iii)   What is the source of the cash flow?
(iv)   Does the cash flow result from a transactions which determine a profit or a loss.

The statement of cash flows shows the **movement in cash and cash equivalents** between the start of the period and the end of the period. Cash is generally considered to be a straightforward item to determine; cash equivalents less so. IAS 7 defines them as 'short-term, highly liquid investments that are readily convertible to known amounts of cash and which are subject to an insignificant risk of changes in value'. The standard does not define 'short-term' but does state that 'an investment normally **qualifies as a cash equivalent only when it has a short maturity** of, say, three months or less from the date of acquisition'.

Three months would not generally be long enough for a significant change in value, and is also consistent with the **purpose of meeting short-term cash commitments**. In limited circumstances, a longer-term deposit with an early withdrawal penalty may be treated as a cash equivalent. The terms of the arrangement need to be considered in each case:

(i)   The **$3m** on deposit for twelve months can be withdrawn early, but the penalty – loss of all interest earned – is so significant as to indicate that the cash is not intended to meet short term cash commitments. Therefore this investment would **not qualify as a cash equivalent.**

(ii)   The $7m deposit also has a twelve-month maturity period, and can be withdrawn with 21 days' notice. There is a penalty for early withdrawal, but this is much less severe than the first deposit, being only a reduction in the rate of interest from 3% to 2%. This is normal for short-term deposits, as stated by the bank, indicating that the entity wishes to keep the funds available for short-term needs. Therefore this deposit **does meet the IAS 7 definition of cash equivalents**.

(c)   **Professional ethics and conflict of interest**

Ethical codes are important to accountants **because ethics have practical application in the accountant's professional life**. The directors of Angel have been dismissive of the importance of ethics, but their arguments can be countered as follows.

Company directors are understandably **motivated by profit** – it is what the company's shareholders expect – and there may appear to be a conflict of interest between profit and ethics, including social ethics. Excessive focus on profit has led in some cases to **aggressive earnings management**, whereby directors use creative accounting techniques to present the results in a favourable light, or to **questionable business practices**, such as outsourcing to countries with poor health and safety records, or which use child labour.

Ethical codes cannot provide ready-made solutions to all potential conflicts, but it **can provide a set of principles on which to base judgements**. A vague wish to 'do the right thing' will be of little use when faced with a decision to report a colleague or member of the client's staff who is acting unethically. The study of ethics can direct the accountant's thinking and reasoning and help him or her make the right decision, even if it does not make that decision any easier. An example of ethical guidance serving this purpose is the ACCA's *Code of Ethics and Conduct,* which requires its members to adhere to a set of fundamental principles in the course of their professional duty, such as confidentiality, objectivity, professional behaviour, integrity, professional competence and due care.

The two goals – profit maximisation and ethical behaviour – **need not conflict**. It is possible that an ethical approach by companies can **improve business performance. Customers may buy from a company that they perceive as environmentally friendly,** or which avoids animal testing, and **employees may remain loyal** to such a company, and both these factors are likely to increase shareholder wealth in the long term. If a company engages constructively with the country or community in which it is based, it may be seen by shareholders and potential shareholders as being a **good long- term investment** rather than in it for short-term profits. As regards manipulation and creative accounting, in the long term, relationships with stakeholders are built on **trust and honesty,** eg, a company that provides transparent **disclosures,** particularly when these go beyond what is required by legislation or accounting standards, will be seen as **responsible and a good potential investment**.

60 Case study question: Jocatt

Text reference. Group statements of cash flow are covered in Chapter 17. Ethical issues are covered in Chapter 2.

Top tips. In tackling part (a), remember that time management is the key to cash flow questions. Set out your proforma and workings and do not spend too long on the fiddly bits. The question also required candidates to understand how a business combination achieved in stages would work under the revised IFRS 3 – you need to know that the fair value of the previously held interest in Tigret, and the fair value of the non-controlling interest in Tigret as a subsidiary, go in the goodwill calculation. Other complications include a retirement benefit scheme, a rights issue and goodwill impairment (because the goodwill is more fiddly, being a piecemeal acquisition). Make sure you allow adequate time for Part (b)(i) and (ii). The examiner has recently stressed that students often don't – you can't hope to do well if you don't answer the whole question. There are 15 marks here for Part (b).

Easy marks. In Part (a) these are available for basic cash flow aspects – working capital calculations, non-controlling interest, tax and investment property additions. Follow our order for the workings – the easy ones come first. In Part (b), don't be tempted to write all you know about the direct method and how it works. The question is quite specific. Part (ii) follows on from Part (i), because one of the key problems with the indirect method is manipulation, and this has ethical implications.

Examiner's comment. Candidates generally performed well on this part of the question. The main areas where candidates found difficulties were:ensuring that the purchase of the subsidiary was dealt with in calculating cash flows across the range of assets and liabilities;the treatment of the past service costs relating to the defined benefit scheme; The calculation of the cash flow on taxation, although many candidates made a good attempt at this calculation

The first part of Part (b) on the indirect method of preparing cash flow statements was poorly answered. However, candidates performed well on the ethical aspects.

	Marks
(a)	
Net profit before tax	1
Retirement benefit expense	2
Depreciation on PPE	1
Depreciation on investment property	1
Amortisation of intangible assets	1
Profit on exchange of land	1
Loss on replacement of investment property	1
Associate's profit	1
Impairment of goodwill	4
Gain on revaluation of investment in equity instruments (Tigret) prior to derecognition	1
Finance costs	1
Decrease in trade receivables	1
Decrease in inventories	1
Increase in trade payables	1
Cash paid to retirement benefit scheme	1
Finance costs paid	1
Income taxes paid	2
Purchase of associate	1
Purchase of PPE	2
Purchase of subsidiary	1
Additions – investment property	1
Proceeds from sale of land	1
Intangible assets	1
Purchase of investments in equity instruments	1
Repayment of long-term borrowings	1
Rights issue NCI	1
Non-controlling interest dividend	1
Dividends paid	1
Net increase in cash and cash equivalents	1
	35
(b)	
(i) Subjective	8
(ii) Subjective	7
	50

(a) JOCATT GROUP
STATEMENT OF CASH FLOWS FOR YEAR ENDED 30 NOVEMBER 20X2

	$m	$m
Cash flows from operating activities		
Profit before taxation	59.0	
Adjustments for:		
Depreciation	27.0	
Amortisation (W1)	17.0	
Impairment of goodwill (W1)	31.5	
Profit on exchange of land*: 15 + 4 − 10	(9.0)	
Gain on investment property* (W1)	(1.5)	
Loss on replacement of investment property	0.5	
Gain on revaluation of investment in equity instruments		
(Tigret – fair value on derecognition less fair value at 1 December 20X1: 5 – 4)	(1.0)	
Retirement benefit expense (W7)	4.0	
Cash paid to defined benefit plan **(W3)**	(7.0)	
Share of profit of associate (per question)	(6.0)	
Interest expense (per question)	6.0	
	120.5	
Decrease in trade receivables (W4)	56.0	
Decrease in inventories (W4)	23.0	
Increase in trade payables (W4)	89.0	
Cash generated from operations	288.5	
Interest paid	(6.0)	
Income taxes paid (W3)	(16.5)	
Net cash from operating activities		266
Cash flows from investing activities		
Acquisition of subsidiary, net of cash acquired: 15 – 7	(8.0)	
Acquisition of associate (W1)	(48.0)	
Purchase of property, plant and equipment (W1)	(98.0)	
Purchase of investment property (per question)	(1.0)	
Purchase of intangible assets **(W6)**	(12.0)	
Purchase of investments in equity instruments (W1)	(5.0)	
Proceeds from sale of land	15.0	
Net cash used in investing activities		(157)
Cash flows used in financing activities		
Proceeds from issue of share capital (W2)	0.0	
Repayment of long-term borrowings (W3)	(4.0)	
Rights issue to non-controlling shareholders (from SOCIE)	2.0	
Dividends paid (from SOCIE or **(W2)**)	(5.0)	
Dividends paid to non-controlling interest shareholders (from SOCIE or (W2))	(13.0)	
Net cash used in financing activities		(20)
Net increase in cash and cash equivalents		89
Cash and cash equivalents at the beginning of the year		143
Cash and cash equivalents at the end of the year		232

*Note. The statement of profit or loss and other comprehensive income in the question shows 'gains on property' of $10.5m, which need to be added back to profit in arriving at cash generated from operations. This is made up of $1.5m gain on investment property (W2) and $9m gain on the exchange of surplus land for cash and plant (Note (vi)) of the question. The double entry for the exchange is:

DEBIT	Cash	$15m	
DEBIT	Plant	$4m	
CREDIT	Land		$10m
CREDIT	Profit or loss		$9m

Separate from this, also shown in W2, is an impairment loss on the old heating system, for which the double entries are:

DEBIT   Profit or loss (old heating system) $0.5m
CREDIT   Investment property (old heating system) $0.5m

DEBIT   Investment property (new heating system) $1m
CREDIT   Cash $1m

Workings

1   *Assets*

	PPE	Investment property	Goodwill	Intangible assets	Associate	Investments in equity instruments
	$m	$m	$m	$m	$m	$m
b/d	254	6.0	68.0	72	0	90
P/L		1.5 β			6	1
OCI	(7)					3 *
Dep'n/ Amort'n/ Impairment	(27)		(31.5) β	(17) β		
Acquisition of sub/assoc	15		(W5) 11.5	18	48 β	
Non-cash additions	4					
Disposals/derecognition	(10)	(0.5)				(5)
Cash paid/(rec'd) β	98	1.0	0.0	(W6) 12	(0)	5
c/d	327	8.0	48.0	85	54	94

* Grossed up for related tax: $2m + $1m

2   *Equity*

	Share capital $m	Retained earnings $m	NCI $m
b/d	275	324	36
P/L		38	10
OCI		(6)	
Acquisition of subsidiary	15		20
Rights issue (5 × 40%)			2
Cash (paid)/rec'd β	0	(5) *	(13) *
c/d	290	351	55

* **Note.** Cash flow given in question, but working shown for clarity.

3   *Liabilities*

	Long-term borrowings $m	Tax payable $m	Pension liability $m
		(41 + 30)	
b/d	71	71.0	22
P/L		11.0	(W7) 4
OCI		1.0	6
Acquisition of subsidiary		(W5)1.5	
Cash (paid)/rec'd β	(4)	(16.5)	(7)
c/d	67	68.0	25
		(35 + 33)	

4   Working capital changes

	Inventories $m	Trade receivables $m	Trade payables $m
b/d	128	113	55
Acquisition of subsidiary		5	
∴ **Increase/(decrease)**	(23)	(56)	89
c/d	105	62	144

5   Goodwill on acquisition of Tigret

	$m	$m
Consideration transferred: $15m + $15m		30.0
Fair value of non-controlling interests		20.0
Fair value of previously held equity interest		5.0
		55.0
Identifiable net assets: 15 + 18 + 5 + 7	45.0	
Deferred tax: ($45m – $40m) × 30%	(1.5)	
		(43.5)
		11.5

6   Intangible assets

The research costs of $2m and the marketing costs of $1m are charged to profit or loss for the year.

The $8m cost of the patents and the $4m development costs = $12m are cash outflows to acquire intangible assets.

7   Pension costs

The total net pension cost charged to profit or loss is:

	$'m
Current service cost	10
Past service cost (recognised immediately)	2
Net interest income on plan assets	(8)
	4

(b)   (i)   Use of the indirect method of preparing statements of cash flow

The **direct method** of preparing cash flow statements discloses **major classes of gross cash receipts and gross cash payments**. It shows the items that affected cash flow and the size of those cash flows. Cash received from, and cash paid to, specific sources such as customers and suppliers are presented. This contrasts with the indirect method, where accrual-basis net income (loss) is converted to cash flow information by means of add-backs and deductions.

An important **advantage** of the direct method is that the users can see and understand the actual **cash flows,** and how they relate to items of income or expense. For example, payments of expenses are shown as cash disbursements and are deducted from cash receipts. In this way, the **user is able to recognise the cash receipts and payments** for the period.

From the point of view of the **user, the direct method is preferable**, because it discloses information, not available elsewhere in the financial statements, which could be of use in estimating future cash flow.

The **indirect method** involves **adjusting the net profit or loss** for the period for:

(1)   Changes during the period in inventories, operating receivables and payables

(2)   Non-cash items, eg depreciation, provisions, profits/losses on the sales of assets

(3)   Other items, the cash flows from which should be classified under investing or financing activities

From the point of view of the **preparer of accounts, the indirect method is easier to use,** and **nearly all companies use it in practice**. The main argument companies have for using the indirect method is that the **direct method is too costly**. The **disadvantage** of the indirect method is that **users find it difficult to understand** and it is therefore more **open to manipulation**. This is particularly true with regard to classification of cash flows. Companies may wish to classify cash inflows as operating cash flows and cash outflows as non-operating cash flows.

The directors' proposal to report the loan proceeds as operating cash flow may be an example of such manipulation. For Jocatt, the indirect method would **not,** as is claimed, **be more useful and informative to users** than the direct method. IAS 7 allows both methods, however, so the indirect method would still be permissible.

(ii)   **Reporting the loan proceeds as operating cash flow**

The directors of Jocatt have an **incentive to enhance operating cash flow**, because they receive extra income if operating cash flow exceeds a predetermined target. Accordingly, their proposal to classify the loan proceeds as operating cash flow should come under scrutiny.

Their proposal should first of all be considered in the light of their claim that the indirect method is more useful to users than the direct method. The opposite is the case, so while both methods are allowed, the directors' **motivation for wishing to use the method that is less clear to users** should be questioned.

The IAS 7 indirect method allows some leeway in classification of cash flows. For example, dividends paid by the entity can be shown as financing cash flows (showing the cost of obtaining financial resources) or operating cash flows (so that users can assess the entity's ability to pay dividends out of operating cash flows). However, the **purpose of such flexibility is to present the position as fairly as possible**. Classifying loan proceeds as operating cash flow does not do this.

Ethical behaviour in the preparation of financial statements, and in other areas, is of **paramount importance**. Directors act unethically if they use 'creative' accounting in accounts preparation to make the figures look better, in particular if their presentation is determined not by finding the best way to apply International Financial Reporting Standards, but, as here, by **self-interest**.

To act ethically, the directors must put the interests of the company and its shareholders first, and must also have regard to other stakeholders such as the loan provider. Accordingly, the **loan proceeds should be reported as cash inflows from financing activities,** not operating activities.

61 Case study question: Warrburt

Text reference. Group statements of cash flow are covered in Chapter 17 of the text. Foreign currency transactions are covered in Chapter 16. Ethics is covered in Chapter 3.

Top tips. This question has been amended from the original. There are many straightforward, non-group aspects to this group statement of cash flows, so make sure you don't get bogged down in the detailed adjustments at the expense of these. The adjustments to the net loss before tax include some more unusual ones, such as the profit on the investment in equity instruments and the exchange loss. (Note that the realised loss of $1.1m would not normally be adjusted, but it is here, because it is not an operating item and so must be transferred to the 'purchase of property, plant and equipment' caption.) We have set up workings for impairment on goodwill and intangibles, even though the amounts are given to you in the question. It is good practice to set up standard workings in case there is something missing from the information in the question, or you have to calculate the figures from scratch.

Don't skimp on Part (b) – it has ten marks.

Easy marks. These are available for setting out the proforma and workings, and also for valid points made in Part (b) on interpretation and Part (c) on ethical matters. Do not spend too much time on the fiddly foreign exchange working at the expense of these much easier marks.

Examiner's comments. Candidates generally performed well on Part (a) of the question producing good answers, which were rewarded with good marks on this part. The main issues, which caused problems, were the new IAS 1 format of the financial statements, which many candidates were not familiar with and the treatment of the benefits paid by the trustees of the defined benefit scheme, which had no cash flow effect. The calculation of the exchange loss on the PPE was problematical for some candidates from the viewpoint of how to treat it in the statement of cash flows. Also the calculation of trade payables often failed to take into account the creditor for the purchase of plant. In Part (b), Many candidates did not use the information in the first part of the question in answering this part but gave general advantages and disadvantages of statements of cash flows. Part (c) question was quite well answered. However, candidates should develop a greater understanding of ethical principles rather than simply the ability to reiterate the ethical codes.

Marking scheme

		Marks
(a)	Net loss before tax	1
	Investment in equity instruments	4
	Retirement benefit	3
	Property, plant and equipment	6
	Insurance proceeds	2
	Associate	4
	Goodwill and intangibles	1
	Finance costs	2
	Taxation	4
	Working capital	4
	Proceeds of share issue	1
	Repayment of borrowings	1
	Dividends	1
	Non-controlling interest	1
		35
(b)	Operating cash flow and discussion	10
(c)	Discussion	5
	Available	50

(a)   WARRBURT GROUP
         STATEMENT OF CASH FLOWS FOR THE YEAR ENDED 30 NOVEMBER 20X8

	$m	$m
Operating activities		
Net loss before tax	(47)	
Adjustments for		
Gain on revaluation of investment in equity instruments		
(Alburt – fair value on disposal less fair value at 1 December 20X7(W1)	(7)	
Retirement benefit expense	10	
Depreciation	36	
Profit on sale of property plant and equipment: $63m – $56m	(7)	
Profit on insurance claim: $3m – $1m	(2)	
Foreign exchange loss (W6) $1.1m + $0.83m	2	
Share of profit of associate	(6)	
Impairment losses: $20m + $12m	32	
Interest expense	9	
	20	
Decrease in trade receivables (W4)	71	
Decrease in inventories (W4)	63	
Decrease in trade payables (W4)	(86)	
Cash generated from operations	68	
Retirement benefit contributions*	(10)	
Interest paid (W5)	(8)	
Income taxes paid (W3)	(39)	
Net cash from operating activities		11
Investing activities		
Purchase of property, plant and equipment: $56m (W1) + $1.1m (W6)	(57)	
Proceeds from sale of property, plant and equipment	63	
Proceeds from sale of investments in equity instruments	45	
Acquisition of associate (W1)	(96)	
Dividend received from associate: (W1)	2	
Net cash used in investing activities		(43)
Financing activities		
Proceeds from issue of share capital (W2)	55	
Repayment of long-term borrowings (W3)	(44)	
Dividends paid	(9)	
Dividends paid to non-controlling shareholders (W3)	(5)	
Net cash used in financing activities		(3)
Net decrease in cash and cash equivalents		(35)
Cash and cash equivalents at beginning of year		323
Cash and cash equivalents at end of year		288

*Note. Only the contributions paid are reported in the cash flow, because this is the only movement of cash. The amounts paid by the trustees are not included, because they are not paid by the company.

Workings

1 *Assets*

	PPE $m	Goodwill $m	Intangible assets $m	Associate $m	Investment in equity instruments $m
b/d	360	100	240	0	150
P/L				6	
OCI (revaluation)	4				30**
Fair value gain on investment in Alburt					7
Dep'n/Impairment/	(36)	**(20)** β	**(12)** β		
Acquisition of associate				**96** β	
Asset destroyed	(1)				
Replacement from insurance company (at fair value)	3				
Disposals	(56)				
Non-cash additions (on credit)*	20				
				8 × 25%	
Cash paid/(rec'd)	**56**	0	0	(2)	**(45)**
c/d	350	80	228	100	142

Notes

* The additions are translated at the historic rate. Adjustment for exchange rate differences are dealt with in (W9).

	$m
Additions (cash) $\dfrac{280}{5}$ =	56
Additions (credit) $\dfrac{100}{5}$	20
Total (excluding destroyed assets replaced): 78 − (3 − 1)	76

** This is the gain on revaluation, which is shown in the statement of profit or loss and other comprehensive income net of deferred tax of $3m (W3), that is at $27m. The gross gain is therefore $30m and is the amount reflected in this working.

2 *Equity*

	Share capital $m	Retained earnings $m	NCI $m
b/d	595	454	53
P/L		(74)	(2)
OCI		(4)*	
Cash (paid)/rec'd	**55** β	(9) **	(5) **
c/d	650	367	46

*Actuarial loss

* *Cash flow given in question, but working shown for clarity

3   *Liabilities*

	Long-term borrowings $m	Tax payable $m	Retirement benefit liability $m
b/d	64	(26 + 42) 68	96
P/L		29	10
OCI		3 + 2 (W1)*	4
		5	
Cash (paid)/rec'd	**(44)** β	**(39)** β	**(10)****
c/d	20	63	100
		(28+ 35)	

* On revaluation gain on PPE + revaluation gain on investments in equity interests

** Only the contributions paid are reported in the cash flow, because this is the only movement of cash. The amounts paid by the trustees are not included, because they are not paid by the company.

4   *Working capital changes*

	Inventories $m	Trade receivables $m	Trade payables $m
b/d	198	163	180.00
Acquisition of subsidiary	–	–	–
Exchange loss (W6)			20.83
∴ **Increase/(decrease)**	**(63)** β	**(71)** β	**(85.83)** β
c/d	135	92	115

5   *Interest payable*

The total net pension cost charged to profit or loss is:

	$m
Balance b/fwd (short-term provisions)	4
Profit or loss for year	9
Cash paid (balancing figure)	**(8)**
Balance c/fwd (short-term provisions)	5

6   *Exchange loss*

At 30 June 20X8:

DEBIT   Property, plant and equipment (W1) $\dfrac{380}{5}$ \$76m

CREDIT   Payables $\dfrac{380}{5}$ \$76m

To record purchase of property, plant and equipment

At 31 October 20X8;

DEBIT   Payables $\dfrac{280}{5}$ \$56m

DEBIT   Profit/loss (loss)   \$1.1m

CREDIT   Cash $\dfrac{280}{4.9}$ \$57.1m

Being payment of 280 million dinars
At 30 November 20X8:

DEBIT   P/L (loss) $0.83

CREDIT   Payables $\left(\dfrac{100}{4.8} = 20.83 \right) - \left(\dfrac{100}{5} = 20 \right)$ $0.83m

Being loss on re-translation of payable at the year end.

Notes

1   The $20.83m was wrongly included in trade payables, so must be removed from the decrease in trade payables in the SOCF.

2   The unrealised loss on retranslation of the payable ($0.83m) must always be adjusted. The realised loss on the cash payment of $1.1 would not normally be adjusted, but it relates to a non-operating item, so is transferred to 'purchase of PPE'.

(b)   **Key issues arising from the statement of cash flows**

The statement of financial position and the statement of profit or loss and other comprehensive income, and the ratios associated with these statements, can provide useful information to users, but it is the **statement of cash flows** which gives the **key insight** into a company's liquidity. Cash is the life-blood of business, and less able to be manipulated than profit. It is particularly important to look at where the cash has come from. If the cash is from trading activity, it is a healthy sign.

Although Warrburt has made a loss before tax of $23m, net cash from operating activities is a modest but healthy $11m. Before working capital changes, the cash generated is $20m. The question arises, however, as to **whether this cash generation can continue if profitability does not improve**.

Of some concern is the fact that **a large amount of cash has been generated by the sale of investments in equity instruments**. This source of cash generation is not sustainable in the long term.

Operating cash flow **does not compare favourably with liabilities** ($115m). In the long term, operating cash flow should finance the repayment of long-term debt, but in the case of Warrburt, working capital is being used to **for investing activities,** specifically the purchase of an associate and of property, plant and equipment. It remains to be seen whether these investments generate future profits that will sustain and increase the operating cash flow.

The company's **current ratio** (515/155 = 3.3) and **acid test ratio** (380/155 = 2.45) are **sound;** it appears that cash is tied up in long-term, rather than short-term investment. An encouraging sign, however, is that the cash used to repay long-term loans has been nearly replaced by cash raised from the issue of share capital. This means that **gearing will reduce**, which is particularly important in the light of possible problems sustaining profitability and cash flows from trading activities.

(c)   **Ethical responsibility of accountant**

Directors may, particularly in times of falling profit and cash flow, wish to **present a company's results in a favourable light.** This may involve manipulation by creative accounting techniques such as window dressing, or, as is proposed here, an **inaccurate classification**.

If the proceeds of the sale of investments in equity instruments and property, plant and equipment are presented in the cash flow statement as part of 'cash generated from operations', the picture is **misleading**. Operating cash flow is crucial, in the long term, for the survival of the company, because it derives from trading activities, which is what the company is there to do. **Sales of assets generate short term cash flow,** and cannot be repeated year-on-year, unless there are to be no assets left to generate trading profits with.

As **a professional, the accountant has a duty,** not only to the company he works for, but to his professional body, stakeholders in the company, and to **the principles of independence and fair presentation of financial statements**. It is essential that the accountant **tries to persuade the directors not to proceed with the adjustments**, which he or she must know violates IAS 7, and may well go against the requirements of local legislation. If, despite his protests, the directors insist on the misleading presentation, then the accountant has a duty to **bring this to the attention of the auditors**.

62 Glowball

Marking scheme

		Marks
(a)	Current reporting requirements	10
(b)	Restoration	5
	Infringement of law	4
	Emissions	4
	Decommissioning activities	4
	Report	4
	Available	31
	Maximum	25

REPORT

To: The Directors   Date: 8 June 20X3
      Glowball

From: Ann Accountant

Environmental Reporting

Introduction

The purpose of this report is to provide information about current reporting requirements and guidelines on the subject of environmental reporting, and to give an indication of the required disclosure in relation to the specific events which you have brought to my attention. We hope that it will assist you in preparing your environmental report.

Current reporting requirements and guidelines

Most businesses have generally ignored environmental issues in the past. However, the use and **misuse** of **natural resources** all lead to environmental costs generated by businesses, both large and small.

There are very few rules, legal or otherwise, to ensure that companies disclose and report environmental matters. Any **disclosures tend to be voluntary**, unless environmental matters happen to fall under standard accounting principles. Environmental matters may be reported in the accounts of companies in the following areas.

IFRS and environmental reporting

There are **no required disclosures** under IFRS. However, if environmental matters fall within the scope of specific accounting principles they must be dealt with under the relevant standard. In particular:

- IAS 1 (revised) *Presentation of financial statements* requires disclosure of facts material to a proper understanding of financial statements.
- IAS 37 *Provisions, contingent liabilities and contingent assets* requires provisions for environmental damage to be recognised.

National and legal requirements

In the UK, the Companies Act 2006 requires disclosure of environmental matters in the Expanded Business Review, now incorporated into the Operating and Financial Review as best practice in Reporting Statement 1. Other countries require environmental reporting under national law.

Voluntary disclosure: sustainability

Most environmental disclosure is voluntary, although lists of companies in particular are under a great deal of pressure to make such disclosures. There have been a number of **initiatives** in the past (CERES, Friends of the Earth Charter) but the most important of these is the **Global Reporting Initiative (GRI)**.

The GRI is a long-term, multi-stakeholder international not-for-profit organisation, with many stakeholders. Its aim is to develop and disseminate globally applicable **Sustainability Reporting Guidelines** for voluntary use. These guidelines cover a number of areas (economic, environmental and social), and the latest guidelines (G4) were published in 2013.

The Guidelines set out the **framework of a sustainability report** and offer two options: the **Core option** and the **Comprehensive option**.

(a)   The **Core option** contains the **essential elements** of a sustainability report. It provides the background against which an organisation communicates the impacts of its economic, environmental and social and governance performance and impacts.

(b)   The **Comprehensive option** builds on the Core option by requiring **additional disclosures**

Organisations choosing the Core option have to disclose **at least one indicator** related to each 'identified material aspect', while organisations choosing the Comprehensive option have to disclose all indicators related to each 'identified material aspect'. For environmental reporting the indicators are: materials; energy; water; biodiversity; emissions; effluents and waste; products and services; compliance; transport; supplier environmental assessment; environmental grievance mechanisms.

Comments on 'environmental events'

(a)   Of relevance to the farmland restoration is IAS 37 *Provisions, contingent liabilities and contingent assets.* Provisions for environmental liabilities should be recognised where there is a **legal or constructive obligation** to rectify environmental damage or perform restorative work. The mere existence of the restorative work does not give rise to an obligation and there is no legal obligation. However, it could be argued that there is a constructive obligation arising from the company's approach in previous years, which may have given rise to an **expectation** that the work would be carried out. If this is the case, a provision of $150m would be required in the financial statements. In addition, this provision and specific examples of restoration of land could be included in the environmental report.

(b)   The treatment of the **fine** is straightforward: it is an obligation to transfer economic benefits. An estimate of the fine should be made and a **provision** set up in the financial statements for $5m. This should be mentioned in the environmental report. The report might also **put the fines in context** by stating how many tests have been carried out and how many times the company has passed the tests. The directors may feel that it would do the company's reputation no harm to point out the fact that the number of prosecutions has been falling from year to year.

(c)   These statistics are good news and need to be covered in the environmental report. However, the emphasis should be on **accurate factual reporting** rather than boasting. It might be useful to provide target levels for comparison, or an industry average if available. The emissions statistics should be split into three categories:

*   Acidity to air and water
*   Hazardous substances
*   Harmful emissions to water

As regards the aquatic emissions, the $70m planned expenditure on **research** should **be mentioned in the environmental report**. It shows a commitment to benefiting the environment. However, **IAS 37 would not permit a provision** to be made for this amount, since an obligation does not exist and the **expenditure is avoidable**. Nor does it qualify as development expenditure under IAS 38.

(d)   The environmental report should mention the steps the company is taking to minimise the harmful impact on the environment in the way it sites and constructs its gas installations. The report should also explain the policy of dismantling the installations rather than sinking them at the end of their useful life.

Currently the company builds up a provision for decommissioning costs over the life of the installation. However, IAS 37 does not allow this. Instead, the **full amount must be provided** as soon as there is an

obligation arising as a result of **past events**, the **settlement** of which is **expected** to result in an **outflow of resources**. The obligation exists right at the beginning of the installation's life, and so the full $407m must be provided for. A corresponding asset is created.

63 Preparation question: Current issues

(a)   **New IFRS 9 business model**

(i)   A financial asset **must** be classified and measured **at fair value through other comprehensive income** if it meets both the following criteria:

(1)   The financial asset is held within a business model whose objective is achieved by **both collecting contractual cash flows and selling financial assets.**

(2)   The contractual terms of the financial asset give rise on specified dates to cash flows that are solely payments of principal and interest on the principal amount outstanding.

(ii)   Yes, this is an exception to the above requirement. The asset may be designated at fair value through profit or loss under the fair value option)

(b)   (i)   **Problems with the old hedging rules**

(1)   **The IAS 39 provisions were not based on consistent principles.** The provisions were rules-based, which led to inconsistency and arbitrariness.

(2)   **The IAS 39 rules did not provide sufficient information on risk management.** Increasingly users of financial statements have said that they wish to understand the risks that an entity faces, and the entity's strategy in managing those risks. Many believed that the IAS 39 requirements did not provide such an understanding.

(3)   **The IAS 39 rules on hedging did not reflect risk management practice.** For example:

- **There were instances where hedge accounting cannot be applied to groups of items, whereas for risk management purposes, items are often hedged on a group basis**. One example of this is equities making up an index such as the FTSE   100. These have an apparent economic link, but under the IAS 39 rules they could not be grouped together for hedging purposes, because they did not have similar risk characteristics.

- IAS 39 did not allow components of non-financial items to be hedged but entities usually hedge components of such items. For instance, an entity may wish to hedge the oil price component of the jet fuel price exposure by entering into a forward contract for crude oil. Under the IAS 39 rules, the entity could only hedge the price of jet fuel itself or the foreign currency risk.

- IAS 39 did not allow net positions to be hedged. However, companies often hedge net positions. For example, they may hedge a net foreign exchange position of $60m that is made up of an asset of $200m and a liability of $140m.

(4)   IAS 39's rules **were confusing and complex.**.

(5)   IAS 39's rules provided **insufficient disclosures** in the financial statements about an entity's risk management activities.

(6)   IAS 39 permitted hedge accounting only if a hedge is highly effective, both prospectively and retrospectively. IAS 39 regarded a hedge as highly effective if the offset is within the range of 80 to 125%. This was a **purely quantitative test** and has been felt to be narrow and arbitrary.

(ii)   **Changes in IFRS 9**

The proposed amendments are intended to 'improve the ability of investors to understand risk management activities and to assess the amounts, timing and uncertainty of future cash flows. The proposals will replace the 'rule-based' requirements for hedge accounting currently in IAS 39, and align the accounting more closely with risk management activities of an entity.

IFRS 9 contains a new, **principles based model** for hedge accounting that aims to **align accounting with risk management activities**. This will combine the following.

(1) A **management view**, that aims to use information produced internally for risk management purposes,

(2) An **accounting view** that seeks to address the risk management issue of the timing of recognition of gains and losses.

(3) An **objective-based assessment** for hedge effectiveness, replacing the somewhat arbitrary 80%-125% 'bright line' test of IAS 39.

IFRS 9 also made changes to changes to:

(4) Eligible hedging instruments and eligible hedged items

(5) Accounting for qualifying fair value hedges. Under IFRS 9

- The gain or loss on the hedging instrument and the hedged item should be recognised in other comprehensive income.

- The ineffective portion of the gain or loss is transferred to profit or loss.

(7) Rebalancing of the hedging relationship

(8) Discontinuing hedge accounting

(9) Accounting for time value of purchased options

(10) Improved disclosure requirements

(c) (i) IFRS 10 states that an investor **controls** an investee if and only if it has all of the following.

Power over the investee

(1) Exposure, or rights, to **variable returns** from its involvement with the investee, and
(2) The **ability to use its power** over the investee to affect the amount of the investor's returns.

Power is defined as **existing rights that give the current ability to direct the relevant activities of the investee**. There is no requirement for that power to have been exercised.

Relevant activities may include:

- Selling and purchasing goods or services
- Managing financial assets
- Selecting, acquiring and disposing of assets
- Researching and developing new products and processes
- Determining a funding structure or obtaining funding.

In some cases assessing power is straightforward, for example, where power is obtained directly and solely from having the majority of voting rights or potential voting rights, and as a result the ability to direct relevant activities.

(ii) The absolute size of Twist's holding and the relative size of the other shareholdings alone are not conclusive in determining whether the investor has rights sufficient to give it power. However, the fact that Twist has **a contractual right to appoint, remove and set the remuneration of management** is sufficient to conclude that it **has power over Oliver**. The fact that Twist has not exercised this right is not a determining factor when assessing whether Twist has power. In conclusion, Twist does control Oliver, and should consolidate it.

(iii) In this case, the size of Copperfield's voting interest and its size relative to the other shareholdings are sufficient to conclude that Copperfield **does not have power**. Only two other investors, Murdstone and Steerforth would need to co-operate to be able to prevent Copperfield from directing the relevant activities of the Spenlow.

(d)   The requirement to consolidate an investment is determined by **control**, not merely by ownership. In most cases, this will involve the parent company owning a majority of the ordinary shares in the subsidiary (to which normal voting rights are attached). There are circumstances, however, when the parent may own only a minority of the voting power in the subsidiary, *but* the parent still has control.

IFRS 10 *Consolidated financial statements,* issued in 2011, retains **control** from its predecessor IAS 27 as the key concept underlying the parent/subsidiary relationship but it has broadened the definition and clarified its application.

IFRS 10 states that an investor **controls** an investee if and only if it has all of the following:

(i)   **Power** over the investee

(ii)   Exposure, or rights, to **variable returns** from its involvement with the investee, and

(iii)   The **ability to use its power** over the investee to affect the amount of the investor's returns.

Power is defined as **existing rights that give the current ability to direct the relevant activities of the investee**. There is no requirement for that power to have been exercised.

Relevant activities may include:

- Selling and purchasing goods or services
- Managing financial assets
- Selecting, acquiring and disposing of assets
- Researching and developing new products and processes
- Determining a funding structure or obtaining funding.

In some cases assessing power is straightforward, for example, where power is obtained directly and solely from having the majority of voting rights or potential voting rights, and as a result the ability to direct relevant activities.

In other cases, assessment is more complex and more than one factor must be considered. IFRS 10 gives the following examples of **rights**, other than voting or potential voting rights, which individually, or alone, can give an investor power.

Rights to appoint, reassign or remove key management personnel who can direct the relevant activities

(i)   Rights to appoint or remove another entity that directs the relevant activities

(ii)   Rights to direct the investee to enter into, or veto changes to transactions for the benefit of the investor

(iii)   Other rights, such as those specified in a management contract.

Applying the above criteria to Red's relationship with Blue:

Red has power to govern the financial and operating policies of Blue, through its **operating guidelines**. It also has the power to prohibit the investment manager from profiting personally from the investments. Red is exposed to and has rights to variable returns from its investment in Blue, as it receives 95% of the profits and 100% of the losses of Blue.

Red therefore **controls** Blue, and **Blue should be consolidated**.

(e)   **Current issues relating to equity accounting**

These fall into two main categories

(i)   **Separate financial statements of the investor.** The option to apply the equity method in separate financial statements had been removed in the 2003 revision of IAS 27 *Consolidated and separate financial statements* as the IASB noted at that time that the information provided by the equity method is reflected in the investor's economic entity financial statements and that there was no need to provide the same information in the separate financial statements. The decision was carried forward to IAS 27 *Separate financial statements* in 2011. However, the IASB reconsidered this decision in the light of feedback and reinstated the option in a 2014 amendment to IAS 27.

Accordingly, investments in subsidiaries, associates and joint ventures in the separate financial statements of the parent is should be:

(1) Accounted for at **cost**, *or*

(2) In accordance with **IFRS 9**, *or*

(3) Using the equity method as described in IAS 28 *Investments in associates and joint ventures*

The amendments also clarify that when a parent ceases to be an investment entity, or becomes an investment entity, it must account for the change from the date when the change in status occurred.

(ii) **ED *Equity method: share of other net asset changes.*** This Exposure Draft was published in November 2012. The objective of the proposed amendments is to provide additional guidance to IAS 28 on the application of the equity method. Specifically; the proposed amendments intend to specify the following.

(1) An investor should recognise, in the investor's equity, its share of the changes in the net assets of the investee that are not recognised in profit or loss or other comprehensive income (OCI) of the investee, and that are not distributions received ('other net asset changes').

(2) The investor must reclassify to profit or loss the cumulative amount of equity that the investor had previously recognised when the investor discontinues the use of the equity method.

64 Fair values and IFRS 13

Text reference. Current issues are covered in Chapter 19. Fair value is covered where relevant in Chapters 4, 5, 12 and elsewhere briefly.

Top tips. This question is very topical, as IFRS 13 was issued in 2011.

Easy marks. Part (a) is fairly open ended, and credit will be given for valid points if you back up your arguments.

(a) **Fair value measurement or historical cost**

The debate between historical cost accounting and fair value measurement centres on **reliability versus relevance**. Very broadly speaking, fair values are perceived as relevant but not reliable. Historical cost accounting is perceived as reliable but not relevant.

Fair value can be said to be more relevant than historical cost because it is based on current market values rather than a value that is in some cases many years out of date. Fair values for an entity's assets, it is argued, will be give a closer approximation to the value of the entity as a whole, and are more useful to a decision maker or an investor.

If there is **more standardisation in fair valuing** – IFRS 13 *Fair value measurement* is a step towards this – then in the future, if not immediately, fair value measurement will have the advantage of being both relevant and reliable.

Historical cost accounting traditionally matches cost and revenue. The objective has been to match the cost of the asset with the revenue it earns over its useful life. It has a number of **disadvantages**.

(i) If the historical cost differs from its fair value on initial recognition, the **matching process in future periods becomes arbitrary**.

(ii) Non-current asset **values are unrealistic**, particularly those of property.

(iii) **Holding gains on inventory are included in profit.** During a period of high inflation the **monetary value of inventories held may increase significantly** while they are being processed. The conventions of historical cost accounting lead to the **realised part of this holding gain** (known as *inventory appreciation*) being **included** in **profit** for the year.

(iv) **Comparisons over time are unrealistic**, because they do not take account of inflation.

(v) **Costs incurred before an asset is recognised are not capitalised.** This is particularly true of development expenditure, and means that the historical cost does not represent the fair value of the consideration given to create the asset.

However, historical cost has a number of **advantages** over fair values, mainly as regards reliability.

(i)   It is **easy to understand**.

(ii)   It is grounded in **real transaction amounts**, and is therefore **objective** and objectively verifiable.

(iii)   There is **less scope for manipulation**.

Until there is **more uniformity and objectivity in fair valuing**, it is likely that historical cost accounting will continue to be used.

(b)   **IFRS 13 changes**

(i)   **Definition.** With the publication of IFRS 13, IFRS and US GAAP now have the same definition of fair value and the measurement and disclosure requirements are now aligned. IFRS 13 defines fair value as **'the price that would be received to sell an asset or paid to transfer a liability in an orderly transaction between market participants at the measurement date.'**

The previous definition used in IFRS was 'the amount for which an asset could be exchanged, or a liability settled, between knowledgeable, willing parties in an arm's length transaction'.

The price which would be received to sell the asset or paid to transfer (not settle) the liability is described as the 'exit price' and this is the definition used in US GAAP. Although the concept of the 'arm's length transaction' has now gone, the market-based current exit price retains the notion of an exchange between unrelated, knowledgeable and willing parties.

(ii)   **Measurement.** Fair value is a market-based measurement, not an entity-specific measurement. It focuses on assets and liabilities and on exit (selling) prices. It also takes into account market conditions at the measurement date. In other words, it looks at the amount for which the holder of an asset could sell it and the amount which the holder of a liability would have to pay to transfer it. It can also be used to value an entity's own equity instruments.

Because it is a market-based measurement, fair value is measured using the assumptions that market participants would use when pricing the asset, taking into account any relevant characteristics of the asset.

It is assumed that the transaction to sell the asset or transfer the liability takes place either:

(1)   In the **principal market** for the asset or liability; or

(2)   In the absence of a principal market, in the **most advantageous market** for the asset or liability. The principal market is the market which is the most liquid (has the greatest volume and level of activity) for that asset or liability. The most advantageous market is the market that maximises the amount that would be received to sell the asset or minimizes the amount that would be paid to transfer the liability (after taking into account transaction costs and transport costs). **In most cases the principal market and the most advantageous market will be the same.**

IFRS 13 acknowledges that when market activity declines an entity must use a valuation technique to measure fair value. In this case the emphasis must be on whether a transaction price is based on an orderly transaction, rather than a forced sale.

(iii)   **Non-financial assets.** For non-financial assets the fair value measurement looks at the use to which the asset can be put. It takes into account the ability of a market participant to generate economic benefits by using the asset in its highest and best use.

(iv)   **Valuation techniques.** IFRS 13 states that valuation techniques must be those which are appropriate and for which sufficient data are available. Entities should maximise the use of relevant **observable inputs** and minimise the use of **unobservable inputs**. The standard establishes a three-level hierarchy for the inputs that valuation techniques use to measure fair value:

Level 1 Quoted prices (unadjusted) in active markets for identical assets or liabilities that the reporting entity can access at the measurement date

Level 2 Inputs other than quoted prices included within Level 1 that are observable for the asset or liability, either directly or indirectly, eg quoted prices for similar assets in active markets or for identical or similar assets in non active markets or use of quoted interest rates for valuation purposes

Level 3 Unobservable inputs for the asset or liability, ie using the entity's own assumptions about market exit value

(v)   **Disclosure.** For assets and liabilities that are measured at fair value on a recurring or non-recurring basis, an entity must disclose the valuation techniques and inputs used to develop those measurements. For recurring fair value measurements using significant **unobservable inputs** (Level 3), it must disclose the effect of the measurements on profit or loss or other comprehensive income for the period.

(c)   **Investment in Greenfield**

The illustrative examples booklet accompanying IFRS 13 mentions the case of a financial asset for which sale is legally or contractually restricted for a specified period. The restriction is a characteristic of the instrument and, therefore, would be transferred to market participants. In this case the fair value of the instrument would be measured on the basis of the quoted price for an otherwise identical unrestricted equity instrument of the same issuer that trades in a public market, adjusted to reflect the effect of the restriction. The adjustment would reflect the amount market participants would demand because of the risk relating to the inability to access a public market for the instrument for the specified period. The adjustment will vary depending on:

(i)   The nature and duration of the restriction

(ii)   The extent to which buyers are limited by the restriction (eg there might be a large number of qualifying investors)

(iii)   Qualitative and quantitative factors specific to both the instrument and the issuer

65 Jones and Cousin

Text reference. This topic is covered in Chapter 19 of the text.

Top tips. In part (b), make full use of the information in the question, but do not simply regurgitate it.

Easy marks. Part (a) is very straightforward book work. Part (b) also has easy marks for style and layout.

Marking scheme

		Marks
(a)	Principle	6
	Mandatory discussion	7
Available/maximum		13
(b)	Principal risks	9
	Treasury policies	3
Available/maximum		12
	Style and presentation	2
Available		27
Maximum		25

(a) In December 2010, the IASB issued an IFRS Practice Statement *Management Commentary*, which is the international equivalent of the UK's Operating and Financial Review. The purpose of the commentary is to provide a context for interpreting a company's **financial position, performance and cash flows**. The principles and objectives of a Management Commentary (MC) are as follows:

   (i) To provide **management's view** of the entity's performance, position and progress;

   (ii) To **supplement and complement** information presented in the financial statements;

   (iii) To include **forward-looking information**; and

   (iv) To include information that possesses the **qualitative characteristics** described in the *Conceptual Framework* (see Chapter 1).

   The Practice Statement says that to meet the objective of management commentary, an entity should include information that is essential to an understanding of:

   (i) The **nature of the business**

   (ii) Management's **objectives and its strategies** for meeting those objectives

   (iii) The entity's most significant **resources, risks and relationships**

   (iv) The **results** of operations and **prospects**

   (v) The critical **performance measures and indicators** that management uses to evaluate the entity's performance against stated objectives

   The arguments for a mandatory MC are largely to do with content and comparability. It is argued that a mandatory MC will make it easier for companies themselves to judge what is required in such a report and the required standard of reporting, thereby making such reports more **robust, transparent and comparable**. If an MC is not mandatory then there may be **uncertainty** as to content and the possibility of **misinformation**. There is also the risk that without a mandatory MC directors may take a **minimalist approach** to disclosure which will make the MC less useful and the information to be disclosed will be in hands of senior executives and directors.

   However, the **arguments against** a mandatory MC are that it could **stifle the development of the MC as a tool** for communication and may lead to a **checklist approach** to producing it. It is argued that a mandatory MC is not required as market forces and the needs of investors should lead to companies feeling the pressure to provide a useful and reliable report. The IASB decided to issue a Practice Statement rather than an IFRS and to leave it to regulators to decide who would be required to publish a management commentary. This approach avoids the **adoption hurdle**, ie that the perceived cost of applying IFRSs might increase, which could otherwise dissuade jurisdictions/countries not having adopted IFRSs from requiring its adoption, especially where requirements differ significantly from existing national requirements.

(b)

Jones and Cousin
Annual Report 20X6
Management Commentary

Introduction

Jones and Cousin is a public quoted company and the group develops, manufactures and markets products in the medical sector. This report is designed to assist members of the group in understanding and assessing the strategies of the group and the potential success of these strategies.

Risks

The group faces a number of risks which will be considered under the headings of:

- Market risk
- Product risk
- Currency risk

Market risk

The market in which the group operates is quite fiercely competitive and contains a number of different competitors including specialised and large international corporations. There is the risk that any technical advances or product innovations by these competitors could adversely affect the group's profits. Also this element of competition also means that there is a risk of loss of market share or lower than expected sales growth which could affect the share price.

The sector in which the group operates is heavily monitored by local governments and the group's share of revenue in a market sector is often determined by government policy. The group is therefore heavily dependent upon governments providing the funds for health care. Any reduction in funds by governments would almost certainly lead to a fall in revenue for the group.

Product risk

The products of the group are essentially a low health risk. However, there is always the possibility of a problem with products which may lead to legal action which would be costly and damage the group's reputation and goodwill. The industry is highly regulated in terms of both medical and environmental laws. Any such claims would have an adverse effect on sales, profit and share price.

There will always be innovations in this market sector and the group is careful to protect its products with patents and will enter into legal proceedings where necessary to protect those patents. There is also the problem of infringing the patents of others. If claims were brought for infringement of patents of other companies this would be costly and damaging and alternative products would have to be found.

There are constantly new products being developed by the group which is costly in terms of research and development expenditure. Product innovation may not always be successful and this highly regulated market may not always gain the regulatory approval required.

Currency risk

The group operates in 27 different countries and earns revenue and incurs costs in several different currencies. Although the dollar is the group's functional currency only 5% of its business is in the country of incorporation. Therefore exchange fluctuations in the main currencies in which it trades may have a material effect on the group's profits and cash flows.

Relationships

The group has a positive ethical programme. It sources its products from a wide range of suppliers largely in the form of long term contracts for the supply of goods. The group has a policy of ensuring that such suppliers are suitable from both qualitative and ethical perspectives.

The group has a set of corporate and social responsibility principles for which the Board of Directors is responsible. The risks that the group bears from these responsibilities are managed by the Managing Director. The group operates in many geographical areas and encourages its subsidiaries to help local communities to reinvest in local educational projects. Great care is taken by the group to ensure that obsolete products are disposed of responsibly and safely. Wherever possible reusable materials are used.

Group policy is to attract and retain employees and to maintain an equal opportunities policy for all employees. To this end employees regularly receive in-house training and are kept informed of management policies.

Treasury policies

The group uses derivative products to protect against both currency risk and interest rate risk. This is done by the used of fixed rate currency swaps and using floating to fixed rate interest rate swaps. All financial instruments are accounted for as cash flow hedges which means that gains and losses are recognised initially in reserves and are only released to profit or loss when the hedged item also affects profit or loss.

66 Lockfine

Marking scheme

		Marks
(a)	1mark per question up to maximum	6
(b)	1mark per question up to maximum	6
(c)	1mark per question up to maximum	6
(d)	1mark per question up to maximum	5
Professional marks		2
Maximum		25

(a) **IFRS 1 and deemed cost**

IFRS 1 *First time adoption of International Financial Reporting Standards* states that an entity may elect to measure an item of property, plant and equipment at the **date of transition to IFRS** at fair value and **use that fair value as its deemed cost at that date**. Fair value is defined in IFRS 1 as amended by IFRS 13 *Fair value measurement* as:

'the price that would be received to sell an asset or paid to transfer a liability in an orderly transaction between market participants at the measurement date.'

An entity adopting IFRS for the first-time may, under IFRS 1 as amended by IFRS 13, elect **to use a previous GAAP revaluation** of an item of property, plant and equipment at or before the date of transition to IFRS as deemed cost at the date of the revaluation under the following conditions.

(i) The revaluation was broadly comparable to fair value.

(ii) The revaluation was broadly comparable to cost or depreciated cost in accordance with IFRS, adjusted to reflect, for example, changes in a general or specific price index.

In addition, IFRS 1 does not give detailed rules about determining fair value, and first-time adopters who use fair value as deemed cost **must only provide limited disclosures**, not a full description of the methods and assumptions used.

In the case of Lockfine, the question to be decided is whether the selling agents' estimates can be used as the fair value to be used, in turn, as deemed cost under IFRS 1.

BPP
LEARNING MEDIA

The selling agents' estimates provide only limited information about the valuation methods and assumptions, and it is doubtful that they can be relied upon for determining fair value in accordance with IAS 16 *Property, plant and equipment* and IFRS 13 *Fair value measurement*. Under IAS 16 measurement of fair value must be **reliable**. While it is correct to use independent valuers, IAS 16 requires that the reporting entity know the **assumptions** that have been made in assessing reliability. In addition, using the average of the highest amounts may not be prudent.

IFRS 1 allows more latitude than IAS 16. Lockfine is **not in breach of IFRS 1 which does not specify detailed rules for this particular case**, and allows fair value as determined on the basis of selling agents' estimates. This is a cost effective approach for entities that do not perform a full retrospective application of the requirements of IAS 16.

(b)   **Fishing rights**

IFRS 1 requires that if an entity which is in the process of adopting IFRS decides to apply IFRS 3 retrospectively to a business combination, it **cannot do so selectively,** but must apply IFRS 3 **consistently to all business combinations** that occur between the date on which it decides to adopt.

IFRS 3 and the date of transition. An entity must have regard to **similar transactions in the period**. When allocating values to the assets and liabilities of the acquired company, the entity needs to have documentation to support its purchase price allocation. Without this, use of other methods of price allocation is not permitted unless the methods are strictly in accordance with IFRS.

Lockfine was **unable to recognise** the fishing rights of the business combination as separately identifiable because it **could not obtain a reliable value** for the rights, so it included the rights within goodwill.

IAS 38 has two criteria, both of which must be met for an entity to recognise an intangible asset, whether purchased or internally generated:

(i)   It is probably that the future economic benefits attributable to the asset will flow to the entity.
(ii)   The cost of the asset can be measured reliably.

The fishing rights **satisfy the first, but not the second of these criteria**. Accordingly the fishing rights were **correctly subsumed within goodwill**. As long as the goodwill presented under the first IFRS financial statements did not require a write down for impairment, it should be the net carrying amount at the date of transition.

Although the fishing rights have a finite life, **they will not be amortised over the period** specified by the rights, because they are included within goodwill. Instead, **the goodwill is reviewed annually for impairment** in accordance with IAS 36 *Impairment of assets*.

(c)   **Electronic map data**

The standard that applies here is IAS 38 *Intangible assets*. Under IAS 38, an intangible asset is an asset with the following characteristics.

(i)   It meets the standard's **identifiability criteria**. This means it must be separable or must arise from contractual or other legal rights

(ii)   It is probable that **future economic benefits** attributable to the asset will flow to the entity. These could be in the form of increased revenues or cost savings.

(iii) The entity has **control**, that is the power to obtain benefits from the asset.

(iv)   Its cost can be **measured reliably**.

It appears that the capitalised expenses of the acquisition and production of the electronic map data **meet these criteria**.

(i)   The electronic maps are identifiable because they are capable of being separated from the entity as a whole and sold (or transferred or licensed), regardless of whether the entity intends to do this.

(ii)   They are controlled by Lockfine.

(iii) It is probable that benefits attributable to the maps will flow to the entity because the electronic maps will generate revenue when used by the fishing fleet.

(iv)   Their value can be measured reliably – Lockfine has a record of the costs.

The **electronic maps** will therefore be **recognised as an intangible asset at cost**. Generally they will subsequently be carried at cost less any amortisation and impairment losses.

Regarding the **database**, Lockfine believes that this has an indefinite useful life and, by implication, should not be amortised but should be tested annually for impairment. IAS 38 regards an intangible asset as having an indefinite useful life when, based on analysis of all the relevant factors, there is no foreseeable limit to the period over which the asset is expected to generate net cash inflows for the entity.

Indefinite does not mean the same as infinite and in the context of IAS 38 has specific implications. In particular, the indefinite useful life should not depend on future planned expenditure in excess of that required to maintain the asset. In this respect, **Lockfine complies with IAS 38**.

In addition, IAS 38 identifies certain factors that may affect the useful life, changing it in this instance from indefinite to finite. These include technological or commercial obsolescence and actions by competitors.

There is no specific requirement for an entity to disclose the IAS 38 criteria for recognition of an intangible asset arising from development, although it does require disclosure of assets which have an indefinite useful life (the carrying amount and reasons for assessing the useful life as indefinite(. However, under IAS 1 *Presentation of financial statements,* entities **must disclose accounting policies that are relevant for an understanding of their financial statements**. The electronic maps and the data base constitute a material amount of total assets, so the accounting policies, including the IAS 38 criteria for development expenditure, need to be disclosed.

(d)   **Restructuring plans**

IAS 37 criteria

IAS 37 *Provisions, contingent liabilities and contingent assets* **contains specific requirements** relating to **restructuring provisions**. The general recognition criteria apply and IAS 37 also states that **a provision should be recognised** if an entity has a **constructive obligation** to carry out a restructuring. A constructive obligation exists where **management has a detailed formal plan** for the restructuring, identifying **as a minimum:**

(i)   The business or part of the business being restructured

(ii)   The principal locations affected by the restructuring

(iii)   The location, function and approximate number of employees who will be compensated for the termination of their employment

(iv)   The date of implementation of the plan

(v)   The expenditure that will be undertaken.

In addition, the plan must have raised a **valid expectation** in those affected that the entity will carry out the restructuring. To give rise to such an expectation and therefore a constructive obligation, the **implementation must be planned to take place as soon as possible**, and the timeframe must be such as to make changes to the plan unlikely.

Plan A

Lockfine proposes recognising a provision in respect of the plan to sell 50% of its off-shore fleet in a year's time and to make 40% of the seamen redundant. However, although the plan has been communicated to the public, the above criteria are not met. **The plan is insufficiently detailed**, and various aspects are not finalised. The figure of 40% is tentative as yet, the **fleets and employees affected have not been identified**, and a decision has not been made on whether the off-shore fleet will be restructured in the future. Some of these issues await further analysis.

The proposal does not, therefore, meet the IAS 37 criteria for a detailed formal plan and an announcement of the plan to those affected by it. Lockfine cannot be said to be committed to this restructuring and so **a provision should not be recognised**.

Plan B

Lockfine has not proposed recognising a provision for the plan to reorganise its headquarters and make 20% of the headquarters' workforce redundant. However, it is likely that this treatment is incorrect, because the plan appears to meet the IAS 37 criteria above:

(i) The locations and employees affected have been **identified**.

(ii) An **announcement** has been made and employee representatives notified – it is not necessary to notify individual employees as their representatives have been told.

(iii) The conclusion of the three month consultation period indicates that the above announcement is sufficiently detailed to give rise to a **valid expectation** that the restructuring will take place, particularly if the discussions have been about the terms of the redundancy.

It will be necessary to c**onsider the above negotiations** – provided these are about details such as the terms of redundancy rather than about changing the plan, then the IAS 37 criteria have been met. Accordingly, a provision needs to be recognised.

67 Seltec

Text references. Financial instruments are covered in Chapter 7, brands in Chapter 4, and business combinations in Chapters 12 to 17. This is a specialised industry question – other specialised industries are covered in Chapter 20 of your text.

Top tips. Note that IFRS 9 simplifies the treatment of embedded derivatives that are financial assets within the scope of the standard – these no longer need to be separated from their host contract. However, the more complex rules still apply to embedded derivatives that are not assets. In Part (b), you need to think carefully about what constitutes a business combination – substance is more important than form.

Easy marks. These are available for the definition of embedded derivatives and basic principles of intangible assets.

Examiner's comment. The examiner was satisfied in the main with candidates' answers, but disappointed that few recognised the embedded derivative. Answers to the final part of the question, on business combinations, were disappointing, the main weakness being the application of the knowledge and the understanding of the nature of the purchase of the entities.

Marking scheme

	Marks
Hedge accounting	5
Futures	5
Embedded derivative	4
Brands	5
Business combinations	4
Professional marks	2
	25

(a)   **Financial instruments**

Derivatives

IAS 32 *Financial instruments: presentation* and IFRS 9 *Financial instruments* define a **derivative** as a financial instrument or other contract that has all three of the following characteristics.

(i)   Its value changes in response to the change in a specified interest rate, financial instrument price, commodity price, foreign exchange rate, index of prices or rates, credit rating or credit index, or other variable (sometimes called the 'underlying').

(ii)   It requires no initial net investment or an initial net investment that is smaller than would be required for other types of contracts that would be expected to have a similar response to changes in market factors.

(iii)   It is settled at a future date.

A contract is **not considered to be a derivative where its purpose is to take physical delivery** in the normal course of business, unless the entity has a practice of settling the contracts on a net basis.

In the case of Seltec, while the company often takes physical delivery of the edible oil, it does so only to sell shortly afterwards, and usually settles on a net basis. Thus the **contracts will be considered to be derivative** contracts rather than contracts for purchase of inventory. Derivatives are accounted for at fair value through profit or loss, unless hedge accounting applies.

Hedge accounting

The rules on hedge accounting are set out in IFRS 9 *Financial instruments* (July 2014). Before a hedging relationship qualifies for hedge accounting, **all** of the following **conditions** must be met.

(i)   The hedging relationship consists **only of eligible hedging instruments and eligible hedged items**.

(ii)   There must be **formal documentation** (including identification of the hedged item, the hedging instrument, the nature of the risk that is to be hedged and how the entity will assess the hedging instrument's effectiveness in offsetting the exposure to changes in the hedged item's fair value or cash flows attributable to the hedged risk).

(iii)   The hedging relationship meets all of the following hedge effectiveness criteria

(1)   There is an **economic relationship** between the hedged item and the hedging instrument, ie the hedging instrument and the hedged item have values that generally move in the opposite direction because of the same risk, which is the hedged risk;

(2)   The **effect of credit risk does not dominate the value** changes that result from that economic relationship, ie the gain or loss from credit risk does not frustrate the effect of changes in the underlyings on the value of the hedging instrument or the hedged item, even if those changes were significant; and

(3)   The **hedge ratio of the hedging relationship** (quantity of hedging instrument vs quantity of hedged item) is the same as that resulting from the quantity of the hedged item that the entity **actually hedges** and the quantity of the hedging instrument that the entity **actually uses** to hedge that quantity of hedged item.

There are two kinds of hedging that Seltec may consider: fair value hedging and cash flow hedging.

A **fair value hedge** is a hedge of the exposure to changes in the fair value of a recognised asset or liability, or an identified portion of such an asset or liability, that is attributable to a particular risk and could affect profit or loss. The **gain or loss** resulting from **re-measuring** the hedging instrument at fair value is **recognised in profit or loss**. The gain or loss on the hedged item attributable to the **hedged risk** should **adjust the carrying amount** of the hedged item and be **recognised in profit or loss**.

A **cash flow hedge**: a hedge of the exposure to variability in cash flows that:

(i)   Is attributable to a particular risk associated with a recognised asset or liability (such as all or some future interest payments on variable rate debt) or a highly probable forecast transaction (such as an anticipated purchase or sale), and that

(ii)   Could affect profit or loss.

The portion of the gain or loss on the hedging instrument that is determined to be an **effective** hedge must be **recognised in other comprehensive income(items that may subsequently be reclassified to profit or loss)** and transferred to profit or loss when the hedged item is recognised in profit or loss. The **ineffective portion** of the gain or loss on the hedging instrument must be **recognised in profit or loss**.

The rules for cash flow hedges are particularly restrictive because it is difficult to isolate and measure the cash flows attributable to the specific risks for the non-financial items. Cash flow hedging results in higher volatility in earnings, so, provided the documentation and other requirements are met, **Seltec may prefer to use fair value hedging**. Seltec must take into account all changes in the price of edible oil of all types and geographical locations that it processes and sells and these must be compared with the changes in the value of the future. The hedge will be ineffective if the contracts have different prices. However, a hedge does not need to be fully effective, and hedge accounting may still be used provided the effectiveness is in the range 80% to 125%.

Embedded derivative

Certain contracts that are not themselves derivatives (and may not be financial instruments) include derivative contracts that are 'embedded' within them. These non-derivatives are called **host contracts** IFRS 9 defines an embedded derivative as a derivative instrument that is combined with a non-derivative host contract to form a single hybrid instrument. Some of the cash flows of the instrument vary in a way that is similar to a stand-alone derivative.

Ordinary derivatives must be accounted for at fair value in the statement of financial position with changes recognised through profit or loss.

IFRS 9 treatment

Where the host contract is a financial asset within the scope of the IFRS 9, the classification and **measurement rules of the standard are applied to the entire hybrid contract**. However, in this case the contract is a financial liability, not a financial asset within the scope of IFRS 9. Accordingly, the following rules apply:

The embedded derivative must be **separated from its host contract** and accounted for as a derivative, provided the following conditions are met.

(i)   The economic characteristics and risks of the embedded derivative are not closely related to the economic characteristics and risks of the host contract.

(ii)   A separate instrument with the same terms as the embedded derivative would meet the definition of a derivative.

(iii) The hybrid (combined) instrument is not measured at fair value with changes in fair value recognised in the profit or loss (a derivative embedded in a financial asset or financial liability need not be separated out if the entity holds the combined instrument at fair value through profit or loss).

If the embedded derivative is separated from its host contract, the **host contract is accounted for under the applicable IFRS**. A contract denominated in a foreign currency contains an embedded derivative unless:

(i)   The foreign currency denominated in the contract is the currency of one of the parties to the contract.

(ii)   The foreign currency is that commonly used in the market in which such transactions take place.

(iii) The foreign currency is that in which the related goods or services are denominated in routine commercial transactions.

In the case of Seltec, **none of the above three exceptions apply**. Seltec's trade in edible oil is generally in dollars, not pound sterling, the pound is not the functional currency of either party, and it is not the currency normally used in transactions in the business environment in which Seltec operates. Finally, the economic characteristics and risks of the embedded derivative are not closely related to the economic characteristics and risks of the host contract, since changes in the price of oil and currency fluctuations have different risks.

In conclusion, IFRS 9 would treat Seltec's contracts as containing an embedded derivative. The currency derivative must be accounted for at fair value through profit or loss.

(b)   **Intangible assets**

An entity should **assess** the useful life of an intangible asset, which may be **finite or indefinite**. An intangible asset has an indefinite useful life when there is **no foreseeable limit** to the period over which the asset is expected to generate net cash inflows for the entity.

Seltec wishes to treat both brands as having indefinite useful lives. However, this may not be appropriate, and there are certain factors that need to be considered:

(i)   Does the brand have long-term potential? The first brand has a proven track record, but the second, named after a famous film star, may last only as long as the film star's popularity, which will not be indefinite.

(ii)   Is Seltec committed to supporting the brand? In the case of the first, it is, but the second is a relatively new product, and it is not clear that Seltec is in for the long haul.

If, as is likely, the **useful life of the second brand is considered to be finite**, its cost less residual should be amortised on a systematic basis over its useful life, using the straight-line method as an approximation if the pattern of benefits cannot be determined reliably.

The **first brand**, which is correctly said to have an **indefinite useful life**, should not be amortised. Its useful life should be reviewed at each reporting period to determine whether the assessment of the useful life as indefinite is still applicable. If not, the change, from indefinite to finite would be accounted for as a change in accounting estimate as per IAS 8. It should also be assessed for impairment in accordance with IAS 36, and otherwise accounted for like the second brand.

Purchase of entities

IFRS 3 *Business combinations* defines a business combination as 'a transaction or event in which an acquirer obtains control of one or more businesses. A business is defined as an integrated set of activities and assets that is capable of being conducted and managed for the purpose of providing a return directly to investors or other owners, members or participants'. Such a return may be in the form of cash, dividends or lower costs.

The two limited liability **companies do not meet the IFRS 3 definition of a business** because they are not self-sustaining and do not generate revenue independently of Seltec. The acquisition **should be treated as a purchase of property**.

68 Ethan

Text reference. Deferred tax is covered in Chapter 6 of your BPP Study Text. Investment property and impairment are covered in Chapter 4, and financial instruments and fair value are covered in Chapter 7.

Top tips. In Part (a), our answer focuses on IFRS 13, because by the time you take your exam, this IFRS will have been examinable for at least two years. Part (b) required application of the fair value option in IFRS 9 *Financial Instruments.* The option is used where such application would eliminate or significantly reduce a measurement or recognition inconsistency between the debt liabilities and the investment properties to which they were related in this question. In Part (c), candidates needed to recognise that, in classifying the B shares as equity rather than as a liability, the entity had not complied with IAS 32 *Financial instruments: presentation.* There were pointers to the shares being classified as a liability, in particular the fact that entity was obliged to pay an annual cumulative dividend on the B shares and did not have discretion over the distribution of such dividend.

Easy marks. There are no obviously easy marks in this question.

Examiner's comment. In Part (a), credit was given if candidates answered the part on fair value in terms of IAS 40 rather than the new IFRS 13. Answers to this question varied in standard, and candidates did not seem to be able to identify the key issues. The nature of the technical knowledge in this question was not high but the need to apply that knowledge was crucial to a good answer. Candidates had difficulty in understanding the nature of the option in Part (b), and yet it is used often in practice, which means it is an important element of the syllabus. In Part (c), few candidates realised that certain characteristics of the B shares indicated that they should be classified as a liability.

	Marks
Impairment testing	5
Deferred taxation	6
Fair value option – IFRS 9	7
Financial liability	5
Communication skills	2
	25

(a) **Fair value**

The **fair value** of an asset is the price that would be received to sell an asset or paid to transfer a liability in an orderly transaction between market participants at the measurement date (IFRS 13 *Fair value measurement*). IFRS 13 states that valuation techniques must be those which are appropriate and for which sufficient data are available. Entities should maximise the use of relevant **observable inputs** and minimise the use of **unobservable inputs**. The standard establishes a three-level hierarchy for the inputs that valuation techniques use to measure fair value.

Level 1 Quoted prices (unadjusted) in active markets for identical assets or liabilities that the reporting entity can access at the measurement date

Level 2 Inputs other than quoted prices included within Level 1 that are observable for the asset or liability, either directly or indirectly, eg quoted prices for similar assets in active markets or for identical or similar assets in non-active markets or use of quoted interest rates for valuation purposes

Level 3 Unobservable inputs for the asset or liability, ie using the entity's own assumptions about market exit value

Although an active market exists for Ethan's investment properties, Ethan uses a discounted cash flow model to measure fair value. This is **not in accordance with IFRS 13**. As the fair value hierarchy suggests, IFRS 13 favours Level 1 inputs, that is market-based measures, over unobservable (Level 3) inputs such as discounted cash flows.

Goodwill and deferred tax

If the **fair value** of the investment properties **is not measured correctly** in accordance with IFRS 13, this means that the **deferred tax liability** on investment properties **may also be incorrect**. In addition, as goodwill is calculated as consideration transferred less fair value of net assets, **goodwill may be incorrect**. This is because deferred tax is calculated on the difference between the carrying amount of the asset and its tax base. So if the carrying amount is incorrect, the deferred tax will be incorrect. The goodwill calculation uses the fair value of **all** net assets, not just the investment properties and the related deferred tax liability, so it is **incorrect to use an increase in the deferred tax liability** as the **basis** for assessing whether goodwill is impaired.

The reasoning behind Ethan's approach is that as the deferred tax liability decreases, the fair value of net assets increases, thereby decreasing goodwill. However, this method of determining whether goodwill is impaired **does not accord with IAS 36** *Impairment of assets.* IAS 36 requires that goodwill should be **reviewed for impairment annually** for any indicators of impairment, which may be internal or external, and are not confined to changes in the deferred tax liability. Where it is not possible to measure impairment for individual assets, the loss should be measured for a **cash generating unit**.

The **recoverable amount** is **defined** as the **higher** of:

(i) The **asset's fair value less costs to sell**. This is the price that would be received to sell the asset in an orderly transaction between market participants at the measurement date under current market conditions, net of costs of disposal.

(ii)   The asset's **value in use**. This is the present value of estimated future cash flows (inflows minus outflows) generated by the asset, including its estimated net disposal value (if any) at the end of its useful life.

If an **asset's carrying amount** is **higher than its recoverable amount**, an **impairment loss** has occurred. The impairment loss should be **written off against profit or loss** for the year, and the corresponding credit (write-off) applied first to goodwill, then to the investment properties, then to other assets pro-rata.

Deferred tax assets on losses

In theory, unused tax losses give rise to a deferred tax asset. However, IAS 12 *Income taxes* states that **deferred tax assets should only be recognised to the extent that they are regarded as recoverable**. They should be regarded as recoverable to the extent that on the basis of all the evidence available it is **probable that there will be suitable taxable profits against which the losses can be recovered**. It is unlikely that future taxable profits of Ethan will be sufficient to realise all of the tax loss because of:

(i)   The announcement that a substantial loss will be incurred this year instead of the expected profit
(ii)   Considerable negative variances against budgets in the past

Consequently, **Ethan should not recognise the deferred tax asset**.

(b)   **IFRS 9 fair value option**

Generally under IFRS 9 *Financial instruments*, the debt issued to finance its investment properties would be accounted for using **amortised cost,** while the properties themselves are at fair value. This is an **accounting mismatch,** that is a recognition or measurement inconsistency between the debt liability and the asset to which it relates. The asset and liability, and the gains and losses arising on them, would be measured on different bases.

The IFRS 9 **fair value option** allows an entity to **designate a liability at initial recognition as being at fair value through profit or loss** if using this option would **eliminate or significantly reduce** an accounting mismatch. Ethan has argued that the basis of measurement of the debt and the investment properties is **similar**, particularly as regards **interest rates**. This argument holds good in respect of the interest, and so the **fair value option would be allowed**.

However, IFRS 9 stipulates that if a liability is designated as being at fair value through profit or loss, **changes in the fair value that are due to changes in the liability's credit risk must be recognised directly in other comprehensive income** rather than profit or loss. Such **changes may not be re-classified** to profit or loss in subsequent years, although a **reserves transfer** is permitted from other components of equity to retained earnings. On the other hand, **if changes in the fair value attributable to the credit risk** of the liability **create or enlarge an accounting mismatch in profit or loss**, then all fair value movements are **recognised in profit or loss.**

(c)   **B shares of subsidiary**

Ethan's accounting treatment of the B shares (as equity instruments) does not comply with IAS 32 *Financial instruments: presentation.* The IAS 32 definition of a financial liability includes any liability that is **a contractual obligation to deliver cash or another financial asset to another entity**. A financial instrument may only be classified as an equity instrument rather than a liability if the instrument does not include an obligation to deliver cash or other financial asset to another entity, or to exchange financial instruments with another entity under conditions that are potentially unfavourable.

In the **subsidiary's books,** the B shares would be treated as a **financial liability.** They contain an **obligation** to deliver cash in the form of a fixed dividend. The dividend is cumulative and must be paid whether or not the subsidiary has sufficient legally distributable profits when it is due, and so **the subsidiary cannot avoid this obligation**.

In the **consolidated financial statements,** the B shares would also be treated as a financial liability, **the intragroup element of this liability (70%) would cancel against the investment in B shares in the parent's (Ethan's) statement of financial position**. The shares **owned by external parties would not cancel;** they would remain **a financial liability**. It **is incorrect to treat them as non-controlling interest** because they are **not equity**.

69 Norman

Marking scheme

		Marks
(a)	Identification of segments	2
	Definition	2
	Reporting information	2
	Normal applicability	5
		11
(b)	Sale of businesses	4
	Vouchers	4
	Grant income	4
	Quality of discussion	2
		14
Maximum		25

(a) **Determining operating segments**

IFRS 8 *Operating segments* states that an operating segment is a reported **separately** if:

(i)   It **meets the definition of an operating segment**, ie:

        (1)   It engages in business activities from which it may **earn revenues** and **incur expenses**,

        (2)   Its operating results are **regularly reviewed by the entity's chief operating decision maker** to make decisions about resources to be allocated to the segment and assess its performance, and

        (3)   **Discrete financial information** is available for the segment,

    and

(ii)   It exceeds **at least one** of the following quantitative thresholds:

        (1)   Reported revenue is **10% or more the combined revenue** of all operating segments (external and intersegment), or

        (2)   The absolute amount of its reported profit or loss is **10% or more of the greater of,** in absolute amount, **all operating segments not reporting a loss, and all operating segments reporting a loss**, or

        (3)   Its assets are **10% or more of the total assets** of all operating segments.

At least **75% of total external revenue** must be reported by operating segments. Where this is not the case, additional segments must be identified (even if they do not meet the 10% thresholds).

Two or more operating segments **below** the thresholds may be aggregated to produce a reportable segment if the segments have similar economic characteristics, and the segments are similar in a **majority** of the following aggregation criteria:

(1)   The nature of the products and services
(2)   The nature of the production process
(3)   The type or class of customer for their products or services
(4)   The methods used to distribute their products or provide their services
(5)   If applicable, the nature of the regulatory environment

Operating segments that do not meet **any of the quantitative thresholds** may be reported separately if management believes that information about the segment would be useful to users of the financial statements.

For Norman, **the thresholds are as follows**:

(i)   Combined revenue is $1,010 million, so 10% is $101 million.
(ii)   Combined reported profit is $165 million, so 10% is $16.5 million.
(iii)   Combined reported loss is $10 million, so 10% is $1 million.
(iv)   Total assets are $3,100 million, so 10% is $310 million.

The **South East Asia segment** meets the criteria, passing all three tests. Its combined revenue is $302 million; its reported profit is $60 million, and its assets are $800 million.

The **European segment** also meets the criteria, but only marginally. Its reported revenue, at $203 million is greater than 10% of combined revenue, and only one of the tests must be satisfied. However, its loss of $10 million is less than the greater of 10% of combined profit and 10% of combined loss, so it fails this test. It also fails the assets test, as its assets, at $300 million are less than 10% of combined assets ($310 million).

IFRS 8 requires further that at least 75% of total external revenue must be reported by operating segments. Currently, only 50% is so reported. Additional operating segments (the 'other regions') must be identified until this 75% threshold is reached.

IFRS 8 may result in a **change** to the way Norman's operating segments are reported, depending on how segments were previously identified.

(b)   **Sale of hotel complex**

The issue here is one of **revenue recognition**, and the accounting treatment is governed by IFRS 15 *Revenue with contracts from customers.* Stage (v) of the standards revenue recognition process requires that **revenue is recognised when (or as)a performance obligation is satisfied**. The entity satisfies a performance obligation by transferring **control** of a promised good or service to the customer. A performance obligation can be satisfied **at a point in time**, such as when goods are delivered to the customer, or **over time**. In the case of the hotel transfer, the issue is that of a performance obligation **satisfied at a point in time.** One of the IFRS 15 indicators of control is that significant risks and rewards of ownership have been transferred to the customer.

It can be argued in some cases where property is sold that the seller, by continuing to be involved, has **not satisfied the performance obligation by transferring control,** partly because the seller has not transferred the risks and rewards of ownership. In such cases, the **sale is not genuine**, but is often in substance a **financing arrangement**. IFRS 15 requires that the substance of a transaction is determined by looking at the transaction as a whole. If two or more transactions are linked, they should be treated as one transaction to better reflect the commercial substance.

Norman continues to operate and manage the hotel complex, receiving the bulk (75%) of the profits, and the residual interest reverts back to Norman; effectively, Norman **retains control** by retaining the risks and rewards of ownership. Conquest does not bear any risk: its minimum annual income is guaranteed at $15m. **The sale should not be recognised**. In substance it is a **financing transaction**. The **proceeds** should be treated as a **loan**, and the payment of **profits** as **interest**.

Discount vouchers

The treatment of the vouchers is governed by IFRS 15 *Revenue with contracts from customers.*. The principles of the standard require that

(i)   The voucher should be accounted for as a **separate component** of the sal.e

(ii)   The promise to provide the discount is a **performance obligation.**

(ii)   The entity must estimate the **stand-alone selling price** of the discount voucher in accordance with paragraph B42 of IFRS 15. The That estimate must reflect the discount that the customer would obtain when exercising the option, adjusted for both of the following:

(1) Any discount that the customer could receive without exercising the option
(2) The likelihood that the option will be exercised.

The vouchers are issued as part of the sale of the room and redeemable against future bookings. The substance of the transaction is that **the customer is purchasing both a room and a voucher**.

Vouchers worth $20 million are eligible for discount as at 31 May 20X8. However, based on past experience, it is likely that only one in five vouchers will be redeemed, that is vouchers worth $4 million. Room sales are $300 million, **so effectively, the company has made sales worth $(300m + 4m) = $304 million in exchange for $300 million**. The **stand-alone price would give a total of $300m for the rooms and $4m for the vouchers.**

To **allocate the transaction price**, step (iv) of IFRS 15's five-step process for revenue recognition, the proceeds need to be split proportionally **pro-rata the stand-alone prices**, that is the discount of $4 million needs to be allocated between the room sales and the vouchers, as follows:

Room sales: $\dfrac{300}{304} \times \$300m = \$296.1m$

Vouchers (balance) = $3.9m

The $3.9 million attributable to the vouchers is only recognised when the performance obligations are fulfilled, that is when the vouchers are redeemed.

Government grant

The applicable standard relating to this transaction is IAS 20 *Accounting for government grants and disclosure of government assistance.* The principle behind the standard is that of accruals or matching: the **grant received must be matched with the related costs**.

Government grants are assistance by government in the form of transfers of resources to an entity in return for past or future compliance with certain conditions relating to the operating activities of the entity. There are two main types of grants:

(i)   **Grants related to assets**: grants whose primary condition is that an entity qualifying for them should purchase, construct or otherwise acquire long-term assets. Subsidiary conditions may also be attached restricting the type or location of the assets or the periods during which they are to be acquired or held. In this case the condition relates to the cost of building the hotels, which must be $500m or more.

(ii)   **Grants related to income**: These are government grants other than grants related to assets.

It is not always easy to match costs and revenues if the terms of the grant are not explicit about the expense to which the grant is meant to contribute. In the case of Norman, the intention of the grant is to create employment in the area, and the building of hotels is for that purpose. However, on balance, the grant can be seen as **capital based,** because the amount is not tied into payroll expenditure or numbers of jobs created, and the repayment clause is related to the cost of the asset (building of hotels). Accordingly, IAS 20 allows two possible approaches:

(i)   Match the grant against the depreciation of the hotels using a deferred income approach.
(ii)   Deduct the grant from the carrying value of the asset.

70 Preparation question: Reconstruction scheme

Text reference. This topic is covered in Chapter 20 of the Study Text.

Top tips. In part (b), the changes to be considered are in the *market* value (or income stream) rather than the *nominal* value of each investor class. You only have sufficient information to look at future income (which will anyway have a considerable influence on market value) so you should look at that. It is also essential to recognise that the ordinary shareholders stand to lose control of the company under the current proposals.

(a)   STATEMENT OF FINANCIAL POSITION OF CONTEMPLATION GROUP
        AS AT 1 JULY 20X2 AFTER RECONSTRUCTION

	$'000
Non-current assets	3,600
Current assets	4,775
	8,375
Ordinary 25c shares (W3)	1,875
8% preference shares of $1 each, fully paid ($3.3m – $0.8m dividend in arrears)	2,500
Reserves (W1)	–
14% 20Y5 loan notes	3,000
Current liabilities	1,000
	8,375

Workings

1   *Reserves*

	$'000
Reserves at 30 June 20X2	(9,425)
Cancellation of previous ordinary shares	10,000
Net effect of issue of ordinary shares to preference shareholders in lieu of accrued arrears of dividend (W2)	300
Issue of new ordinary shares to holders of previous ordinary shares	(875)
	Nil

2   *Net effect of elimination of accrued preference dividend arrears*

	$'000
Cancellation of dividend arrears (8% × 4 × $2.5m)	800
Issue of new shares	500
Net effect: loss in nominal value of holding	300

3   *Ordinary shares*

	No	$'000
Issued to loan note holders	2,000,000	500
Issued to preference shareholders	2,000,000	500
Issued to existing ordinary shareholders	3,500,000	875
	7,500,000	1,875

Note. The purpose of the reconstruction is to eliminate the negative reserves and allow the company to start again. The table below shows the effect of each of the four adjustments ((a) to (d) in the question) in achieving this.

Ref	Item	Debit $'000	Credit $'000
(a)	Ordinary share capital cancelled	10,000	
(b)	11% loan notes retired	3,500	
	14% loan notes issued		3,000
	2,000,000 25c shares issued		500

(c)	Cancellation of dividend arrears (8% × 4 × $2.5m)	800	
	Issue of new shares		500
(d)	Issue of shares to existing shareholders 3.5m × 25c		875
	Elimination of negative reserves balance		9,425
		14,300	14,300

(b) (i) **Loan note holders**

	$'000
Cancellation of previous loan notes	3,500
Issue of new loan notes	3,000
Issue of new shares	500
Net effect on nominal value of holding	Nil

Loan note interest (before tax is paid by the recipient) would be $385,000 pa ($3.5m × 11%) if no reconstruction was effected and $420,000 ($3m × 14%) if the scheme is agreed. In addition, the loan note holders would be entitled to a share of earnings from their ordinary shares. (Maximum $273,867: see below.)

Loan note holders as fixed chargeholders would be repaid in full in the event of a liquidation and must therefore balance the risk of the company's failure in the future, when its assets may have declined in value, thus reducing their usefulness as security, against the forecast increase in return. They must also assess the effect of an extra few years' delay in redemption, which increases the risk. If loan note holders have confidence in the new strategy, then they are better off under the reconstruction.

(ii) **Preference shareholders**

	$'000
Cancellation of dividend arrears (8% × 4 × $2.5m)	800
Issue of new shares	500
Net effect: loss in nominal value of holding	300

No preference dividend could be paid if the reconstruction scheme does not go ahead as all profits for the foreseeable future would be applied in reducing retained losses. If the scheme is agreed, the annual dividend could be restored immediately and, as above, there would be an equity interest with a maximum dividend of $273,867 (see below).

Preference shareholders are assured of repayment of their capital at the moment but may not be in the future if losses are made again. If they are prepared to accept the risk that the new strategy may fail, then they are better off under the reconstruction.

(iii) **Existing ordinary shareholders**

	$'000
Cancellation of previous shares	(10,000)
Cancellation of previous negative reserves: 9,425 – 800*	8,625
Issue of new shares	875
Net effect: loss of nominal value of equity	(500)

Note. The $800,000 accrued arrears of preference dividends has been excluded from the figure for negative reserves because they are dealt with in (ii) above and do not affect the ordinary shareholders.

Ordinary shareholders will receive no dividend for many years if the scheme is not accepted. If it is accepted, then for the first few years, earnings will be as follows.

	$
Post-tax profits before interest	1,500,000
Loan note interest (less tax relief) 14% × 65% × $3m	273,000
	1,227,000
Preference dividend	200,000
Earnings	1,027,000

However, of this 1,000/(1,000 + 875) (part (a) (W3)) will be attributable to the new shares issued to loan note holders and preference shareholders (500/1,875 × $1,027,000 = $273,867 each). Therefore, the existing shareholders will receive a maximum dividend of 875/(1,875) × $1,027,000 = $479,267. It is, of course, exceedingly unlikely that the company will distribute its entire post-tax profit, and so the actual dividend would probably be lower.

(c) To: A Grieved
     From: Financial Adviser
     Date: 28 June 20X2
     Subject: *Proposed scheme of reconstruction*

You have commented that you feel the proposed scheme is 'unfair': presumably you mean to the existing ordinary shareholders. This claim can be examined by looking at the outcome for you as an ordinary shareholder in each of the three options open to the directors:

(i)   To liquidate the company;
(ii)   To continue without reconstructing;
(iii) To adopt the proposed reconstruction.

(i)   If the company is liquidated, the net assets would amount to the following.

	$'000
Realisation of assets (gross) ($3.1m + $3.5m)	6,600
Less loan notes	3,500
Less arrears of preference dividends	800
Net assets	2,300

This would be entirely absorbed by the claims of the preference shareholders ($2.5m). Thus there would be nothing left over for distribution to ordinary shareholders.

(ii)   If no reconstruction takes place the profits after tax and interest will amount to approximately $1.25m ($1.5m profit before interest – [65% × 11% × $3.5m) interest) per annum. Thus it will be some seven years before the deficit on the profit and loss account is cleared and a further year to clear the arrears of preference dividends. Thus, the ordinary shareholders cannot expect a dividend for over eight years. The present value of such a dividend stream is minimal.

(iii) The net interest of the original ordinary shareholders in the reconstructed company is: 3,500,000 shares × 25c = $875,000.

       There are no reserves.

       In addition, the original shareholders can expect to receive dividends or a share in retained earnings from the time of the reconstruction.

So, while the original ordinary shareholders have given up more than the preference shareholders and the loan note holders (who have lost nothing) the reconstruction offers more than the possible alternative options.

Thus, from the point of view of income, the proposed scheme seems the best option under discussion.

However, you should also consider the fact that your control over the company has been seriously diluted. Over half the equity after the reconstruction ie 54% (4m shares/7.5m shares (W3) would be owned by the loan note holders and preference shareholders, who would also still own their loan notes and preference shares. The scheme could be amended so that control remains in the hands of the existing shareholders, who are, after all, not cushioned by holding loan notes or preference shares. If preference shareholders were given fewer ordinary shares, the scheme would be more equitable. The loan note holders would be unlikely to agree to any scaling down of their share allocation.

Nevertheless, with this proviso, it seems that the scheme is fair to ordinary shareholders who otherwise have no hope of dividends or repayment of capital in the event of a liquidation.

Please let me have your comments on the attached draft letter to the directors of Swanee as soon as possible. If they can be persuaded to agree to the suggested scaling down of new equity, then I would advise you to accede to the proposal.

(d)   The Directors
       Contemplation Limited
       Anytown   28 June 20X2

       Dear Sirs,

       We are acting for A Grieved, the holder of 10% of the ordinary capital of Contemplation Limited, and refer to the proposals for reconstructing the company.

       We consider that this proposal is unfairly advantageous to the existing shareholders. The loan note holders would increase their return from their investment from $385,000 pa (interest only) to $693,867 ($420,000 interest plus $273,867 share of the projected earnings).

       The preference shareholders' return will also increase dramatically from a notional $200,000 pa (unlikely to be paid in the foreseeable future) to $473,867 pa ($200,000 preference dividend and $273,867 share of earnings).

       This seems excessive in view of the reduced financial and business risk which would result from the reconstruction. We would suggest that an increase in return of 50% to $577,500 would adequately compensate the loan note holders for the additional risk of holding equity rather than loans. Consequently we would suggest that, in addition to the new 14% loan notes an issue of 1,150,193 shares would be more appropriate.

       In view of the power of loan note holders, we accept that they may not accept a revision to the scheme that reduces the total nominal value of their investment in the company. The preference shareholders, however, are in a different category. There seems no justification for issuing to them such a high proportion of the new 25c shares. If they were to be given 730,282 shares (assuming the above scaling down was not accepted), their projected return would still increase by 50% and the existing ordinary shareholders would retain control of the company.

       We look forward to your comments on the above suggestions.

       Yours faithfully,

       F Adviser & Co

71 Plans

> **Text reference.** This topic is covered in Chapter 20 of the Study Text.
>
> **Top tip.** The Examiner has mentioned internal reconstructions as an area he may test.

Key considerations and accounting impacts

There are a number of reasons why a group may re-organise, for example:

- Companies may be transferred to another business during a **divisionalisation process**
- To **create efficiencies** of group structure for **tax purposes**

The impact of each of the proposed structures is discussed below.

Plan 1: share for share exchange

If the purchase consideration is in the form of shares, then a share premium account will need to be set up in the books of Y. This share premium account must comprise the minimum premium value, which is the excess of the book value of the investment over the nominal value of the shares issued: $70m − $50m = $20m.

The impact on the individual company accounts and on the group accounts is as follows:

	Note	X $m	Y $m	Z $m	Group $m
Property, plant and equipment		600	200	45	845
Goodwill					10
Cost of investment in Y	1	130			
Cost of investment in Z	2		70		
Net current assets		160	100	20	280
		890	370	65	1,135

	Note	X $m	Y $m	Z $m	Group $m
Share capital	3	120	110	40	120
Share premium	4		20		
Retained earnings	5	770	240	25	1,015
		890	370	65	1,135

Notes

1 *Cost of investment in Y*

This is increased by the total value of the shares issued: $50m + $20m = $70m.

2 *Cost of investment in Z*

Transferred to Y. The book value of the investment is preserved.

3 *Share capital*

Y's share capital is increased by the nominal value of the shares issued, $50m.

4 *Share premium*

This is as discussed above.

5 *Retained earnings*

Goodwill arising on the purchase of Z is $10m ($70m – ($40m + $20m)). The group retained earnings are calculated as follows.

	X $m	Y $m	Z $m
Per question	770	240	25
Retained earnings at acquisition		–	(20)
	770	240	5
Share of post-acquisition retained earnings of Y (240 × 100%)	240		
Share of post-acquisition retained earnings of Z (5 × 100%)	5		
	1,015		

Plan 2: cash purchase

The group accounts are not affected by the change as the reorganisation is internal. It has no impact on the group as a single entity.

If the purchase consideration is in the form of cash, a gain or loss on the sale of Z will arise in the books of X. This does not count as a distribution as the cash price of $75m is not in excess of the fair value of the net assets of Z, $80m. The effect on the accounts would be as follows:

	Note	X $m	Y $m	Z $m	Group $m
Property, plant and equipment		600	200	45	845
Goodwill					10
Cost of investment in Y		60			
Cost of investment in Z	1		75		
Net current assets	2	235	25	20	280
		895	300	65	1,135
Share capital		120	60	40	120
Retained earnings	3	775	240	25	1,015
		895	300	65	1,135

Notes

1   *Cost of investment in Z*

    This is the cash consideration of $75m.

2   *Net current assets*

    X's cash increases by $75m and Y's cash decreases by $75m.

3   *Retained earnings*

    X's retained earnings have been increased by $5m, being the profit on the sale of the investment in Z. This is eliminated on consolidation as it is an intragroup transaction. The consolidated retained earnings are calculated in exactly the same way as in the share for share exchange.

Summary and conclusion

There are advantages and disadvantages to each of the two plans. Before we could make a recommendation we would need more information about *why* the group wishes to restructure.

Neither plan changes the group financial statements. From an internal point of view it results in a closer relationship between Y and Z. This may be advantageous if Y and Z are close geographically or in terms of similarity of business activities. Alternatively, it might be advantageous for tax reasons.

72 Decany

Text reference. Group reorganisations are covered in Chapter 14. IAS 27 is covered in Chapter 12. IAS 37 is covered in Chapter 9.

Top tips. This question tested group reorganisations for the first time under the revised syllabus. In part (a)(i) you had to process the effects of the group reorganisation in the three affected companies of the group, which was straightforward. This part of the question did not require detailed knowledge of IFRS but the ability to apply accounting techniques. The preparation of the group financial statements was not required, and you should not have wasted time trying to do this. Part (a)(ii) required a specialist knowledge of IAS 27, now called *Separate financial statements*. Note that the examiner has said this could come up again. Part (b) is a likely common add-on to this type of question.

Easy marks. Don't be put off by the fact that this is a re-construction scheme. There are some fairly straightforward accounts preparation aspects.

Examiner's comment. Candidates performed quite well on the numerical part of the question but often seemed to find it difficult to apply the requirements and often made basic mistakes due to not reading the question thoroughly. For example, the holding company sold an investment in a subsidiary to another subsidiary. Many candidates left the investment sold in the financial statements of the holding company. Part (a)(ii) was poorly answered. The distinction between pre- and post-acquisition profits is no longer required and the payment of such dividends requires the entity to consider whether there is an indicator of impairment. This is a point fundamental to the preparation of group accounting and will be examined again. Answers to Part (b) were disappointing because many candidates did not realise that the reconstruction only masked the problem facing the group. It did not solve or alter the business risk currently being faced by the group.

			Marks
(a)	(i)	Decany	5
		Ceed	5
		Rant	3
			13
	(ii)	IAS 27	5
(b)		Discussion – subjective	5
		Professional marks	2
			25

(a)   (i)   **Individual entity statements of financial position after the restructuring plan**

	Note	Decany $m	Ceed $m	Rant $m
Non-current assets				
Property, plant and equipment at depreciated cost/valuation		600	170 + 15 = 185.0	45 – 10 = 35
Cost of investment in Ceed		130		11
Cost of investment in Rant	1		98.0	
Loan receivable	2	98		
Current assets	2	155 + 25 = 180	130 – 98 = 32.0	20 + 98 = 118
		1,008	315.0	164
Equity and reserves				
Share capital		140	70 + 5 = 75.0	35
Share premium	3		6.0	
Retained earnings	5	776	185.5	10
		916	266.5	45
Non-current liabilities				
Long-term loan	6	5	4.0	106
Provisions	7	2	9.5	
Current liabilities				
Dividend payable			25.0	
Trade payables		85	10.0	13
		1,008	315.0	164

Notes

1   *Sale of shares in Rant*

In Creed's books:

DEBIT	Investment in Rant	$98m
CREDIT	Cash	$98

This is the cash consideration of $98m.

Decany has made a profit on the sale of rant of $98m – $95m = $3m, which is added to Decany's retained earnings. In Decany's books:

DEBIT	Cash	$98m	
CREDIT	Investment in Rant		$95m
CREDIT	Profit or loss (and retained earnings)		$3m

2   *Loan receivable*

Decany now has a loan receivable of $98m and Ceed's cash decreases by $98m. In Decany's books:

DEBIT	Loan receivable	$98m
CREDIT	Cash (current assets)	$98m

In Rant's books:

DEBIT	Cash (current assets)	$98m
CREDIT	Loan payable	$98m

3   *Sale of land by Rant to Creed/calculation of share premium*

The value of the shares issued to Decany is the land less the mortgage, ie $11m. The difference between this and the nominal value is the share premium.

In Ceed's books:

DEBIT	Land	$15m
CREDIT	Mortgage liability (long-term loan)	$4m
CREDIT	Share capital	$6m
CREDIT	Share premium (balancing figure)	$5m

In Rant's books:

DEBIT	Investment in Ceed	$11m
DEBIT	Mortgage liability (long-term loan)	$4m
CREDIT	Land	$10m
CREDIT	Profit or loss (and retained earnings)	$5m

4   *Dividend payable by Ceed to Decany*

In Creed's books:

DEBIT	Retained earnings	$25m
CREDIT	Dividend payable	$25m

In Creed's books:

DEBIT	Dividend receivable (current assets)	$25m
CREDIT	Retained earnings	$25m

5   *Retained earnings*

	Decany $m	Ceed $m	Rant $m
Per question	750	220.0	5
Dividend from Ceed to Decany	25	(25.0)	–
Profit on sale of Rant	3	–	–
Profit on sale or land			5
Provision for restructuring (note 6)	(2)	(9.5)	–
	776	185.5	10

6   *Long-term loan (Rant)*

	$m
Per question	12
Loan payable (note 2)	98
Mortgage liability (note 3)	(4)
	106

7   *Redundancy costs and provision for restructuring*

The fact that there is a detailed plan for restructuring with employees identified for redundancy creates a constructive obligation under IAS 37 *Provisions, contingent liabilities and contingent assets*, and accordingly a provision should be made for redundancy costs and restructuring. Creed will incur the redundancy costs, which should be recognised in its financial statements at the present value of the future cash flows:

	$m
4m × 1/1.03	3.9
6m × 1/1.03^2	5.6
	9.5

The provision of $9.5m will be shown in Creed's financial statements, and the overall restructuring provision of $2m in the financial statements of Decany.

(ii) **IAS 27 rules on reorganisation and payment of dividends between group companies**

IAS 27 *Separate financial statements* was issued in 2011 and carries forward a change made to IAS 27 *Consolidated and separate financial statements* in 2008 in respect of group reorganisations. In limited reorganisations IAS 27 effectively allows the **cost of an investment in a subsidiary to be based on the previous carrying amount of the subsidiary rather than on its fair value**. This is only allowed when a new parent (Ceed) is inserted above an existing parent of a group or entity (Rant), and where the following **criteria** are satisfied.

(1) The new parent (Ceed) obtains control of the original parent or entity (Rant) by issuing equity instruments in exchange for existing equity instruments of the original parent or entity.

(2) The assets and liabilities of the new group and the original group are the same immediately before and after the reorganisation.

(3) The owners of the original parent or entity (Decany) before the reorganisation have the same absolute and relative interests in the net assets of the original group and the new group immediately before and after the reorganisation.

The reorganisation of the Decany group appears to meet all the above criteria. (In respect of (3), Rant has not acquired a further interest in Ceed as a result of the transfer of land because the shares in Ceed issued to Rant are non-voting.)

A further amendment carried forward in the revised IAS 27 was the removal of the 'cost method'. This required an entity to recognise distributions as income only if they came from post-acquisition retained earnings. Distributions received in excess of such retained earnings were regarded as a recovery of investment and were recognised as a reduction in the cost of the investment. Now, however, IAS 27 requires all dividends **in profit or loss in its separate financial statements when its right to receive the dividend is established**. The distinction between pre- and post-acquisition profits, which had been problematic, is no longer required.

If such dividends are paid, the entity is required to consider whether there is has been an **impairment**. Applying IAS 36 *Impairment of assets,* impairment is indicated in the following cases.

(1) The dividend exceeds the total comprehensive income of the subsidiary, jointly controlled entity or associate in the period the dividend is declared.

(2) The carrying amount of the investment in the separate financial statements exceeds the carrying amounts in the consolidated financial statements of the investee's net assets, including associated goodwill.

Neither of these apply in the case of Creed, and so there is no indication that Creed is impaired.

(b) **Impact of reconstruction plan**

The reconstruction plan has no impact on the group financial statements as all the intra-group transactions will be eliminated on consolidation. From an internal point of view it results in **a closer relationship between Creed and Rant**. This may be advantageous if Creed and Rant are close geographically or in terms of similarity of business activities. Alternatively, it might be advantageous for tax reasons.

Regarding the restructuring plan, IAS 37 *Provisions, contingent liabilities and contingent assets* **contains specific requirements** relating to **restructuring provisions**. The general recognition criteria apply and IAS 37 also states that **a provision should be recognised** if an entity has a **constructive obligation** to carry out a restructuring. A constructive obligation exists where **management has a detailed formal plan** for the restructuring, identifying **as a minimum:**

(i)   The business or part of the business being restructured

(ii)   The principal locations affected by the restructuring

(iii) The location, function and approximate number of employees who will be compensated for the termination of their employment

(iv)   The date of implementation of the plan

(v)   The expenditure that will be undertaken.

It appears that these criteria have been met. However, the amount of $2m in Decany's financial statements seems rather large, considering that the redundancy is provided separately in the accounts of Ceed, and the restructuring does not involve any relocation.

The plan shows the companies in a **more favourable light** in that Rant's **short-term cash flow problem is eliminated**. Rant now has cash available. However, it is showing a much increased long-term loan. In the financial statements of Rant, the investment in Ceed must be accounted as a financial asset under IFRS 9 *Financial instruments.*

It is possible that the purchase consideration for rant of $98m could be seen as **a transaction at an overvalue**. It creates a profit of $3m, which could be seen as artificial. The question also arises as to whether this $3m should be recognised, and of whether it should be viewed as a distribution. Should problems arise in connection with local legislation, a share exchange might be a less problematic plan than a cash purchase.

The question may also arise as to whether Ceed has effectively **made a distribution**. This could happen where the purchase consideration was well in excess of the fair value of Rant. An alternative to a cash purchase would be a share exchange. In this case, local legislation would need to be reviewed in order to determine the requirements for the setting up of any share premium account.

73 Lucky Dairy

Text reference. IAS 41 is covered in Chapter 20 of your Study Text. IAS 37 is covered in Chapter 9 and IFRS 5 in Chapter 15.

Top tips. In this question you were required to deal with a scenario that had as its main theme IAS 41 *Agriculture.* You should not, however, make the mistake of thinking that this question is just about IAS 41; it required a knowledge of several other standards including IAS 37 and IFRS 5.

Examiner's comment. Some candidates had not studied the area and guessed at the answer which generally led to poor marks. However many candidates produced excellent answers although some seemed to think that the question was solely on IAS 41.

The dairy herd

The dairy herd is a **biological asset** as defined by IAS 41 *Agriculture.* IAS 41 states that a biological asset should be **measured at fair value less estimated point of sale costs** unless its fair value cannot be measured reliably. **Gains and losses** arising from a change in fair value should be **included in profit or loss** for the period.

In this case, fair value is based on market price and point of sale costs are the costs of transporting the cattle to the market. Cattle stock for the Ham and Shire regions is valued on this basis.

IAS 41 encourages companies to **analyse the change in fair value** between the movement due to **physical changes** and the movement due to **price changes** (see the table below). It also encourages companies to provide a quantified description of each group of biological assets. Therefore the value of the cows and the value of the heifers should be **disclosed separately** in the balance sheet.

Valuing the dairy herd for the Dale Region is less straightforward as its **fair value cannot be measured reliably at the date of purchase**. In this situation IAS 41 requires the herd to be valued at **cost less any impairment losses**. The standard also requires companies to provide an **explanation of why** fair value cannot be measured reliably and the **range of estimates** within which fair value is likely to fall.

Valuation of cattle stock, excluding Dale region

	Cows $'000	Heifers $'000	Total $'000
Fair value of herd at 1 June 20X1 (50,000 × 50)	2,500		2,500
Purchase 1 December 20X1 (25,000 × 40)		1,000	1,000
Increase in fair value less estimated point of sale costs due to price change:			
(50,000 × (55 – 50)/25,000 × (42 – 40))	250	50	300
Increase in fair value less estimated point of sale costs due to physical change:			
(50,000 × (60 – 55)/25,000 × (46 – 42))	250	100	350
Fair value less estimated point of sale costs at			
31 May 20X2 (50,000 × 60/25,000 × 46)	3,000	1,150	4,150

Valuation of cattle stock in Dale Region

	$'000
Cost at 1 June 20X1	
Cows (20,000 × 50)	1,000
Heifers (10,000 × 40)	400
	1,400
Less impairment loss	(200)
	1,200

Note. The herd is impaired because its recoverable amount is $1.2 million. This is the higher of fair value less costs to sell of $1 million (the amount that the Lucky Dairy has been offered) and value in use of $1.2 million (discounted value of the milk to be produced).

	$'000
Estimated fair value at 31 May 20X2 (for disclosure only):	
Cows (20,000 × 60)	1,200
Heifers (10,000 × 55)	550
	1,750

Milk

The milk is **agricultural produce** as defined by IAS 41 and should normally be measured at **fair value less estimated point of sale costs at the time of milking**. In this case the company is holding ten times the amount of inventory that it would normally hold and it is probable that much of this milk is unfit for consumption. The company should estimate the amount of milk that will not be sold and **write down** the inventory accordingly. The write down should be disclosed separately in the income statement as required by IAS 1 *Presentation of financial statements*.

Government grant

Under IAS 41, the government grant should be recognised as income **when it becomes receivable**. As it was only on 6 June 20X2 that the company received official confirmation of the amount to be paid, the income **should not be recognised in the current year**. The amount may be sufficiently material to justify disclosure as a non-adjusting event after the balance sheet date.

Legal proceedings and additional compensation

The lawyers have indicated that the company will probably be found liable for passing on the disease to consumers. There is a **present obligation as the result of a past obligating event** and therefore a **provision for $2 million should be recognised**, as required by IAS 37 *Provisions, contingent liabilities and contingent assets*.

IAS 37 states that **reimbursement** should only be recognised when it is **virtually certain** to be received. It is **only possible** that the company will receive compensation for the legal costs and therefore this **cannot be recognised**. However, the compensation should be **disclosed** as a contingent asset in the financial statements.

Planned sale of Dale farms

The Board of Directors has **approved the planned closure**, but there has **not yet been a public announcement**. Despite the fact that a local newspaper has published an article on the possible sale, the company **has not created a valid expectation** that the sale will take place and in fact **it is not certain** that the sale will occur. Therefore there is **no 'constructive obligation'** and under IAS 37 **no provision should be made** for redundancy or any other costs connected with the planned sale.

Under IFRS 5 *Non-current assets held for sale and discontinued operations* Dale must be treated as a **continuing operation** for the year ended 31 May 20X2 as the sale has not taken place. As management are **not yet fully committed** to the sale **neither the operation as a whole nor any of the separate assets of Dale can be classified as 'held for sale'.**

74 IFRSs and SMEs

Text reference. SMEs are covered in Chapter 21 of your Study Text.

Top tips. This question required candidates to discuss the need to develop a set of IFRSs especially for small to medium-sized enterprises (SMEs). Do not be tempted to waffle or repeat yourself. Since this question was set, the IASB has published an IFRS for SMEs.

Easy marks. This is a knowledge-based question, so all marks are easy if you know it.

Examiner's comment. This question was generally well answered and the topic will feature in future exams.

Marking scheme

		Marks
(a)	Subjective	7
(b)	Purpose	3
	Definition of entity	4
	How to modify	6
	Items not dealt with	3
	Full IFRS	3
Available		26
Maximum		25

(a) Originally, International Accounting Standards (IASs) issued by the International Accounting Standards Committee (IASC) were **designed to be suitable for all types of entity**, including small and medium entities (SMEs) and entities in developing countries. Large listed entities based their financial statements on national GAAP which normally **automatically complied** with those IASs due to choices permitted in the past. In recent years, IASs and IFRSs have become **increasingly complex and prescriptive**. They are now designed **primarily** to meet the information needs of **institutional investors in large listed entities** and their advisers. In many countries, IFRSs are **used mainly by listed companies**.

There is a case for continued use of full IFRSs by SMEs. It can be argued that the **main objectives** of general purpose financial statements **are the same for all types of company**, of whatever size. Compliance with full IFRSs ensures that the financial statements of SMEs **present their financial performance fairly** and gives them greater **credibility**. It also ensures their **comparability** with those of other entities.

There were also many arguments for developing a separate set of standards for SMEs, and these have been taken into account (see below) Full IFRSs have become very **detailed and onerous** to follow. The **cost** of complying may **exceed the benefits** to the entity and the users of its financial statements. At present, an entity cannot describe their financial statements as IFRS financial statements unless they have complied with every single requirement.

SME financial statements are normally **used by a relatively small number of people**. Often, the **investors** are also **involved in day to day management**. The **main external users** of SME financial statements tend to be **lenders and the tax authorities**, rather than institutional investors and their advisers. These users have **different information needs** from those of investors. For these users, the accounting treatments and the detailed disclosures required may sometimes **obscure the picture** given by the financial statements. In some cases, **different, or more detailed information may be needed**. For example, related party transactions are often very significant in the context of SME activities and expanded disclosure may be appropriate.

The *IFRS for Small and Medium-Sized Entities* (IFRS for SMEs) was published in July 2009, and therefore falls to be examinable in 2010. It is only 230 pages, and has **simplifications** that reflect the needs of users of SMEs' financial statements and cost-benefit considerations. It is designed to facilitate financial reporting by small and medium-sized entities in a number of ways:

(i)   It provides significantly **less guidance** than full IFRS.

(ii)   Many of the **principles** for recognising and measuring assets, liabilities, income and expenses in full IFRSs are **simplified**.

(iii)   Where full IFRSs allow accounting policy choices, the IFRS for SMEs **allows only the easier** option.

(iv)   **Topics not relevant** to SMEs are **omitted**.

(v)   Significantly **fewer disclosures** are required.

(vi)   The standard has been written in **clear language** that can easily be translated.

(b)   **Issues in developing IFRSs for SMEs**

(i)   **The purpose of the standards and type of entity to which they should apply**

The main objective of accounting standards for SMEs is that they should provide the users of SME financial statements with **relevant, reliable and understandable information**. The standards should be **suitable for SMEs globally** and should **reduce the financial reporting burden** on SMEs. It is generally accepted that SME standards should be built on the **same conceptual framework** as full IFRSs.

It could also be argued that SME standards should **allow for easy transition** to full IFRS as some SMEs will become listed entities or need to change for other reasons. This would mean that SME standards **could not be separately developed from first principles** (as many would prefer) but instead would be a **modified version of full IFRS**. Some argue that ease of transition is not important as relatively few SMEs will need to change to IFRS in practice.

The **definition** of an SME could be based on **size** or on **public accountability** or on a combination of the two. There are several disadvantages of basing the definition on size limits alone. Size limits are **arbitrary** and **different limits are likely to be appropriate in different countries**. Most people believe that SMEs are **not simply smaller versions of listed entities**, but differ from them in more fundamental ways.

The most important way in which SMEs differ from other entities is that they are **not usually publicly accountable**. Using this as the basis of a definition raises other issues: which types of company are publicly accountable? Obviously the **definition would include** companies which have **issued shares** or other instruments **to the public**. It has been suggested that this category should also include companies **holding assets in a fiduciary capacity** (such as banks or providers of pensions), companies that provide **essential public services** (utility companies) and any entity with **economic significance in its country** (which in turn would have to be defined). This would mean that SME standards could potentially be used by a very large number of entities covering a very large range in terms of size.

There is a case for allowing **national standard setters** to **impose size limits** or otherwise **restrict** the types of entities that could use SME standards. There is also a case for allowing national standard setters to **define 'publicly accountable'** in a way that is appropriate for their particular jurisdiction.

The *IFRS for SMEs* published in July 2009 does not use size or quantitative thresholds, but qualification is determined by public accountability. It is up to legislative and regulatory authorities and standard-setters in individual jurisdictions to decide who may or must use the IFRS for SMEs.

(ii) **How existing standards could be modified to meet the needs of SMEs**

The starting point for modifying existing standards should be the most likely **users** of SME financial statements and their **information needs**. SME financial statements are mainly used by **lenders** and **potential lenders, the tax authorities** and **suppliers**. In addition, the **owners and management** (who are often the same people) may be dependent on the information in the financial statements. SME financial statements must **meet the needs** of their users, but the **costs** of providing the information **should not outweigh the benefits**.

There is considerable scope for **simplifying disclosure and presentation requirements**. Many of the existing requirements, for example those related to financial instruments, discontinued operations and earnings per share, are **not really relevant** to the users of SME financial statements. In any case, lenders and potential lenders are normally able to ask for additional information (including forecasts) if they need it.

The SME standards are a **simplified version of existing standards**, using only those principles that are likely to be relevant to SMEs. The IASB has proposed that the **recognition and measurement principles** in full IFRSs should **remain unchanged** unless there is a good argument for modifying them. Clearly the SME standards will have to be sufficiently rigorous to produce information that is relevant and reliable. However, many believe that there is a **case for simplifying** at least some of the more **complicated measurement requirements** and that it will be difficult to reduce the financial reporting burden placed on SMEs otherwise.

(iii) **How items not dealt with by SME standards should be treated**

Because SME standards **do not cover all possible transactions** and events, there will be occasions where an SME has to **account for an item that the standards do not deal with**. There are several alternatives.

(a) The entity is **required to apply the relevant full IFRS**, while still following SME standards otherwise.

(b) Management can **use its judgement** to develop an accounting policy based on the relevant full IFRS, or the *Framework*, or other IFRSs for SMEs and the other sources of potential guidance cited in IAS 8.

(c) The entity could continue to follow its **existing practice**.

In theory, the **first alternative is the most appropriate** as this is the most likely to result in relevant, reliable and comparable information. The argument against it is that SMEs may then effectively have to comply with **two sets of standards**.

Another issue is whether an SME should be able to **opt to comply** with a specific full IFRS or IFRSs while still following SME standards otherwise. There is an argument that SMEs should be able to, for example, make the additional disclosures required by a full IFRS if there is a good reason to do so. The argument against optional reversion to full IFRSs is that it would lead to **lack of comparability**. There would also need to be safeguards against entities attempting to 'pick and mix' accounting standards.

75 Whitebirk

Marking scheme

			Marks
(a)		Subjective assessment including professional	11
(b)	(i)	Business combination	4
	(ii)	Research and development expenditure	3
	(iii)	Investment property	2
	(iv)	Intangible	2
			22

(a)   **Modifications to reduce the burden of reporting for SMEs**

The *IFRS for SMEs* is only 230 pages, and has **simplifications** that reflect the needs of users of SMEs' financial statements and cost-benefit considerations. It is designed to facilitate financial reporting by small and medium-sized entities in a number of ways:

   (i)   It provides significantly **less guidance** than full IFRS. A great deal of the guidance in full IFRS would not be relevant to the needs of smaller entities.

   (ii)   Many of the **principles** for recognising and measuring assets, liabilities, income and expenses in full IFRSs are **simplified**. For example, goodwill and intangibles are always amortised over their estimated useful life (or ten years if it cannot be estimated). Research and development costs must be expensed. With defined benefit pension plans, all actuarial gains and losses are to be recognised immediately in other comprehensive income. All past service costs are to be recognised immediately in profit or loss. To measure the defined benefit obligation, the projected unit credit method must be used.

   (iii) Where full IFRSs allow accounting policy choices, the *IFRS for SMEs* **allows only the easier option**. Examples of alternatives not allowed in the *IFRS for SMEs* include: revaluation model for intangible assets and property, plant and equipment, proportionate consolidation for investments in jointly-controlled entities and choice between cost and fair value models for investment property (measurement depends on the circumstances).

   (iv)   **Topics not relevant** to SMEs are **omitted**: earnings per share, interim financial reporting, segment reporting, insurance and assets held for sale.

   (v)   Significantly **fewer disclosures** are required.

   (vi)   The standard has been written in **clear language** that can easily be translated.

   The above represents a considerable reduction in reporting requirements – perhaps as much as 90% – compared with listed entities. Entities will naturally wish to use the *IFRS for SMEs* if they can, but **its use is restricted**.

The restrictions are **not related to size**. There are several disadvantages of basing the definition on size limits alone. Size limits are **arbitrary** and **different limits are likely to be appropriate in different** countries. Most people believe that SMEs are **not simply smaller versions of listed entities**, but differ from them in more fundamental ways.

The most important way in which SMEs differ from other entities is that they are **not usually publicly accountable**. Accordingly, there are **no quantitative thresholds** for qualification as a SME; instead, the scope of the IFRS is determined by a **test of public accountability**. The IFRS is suitable for all entities except those whose securities are publicly traded and financial institutions such as banks and insurance companies.

Another way in which the use of the *IFRS for SMEs* is restricted is that **users cannot cherry pick** from this IFRS and full IFRS. If an entity adopts the *IFRS for SMEs,* it **must adopt it in its entirety**.

(b)   (i)   **Business combination**

IFRS 3 *Business combinations* allows an entity to adopt the full or partial goodwill method in its consolidated financial statements. The *IFRS for SMEs* **only allows the partial goodwill method**. This avoids the need for SMEs to determine the fair value of the non-controlling interests not purchased when undertaking a business combination.

In addition, IFRS 3 *Business combinations* requires goodwill to be tested annually for impairment. The *IFRS for SMEs* **requires goodwill to be amortised instead**. This is a much simpler approach and the *IFRS for SMEs* specifies that if an entity is unable to make a reliable estimate of the useful life, it is presumed to be ten years, simplifying things even further.

Goodwill on Whitebirk's acquisition of Close will be calculated as:

	$'000
Consideration transferred	5,700
Non-controlling interest: 10% × $6m	600
	6,300
Less fair value of identifiable net assets acquired	(6,000)
Goodwill	300

This goodwill of $0.3m will be amortised over ten years, that is $30,000 per annum.

(ii)   **Research and development expenditure**

The *IFRS for SMEs* requires all internally generated research and development expenditure to be **expensed through profit or loss.** This is simpler than full IFRS – IAS 38 *Intangible Assets* requires internally generated assets to be capitalised if certain criteria (proving future economic benefits) are met, and it is often difficult to determine whether or not they have been met.

Whitebirk's total expenditure on research ($0.5m) and development ($1m) must be written off to profit or loss for the year, giving a charge of $1.5m.

(iii)   **Investment property**

Investment properties must be held at fair value through profit or loss under the *IFRS for SMEs* where their fair value can be measured without undue cost or effort, which appears to be the case here, given that an estate agent valuation is available. Consequently a gain of $0.2m ($1.9m – $1.7m) will be reported in Whitebirk's profit or loss for the year.

(iv)   **Intangible asset**

IAS 36 *Impairment of assets* requires annual impairment tests for indefinite life intangibles, intangibles not yet available for use and goodwill. This is a complex, time-consuming and expensive test.

The *IFRS for SMEs* only requires impairment tests where there are indicators of impairment. In the case of Whitebirk's intangible, there are no indicators of impairment, and so an impairment test is not required.

Mock exams

ACCA

Paper P2

Corporate Reporting (International)

Mock Examination 1

Question Paper	
Time allowed	
Reading and planning	**15 minutes**
Writing	**3 hours**
This paper is divided into two sections	
Section A	This ONE question is compulsory and MUST be attempted
Section B	TWO questions ONLY to be answered

DO NOT OPEN THIS PAPER UNTIL YOU ARE READY TO START UNDER EXAMINATION CONDITIONS

SECTION A – This ONE question is compulsory and MUST be attempted

Question 1

The following draft statements of financial position relate to Ribby, Hall, and Zian, all public limited companies, as at 31 May 20X8.

	Ribby $m	Hall $m	Zian Dinars m
Assets			
Non-current assets:			
Property, plant and equipment	250	120	360
Investment in Hall	98	–	–
Investment in Zian	30	–	–
Financial assets	10	5	148
Current assets	22	17	120
Total assets	410	142	628
Equity			
Ordinary shares	60	40	209
Other components of equity	30	10	–
Retained earnings	120	80	307
Total equity	210	130	516
Non-current liabilities	90	5	40
Current liabilities	110	7	72
Total equity and liabilities	410	142	628

The following information needs to be taken account of in the preparation of the group financial statements of Ribby.

(a) Ribby acquired 70% of the ordinary shares of Hall on 1 June 20X6 when Hall's other components of equity were $10 million and retained earnings were $60 million. The fair value of the net assets of Hall was $120 million at the date of acquisition. Ribby acquired 60% of the ordinary shares of Zian for 330 million dinars on 1 June 20X6 when Zian's retained earnings were 220 million dinars. The fair value of the net assets of Zian on 1 June 20X6 was 495 million dinars. The excess of the fair value over the net assets of Hall and Zian is due to an increase in the value of non-depreciable land. There have been no issues of ordinary shares since acquisition and goodwill on acquisition is not impaired for either Hall or Zian.

(b) Zian is located in a foreign country and imports its raw materials at a price which is normally denominated in dollars. The product is sold locally at selling prices denominated in dinars, and determined by local competition. All selling and operating expenses are incurred locally and paid in dinars. Distribution of profits is determined by the parent company, Ribby. Zian has financed part of its operations through a $4 million loan from Hall which was raised on 1 June 20X7. This is included in the financial assets of Hall and the non-current liabilities of Zian. Zian's management have a considerable degree of authority and autonomy in carrying out the operations of Zian and other than the loan from Hall, are not dependent upon group companies for finance.

(c) Ribby has a building which it purchased on 1 June 20X7 for 40 million dinars and which is located overseas. The building is carried at cost and has been depreciated on the straight-line basis over its useful life of 20 years. At 31 May 20X8, as a result of an impairment review, the recoverable amount of the building was estimated to be 36 million dinars.

(d) Ribby has a long-term loan of $10 million which is owed to a third party bank. At 31 May 20X8, Ribby decided that it would repay the loan early on 1 July 20X8 and formally agreed this repayment with the bank prior to the year end. The agreement sets out that there will be an early repayment penalty of $1 million.

(e) The directors of Ribby announced on 1 June 20X7 that a bonus of $6 million would be paid to the employees of Ribby if they achieved a certain target production level by 31 May 20X8. The bonus is to be paid partly in cash and partly in share options. Half of the bonus will be paid in cash on 30 November 20X8 whether or not the employees are still working for Ribby. The other half will be given in share options on the same date, provided that the employee is still in service on 30 November 20X8. The exercise price and number of options will be fixed by management on 30 November 20X8. The target production was met and management expect 10% of employees to leave between 31 May 20X8 and 30 November 20X8. No entry has been made in the financial statements of Ribby.

(f) Ribby operates a defined benefit pension plan that provides a pension of 1·2% of the final salary for each year of service, subject to a minimum of four years service. On 1 June 20X7, Ribby improved the pension entitlement so that employees receive 1.4% of their final salary for each year of service. This improvement applied to all prior years service of the employees. As a result, the present value of the defined benefit obligation on 1 June 20X7 increased by $3.5 million as follows:

	$m
Employees with more than four years' service	3.0
Employees with less than four years service (average service of two years)	0.5
	3.5

Ribby had not accounted for the improvement in the pension plan.

(g) Ribby is considering selling its subsidiary, Hall. Just prior to the year end, Hall sold inventory to Ribby at a price of $6 million. The carrying value of the inventory in the financial records of Hall was $2 million. The cash was received before the year end, and as a result the bank overdraft of Hall was virtually eliminated at 31 May 20X8. After the year end the transaction was reversed, and it was agreed that this type of transaction would be carried out again when the interim financial statements were produced for Hall, if the company had not been sold by that date.

(h) The following exchange rates are relevant to the preparation of the group financial statements:

	Dinars to $
1 June 20X6	11
1 June 20X7	10
31 May 20X8	12
Average for year to 31 May 20X8	10.5

(i) It is the group's policy to value the non-controlling interest at acquisition at fair value. The fair value of the non-controlling interest in Hall on 1 June 20X6 was $42million. The fair value of the non-controlling interest in Zian on 1 June 20X6 was 220 million dinars.

Required

(a) Discuss and apply the principles set out in IAS 21 *The effects of changes in foreign exchange rates* in order to determine the functional currency of Zian. **(8 marks)**

(b) Prepare a consolidated statement of financial position of the Ribby Group at 31 May 20X8 in accordance with International Financial Reporting Standards. **(35 marks)**

(c) Discuss how the manipulation of financial statements by company accountants is inconsistent with their responsibilities as members of the accounting profession, setting out the distinguishing features of a profession and the privileges that society gives to a profession. (Your answer should include reference to the above scenario.) **(7 marks)**

(Total = 50 marks)

SECTION B – TWO questions ONLY to be attempted

Question 2

`12/12`

Coate, a public limited company, is a producer of ecologically friendly electrical power (green electricity).

(a) Coate's revenue comprises mainly the sale of electricity and green certificates. Coate obtains green certificates under a national government scheme. Green certificates represent the environmental value of green electricity. The national government requires suppliers who do not produce green electricity to purchase a certain number of green certificates. Suppliers who do not produce green electricity can buy green certificates either on the market on which they are traded or directly from a producer such as Coate. The national government wishes to give incentives to producers such as Coate by allowing them to gain extra income in this way.

Coate obtains the certificates from the national government on satisfactory completion of an audit by an independent organisation, which confirms the origin of production. Coate then receives a certain number of green certificates from the national government depending on the volume of green electricity generated. The green certificates are allocated to Coate on a quarterly basis by the national government and Coate can trade the green certificates.

Coate is uncertain as to the accounting treatment of the green certificates in its financial statements for the period ended 30 November 20X2 and how to treat the green certificates which were not sold at the end of the reporting period. **(7 marks)**

(b) During the year ended 30 November 20X2, Coate acquired an overseas subsidiary whose financial statements are prepared in a different currency to Coate. The amounts reported in the consolidated statement of cash flows included the effect of changes in foreign exchange rates arising on the retranslation of its overseas operations. Additionally, the group's consolidated statement of cash flows reported as a loss the effect of foreign exchange rate changes on cash and cash equivalents as Coate held some foreign currency of its own denominated in cash. **(5 marks)**

(c) Coate also sold 50% of a previously wholly owned subsidiary, Patten, to a third party, Manis. Manis is in the same industry as Coate. Coate has continued to account for the investment in Patten as a subsidiary in its consolidated financial statements. The main reason for this accounting treatment was the agreement that had been made with Manis, under which Coate would exercise general control over Patten's operating and financial policies. Coate has appointed three out of four directors to the board. The agreement also stated that certain decisions required consensus by the two shareholders.

Under the shareholder agreement, consensus is required with respect to:

(i) Significant changes in the company's activities

(ii) Plans or budgets that deviate from the business plan

(iii) Accounting policies; acquisition of assets above a certain value; employment or dismissal of senior employees; distribution of dividends or establishment of loan facilities

Coate feels that the consensus required above does not constitute a hindrance to the power to control Patten, as it is customary within the industry to require shareholder consensus for decisions of the types listed in the shareholders' agreement. **(6 marks)**

(d) In the notes to Coate's financial statements for the year ended 30 November 20X2, the tax expense included an amount in respect of 'Adjustments to current tax in respect of prior years' and this expense had been treated as a prior year adjustment. These items related to adjustments arising from tax audits by the authorities in relation to previous reporting periods.

The issues that resulted in the tax audit adjustment were not a breach of tax law but related predominantly to transfer pricing issues, for which there was a range of possible outcomes that were negotiated during 20X2 with the taxation authorities. Further at 30 November 20X1, Coate had accounted for all known issues arising from the audits to that date and the tax adjustment could not have been foreseen as at 30 November 20X1, as the audit authorities changed the scope of the audit. No penalties were expected to be applied by the taxation authorities. **(5 marks)**

Required

Discuss how the above events should be accounted for in the individual or, as appropriate, the consolidated financial statements of Coate.

Note. The mark allocation is shown against each of the four events above.

Professional marks will be awarded in Question 2 for the clarity and quality of the presentation and discussion.

(2 marks)

(Total = 25 marks)

Question 3

Blackcutt is a local government organisation whose financial statements are prepared using International Financial Reporting Standards.

(a) Blackcutt wishes to create a credible investment property portfolio with a view to determining if any property may be considered surplus to the functional objectives and requirements of the local government organisation. The following portfolio of property is owned by Blackcutt.

Blackcutt owns several plots of land. Some of the land is owned by Blackcutt for capital appreciation and this may be sold at any time in the future. Other plots of land have no current purpose as Blackcutt has not determined whether it will use the land to provide services such as those provided by national parks or for short-term sale in the ordinary course of operations.

The local government organisation supplements its income by buying and selling property. The housing department regularly sells part of its housing inventory in the ordinary course of its operations as a result of changing demographics. Part of the inventory, which is not held for sale, is to provide housing to low-income employees at below market rental. The rent paid by employees covers the cost of maintenance of the property. **(7 marks)**

(b) Blackcutt has outsourced its waste collection to a private sector provider called Waste and Co and pays an annual amount to Waste and Co for its services. Waste and Co purchases the vehicles and uses them exclusively for Blackcutt's waste collection. The vehicles are painted with the Blackcutt local government organisation name and colours. Blackcutt can use the vehicles and the vehicles are used for waste collection for nearly all of the asset's life. In the event of Waste and Co's business ceasing, Blackcutt can obtain legal title to the vehicles and carry on the waste collection service. **(6 marks)**

(c) Blackcutt owns a warehouse. Chemco has leased the warehouse from Blackcutt and is using it as a storage facility for chemicals. The national government has announced its intention to enact environmental legislation requiring property owners to accept liability for environmental pollution. As a result, Blackcutt has introduced a hazardous chemical policy and has begun to apply the policy to its properties. Blackcutt has had a report that the chemicals have contaminated the land surrounding the warehouse. Blackcutt has no recourse against Chemco or its insurance company for the clean-up costs of the pollution. At 30 November 20X6, it is virtually certain that draft legislation requiring a clean up of land already contaminated will be enacted shortly after the year end. **(4 marks)**

(d) On 1 December 20X0, Blackcutt opened a school at a cost of $5 million. The estimated useful life of the school was 25 years. On 30 November 20X6, the school was closed because numbers using the school declined unexpectedly due to a population shift caused by the closure of a major employer in the area. The school is to be converted for use as a library, and there is no expectation that numbers using the school will increase in the future and thus the building will not be reopened for use as a school. The current replacement cost for a library of equivalent size to the school is $2.1 million. Because of the nature of the non-current asset, value-in-use and net selling price are unrealistic estimates of the value of the school. The change in use would have no effect on the estimated life of the building. **(6 marks)**

Required

Discuss how the above events should be accounted for in the financial statements of Blackcutt.

Note. The mark allocation is shown against each of the four events above.

Professional marks will be awarded in Question 3 for the clarity and quality of the presentation and discussion.

(2 marks)

(Total = 25 marks)

Question 4

12/12

The International Accounting Standards Board has recently completed a joint project with the Financial

Accounting Standards Board (FASB) on fair value measurement by issuing IFRS 13 *Fair value measurement.* IFRS 13 defines fair value, establishes a framework for measuring fair value and requires significant disclosures relating to fair value measurement.

The IASB wanted to enhance the guidance available for assessing fair value in order that users could better gauge the valuation techniques and inputs used to measure fair value. There are no new requirements as to when fair value accounting is required, but the IFRS gives guidance regarding fair value measurements in existing standards. Fair value measurements are categorised into a three-level hierarchy, based on the type of inputs to the valuation techniques used. However, the guidance in IFRS 13 does not apply to transactions dealt with by certain specific standards.

Required

(a) (i) Discuss the main principles of fair value measurement as set out in IFRS 13. **(7 marks)**

(ii) Describe the three-level hierarchy for fair value measurements used in IFRS 13. **(6 marks)**

(b) Jayach, a public limited company, is reviewing the fair valuation of certain assets and liabilities in light of the introduction of IFRS 13.

It carries an asset that is traded in different markets and is uncertain as to which valuation to use. The asset has to be valued at fair value under International Financial Reporting Standards. Jayach currently only buys and sells the asset in the Australasian market. The data relating to the asset are set out below.

Year to 30 November 20X2	Asian market	European market	Australasian market
Volume of market – units	4 million	2 million	1 million
Price	$19	$16	$22
Costs of entering the market	$2	$2	$3
Transaction costs	$1	$2	$2

Additionally, Jayach had acquired an entity on 30 November 20X2 and is required to fair value a decommissioning liability. The entity has to decommission a mine at the end of its useful life, which is in three years' time. Jayach has determined that it will use a valuation technique to measure the fair value of the liability. If Jayach were allowed to transfer the liability to another market participant, then the following data would be used.

Input	Amount
Labour and material cost	$2 million
Overhead	30% of labour and material cost
Third party mark-up – industry average	20%
Annual inflation rate	5%
Risk adjustment – uncertainty relating to cash flows	6%
Risk-free rate of government bonds	4%
Entity's non-performance risk	2%

Jayach needs advice on how to fair value the liability.

Required

Discuss, with relevant computations, how Jayach should fair value the above asset and liability under IFRS 13. **(10 marks)**

Professional marks will be awarded in question 4 for the clarity and quality of the presentation and discussion.

(2 marks)

(Total = 25 marks)

Answers

DO NOT TURN THIS PAGE UNTIL YOU HAVE
COMPLETED THE MOCK EXAM

A PLAN OF ATTACK

If this were the real Corporate Reporting exam and you had been told to turn over and begin, what would be going through your mind?

The answer may be 'I can't do this to save my life'! You've spent most of your study time on groups and current issues (because that's what your tutor/BPP Study Text told you to do), plus a selection of other topics, and you're really not sure that you know enough. The good news is that this may get you through. The first question, in Section A, is very likely to be on groups. In Section B you have to choose three out of four questions, and at least one of those is likely to be on current issues – a new IFRS, ED or discussion paper. So there's no need to panic. First spend **five minutes or so looking at the paper**, and develop a **plan of attack**.

Looking through the paper

The compulsory question in Section A is, as a case study on groups, in this case a complex group. You also have a fairly easy bit on corporate citizenship. In Section B you have three questions on a variety of topics:

- Question 2 is a scenario question covering IAS 20, IAS 7, IFRS 10 definition of control and adjustment for tax liability
- Question 3 is a specialised industry question covering investment property, leasing, provisions and impairment
- Question 4 is on the topical issue of fair value measurement under IFRS 13

You only have to answer two out of these three questions. You don't have to pick your optional questions right now, but this brief overview should have convinced you that you have enough choice and variety to have a respectable go at Section B. So let's go back to the compulsory question in Section A.

Compulsory question

Question 1 requires you to **prepare a consolidated statement of financial position for a group with two subsidiaries, one a foreign subsidiary**. Don't be put off by the foreign currency aspects – the translation process is actually quite mechanical. However, there are easy marks to be gained for basic consolidation techniques such as intragroup trading. Part (a) is a good source of easy marks too.

Optional questions

Deciding between the optional questions is obviously a personal matter – it depends how you have spent your study time.

In our opinion, Questions 3 and 4 are more straightforward than Question 2. Question 4 allows plenty of scope for earning marks through textbook knowledge of principles, and question 3 has the advantage over Question 2 covering more mainstream topics. Question 2 has a rather obscure Part (b), although you could make up the marks elsewhere. The secret is to plan your answer; break it down into bite sized subsections, clearly labelled to help your marker to quickly conclude you understand the problem and have a logical answer.

Allocating your time

BPP's advice is always allocate your time **according to the marks for the question** in total and for the parts of the question. But **use common sense.** If you're doing Question 4 but have no idea about the numbers for fair value, jot down something (anything!) and spent more time on Part (a), where most of the easy marks are to be gained.

Forget about it!

And don't worry if you found the paper difficult. More than likely other candidates will too. The paper is marked fairly leniently and always has a good pass rate. If this were the real thing, you would need to **forget** the exam the minute you left the exam hall and **think about the next one**. Or, if it's the last one, **celebrate**!

BPP LEARNING MEDIA

Question 1

Marking scheme

		Marks
(a)	Consideration of factors	6
	Conclusion	2
		8
(b)	Translation of Zian	6
	Loan	2
	Goodwill: Zian	4
	Non-controlling interest	4
	Building	3
	Early repayment of loan	1
	Pension	2
	Inventory	1
	Bonus	3
	Goodwill: Hall	2
	Retained earnings: Hall	2
	Zian	1
	Ribby	3
	Other components of equity	1
		35
(c)	Accounting	3
	Ethical discussion	4
		7
	Maximum	50

(a) **Factors to consider in determining functional currency of Zian**

IAS 21 *The effects of changes in foreign exchange rates* defines functional currency as 'the currency of the primary economic environment in which the entity operates'. Each entity, whether an individual company, a parent of a group, or an operation within a group, should determine its functional currency and **measure its results and financial position in that currency**.

An entity should consider the following factors:

(i)   Is it the currency that mainly **influences sales prices** for goods and services (this will often be the currency in which sales prices for its goods and services are denominated and settled)?

(ii) Is it the currency of the country whose **competitive forces and regulations** mainly determine the sales prices of its goods and services?

(iii) Is it the currency that **mainly influences labour, material and other costs** of providing goods or services? (This will often be the currency in which such costs are denominated and settled.)

Applying the first of these, it appears that **Zian's functional currency is the dinar**. Zian **sells its products locally** and its prices are determined by local competition. However, point (ii) on operating costs suggests that the **functional currency is the dollar**. Zen **imports goods which are paid for in dollars**, and while selling and operating costs are paid in dinars, it is the currency that determines the pricing of transactions that is important.

Other factors may also provide evidence of an entity's functional currency:

(i)   It is the currency in which **funds from financing activities** are generated.
(ii) It is the currency in which **receipts from operating activities** are usually retained.

Zian finances its operations in part by means of a $4m loan from Hall. However, it **does not depend on Hall, or other group companies for finance**. Furthermore, Zian operates with a considerable degree of autonomy, and is not under the control of the parent as regards finance or management. It also generates sufficient cash lows to meet its cash needs. These aspects point away from the dollar as the functional currency.

The position is **not clear cut**, and there are arguments on both sides. However, **on balance it is the dinar** that should be considered as the functional currency, since this most faithfully represents the economic reality of the transactions, both operating and financing, and the autonomy of Zian in relation to the parent company.

(b)   RIBBY GROUP
CONSOLIDATED STATEMENT OF FINANCIAL POSITION AS AT 31 MAY 20X8

	$m
Non-current assets	
Property, plant and equipment: 250 + 120 + 30 (W2) + 10 (W7) + 5.5 (W7) – 0.8 (W9)	414.7
Goodwill: 20 (W2) + 4.6 (W4)	24.6
Financial assets: 10 + 5 + 12.3 (W2) – 4 (W8)	23.3
	462.6
Current assets: 22 + 17 + 10 (W2) + 6 (W13) – 4 (W13)	51.0
	513.6
Equity	
Ordinary shares	60.0
Other components of equity*: 30 + 1.8	31.8
Retained earnings (W5)	122.6
	214.4
Non-controlling interests (W6)	67.7
	282.1
Non-current liabilities	
90 + 5 + 4 (W2) – 4 (W8) – 10 (W10) + 3.5 (W12)	88.5
Current liabilities	
110 + 7 + 6 (W2) + 10 (W10) + 1 (W10) + 3 (W11) + 6 (W13)	143.0
	513.6

*Note. Hall's 'other components of equity' are all pre-acquisition.

Workings

1   *Group structure*

                                        Ribby

    1.6.20X6   70%   60%   1.6.20X6
    Cost $98m   Cost $30m (330m dinars)

            Hall ($)   Zian (dinars)

    Retained earnings: $60m   Retained earnings: 220m dinars
    Other components of equity: $10m   Fair value NA: 495m dinars

2   *Translation of SOFP of Zian at 31 May 20X8*

	Dinars (m)	Rate	$m
Property, plant and equipment	360	12	30.0
Financial assets	148	12	12.3
Current assets	120	12	10.0
	628		52.3
Share capital	209	11	19.0
Retained earnings			
Pre-acqn	220	11	20.0
	429		39.0
Post-acqn. (307 – 220 – 8 (W8)	79	ß	3.3
	508		42.3
Non-current liabilities 40 + 8 (W8)	48	12	4.0
Current liabilities	72	12	6.0
	628		52.3

3   *Goodwill: Hall*

	$m	$m
Consideration transferred		98
Fair value of non-controlling interests		42
Fair value of identifiable net assets at acq'n (per question)		(120)
		20

4   *Goodwill: Zian*

	Dinars (m)	Rate	$m
Consideration transferred (30 × 11)	330		30.0
Non-controlling interests	220		20.0
		11	
Less: fair value of net assets at acq'n per question	(495)		(45.0)
At 1 June 20X6	55		5.0
Impairment loss	(0)		(0.0)
Exchange loss	–		(0.4)
At 31 May 20X8	55	12	4.6

5 *Retained earnings*

	Ribby $m	Hall $m	Zian $m
Per question/as translated (W2)	120.0	80.0	23.3
Adjustments			
Fair value movement (W7)			(0.5)
Impairment (W9)	(0.8)		
Loan penalty (W10)	(1.0)		
Bonus/share options (W11)	(4.8)		
Past service cost (W12)	(3.5)		
Unrealised profit in inventory (W13)		(4)	
Pre-acquisition: per question		(60)	
as translated (W2)			(20.0)
		16	2.8
Group share: Hall: 16 × 70%	11.2		
Zian: 2.8 × 60%	1.7		
Exchange loss on goodwill ((W4) 0.4 × 60%)	(0.2)		
	122.6		

6 *Non-controlling interests*

	Hall $m	Zian $m
NCI at acquisition (W3)/(W4)	42.0	20.0
NCI share of post acquisition retained earnings:		
Hall ((W5) 16 × 30%)	4.8	
Zian ((W5) 2.8 × 40%)		1.1
Exchange loss on goodwill ((W4) 0.4 × 40%)		(0.2)
	46.8	20.9

67.7

7 *Fair value adjustments*

Hall:

	Acquisition 1 June 20X6 $m	Movement 2 years $m	Year end 31 May 20X8 $m
Land: 120 – 40 (SC) – 60 (RE) – 10 (other)	10	–	10

Zian:

	Acquisition 1 June 20X6	Movement (exchange diff)	Year-end 31 May 20X8 $m
Land (in dinars (m))			
495 – 209 (SC) – 220 (RE) = 66			
In dollars: 66/11 (66/12)	6	(0.5)	5.5

Note: The land is non-depreciable so the movement for Zian is the change in exchange rate.

8 *Intragroup loan*

	Dinar
Initial value 1 June 20X7 ($4m × 10)	40
Year-end value 31 May 20X8 ($4m × 12)	48
Foreign exchange loss	8

Adjust in Zian's books (W6)

DEBIT Profit and loss (retained earnings)   8 dinars
CREDIT Non-current liabilities   8 dinars

The intra-group loan will be eliminated from the consolidated SOFP.

DEBIT Non-current liabilities $4m
CREDIT Financial assets $4m

9   *Impairment loss on building*

	$
Cost at 1 June 20X7: 40m dinar/10	4.0
Depreciation: 4m/20	(0.2)
	3.8
Impairment loss (bal. fig.)	(0.8)
Impaired value at 31 May 20X8: 36m dinar/12	3.0

10   *Early repayment of loan*

The decision to repay the loan early has two implications:

(i)   The loan must be transferred from non-current liabilities to current liabilities.

(ii)   A penalty for early re-payment. The double entries are:

DEBIT   Non-current liabilities $10m
CREDIT   Current liabilities $10m

Being transfer to current liabilities

DEBIT   Profit or loss for the year $1m
CREDIT   Current liabilities $1m

Being accrual of early repayment penalty

11   *Bonus and share options*

Half the bonus is to be paid in cash, so a liability of $(6m × ½) = $3m must be accrued.

The remainder of the bonus is to be paid in share options. The grant date will be 30 November 20X8, as this is when the terms of the share options become fixed. However, the services must be recognised as received, and so 12 months of the 18 month service period up to the grant date must be recognised.

The double entry is as follows:

DEBIT   Profit or loss (retained earnings) $4.8m

CREDIT   Current liabilities (cash bonus (6m × ½)) $3m

CREDIT   Other components of entity $90\% \times \$6m \times \frac{1}{2} \times \frac{12 \text{ months}}{18 \text{ months}}$ $1.8m

12   *Past service cost*

The past service cost of $3m relates to a benefit has already been vested, while the remaining $0.5m relates to an entitlement that has not yet fully vested, as it is given in return for services over the remaining two-year period. However, following the 2011 revision of IAS 19, all past service costs must be charge to profit or loss.

The double entry is as follows:

On 1 June 20X7:

DEBIT   Profit or loss (retained earnings) $3.5m
CREDIT   Present value of obligation (non-current liabilities) $3.5m

13   *Sale of inventory*

This transaction is known as 'window dressing'. It should not be shown as a sale; the sale must be cancelled and the inventory re-instated at $2m (cost) rather than $6m sales price.

The entries for the cancellation of the sale are:

DEBIT	Sales	$6m	
CREDIT	Cash (current liabilities)		$6m

For the cancellation of the purchase:

DEBIT	Cash (current assets)	$6m	
CREDIT	Purchases		$6m

The above entries have no effect on retained earnings, but the elimination of unrealised profit, reducing inventory from $6m to $2m, will affect it.

DEBIT	Closing inventory/cost of sales (Hall's books): 6 – 2	$4m	
CREDIT	Inventory (current asset)		$4m

(c) **Ethical implications of sale of inventory**

Members of the accounting profession enjoy a number of privileges. These include:

(i) Special status and respect within the community.

(ii) Self-regulation, that is regulation by the accountants' professional body

(iii) An exclusive right to certain functions. For example, auditors must be members of certain professional bodies.

Like other professions, the accounting profession has **features that distinguish it** from non-professional jobs. The most important of these is specialist knowledge, but also recognition as being committed to the good of society, rather than just commercial gain.

To **earn this status and these privileges**, accountants should, as a minimum:

(a) Be committed to the presentation of true, fair and accurate financial statements.

(b) Show independence and objectivity in applying financial reporting standards.

(c) Be committed to an ethical approach to business, and apply this in the preparation of financial statements.

Ethical behaviour in the preparation of financial statements, and in other areas, is of **paramount importance**. This applies equally to preparers of accounts, to auditors and to accountants giving advice to directors. Company accountants act unethically if they use 'creative' accounting in accounts preparation to make the figures look better.

In treating the inventory as sold, Ribby is indulging in '**window dressing**'. This is not a genuine sale; its purpose is purely **to show Ribby's subsidiary Hall in a better financial position** than is truly the case, in order to increase the likelihood of the sale of Hall. The 'sale' of inventory would increase cash and retained earnings by $4m, boosting the appearance of both profitability and liquidity. This would **mislead a potential buyer**. Nor would this manipulation be a 'one-off'; if the subsidiary is not sold, the transaction would be carried out again in the interim accounts. Neither the final accounts for 31 May 20X8, nor the interim accounts would give a fair presentation of the true picture.

The treatment of the inventory is therefore **unethical**, and should be reversed when preparing the consolidated financial statements.

Question 2

Marking scheme

	Marks
(a) 1 mark per point up to maximum	7
(b) 1 mark per point up to maximum	5
(c) 1 mark per point up to maximum	6
(d) 1 mark per point up to maximum	5
Professional marks	2
	25

(a)   **Green certificates**

The applicable standard relating to the green certificates is IAS 20 *Accounting for government grants and disclosure of government assistance*.

The principle behind the standard is that of accruals or matching: the **grant received must be matched with the related costs**.

Government grants are assistance by government in the form of transfers of resources to an entity in return for past or future compliance with certain conditions relating to the operating activities of the entity. A government grant is recognised only when there is reasonable assurance that the entity will comply with the conditions attaching to it and the grants will be received. In the case of the green certificates, the condition that must be complied with is the environmentally friendly production of electricity, as verified by the an independent audit.

There are two main types of grants:

(i)   **Grants related to assets.** These are grants whose primary condition is that an entity qualifying for them should purchase, construct or otherwise acquire long-term assets. Subsidiary conditions may also be attached restricting the type or location of the assets or the periods during which they are to be acquired or held.

(ii)   **Grants related to income.** These are government grants other than grants related to assets.

Since Coate can trade the green certificates, they are not long-term assets, and therefore fall into the category of **grants related to income**. They must be matched against the related costs of production of 'green electricity', as they are a form of government compensation for these costs.

There are two possible ways of presenting the grants (green certificates).

(i)   As a credit in profit or loss, either separately or under a general heading such as 'other income', or
(ii)   As a deduction from the related expense.

The **green certificates** are items held for sale in the ordinary course of business, and therefore should be recognised as **inventories** in accordance with IAS 2 *Inventories*. Green certificates that are unsold at the end of the reporting period are included in inventory and charged to production as **part of the cost of sales**.

A **deferred income approach** is used to match the grant to the related cost as follows.

To record the quarterly receipt of the grant

| DEBIT | Certificate (SOFP) | $ Fair value of certificate at receipt |
| CREDIT | Deferred income (SOFP) | $ Fair value of certificate at receipt |

On the sale of a certificate: contribution to cost of production

When the certificate is sold its fair value may be recognised in profit or loss. It is treated as a deduction from cost of sales because it is a contribution to the cost of generating the 'green electricity'.

| DEBIT | Deferred income (SOFP) | $ Fair value of certificate at receipt |
| CREDIT | Cost of sales (SPLOCI) | $ Fair value of certificate at receipt |

On the sale of a certificate: surplus/deficit

The certificate may be sold for more or less than its fair value at the time it was received from the government. This surplus/deficit is taken to/deducted from revenue in the SPLOCI.

DEBIT	Bank/receivable (SOFP)	$ Fair value of trade
CREDIT	Certificate (SOFP)	$ Fair value of certificate at receipt
DEBIT/CREDIT	Revenue (SPLOCI)	$ Balance (deficit/surplus)

Following IAS 1 *Presentation of financial statements,* Coates is required to **disclose its accounting policy** in relation to government grants. IAS 20 specifically requires disclosure of **the nature and extent of the government assistance given and any conditions not yet fulfilled or related contingencies**. The disclosures of unfulfilled conditions are unlikely to be extensive because an audit must be completed to show that the conditions have been fulfilled.

(b)   **Foreign exchange and cash flows**

According to IAS 7 *Statement of cash flows*, **unrealised foreign exchange gains and losses are not cash flows**. However, IAS 7 requires that the components making up the total opening and closing balances of cash and cash equivalents in the statement of cash flows should be disclosed in order to **reconcile cash and cash equivalents at the beginning and end of the period**.

Individual accounts (foreign cash balances)

Coates holds **foreign currency cash and cash equivalent** balances. As these are **monetary items**, IAS 21 *The effects of changes in foreign exchange rates* requires them to be **retranslated at the closing rate** at the reporting date. Exchange **gains and losses are recorded in profit or loss** in Coates's **individual** financial statements

In the **consolidated statement of cash flows**, if the **indirect method** is adopted, these exchange differences are **removed from profit before tax** as an adjustment within 'operating activities'. Instead they are shown at the foot of the consolidated statement of cash flows (as a separate heading from operating, investing and financing activities) as **part of the reconciliation** between opening and closing cash and cash equivalent balances.

Group accounts (overseas subsidiary)

IAS 21 requires the **assets and liabilities** (both monetary and non-monetary) of the overseas subsidiary to be **translated at the closing rate in the consolidated financial statements**. **Income and expenses** are translated at the rate ruling at the date of the transaction or the **average rate** as a close approximation. **Exchange differences** arising on retranslation of opening net assets and profit are recorded in **other comprehensive income** and then held as a separate component of equity. **On disposal** of the subsidiary, the gains or losses are **reclassified from other comprehensive income to profit or loss for the year**.

As the subsidiary was acquired during the current year, its cash and cash equivalents at the date of acquisition would have been recorded as a **cash flow within 'investing activities'**. As its year end cash and cash equivalents balance would have also been included in the closing cash and cash equivalents balance at the foot of the group statement of cash flows translated at the closing rate, the exchange difference arising from the **movement in exchange rates** between the acquisition date and the year-end will have to be shown **separately at the foot of the statement of cash flows** as part of the movement in cash and cash equivalents.

(c)   **Treatment of former subsidiary**

Coate wishes to continue to consolidate its investment in Patten, of which it has sold 50% to Manis. The requirement (or in this case permission) to consolidate an investment is determined by **control**, not merely by ownership. In most cases, this will involve the parent company owning a majority of the ordinary shares in the subsidiary (to which normal voting rights are attached). There are circumstances, however, when the parent may own an equal share or only a minority of the voting power in the subsidiary, *but* the parent still has control. Coate is arguing that it still has control over Patten because of the agreement made with Manis that Coate would exercise general control over Patten's operating and financial policies. Whether this is the case will be determined in accordance with IRS 10 *Consolidated financial statements*.

IFRS 10 states that an investor **controls** an investee if and only if it has all of the following.

(i)   **Power** over the investee
(ii)   Exposure, or rights, to **variable returns** from its involvement with the investee, and
(iii)   The **ability to use its power** over the investee to affect the amount of the investor's returns.

Power is defined as **existing rights that give the current ability to direct the relevant activities of the investee**. In some cases assessing power is straightforward, for example, where power is obtained directly and solely from having the majority of voting rights or potential voting rights, and as a result the ability to direct relevant activities. In other cases, assessment is more complex and more than one factor must be considered. Coate has only 50% of the voting rights of Patten, and so other factors come into play here.

IFRS 10 gives the following examples of **rights**, other than voting or potential voting rights, which individually, or alone, can give an investor power.

(i)   Rights to appoint, reassign or remove key management personnel who can direct the relevant activities

(ii)   Rights to appoint or remove another entity that directs the relevant activities

(iii)   Rights to direct the investee to enter into, or veto changes to transactions for the benefit of the investor

(iv)   Other rights, such as those specified in a management contract

Coates does not appear to have these rights over Patten. While the shareholder agreement gives Coates influence over Patten, the requirement for consensus with Manis relates to **decisions made in the ordinary course of business,** such as significant changes in the company's activities or budgets, appointment and dismissal of senior employees. Coates argues that it is customary within the industry to require shareholder consensus for such decisions, but the **extent of the restrictions precludes control by Coates**. Rather, the consensus requirements suggest **joint control,** and indicate that this is a joint arrangement, as per IFRS 11 *Joint arrangements*. IFRS 11 defines joint control as:

> The contractually agreed sharing of control of an arrangement, which exists only when decisions about the relevant activities require the unanimous consent of the parties sharing control

There are two types of joint arrangements: joint ventures and jointly controlled entities. Patten is a **separate vehicle**. As such, it could be either a joint operation or joint venture, so other facts must be considered.

There are no facts that suggest that Coates and Manis have rights to the assets of Patten in the consolidated financial statements nor an obligation for its liabilities. Therefore, as each party has an interest in the **net assets** of Patten, Patten should be treated as a **joint venture** (rather than a joint operation). Manis must be **de-consolidated from the Coates group,** and **equity accounted for** as a **joint venture** instead.

(d)   **Tax adjustment**

According to IAS 12 *Income taxes* the tax expense in the statement of profit or loss and other comprehensive income includes the tax charge for the year, any under or overprovision of income tax from the previous year and any increase or decrease in the deferred tax provision:

	$
Current tax expense	X
Under/overprovisions relating to prior periods	X/(X)
Increases/decreases in the deferred tax balance	X/(X)
	X

While the correction of an over or under provision relates to a prior period, this is **not a prior period adjustment** as defined in IAS 8 *Accounting policies, changes in accounting estimates and errors* and as assumed by Coates. Rather, it is a **change in accounting estimate**.

Changes in accounting estimates result from new information or new developments and, accordingly, are **not corrections of errors**. A prior period error, which would require a prior period adjustment is **an omission or misstatement arising form failure to use reliable information** that was available or could have been obtained at the time of the authorisation of the financial statements. This is **not the case here**. Coates had accounted for all known issues at the previous year end (30 November 20X1), and could not have foreseen that the tax adjustment would be required. No penalties were applied by the taxation authorities, indicating that there were no fundamental errors in the information provided to them. Correction of an over- or under-provision for taxation is routine, since taxation liabilities are difficult to estimate.

The effect of a change in accounting estimate must be **applied by the company prospectively** by including it in profit or loss in the period of change, with separate disclosure of the adjustment in the financial statements.

Question 3

Marking scheme

	Marks
(a) 1 mark per point up to maximum	7
(b) 1 mark per point up to maximum	6
(c) 1 mark per point up to maximum	4
(d) 1 mark per point up to maximum	6
Professional marks	2
	25

(a)   **Investment property**

IAS 40 *Investment property* applies to the accounting for property (land and/or buildings) **held to earn rentals or for capital appreciation or both**. Examples of investment property given in the standard include, but are not limited to:

(i)   Land held for **long-term capital appreciation**

(ii)   Land held for **undetermined future use**

Assets which IAS 40 states are not investment property, and which are therefore **not covered** by the standard include:

(i) Property held for use in the **production or supply of goods or services** or for administrative purposes

(ii) Property held for **sale in the ordinary course of business** or in the process of construction of development for such sale

Owner-occupied property, property being **constructed on behalf of third parties** and property leased to a third party **under a finance lease** are also specifically **excluded** by the IAS 40 definition.

If the entity provides **ancillary services** to the occupants of a property held by the entity, the appropriateness of classification as investment property is determined by the significance of the services provided. If those services are a relatively insignificant component of the arrangement as a whole (for instance, the building owner supplies security and maintenance services to the lessees), then the entity may treat the property as investment property. **Where the services provided are more significant** (such as in the case of an owner-managed hotel), the property should be classified as **owner-occupied**.

Applying IAS 40 to Blackcutt's properties, **the land owned for capital appreciation** and which may be sold any time in the future **will qualify as investment property**. Likewise, the **land whose use has not yet been determined** is also covered by the IAS 40 definition of investment property: as it has no current purpose it is deemed to be held for capital appreciation.

Investment property should be recognised as an asset where it is probable that the future economic benefits associated with the property will flow to the entity and the value can be measured reliably. IAS 40 permits an entity to choose between the cost model and the fair value model. Where the fair value model applies, the property is valued in accordance with IFRS 13 *Fair value measurement*. Gains or losses arising from changes in the fair value of investment property are recognised in profit or loss for the year.

The **houses routinely bought and sold** by Blackcutt in the ordinary course of its operations will **not qualify as investment property**, but will be treated under IAS 2 *Inventories*.

The **part of the housing inventory** not held for sale but **used to provide housing to low-income employees does not qualify as investment property** either. The properties are **not held for capital appreciation**, and because the rent is **below market rate** and only covers the maintenance costs, **they cannot be said to be held for rentals**. The **rental income is incidental** to the purposes for which the property is held, which is to provide housing services. As with the example of the owner-managed hotel above, the services are significant, and the property should be classified as **owner occupied**. Further indication that it is owner occupied is provided by the fact that it is rented out to **employees of the organisation**. It will be accounted for under IAS 16 *Property, plant and equipment*.

(b) **Lease**

The issue here is whether the arrangement with the private sector provider Waste and Co is, or contains, a lease, even if it does not take the legal form of a lease. The **substance of the arrangement should be considered** in connection with the *Conceptual Framework for Financial Reporting* and IAS 17 *Leases*. Key factors to consider are as follows.

(i) Who obtains most of the **benefit** from the asset?
(ii) Who **controls** the asset by operating it or directing others to do so?
(iii) Who has the **right to use** the asset or to direct others to do so?
(iv) Who has the **risks and rewards** associated with the asset?

The answer in each case is **Blackcutt**.

(i) Waste and Co purchases the vehicles and uses them exclusively for Blackcutt. If Waste and Co goes out of business, Blackcutt can re-possess the vehicles and continue to use them for waste collection.

(ii) Blackcutt controls the vehicles, since it stipulates how they are painted, and ostensibly owns them because they must be painted with Blackcutt's name.

(iii) Blackcutt can use the vehicles and uses them exclusively for waste collection for nearly all their life.

(iv) Following on from this, Blackcutt has the risks and rewards associated with the asset.

The arrangement is in substance **a lease**. As Blackcutt has **substantially all the risks and rewards of ownership,** the arrangement should be treated as a **finance lease**. The vehicles should be recorded in assets in Blackcutt's statement of financial position, with a corresponding lease liability. The value of the lease may be determined by considering the fair value of acquiring the vehicle. The service element relating to the waste collection may be considered separately.

(c) **Provision**

Under IAS 37 *Provisions, contingent liabilities and contingent assets,* provisions must be recognised in the following circumstances, and must not be recognised if they do not apply.

(i) There is a **legal** or **constructive obligation** to transfer benefits as a result of **past events**.

(ii) It is probably that **an outflow of economic resources** will be required to **settle** the **obligation**.

(iii) A **reliable estimate** of the amount required to settle the obligation can be made.

A legal or constructive obligation is one created by an **obligating event.** Here the obligating event is the **contamination of the land**, because of the virtual certainty of legislation requiring the clean-up. As Blackcutt has no recourse against Chemco or its insurance company this past event will certainly give rise to a **transfer of economic benefits from** Blackcutt.

Consequently, Blackcutt **must recognise a provision** for the best estimate of the clean-up costs. It should **not set up a corresponding receivable**, since no reimbursement may be obtained from Chemco or its insurance company.

(d) **Impairment of building**

The basic principle of IAS 36 *Impairment of assets* is that an asset should be carried at no more than its recoverable amount, that is the amount to be recovered through use or sale of the asset. If an **asset's value** is **higher than its recoverable amount**, an **impairment loss** has occurred. The impairment loss should be **written off** against profit or loss for the year.

Entities must determine, at each reporting date, whether there are any indications that impairment has occurred. In this case, **impairment is indicated** because the use to which the building is to be put has changed significantly (from a school to a library), a situation which will continue for the foreseeable future.

The **recoverable amount** is **defined** as the **higher** of the **asset's fair value less costs to sell** and the asset's **value in use.** However, these values are unavailable because of the specialised nature of the asset, and the only information available is depreciated replacement cost. Using a **depreciated replacement cost approach**, the impairment loss would be calculated as follows.

Asset	Cost/replacement cost	Accumulated depreciation 6/25	Carrying amount/ replacement cost
	$'000	$'000	$'000
School	5,000	(1,200)	3,800
Library	2,100	(504)	(1,596)
Impairment loss			2,204

Blackcutt should therefore recognise an **impairment loss of $2.204m** in profit or loss for the year.

Question 4

Marking scheme

		Marks
(a)	(i) 1 mark per point up to maximum	7
	(ii) IFRS 13 hierarchy	6
(b)	1 mark per point up to maximum	6
	Calculations	4
Professional marks		2
		25

(a) (i) **IFRS 13 principles of fair value measurement**

IFRS 13 *Fair value measurement* defines fair value as **'the price that would be received to sell an asset or paid to transfer a liability in an orderly transaction between market participants at the measurement date.'**

The previous definition used in IFRS was 'the amount for which an asset could be exchanged, or a liability settled, between knowledgeable, willing parties in an arm's length transaction'.

The price which would be received to sell the asset or paid to transfer (not settle) the liability is described as the 'exit price', the definition also used in US GAAP. Although the concept of the 'arm's length transaction' has now gone, the market-based current exit price retains the notion of an exchange between unrelated, knowledgeable and willing parties.

Fair value is a **market-based measurement,** not an entity-specific measurement. It **focuses on assets and liabilities and on exit (selling) prices**. It also takes into account market conditions at the measurement date. In other words, it looks at the amount for which the holder of an asset could sell it and the amount which the holder of a liability would have to pay to transfer it. It can also be used to value an entity's own equity instruments.

Because it is a market-based measurement, fair value is measured using the assumptions that market participants would use when pricing the asset, taking into account any relevant characteristics of the asset.

It is assumed that the transaction to sell the asset or transfer the liability takes place either:

(1)   In the **principal market** for the asset or liability; or

(2)   In the absence of a principal market, in the **most advantageous market** for the asset or liability.

The **principal market** is the market which is the **most liquid** (has the greatest volume and level of activity for that asset or liability). In most cases the principal market and the most advantageous market will be the same.

Fair value is **not adjusted for transaction costs.** Under IFRS 13, these are **not a feature of the asset or liability,** but may be taken into account when **determining the most advantageous market.**

Fair value measurements are based on an asset or a liability's **unit of account**, which is specified not by IFRS 13, but by each IFRS where a fair value measurement is required. For most assets and liabilities, the unit of account is the individual asset or liability, but in some instances may be a group of assets or liabilities.

IFRS 13 acknowledges that when **market activity declines**, an entity must use a **valuation technique** to measure fair value. In this case the emphasis must be on whether a transaction price is based on an orderly transaction, rather than a forced sale.

The IFRS identifies **three valuation approaches**.

(1)   **Market approach.** A valuation technique that uses prices and other relevant information generated by market transactions involving identical or comparable (ie similar) assets, liabilities or a group of assets and liabilities, such as a business.

(2)   **Cost approach.** A valuation technique that reflects the amount that would be required currently to replace the service capacity of an asset (often referred to as current replacement cost).

(3)   **Income approach.** Valuation techniques that convert future amounts (eg cash flows or income and expenses) to a single current (ie discounted) amount. The fair value measurement is determined on the basis of the value indicated by current market expectations about those future amounts.

For **non-financial assets** the fair value measurement looks at the use to which the asset can be put. It takes into account the ability of a market participant to generate economic benefits by using the asset in its **highest and best use**.

(ii)   **IFRS 13 three-level hierarchy for fair value measurement**

IFRS 13 states that valuation techniques must be those which are appropriate and for which sufficient data are available. Entities should maximise the use of relevant **observable inputs** and minimise the use of **unobservable inputs**. The standard establishes a three-level hierarchy for the inputs that valuation techniques use to measure fair value:

Level 1   **Quoted prices** (unadjusted) in active markets for identical assets or liabilities that the reporting entity can access at the measurement date. If there is a quoted price in an active market, an entity uses that rice without adjustment to measure fair value. An example is prices on a stock exchange. Active markets are ones where transactions take place with sufficient frequency and volume for pricing information to be provided.

| | | Level 2 | **Inputs other than quoted prices** included within Level 1 that are observable for the asset or liability, either directly or indirectly, eg quoted prices for similar assets in active markets or for identical or similar assets in non-active markets or use of quoted interest rates for valuation purposes. |

Level 2 — **Inputs other than quoted prices** included within Level 1 that are observable for the asset or liability, either directly or indirectly, eg quoted prices for similar assets in active markets or for identical or similar assets in non-active markets or use of quoted interest rates for valuation purposes.

Level 3 — **Unobservable inputs** for the asset or liability, ie using the entity's own assumptions about market exit value. For example, cash flow forecasts may be used to value an entity that is not listed.

Each fair value measurement is categorized based on the lowest level input that is significant to it.

Entities may use more than one valuation technique to measure fair value in a given situation. A **change of valuation technique** is **considered to be a change of accounting estimate** in accordance with IAS 8. However, the disclosures in IAS 8 for a change in accounting estimate are **not required** for revisions resulting from a change in valuation technique or its application.

(b) (i) **Fair value of asset**

Year to 30 November 20X2	Asian market	European market	Australasian market
Volume of market – units	4m	2m	1m
	$		$
Price	19	16	22
Costs of entering the market	(2)	(2)	n/a*
Potential fair value	17	14	22
Transaction costs	(1)	(2)	(2)
Net profit	16	12	20

*****Notes**

(1) Because Jayach currently buys and sells the asset in the Australasian market, the **costs of entering that market** are not incurred and therefore **not relevant**.

(2) Fair value is **not adjusted for transaction costs.** Under IFRS 13, these are not a feature of the asset or liability, but may be taken into account when determining the most advantageous market.

(3) The **Asian market is the principal market** for the asset because it is the market with the greatest volume and level of activity for the asset. If information about the Asian market is available and Jayach can access the market, then Jayach should base its fair value on this market. Based on the Asian market, the **fair value of the asset would be $17**, measured as the price that would be received in that market ($19) less costs of entering the market ($2) and ignoring transaction costs.

(4) If **information** about the Asian market is **not available**, or if Jayach **cannot access the market**, Jayach must measure the fair value of the asset using the price in the **most advantageous market**. The most advantageous market is the market that maximises the amount that would be received to sell the asset, after taking into account both transaction costs and usually also costs of entry, that is the net amount that would be received in the respective markets. The most advantageous market here is therefore the **Australasian market**. As explained above, costs of entry are not relevant here, and so, based on this market, the **fair value would be $22**.

It is assumed that market participants are independent of each other and knowledgeable, and able and willing to enter into transactions.

(ii) **Fair value of decommissioning liability**

Because this is a business combination, Jayach must measure the liability at fair value in accordance with IFRS 13, rather than using the best estimate measurement required by IAS 37 *Provisions, contingent liabilities and contingent assets*. In most cases there will be no observable market to provide pricing information. If this is the case here, Jayach will use **the expected present value technique** to measure the fair value of the decommissioning liability. If Jayach were contractually committed to transfer its decommissioning liability to a market participant, it would conclude that a market participant would use the inputs as follows, arriving at a **fair value of $3,215,000**.

Input	Amount
	$'000
Labour and material cost	2,000
Overhead: 30% × 2,000	600
Third party mark-up – industry average: 2,600 × 20%	520
	3120
Inflation adjusted total (5% compounded over three years): $3,120 \times 1.05^3$	3,612
Risk adjustment – uncertainty relating to cash flows: 3,612 × 6%	217
	3,829
Discount at risk-free rate plus entity's non-performance risk (4% + 2% = 6%): $3,829 \div 1.06^3$	3,215

ACCA

Paper P2

Corporate Reporting (International)

Mock Examination 2

Question Paper	
Time allowed	
Reading and planning	**15 minutes**
Writing	**3 hours**
This paper is divided into two sections	
Section A	This ONE question is compulsory and MUST be attempted
Section B	TWO questions ONLY to be answered

SECTION A – This ONE question is compulsory and MUST be attempted

Question 1

Beth, a public limited company, has produced the following draft statements of financial position as at 30 November 20X7. Lose and Gain are both public limited companies:

	Beth $m	Lose $m	Gain $m
Assets			
Non current assets			
Property, plant and equipment	1,700	200	300
Intangible assets	300		
Investment in Lose (at cost)	200		
Investment in Gain	180		
	2,380	200	300
Current assets			
Inventories	800	100	150
Trade receivables	600	60	80
Cash	500	40	20
	1,900	200	250
Total assets	4,280	400	550
Share capital of $1	1,500	100	200
Other reserves	300		
Retained earnings	400	200	300
Total equity	2,200	300	500
Non-current liabilities	700		
Current liabilities	1,380	100	50
Total liabilities	2,080	100	50
Total equity and liabilities	4,280	400	550

The following information is relevant to the preparation of the group financial statements of the Beth Group.

(i)	Date of acquisition	Holding acquired %	Retained earnings at acquisition $m	Purchase consideration $m
Lose:	1 December 20X5	20	80	40
	1 December 20X6	60	150	160
Gain:	1 December 20X6	30	260	180

Lose and Gain have not issued any share capital since the acquisition of the shareholdings by Beth. The fair values of the net assets of Lose and Gain were the same as their carrying amounts at the date of the acquisitions.

Beth did not have significant influence over Lose at any time before gaining control of Lose, but does have significant influence over Gain. There has been no impairment of goodwill on the acquisition of Lose since its acquisition, but the recoverable amount of the net assets of Gain has been deemed to be $610 million at 30 November 20X7.

It is the group's policy to value its non-controlling interests at fair value. The fair value of the non-controlling interest in Lose at 1 December 20X6 was $53.33m.

The fair value of the 20% holding in Lose on 30th November 20X6 was also $53.33m.

(ii) Lose entered into an operating lease for a building on 1 December 20X6. The building was converted into office space during the year at a cost to Lose of $10 million. The operating lease is for a period of six years, at the end of which the building must be returned to the lessor in its original condition. Lose thinks that it would cost $2 million to convert the building back to its original condition at prices at 30 November 20X7.

The entries that had been made in the financial statements of Lose were the charge for operating lease rentals ($4 million per annum) and the improvements to the building. Both items had been charged to the profit or loss. The improvements were completed during the financial year.

(iii) On 1 October 20X7, Beth sold inventory costing $18 million to Gain for $28 million. At 30 November 20X7, the inventory was still held by Gain. The inventory was sold to a third party on 15 December 20X7 for $35 million.

(iv) Beth had contracted to purchase an item of plant and equipment for 12 million euros on the following terms:

Payable on signing contract (1 September 20X7)	50%
Payable on delivery and installation (11 December 20X7)	50%

The amount payable on signing the contract (the deposit) was paid on the due date and is refundable. The following exchange rates are relevant:

20X7	Euros to 1 dollar
1 September	0.75
30 November	0.85
11 December	0.79

The deposit is included in trade receivables at the rate of exchange on 1 September 20X7. A full year's charge for depreciation of property, plant and equipment is made in the year of acquisition using the straight line method over six years.

(v) Beth sold some trade receivables which arose during November 20X7 to a factoring company on 30 November 20X7. The trade receivables sold are unlikely to default in payment based on past experience but they are long dated with payment not due until 1 June 20X8. Beth has given the factor a guarantee that it will reimburse any amounts not received by the factor. Beth received $45 million from the factor being 90% of the trade receivables sold. The trade receivables are not included in the statement of financial position of Beth and the balance not received from the factor (10% of the trade receivables factored) of $5 million has been written off against retained earnings.

(vi) Beth granted 200 share options to each of its 10,000 employees on 1 December 20X6. The shares vest if the employees work for the Group for the next two years. On 1 December 20X6, Beth estimated that there would be 1,000 eligible employees leaving in each year up to the vesting date. At 30 November 20X7, 600 eligible employees had left the company. The estimate of the number of employees leaving in the year to 30 November 20X8 was 500 at 30 November 20X7. The fair value of each share option at the grant date (1 December 20X6) was $10. The share options have not been accounted for in the financial statements.

(vii) The Beth Group operates in the oil industry and contamination of land occurs including the pollution of seas and rivers. The Group only cleans up the contamination if it is a legal requirement in the country where it operates. The following information has been produced for Beth by a group of environmental consultants for the year ended 30 November 20X7:

Cost to clean up contamination	Law existing in country
$m	
5	No
7	To come into force in December 20X7
4	Yes

The directors of Beth have a widely publicised environmental attitude which shows little regard for the effects on the environment of their business. The Group does not currently produce a separate environmental report and no provision for environmental costs has been made in the financial statements. Any provisions would be shown as non-current liabilities. Beth is likely to operate in these countries for several years.

Other information

Beth is currently suffering a degree of stagnation in its business development. Its domestic and international markets are being maintained but it is not attracting new customers. Its share price has not increased whilst that of its competitors has seen a rise of between 10% and 20%. Additionally it has recently received a significant amount of adverse publicity because of its poor environmental record and is to be investigated by regulators in several countries. Although Beth is a leading supplier of oil products, it has never felt the need to promote socially responsible policies and practices or make positive contributions to society because it has always maintained its market share. It is renowned for poor customer support, bearing little regard for the customs and cultures in the communities where it does business. It had recently made a decision not to pay the amounts owing to certain small and medium entities (SMEs) as the directors feel that SMEs do not have sufficient resources to challenge the non-payment in a court of law. The management of the company is quite authoritarian and tends not to value employees' ideas and contributions.

Required

(a) Prepare the consolidated statement of financial position of the Beth Group as at 30 November 20X7 in accordance with International Financial Reporting Standards. **(35 marks)**

(b) Describe to the Beth Group the possible advantages of producing a separate environmental report.

(8 marks)

(c) Discuss the ethical and social responsibilities of the Beth Group and whether a change in the ethical and social attitudes of the management could improve business performance. **(7 marks)**

(Total = 50 marks)

SECTION B – TWO questions ONLY to be attempted

Question 2

(a) In its annual financial statements for the year ended 31 March 20X3, Verge, a public limited company, had identified the following operating segments.

    (i) Segment 1 local train operations
    (ii) Segment 2 inter-city train operations
    (iii) Segment 3 railway constructions

The company disclosed two reportable segments. Segments 1 and 2 were aggregated into a single reportable operating segment. Operating segments 1 and 2 have been aggregated on the basis of their similar business characteristics, and the nature of their products and services. In the local train market, it is the local transport authority which awards the contract and pays Verge for its services. In the local train market, contracts are awarded following a competitive tender process, and the ticket prices paid by passengers are set by and paid to the transport authority. In the inter-city train market, ticket prices are set by Verge and the passengers pay Verge for the service provided. **(5 marks)**

(b) Verge entered into a contract with a government body on 1 April 20X1 to undertake maintenance services on a new railway line. The total revenue from the contract is $5 million over a three-year period. The contract states that $1 million will be paid at the commencement of the contract but although invoices will be subsequently sent at the end of each year, the government authority will only settle the subsequent amounts owing when the contract is completed. The invoices sent by Verge to date (including $1 million above) were as follows:

Year ended 31 March 20X2 $2.8 million
Year ended 31 March 20X3 $1.2 million

The balance will be invoiced on 31 March 20X4. Verge has only accounted for the initial payment in the financial statements to 31 March 20X2 as no subsequent amounts are to be paid until 31 March 20X4. The amounts of the invoices reflect the work undertaken in the period. Verge wishes to know how to account for the revenue on the contract in the financial statements to date.

Market interest rates are currently at 6%. **(6 marks)**

(c) In February 20X2, an inter-city train did what appeared to be superficial damage to a storage facility of a local company. The directors of the company expressed an intention to sue Verge but in the absence of legal proceedings, Verge had not recognised a provision in its financial statements to 31 March 20X2. In July 20X2, Verge received notification for damages of $1.2m, which was based upon the estimated cost to repair the building. The local company claimed the building was much more than a storage facility as it was a valuable piece of architecture which had been damaged to a greater extent than was originally thought. The head of legal services advised Verge that the company was clearly negligent but the view obtained from an expert was that the value of the building was $800,000. Verge had an insurance policy that would cover the first $200,000 of such claims. After the financial statements for the year ended 31 March 20X3 were authorised, the case came to court and the judge determined that the storage facility actually was a valuable piece of architecture. The court ruled that Verge was negligent and awarded $300,000 for the damage to the fabric of the facility. **(6 marks)**

(d) Verge was given a building by a private individual in February 20X2. The benefactor included a condition that it must be brought into use as a train museum in the interests of the local community or the asset (or a sum equivalent to the fair value of the asset) must be returned. The fair value of the asset was $1.5 million in February 20X2. Verge took possession of the building in May 20X2. However, it could not utilise the building in accordance with the condition until February 20X3 as the building needed some refurbishment and adaptation and in order to fulfil the condition. Verge spent $1 million on refurbishment and adaptation.

BPP
LEARNING MEDIA

On 1 July 20X2, Verge obtained a cash grant of $250,000 from the government. Part of the grant related to the creation of 20 jobs at the train museum by providing a subsidy of $5,000 per job created. The remainder of the grant related to capital expenditure on the project. At 31 March 20X3, all of the new jobs had been created. **(6 marks)**

Required

Advise Verge on how the above accounting issues should be dealt with in its financial statements for the years ending 31 March 20X2 (where applicable) and 31 March 20X3.

Note. The mark allocation is shown against each of the four issues above.

Professional marks will be awarded in this question for clarity and quality of presentation. **(2 marks)**

(Total = 25 marks)

Question 3

(a)   Janne is a real estate company, which specialises in industrial property. Investment properties including those held for sale constitute more than 80% of its total assets.

It is considering leasing land from Maret for a term of 30 years. Janne plans to use the land for its own office development but may hold the land for capital gain. The title will remain with Maret at the end of the initial lease term. Janne can lease the land indefinitely at a small immaterial rent at the end of the lease or may purchase the land at a 90% discount to the market value after the initial lease term. Janne is to pay Maret a premium of $3 million at the commencement of the lease, which equates to 70% of the value of the land. Additionally, an annual rental payment is to be made, based upon 4% of the market value of the land at the commencement of the lease, with a market rent review every five years. The rent review sets the rent at the higher of the current rent or 4% of the current value of the land. Land values have been rising for many years.

Additionally, Janne is considering a suggestion by Maret to incorporate a clean break clause in the lease which will provide Janne with an option of terminating the agreement after 25 years without any further payment and also to include an early termination clause after ten years that would require Janne to make a termination payment which would recover the lessor's remaining investment.   **(12 marks)**

(b)   Janne measures its industrial investment property using the fair value method, which is measured using the 'new-build value less obsolescence'. Valuations are conducted by a member of the board of directors. In order to determine the obsolescence, the board member takes account of the age of the property and the nature of its use. According to the board, this method of calculation is complex but gives a very precise result, which is accepted by the industry. There are sales values for similar properties in similar locations available as well as market rent data per square metre for similar industrial buildings.   **(5 marks)**

(c)   Janne operates through several subsidiaries and reported a subsidiary as held for sale in its annual financial statements for both 20X2 and 20X3. On 1 January 20X2, the shareholders had, at a general meeting of the company, authorised management to sell all of its holding of shares in the subsidiary within the year. Janne had shown the subsidiary as an asset held for sale and presented it as a discontinued operation in the financial statements at 31 May 20X2. This accounting treatment had been continued in Janne's 20X3 financial statements.

Janne had made certain organisational changes during the year to 31 May 20X3, which resulted in additional activities being transferred to the subsidiary. Also during the year to 31 May 20X3, there had been draft agreements and some correspondence with investment bankers, which showed in principle only that the subsidiary was still for sale.   **(6 marks)**

Required

Advise Janne on how the above accounting issues should be dealt with in its financial statements.

Note. The mark allocation is shown against each of the three issues above.

Professional marks will be awarded in this question for clarity and quality of presentation.   **(2 marks)**
(Total = 25 marks)

Question 4

The transition to International Financial Reporting Standards (IFRSs) involves major change for companies as IFRSs introduce significant changes in accounting practices that were often not required by national generally accepted accounting practice. It is important that the interpretation and application of IFRSs is consistent from country to country. IFRSs are partly based on rules, and partly on principles and management's judgement. Judgement is more likely to be better used when it is based on experience of IFRSs within a sound financial reporting infrastructure. It is hoped that national differences in accounting will be eliminated and financial statements will be consistent and comparable worldwide.

Required

(a)   Discuss how the changes in accounting practices on transition to IFRSs and choice in the application of individual IFRSs could lead to inconsistency between the financial statements of companies.   **(17 marks)**

(b)   Discuss how management's judgement and the financial reporting infrastructure of a country can have a significant impact on financial statements prepared under IFRS.   **(6 marks)**

Appropriateness and quality of discussion.   **(2 marks)**

(Total = 25 marks)

Answers

DO NOT TURN THIS PAGE UNTIL YOU HAVE
COMPLETED THE MOCK EXAM

A PLAN OF ATTACK

Managing your nerves

As you turn the pages to start this exam a number of thoughts are likely to cross your mind. At best, examinations cause anxiety so it is important to stay focused on your task for the next three hours! Developing an awareness of what is going on emotionally within you may help you manage your nerves. Remember, you are unlikely to banish the flow of adrenaline, but the key is to harness it to help you work steadily and quickly through your answers.

Working through this mock exam will help you develop the exam stamina you will need to keep going for three hours.

Managing your time

Planning and time management are two of the key skills which complement the technical knowledge you need to succeed. To keep yourself on time, do not be afraid to jot down your target completion times for each question, perhaps next to the title of the question on the paper.

Focusing on scoring marks

When completing written answers, remember to communicate the critical points, which represent marks, and avoid padding and waffle. Sometimes it is possible to analyse a long sentence into more than one point. Always try to maximise the mark potential of what you write.

As you read through the questions, jot down on the question paper, any points you think you might forget. There is nothing more upsetting than coming out of an exam having forgotten to write a point you knew!

Also remember you can only score marks for what is on paper; you must write down enough to help the examiner to give you marks!

Structure and signpost your answers

To help you answer the examiner's requirements, highlight as you read through the paper the key words and phrases in the examiner's requirements.

Also, where possible try to use headings and subheadings, to give a logical and easy-to-follow structure to your response. A well structured and signposted answer is more likely to convince the examiner that you know your subject.

Your approach

This paper has two sections. The first section contains one question which is compulsory. The second has three questions and you must answer two of them.

You have a choice.

- Read through and answer the Section A question before moving on to Section B.
- Go through Section B and select the two questions you will attempt. Then go back and answer the question in Section A first.
- Select the two questions in Section B, answer them and then go back to Section A.

You will have fifteen minutes before the start of the exam to go through the questions you are going to do.

Time spent at the start of each question confirming the requirements and producing a plan for the answers is time well spent.

Question selection

When selecting the two questions from Section B make sure that you read through all of the requirements. It is painful to answer part (a) of a question and then realise that parts (b) and (c) are beyond you, by then it is too late to change your mind and do another question.

When reviewing the requirements look at how many marks have been allocated to each part. This will give you an idea of how detailed your answer must be.

Generally, you need to be aware of your strengths and weaknesses and select accordingly.

Doing the exam

Actually doing the exam is a personal experience. There is not a single *right way*. As long as you submit complete answers to question 1 and any two from questions 2 to 4 after the three hours are up, then your approach obviously works.

Looking through the paper

The compulsory case study question is, as will always be the case, on groups, in this case a business combination achieved in stages. You also have an associate, some foreign currency, debt factoring and ethical issues. In Section B you have three questions on a variety of topics:

* Question 2 (international and UK) is a four-part scenario involving a train operator, testing segment reporting, revenue recognition, provisions and property-related matters (IAS 16, IAS 20 and IAS 1).
* Question 3, the specialised industry question, is set in the property industry. It required an in-depth analysis of whether a lease was a finance lease, a discontinued operation and, for the international stream only, consideration of fair value of an investment property (IFRS 13).
* Question 4 is on the challenges of a move to IFRS.

You only have to answer three out of these four questions. You don't have to pick your optional questions right now, but this brief overview should have convinced you that you have enough choice and variety to have a respectable go at Section B. So let's go back to the compulsory question in Section A.

Compulsory question

Question 1 requires you to prepare a consolidated statement of financial position for a group in which there has been a business combination achieved in stages. Additional adjustments include debt factoring, a provision, capitalisation of leasehold expenses and a foreign currency contract. The key with this question, which you cannot avoid doing, is not to panic. There is a lot of number crunching, and you might not be able to complete the question. The thing to do is to set out your proformas and then patiently, but briskly, work through the workings, doing as much as you can. By using a strategy of picking the low hanging 'fruit' you could get 80% of the group aspects right which enables you to put 22 marks in the bank!

Optional questions

Deciding between the optional questions is obviously a personal matter – it depends how you have spent your study time.

Question 3 is rather more difficult than Question 2, in our opinion, because of the greater depth required for Part (a) on the finance lease (nearly half the marks for the whole question).

One thing is clear – the optional questions all contain a discursive element and are all based around a scenario. The Examiner has said that the emphasis in this paper is on giving advice in a practical situation.

The secret is to plan your answer; break it down into bite sized subsections, clearly labelled to help your examiner to quickly conclude you understand the problem and have a logical answer.

Allocating your time

The golden rule is always allocate your time according to the marks for the question in total and for the parts of the question. But be sensible. If (for example) you have committed yourself to answering Question 5, but can think of nothing to say about fair value, you may be better off trying to pick up some extra marks on the questions you can do.

Afterwards

Don't be tempted to do a post mortem on the paper with your colleagues. It will only worry you and them and it's unlikely you'll be able to remember exactly what you wrote anyway. If you really can't resist going over the topics covered in the paper, allow yourself a maximum of half an hour's 'worry time', then put it out of your head! Relax as it's all out of your hands now!

Question 1

Text reference. Business combinations achieved in stages are covered in Chapter 14; ethics in Chapter 2; the environment in Chapter 3.

Top tips. There is a lot of information in this question, but do not let this put you off. As so many marks are available for consolidation aspects, the key is to establish the group structure and work out the goodwill. This needs to be calculated only once: when Lose gains control. Note that the group aspects can be dealt with separately from the adjustments.

Easy marks. Marks are available for standard consolidation calculations, for example five marks for goodwill in Lose, which is easy once you have established the group structure. Parts (b) and (c) are fairly open ended.

Examiner's comment. In Part (a),the piecemeal acquisition was well answered, but not the effect of the above on the group reserve. Many candidates did not correctly deal with the elimination of inter group profit between the associate and the holding company generally taking out the whole of the profit rather than 30% of it. Several candidates did not consider the impairment of the associate. Many did not realise that if a payment to the supplier is a deposit and is refundable, then the amount is deemed to be a monetary amount which should be retranslated at the year end. Similarly, many candidates did not realise that the factored trade receivables should not have been derecognised and therefore should remain on the SOFP. The calculation of the share options was generally well done but the calculation of the non-controlling interest was surprisingly poorly done considering that there was relatively little adjustment required to the subsidiary's closing reserves. Candidates often had differing views as to the nature of the environmental provision and markers were instructed to give credit for a well argued case. Parts (b) and (c) of the question were quite well answered although many candidates did not spend long enough on them. The main problem with the answers to this part was failure to consider the ethical issues involved. Two professional marks were awarded for the quality of the appraisal and analysis of the position of the company in respect of its environmental and social policy. This would mean not simply regurgitating the facts of the case but having the ability to conceptualise the facts and produce key conclusions from those facts.

Marking scheme

		Marks
(a)	Goodwill – Lose	5
	Non-controlling interest	1
	Group reserves	2
	Associate and impairment	5
	Intra-group profit	2
	Foreign currency	4
	Debt factoring	4
	Share options	4
	Provision	3
	Operating lease	3
	Other statement of financial position items	2
	Maximum	35
(b)	Benefits of environmental report – Maximum	8
(c)	Discussion of ethical and social responsibility – subjective, maximum	7
	Maximum	50

(a)   BETH GROUP
       CONSOLIDATED STATEMENT OF FINANCIAL POSITION
       AS AT 30 NOVEMBER 20X7

	$m
Non-current assets	
Property, plant and equipment: 1,700 + 200 + (W6) 10 + 2 – 2	1,910
Goodwill (W2)	17
Other intangible assets	300
Investment in associate (W3)	183
	2,410
Current assets	
Inventories: 800 + 100	900
Trade receivables: 600 + 60 – 1 (W8) + 50 (W9)	709
Cash: 500 + 40	540
	2,149
Total assets	4,559
Equity and liabilities	
Equity attributable to owners of the parent	
Share capital	1,500
Retained earnings (W4)	447
Other reserves: 300 + 9 (W10)	309
	2,256
Non-controlling interests (W5)	65
	2,321
Non-current liabilities: 700 + 2 (W7) + 11 (W11)	713
Current liabilities: 1,380 + 100 + 45 (W9)	1,525
Total equity and liabilities	4,559

Workings

1   *Group structure*

	1 Dec X5		1 Dec X6	Beth			1 Dec X6
	20%	+	60% = 80%				30%
Pre-acquisition retained earnings	$80m		$150m			Pre-acquisition retained earnings	$260m

2   *Goodwill: Lose (at date control obtained)*

	$m	$m
Consideration transferred		160.00
Non-controlling interests		53.33
Fair value of previously held equity interest		53.33
Fair value of identifiable assets acquired and liabilities assumed		
Share capital	100	
Retained earnings	150	
		(250.00)
		16.66

3   *Investment in associate*

	$m
Cost	180
Share of post acquisition retained earnings (W4)	12
Unrealised profit in inventories (W6)	(3)
Impairment loss (to profit or loss/retained earnings) (bal fig)	(6)
Recoverable amount: $610 × 30%	183

4 Retained earnings

	Beth	Lose 80%	Gain
	$m	$m	$m
Per question	400.00	200	300
Profit on derecognition of investment*	13.33		
Unrealised profit (W6)	(3.00)		
Operating lease (W7): 10 – 2		8	
Foreign currency (W8)	(1.00)		
Debt factoring reversal (W9)	5.00		
Share-based payment (W10)	(9.00)		
Provision (W11)	(11.00)		
Pre-acquisition		(150)	(260)
		58	40
Group share			
Lose: 58 × 80%	46.40		
Gain: 40 × 30%	12.00		
Impairment (W3)	(6.00)		
	446.73		rounded up to 447

*Profit on derecognition of investment:

	$m
Fair value at date control obtained	53.33
Cost	(40.00)
	13.33

5 Non-controlling interests: Lose

	$m
NCI at acquisition	53.33
NCI share of post acquisition retained earnings ((W4) 58 × 20%)	11.60
	64.93

Non-controlling interest: $64.93m rounded up to $65m.

6 Unrealised profit on intra-group trading with associate (Gain)

	$m
Inventories: selling price	28
Cost	(18)
Profit	10

IAS 28 requires that Beth's share of this profit should be eliminated. Beth's share is 30% × $10m = $3m.

DEBIT	Cost of sales/retained earnings (Beth)	$3m	
CREDIT	Investment in associate		$3m

Note. The unrealised profit is eliminated from retained earnings in the books of the seller (Beth) and from inventories in the books of the holder (Gain), ie the investment in associate.

7 Lease

IAS 16 *Property, plant and equipment* requires that Lose should capitalise the leasehold improvements of $10m and depreciate them over the term of the lease. The requirement in the lease to return the building in its original condition is an obligation arising from past events, so a provision of $2m should be made for the estimated costs.

Capitalise leasehold improvements

DEBIT	Property, plant and equipment	$10m	
CREDIT	Cost of sales /retained earnings		$10m

Provide for conversion costs

DEBIT	Property, plant and equipment	$2m	
CREDIT	Non-current liability		$2m

Adjust for depreciation

DEBIT	Cost of sales/retained earnings	$2m	
	$(10 + 2) \div 6$		
CREDIT	Property, plant and equipment		$2m

Note. The PPE adjustment will affect non-controlling interest in Lose.

8   *Foreign currency contract*

The payment to the supplier is a refundable deposit. It is deemed to be a monetary amount and is re-translated at the year end.

At 1 September 20X7	$m
€12m × 50% ÷ 0.75	= 8.00

At y/e (30 November 20X7)	
€12m × 50% ÷ 0.85	= 7.06
Loss	= 0.94 (rounded to $1m)

DEBIT	Retained earnings	$1m	
CREDIT	Receivables		$1m

9   *Debt factoring*

Under IFRS 9 *Financial instruments* a financial asset must be de-recognised:

(i)   If the contractual rights to the cash flows have expired

(ii)   If the financial asset has been transferred, together with the risks and rewards

Condition (ii) has not been met. Beth still bears the risks and rewards of ownership. Accordingly, the receivable must be reinstated.

DEBIT	Receivables	$50m	
CREDIT	Retained earnings		$5m
CREDIT	Loan (current liabilities)		$45m

10   *Share options*

Following IFRS 2, a charge must be made to profit or loss and a corresponding credit to equity, as follows.

200 options × (10,000 − (600+500)) × ½ × $10
= $8.9m, rounded to $9m

DEBIT	Retained earnings	$9m	
CREDIT	Equity (Share-based payment reserve/other reserves)		$9m

11   *Provision for contamination clear up*

Following IAS 37, a provision must be recognised if and only if:

(i)   A present obligation (legal or constructive) has arisen as a result of a past event

(ii)   Payment is probable

(iii)   The amount can be measured reliably

In this case, a provision must be made for the costs of contamination only where there is a legal obligation to clean it up. A moral obligation does not justify a provision. $4m relates to costs where there is an existing law. $7m relates to a law that will come in December 20X7, but it is assumed that the law will apply retrospectively. The total provision that must be made is $(7+4)m = $11m.

DEBIT	Profit and loss/retained earnings	$11m	
CREDIT	Non-current liability		$11m

(b) **Advantages of a separate environmental report**

Most countries do not have any legal requirements to produce an environmental report, and until fairly recently, environmental reporting was not seen as important. However, there would be a number of advantages for Beth in producing an environmental report.

(i) Producing a separate report will force Beth to **improve its practices** on environmental matters, an area the group has neglected.

(ii) Customers will see the efforts the group is making, and this will **increase customer confidence** in the group and its products.

(iii) The oil industry has a negative image when it comes to environmental matters. If Beth can be shown to be making an effort, and giving a detailed report on the changes made, this will **give the group an edge over its competitors**.

(iv) Beth has a **poor reputation as a good corporate citizen**. This needs to be put right and **be seen to be put right**.

(v) The group is facing potential litigation. If it takes steps to improving environmental performance and reporting on this, it can **improve relationships with regulators,** and therefore reduce the potential threat.

(vi) Beth operates in a number of different countries, and so needs to **improve its international reputation**. The international trend is towards improving environmental performance and increased provision of environmental information. Sustained efforts in this area will enhance the group's standing in the international arena.

(vii) Environmental performance covers areas such as waste management, resources and costs. Improvements in these areas will bring **economies and efficiencies** which will improve the group's profitability.

(viii) **Management information systems will be enhanced** in order to provide environmental information.

(ix) A good quality environmental report will make Beth **attractive to investors** and financial analysts, who are keen to see evidence of sustainability.

(x) Companies Beth supplies and contracts with may have to demonstrate to their own investors that they are dealing with reputable suppliers and contractors. Good environmental practices and reporting will **make Beth a more attractive supplier and contractor** to deal with.

A separate environmental report on its own is clearly not enough to give these benefits – the report must be underpinned by **sustained action**.

(c) **Ethical and social responsibilities**

Ethics and corporate social responsibility are important in themselves, but also because they can improve business performance. At present the company is stagnating, because it has focused on maintaining market share and on its own shareholders at the expense of other stakeholders. Corporate social responsibility is concerned with a company's **accountability to a wide range of stakeholders**, not just shareholders. For Beth, the most significant of these include:

(i) Regulators
(ii) Customers
(iii) Creditors
(iv) Employees

Regulators

The relationship with regulators is not good, mainly because of a poor reputation on environmental matters. Beth just does the bare minimum, for example cleaning up contamination only when legally obliged to do so. Adopting **environmentally friendly policies** and reporting in detail on these in an environmental report will go some way towards mending the relationship. **Litigation costs**, which have a direct impact on profit, can be **avoided.**

Customers

Currently Beth provides poor customer support, and makes no effort to understand the customs and cultures of the countries in which it operates. Moreover, it makes no positive contributions and does not promote socially responsible policies. This attitude could easily **alienate its present customers and deter new ones**. A **competitor** who does make positive contributions to the community, for example in sponsoring education or environmental programmes, will be **seen as having the edge** and could take customers away from Beth. Corporate social responsibility involves **thinking long-term** about the community rather than about short-term profits, but in the long term, profits could suffer if socially responsible attitudes are not adopted.

Creditors

Suppliers are key stakeholders, who must be handled responsibly if a reputation in the wider business community is not to suffer. **Beth's policy of not paying small and medium-sized companies is very short-sighted**. While such companies may not be in a position to sue for payment, the effect on goodwill and reputation will be very damaging in the long term. Suppliers may be put off doing business with Beth. Perhaps a key component can only be sourced from a small supplier, who will not sell to Beth if word gets around that it does not pay. This **unethical and damaging policy must be discontinued** and relationships with all suppliers fostered.

Employees

Employees are very important stakeholders. Beth's authoritarian approach to management and its refusal to value employees or listen to their ideas, is **potentially damaging to business performance**. High staff turnover is costly as new staff must be recruited and trained. Employees who do not feel valued will not work as hard as those who do. In addition, **employees may have some good ideas** to contribute that would benefit performance; at the moment Beth is missing out on these ideas.

Acting responsibly and ethically is not just right; it is also profitable.

Question 2

Marking scheme

		Marks
(a)	Segment explanation up to	5
(b)	IAS 18 explanation and calculation	6
(c)	IAS 37 explanation and calculation	6
(d)	IAS 1/16/20 explanation and calculation	6
	Professional marks	2
	Available	25

(a) **Operating segments**

IFRS 8 *Operating segments* requires operating segments as defined in the standard to be reported separately if they exceed at least one of certain qualitative thresholds. Two or more operating segments **below** the thresholds may be **aggregated** to produce a reportable segment if the segments have **similar economic characteristics,** and the segments are similar in a **majority** of the following aggregation criteria:

(i)   The nature of the products and services
(ii)   The nature of the production process
(iii)   The type or class of customer for their products or services
(iv)   The methods used to distribute their products or provide their services
(v)   If applicable, the nature of the regulatory environment

Verge has aggregated segments 1 and 2, but this aggregation may not be permissible under IFRS 8. While the products and services are similar, the **customers for those products and services are different.** Therefore the fourth aggregation criteria has not been met.

In the local market, the decision to award the contract is in the hands of the local authority, which also sets prices and pays for the services. The **company is not exposed to passenger revenue risk**, since a contract is awarded by competitive tender. It could be argued that the local authority is the major customer in the local market.

By contrast, in the inter-city train market, the **customer ultimately determines whether a train route is economically viabl**e by choosing whether or not to buy tickets. Verge sets the ticket prices, but will be influenced by customer behaviour or feedback. The **company is exposed to passenger revenue risk**, as it sets prices which customers may or may not choose to pay.

It is possible that the fifth criteria, regulatory environment, is not met, since the local authority is imposing a different set of rules to that which applies in the inter-city market.

In conclusion, the two segments have different economic characteristics and so **should be reported as separate segments** rather than aggregated.

(b) **Maintenance contract**

The applicable standards here are IFRS 15 *Revenue from contracts with customers* and IAS 8 *Accounting policies, changes in accounting estimates and errors.*

Recognition of revenue from the maintenance contract

IFRS 15 *Revenue from contracts with customers* states that the entity must **determine the transaction price** (Step (iii) of the IFRS 15 five-step process for revenue recognition). The transaction price is the amount of consideration a company expects to be entitled to from the customer in exchange for transferring goods or services and must take account of the time value of money, if material.

Under IFRS 15, an entity must **adjust the promised amount of consideration for the effects of the time value of money if the timing of payments** agreed to by the parties to the contract (either explicitly or implicitly) **provides the customer or the entity with a significant benefit of financing** the transfer of goods or services to the customer. In those circumstances, the contract contains a **significant financing component**. A significant financing component may exist regardless of whether the promise of financing is explicitly stated in the contract or implied by the payment terms agreed to by the parties to the contract.

Where the inflow of cash or cash equivalents is **deferred,** the amount of the inflow must be **discounted** because the fair value is less than the nominal amount. In effect, this is partly a financing transaction, with Verge providing interest-free credit to the government body. The **market rate of interest**, here 6%, must be used to calculate the discounted amount, and the difference between this and the cash eventually received recognised as interest income.

IFRS 15 revenue recognition process (Step (v)) would treat this as a **performance obligation satisfied over time** because the customer simultaneously receives and consumes the benefits as the performance takes place. Verge must therefore **recognise revenue from the contract as the services are provided,** that is.

as work is performed throughout the contract's life, and not as the cash is received. The invoices sent by Verge reflect the work performed in each year, but the amounts must be **discounted in order to report the revenue at fair value**. The exception is the $1 million paid at the beginning of the contract. This is paid in advance and therefore not discounted, but it is invoiced and recognised in the year ended 31 March 20X2. The remainder of the amount invoiced in the year ended 31 March 20X2 ($2.8m − $1m = $1.8m) is discounted at 6% for two years.

In the year ended 31 March 20X3, the invoiced amount of $1.2m will be discounted at 6% for only one year. There will also be interest income of $96,000, which is the **unwinding of the discount** in 20X2.

Recognised in y/e 31 March 20X2

	$m
Initial payment (not discounted)	1.0
Remainder invoiced at 31 March 20X2: $1.8 \times \dfrac{1}{1.06^2}$	1.6
Revenue recognised	2.6

Recognised in y/e 31 March 20X3

Revenue: $\$1.2m \times \dfrac{1}{1.06} = \$1.13m$

Unwinding of the discount on revenue recognised in 20X2 $1.6m \times 6\% = \$96,000$
Correction of prior period error

The accounting treatment previously used by Verge was incorrect because it did not comply with IAS 18. Consequently, the change to the new, correct policy is **the correction of an error rather than a change of accounting policy**.

Prior period errors, under IAS 8 *Accounting policies, changes in accounting estimates and errors*, result from failure to use or misuse of information that:

(i)   Was available when financial information for the period(s) in question was available for issue; and

(ii)   Could reasonably be expected to have been obtained and taken into account in the preparation and presentation of those financial statements.

IAS 18 includes the effects of mistakes in applying accounting policies, mathematical mistakes and oversights. Only including $1m of revenue in the financial statements for the year ended 31 March 20X2 is clearly a mistake on the part of Verge. As a prior period error, it **must be corrected retrospectively**. This involves **restating the comparative figures** in the financial statements for 20X3 (ie, the 20X2 figures) and **restating the opening balances** for 20X3 so that the financial statements are presented as if the error had never occurred.

(c)   **Legal claim**

A **provision** is defined by IAS 37 *Provisions, contingent liabilities and contingent assets* as **a liability of uncertain timing or amount**. IAS 37 states that a provision should only be recognised if:

•   There is a **present obligation** as the result of a **past event**
•   An **outflow of resources embodying economic benefits is probable**, and
•   A **reliable estimate** of the amount can be made

If these conditions apply, a provision must be recognised.

The past event that gives rise, under IAS 37, to a present obligation, is known as the **obligating event.** The obligation may be legal, or it may be constructive (as when past practice creates a valid expectation on the part of a third party). The entity must have **no realistic alternative but to settle** the obligation.

Year ended 31 March 20X2

In this case, the obligating event is the damage to the building, and it took place in the year ended 31 March 20X2. As at that date, no legal proceedings had been started, and the damage appeared to be superficial. While Verge should recognise an obligation to pay damages, at 31 March 20X2 **the amount of any provision would be immaterial**. It would a best estimate of the amount required to settle the obligation at that date,

taking into account all relevant risks and uncertainties, and at the year end the amount does not look as if it will be substantial.

Year ended 31 March 20X3

IAS 37 requires that **provisions should be reviewed at the end of each accounting period for any material changes** to the best estimate previously made. The legal action will cause such a material change, and Verge will be required to reassess the estimate of likely damages. While the local company is claiming damages of $1.2m, Verge is not obliged to make a provision for this amount, but rather should **base its estimate on the legal advice** it has received and the opinion of the expert, both of which put the value of the building at $800,000. This amount should be provided for as follows.

DEBIT   Profit or loss for the year $800,000
CREDIT   Provision for damages $800,000

Some or all of the expenditure needed to settle a provision may be expected to be recovered form a third party, in this case the insurance company. If so, the **reimbursement should be recognised only when it is virtually certain that reimbursement will be received if the entity settles the obligation**.

- The reimbursement should be treated as a **separate asset,** and the amount recognised should **not be greater than the provision itself**.

- The provision and the amount recognised for reimbursement **may be netted off in profit or loss** for the year.

There is no reason to believe that the insurance company will not settle the claim for the first $200,000 of damages, and so the company **should accrue for the reimbursement** as follows.

DEBIT   Receivables $200,000
CREDIT   Profit or loss for the year $200,000

Verge lost the court case and is required to pay $300,000. This was after the financial statements were authorised, however, and so it is **not an adjusting event** per IAS 10 *Events after the reporting period*. Accordingly the amount of the provision as at 31 March 20X3 does not need to be adjusted.

(d) **Gift of building**

The applicable standards here are IAS 16 *Property, plant and equipment,* and IAS 20 *Accounting for government grants and disclosure of government assistance,* within the framework of IAS 1 *Presentation of financial statements.* IAS 1 requires that all items of income and expense recognised in a period should be included in profit or loss for the period unless a standard or interpretation requires or permits a different treatment.

IAS 16: recognition of building

IAS 16 states that the **cost** of an item of property, plant and equipment should be **recognised when two conditions** have been fulfilled:

- It is probable that future economic benefits associated with the item will flow to the entity.
- The cost of the item can be measured reliably.

These conditions are normally fulfilled when the risks and rewards have transferred to the entity, and they may be assumed to transfer **when the contract is unconditional and irrevocable**. As at 31 March 20X2, the condition of use has **not been complied** with and Verge has not taken possession of the building.

The building may, however, be recognised in the year ended 31 March 20X3, as the conditions of donation were met in February 20X3. The **fair value** of the building of $1.5m must be recognised as income in **profit or loss** for the year, as it was a gift. The **refurbishment and adaptation cost must also be included** as part of the cost of the asset in the statement of financial position, because, according to IAS 16, the cost includes **directly attributable costs of bringing the asset to the location and condition necessary** for it to be capable of operating in a manner intended by management. The transactions should be recorded as follows.

DEBIT   Property, plant and equipment $2.5m
CREDIT   Profit or loss for the year $1.5m
CREDIT   Cash/payables $1m

In addition, the building would be depreciated in accordance with the entity's accounting policy, which could (depending on the policy) involve time apportioning over one or two months (February and March 20X3), depending on when in February the building came into use as a museum.

IAS 20: Government grant

The principle behind IAS 20 *Accounting for government grants and disclosure of government assistance* is that of accruals or matching: the **grant received must be matched with the related costs** on a systematic basis. Grants receivable as compensation for costs already incurred, or for immediate financial support with no future related costs, should be recognised as income in the period in which they are receivable.

Government grants are assistance by government in the form of transfers of resources to an entity in return for past or future compliance with certain conditions relating to the operating activities of the entity. There are two main types of grants:

(i) **Grants related to assets**: grants whose primary condition is that an entity qualifying for them should purchase, construct or otherwise acquire long-term assets.

(ii) **Grants related to income**: These are government grants other than grants related to assets.

It is not always easy to match costs and revenues, but in this case the terms of the grant are explicit about the expense to which the grant is meant to contribute. **Part of the grant** relates to the **creation of jobs** and this amount (20 × $5,000 = $100,000) should be **taken to income.**

The **rest of the grant** ($250,000 – $100,000 = $150,000) should be recognised as **capital-based grant** (grant relating to assets). IAS 20 would **two possible approaches** for the capital-based portion of the grant.

(i) Match against the depreciation of the building using a deferred income approach.
(ii) Deduct from the carrying value of the building, resulting in a reduced depreciation charge.

The double entry would be:

DEBIT	Cash	$250,000	
CREDIT	Profit or loss		$100,000
CREDIT	Deferred income/PPE (depending on the accounting policy)		$150,000

If a deferred income approach is adopted, the **deferred income would be released over the life of the building and matched against depreciation**. Depending on the policy, both may be time apportioned because conditions were only met in February 20X3.

Question 3

Marking scheme

		Marks
(a)	Leases explanation up to	12
(b)	Investment properties explanation	5
(c)	IFRS 5 explanation	6
	Professional marks	2
	Available	25

(a) **Lease of land from Maret**

The relevant considerations here are the **lease classification criteria** in IAS 17 *Leases,* and the fact that **land normally has an indefinite economic life**. IAS 17 distinguishes between operating leases and finance leases. A finance lease is a lease that **transfers substantially all the risks and rewards incidental to ownership of an asset**. All other leases are classified as operating leases. A lease of land with a long term may be classified as a finance lease, even if title is not transferred to the lessee, as here. The classification, which is made at the inception of the lease, depends on the **substance** rather than the form, and includes the following situations, which are relevant here.

(i) The lease transfers ownership of the asset to the lessee by the end of the lease term;

(ii) The lessee has the ability to continue to lease for a secondary period at a rent that is substantially lower than market rent;

(iii) The lessee has the option to purchase the asset at a price which is expected to be sufficiently lower than fair value at the date the option becomes exercisable that, at the inception of the lease, it is reasonably certain that the option will be exercised;

(iv)   At the inception of the lease, the present value of the minimum lease payments amounts to at least substantially all of the fair value of the leased asset and

(v)   The lease term is for the major part of the economic life of the asset even if title is not transferred.

Considering points (i),(ii) and (iii) the lease does not automatically transfer ownership by the end of the lease term. However, Janne has the **option**, of leasing the land indefinitely for a minimal rent, or purchasing it at price significantly lower than the market price. This indicates that Maret expects to achieve its return on investment mainly through the lease payments, after which it effectively ceases to have the risks and rewards of ownership. This **would indicate that the lease is a finance lease**. Conversely, **the lack of a purchase option if the lease is extended at an immaterial rent may indicate an operating lease**: if Maret does not expect to achieve its return on investment through Janne's lease payments, and is hoping to achieve this through a subsequent lease or sale. If so, then the lease will not be for a major part of the asset's economic life as land has an indefinite economic life, and this would also point to the lease being an operating lease.

Considering next the issue of the **minimum lease payments**, it should be noted that there is a contingent rent, based on the market value of the land. A contingent rent is one that is not fixed at the inception of the lease but is dependent on a future uncertain event. **IAS 17 excludes contingent rents from minimum lease payments** as used in calculating whether point (iv) above applies, and requires them to be accounted for as income or expense in the period in which they are incurred. If the nature of the contingency on which the rents are based suggests that risks and rewards of ownership have not been transferred to the lessee, then contingent rents may indicate that the lease is an operating lease. Here the contingency (value of the land) suggests that Janne does bear some of the risks and rewards of ownership.

More importantly, the lease premium is 70% of the fair value of the land and the rent is at least 4% of the value of the land for 30 years, and so the **minimum lease payment criterion has been met.** In addition, the lessor has ensured that it will achieve the return on the investment by stipulating a revision of the rent every five years.

In conclusion, it would appear that the **lease of the land is a finance lease**. The accounting treatment is as follows.

(i)   Capitalise the upfront premium and the present value of the lease payments at the beginning of the lease as property, plant and equipment.

(ii)   Show the present value of the annual lease payments as a liability.

(iii)   Recognise the interest expense over the lease term so as to produce a constant periodic rate of interest on the remaining balance of the liability.

If Janne decides to **hold the land for capital gain**, then the lease may meet the definition of an **investment property**. If so, IAS 40 *Investment property* will apply, and Janne will need to account for the land using either the fair value model or the cost model.

Maret has suggested a 'clean break' clause. If a lease contains a **clean break clause,** that is, Janne would be free to walk away from the lease agreement after a certain time without penalty. In such cases **the lease term** for accounting purposes will normally be **the period between the commencement of the lease and the earliest point at which the break option is exercisable by the lessee**. If there is a penalty for early termination (before the stipulated time), and the penalty is such as to recover the lessor's investment, then the termination clause is normally disregarded for the purpose of determining the lease term. In this case the **implication of Maret's proposals is that its return on investment would be achieved after 25 years** – any earlier and the compensation payable must cover it. This points to the lease being a **finance lease**.

(b)   **Fair value**

IAS 40 *Investment property* allows two methods for valuing investment property: the fair value model and the cost model. If the fair value method is adopted, **then the investment property must be valued in accordance with IFRS 13** *Fair value measurement.* This is a recent standard, giving a common framework for guidance on measuring fair value. It defines fair value as: 'the price that would be received to sell an asset or paid to transfer a liability in an orderly transaction between market participants at the measurement date'.

Fair value is a market-based measurement rather than specific to the entity, so a company is not allowed to choose its own way of measuring fair value. IFRS 13 states that valuation techniques must be those which are appropriate and for which sufficient data are available. Entities should maximise the use of relevant **observable inputs** and minimise the use of **unobservable inputs**. The standard establishes a three-level hierarchy for the inputs that valuation techniques use to measure fair value.

Level 1 Quoted prices (unadjusted) in active markets for identical assets or liabilities that the reporting entity can access at the measurement date

Level 2 Inputs other than quoted prices included within Level 1 that are observable for the asset or liability, either directly or indirectly, eg quoted prices for similar assets in active markets or for identical or similar assets in non-active markets or use of quoted interest rates for valuation purposes

Level 3 Unobservable inputs for the asset or liability, ie using the entity's own assumptions about market exit value

Although the directors claim that 'new-build value less obsolescence' is accepted by the industry, it **may not be in accordance with IFRS 13**. As the fair value hierarchy suggests, IFRS 13 favours Level 1 inputs, that is market-based measures, over unobservable (Level 3) inputs. Due to the nature of investment property, which is often unique and not traded on a regular basis, fair value measurements are likely to be categorised as Level 2 or Level 3 valuations.

IFRS 13 mentions three valuation techniques: the market approach, the income approach and the cost approach. A market or income approach would usually be more appropriate for an investment property than a cost approach. The 'new-build value less obsolescence' (cost approach) does not take account of the Level 2 inputs such as sales value (market approach) and market rent (income approach). Nor does it take account of reliable estimates of future discounted cash flows, or values of similar properties.

In conclusion, **Janne must apply IFRS 13** to the valuation of its investment property, taking account of Level 2 inputs.

(c)   **Disposal group held for sale**

IFRS 5 classifies a disposal group as held for sale where its carrying amount will be recovered principally through sale rather than use. The held for sale criteria in IFRS 5 *Non-current assets held for sale and discontinued operations* are very strict, and often decision to sell an asset or disposal group is made well before they are met.

IFRS requires an asset or disposal group to be classified as held for sale where it is **available for immediate sale** in its **present condition** subject only to **terms that are usual** and customary and the sale is **highly probable**.

The standard does not give guidance on **terms that are usual and customary** but the guidance notes give examples. Such terms may include, for example, a specified period of time for the seller to vacate a headquarters building that is to be sold, or it may include contracts or surveys. However, they would not include terms imposed by the seller that are not customary, for example, a seller could not continue to use its headquarters building until construction of a new headquarters building had taken place.

For a sale to be **highly probable**:

*   Management must be **committed** to the sale.
*   An **active programme to locate a buyer** must have been initiated.
*   The asset must be **marketed at a price** that is **reasonable in relation to its own fair value**
*   The sale must be **expected to be completed within one year** from the date of classification.
*   It is **unlikely** that **significant changes** will be made to the plan **or the plan withdrawn**.

In **exceptional circumstances**, a disposal group may be classified as held for sale or **discontinued after a period of 12 months**:

(i)   Circumstances arose during the initial twelve-month period that were previously considered unlikely, and the disposal group was not sold.

(ii)   During the twelve-month period, the entity took steps to respond to the change in circumstances by actively marketing the disposal group at a price that is reasonable in the light of the change in circumstances, and the held-for-sale criteria are met.

The draft agreements and correspondence with bankers are **not specific enough** to prove that the subsidiary met the IFRS 5 criteria at the date it was classified. In addition, the **organisational changes** made by Janne in the year to 31 May 20X3 are a **good indication that the subsidiary was not available for sale in its present condition at the point of classification**. Additional activities have been transferred to the subsidiary, which is not an insignificant change.

Finally, the shareholders' authorisation was given for a year from 1 January 20X2. There is **no evidence that this authorisation was extended beyond 1 January 20X3**. The **subsidiary should therefore be treated as a continuing operation** in the financial statements for the year ended 31 May 20X2 and 31 May 20X3.

Question 4

Marking scheme

		Marks
(a)	Changes from national GAAP	2
	Complexity	1
	Recognition, measurement, disclosure	2
	Alternative forms of presentation	1
	Inconsistent principles	2
	Alternative accounting treatments	3
	Little industry related guidance	1
	IFRS I	2
	Interpretation of IFRS	2
	Adoption date	1
		17
(b)	Management judgements	2
	Disclosure of sensitivity	1
	Regulatory infrastructure	2
	Training/markets	1
	Communication	2
		8
	Maximum	25

(a) **The challenge**

Implementation of International Financial Reporting Standards entails **a great deal of work** for many companies, particularly those in countries where local GAAP has not been so onerous. For example, many jurisdictions will not have had such detailed rules about recognition, measurement and presentation of financial instruments, and many will have had no rules at all about share-based payment.

A challenge for preparers of financial statements is also **a challenge for users**. When financial statements become far more complex under IFRS than they were under local GAAP, users may find them hard to understand, and consequently of little relevance.

Presentation

Many developed countries have legislation requiring set formats and layouts for financial statements. For example, in the UK there is the Companies Act 2006. IFRS demands that presentation is in accordance with IAS 1 *Presentation of financial statements,* but this standard allows alternative forms of presentation. In choosing between alternatives, **countries tend to adopt the format that is closest to local GAAP**, even if this is not necessarily the best format. For example, UK companies are likely to adopt the two-statement format for the statement of profit or loss and other comprehensive income, because this is closest to the old profit and loss account and statement of total recognised gains and losses.

Concepts and interpretation

Although later IAS and IFRS are based to an extent on the IASB *Conceptual Framework,* there is **no consistent set of principles** underlying them. The *Conceptual Framework* itself is being revised, and there is controversy over the direction the revision should take. Consequently, preparers of accounts are likely to think in terms of the conceptual frameworks – if any – that they have used in developing local GAAP, and these may be different from that of the IASB. German accounts, for example, have traditionally been aimed at the tax authorities.

Where IFRS themselves give clear guidance, this may not matter, but where there is uncertainty, preparers of accounts will fall back on their traditional conceptual thinking.

Choice of accounting treatment

Although many so-called 'allowed alternatives' have been eliminated from IFRS in recent years, choice of treatment remains. For example, IAS 16 *Property, plant and equipment* gives a choice of either the cost model or the revaluation model for a class of property, plant or equipment.

It could be argued that choice is a good thing, as companies should be able to select the treatment that most fairly reflects the underlying reality. However, in the context of change to IFRS, there is a danger that companies **will choose the alternative that closely matches the approach followed under local GAAP, or the one that is easier to implement**, regardless of whether this is the best choice.

Choice of recognition or measurement method

An example of **potential inconsistency** is IAS 21 *The effects of changes in foreign exchange rates.* The identification of the functional currency under this standard can be a subjective process, with arguments on either side. Revenue recognition is also an aspect of accounting that can cause considerable variation between companies and between countries, even if they all adopt IAS 18 *Revenue,* because this standard allows variations in recognition methods. For example some companies with customer loyalty programmes may defer part of the revenue received.

Inconsistency of timing and exemptions taken

IFRSs have provision for early adoption, and this can affect comparability, although impact of a new standard must be disclosed under IAS 8 *Accounting policies, changes in accounting estimates and errors.* Further, IFRS 1 *First time adoption of International Financial Reporting Standards* permits a number of exemptions during the periods of transition to IFRS. This gives scope for manipulation, if **exemptions are 'cherry-picked'** to produce a favourable picture.

(b) **Impact of management judgement on IFRS financial statements**

The extent of the impact will vary, depending on how developed local GAAP was before the transition. However, in general it is likely that **management judgement will have a greater impact** on financial statements prepared under IFRS than under local GAAP. The main reasons for this are as follows.

(i) The **volume** of rules and number of areas addressed by IFRS is likely to be greater than that under local GAAP.

(ii) Many issues are perhaps **addressed for the first time**, for example share-based payment.

(iii) IFRSs are likely to be **more complex** than local standards.

(iv) IFRSs allow **choice** in many cases, which leads to subjectivity.

(v) Selection of **valuation method** requires judgement, and many IFRS leave the choice of method open. This affects areas such as pensions, impairment, intangible assets acquired in business combinations, onerous contracts and share-based payment.

Financial reporting infrastructure

As well as sound management judgement, implementation of IFRS requires a sound financial reporting infrastructure. Key aspects of this include the following.

(i) A **robust regulatory framework**. For IFRS to be successful, they must be rigorously enforced.

(ii) **Trained and qualified staff**. Many preparers of financial statements will have been trained in local GAAP and not be familiar with the principles underlying IFRS, let alone the detail. Some professional bodies provide conversion qualifications – for example, the ACCA's Diploma in International Financial Reporting – but the availability of such qualifications and courses may vary from country to country.

(iii) **Availability and transparency of market information**. This is particularly important in the determination of fair values, which are such a key component of many IFRSs.

(iv) **High standards of corporate governance and audit**. This is all the more important in the transition period, especially where there is resistance to change.

Overall, there are significant advantages to the widespread adoption of IFRS, but if the transition is to go well, there must be a realistic assessment of potential challenges.

ACCA

Paper P2

Corporate Reporting (International)

Mock Examination 3

December 2014

Question Paper	
Time allowed	
Reading and planning	**15 minutes**
Writing	**3 hours**
This paper is divided into two sections	
Section A	This ONE question is compulsory and MUST be attempted
Section B	TWO questions ONLY to be answered

DO NOT OPEN THIS PAPER UNTIL YOU ARE READY TO START UNDER EXAMINATION CONDITIONS

SECTION A – This ONE question is compulsory and MUST be attempted

Question 1

(a)   Joey, a public limited company operates in the media sector. Joey has investments in two companies. The draft statements of financial position at 30 November 20X4 are as follows.

	Joey $m	Margy $m	Hulty $m
Assets			
Non-current assets			
Property, plant and equipment	3,295	2,000	1,200
Investments in subsidiaries and other investments			
Margy	1,675		
Hulty	700		
	5,670	2,000	1,200
Current assets	985	861	150
Total assets	6,655	2,861	1,350
Equity and liabilities			
Share capital	850	1,020	600
Retained earnings	3,340	980	350
Other components of equity	250	80	40
Total equity	4,440	2,080	990
Non-current liabilities	1,895	675	200
Current liabilities	320	106	160
Total liabilities	2,215	781	360
Total equity and liabilities	6,655	2,861	1,350

The following information is relevant to the preparation of the group financial statements.

(i)   On 1 December 20X1, Joey acquired 30% of the ordinary shares of Margy for a cash consideration of $600 million when the fair value of Margy's identifiable net assets was $1,840 million. Joey treated Margy as an associate and has equity accounted for Margy up to 1 December 20X3. Joey's share of Margy's undistributed profit amounted to $90 million and its share of a revaluation gain amounted to $10 million. On 1 December 20X3, Joey acquired a further 40% of the ordinary shares of Margy for a cash consideration of $975 million and gained control of the company. The cash consideration has been added to the equity accounted balance for Margy at 1 December 20X3 to give the carrying amount at 30 November 20X4.

At 1 December 20X3, the fair value of Margy's identifiable net assets was $2,250 million. At 1 December 20X3, the fair value of the equity interest in Margy held by Joey before the business combination was $705 million and the fair value of the non-controlling interest of 30% was assessed as $620 million. The retained earnings and other components of equity of Margy at 1 December 20X3 were $900 million and $70 million respectively. It is group policy to measure the non-controlling interest at fair value.

(ii)   At the time of the business combination with Margy, Joey has included in the fair value of Margy's identifiable net assets, an unrecognised contingent liability of $6 million in respect of a warranty claim in progress against Margy. In March 20X4, there was a revision of the estimate of the liability to $5 million. The amount has met the criteria to be recognised as a provision in current liabilities in the financial statements of Margy and the revision of the estimate is deemed to be a measurement period adjustment.

(iii) Additionally, buildings with a carrying amount of $200 million had been included in the fair valuation of Margy at 1 December 20X3. The buildings have a remaining useful life of 20 years at 1 December 20X3. However, Joey had commissioned an independent valuation of the buildings of Margy which was not complete at 1 December 20X3 and therefore not considered in the fair value of the identifiable net assets at the acquisition date. The valuations were received on 1 April 20X4 and resulted in a decrease of $40 million in the fair value of property, plant and equipment at the date of acquisition. This decrease does not affect the fair value of the non-controlling interest at acquisition and has not been entered into the financial statements of Margy. Buildings are depreciated on the straight-line basis and it is group policy to leave revaluation gains on disposal in equity. The excess of the fair value of the net assets over their carrying value, at 1 December 20X3, is due to an increase in the value of non-depreciable land and the contingent liability.

(iv) On 1 December 20X3, Joey acquired 80% of the equity interests of Hulty, a private entity, in exchange for cash of $700 million. Because the former owners of Hulty needed to dispose of the investment quickly, they did not have sufficient time to market the investment to many potential buyers. The fair value of the identifiable net assets was $960 million. Joey determined that the fair value of the 20% non-controlling interest in Hulty at that date was $250 million. Joey reviewed the procedures used to identify and measure the assets acquired and liabilities assumed and to measure the fair value of both the non-controlling interest and the consideration transferred. After that review, Hulty determined that the procedures and resulting measures were appropriate. The retained earnings and other components of equity of Hulty at 1 December 20X3 were $300 million and $40 million respectively. The excess in fair value is due to an unrecognised franchise right, which Joey had granted to Hulty on 1 December 20X2 for five years. At the time of the acquisition, the franchise right could be sold for its market price. It is group policy to measure the non-controlling interest at fair value.

All goodwill arising on acquisitions has been impairment tested with no impairment being required.

(v) Joey is looking to expand into publishing and entered into an arrangement with Content Publishing (CP), a public limited company, on 1 December 20X3. CP will provide content for a range of books and online publications.

CP is entitled to a royalty calculated as 10% of sales and 30% of gross profit of the publications. Joey has sole responsibility for all printing, binding, and platform maintenance of the online website. The agreement states that key strategic sales and marketing decisions must be agreed jointly. Joey selects the content to be covered in the publications but CP has the right of veto over this content. However on 1 June 20X4, Joey and CP decided to set up a legal entity, JCP, with equal shares and voting rights. CP continues to contribute content into JCP but does not receive royalties. Joey continues the printing, binding and platform maintenance. The sales and cost of sales in the period were $5 million and $2 million respectively. The whole of the sale proceeds and the costs of sales were recorded in Joey's financial statements with no accounting entries being made for JCP or amounts due to CP. Joey currently funds the operations. Assume that the sales and costs accrue evenly throughout the year and that all of the transactions relating to JCP have been in cash.

(vi) At 30 November 20X3, Joey carried a property in its statement of financial position at its revalued amount of $14 million in accordance with IAS 16 *Property, plant and equipment*. Depreciation is charged at $300,000 per year on the straight line basis. In March 20X4, the management decided to sell the property and it was advertised for sale. By 31 March 20X4, the sale was considered to be highly probable and the criteria for IFRS 5 *Non-current assets held for sale and discontinued operations* were met at this date. At that date, the asset's fair value was $15·4 million and its value in use was $15·8 million. Costs to sell the asset were estimated at $300,000. On 30 November 20X4, the property was sold for $15·6 million. The transactions regarding the property are deemed to be material and no entries have been made in the financial statements regarding this property since 30 November 20X3 as the cash receipts from the sale were not received until December 20X4.

Required

Prepare the group consolidated statement of financial position of Joey as at 30 November 20X4.

(35 marks)

(b)   The Joey Group wishes to expand its operations. As part of this expansion, it has granted options to the employees of Margy and Hulty over its own shares as at 7 December 20X4. The awards vest immediately. Joey is not proposing to make a charge to the subsidiaries for these options.

Joey does not know how to account for this transaction in its own, the subsidiaries, and the group financial statements.

Required

Explain to Joey how the above transaction should be dealt with in its own, the subsidiaries', and the group financial statements.   **(8 marks)**

(c)   Joey's directors feel that they need a significant injection of capital in order to modernise plant and equipment as the company has been promised new orders if it can produce goods to an international quality. The bank's current lending policies require borrowers to demonstrate good projected cash flow, as well as a level of profitability which would indicate that repayments would be made. However, the current projected cash flow statement would not satisfy the bank's criteria for lending. The directors have told the bank that the company is in an excellent financial position, that the financial results and cash flow projections will meet the criteria and that the chief accountant will forward a report to this effect shortly. The chief accountant has only recently joined Joey and has openly stated that he cannot afford to lose his job because of his financial commitments.

Required

Discuss the potential ethical conflicts which may arise in the above scenario and the ethical principles which would guide how a professional accountant should respond in this situation.   **(7 marks)**

(Total = 50 marks)

Section B – TWO questions ONLY to be attempted

Question 2

(a) Coatmin is a government-controlled bank. Coatmin was taken over by the government during the recent financial crisis. Coatmin does not directly trade with other government-controlled banks but has underwritten the development of the nationally owned railway and postal service. The directors of Coatmin are concerned about the volume and cost of disclosing its related party interests because they extend theoretically to all other government-controlled enterprises and banks. They wish general advice on the nature and importance of the disclosure of related party relationships and specific advice on the disclosure of the above relationships in the financial statements.. **(5 marks)**

(b) At the start of the financial year to 30 November 20X3, Coatmin gave a financial guarantee contract on behalf of one of its subsidiaries, a charitable organisation, committing it to repay the principal amount of $60 million if the subsidiary defaulted on any payments due under a loan. The loan related to the financing of the construction of new office premises and has a term of three years. It is being repaid by equal annual instalments of principal with the first payment having been paid. Coatmin has not secured any compensation in return for giving the guarantee, but assessed that it had a fair value of $1·2 million. The guarantee is measured at fair value through profit or loss. The guarantee was given on the basis that it was probable that it would not be called upon. At 30 November 20X4, Coatmin became aware of the fact that the subsidiary was having financial difficulties with the result that it has not paid the second instalment of principal. It is assessed that it is probable that the guarantee will now be called. However, just before the signing of the financial statements for the year ended 30 November 20X4, the subsidiary secured a donation which enabled it to make the second repayment before the guarantee was called upon. It is now anticipated that the subsidiary will be able to meet the final payment. Discounting is immaterial and the fair value of the guarantee is higher than amount of the loss allowance determined in accordance with the IFRS 9 (revised July 2014) rules on expected credit losses. Coatmin wishes to know the principles behind accounting for the above guarantee under IFRS and how the transaction would be accounted for in the financial records.

(7 marks)

(c) Coatmin's creditworthiness has been worsening but it has entered into an interest rate swap agreement which acts as a hedge against a $2 million 2% bond issue which matures on 31 May 20X6. Coatmin wishes to know the circumstances in which it can use hedge accounting. In particular, it needs advice on hedge effectiveness and whether this can be calculated. **(7 marks)**

(d) Coatmin provides loans to customers and funds the loans by selling bonds in the market. The liability is designated as at fair value through profit or loss. The bonds have a fair value increase of $50 million in the year to 30 November 20X4 of which $5 million relates to the reduction in Coatmin's creditworthiness. The directors of Coatmin would like advice on how to account for this movement.

(4 marks)

Required

Discuss, with suitable calculations where necessary, the accounting treatment of the above transactions in the financial statements of Coatmin.

Note. The mark allocation is shown against each of the questions above.

Professional marks will be awarded in question 2 for clarity and quality of the presentation. **(2 marks)**

(Total = 25 marks)

Question 3

(a)   Kayte operates in the shipping industry and owns vessels for transportation. In June 20X4, Kayte acquired Ceemone whose assets were entirely investments in small companies. The small companies each owned and operated one or two shipping vessels. There were no employees in Ceemone or the small companies. At the acquisition date, there were only limited activities related to managing the small companies as most activities were outsourced. All the personnel in Ceemone were employed by a separate management company. The companies owning the vessels had an agreement with the management company concerning assistance with chartering, purchase and sale of vessels and any technical management. The management company used a shipbroker to assist with some of these tasks.

     Kayte accounted for the investment in Ceemone as an asset acquisition. The consideration paid and related transaction costs were recognised as the acquisition price of the vessels. Kayte argued that the vessels were only passive investments and that Ceemone did not own a business consisting of processes, since all activities regarding commercial and technical management were outsourced to the management company. As a result, the acquisition was accounted for as if the vessels were acquired on a stand-alone basis.

     Additionally, Kayte had borrowed heavily to purchase some vessels and was struggling to meet its debt obligations. Kayte had sold some of these vessels but in some cases, the bank did not wish Kayte to sell the vessel. In these cases, the vessel was transferred to a new entity, in which the bank retained a variable interest based upon the level of the indebtedness. Kayte's directors felt that the entity was a subsidiary of the bank and are uncertain as to whether they have complied with the requirements of IFRS 3 *Business combinations* and IFRS 10 *Consolidated financial statements* as regards the above transactions. **(12 marks)**

(b)   Kayte's vessels constitute a material part of its total assets. The economic life of the vessels is estimated to be 30 years, but the useful life of some of the vessels is only 10 years because Kayte's policy is to sell these vessels when they are 10 years old. Kayte estimated the residual value of these vessels at sale to be half of acquisition cost and this value was assumed to be constant during their useful life. Kayte argued that the estimates of residual value used were conservative in view of an immature market with a high degree of uncertainty and presented documentation which indicated some vessels were being sold for a price considerably above carrying value. Broker valuations of the residual value were considerably higher than those used by Kayte. Kayte argued against broker valuations on the grounds that it would result in greater volatility in reporting.

     Kayte keeps some of the vessels for the whole 30 years and these vessels are required to undergo an engine overhaul in dry dock every 10 years to restore their service potential, hence the reason why some of the vessels are sold. The residual value of the vessels kept for 30 years is based upon the steel value of the vessel at the end of its economic life. At the time of purchase, the service potential which will be required to be restored by the engine overhaul is measured based on the cost as if it had been performed at the time of the purchase of the vessel. In the current period, one of the vessels had to have its engine totally replaced after only eight years. Normally, engines last for the 30-year economic life if overhauled every 10 years. Additionally, one type of vessel was having its funnels replaced after 15 years but the funnels had not been depreciated separately. **(11 marks)**

Required

Discuss the accounting treatment of the above transactions in the financial statements of Kayte.

Note. The mark allocation is shown against each of the elements above.

Professional marks will be awarded in question 3 for clarity and quality of presentation. **(2 marks)**

(Total = 25 marks)

Question 4

(a) An assessment of accounting practices for asset impairments is especially important in the context of financial reporting quality in that it requires the exercise of considerable management judgement and reporting discretion. The importance of this issue is heightened during periods of ongoing economic uncertainty as a result of the need for companies to reflect the loss of economic value in a timely fashion through the mechanism of asset write-downs. There are many factors which can affect the quality of impairment accounting and disclosures. These factors include changes in circumstance in the reporting period, the market capitalisation of the entity, the allocation of goodwill to cash generating units, valuation issues and the nature of the disclosures.

Required

Discuss the importance and significance of the above factors when conducting an impairment test under IAS 36 *Impairment of assets*. **(13 marks)**

(b) (i) Estoil is an international company providing parts for the automotive industry. It operates in many different jurisdictions with different currencies. During 20X4, Estoil experienced financial difficulties marked by a decline in revenue, a reorganisation and restructuring of the business and it reported a loss for the year. An impairment test of goodwill was performed but no impairment was recognised. Estoil applied one discount rate for all cash flows for all cash generating units (CGUs), irrespective of the currency in which the cash flows would be generated. The discount rate used was the weighted average cost of capital (WACC) and Estoil used the 10-year government bond rate for its jurisdiction as the risk free rate in this calculation. Additionally, Estoil built its model using a forecast denominated in the functional currency of the parent company. Estoil felt that any other approach would require a level of detail which was unrealistic and impracticable. Estoil argued that the different CGUs represented different risk profiles in the short term, but over a longer business cycle, there was no basis for claiming that their risk profiles were different.

(ii) Fariole specialises in the communications sector with three main CGUs. Goodwill was a significant component of total assets. Fariole performed an impairment test of the CGUs. The cash flow projections were based on the most recent financial budgets approved by management. The realised cash flows for the CGUs were negative in 20X4 and far below budgeted cash flows for that period. The directors had significantly raised cash flow forecasts for 20X5 with little justification. The projected cash flows were calculated by adding back depreciation charges to the budgeted result for the period with expected changes in working capital and capital expenditure not taken into account.

Required

Discuss the acceptability of the above accounting practices under IAS 36 *Impairment of assets*.

(10 marks)

Professional marks will be awarded in question 4 for clarity and quality of presentation. **(2 marks)**

(Total = 25 marks)

Answers

DO NOT TURN THIS PAGE UNTIL YOU HAVE
COMPLETED THE MOCK EXAM

A PLAN OF ATTACK

Managing your nerves

As you turn the pages to start this exam a number of thoughts are likely to cross your mind. At best, examinations cause anxiety so it is important to stay focused on your task for the next three hours! Developing an awareness of what is going on emotionally within you may help you manage your nerves. Remember, you are unlikely to banish the flow of adrenaline, but the key is to harness it to help you work steadily and quickly through your answers.

Working through this mock exam will help you develop the exam stamina you will need to keep going for three hours.

Managing your time

Planning and time management are two of the key skills which complement the technical knowledge you need to succeed. To keep yourself on time, do not be afraid to jot down your target completion times for each question, perhaps next to the title of the question on the paper.

Focusing on scoring marks

When completing written answers, remember to communicate the critical points, which represent marks, and avoid padding and waffle. Sometimes it is possible to analyse a long sentence into more than one point. Always try to maximise the mark potential of what you write.

As you read through the questions, jot down on the question paper, any points you think you might forget. There is nothing more upsetting than coming out of an exam having forgotten to write a point you knew!

Also remember you can only score marks for what is on paper; you must write down enough to help the examiner to give you marks!

Don't write in the answer booklet during the 15 minutes of reading time!

Structure and signpost your answers

To help you answer the examiner's requirements, highlight as you read through the paper the key words and phrases in the examiner's requirements.

Also, where possible try to use headings and subheadings, to give a logical and easy-to-follow structure to your response. A well structured and signposted answer is more likely to convince the examiner that you know your subject.

Your approach

This paper has two sections. The first section contains one long case study question which is compulsory. The second has three questions and you must answer two of them.

You have a choice.

- Read through and answer the Section A question before moving on to Section B.
- Go through Section B and select the two questions you will attempt. Then go back and answer the question in Section A first.
- Select the two questions in Section B, answer them and then go back to Section A.

You are allowed 15 minutes before the start of the exam to go through the questions you are going to do.

Time spent at the start of each question confirming the requirements and producing a plan for the answers is time well spent.

Question selection

When selecting the two questions from Section B make sure that you read through all of the requirements. It is painful to answer part (a) of a question and then realise that parts (b) and (c) are beyond you, by then it is too late to change your mind and do another question.

When reviewing the requirements look at how many marks have been allocated to each part. This will give you an idea of how detailed your answer must be.

Generally, you need to be aware of your strengths and weaknesses and select accordingly.

Doing the exam

Actually doing the exam is a personal experience. There is not a single *right way*. As long as you submit complete answers to question 1 and any two from questions 2 to 4 after the three hours are up, then your approach obviously works.

Looking through the paper

The compulsory question is a case study. It has two acquisitions, one in stages and one with a gain on a bargain purchase, and adjustments for a non-current asset held for sale and a joint venture plus a written part on share-based payment and ethics. In Section B you have three questions on a variety of topics:

- Question 2 is a scenario question covering related parties and financial instruments.
- Question 3 is a specialised industry question set in the shipping industry, and covering business combinations and control, and IAS 16.
- Question 4 was a discussion of impairment and application to a scenario, but not the usual current issues question.

You only have to answer two out of these three questions. You don't have to pick your optional questions right now, but this brief overview should have convinced you that you have enough choice and variety to have a respectable go at Section B. So let's go back to the compulsory question in Section A.

Compulsory question

Part (a) requires a consolidated statement of financial position, with plenty of opportunity to pass, even if you don't get all the complexities. The main thing is to get the group structure right. Just keep going, set out your workings clearly, and above all make sure you complete the question. Don't get bogged down in the joint venture. Part (b) is on a standard, IFRS 2 *Share-based payment,* that comes up quite regularly, with marks available for sensible points. Part (c) is subjective and credit will be given for valid arguments.

Optional questions

Deciding between the optional questions is obviously a personal matter – it depends how you have spent your study time.

In our opinion, questions 3 and 4 are more straightforward than question 2. Question 4 allows plenty of scope for earning marks through textbook knowledge of principles, and question 3 has the advantage over question 2 covering more mainstream topics. Question 2 should really be avoided – it deals with some very technical points with no easy way in.

Use the information in the scenario

It is there for a purpose! Many students lose marks because they do not do this.

Allocating your time

The golden rule is always allocate your time according to the marks for the question in total and for the parts of the question. But be sensible. If, for example, you have committed yourself to answering Question 2, but are stuck on the impairment, you may be better off trying to pick up some extra marks on the questions you can do.

Afterwards

Don't be tempted to do a post mortem on the paper with your colleagues. It will only worry you and them and it's unlikely you'll be able to remember exactly what you wrote anyway. If you really can't resist going over the topics covered in the paper, allow yourself a maximum of half an hour's 'worry time', then put it out of your head! Relax as it's all out of your hands now!

Question 1

Marking scheme

		Marks
(a)	Property, plant and equipment	5
	Goodwill	6
	Assets held for sale	5
	Current assets/total non-current liabilities	1
	Retained earnings	6
	Other components of equity	3
	Non-controlling interest	3
	Current liabilities	1
	Joint venture	5
		35
(b)	Subjective assessment of discussion – up to 2 marks per element	8
(c)	Subjective assessment – 1 mark per point	7
	Available	50

(a)   JOEY GROUP
      CONSOLIDATED STATEMENT OF FINANCIAL POSITION AS AT 30 NOVEMBER 20X4

	$m
Assets	
Non-current assets	
Property, plant and equipment: 3,295 + 2,000 + 1,200 − 38 (W2) + 266 (W9)	
− 14 (W2)	6,709.00
Goodwill (W2)	89.00
Intangible asset: franchise right (W7)	15.00
Joint venture (W9)	0.75
	6,813.75
Current assets: 985 + 861 + 150 + 15.3 (W8)	2,011.30
Total assets	8,825.05
Equity and liabilities	
Equity attributable to owners of the parent	
Share capital	850.00
Retained earnings (W3)	3,450.25
Other components of equity (W5)	258.50
	4,558.75
Non-controlling interests (W6)	908.10
	5,466.85
Non-current liabilities: 1,895 + 675 + 200	2,770.00
Current liabilities: 320 + 106 + 160 + 0.7 (W9) + 1.5 (W9)	588.20
Total equity and liabilities	8,825.05

Workings

1   *Group structure*

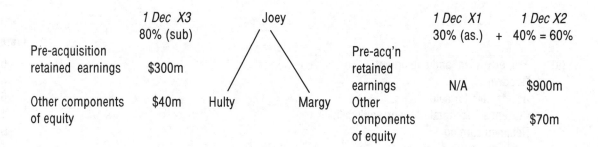

	1 Dec X3 80% (sub)	Joey		1 Dec X1 30% (as.)	1 Dec X2 + 40% = 60%
Pre-acquisition retained earnings	$300m	Hulty Margy	Pre-acq'n retained earnings	N/A	$900m
Other components of equity	$40m		Other components of equity		$70m

2   *Goodwill*

	Hulty $m	Hulty $m	Margy $m	Margy $m
Consideration transferred		700		975
Non-controlling interest (at fair value)		250		620
Fair value of previously held equity interest				705
Less fair value of net assets at acquisition				
Share capital	600		1,020	
Retained earnings	300		900	
Other components of equity	40		70	
Fair value adjustments:				
Land (W7)	-		266	
Contingent liability (note 3)	-		(6)	
Franchise right (W7)	20		–	
		(960)		(2,250)
Gain on bargain purchase (note (i))		(10)*		50
Add decrease in FV of buildings (note (ii))				40
Measurement period adjustment - contingent liability: $6m – $5m (note (iii))				(1)
Goodwill				89

Notes

(i)   This is a gain on a bargain purchase and should be recorded in profit or loss for the year attributable to the parent (W3).

(ii)   The carrying amount of property, plant and equipment as of 30 November 20X4 is decreased by $40m less excess depreciation charged of $2m, ie$38m. This will increase the carrying amount of goodwill by $40m and depreciation expense for 20X4 is decreased by $2m. The decrease in depreciation is split between the retained earnings of the parent ($1·4m) and NCI ($0·6m).

(iii) In accordance with IFRS 3 *Business combinations*, contingent liabilities subsequent to the date of acquisition must be measured at the higher of the amount that would be recognised under IAS 37 *Provisions, contingent liabilities and contingent assets* and the amount initially recognised, less any cumulative amortisation. These requirements apply only for the period in which the item is considered to be a contingent liability. In this case the contingent liability has subsequently met the requirements to be classified as a provision and will be measured in accordance with IAS 37, rather than IFRS 3.

3   *Retained earnings*

	Joey $m	Hulty $m	Margy $m
Per question	3,340.00	350	980
Fair value movement: depn. reduction (W7)			2
amortisation (W7)		(5)	
Liability adjustment			5
Gain on bargain purchase (W2)	10.00		
Profit on derecognition of associate (W4)	5.00		
Asset held for sale: 0.2 – 0.1 – 0.3 (W8)	(0.20)		
Joint operation (W9)	(0.70)		
Joint venture: 0.75 – 1.5 (W9)	(0.75)		
Pre-acquisition		(300)	(900)
		45	87
Group share			
Hulty: 80% × 45	36.00		
Margyy: 70% × 87	60.90		
	3,450.25		

4   Profit on derecognition of 30% associate

	$m
Fair value at date control obtained (per question	705
Carrying amount of associate: 600 cost + 90 (post-acqn. RE) + 10 (post acqn OCE)	(700
	5

5   Other components of equity

	Joey $m	Hulty $m	Margy $m
Per question	250.0	40	80
Asset held for sale	1.5		
Pre-acquisition		(40)	(70)
:		0	10
Group share post acqn			
Hulty: 80% × 0	0.0		
Margyy: 70% × 10	7.0		
	258.5		

6   Non-controlling interests

	Hulty $m	Margy $m
At date of control (FV)	250	620.0
Post-acquisition share of retained earnings		
Hulty: 45 (W3) × 20%	9	
Margy: 87 (W3) × 30%		26.1
Post-acquisition share of other components of equity		
Hulty: 0(W5) × 20%	0	
Margy: 10(W5) × 30%		3.0
	259	649.1

908.1

7   Fair value adjustments

Hulty:

	At acqn 1 Dec 20X3 $m	Movement (over 4 years) $m	At year end 30 Nov 20X4 $m
Franchise: 960 − (600 + 300 + 40)	20	(5)	15

Margy:

	At acqn 1 Dec 20X3	Movement (reduced depn.)	At year end 30 Nov 20X4
Land: 2,250 − (1,020 + 900 + 70) + 6*	266	-	266
Property, plant & equipment	(40)	2	(38)
	Goodwill (FV of NA)	Retained earnings	PPE in year end

*Contingent liability

8   Asset held for sale

At 31 March 20X4, the criteria in IFRS 5 *Non-current assets held for sale and discontinued operations* have been met, and the property may be classified as held for sale. In accordance with IFRS 5, an asset held for sale should be measured at the **lower of** its **carrying amount** and **fair value less costs to sell**. Immediately before classification of the asset as held for sale, the entity must recognise impairment in accordance with applicable IFRS. Any impairment loss is generally recognised in profit or loss. The steps are as follows.

Step 1   Calculate carrying value under applicable IFRS, here IAS 16 *Property, plant and equipment*.

At 31 March 20X4, the date of classification as held for sale, depreciation to date is calculated as $300,000 \times 4/12 = \$100,000$. The carrying value of the property is therefore $13.9m. The journal entries are:

DEBIT Profit or loss (W3) $0.1m
CREDIT   PPE $0.1m

The difference between the carrying value and the fair value at 31 March 20X4 is material, so the property is revalued to its fair value of $15.4m

DEBIT   PPE $(15.4 – 13.9)m $1.5m
CREDIT   Other comprehensive income (W5) $1.5m

Step 2   Consider whether the property is impaired by comparing its carrying amount, the fair value of $15.4m, with its recoverable amount. The recoverable amount is the higher of value in use (given as $15.8m) and fair value less costs to sell ($15.4m – $3m = $15.1m.) The property is not impaired because the recoverable amount (value in use) is higher than the carrying amount (fair value). No impairment loss is recognised.

Step 3   Classify as held for sale. Compare the carrying amount ($15.4m) with fair value less costs to sell ($15.1m). Measure at the lower of carrying value and fair value less costs to sell, here $15.1m, giving an initial write-down of $300,000.

DEBIT Profit or loss (W3) $0.3m
CREDIT   PPE $0.3m

Step 4   On 30 November 20X4, the property is sold for $15.6m, which, after deducting costs to sell of $0.3m gives a profit or $0.2m.

DEBIT Receivables $15.3m
CREDIT   PPE $15.1m
CREDIT   Profit or loss (W3) $0.2m

---

9   *Joint operation and joint venture*

The arrangement with Content Publishing qualifies as a joint arrangement under IFRS 11 *Joint arrangements,* because key strategic and marketing decisions are taken jointly. For the period to 31 May 20X4, the arrangement is not structured through a separate vehicle, and so must be classified under IFRS 11 as a joint operation.

The treatment of the joint operation is set out in IFRS 11. Joey must recognise on a line-by-line basis its assets, liabilities, revenues and expenses plus its share of the joint assets, liabilities, revenue and expenses. The figures are calculated as follows:

Profit or loss of joint operation for the six months ending 31 May 20X4:

	$m
Revenue: $5 \times 6/12$	2.50
Cost of sales: $2 \times 6/12$	(1.00)
Gross profit	1.50

Joey's share is therefore:

	$m
Revenue: $90\% \times \$2.5m$	2.25
Cost of sales: printing, binding, platform maintenance, all Joey	(1.00)
Gross profit	1.25
Profit royalty to CP: $30\% \times \$1.5m$	(0.45))
Net profit	0.80

Joey must adjust the profit for the period to 31 May 20X4 by the amounts owing to CP as follows:

DEBIT Profit or loss (0.45 + (2.5 × 10%) $0.7m
CREDIT   Accounts payable (CP) $0.7m

From 1 June 20X4 the arrangement qualifies as a joint venture under IFRS 11, since Joey has a share of the net assets rather than rights to the individual assets and liabilities. The profit of the new entity must be removed as follows:

DEBIT Profit or loss $1.5m
CREDIT   JCP profit for the period $1.5m

Joey's share of JCP's profit must be equity accounted as follows:

DEBIT Investment in joint venture   (($5m – $2m) × 6/12 × 50%) $0.75m
CREDIT   Profit or loss $0.75m

(b) **Share-based payment**

This arrangement will be governed by IFRS 2 *Share-based payment,* which includes within its scope **transfers of equity instruments of an entity's parent in return for goods or services.** Clear guidance is given in the standard as to **when to treat group share-based payment transactions as equity settled and when to treat them as cash settled.**

To determine the accounting treatment, the group entity receiving the goods and services must **consider its own rights and obligations as well as the awards granted.** The amount recognised by the group entity receiving the goods and services will not necessarily be consistent with the amount recognised in the consolidated financial statements.

Group share-based payment transactions **must be treated as equity** settled if either of the following apply:

(i) The entity **grants rights to its own equity instruments**.

(ii) The entity has **no obligation to settle the** share-based payment transactions.

Treatment in consolidated financial statements

Because the group receives all of the services in consideration for the group's equity instruments, the transaction is treated as **equity settled**. The fair value of the share-based payment at the grant date is **charged to profit or loss over the vesting period with a corresponding credit to equity.**

Treatment in subsidiaries' financial statements

The subsidiaries do not have an obligation to settle the awards, so the grant is treated as an **equity settled** transaction. The fair value of the share-based payment at the grant date is **charged to profit or loss over the vesting period with a corresponding credit to equity.** The parent, Joey, is compensating the employees of the subsidiaries, Margy and Hulty, with no expense to the subsidiaries, and therefore the **credit in equity is treated as a capital contribution**. Because the shares vest immediately, the expense recognised in Margy and Hulty's statement of profit or loss will be the full cost of the fair value at grant date.

Treatment in parent's separate financial statements

There are no employees providing services to the parent, Joey, and therefore there is **no share-based payment charge**. Joey should recognised an increase in its investment in the subsidiaries and a credit to equity.

Potential IAS 24 disclosures

Joey should consider whether any of the employees are **key management personnel**. If so, the disclosure requirements of IAS 24 *Related party disclosures* should be applied.

(c) **Ethical issue and potential conflict of interest**

Ethical standards are important to accountants **because ethics have practical application in the accountant's professional life.**

Company directors are understandably **motivated by profit** – it is what the company's shareholders expect – and there may appear to be a conflict of interest between profit and ethics, including social ethics. Excessive focus on profit has led in some cases to **aggressive earnings management**, whereby directors use creative accounting techniques to present the results in a favourable light, or to **questionable business practices**, such as outsourcing to countries with poor health and safety records, or which use child labour.

Ethical codes cannot provide ready-made solutions to all potential conflicts, but it **can provide a set of principles on which to base judgements**. A vague wish to 'do the right thing' will be of little use when faced with a decision to report a colleague or member of the client's staff who is acting unethically. The study of ethics can direct the accountant's thinking and reasoning and help him or her make the right decision, even if it does not make that decision any easier. An example of ethical guidance serving this purpose is the ACCA's *Code of Ethics and Conduct,* which requires its members to adhere to a set of fundamental principles in the course of their professional duty, such as confidentiality, objectivity, professional behaviour, integrity, professional competence and due care.

In this particular case there is a **twofold conflict of interest:**

(i) The chief accountant is under pressure to provide the bank with a projected cash flow statement that will meet the bank's criteria when in fact the projections do not meet the criteria. The chief accountant's financial commitments mean that that he cannot afford to lose his job. **His ethical and professional standards are at odds with the pressures of his personal circumstances.**

(ii) The **directors have a duty to the company's shareholders and employees, and a duty to present fairly any information the bank may rely on**. Joey's need for a significant injection of capital, arising from the directors' wish to modernise plant and equipment is at odds with this. In fact it could be argued that there is a **conflict between the short-term interests of the company** (the need to modernise) **and its long-term interests** (the detriment to the company's reputation if its directors do not act ethically).

The **chief accountant is faced with an immediate ethical dilemma** and must apply his moral and ethical judgement. As a professional, he has a responsibility to present the truth fairly, and not to indulge in 'creative accounting' in response to pressure. **He should therefore put the interests of the company and professional ethics first,** and insist that the report to the bank is an honest reflection of the current financial position.

Question 2

Text reference. Related parties are covered in Chapter 11 of your Study Text and financial instruments are covered in Chapter 7.

Top tips. Part (c) has been amended to reflect the July 2014 version of IFRS 9. Part (a) tested an exemption from IAS 24 (for government-related activities), rather than the more mainstream aspect, but as the examiner stated, you would have been given credit for discussion of the relevant principles. Part (b) also tested an exemption from the mainstream – financial guarantee contracts, which are not required to be classified as subsequently measured at amortised cost. Pay attention to 'clues' in the question – the fact that the guarantee is being measured at FVTPL suggests that it is a financial instrument rather than a provision. Part (d) on credit risk is topical, but candidates may have struggled with the interest rate swap in part (c) of the original question, now amended for IFRS 9.

Easy marks. There are marks for textbook explanations on hedging in Part (c), but in general this is a tricky question.

Marking scheme

		Marks
(a)	IAS 24	5
(b)	IFRS 9 explanation	3
	Guarantee calculations	4
(c)	Hedging discussion	4
	Effectiveness discussion	3
(d)	Credit risk entries	4
Professional marks		2
		25

(a) **Related parties**

The applicable standard relating to the activities is IAS 24 *Related party disclosures.* The standard requires disclosure of transactions with related parties. The definition of related parties is very detailed and includes parents, subsidiaries, and key management personnel of the entity or of a parent of the entity. Post-employment benefit plans are also included.

Where related party transactions have taken place, management must disclose the following:

(i) The name of its **parent** and, if different, the **ultimate controlling party** irrespective of whether there have been any transactions.

(ii) Total **key management personnel compensation** (broken down by category)

(iii) **If the entity has had related party transactions**:

(1) nature of the related party **relationship**

(2) information about the **transactions and outstanding balances, including commitments and bad and doubtful debts** necessary for users to understand the potential effect of the relationship on the financial statements.

No disclosure is required of intragroup related party transactions in the consolidated financial statements (since they are eliminated).Items of a **similar** nature may be disclosed **in aggregate** except where separate disclosure is necessary for understanding purposes.

A g**overnment-related entity** is an entity over which a government has control, joint control or significant influence. In the wake of the financial crisis, more financial institutions were caught by the rules, because the financial support provided by governments of many countries to banks and other financial institutions resulted in control or significant influence. In principle, a government-controlled bank such as Coatmin could be required to disclosed details of its transactions, deposits and commitments with the central bank and with other government-controlled banks.

However, an **exemption** is available from full disclosure of transactions, outstanding balances and commitments with the government or with other entities related to the same government.

If the exemption is applied, IAS 24 requires disclosure of:

(a)   The **name of the government** and **nature of the relationship**, and

(b)   The nature and amount of each **individually significant transaction** (plus a qualitative or quantitative indication of the extent of other transactions which are collectively, but not individually, significant).

These disclosures provide more meaningful information about the nature of the entity's relationship and transactions with government than do the usual IAS 24 disclosures.

(b)   **Financial guarantee contract**

IFRS 9 *Financial instruments* (revised July 2014) requires entities to classify all financial liabilities as subsequently measured at amortised cost using the effective interest method, with the following exceptions.

(i)   Financial liabilities **at fair value through profit or loss**. Such liabilities, including derivatives that are liabilities, must be subsequently measured at fair value.

(ii)   Financial liabilities that arise **when a transfer of a financial asset does not qualify for derecognition** or when the continuing involvement approach applies

(i)   **Financial guarantee contracts.** After initial recognition, an issuer of such a contract must subsequently measure it at the higher of:

(1)   The amount of the loss allowance determined in accordance with the IFRS 9 rules on expected credit losses, and

(2)   The amount initially recognised less, when appropriate, the cumulative amount of income recognised in accordance with the principles of IFRS 15 *Revenue from contracts with customers*.

If an entity chooses to measure a financial guarantee contract (or loan commitment) **at fair value through profit or loss,** as here, **all fair value movements go through profit or loss** with no transfer to other comprehensive income. Changes in the credit risk of liabilities relating to financial guarantee contracts are not required to be presented in other comprehensive income under IFRS 9 (revised July 2014).

Assuming that discounting is not material, the accounting entries will be as follows.

At 1 December 20X2

DEBIT	Profit or loss	$1.2m	
CREDIT	Financial liabilities		$1.2m

To record the loss incurred in giving the guarantee

At 30 November 20X3

DEBIT	Financial liabilities	$0.4m	
CREDIT	Profit or loss		$0.4m

To amortise the initial fair value over the life of the guarantee.

This reflects the reduction in exposure arising from the fact that the subsidiary has made the first repayment.

At 30 November 20X4

DEBIT	Profit or loss ($40m – $8m)	$39.2m	
CREDIT	Financial liabilities		$39.2m

To provide for the calling of the guarantee

DEBIT	Financial liabilities	$39.6m	
CREDIT	Profit or loss		$39.6m

To record movement from expected credit loss allowance to measurement at amortised initial value

The above change was made in the light of the subsidiary's receipt of the donation enabling it to make the second repayment, which means a change in probability that the guarantee will be called. This is an event after the reporting period which provides further evidence of conditions existing at the end of the reporting period, and so is an adjusting event.

(c)   **Hedging**

IFRS 9 *Financial instruments* (revised July 2014) allows hedge accounting but only if **all** of the following **conditions** are met.

(i)   The hedging relationship consists **only of eligible hedging instruments and eligible hedged items**.

(ii)   There must be **formal documentation** (including identification of the hedged item, the hedging instrument, the nature of the risk that is to be hedged and how the entity will assess the hedging instrument's effectiveness in offsetting the exposure to changes in the hedged item's fair value or cash flows attributable to the hedged risk).

(iii)   The hedging relationship meets all of the IFRS 9 hedge effectiveness criteria.

IFRS 9 defines **hedge effectiveness** as the degree to which changes in the fair value or cash flows of the hedged item attributable to a hedged risk are offset by changes in the fair value or cash flows of the hedging instrument. The directors of Coatmin have asked whether hedge effectiveness can be calculated. It is possible that they have in mind the somewhat arbitrary 80%-125% 'bright line' test of IAS 39, the forerunner of IFRS 9. IFRS 9 replaces this with an **objective-based assessment** for hedge effectiveness, under which the following criteria must be met.

(i)   There is an **economic relationship** between the hedged item and the hedging instrument, ie the hedging instrument and the hedged item have values that generally move in the opposite direction because of the same risk, which is the hedged risk;

(ii)   The **effect of credit risk does not dominate the value** changes that result from that economic relationship, ie the gain or loss from credit risk does not frustrate the effect of changes in the underlyings on the value of the hedging instrument or the hedged item, even if those changes were significant; and

(iii)   The **hedge ratio of the hedging relationship** (quantity of hedging instrument vs quantity of hedged item) is the same as that resulting from the quantity of the hedged item that the entity **actually hedges** and the quantity of the hedging instrument that the entity **actually uses** to hedge that quantity of hedged item.

While the above criteria will certainly involve calculations, the assessment is more sophisticated and arguably more realistic.

(d)   **Liability**

IFRS 9 *Financial instruments* (revised July 2014) requires that financial liabilities which are **designated as measured at fair value through profit or loss are treated differently**. In this case the gain or loss in a period must be classified into:

- Gain or loss **resulting from credit risk**, and
- **Othe**r gain or loss.

This provision of IFRS 9 was in response to an anomaly regarding changes in the credit risk of a financial liability.

Changes in a financial liability's credit risk affect the fair value of that financial liability. This means that when an entity's creditworthiness deteriorates, the fair value of its issued debt will decrease (and *vice versa*). IFRS 9 requires the gain or loss as a result of credit risk to be recognised in other comprehensive income, unless it creates or enlarges an **accounting mismatch**, in which case it is recognised in profit or loss. The other gain or loss (not the result of credit risk) is recognised in profit or loss.

On derecognition any gains or losses recognised in other comprehensive income are **not** transferred to **profit or loss**, although the cumulative gain or loss may be transferred within equity.

Coatmin should split the fair value increase as follows:

STATEMENT OF PROFIT OR LOSS AND OTHER COMPREHENSIVE INCOME (EXTRACT)
FOR THE YEAR ENDED 30 NOVEMBER 20X4
Profit or loss for the year

	$'000
Liabilities at fair value	
Change in fair value not attributable to change in credit risk	45
Profit (loss) for the year	45
Other comprehensive income (not reclassified to profit or loss)	
Fair value loss on financial liability attributable to change in credit risk	5
Total comprehensive income	50

Question 3

Text reference. Specialised industries are covered in general terms in Chapter 20 of your Study Text. IFRS 3 and IFRS 10 (control) are covered in Chapter 12. IAS 16 is covered in Chapter 3.

Top tips. Part (b) required candidates to consider the IFRS 3 definition of a business, which has not been tested before, although there were pointers in the scenario to suggest that the accounting treatment was incorrect, and that IFRS 3 principles of control, well within the mainstream, should have been applied. Part (b) was more demanding. While covering IAS 16, a standard that will be assumed knowledge for P2, the application was challenging, but fair.

Easy marks. The discussion of control should have presented few problems.

Examiner's comment. Generally candidates answered the question quite well. Componentisation regularly features in this examination as it is a major problem for entities worldwide. Marks were allocated on a basis of one mark per valid point which indicates that there is a minimum amount which candidates need to write in order to gain a pass mark in this question

ACCA Examiner's answer. The Examiner's answer to this question is included at the back of this Kit.

Marking scheme

		Marks
(a)	IFRS 3/IFRS 10 – 1 mark per point up to	12
(b)	IAS 16 and application – 1 mark per point up to	11
Professional marks		2
		25

(a) **Acquisition of Ceemone**

Compliance with IFRS 3

Kayte has accounted for its investment in Ceemone as an asset acquisition, but this is **incorrect**. The investment **should have been accounted for as a business combination** in accordance with IFRS 3 *Business combinations*. This has the following implications.

(i)   Transaction costs must be expensed.

(ii)   The vessels must be recognised at fair value.

(iii)   Any deferred tax must be recognised at nominal value.

(iv)   Goodwill must be recognised, being the difference between the fair value of the consideration transferred and the fair value of the identifiable assets acquired and the liabilities assumed.

IFRS 3 gives a **definition of a business**, which needs to be applied in determining whether a transaction is a business combination:

> 'An integrated set of activities and assets that is capable of being conducted and managed for the purpose of providing a return in the form of dividends, lower costs or other economic benefits directly to investors or other owners, members or participants.'

A business generally has three elements.

(i) **Inputs**. An economic resource (e.g. non-current assets, intellectual property) that creates outputs when one or more processes are applied to it. In the case of Ceemone, the inputs would be shares in vessel-owning companies, charter arrangements, outsourcing arrangements with a management company and relationships with a shipping broker.

(ii) **Process**. A system, standard, protocol, convention or rule that when applied to an input or inputs, creates outputs (e.g. strategic management, operational processes, resource management). For Ceemone, this would encompass financing the business, purchases and sales of the vessels and activities relating to chartering and operating the vessels.

(iii) **Outputs**. The result of inputs and processes applied to those inputs. The charter agreements would enable Ceemone to generate revenue and other economic benefits for Kayte. (IFRS 3 states that outputs are not required in order to qualify as a business.)

It is **not relevant that some activities were outsourced** to the management company. IFRS 3 states:

> 'Determining whether a particular set of assets and activities is a business should be based on whether the integrated set is capable of being conducted and managed as a business by a market participant. Thus, in evaluating whether a particular set is a business, it is not relevant whether a seller operated the set as a **business** or whether the acquirer intends to operate the set as a business.'

Ceemone could choose to conduct and manage the integrated set of assets and activities as a business. In summary, **the acquisition includes all the elements which constitute a business** in accordance with IFRS 3 and must be accounted for as a business combination.

IFRS 10 and control

The directors of Kayte believe that the entity to which the vessels have been transferred and in which the bank holds a variable interest is a **subsidiary of the bank**. In determining this, IFRS 10 *Consolidated financial statements* looks at the substance of the transaction rather than its legal form. The key point is whether an investor has **control** over an investee.

IFRS 10 *Consolidated financial statements* requires an acquirer to be identified in all business combinations, even where the business combination looks like a merger of equals. The acquirer is the combining entity which obtains **control** of the entity with which it is combined. It is not always easy to determine which party is the acquirer, and IFRS 10 gives guidance on the matter. The key point is **control,** rather than mere ownership, but this may not be easy to assess.

IFRS 10 states that an investor **controls** an investee if and only if it has all of the following.

(i) **Power** over the investee
(ii) Exposure, or rights, to **variable returns** from its involvement with the investee, and
(iii) The **ability to use its power** over the investee to affect the amount of the investor's returns.

Power is defined as **existing rights that give the current ability to direct the relevant activities of the investee**. There is no requirement for that power to have been exercised.

It is likely that the bank has power over the entity, and it may be exposed to variable returns from its involvement with the entity. The bank's interest depends on the entity's level of indebtedness, and so it can be said to have the ability to use its power to effect the amount of the investor's returns. The **bank may therefore be regarded as having a measure of control.** However, the extent of this control is not clear and will depend on the constitution of the entity.

(b)   **Vessels**

Vessels sold at ten years old

Kayte's estimate of the residual life of these vessels is **based on acquisition cost.** This is **unacceptable** under IAS 16 *Property, plant and equipment.* IAS 16 defines residual value as:

> 'The estimated amount that an entity would currently obtain from disposal of the asset, after deducting the estimated costs of disposal, if the asset were already of the age and in the condition expected at the end of its useful life.'

IAS 16 requires that property, plant and equipment must be depreciated so that its depreciable amount is allocated on a systematic basis over its useful life. Depreciable amount is the cost of an asset less its residual value. IAS 16 stipulates that the **residual value must be reviewed at least each financial year-end** and, if expectations differ from previous estimates, any change is accounted for prospectively as a change in estimate under IAS 8 *Accounting policies, changes in accounting estimates and errors.*

Kayte's model implies that the residual value of the vessels remains constant through the vessels' useful life. However, the **residual value should be adjusted,** particularly as the date of sale approaches and the residual value approaches proceeds of disposal less costs of disposal at the end of the asset's useful life.

Following IAS 16, if the residual value is greater than an asset's carrying amount, the depreciation charge is zero until such time as the residual value subsequently decreases to an amount below the asset's carrying amount. The residual value should be the value at the reporting date as if the vessel were already of the age and condition expected at the end of its useful life. Depreciable amount is affected by an increase in the residual value of an asset because of past events, but not by expectation of changes in future events, other than the expected effects of wear and tear.

In this case it appears that the **useful life of the vessels (ten years) is shorter than the economic life (30 years).** IAS 16 does not give guidance about the appropriate treatment in such cases. In the absence of such guidance, **broker valuations could be used.** The resulting volatility is not an argument against the use of such valuations.

Vessels kept for 30 years

Kayte **correctly uses a residual value for these vessels based upon the scrap value of steel.** The depreciable amount of the vessels is therefore the cost less the scrap value of steel, and the vessels should be depreciated over the 30-year period.

The **engine does not need to be treated as a separate component** of the asset, because as long as it is maintained every ten years, it will have the same 30-year life as the vessel. The **cost of major, planned maintenance is likely to increase over the life of the vessel** because of its age and the effects of inflation. This cost will need to be capitalised as incurred, and as a result the depreciation charge may be greater in the later years of the assets' useful life.

The **cost of the engine overhaul**, as major planned maintenance, needs to be **capitalised as a new asset**. It is then **depreciated over the ten years until the next overhaul.** Generally the depreciation of the original amount capitalised in respect of the vessel will be **calculated to have a net book value of nil when the overhaul is undertaken.**

Vessel with engine completely replaced after eight years

In the case of this vessel, work was required earlier than expected. The **overhaul costs and any remaining net book value** of the old engine should be **expensed immediately.**

Funnels

In determining which parts of the vessel, if any, to treat as separate components, the entity needs to consider all major maintenance events that are likely to occur. It may not always be possible to identify these until later, when it may transpire that **not all components were identified.** This is true of the funnels, which were not initially identified as separate components. They now need to be thus identified and it will be necessary to **determine what the net book value would have been had they been initially identified.** The initial cost of the funnels can be determined by reference to replacement cost, and the associated depreciation charge determined using the rate for the vessel (over thirty years). There will therefore be a significant net book value to be written off at the time the replacement funnels are capitalised.

Question 4

Marking scheme

		Marks
(a)	Subjective – 1 mark per point	13
(b)	Subjective	10
Professional marks		2
		25

(a)   Entities must determine, **at each reporting date**, whether there are any indications that impairment has occurred. Indicators of impairment may be internal or external. The following factors need to be considered when conducting an impairment test under IAS 36 *Impairment of assets*.

   (i)   **Changes in circumstances in the reporting period**

        Circumstances may change due to internal factors, for example matters as physical damage, adverse changes to the methods of use of the asset, management restructuring and over-estimation of cash flows, and external factors, such as **adverse changes** in the **markets** or **business** in which the asset is used, or adverse changes to the **technological, economic or legal environment** of the business.

        If such indicators come to light between the date of the impairment test and the end of the next reporting period, **more than one impairment test may be required** in the accounting period. In addition, tests for impairment of goodwill and some other intangible assets may be performed at any time during the accounting period, provided it is performed at the same time each year. Not all goodwill is tested at the year end – some entities test it at an interim period. Should impairment indicators arise after the annual impairment test has been performed, it may be necessary to test goodwill for impairment at the year end and at a subsequent interim reporting date as well.

        A possible indicator of impairment is volatility in financial statements; for example sharp changes in commodity prices may cause the assets of mining and energy companies to be impaired. In such cases, the assets affected should be tested in the interim period.

   (ii) **Market capitalisation**

        A strong indicator of impairment is when the **carrying amount** of an entity's assets exceeds the entity's **market capitalisation,** suggesting that the entity is overvalued. However, there **may not be a direct correlation** between the market capitalisation and the impairment loss arising from a lower return generated on the entity's assets –the market may have taken other factors into account. The discrepancy does, however, **highlight the need for the entity to examine its cash-generating units,**

and possibly to test goodwill for impairment. The reason for the shortfall must be examined and understood, even though IAS 36 does not require a formal reconciliation between an entity's market capitalisation, its fair value less costs to sell and its value in use.

(iii) **Allocating goodwill to cash-generating units**

Goodwill arising on an acquisition is required to be allocated to each of the acquirer's cash-generating units (CGUs), or to a group of CGUs, that are expected to benefit from the synergies of the combination. **If CGUs are subsequently revised or operations disposed of, IAS 36 requires goodwill to be reallocated, based on relative values, to the units affected.**

The difficulty with this is that IAS 36 **does not give guidance as to what is meant by relative value.** While **fair value less costs to sell** (FVLCS) could be used, this is not mandated by the standard. However, the entity may still need to carry out a valuation process on the part retained. **Value in use**(VIU) is a possibility, but the measure needs to be one that can be applied equally to both the part retained and the part disposed of. VIU has the obvious problem that it will be much the same as FVLCS for the operations disposed of, but there could be significant differences between VIU and FVLCS for the part retained. Alternatively, there could be reasonable ways of estimating relative value by using an **appropriate industry or business surrogate**, for example revenue, profits, industry KPIs.

(iv) **Valuation issues**

The basic principle of IAS 36 *Impairment of assets* is that an asset should be carried at no more than its recoverable amount, that is the amount to be recovered through use or sale of the asset. If an **asset's value** is **higher than its recoverable amount**, an **impairment loss** has occurred. The impairment loss should be **written off** against profit or loss for the year.

The **recoverable amount** is **defined** as the **higher** of the **asset's fair value less costs of disposal** and the asset's **value in use**. Measuring both of these requires the use of **estimates and assumptions,** some of which **may be problematic**.

(1) **Fair value less costs of disposal** is defined as the price that would be received to sell the asset in an orderly transaction between market participants at the measurement date under current market conditions, net of costs of disposal. IAS 36 gives a 'hierarchy of evidence' for this, with 'price in a binding sale agreement' at the top, only likely to be available if the asset is held for sale, and allowing, in the absence of any active market, estimates based on **a discounted cash flow (DCF) model, which may not be reliable.**

(2) Determining the types of **future cash flows which should be included in the measurement of VIU can also be difficult**. Under IAS 36 an asset or CGU must be tested in its current status, not the status that management wishes it was in or hopes to get it into in the near future. Therefore, the standard requires VIU to be measured at the net present value of the future cash flows the entity expects to derive from the asset or CGU in its current condition over its remaining useful life. This means that it is not appropriate to take account of management plans for enhancing the performance of the asset or CGU, even though these may bring about an increase in value. .

(3) While the cash flows used in testing for impairment are specific to the entity, the **discount rate is supposed to appropriately reflect the current market assessment of the time value of money and the risks specific to the asset or cash generating unit.** When a specific rate for an asset or cash generating unit is not directly available from the market, which is usually the case, the discount rate to be used is a surrogate. An estimate should be made of a **pre-tax rate that reflects the current market assessment of the time value of money and the risks specific to the asset** that have **not been adjusted** for in the estimate of future cash flows. According to IAS 36, this rate is the return that the investors would require if they chose an investment that would generate cash flows of amounts, timing and risk profile equivalent to those that the entity expects to derive from the assets.

Rates that should be considered are the entity's weighted average cost of capital (WACC), the entity's incremental borrowing rate or other market rates. The objective must be to obtain a rate which is sensible and justifiable..

(4)   The test is further complicated by the **impact of taxation.** IAS 36 requires that VIU be measured using pre-tax cash flows and a pre-tax discount rate, but WACC is a post-tax rate, as are most observable equity rates used by valuers.

(5)   There is a need for **consistency in determining the recoverable amount and carrying amount which are being compared.** For example, in the case of pensions, there can be significant differences between the measurement basis of the pension asset or (more likely) liability and the cash flows that relate to pensions.

(6)   IAS 36 requires that **corporate assets** must be allocated to a cash-generating unit on a 'reasonable and consistent basis, but does not expand on this.

(v)   **Disclosures**

With regard to the impairment loss recognised in respect of each cash generating unit, IAS 36 would disclosure of:

(1)   The amount of the loss
(2)   The events and circumstances that led to the loss
(3)   A description of the impairment loss by class of asset

It is **no defence** to maintain that this information was **common knowledge in the market**. The disclosures are still needed.

(b)   (i)   **Discount rate**

Estoil has **not complied with IAS 36** *Impairment of assets* in its use of one discount rate for all cash-generating units (CGUs) regardless of the currency of the country in which the cash flows are generated. IAS 36 requires that **future cash flows must be estimated in the currency in which they will be generate**d and then discounted using a discount rate appropriate for that currency. The present value thus calculated must be **translated using the spot exchange rate at the date of the value in use calculation.**

The currency in which the estimated cash flows are denominated has an impact on many of the inputs to the weighted average cost of capital (WACC) calculation, including the risk-free interest rate. **Estoil was incorrect in using the ten-year government bond rate for its own jurisdiction** as the risk-free rate because government bond rates differ between countries due to different expectations about future inflation, and so there may be a discrepancy between the expected inflation reflected in the estimated cash flows and the risk-free rate.

IAS 36 requires that the **discount rate should appropriately reflect the current market assessment of the time value of money and the risks specific to the asset or cash generating unit.** Applying one discount rate for all the CGUs does not achieve this. The WACC of the CGU or of the company of which the CGU is currently part should generally be used to determine the discount rate. The company's WACC may only be used for all CGUS if the risks associated with the individual CGUs do not materially diverge from the remainder of the group, and this is **not evident** in the case of Estoil.

(ii)   **Cash flow forecasts**

IAS 36 requires that any cash flow projections are based upon **reasonable and supportable assumptions** over a maximum period of five years unless it can be proven that longer estimates are reliable. The assumptions should **represent management's best estimate of the range of economic conditions expected to obtain over the remaining useful life of the asset.** Management must also assess the reasonableness of the assumptions by examining the reasons for any differences between past forecasted cash flows and actual cash flows. **The assumptions that form the basis for current cash flow projections must be consistent with past actual outcomes.**

Fariole has **failed to comply** with the requirements of IAS 36 in the preparation of its cash flow forecasts. Although the realised cash flow **forecasts for 20X4 were negative** and well below projected cash flows, **the directors significantly increased budgeted cash flows for**

20X5. This increase was **not justified,** and casts doubts on Fariole's ability to budget realistically.

IAS 36 requires estimates of future cash flows to include:

(1)   Projections of cash inflows from the continuing use of the asset

(2)   Projections of cash outflows which are necessarily incurred to generate the cash inflows from continuing use of the asset

(3)   Net cash flows to be received (or paid) for the disposal of the asset at the end of its useful life.

Forecast cash outflows must include those relating to the day-to-day servicing of the asset. This will **include future cash outflows needed to maintain the level of economic benefits expected to be generated by the asset in its current condition.** Fariole has not taken into account expected changes in working capital and capital expenditure, but it is very likely that investments in working capital and capital expenditure would be necessary to maintain the assets of the CGUs in their current condition.

In conclusion, the **cash flow forecasts used by Fariole are not in accordance with IAS 36.**

ACCA's exam answers:
June and December 2014 papers

Note: The ACCA examiner's answers are correct at the time of going to press but may be subject to some amendments before the final versions are published.

1   (a)   (i)   Marchant Group: Statement of profit or loss and other comprehensive income for the year
ended 30 April 2014

	$m
Revenue	538
Cost of sales	(383)
Gross profit	155
Other income	45.7
Administrative costs	(30)
Other expenses	(74.69)
Share of profits of associates	1.5
Operating profit	97·51
Finance costs	(10)
Finance income	15
Profit before tax	102.51
Income tax expense	(30.5)
Profit for the year	72.01

Other comprehensive income:	
Items which will not be reclassified to profit or loss	
Changes in revaluation surplus	2.8
Remeasurements – defined benefit plan	(2)
Total items which will not be reclassified subsequently to profit or loss	0.8
Items which may be reclassified subsequently to profit or loss	
Losses on cash flow hedge	(3)
Other comprehensive loss for the year	(2.2)
Total comprehensive income for the year	69.81

Profit/loss attributable to: (w7)	
Owners of the parent	60.21
Non-controlling interest	11.8
	72.01

Total comprehensive income attributable to:	
	$m
Owners of the parent	59.21
Non-controlling interest	10.6
	69·81

Working 1

(Note that this is purely a working and does not purport to show necessarily what would be reported in the individual accounts)

	Marchant $m	Nathan $m	Option $m	Adjustment $m	Total $m
Revenue	400	115	35	(12)	538
Cost of sales	(312)	(65)	(18)	12	(383)
Gross profit	88	50	17		155
Other income (21 – 5·3 + 22) W2/W3	37.7	7	1		45.7
Administrative costs	(15)	(9)	(6)		(30)
Other expenses	(35)	(19)	(4)		
Impairment of goodwill	(5)				
Share of profits of associates	1.5				
Net service cost	(7.2)				
PPE expense	(2.36)				
Share options	(2.13)				(73.19)
Operating profit	60.51	29	8		97.51
Finance costs	(5)	(6)	(2)		(10)
Cash flow hedge to OCI		3			
Finance income	6	5	4		15
Profit before tax	61.51	31	10		102.51
Income tax expense	(19)	(9)	(2.5)		(30.5)
Profit for the year	42.51	22	7.5		72.01
Other comprehensive income					
Remeasurements defined benefit plan	(2)				(2)
Revaluation surplus ($10m – $5m (W2))	5				5
Revaluation adjustment	(2.2)				(2.2)
Cash flow hedge (finance costs reduced by same amount)		(3)			(3)
Other comprehensive income/loss for year	0.8	(3)			(2.2)
Total comprehensive income for year	43.31	19	7.5		69.81

Note that the share of the associates' profit should be disclosed on the face of the statement of profit or loss. Therefore other expenses will be $73·19m plus $1·5m, i.e. $74·69m.

Working 2 Nathan

	$m	$m
Fair value of consideration for 60% interest	80	
Fair value of non-controlling interest	45	125
Fair value of identifiable net assets acquired		(110)
Goodwill		15

Goodwill impairment

After goodwill has been impaired (20% of $15m, i.e. $3m), any subsequent increase in the recoverable amount is likely to be internally generated goodwill rather than a reversal of purchased goodwill impairment. IAS 38 *Intangible Assets* prohibits the recognition of internally generated goodwill, thus any reversal of impairment is not recognised.

Hence $5 million needs to be charged to profit or loss to undo the reversal.

Total impairment is still $3 million.

The gains recorded regarding the investment in Nathan will be follows:

Gain on investment in Nathan ($95m – $90m)	$5m
Gain on sale of holding in Nathan ($18 – (8%/60% of $95m))	$5.3m

No gain or loss is recognised in profit or loss on the sale of Nathan in the group accounts as the sale is shown as a movement in equity. Therefore it is eliminated. Additionally, the gain on the revaluation of the investment in Nathan will also be eliminated on consolidation as the calculation of goodwill will be based on the fair value of the consideration at the date of acquisition and not at the date of the current financial statements.

Working 3 Option

	$m	$m
Fair value of consideration for 60% interest	70	
Fair value of non-controlling interest	28	98
Fair value of identifiable net assets acquired		(86)
Goodwill		12

As Marchant has sold a controlling interest in Option, a gain or loss on disposal should be calculated. Additionally, the results of Option should only be consolidated in the statement of profit or loss and other comprehensive income for the six months to 1 November 2013. Thereafter Option should be equity accounted.

The gain recognised in profit or loss would be as follows:

	$m
Fair value of consideration	50
Fair value of residual interest to be recognised as an associate	40
Value of NCI	34
	124
Less: net assets and goodwill derecognised	
net assets	(90)
goodwill	(12)
Gain on disposal to profit or loss	22

The share of the profits of the associate would be 20% of a half year's profit ($15m/2), i.e. $1·5 million.

Working 4 Defined benefit plan

Pension cost recognised for the year would be	$m
Current service cost	4
Net interest cost (10% of $50m – $48m)	0.2
Past service cost	3
Net service cost recognised in profit or loss	7.2
Remeasurements in OCI	2
Net cost for year recognised in total comprehensive income	9.2

IAS 19 does not specify where service cost and net interest cost should be presented. Therefore it is acceptable to include the net interest cost in finance costs. IAS 19 states that past service cost should be recognised immediately and the past service cost will be included in the defined benefit obligation at 1 May 2013. Therefore there is no need to calculate an interest cost on the past service cost.

Working 5 Property, plant and equipment

	$m
Carrying amount at 1 May 2013	13
Depreciation for year ($13m/9)	(1.44)
Carrying amount at 30 April 2014	11.56
Fall in value charged to revaluation surplus ($13m – ($12m – ($12m/10)))	(2.2)
Fall in value charged to profit or loss	(2.36)
Carrying amount after revaluation 30 April 2014	7

Working 6 Share options

Year	Expense for year $m	Cumulative expense $m	Calculation
30 April 2013	1.07	1.07	4 directors × $100 × 8,000 × 1/3
30 April 2014	2.13	3.2	6 directors × $100 × 8,000 × 2/3

Working 7 Non-controlling interest (NCI)

NCI in profits for year is (40% of $22m + 40% of $15 million/2) = $11.8 million
NCI in TCI (40% of 19 + 40% of $15 million/2) = $10.6 million

Working 8

The loss on the sale of the inventory is not eliminated from group profit or loss. Because the sale is at fair value, the inventory value must have been impaired and therefore the loss on sale must remain realised. However, the revenue and cost of sales of $12 million will be eliminated.

(ii) Once control has been achieved, further transactions whereby the parent entity acquires further equity interests from non-controlling interests, or disposes of equity interests but without losing control, are accounted for as equity transactions, that is transactions with owners in their capacity as owners. Thus it follows that:

- the carrying amounts of the controlling and non-controlling interests are adjusted to reflect the changes in their relative interests in the subsidiary;

- any difference between the amount by which the non-controlling interests is adjusted and the fair value of the consideration paid or received is recognised directly in equity and attributed to the owners of the parent; and

- there is no consequential adjustment to the carrying amount of goodwill, and no gain or loss is recognised in profit or loss.

Sale of equity interest in Nathan

	$m
Fair value of consideration received	18
Amount recognised as non-controlling interest (net assets per question at year end ($120m + fair value adjustment PPE at acquisition $14m + goodwill (15 – 3)) × 8%)	(11.7)
Positive movement in parent equity	6.3

The fair value adjustment is $110m – ($25m + $65m + $6m). The income should be shown as a movement in equity not in income. Hence it does not affect the consolidated statement of profit or loss and other comprehensive income.

(b) IFRSs utilise the 'fair value' concept and 'present value' more frequently than some other accounting frameworks. However, it is not a complete fair value system. The IASB has a preference for a mixed system of measurements using a combination of fair value and measurements at depreciated historical cost. IASB bases its standards on the business model of the entity and on the probability of realising the asset and liability-related cash flows through operations or transfers. Fair values, when used in the financial statements, affect the performance measurement and the net assets position and improve the disclosure of risks and of value which may be realisable. IFRS 13 *Fair Value*

Measurement was developed to solve the problems in the application of the fair value concept. However, IFRSs do not require that all assets and liabilities are valued at fair value. The financial statements of many entities will measure most items at depreciated historical cost, except where entities grow through acquisition when acquired assets and liabilities are valued at fair value on the acquisition date. However, a revaluation through other comprehensive income is allowed provided it is carried out regularly under IAS 16 *Property, Plant and Equipment* and, in addition, IAS 40 *Investment Property* allows as an option the measurement of investment properties at fair value with corresponding changes in earnings as this better reflects the business model of some property companies. However, the historical cost basis is still regularly used by entities holding investment properties. IAS 38 *Intangible Assets* allows the measurement of intangible assets at fair value, with corresponding changes in equity, but only if there is an active market, and thus a reliable valuation, for these assets.

IFRS 9 *Financial Instruments* replaces the multiple classification and measurement models for financial assets in IAS 39 with a single model which has only two classification categories: amortised cost and fair value. Classification under IFRS 9 is driven by the entity's business model for managing the financial assets and the contractual characteristics of the financial assets.

A financial asset is measured at amortised cost if two criteria are met:

(a)   the objective of the business model is to hold the financial asset for the collection of the contractual cash flows; and

(b)   the contractual cash flows under the instrument solely represent payments of principal and interest.

The new standard removes the requirement to separate embedded derivatives from financial asset hosts. It requires a hybrid contract to be classified in its entirety at either amortised cost or fair value.

As regards derivative financial instruments (swaps, options, future contracts), most of these contracts do not have a cost when signed, and their historical cost is not relevant and obviously it is useless to measure the extent of the commitments undertaken. A market value measurement with matching changes in profit or loss is therefore needed to reflect the risks. This can generate some volatility. Liabilities, except for derivative financial instruments, are recorded at amortised cost. A fair value option is available for financial liabilities, to be used only when some inconsistency should be avoided. In practice, only banks make a limited use of this option for their market transactions.

The fact that IFRSs make some use of fair values in the measurement of assets and liabilities is often misunderstood as meaning that financial statements prepared under IFRSs reflect the aggregate financial value of an entity. The IASB identifies the objective of general purpose financial reporting as being the provision of financial information about the reporting entity which is useful to existing and potential investors, lenders and other creditors in making decisions about providing resources to the entity. The Conceptual Framework states that general purpose financial reports are not designed to show the value of a reporting entity. The purpose of IFRS financial statements is not to disclose the selling value of the entity, even when some of the identifiable assets and liabilities are recorded at fair value. As IFRSs do not allow an entity to recognise intangible assets generated internally by business operations, any attempt to state the aggregate value of the business would be incomplete.

An entity's net assets are reported at market value only when it is acquired by another entity and consolidated in group accounts.

(c)   A lease is classified as a finance lease if it transfers substantially all the risks and rewards incident to ownership. All other leases are classified as operating leases and classification is made at the inception of the lease. Whether a lease is a finance lease or an operating lease depends on the substance of the transaction rather than the legal form. Thus in many circumstances, the classification of a lease can be quite subjective. In the case of a lease of land, this is particularly subjective as the title to the land may not pass to the lessee at the end of the agreement but the lease may still be classed as a finance lease where the present value of the residual value of the land is negligible and the risks and rewards pass to the lessee. Thus, it appears that at first sight this is a difference in a professional opinion, which can be solved by the financial controller seeking advice.

If the features of the lease appear to meet IAS 17 *Leases* criteria for classification as a finance lease and the treatment used is part of a strategy to understate the liabilities of the entity in order to raise a loan, then an ethical dilemma arises. Professional accountants are capable of making judgements, applying their skills and reaching informed decisions in situations where the general public cannot. The judgements made by professional accountants should be independent and not affected by business pressures. The code of ethics is very important because it sets out boundaries outside which accountants should not stray. The financial director should not place the financial controller under undue pressure in order to influence his decisions. If the financial controller is convinced that the lease is a finance lease, then disclosure of this fact should be made to the internal governance authority. The financial controller will have the knowledge that his actions were ethical.

2   (a)   The functional currency is the currency of the primary economic environment in which the entity operates, which is normally the one in which it primarily generates and expends cash. An entity's management considers the following primary indicators in determining its functional currency:

   (a)   the currency which mainly influences sales prices for goods and services;

   (b)   the currency of the country whose competitive forces and regulations mainly determine the sales prices of goods and services; and

   (c)   the currency which mainly influences labour, material and other costs of providing goods and services.

   Further secondary indicators which may also provide evidence of an entity's functional currency are the currency in which funds from financing activities are generated and in which receipts from operating activities are retained.

   Additional factors are considered in determining the functional currency of a foreign operation and whether its functional currency is the same as that of the reporting entity. These are:

   (a)   the autonomy of a foreign operation from the reporting entity;
   (b)   the level of transactions between the two;
   (c)   whether the foreign operation generates sufficient cash flows to meet its cash needs; and
   (d)   whether its cash flows directly affect those of the reporting entity.

   When the functional currency is not obvious, management uses its judgement to determine the functional currency which most faithfully represents the economic effects of the underlying transactions, events and conditions.

   In the case of Aspire, the subsidiary does not make any decisions as to the investment of funds, and consideration of the currency which influences sales and costs is not relevant. Although the costs are incurred in dollars, they are not material to any decision as to the functional currency. Therefore it is important to look at other factors to determine the functional currency. The subsidiary has issued 2 million dinars of equity capital to Aspire, which is a different currency to that of Aspire, but the proceeds have been invested in dinar denominated bonds at the request of Aspire. The subsidiary has also raised 100,000 dinars of equity capital from external sources but this amount is insignificant compared to the equity issued to Aspire. The income from investments is either remitted to Aspire or reinvested on instruction from Aspire. The subsidiary has a minimum number of staff and does not have any independent management. The subsidiary is simply a vehicle for the parent entity to invest in dinar related investments. Aspire may have set up the entity so that any exposure to the dinar/dollar exchange rate will be reported in other comprehensive income through the translation of the net investment in the subsidiary. There does not seem to be any degree of autonomy as the subsidiary is merely an extension of Aspire's activities. Therefore the functional currency would appear to be the dollar.

   In contrast, the dinar represents the currency in which the economic activities of the subsidiary are primarily carried out as is the case regarding the financing of operations and retention of any income not remitted. However, the investment of funds could have been carried out directly by Aspire and therefore the parent's functional currency should determine that of the subsidiary.

   (b)   Where a foreign branch's taxable profit is determined in a foreign currency, changes in exchange rates may give rise to temporary differences. This can arise where the carrying amounts of the non-monetary assets are translated at historical rates and the tax base of those assets are translated at the rate at the reporting date. An entity may translate the tax base at the year-end rate as this rate gives the best measure of the amount which will be deductible in future periods. The resulting deferred tax is charged or credited to profit or loss.

Property	Dinars (000)	Exchange rate	Dollars (000)
Cost	6,000	5	1,200
Depreciation for year	(500)		(100)
Net book amount	5,500		1,100
Tax base			
Cost	6,000		
Tax depreciation	(750)		
	5,250	6	875
Temporary difference			225
Deferred tax at 20%			45

The deferred tax arising will be calculated using the tax rate in the overseas country. The deferred tax arising is therefore $45,000, which will increase the tax charge in profit or loss. If the historical rate had been used, the tax base would have been $1.05 million (5.25m/5) which would have led to a temporary difference of $50,000 and a deferred tax liability of $10,000, which is significantly lower than when the closing rate is used.

(c)   The goodwill arising when a parent acquires a multinational operation with several currencies is allocated to each level of functional currency. Goodwill arising on acquisition of foreign operations and any fair value adjustments are both treated as the foreign operation's assets and liabilities. They are expressed in the foreign operation's functional currency and translated at the closing rate. Exchange differences arising on the retranslation of foreign entities' financial statements are recognised in other comprehensive income and accumulated as a separate component of equity

Exchange rate at 1 May 2013	$1= 5 dinars
Exchange rate at 30 April 2014	$1 =6 dinars
Net assets at fair value	1,100m dinars
Translated at 1 May 2013	$220m
Purchase consideration	$200m
NCI (250m dinars/5)	$50m
Goodwill	$30m
Goodwill treated as foreign currency asset at 1 May 2013 ($30m × 5)	150m dinars
Goodwill translated at closing rate at 30 April 2014 (150m dinars/6)	$25m
Translation adjustment for goodwill in equity	($5m)

An exchange loss of $5 million will be charged in other comprehensive income together with any gain or loss on the retranslation of the net assets of the operations.

(d)   The loan balance, as a monetary item, is translated at the spot exchange rate at the year-end date. Interest is translated at the average rate because it approximates to the actual rate. Because the interest is at a market rate for a similar two-year loan, Aspire measures the loan on initial recognition at the transaction price translated into the functional currency. Because there are no transaction costs, the effective interest rate is 8%.

On 1 May 2013, the loan is recorded on initial recognition as follows:

Dr Cash	$1 million
Cr Loan payable – financial liability	$1 million

Year ended 30 April 2014
Aspire records the interest expense as follows:

Dr Profit or loss – interest expense	$71,429
Cr Loan payable – financial liability	$71,429

To recognise interest payable for the year ended 30 April 2014 (0.4 million dinars/5.6).

On 30 April 2014 the interest is paid and the following entry is made:

Dr Loan payable – financial liability	$66,666
Cr Cash	$66,666

To recognise the payment of 2014 interest on financial liability (0.4 million dinars/6).

At 30 April 2014 the loan is recorded at 5 million dinars/6, i.e. $833,333, which gives rise to an exchange gain of $166,667. In addition to this, a further exchange gain of $4,763 arises on the translation of the interest paid ($71,429 – $66,666). The total exchange gain is therefore $171,430.

3　(a)　Minco needs to consider whether its revenue recognition policy is in compliance with IAS 18 *Revenue*. The criteria for revenue recognition required by paragraph 14 of IAS 18 do not appear to be met, and no revenue should be accounted for as of the date of the transfer of land to the housing association. Revenue arising from the sale of goods should be recognised when all of the following criteria have been satisfied (IAS 18.14):

(a)　the seller has transferred to the buyer the significant risks and rewards of ownership;

(b)　the seller retains neither continuing managerial involvement to the degree usually associated with ownership nor effective control over the goods sold;

(c)　the amount of revenue can be measured reliably;

(d)　it is probable that the economic benefits associated with the transaction will flow to the seller; and

(e)　the costs incurred or to be incurred in respect of the transaction can be measured reliably.

It is important to consider whether the risks for the project have been transferred to the association and whether Minco has control over the project during the construction period. Even if the risk associated with the land is different to the risk associated with the project directly. Minco should assess the risks for the entire project since it is exposed to material risks during the construction period. Minco provides a guarantee as regards the maintenance costs, is liable for certain increases in the interest rate over expectations, and is responsible for financing variations in the procurement and construction contract which the contractor would not cover. Further, Minco guarantees the payment for the housing association's debt on the building loan. Minco is exposed to risk as if it had built the housing units itself because it gives guarantees in respect of the construction process.

Minco also determines the membership of the board of the housing association and thus there is a question mark over whether the board is independent from Minco. Minco guarantees that the housing association would not be liable if budgeted construction costs are exceeded, so the entity is exposed to financial risk in the construction process.

Minco has retained the significant risks and had effective control of the land it had sold and also the entire construction process. Consequently, the revenue recognition criteria in paragraph 14 of IAS 18 are not met on the transfer of the land and Minco should account for the whole project as if it had built the housing units itself. Accordingly, revenue should be recognized when the housing units are finished and delivered to the buyer of the rights in accordance with IAS 18 which appears to be when the project is completed.

(b)　The different payments to the tennis player are not interrelated. Therefore, any interdependencies and interrelations between different forms of payments or specific services and payments need not be examined in order to determine an appropriate expense recognition pattern. The contract relates to advertising and promotional expenditure to improve Minco's brand image by the tennis player. Therefore, in accordance with IAS 38 *Intangible Assets*, the costs must be expensed when the entity has received the service. Any amounts paid in advance of the service being received are recognised as prepayments and expensed when that service is received. The signing bonus of $20,000 is paid to the player on commencement of the contract. In return, the player is obliged to advertise Minco and take part in photo/film sessions. The signing bonus relates to the full contract term and a prepayment of $20,000 is recognised on commencement and is expensed on a straight line basis over the three-year contract period. However, if, from the terms of the contract, separate services can be identified and measured reliably, Minco should allocate the costs and recognise expenses once the separate service is rendered. If the contract is terminated prior to the end of the contract period, any amount not recovered from the player would be expensed immediately.

The player receives the annual retainer at the end of each year, provided she has competed in all of the specified tournaments for that year. Minco has a contractual obligation to deliver cash to the player and, hence, recognises a financial liability during the period, which must be accounted for in accordance with IFRS 9 *Financial Instruments*. The liability is recognised at the point where Minco has an obligation which arises on the date when the player has competed in all the specified tournaments. The financial liability is recognised at the present value of the expected cash flows.

The player also receives additional performance-related payments for success in the tournaments. As these payments relate to specific events, they are treated as executory contracts. They are accrued and expensed when the player has won a tournament.

(c)   As regards the improvements to the building through adding an extra floor, Minco should capitalise the costs of the floor in accordance with IAS 16 *Property, Plant and Equipment* and amortise these costs over the six years of the lease. However, Minco has an obligation to remove the floor at the end of the lease. The obligation arises because the completion of the floor creates an obligation event. A provision should be made for the present value of the cost of removal of the floor in six years' time. At the same time an asset should be recognised for the cost. The cost should be recovered from the benefits generated by the new floor over the remainder of the lease. The asset should be amortised over the six-year period. In effect, this is in substance a decommissioning activity.

As regards the disrepair of the building, the estimated costs should be spread over the six years of the agreement. IAS 37 *Provisions, Contingent Liabilities and Contingent Assets* would indicate that Minco has a present obligation arising from the lease agreement because the landlord can recharge the costs of any repair to Minco. The obligating event is the wear and tear to the building which will arise gradually over the tenancy period and its repair can be enforced through the legal agreement. The obligation relates to wear and tear and is not related to future operating costs. The wear and tear will result in an outflow of economic benefits and a reliable estimate of the yearly obligation arising from this will be made, although it will not necessarily equate to one sixth per year. As regards the roof repair, it is clear from the lease that an obligation exists and therefore a provision should be made for the whole of the rectification work when the need for the repair was identified.

(d)   IAS 34 *Interim Financial Reporting* requires an entity to apply the same accounting policies in its interim financial statements as are applied in its annual financial statements. Measurements should be made on a 'year to date' basis. In valuing the property, Minco should use the provisions of IFRS 5 *Assets held for Sale and Discontinued Operations*. Immediately before the initial classification of the asset as held for sale, the carrying amount of the asset should be measured in accordance with applicable IFRSs. After classification as held for sale, the property should be measured at the lower of carrying amount and fair value less costs to sell. Impairment must be considered both at the time of classification as held for sale and subsequently in accordance with the applicable IFRSs. Any impairment loss is recognised in profit or loss unless the asset has previously been measured at a revalued amount under IAS 16 or IAS 38, in which case the impairment is treated as a revaluation decrease. A gain for any subsequent increase in fair value less costs to sell of an asset is recognised in the profit or loss to the extent that it is not in excess of the cumulative impairment loss which has been recognised in accordance with IFRS 5 or previously in accordance with IAS 36.

At the time of classification as held for sale, depreciation needs to be charged for the four months to 1 October 2013. This will be based upon the year end value at 31 May 2013 of $2.65 million. The property has 10 years life remaining based upon the depreciation to date and assuming a zero residual value, the depreciation for the four months will be approximately $0.1 million. Thus, at the time of classification as held for sale, after charging depreciation for the four months of $0.1 million, the carrying amount is $2.55 million ($4m – $1 – $0.1m – $0.35m) and fair value less costs to sell is assessed at $2.4 million. Accordingly, the initial write-down on classification as held for sale is $150,000 and the property is carried at $2.4 million. On 1 December 2013 in the interim financial statements, the property market has improved and fair value less costs to sell is reassessed at $2.52 million. The gain of $120,000 is less than the cumulative impairment losses recognised to date ($350,000 plus $150,000, i.e. $500,000). Accordingly, it is credited in profit or loss and the property is carried at $2.52 million. On 31 May 2014, the property market has continued to improve, and fair value less costs to sell is now assessed at $2.95 million. The further gain of $430,000 is, however, in excess of the cumulative impairment losses recognised to date ($350,000 plus $150,000 – $120,000 – $430,000, i.e. $50,000). Accordingly, a restricted gain of $380,000 is credited in profit or loss and the property is carried at $2.9 million. Subsequently, the property is sold for $3 million at which point a gain of $100,000 is recognised. This sale would be a non-adjusting event under IAS 10 *Events after the Reporting Period* if deemed to be material.

4   (a)   (i)   IAS 32 *Financial Instruments: Presentation* establishes principles for presenting financial instruments as liabilities or equity. To determine whether a financial instrument should be classified as debt or equity, IAS 32 uses principles-based definitions of a financial liability and of equity. In contrast to the requirements of generally accepted accounting practice in many jurisdictions around the world, IAS 32 does not classify a financial instrument as equity or financial liability on the basis of its legal form. The key feature of debt is that the issuer is obliged to deliver either cash or another financial asset to the holder. The contractual obligation may arise from a requirement to repay principal or interest or dividends. Such a contractual obligation may be established explicitly or indirectly through the terms of the agreement. For example, a bond which requires the issuer to make interest payments and redeem the bond for cash is classified as debt. In contrast, equity is any contract which evidences a residual interest in the entity's assets after deducting all of its liabilities. A financial instrument is an equity instrument only if the instrument includes no contractual obligation to deliver cash or another financial asset to another entity and if the instrument will or may be settled in the issuer's own equity instruments. For example, ordinary shares, where all the payments are at the discretion of the issuer, are classified as equity of the issuer. The classification is not quite as simple as it seems. For example, preference shares required to be converted into a fixed number of ordinary shares on a fixed date or on the occurrence of an event which is certain to occur, should be classified as equity.

A contract is not an equity instrument solely because it may result in the receipt or delivery of the entity's own equity instruments. The classification of this type of contract is dependent on whether there is variability in either the number of equity shares delivered or variability in the amount of cash or financial assets received. A contract which will be settled by the entity receiving or delivering a fixed number of its own equity instruments in exchange for a fixed amount of cash or another financial asset is an equity instrument. However, if there is any variability in the amount of cash or own equity instruments which will be delivered or received, then such a contract is a financial asset or liability as applicable.

For example, where a contract requires the entity to deliver as many of the entity's own equity instruments as are equal in value to a certain amount of cash, the holder of the contract would be indifferent whether it received cash or shares to the value of that amount. Thus this contract would be treated as debt.

Other factors, which may result in an instrument being classified as debt, are:

- redemption is at the option of the instrument holder
- there is a limited life to the instrument
- redemption is triggered by a future uncertain event which is beyond the control of both the holder and issuer of the instrument
- dividends are non-discretionary

Similarly, other factors, which may result in the instrument being classified as equity, are whether the shares are non-redeemable, whether there is no liquidation date or where the dividends are discretionary.

(ii)   The classification of a financial instrument by the issuer as either debt or equity can have a significant impact on the entity's gearing ratio, reported earnings, and debt covenants. Equity classification can avoid such impact but may be perceived negatively if it is seen as diluting existing equity interests. The distinction between debt and equity is also relevant where an entity issues financial instruments to raise funds to settle a business combination using cash or as part consideration in a business combination. Understanding the nature of the classification rules and potential effects is critical for management and must be borne in mind when evaluating alternative financing options. Liability classification normally results in any payments being treated as interest and charged to profit or loss, which may affect the entity's ability to pay dividends on its equity shares.

(b) **Cavor**

An obligation must be established through the terms and conditions of the financial instrument. IAS 32 uses principles-based definitions of a financial liability and of equity. IAS 32 uses substance over form as a principle to classify a financial instrument between equity and financial liability. IAS 32 restricts the role of 'substance' to consideration of the contractual terms of an instrument. Anything outside the contractual terms is not therefore relevant to the classification process under IAS 32. The B shares of Cavor should be classified as equity as there is no contractual obligation to pay the dividends or to call the instrument. Dividends can only be paid on the B shares if dividends have been declared on the A shares and they are payable at the same rate as the A shares which will be variable. There is no contractual obligation to declare A share dividends.

The classification of the B share options in Cavor is dependent on whether there is variability in either the number of equity shares delivered or variability in the amount of cash or financial assets received. As there is no variability and the contract will be settled by the entity issuing a fixed number of its own equity instruments in exchange for a fixed amount of cash, then the share options are classified as an equity instrument.

Lidan

The contractual obligation may arise from a requirement to repay principal or interest or dividends. Such a contractual obligation need not be explicit. It may instead be established indirectly through the terms and conditions of the financial instrument and the liability classification is not avoided by a share settlement alternative which is uneconomic in comparison to the cash obligation. The B shares of Lidan will be classified as a liability. This is because the value of the own share settlement alternative substantially exceeds that of the cash settlement option, meaning that the entity is implicitly obliged to redeem the option for a cash amount of $1 per share. Additionally, IAS 32 also states that where a derivative contract has settlement options, it is a financial asset or liability unless all of the settlement alternatives result in it being an equity instrument. This would also lead to the conclusion that the B shares are a financial liability.

Marking scheme

				Marks
1	(a)	Impairment adjustment		4
		Nathan		6
		Option		6
		Inventory		1
		Share options		4
		PPE		3
		Employee benefits		4
		NCI		2
		Sale of equity interest in Nathan		5
				35
	(b)	1 mark per point up to maximum		9
	(c)	1 mark per point up to maximum		6
				50
2	(a)	1 mark per point up to maximum		7
	(b)	1 mark per point up to maximum		6
	(c)	1 mark per point up to maximum		5
	(d)	1 mark per point up to maximum		5
		Professional marks		2
				25
3	(a)	1 mark per point up to maximum		7
	(b)	1 mark per point up to maximum		5
	(c)	1 mark per point up to maximum		5
	(c)	1 mark per point up to maximum		6
		Professional marks		2
				25
4	(a)	(i)	1 mark per point up to maximum	9
		(ii)	Effects	5
	(b)		1 mark per point up to maximum	9
		Professional marks		2
				25

1   (a)   **Joey**

Consolidated statement of financial position at 30 November 2014

	$m
Assets:	
Non-current assets	
Property, plant and equipment (W8)	6,709
Goodwill (W1)	89
Intangible assets – franchise right (W2)	15
Investment in joint venture (W10)	0.75
	6,813.75
Current assets (W6)	2,011.3
Total assets	8,825.05
Equity and liabilities:	
Equity attributable to owners of parent	
Share capital	850
Retained earnings (W4)	3,450.25
Other components of equity (W5)	258.5
	4,558.75
Non-controlling interest (W7)	908.1
Non-current liabilities (W9)	2,770
Current liabilities (W9)	588.2
Total liabilities	3,358.2
Total equity and liabilities	8,825.05

Working 1 Goodwill on acquisition of Margy

	$m	$m
Fair value of consideration for 40% interest		975
Non-controlling interest – fair value		620
Previously held interest of 30% – fair value		705
Fair value of identifiable net assets acquired:		
Share capital	1,020	
Retained earnings	900	
OCE	70	
FV adjustment – land	266	
– contingent liability	(6)	
		(2,250)
Add decrease in fair value of buildings		40
Measurement period adjustment – contingent liability		(1)
($6m – $5m)		
Goodwill		89

Tutorial note

The carrying amount of Margy at 1 December 2013 is (cash $600 + profit $90m + revaluation gain $10m) $700 million and this interest is fair valued at the date of acquisition to $705 million, giving a revaluation gain of $5 million which goes to profit or loss. The previous revaluation gain of $10 million would not be reclassified to profit or loss even if the interest in Margy were disposed of.

The carrying amount of property, plant and equipment as of 30 November 2014 is decreased by $40 million less the excess depreciation charged of $2 million, i.e. $38 million. The carrying amount of goodwill is increased by $40 million and depreciation expense for 2014 is decreased by $2 million. This latter decrease in expense is split between retained earnings ($1.4m) and NCI ($0.6m).

BPP
LEARNING MEDIA

IFRS 3 Business Combinations requires Joey to measure contingent liabilities subsequent to the date of acquisition at the higher of the amount which would be recognised in accordance with IAS 37 Provisons, Contingent Liabilities and Contingent

Assets, and the amount initially recognised, less any appropriate cumulative amortisation in accordance with IAS 18 Revenue. These requirements should be applied only for the period in which the item is considered to be a contingent liability. In this case, the contingent liability has subsequently met the requirements to be reclassified as a provision, and will be measured in accordance with IAS 37 rather than IFRS 3.

As a result the liability has been measured at March 2014 at $5 million, and recognised through profit or loss during the year ended 30 November 2014. This represents a pre-combination loss which must be credited back to NCI and group reserves. Therefore NCI is credited with $1.5 million and retained earnings with $3.5 million.

Working 2 Hulty

Joey measures the gain on its purchase of the 80% interest in Hulty as follows:

	$m	$m
Purchase consideration – Hulty		700
Non-controlling interest		250
Less fair value of identifiable net assets:		
Share capital	600	
Retained earnings	300	
OCE	40	
FV – franchise right	20	
		(960)
Gain on bargain purchase		(10)

The gain of $10 million is recognised in profit or loss. Additionally, Joey recognises an identified intangible asset for the reacquired right at its fair value of $20 million. This right will be amortised over the remaining term of the franchise agreement of four years. Thus $5 million will be credited to the franchise right account (to give a balance of $15 million) and debited to retained earnings $4 million and NCI $1 million.

Working 3 Asset held for sale

IFRS 5 *Non-current Assets Held for Sale and Discontinued Operations* criteria are met at 31 March 2014. Therefore, Joey should depreciate the property until the date of reclassification as held for sale. Thus, the depreciation charge is $300,000 × 4/12 = $100,000. The carrying value of the property is therefore $13.9 million.

The property should be revalued to its fair value at that date of $15.4 million as the difference between the property's carrying amount at that date and its fair value is deemed to be material. The revaluation increase of $1.5 million is recognised in other comprehensive income in accordance with IAS 16 *Property, Plant and Equipment.*

Joey should consider whether the property is impaired by comparing its carrying amount (fair value) with its recoverable amount (higher of value in use and fair value less costs to sell). No impairment loss is recognised because value in use of $15.8 million is higher than fair value less costs to sell of $15.1 million. The property should be reclassified as held for sale and remeasured to fair value less costs to sell ($15.1 million), which results in the recognition of a loss of $300,000 which should be recognised in profit or loss.

When the property is disposed of on 30 November 2014, a profit on disposal of $200,000 is recognised (net proceeds of $15.3 million less carrying amount of $15.1 million). Any remaining revaluation reserve relating to the property is not recognised in profit or loss, nor transferred to retained earnings in accordance with IAS 16 because of group policy.

Accounting entries

Dr Profit or loss	$100,000
Cr Property	$100,000

The depreciation up to the date of reclassification as held for sale.

Dr Property $1.5 million
Cr OCI $1.5 million

The increase in the value of the property to fair value at the date of the reclassification.

Dr Profit or loss $300,000
Cr Property $300,000

Loss arising on reclassification.

Dr Accounts receivable $15.3 million
Cr Property $15.1 million
Cr Profit or loss $0.2 million

The disposal of the property at the year end.

Working 4 Retained earnings

	$m
Joey	
Balance at 30 November 2014	3,340
Revaluation gain – Margy	5
Depreciation reduction (70% × 2)	1.4
Liability adjustment (70% × 5)	3.5
Amortisation – franchise right (80% × 5)	(4)
Gain on bargain purchase	10
Asset held for sale – depreciation up to reclassification (W3)	(0.1)
Asset held for sale – remeasurement (W3)	(0.3)
Asset held for sale – gain on sale (W3)	0.2
Joint operation (W10)	(0.7)
Joint venture (W10)	0.75
Joint venture (W10)	(1.5)
Post-acquisition reserves: Margy (70% of (980 – 900))	56
Hulty (80% of (350 – 300))	40
	3,450.25

Working 5 Other components of equity

	$m
Balance at 30 November 2014 – Joey	250
Asset held for sale (W3)	1.5
Post-acquisition reserves: Margy post acquisition (70% of 80 – 70)	7
Hulty (80% × (40 – 40))	0
	258.5

Working 6 Current assets

	$m
Balance at 30 November 2014	
Joey	985
Margy	861
Hulty	150
Sale of property (W3)	15.3
	2,011.3

Working 7 Non-controlling interest

	$m
Margy (W1)	620
Hulty (W2)	250
Post-acquisition retained earnings – Margy (30% of 980 – 900)	24
Post-acquisition retained earnings – Hulty (20% of 350 – 300)	10
OCE – post acquisition – Margy (30% of 80 – 70)	3
OCE – post acquisition – Hulty (20% of 40 – 40)	0
Depreciation reduction (30% × 2)	0.6
Franchise right – amortisation (20% × 5)	(1)
Liability adjustment (30% × 5)	1.5
	908·1

Working 8 Property, plant and equipment

	$m	$m
Balance at 30 November 2014		
Joey	3,295	
Margy	2,000	
Hulty	1,200	
		6,495
Decrease in value of building – Margy (W1)	(38)	
Increase in value of land – Margy (W1)	266	
Asset held for sale – depreciation prior to reclassification (W3)	(0.1)	
Asset held for sale – remeasurement prior to reclassification	1.5	
Asset held for sale – remeasurement after reclassification	(0.3)	
Asset held for sale – disposal	(15·1)	214
		6,709

Working 9 Liabilities

	$m	$m
Non-current liabilities – balance at 30 November 2014		
Joey	1,895	
Margy	675	
Hulty	200	
		2,770

	$m	$m
Current liabilities – balance at 30 November 2014		
Joey	320	
Margy	106	
Hulty	160	
Joint operation – CP	0.7	
Joint venture	1.5	
		588·2

Working 10 Joint venture

For the period to 31 May 2014, the requirement for unanimous key strategic decisions means this is a joint venture. Since there is no legal entity, it would be classified as a joint operation. Joey would account for its direct rights to the underlying results and assets.

Up until 31 May 2014, the joint operation had the following results:

	$m
Revenue (5 × 6/12)	2.5
Cost of sales (2 × 6/12)	(1)
Gross profit	1.5

What belongs to Joey is therefore:

	$m
Sales (90% × 2.5)	2.25
Cost of sales (printing, binding, platform – all by Joey)	(1)
Gross profit	1.25
Profit royalty to CP (calculated as 30% of $1·5m)	(0.45)
Net profit	0.8

Therefore Joey should adjust the accounting for the period to 31 May 2014 as follows:

Dr Profit or loss ($0.45m above + ($2.5m × 10%), i.e. $0.25 million)	$0.7 million
Cr Accounts payable CP	$0.7 million

From 1 June 2014, Joey has a share of the net assets rather than direct rights; the joint operation would be classified as a joint venture and must be equity accounted. Therefore the adjustment to the current accounting will be:

Remove profit of new entity JCP:

Dr Profit or loss	$1.5 million
Cr JCP – profit for period	$1.5 million

Recognise Joey's equity-accounted share of JCP's profit:

Dr Investment in joint venture (($5m – $2m)/2 × 50%)	$0.75 million
Cr Profit or loss	$0.75 million

(b) IFRS 2 *Share-based Payment* includes within its scope transfers of equity instruments of an entity's parent in return for goods or services. The standard provides a clear basis to determine the classification of awards in both consolidated and separate financial statements by setting out the circumstances in which group share-based payment transactions are treated as equity settled and cash settled. The entity receiving goods or services should assess its own rights and obligations as well as the nature of awards granted in order to determine the accounting treatment. The amount recognised by the group entity receiving the goods or services will not necessarily be consistent with the amount recognised in the consolidated financial statements. Group share-based payment transactions are treated as equity settled when:

(i) the awards granted are the entity's own equity instruments, or
(ii) the entity has no obligation to settle the share-based payment transaction.

In the group accounts, the transaction is treated as equity settled as the group is receiving all of the services in consideration for the group's equity instruments. An expense is charged in the group statement of profit or loss for the fair value of the share-based payment at the grant date over the vesting period, with a corresponding credit in equity.

In the subsidiaries' accounts, the grant is treated as an equity settled transaction as the subsidiaries do not have an obligation to settle the award. An expense is charged in the subsidiaries' statements of profit or loss for the fair value of the share-based payment at the grant date over the vesting period, with a corresponding credit in equity. The credit in equity is treated as a capital contribution as Joey is compensating the employees of Margy and Hulty with no expense to the subsidiaries. In this case the shares vest immediately, therefore the expense recognised in Margy's and Hulty's statement of profit or loss will be the full cost of the grant date fair value.

In the separate accounts of Joey, there is no share-based payment charge as there are no employees providing services to the parent. Joey would recognise an increase in its investment in the subsidiaries and a credit to equity.

The disclosure requirements of IAS 24 *Related Party Disclosures* by Joey should be applied if any of the employees are key management personnel.

(c)   Joey needs a significant injection of capital in order to modernise plant and equipment and the bank requires the company to demonstrate good projected cash flow and profitability. However, the projected cash flow statement does not satisfy the bank's criteria and the directors have told the bank that the financial results will meet the criteria. Thus there is pressure on the chief accountant to forward a financial report which meets the bank's criteria. The chief accountant cannot afford to lose his job because of his financial commitments and this in itself creates an ethical dilemma for the accountant, as not only is there self-interest of the accountant involved but also the interests of the company and its workforce. The accountant has to rely upon his moral and ethical judgement in these circumstances.

Ethical standards are used by members of a profession to decide the right course of action in given circumstances. Ethics rely on logical and rational reasoning to reach a decision, morals are a behavioural code of conduct to which an individual ascribes and ethical rules create an obligation to undertake a particular course of action. Conflict can arise between personal and ethical values but when an individual becomes a member of a profession, there is a recognition that there is acceptance of the standards of that profession which include its code of ethics and values. The ethical rules of the accounting profession represent an attempt to codify principles. A profession is distinguished by having a specialised body of knowledge, a social commitment, the ability to regulate itself and high social status. The profession should seek to promote or preserve public interest. Professional accountants make a bargain with society in which they promise to serve the public interest which may, at times, be at their own expense. Accountants, as professionals, cannot rely exclusively on rules to define how they will act ethically. Members of the profession have a responsibility to present the truth in a fair and honest fashion and in a spirit of public service. In such circumstances, accountants should think carefully before seeking creative accounting solutions to particular problems. Thus, in this case, the chief accountant should insist that the report to the bank is a true reflection of the current financial position, irrespective of the consequences for himself.

2   (a)   Under IAS 24 *Related Party Disclosures*, disclosures are required in respect of an entity's transactions with related parties. Related parties include parents, subsidiaries, members of key management personnel of the entity or of a parent of the entity and post-employment benefit plans.

Where there have been related party transactions during the period, management discloses the nature of the relationship, as well as information about the transactions and outstanding balances, including commitments, necessary for users to understand the potential impact of the relationship on the financial statements. Disclosure is made by category of related party and by major type of transaction. Management only discloses that related party transactions were made on terms equivalent to those which prevail in arm's length transactions if such terms can be substantiated.

Government-related entities are defined as entities which are controlled, jointly controlled or significantly influenced by the government. The financial crisis widened the range of entities subject to the related party disclosure requirements. The financial support provided by governments to financial institutions in many countries meant that the government controls significantly influenced some of those entities. A government-controlled bank would, in principle, be required to disclose details of its transactions, deposits and commitments with all other government-controlled banks and with the central bank.

However, IAS 24 has an exemption from all of the disclosure requirements of IAS 24 for transactions between government-related entities and the government, and all other government-related entities. Coatmin is exempt from the disclosure requirements in relation to related party transactions and outstanding balances, including commitments, with:

(a)   a government which has control, joint control or significant influence over the reporting entity; and

(b)   another entity which is a related party because the same government has control, joint control or significant influence over both the reporting entity and the other entity.

Those disclosures are replaced with a requirement to disclose:

(a)   the name of the government and the nature of their relationship; and

(b)   (i)   the nature and amount of any individually significant transactions; and
        (ii)   the extent of any collectively significant transactions qualitatively or quantitatively.

The disclosures provide more meaningful information about the nature of an entity's relationship with the government and material transactions.

(b)   IFRS 9 *Financial Instruments* says that an entity should classify all financial liabilities as subsequently measured at amortised cost using the effective interest method, except for:

(a)   financial liabilities at fair value through profit or loss. Such liabilities, including derivatives which are liabilities, shall be subsequently measured at fair value.

(b)   financial liabilities which arise when a transfer of a financial asset does not qualify for de-recognition or when the continuing involvement approach applies.

(c)   financial guarantee contracts as defined in the standard. After initial recognition, an issuer of such a contract shall subsequently measure it at the higher of:

        (i)   the amount determined in accordance with IAS 37 *Provisions, Contingent Liabilities and Contingent Assets*, and

        (ii)   the amount initially recognised less, when appropriate, cumulative amortisation recognised in accordance with IAS 18 *Revenue*.

In addition, financial guarantees and loan commitments which entities choose to measure at fair value through profit or loss will have all fair value movements in profit or loss, with no transfer to OCI. Changes in the credit risk of liabilities relating to loan commitment and financial guarantee contracts are not required to be presented in other comprehensive income.

The accounting entries on the assumption that discounting would not be material will therefore be:

1 December 2012

Dr Profit or loss	$1.2 million
Cr Financial liabilities	$1.2 million

To record the loss incurred in giving the guarantee.

30 November 2013

Dr Financial liabilities	$0.4 million
Cr Profit or loss	$0.4 million

To amortise the initial fair value over the life of the guarantee, reflecting the reduction in exposure as a result of the first

repayment by the subsidiary.

30 November 2014

Dr Profit or loss	$39.2 million
Cr Financial liabilities	$39.2 million

To provide for the calling of the guarantee – the difference between the possible $40 million call and the carrying amount of the guarantee of $0.8 million.

Dr Financial liabilities	$39.6 million
Cr Profit or loss	$39.6 million

To move from the provision back to measurement at amortised initial value following event after the reporting period change in probabilities of the guarantee being called.

BPP
LEARNING MEDIA

An event after the reporting period is an event, which could be favourable or unfavourable, which occurs between the end of the reporting period and the date when the financial statements are authorised for issue. The above is an adjusting event which is an event after the reporting period which provides further evidence of conditions which existed at the end of the reporting period.

(c) IAS 39 *Financial Instruments: Recognition and Measurement* permits hedge accounting under certain circumstances provided that the hedging relationship is:

(a) formally designated and documented, including the entity's risk management objective and strategy for undertaking the hedge, identification of the hedging instrument, the hedged item, the nature of the risk being hedged, and how the entity will assess the hedging instrument's effectiveness; and

(b) expected to be highly effective in achieving offsetting changes in fair value or cash flows attributable to the hedged risk as designated and documented, and effectiveness can be reliably measured; and

(c) assessed on an ongoing basis and determined to have been highly effective.

A hedging instrument is an instrument whose fair value or cash flows are expected to offset changes in the fair value or cash flows of a designated hedged item. All derivative contracts with an external counterparty may be designated as hedging instruments except for some written options. A non-derivative financial asset or liability may not be designated as a hedging instrument except as a hedge of foreign currency risk. For hedge accounting purposes, only instruments which involve a party external to the reporting entity can be designated as a hedging instrument. This applies to intragroup transactions as well with the exception of certain foreign currency hedges of forecast intragroup transactions. However, they may qualify for hedge accounting in individual financial statements.

IAS 39 requires hedge effectiveness to be assessed both prospectively and retrospectively in order to qualify for hedge accounting at the inception of a hedge and, at a minimum, at each reporting date. The changes in the fair value of the hedged item, in this case, attributable to the hedged risk must be expected to be highly effective in offsetting the changes in the fair value of the hedging instrument on a prospective basis, and on a retrospective basis where actual results are within a range of 80% to 125%. All hedge ineffectiveness is recognised immediately in profit or loss including ineffectiveness within the 80% to 125% window.

	Fair value 1 December 2013	Fair value 30 November 2014	Change in value
	$000	$000	$000
Fixed interest bond	2,000	1,910	90
Interest rate swap	Nil	203	203
Effectiveness			226% or 44%

Therefore hedge accounting is not permitted as the results of the effectiveness test fall outside the acceptable range of 80% to 125%. The main reason for the difference in the fair value movements is likely to be Coatmin's deteriorating creditworthiness. IAS 39 allows an entity to designate any portion of the risk in a financial asset as the hedged item. Hedge effectiveness is easier to achieve if the hedged risk matches the hedging instrument as closely as possible. Coatmin should redesignate the risk being hedged and try to exclude the credit risk from the hedging relationship. Maybe it could hedge changes in the bond's fair value to changes in the risk free interest rate.

(d) IFRS 9 requires gains and losses on financial liabilities designated as at fair value through profit or loss to be split into the amount of change in the fair value which is attributable to changes in the credit risk of the liability, which is shown in other comprehensive income, and the remaining amount of change in the fair value of the liability which is shown in profit or loss. IFRS 9 allows th recognition of the full amount of change in the fair value in the profit or loss only if the recognition of changes in the liability's credit risk in other comprehensive income would create an accounting mismatch in profit or loss. This is determined at initial recognition and is not reassessed. Amounts presented in other comprehensive income are not subsequently transferred to profit or loss, and the entity may only transfer the cumulative gain or loss within equity. Thus Coatmin should charge $5 million to OCI and $45 million to profit or loss.

3   (a)   The accounting for the transaction as an asset acquisition does not comply with the requirements of IFRS 3 *Business Combinations* and should have been accounted as a business combination. This would mean that transaction costs would be expensed, the vessels recognised at fair value, any deferred tax recognised at nominal value and the difference between these amounts and the consideration paid to be recognised as goodwill.

In accordance with IFRS 3, an entity should determine whether a transaction is a business combination by applying the definition of a business in IFRS 3. A business is an integrated set of activities and assets which is capable of being conducted and managed for the purpose of providing a return in the form of dividends, lower costs or other economic benefits directly to investors or other owners, members or participants. A business consists of inputs and processes applied to those inputs which have the ability to create outputs. Although businesses usually have outputs, outputs are not required to qualify as a business.

When analysing the transaction, the following elements are relevant:

(i)   Inputs: Shares in vessel owning companies, charter arrangements, outsourcing arrangements with a management company, and relationships with a shipping broker.

(ii)   Processes: Activities regarding chartering and operating the vessels, financing the business, purchase and sales of vessels.

(iii)   Outputs: Ceemone would generate revenue from charter agreements and has the ability to gain economic benefit from the vessels.

IFRS 3 states that whether a seller operated a set of assets and activities as a business or intends to operate it as a business is not relevant in evaluating whether it is a business. It is not relevant therefore that some activities were outsourced as Ceemone could chose to conduct and manage the integrated set of assets and activities as a business. As a result, the acquisition included all the elements which constitute a business, in accordance with IFRS 3.

IFRS 10 *Consolidated Financial Statements* sets out the situation where an investor controls an investee. This is the case, if and only if, the investor has all of the following elements:

(i)   power over the investee, that is, the investor has existing rights which give it the ability to direct the relevant activities (the activities which significantly affect the investee's returns);

(ii)   exposure, or rights, to variable returns from its involvement with the investee;

(iii)   the ability to use its power over the investee to affect the amount of the investor's returns.

Where a party has all three elements, then it is a parent; where at least one element is missing, then it is not. In every case, IFRS 10 looks to the substance of the arrangement and not just to its legal form. Each situation needs to be assessed

individually. The question arises in this case as to whether the entities created are subsidiaries of the bank. The bank is likely

to have power over the investee, may be exposed to variable returns and certainly may have the power to affect the amount

of the returns. Thus the bank is likely to have a measure of control but the extent will depend on the constitution of the entity.

(b)   Kayte's calculation of the residual value of the vessels with a 10-year useful life is unacceptable under IAS 16 *Property, Plant and Equipment* because estimating residual value based on acquisition cost does not comply with the requirements of

IAS 16. Kayte should prepare a new model to determine residual value which would take account of broker valuations at the end of each reporting period and which would produce zero depreciation charge when estimated residual value was higher than the carrying amount.

IAS 16 paragraph 6 defines residual value as the estimated amount which an entity would currently obtain from disposal of the asset, after deducting the estimated costs of disposal, if the asset were already at the age and in the condition expected at the end of its useful life.

IAS 16 requires the residual value to be reviewed at least at the end of each financial year end with the depreciable amount of an asset allocated on a systematic basis over its useful life. IAS 16 specifies that the depreciable amount of an asset is determined after deducting its residual value.

Kayte's original model implied that the residual value was constant for the vessel's entire useful life. The residual value has to be adjusted especially when an expected sale approaches, and the residual value has to come closer to disposal proceeds minus disposal costs at the end of the useful life. IAS 16 says that in cases when the residual value is greater than the asset's carrying amount, the depreciation charge is zero unless and until its residual value subsequently decreases to an amount below the asset's carrying amount. The residual value should be the value at the reporting date as if the vessel were already of the age and in the condition expected at the end of its useful life. An increase in the expected residual value of an asset because of past events will affect the depreciable amount, while expectation of future changes in residual value other than the effects of expected wear and tear will not. There is no guidance in IAS 16 on how to estimate residual value when the useful life is considered to be shorter than the economic life. Undesirable volatility is not a convincing argument to support the accounting treatment, and broker valuations could be a useful starting point to estimate residual value.

As regards the vessels which are kept for the whole of their economic life, a residual value based upon the scrap value of steel is acceptable. Therefore the vessels should be depreciated based upon the cost less the scrap value of steel over the 30-year period. The engine need not be componentised as it will have the same 30-year life if maintained every 10 years. It is likely that the cost of major planned maintenance will increase over the life of a vessel due to inflation and the age of the vessel. This additional cost will be capitalised when incurred and therefore the depreciation charge on these components may be greater in the later stages of a vessel's life.

When major planned maintenance work is to be undertaken, the cost should be capitalised. The engine overhaul will be capitalised as a new asset which will then be depreciated over the 10-year period to the next overhaul. The depreciation of the original capitalised amount will typically be calculated such that it had a net book value of nil when the overhaul is undertaken.

This is not the case with one vessel, because work was required earlier than expected. In this case, any remaining net book value of the old engine and overhaul cost should be expensed immediately.

The initial carve out of components should include all major maintenance events which are likely to occur over the economic life of the vessel. Sometimes, it may subsequently be found that the initial allocation was insufficiently detailed, in that not all components were identified. This is the case with the funnels. In this situation it is necessary to determine what the net book value of the component would currently be had it been initially identified. This will sometimes require the initial cost to be determined by reference to the replacement cost and the associated accumulated depreciation charge determined using the rate used for the vessel. This is likely to leave a significant net book value in the component being replaced, which will need to be written off at the time the replacement is capitalised.

4   (a)   All assets, including goodwill and intangible assets, have to be tested for impairment at the end of each reporting period, if there are indicators of impairment. The main issues in relation to IAS 36 *Impairment of Assets* are as follows:

Changes in circumstances

Changes in circumstances between the date of the impairment test and the next reporting period end may give rise to impairment indicators. If so, more than one impairment test may be required in an annual period. Where an annual impairment test is required for goodwill and certain other intangible assets, IAS 36 allows the impairment test to be performed at any time during the period, provided it is performed at the same time every year.

Many entities test goodwill at an interim period in the year. In times of high uncertainty, goodwill may have to be tested for impairment at year end and at a subsequent interim reporting date as well, if indicators of impairment arise after the annual test has been performed.

If an entity has to test for impairment at the end of the reporting date as well as at the scheduled annual date, it does not necessarily mean that the whole budget process needs to be redone, as top-down adjustments may be sufficient to assess any changes in the period since the latest goodwill impairment review.

Volatility in financial statements may indicate impairment. For example, falls or rises in commodity prices may affect impairment indicators for energy and mining entities, and require those assets to be tested for impairment in the next interim financial statements.

Market capitalisation as a special impairment indicator

Market capitalisation is a powerful indicator as, if it shows a lower figure than the book value of net assets, it inescapably suggests the market considers that the business is overvalued. However, the market may have taken account of factors other than the return which the entity is generating on its assets. A market capitalisation below book equity will not necessarily lead to an equivalent impairment loss. Entities should examine their cash generating units (CGUs) in these circumstances and may have to test goodwill for impairment. IAS 36 does not require a formal reconciliation between market capitalisation of the entity, fair value less costs to sell (FVLCS) and value in use (VIU). However, entities need to be able to understand the reason for the shortfall.

Allocating and reallocating goodwill to cash generating unit (CGU)

Given the complexity, sensitivity and need for significant judgement, companies experience issues assessing goodwill for impairment. The identification of CGUs and the allocation of acquired goodwill is unique to each entity and requires significant judgement. This allocation process in itself determines the appropriate carrying amount to test and should be a reasonable and supportable method.

Acquired goodwill is allocated to each of the acquirer's CGUs, or to a group of CGUs, which are expected to benefit from the synergies of the combination. If CGUs are subsequently revised or operations disposed of, IAS 36 requires goodwill to be reallocated, based on 'relative values', to the units affected. However, the standard does not expand on what is meant by 'relative value'. It does not mandate FVLCS as the basis, but it might mean that the entity has to carry out a valuation process on the part retained. There could be reasonable ways of estimating relative value by using an appropriate industry or business surrogate (for example, revenue, profits, industry KPIs).

Valuation issues

IAS 36 requires the recoverable amount of an asset or CGU to be measured as the higher of the asset's or CGU's FVLCS and VIU. Measuring the FVLCS and VIU of an asset or CGU requires the use of assumptions and estimates.

The following issues are proving particularly troublesome:

(a)   The use of a discounted cash flow (DCF) methodology to estimate FVLCS.

(b)   Determining the types of future cash flows which should be included in the measurement of VIU, in particular, those relating to restructuring programmes. IAS 36 requires an asset or CGU to be tested in its current status, not the status which management wishes it was in or hopes to get it into in the near future. Therefore, the standard requires VIU to be measured at the net present value of the future cash flows the entity expects to derive from the asset or CGU in its current condition over its remaining useful life. This means ignoring many management plans for enhancing the performance of the asset or CGU.

(c)   Determining the appropriate discount rate to apply. Unlike the cash flows used in an impairment test which are entity-specific, the discount rate is supposed to appropriately reflect the current market assessment of the time value of money and the risks specific to the asset or CGU.

When a specific rate for an asset or CGU is not directly available from the market, which is usually the case, the entity's weighted average cost of capital (WACC) can be used as a starting point. While not prescribed, WACC is by far the most commonly used base for the discount rate. However, the appropriate way to calculate the WACC is a complex subject, but the objective must be to obtain a rate, which is sensible and justifiable. In any event the rate can be subjective.

(d)   The impact of taxation on the impairment test, given the requirement in IAS 36 to measure VIU using pre-tax cash flows and discount rates. VIU, as defined by IAS 36, is primarily an accounting concept and not necessarily a business valuation of the asset or CGU. For calculating VIU, IAS 36 requires pre-tax cash flows and a pre-tax discount rate.

WACC is a post-tax rate, as are most observable equity rates used by valuers. Because of the issues in calculating an appropriate pre-tax discount rate and because it aligns more closely with their normal business valuation approach, some entities attempt to perform a VIU calculation based on a post-tax rate and post-tax cash flows.

(e)   Ensuring that the recoverable amount and carrying amount which are being compared are consistently determined. For example, pensions are mentioned by IAS 36 as items which might be included in the recoverable amount of a CGU. In practice, this could be fraught with difficulty, and entities will have to reflect the costs of providing pensions to employees and may need to make a pragmatic allocation to estimate a pension cost as part of the employee cost cash flow.

(f)   The incorporation of corporate assets into the impairment test. If possible, the corporate assets are to be allocated to individual CGUs on a 'reasonable and consistent basis'. This is not expanded upon in IAS 36 and affords some flexibility, but can lead to inconsistency. The same criteria must be applied at all times.

Impairment disclosures

Disclosure is a key communication to investors by management. Disclosures which describe the factors which could result in impairment become even more important when value has been eroded. Goodwill impairment disclosures are a requirement, but can be a problem. The key question is whether sufficient disclosure has been made about the uncertainty of the impairment calculation. Sensitivity disclosures about adverse situations, such as those triggered by volatile prices, provide useful information and whether a possible change in a key assumption, such as the discount rate, could lead to recoverable amount being equal to carrying amount, or result in impairment losses.

(b)   (i)   The discount rate used by Estoil has not been calculated in accordance with the requirements of IAS 36 *Impairment of Assets*. According to IAS 36, the future cash flows are estimated in the currency in which they will be generated and then discounted using a discount rate appropriate for that currency. IAS 36 requires the present value to be translated using the spot exchange rate at the date of the value in use calculation. Furthermore, the currency in which the estimated cash flows are denominated affects many of the inputs to the WACC calculation, including the risk free interest rate.

Estoil has used the 10-year government bond rate for its jurisdiction as the risk free rate in the calculation of the discount rate. As government bond rates differ between countries due to different expectations about future inflation, value in use could be calculated incorrectly due to the disparity between the expected inflation reflected in the estimated cash flows and the risk free rate.

According to IAS 36, the discount rate should reflect the risks specific to the asset. Accordingly, one discount rate for all the CGUs does not represent the risk profile of each CGU. The discount rate generally should be determined using the WACC of the CGU or of the company of which the CGU is currently part. Using a company's WACC for all CGUs is appropriate only if the specific risks associated with the specific CGUs do not diverge materially from the remainder of the group. In the case of Estoil, this is not apparent.

(ii)   It appears that the cash flow forecasts were not prepared based on the requirements of IAS 36. IAS 36 states that cash flow projections used in measuring value in use shall be based on reasonable and supportable assumptions which represent management's best estimate of the range of economic conditions which will exist over the remaining useful life of the asset. IAS 36 also states that management must assess the reasonableness of the assumptions by examining the causes of differences between past cash flow projections and actual cash. Management should ensure that the assumptions on which its current cash flow projections are based are consistent with past actual outcomes. Despite the fact that the realised cash flows for 2014 were negative and far below projected cash flows, the directors had significantly raised budgeted cash flows for 2015 without justification. There are serious doubts about Fariole's ability to establish realistic budgets.

According to IAS 36, estimates of future cash flows should include:

(i)   projections of cash inflows from the continuing use of the asset;

(ii)   projections of cash outflows which are necessarily incurred to generate the cash inflows from continuing use of the asset; and

(iii) net cash flows to be received (or paid) for the disposal of the asset at the end of its useful life.

IAS 36 states that projected cash outflows should include those required for the day-to-day servicing of the asset which includes future cash outflows to maintain the level of economic benefits expected to arise from the asset in its current condition. It is highly unlikely that no investments in working capital or operating assets would need to be made to maintain the assets of the CGUs in their current condition. Therefore, the cash flow projections used by Fariole are not in compliance with IAS 36.

			Marks
1	(a)	Property, plant and equipment	5
		Goodwill	6
		Assets held for sale	5
		Current assets/total non-current liabilities	1
		Retained earnings	6
		Other components of equity	3
		Non-controlling interest	3
		Current liabilities	1
		Joint venture	5
			35
	(b)	Subjective assessment of discussion	8
		Up to 2 marks per element	
	(c)	Subjective assessment – 1 mark per point	7
			50
2	(a)	IAS 24.5	
	(b)	IFRS 9 explanation	3
		Guarantee calculations	4
	(c)	Hedging discussion	4
		Effectiveness discussion	3
	(d)	Credit risk entries	4
		Professional marks	2
			25
3	(a)	IFRS 3/IFRS 10 – 1 mark per point up to	12
	(b)	IAS 16 and application – 1 mark per point up to	11
		Professional marks	2
			25
4	(a)	Subjective issues – 1 mark per point	13
	(b)	Subjective	10
		Professional marks	2
			25

Mathematical tables

Present value table

Present value of $1 = (1+r)^{-n}$ where r = discount rate, n = number of periods until payment.

This table shows the present value of £1 per annum, receivable or payable at the end of *n* years.

Periods (n)	||||| Discount rates (r)									
	1%	2%	3%	4%	5%	6%	7%	8%	9%	10%
1	0.990	0.980	0.971	0.962	0.952	0.943	0.935	0.926	0.917	0.909
2	0.980	0.961	0.943	0.925	0.907	0.890	0.873	0.857	0.842	0.826
3	0.971	0.942	0.915	0.889	0.864	0.840	0.816	0.794	0.772	0.751
4	0.961	0.924	0.888	0.855	0.823	0.792	0.763	0.735	0.708	0.683
5	0.951	0.906	0.863	0.822	0.784	0.747	0.713	0.681	0.650	0.621
6	0.942	0.888	0.837	0.790	0.746	0.705	0.666	0.630	0.596	0.564
7	0.933	0.871	0.813	0.760	0.711	0.665	0.623	0.583	0.547	0.513
8	0.923	0.853	0.789	0.731	0.677	0.627	0.582	0.540	0.502	0.467
9	0.914	0.837	0.766	0.703	0.645	0.592	0.544	0.500	0.460	0.424
10	0.905	0.820	0.744	0.676	0.614	0.558	0.508	0.463	0.422	0.386
11	0.896	0.804	0.722	0.650	0.585	0.527	0.475	0.429	0.388	0.350
12	0.887	0.788	0.701	0.625	0.557	0.497	0.444	0.397	0.356	0.319
13	0.879	0.773	0.681	0.601	0.530	0.469	0.415	0.368	0.326	0.290
14	0.870	0.758	0.661	0.577	0.505	0.442	0.388	0.340	0.299	0.263
15	0.861	0.743	0.642	0.555	0.481	0.417	0.362	0.315	0.275	0.239
16	0.853	0.728	0.623	0.534	0.458	0.394	0.339	0.292	0.252	0.218
17	0.844	0.714	0.605	0.513	0.436	0.371	0.317	0.270	0.231	0.198
18	0.836	0.700	0.587	0.494	0.416	0.350	0.296	0.250	0.212	0.180
19	0.828	0.686	0.570	0.475	0.396	0.331	0.277	0.232	0.194	0.164
20	0.820	0.673	0.554	0.456	0.377	0.312	0.258	0.215	0.178	0.149

Periods (n)	||||| Discount rates (r)									
	11%	12%	13%	14%	15%	16%	17%	18%	19%	20%
1	0.901	0.893	0.885	0.877	0.870	0.862	0.855	0.847	0.840	0.833
2	0.812	0.797	0.783	0.769	0.756	0.743	0.731	0.718	0.706	0.694
3	0.731	0.712	0.693	0.675	0.658	0.641	0.624	0.609	0.593	0.579
4	0.659	0.636	0.613	0.592	0.572	0.552	0.534	0.516	0.499	0.482
5	0.593	0.567	0.543	0.519	0.497	0.476	0.456	0.437	0.419	0.402
6	0.535	0.507	0.480	0.456	0.432	0.410	0.390	0.370	0.352	0.335
7	0.482	0.452	0.425	0.400	0.376	0.354	0.333	0.314	0.296	0.279
8	0.434	0.404	0.376	0.351	0.327	0.305	0.285	0.266	0.249	0.233
9	0.391	0.361	0.333	0.308	0.284	0.263	0.243	0.225	0.209	0.194
10	0.352	0.322	0.295	0.270	0.247	0.227	0.208	0.191	0.176	0.162
11	0.317	0.287	0.261	0.237	0.215	0.195	0.178	0.162	0.148	0.135
12	0.286	0.257	0.231	0.208	0.187	0.168	0.152	0.137	0.124	0.112
13	0.258	0.229	0.204	0.182	0.163	0.145	0.130	0.116	0.104	0.093
14	0.232	0.205	0.181	0.160	0.141	0.125	0.111	0.099	0.088	0.078
15	0.209	0.183	0.160	0.140	0.123	0.108	0.095	0.084	0.074	0.065
16	0.188	0.163	0.141	0.123	0.107	0.093	0.081	0.071	0.062	0.054
17	0.170	0.146	0.125	0.108	0.093	0.080	0.069	0.060	0.052	0.045
18	0.153	0.130	0.111	0.095	0.081	0.069	0.059	0.051	0.044	0.038
19	0.138	0.116	0.098	0.083	0.070	0.060	0.051	0.043	0.037	0.031
20	0.124	0.104	0.087	0.073	0.061	0.051	0.043	0.037	0.031	0.026

Cumulative present value table

This table shows the present value of £1 per annum, receivable or payable at the end of each year for *n* years.

Periods (n)	Discount rates (r)									
	1%	2%	3%	4%	5%	6%	7%	8%	9%	10%
1	0.990	0.980	0.971	0.962	0.952	0.943	0.935	0.926	0.917	0.909
2	1.970	1.942	1.913	1.886	1.859	1.833	1.808	1.783	1.759	1.736
3	2.941	2.884	2.829	2.775	2.723	2.673	2.624	2.577	2.531	2.487
4	3.902	3.808	3.717	3.630	3.546	3.465	3.387	3.312	3.240	3.170
5	4.853	4.713	4.580	4.452	4.329	4.212	4.100	3.993	3.890	3.791
6	5.795	5.601	5.417	5.242	5.076	4.917	4.767	4.623	4.486	4.355
7	6.728	6.472	6.230	6.002	5.786	5.582	5.389	5.206	5.033	4.868
8	7.652	7.325	7.020	6.733	6.463	6.210	5.971	5.747	5.535	5.335
9	8.566	8.162	7.786	7.435	7.108	6.802	6.515	6.247	5.995	5.759
10	9.471	8.983	8.530	8.111	7.722	7.360	7.024	6.710	6.418	6.145
11	10.37	9.787	9.253	8.760	8.306	7.887	7.499	7.139	6.805	6.495
12	11.26	10.58	9.954	9.385	8.863	8.384	7.943	7.536	7.161	6.814
13	12.13	11.35	10.63	9.986	9.394	8.853	8.358	7.904	7.487	7.103
14	13.00	12.11	11.30	10.56	9.899	9.295	8.745	8.244	7.786	7.367
15	13.87	12.85	11.94	11.12	10.38	9.712	9.108	8.559	8.061	7.606
16	14.718	13.578	12.561	11.652	10.838	10.106	9.447	8.851	8.313	7.824
17	15.562	14.292	13.166	12.166	11.274	10.477	9.763	9.122	8.544	8.022
18	16.398	14.992	13.754	12.659	11.690	10.828	10.059	9.372	8.756	8.201
19	17.226	15.678	14.324	13.134	12.085	11.158	10.336	9.604	8.950	8.365
20	18.046	16.351	14.877	13.590	12.462	11.470	10.594	9.818	9.129	8.514

Periods (n)	Discount rates (r)									
	11%	12%	13%	14%	15%	16%	17%	18%	19%	20%
1	0.901	0.893	0.885	0.877	0.870	0.862	0.855	0.847	0.840	0.833
2	1.713	1.690	1.668	1.647	1.626	1.605	1.585	1.566	1.547	1.528
3	2.444	2.402	2.361	2.322	2.283	2.246	2.210	2.174	2.140	2.106
4	3.102	3.037	2.974	2.914	2.855	2.798	2.743	2.690	2.639	2.589
5	3.696	3.605	3.517	3.433	3.352	3.274	3.199	3.127	3.058	2.991
6	4.231	4.111	3.998	3.889	3.784	3.685	3.589	3.498	3.410	3.326
7	4.712	4.564	4.423	4.288	4.160	4.039	3.922	3.812	3.706	3.605
8	5.146	4.968	4.799	4.639	4.487	4.344	4.207	4.078	3.954	3.837
9	5.537	5.328	5.132	4.946	4.772	4.607	4.451	4.303	4.163	4.031
10	5.889	5.650	5.426	5.216	5.019	4.833	4.659	4.494	4.339	4.192
11	6.207	5.938	5.687	5.453	5.234	5.029	4.836	4.656	4.486	4.327
12	6.492	6.194	5.918	5.660	5.421	5.197	4.988	4.793	4.611	4.439
13	6.750	6.424	6.122	5.842	5.583	5.342	5.118	4.910	4.715	4.533
14	6.982	6.628	6.302	6.002	5.724	5.468	5.229	5.008	4.802	4.611
15	7.191	6.811	6.462	6.142	5.847	5.575	5.324	5.092	4.876	4.675
16	7.379	6.974	6.604	6.265	5.954	5.668	5.405	5.162	4.938	4.730
17	7.549	7.120	6.729	6.373	6.047	5.749	5.475	5.222	4.990	4.775
18	7.702	7.250	6.840	6.467	6.128	5.818	5.534	5.273	5.033	4.812
19	7.839	7.366	6.938	6.550	6.198	5.877	5.584	5.316	5.070	4.843
20	7.963	7.469	7.025	6.623	6.259	5.929	5.628	5.353	5.101	4.870